THE DEBATE ON THE TRIAL OF THE TEMPLARS (1307–1314)

The Debate on the Trial of the Templars (1307–1314)

Edited by

JOCHEN BURGTORF
California State University, Fullerton, USA

PAUL F. CRAWFORD
California University of Pennsylvania, USA

HELEN J. NICHOLSON
Cardiff University, Wales

ASHGATE

Published by
Ashgate Publishing Limited
Wey Court East
Union Road
Farnham
Surrey, GU9 7PT
England

Ashgate Publishing Company
Suite 420
101 Cherry Street
Burlington
VT 05401-4405
USA

www.ashgate.com

British Library Cataloguing in Publication Data
The Debate on the Trial of the Templars (1307–1314).
1. Templars – Trials, litigation, etc. 2. Trials (Heresy) – France. 3. Inquisition – France. I. Burgtorf, Jochen. II. Crawford, Paul F., 1961– .III. Nicholson, Helen J., 1960– .
345.4'40288–dc22

Library of Congress Cataloging-in-Publication Data
Burgtorf, Jochen.
The Debate on the Trial of the Templars, 1307–1314 / Jochen Burgtorf, Paul F. Crawford, and Helen Nicholson.
p. cm.
Includes bibliographical references and index.
1. Templars – France – Trials, litigation, etc. 2. Trials (Heresy) – France. 3. Trials (Heresy) – Europe – History. 4. Inquisition – Europe – History. 5. Philip IV, King of France, 1268–1314. 6. Edward II, King of England, 1284–1327. 7. Hospitalers – History – To 1500. 8. Military religious orders – History – To 1580. 9. Grail – Legends – History and criticism. I. Crawford, Paul F. II. Nicholson, Helen. III. Title.
KJV131.T46B85 2010
345.44'0288–dc22 2010010026

ISBN 9780754665700 (hbk)
ISBN 9781409410096 (ebk)

Mixed Sources
Product group from well-managed forests and other controlled sources
www.fsc.org Cert no. SA-COC-1565
© 1996 Forest Stewardship Council
FSC

Printed and bound in Great Britain by
MPG Books Group, UK

Contents

PART IV: THE TRIAL IN THE BRITISH ISLES

PART V: THE TRIAL IN OTHER COUNTRIES

PART VI: GENERAL ASPECTS AND THE AFTERMATH

Notes on Contributors

Malcolm Barber is professor emeritus of medieval European history at the University of Reading (UK). His publications include *The Trial of the Templars* (2nd edn, 2006) and *The New Knighthood: A History of the Order of the Temple* (1994). He is also the editor of *The Military Orders: Fighting for the Faith and Caring for the Sick* (1994).

Elena Bellomo works in the Dipartimento di Scienze dell'Antichità, del Medioevo e Geografico-Ambientali at the University of Genoa (Italy). Her publications on medieval Genoa, the First Crusade and the Templars include *A servizio di Dio e del Santo Sepolcro: Caffaro e l'Oriente latino* (2003) and *The Templar Order in North-West Italy: 1142–c.1330* (2008).

David Bryson is a fellow of the School of Historical Studies at the University of Melbourne (Australia). He has published numerous articles on the Templars and Hospitallers in southwestern France, including 'The Hospitaller and Templar houses of Périgord' and 'Murder in the Preceptory?', in *The Military Orders*, vols 3 and 4 (2008).

Jochen Burgtorf is professor of medieval history at California State University, Fullerton (USA). He is the author of *The Central Convent of Hospitallers and Templars: History, Organization and Personnel (1099/1120–1310)* (2008) and has co-edited (with Helen J. Nicholson) *International Mobility in the Military Orders (Twelfth to Fifteenth Centuries)* (2006).

Paul F. Crawford is assistant professor of ancient and medieval history at California University of Pennsylvania (USA). His publications include the first English translation of *The 'Templar of Tyre': Part III of the 'Deeds of the Cypriots'* (2003), as well as 'The Military Orders and the Last Decade of the Thirteenth Century', in *Epeterida* (2007).

Peter W. Edbury is professor of medieval history and director of the Centre for the Crusades at Cardiff University, Wales (UK). He has written extensively on the Latin kingdom of Jerusalem and Lusignan Cyprus. His publications include *The Kingdom of Cyprus and the Crusades, 1191–1374* (1991) and the edition of John of Ibelin's *Le Livre des Assises* (2003).

Alan Forey has taught at the universities of Oxford, St. Andrews and Durham (UK). His publications include *The Military Orders from the Twelfth to the Early Fourteenth Centuries* (1992) and *The Fall of the Templars in the Crown of Aragon* (2001). He is now working on western conversions to Islam from the eleventh to the fifteenth centuries, and papal attitudes to the Spanish reconquest.

Luis García-Guijarro Ramos lectures in medieval history at the University of Zaragoza, campus of Huesca (Spain). He has researched into various aspects of military and monastic orders in medieval Spain as well as crusader historiography. His publications include *Papado, Cruzados y Órdenes Militares, siglos XI–XIII* (1995).

Anne Gilmour-Bryson is a principal fellow at the University of Melbourne (Australia) and has taught at Trinity Western University, British Columbia (Canada). Her publications on the Templar trial include *The Trial of the Templars in the Papal State and the Abruzzi* (1982) and *The Trial of the Templars on Cyprus: A Complete English Edition* (1998).

Jeffrey S. Hamilton is professor and chair of the Department of History at Baylor University (USA). His publications include *Piers Gaveston, Earl of Cornwall 1307–1312* (1988) and *The Royal Charter Witness Lists of Edward II 1307–1326* (2001). He was also the editor of vol. 4 of the journal *Fourteenth Century England* (2006).

Filip Hooghe works as a historical researcher for the Society of Local History in Klein-Brabant (Belgium), specializing in the medieval history of farms and castles. He obtained his masters degree in history at the Catholic University of Leuven. His publications include *Het Tempeliershof en de Rozendaalhoeve: Een nieuwe kijk op de geschiedenis van Weert* (2004).

Thomas Krämer is currently completing a Ph.D. dissertation at the Free University of Berlin (Germany) on conflicts and conflict resolution involving the military orders and the secular clergy of southern France and southern Germany. His publications include 'L'ordre teutonique dans le Midi', in *Cahiers de Fanjeaux* (2006).

Anthony Luttrell has taught and researched at numerous universities and institutes in Europe and the United States of America. His publications include six volumes in the Variorum Collected Studies series, most recently *Studies on the Hospitallers after 1306* (2007). He is also the co-editor of *La Commanderie: Institution des ordres militaires dans l'Occident médiéval* (2002).

Nicholas Morton received his Ph.D. from Royal Holloway, University of London (UK), and now teaches at Nottingham Trent University. His book *The Teutonic Knights in the Holy Land, 1190–1291* was published in 2009. His wider research interests include the employment of Old Testament imagery in crusading literature and the Latin East in the thirteenth century.

Helen J. Nicholson is reader in history at Cardiff University, Wales (UK), and has published on the military orders, crusades and various related subjects. Her most recent book is *The Knights Templar on Trial: The Trial of the Templars in the British Isles, 1308–1311* (2009). She is currently completing an edition of the Templar trial proceedings in the British Isles.

Simon Phillips is a research fellow at the University of Cyprus. His research interests focus on the military orders and late medieval ecclesiastical history. He recently published *The Prior of the Knights Hospitaller in Late Medieval England* (2009) and is currently working on Hospitaller documents concerning late medieval Cyprus.

Clive Porro is working on a Ph.D. dissertation at Queen Mary, University of London (UK), on 'The Order of Christ in Fourteenth-Century Portugal'. He is the head of Information Rights in the Department for Environment, Food and Rural Affairs, Whitehall (since 2006), and previously served as a clerk to the Public Administration Select Committee in the House of Commons.

Alain Provost is 'maître de conférences' in medieval history at the University of Artois in Arras (France). His Ph.D. dissertation on the trial of Guichard, bishop of Troyes, was completed at the University of Paris IV-Sorbonne. His research interests include the legal and institutional history of the kingdom of France in the late thirteenth and early fourteenth centuries.

Sebastián Salvadó is working on a Ph.D. dissertation at Stanford University (USA) on 'The Thirteenth-Century Templar Breviary of Acre (Paris, Bibliothèque nationale de France, fonds latin 10478)'. He is interested in the inter-relationship between liturgical chants, texts and artworks in the crusader contexts of Aragon-Catalonia and the Latin East.

Magdalena Satora is working on a Ph.D. dissertation at the Nicolaus Copernicus University of Toruń (Poland) on the diplomatic activities of the European royal courts during the trial of the Templars. Her article included in this volume is based on her M.A. thesis written at the same institution.

Jochen G. Schenk is a fellow at the German Historical Institute in London (UK) and a research associate of Wolfson College, Cambridge. He received his Ph.D. from Cambridge University and is working on a religious history of the military orders. His publications include 'Forms of Lay Association with the Order of the Temple', in *Journal of Medieval History* (2008).

Bernard Schotte works in the Department of Historical Monuments and Urban Renewal of the city of Bruges (Belgium), has published various articles on the history of Bruges and is a founding member of a Belgian study group on the Templars and Hospitallers. He studied history at the University of Ghent.

Maria Starnawska works at the Historical Institute of the Academy of Podlasie in Siedlce (Poland). Her research focuses on the history of the military orders and the cult of relics in medieval Poland. Her English-language publications include 'Military Orders and the Beginning of Crusades in Prussia', in *The Crusades and the Military Orders* (2001).

Dale R. Streeter is an assistant professor at Eastern New Mexico University (USA) where he teaches pre-modern European history. His research focuses on the bishops of France in the fourteenth century. His publications include 'Episcopal Careers and the University in Fourteenth-Century France', in *Medieval Prosopography* (2001).

Kristjan Toomaspoeg works as a researcher and 'professore aggregato' at the University of Salento in Lecce (Italy). He received his Ph.D. from the University of Paris X-Nanterre. His publications include *Les Teutoniques en Sicile (1197–1492)* (2003) and his research interests extend to the relations between northern and southern Europe in the middle ages.

Ignacio de la Torre is currently a professor of finance at Instituto de Empresa Business Schhol (Madrid). His publications include a monograph on the Templars and the origin of banking, *Los templarios y el origen de la banca* (2004), and several articles on financial aspects of the Order of the Temple.

Theresa M. Vann is the Joseph S. Micallef curator of the Malta Study Center at the Hill Museum & Manuscript Library in Collegeville, Minnesota (USA). Her research focuses on the military orders as well as medieval Spain. Her publications include numerous articles as well as the collection *Queens, Regents and Potentates* (1993).

Christian Vogel works at the Universität des Saarlandes, Saarbrücken, Germany, as Wissenschaftlicher Mitarbeiter am Lehrstuhl für Geschichte des Mittelalters. He previously worked as a project researcher at Heinrich-Heine-University Duesseldorf. His publications include a study on the statutes of the Templars, *Das Recht der Templer* (2007).

John Walker is a lecturer in the History Department at Hull University (UK). He received his Ph.D. from St. Andrews University, and his dissertation studied the English patrons of the Templars and the order of St. Lazarus. His research interests include the history of Yorkshire during the middle ages and the after-history of the Templars.

List of Abbreviations

CH	*Cartulaire général de l'ordre des Hospitaliers de Saint-Jean de Jérusalem, 1100–1310*, ed. Joseph Delaville Le Roulx, 4 vols (Paris, 1884–1906)
CUP	*Chartularium universitatis Parisiensis*, ed. Heinrich Denifle and Emil Chatelain, 4 vols (Paris, 1889–97)
EUT	Hans Prutz, *Entwicklung und Untergang des Tempelherrenordens* (Berlin, 1888)
MGH	Monumenta Germaniae Historica
MO, 1	*The Military Orders: Fighting for the Faith and Caring for the Sick*, ed. Malcolm Barber (Aldershot, 1994)
MO, 2	*The Military Orders*, vol. 2: *Welfare and Warfare*, ed. Helen Nicholson (Aldershot, 1998)
MO, 3	*The Military Orders*, vol. 3: *History and Heritage*, ed. Victor Mallia-Milanes (Aldershot, 2008)
PT	*Le procès des Templiers*, ed. Jules Michelet, 2 vols (Paris, 1841–51)
PUT	*Papsttum und Untergang des Templerordens*, ed. Heinrich Finke, 2 vols (Münster, 1907)
Reg. Clem. V	*Regestum Clementis papae V*, ed. cura et studio monachorum ordinis S. Benedicti, 9 vols in 7 (Rome, 1885–92)
RHC	Recueil des historiens des croisades
Oc	Historiens occidentaux
Doc arm	Documents arméniens
ROL	*Revue de l'Orient latin*
RT	*La règle du Temple*, ed. Henri de Curzon (Paris, 1886)
UT	*Der Untergang des Templerordens mit urkundlichen und kritischen Beiträgen*, ed. Konrad Schottmüller, 2 vols (Berlin, 1887; repr. Liechtenstein, 1991)

List of Figures

Maps, showing locations mentioned in the text

Illustrations in text

Maps

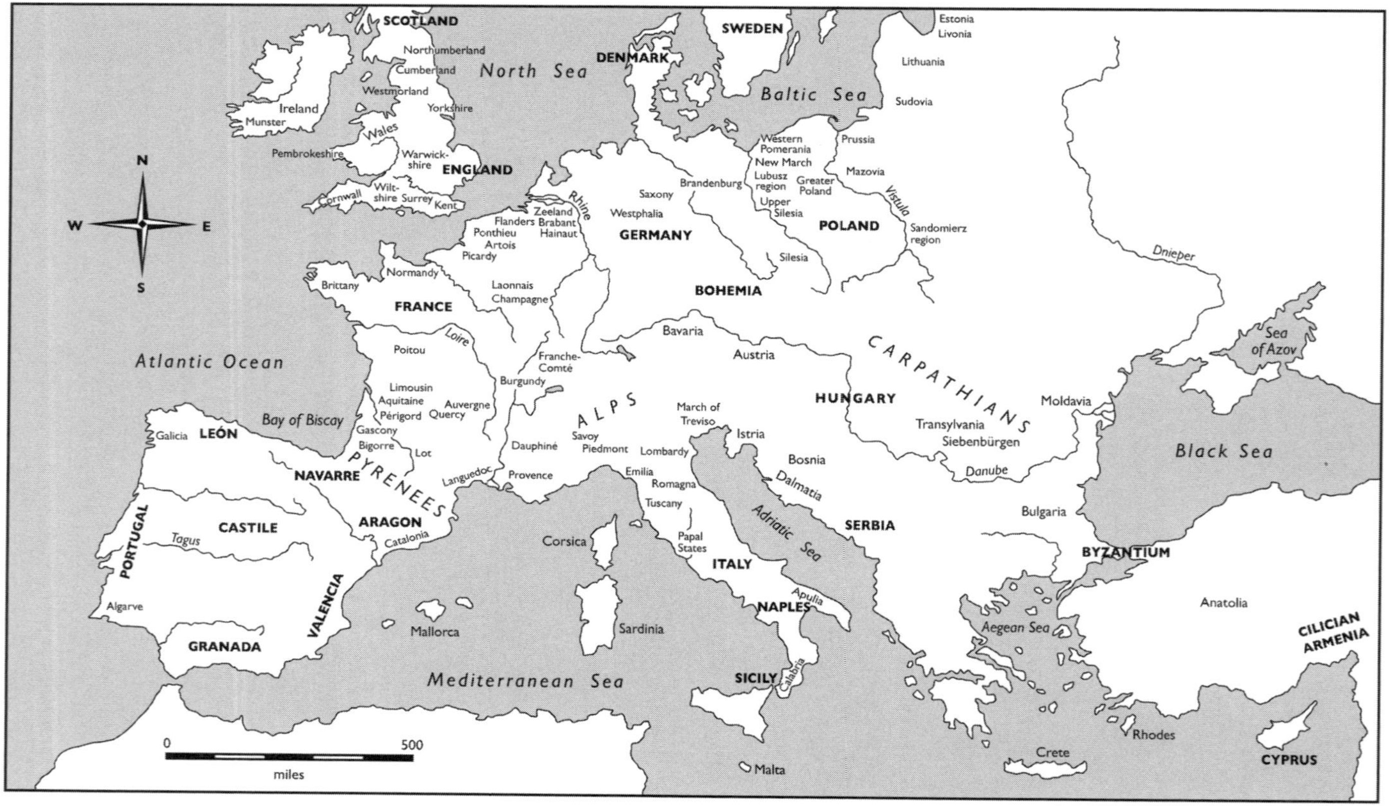

Map 1 Europe, showing locations mentioned in the text

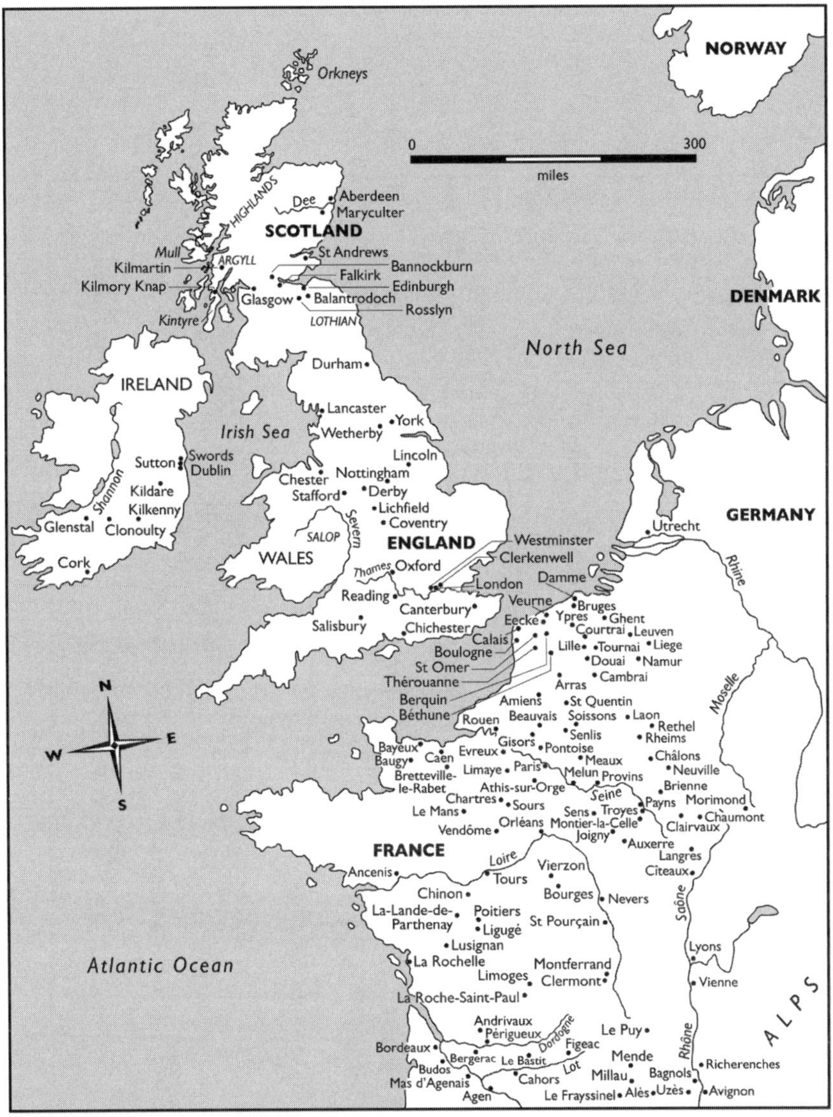

Map 2 Northwestern Europe, showing locations mentioned in the text

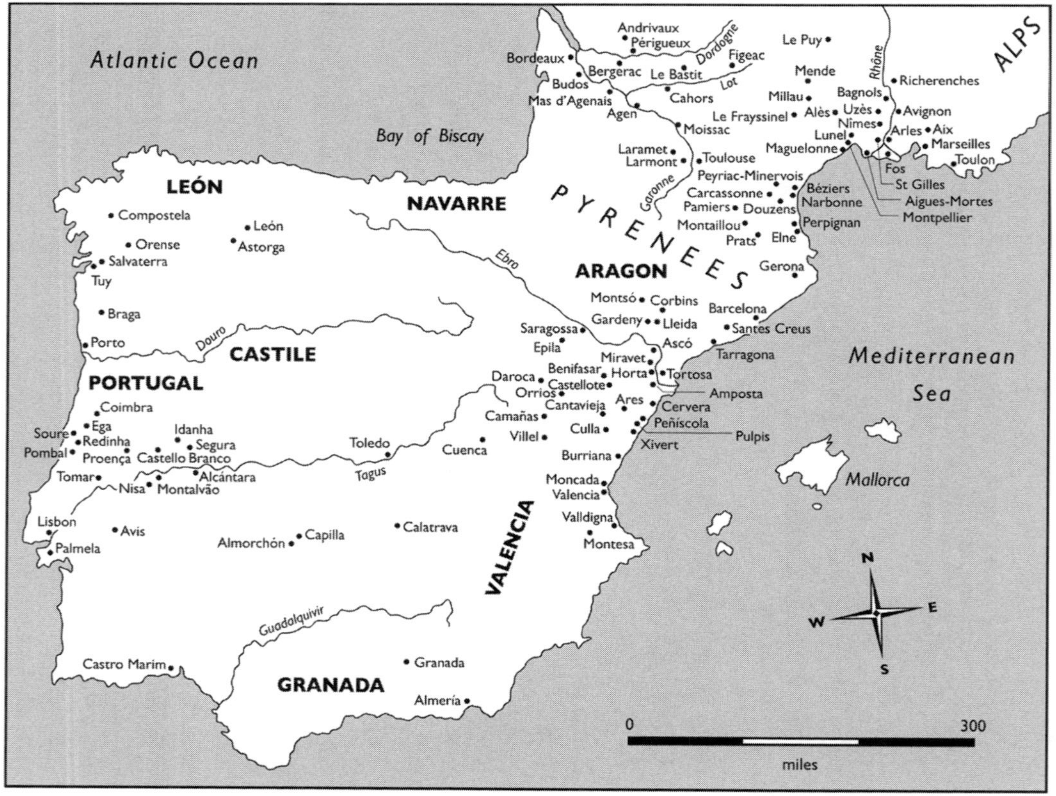

Map 3 southwestern Europe, showing locations mentioned in the text

Map 4 Central Europe, showing locations mentioned in the text

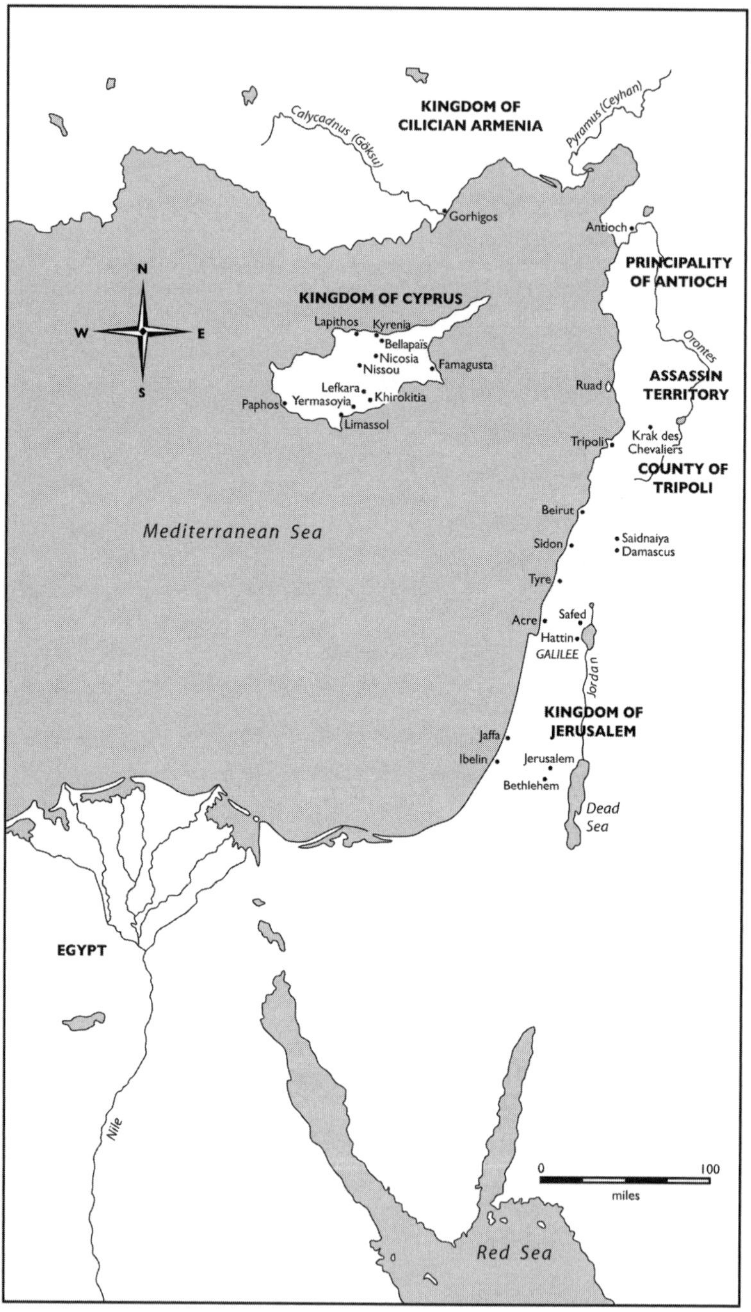

Map 5 The eastern Mediterranean, showing locations mentioned in the text

Preface

Jochen Burgtorf, Paul F. Crawford and Helen J. Nicholson

The year 2007 was the 700th anniversary of the arrest of the Templars and the beginning of the trial of the order (1307–12). In commemoration of this event, Jochen Burgtorf, Paul Crawford and Helen Nicholson organised a series of conference sessions on the trial of the Templars, at both the International Congress on Medieval Studies at the University of Western Michigan, Kalamazoo, USA (3–6 May 2007), and the International Medieval Congress at the University of Leeds, England (9–12 July 2007). Themes included the religious, political and social context of the trial, the papacy, royalty, biography of individual participants, regional aspects, procedural aspects, the aftermath of the trial and the 'surviving' Templars, as well as the historiography of the trial, both contemporary and later. We brought together an international group of young as well as experienced scholars in order to examine these themes.

The conference sessions were very successful. As the fruits of research on the trial of the Templars across Europe were brought together and discussed, it became clear that there is much new and exciting material being discovered about the background, proceedings and aftermath of the trial. The presentation of the papers was followed by lively debate. We are delighted that it has been possible to bring the majority of these papers together in the present volume, making these discoveries available to a wider audience. We thank the editorial committee (Malcolm Barber, Peter W. Edbury, Alan Forey and Anthony Luttrell) for their invaluable comments. We are also very grateful to Malcolm Barber, whose book *The Trial of the Templars* (1978; 2nd edn 2006) remains the standard study of the trial in English, for writing the introduction to this collection. The present volume assembles the research of 29 scholars from different academic generations as well as residents of 10 different countries (Belgium, Canada, Cyprus, France, Germany, Great Britain, Italy, Poland, Spain and the United States of America).

In editing this volume, we have endeavoured to reflect the demands of different national scholarships. The names of individuals have usually been given in the vernacular form preferred by each scholar. Thus, King James II of Aragon is also referred to as Jaume II and Jaime II; Esquieu de Floyran is also Esquieu de Floyrac and Enguerran de Floyran. Rather than cause an international dispute by insisting on one spelling or another, we have allowed the contributors to use their own preferred versions; the index should act as a concordance between the different spellings of these names. Contributors have differed over whether to prefer the term 'preceptor' or 'commander' for the Templars' officials, and 'preceptory' or 'commandery' for their administrative centres, and – given that these terms have identical meanings, but originate in different languages – we have not attempted to impose a single version.

We would like to thank the editors at Ashgate Publishing for their help in the production of this volume. We are especially grateful to Kelly Donovan of California State University, Fullerton, for producing the maps. We also thank Kyle Walker (Fullerton) for his assistance in compiling the index. The original conference sessions were sponsored by the Hill Museum & Manuscript Library in Collegeville, Minnesota (USA), and we thank them for their support.

Fullerton, CA; California, PA; Cardiff, Wales: May 2010

Introduction

Malcolm Barber

Like that staple opening of so many films, it began with a funeral. On 12 October 1307, James of Molay, master of the Temple, was one of a number of distinguished personages who held the cords of the pall spread over the coffin of Catherine of Courtenay, wife of Charles of Valois, brother of King Philip the Fair of France, during her funeral ceremony in the cathedral of Notre-Dame in Paris. Molay's role was an entirely appropriate reflection of his status and importance: he was the head of a great military order with preceptories (also known as commanderies) and estates in every country in Latin Christendom, an order which for nearly two centuries had taken a leading role in the war against the Islamic enemy both in the East and in Iberia. He was, indeed, a figure of European stature, consulted by the pope and apparently trusted by the French king, the most powerful monarch in the West.

Yet, by 24 October, Molay was a prisoner of that same king and had confessed to the inquisitor of France that he was, in fact, the master of an institution which had betrayed the Christian faith. He himself had denied Christ and spat on a crucifix, assertions he repeated before a special assembly of canons and university theologians the next day. In less than two weeks Molay had been transformed from a proud and honoured guest at the court of Philip the Fair into a blasphemer and an apostate, forced into a public humiliation so profound that neither he nor his order ever recovered from it.

The trial of the Templars is one of the most sensational events of the high middle ages. Contemporaries expressed astonishment when, on the 13th, the day after the funeral, all the members of the order in France were suddenly arrested and accused of what amounted to the renunciation of the faith that they were supposed to be defending with their lives. They had, the French government alleged, all been received into the order in ceremonies in which they denied Christ, spat on a crucifix and engaged in obscene kissing with their receptor and, thereafter, they had been obliged to take part in acts of sodomy with other brothers and to worship idols. Molay was not alone: during November and December, French royal officials succeeded in gaining admissions of guilt from nearly all the Templars in their custody, and it looked as if the order was doomed.

However, the trial was prolonged because of unexpected resistance, first from the pope, Clement V, and then from the Templars themselves, led by the order's former procurator at the papal court, Peter of Bologna. Clement V intervened because he regarded the affair as an affront to his jurisdiction and dignity, for he had not been consulted about the arrests but, as he could not reverse the process, he decided to attempt to take over the proceedings himself, ordering arrests in other countries and conducting his own inquiries. The papal intervention had a quite startling effect, for some of the Templars withdrew their confessions, claiming they had been made under coercion. Thus, early in 1308, the pope suspended the proceedings, and it was only after massive pressure from the French crown, culminating in a direct confrontation at Poitiers in May and June 1308, that he could be induced to restart them. This time they took the form of a papal commission to inquire into the order as a whole, and a series of local, episcopal inquiries, which were to investigate individuals at the diocesan level.

The operation of the papal commission in Paris offered the Templars another opportunity and there, in the spring of 1310, they mounted such an effective defence that the French government had to resort to further intimidation in the form of execution by burning of various groups of Templars who had the misfortune to be held in dioceses where the bishops were closely allied to the French monarchy. Even then, there were Templars willing to offer a defence before the commission, but the French government's control of the personnel of the order meant that few of them had the chance to speak out again. The end came in the spring of 1312 at the council of Vienne, when the pope, having gathered reports from across Christendom, declared that the order was too defamed to continue and thus suppressed it, although he did not condemn it on the original charges. Its property was to be transferred to the Hospitallers – by this time established in Rhodes – so that it could continue to be used in the cause of the recovery of the Holy Land, which the pope claimed had been the original intention of the donors.

It had been a long and bitter road for James of Molay, who had not been able to present an effective defence, partly because he was deluded by the promise that his case was reserved for the pope. When, early in 1314, it became obvious that he would never obtain any effective help from Clement, he made his last stand, declaring that the order was innocent in the certain knowledge that this would result in his death. On 18 March, he and Geoffrey of Charney, preceptor of Normandy, were burnt to death as relapsed heretics on the Ile-des-Javiaux in the centre of Paris.

Most of the French Templars were caught unawares on the morning of 13 October 1307. The secrecy which had preceded the action was an essential prerequisite for its success but, both for contemporaries and for historians, it has meant that understanding and interpretation of the trial has, for seven centuries, remained a matter of debate. Nevertheless, however sudden the arrests, the trial had to have a context. Careful consideration has been given to the years between 1291 and 1307 in particular, for in May 1291, the Latin Christians had been driven off the Syrian mainland by the Mamluks, losing Acre, their greatest city, amid scenes of terrible slaughter. Inevitably, there were recriminations, propelled not only by grief at the loss, but also by the desire to evade responsibility for the disaster. Given their role, the military orders of the Temple and the Hospital were certain to be a focus of discontent, and there were many schemes for reform, the most popular of which was a union of the orders and the appointment of new leadership.

However, although contemporaries were anxious to point out the deficiencies of the orders, their criticisms do not accord with the accusations made against the Temple in 1307. If such internal practices did indeed undermine the ability of the brothers to fulfil their functions, it does seem as if they must have been kept secret by a large number of people for some indeterminate time before 1307. Alan Forey examines this basic question, exposing the inconsistencies in the arguments about the existence of such a culture within the order [1]. Even historians convinced that the Templars were largely innocent have found it difficult to accept that none of the accusations had any basis in fact and therefore have believed that something must have been wrong, perhaps in a minority of houses. Yet Forey's paper demonstrates the circularity of such arguments; he can find no evidence other than that derived from the depositions made at the trial, the nature of which, as the paper by Thomas Krämer shows [6], was heavily moulded by inquisitorial procedures.

This, though, is to pose the question within the parameters set by the French government. It is possible that the faults of the order were such that, as Jonathan Riley-Smith has said, even if the trial had never taken place, the order would, sooner or later, have had to be abolished.[1] Anthony Luttrell's attempt to construct a precise chronology for the election of James of Molay as master in the crucial period immediately following the fall of Acre gains a particular relevance in this light, since at the time of the arrests Molay had been master for 15 years, and therefore carried a heavy responsibility for the state of the order in 1307 [2]. If, as Luttrell believes likely, there were severe internal tensions at the time of the election, it may be that Molay had been unable to heal fissures within the order and that this, in turn, had weakened its ability to function effectively. In the end, it is not possible to come to a definitive conclusion, partly because some of the evidence once again has to be drawn from trial depositions, but it is possible that, had the French government been in a position to express any preference in the election, Molay would not have been seen as the ideal candidate. If, in 1291 or 1292, Molay had defeated a pro-French faction within the Temple, this may have had some influence within French government circles in 1307.

All large and privileged ecclesiastical institutions were, of course, likely to come into conflict with secular powers at some stage in their history, especially as rulers sought to develop their administrations and to maximise their financial returns. Nicholas Morton shows that clashes were sometimes unavoidable [3]. Hermann of Salza, master of the Teutonic Knights, for example, tried and failed to tread a middle path between Emperor Frederick II and Pope Gregory IX in 1229, yet the pope, intent on pursuing his own agenda, had no sympathy for the awkward position of the master, apparently having already decided that the Teutonic Knights were imperial partisans. Yet, both the Teutonic Knights and

[1] Jonathan Riley-Smith, 'The Structures of the Orders of the Temple and the Hospital', in *The Medieval Crusade*, ed. Susan J. Ridyard (Woodbridge, 2004), p. 143.

the Hospitallers avoided the fate of the Templars, perhaps because they were more difficult to attack. It may well be that in the counsels of Philip IV, a potent argument for immediate action in the autumn of 1307, even though a papal inquiry remained unfinished, was that the Templar leaders were present in Paris. At any time they may have set out for their headquarters in Cyprus, taking them beyond the French government's reach. In contrast, neither of the other two masters was accessible at the time. Here may be one of the reasons for the victimisation of the Temple, given that criticism of the military orders was not exclusively aimed at the Templars. Indeed, Bernard Schotte has found evidence that Hospitallers as well as Templars took part in the Flemish rebellion against France in 1302–3, a humiliating experience for the French crown, which involved the severe defeat at the battle of Courtrai in July 1302 [4].

A political explanation for the French government's attack on the Temple, has, however, always been a minority view. Until relatively recently, when there has been a shift of emphasis towards an analysis of Philip IV's religious and, indeed, superstitious beliefs, it has been more usual to seek the answer in the financial difficulties of the French government. Ignacio de la Torre concentrates upon the crown's need for silver, most importantly to enable it to reissue better quality coins in 1306 after several years of debasement [5]. Given the shortage of silver and its consequent high price, this was very difficult to achieve and, indeed, the move was complicated by the government's lack of understanding of the wider economic impact. As Theresa Vann points out, the pontifical enquiry of 1373 shows that the Templars had one-half to two-thirds more property in France than the Hospitallers [27] which, together with the accumulation of specie in the Templar bank, made the Templars the more likely target for expropriation.

The arrest of the Templars in France produced a wide variety of documentation, including papal bulls, letters, speeches, diplomatic reports, propaganda tracts, letters of convocation for the French Estates, consultations with university masters, and, most conspicuously, the proceedings of the actual trial, at the core of which were the depositions of the brothers themselves. These depositions can be used in a number of different ways. Taking the records from the *sénéschausée* of Nîmes-Beaucaire, which have not attracted as much attention as those of Paris and elsewhere, Thomas Krämer emphasises how the structure of the interrogation determined the nature of the answers, often very similar both because of the pressure exerted upon the witnesses and the methodology of the inquisitors [6]. Set within the context of imprisonment and torture, the depositions are more the result of the application of a 'system' than a means of providing direct evidence of truth or falsehood. Modern research into the effects of psychological pressure and torture can help historians in their analysis of the confessions arrayed before them. Parallels with the work of James Given on the operation of the inquisitors in Languedoc during the thirteenth century are instructive.[2]

[2] James Given, *Inquisition and Medieval Society: Power, Discipline and Resistance in Languedoc* (Ithaca, NY, and London, 1997).

This does not, of course, invalidate all the information which can be derived from the depositions, but rather induces caution in accepting the contents at face value. This is fundamental in any study of inquisitorial records as the debate about the validity of the material drawn from the Fournier registers by Emmanuel Le Roy Ladurie has shown.[3] The depositions can be used as the fulcrum for research into specific themes. David Bryson has taken the testimony of Ponsard of Gizy (27 November 1309), in which Ponsard accuses certain persons of 'treachery' against the Temple, as the starting-point for an investigation into the background of these men, several times referred to in the course of the trial as the originators of the suspicions against the order [8]. Jochen Schenk follows up references to family connections within the order, a matter not directly interesting to the inquisitors, but one which can help historians to understand the nature of the order in the thirteenth century [12]. This is effective use of the evidence for purposes other than the trial itself, but it also raises questions about the ubiquity of Templar secrecy, implying that this would only have been possible if whole extended families had remained silent about abuses for generations [1]. Confirmation can be found in Christian Vogel's study of runaways and renegades [25]. His examples of Templars who had left the order, either through flight or expulsion, show that, while such matters were not always handled in strict accordance with the Rule, none suggests that the problem of desertion was becoming worse in the later thirteenth century or that they had fled to escape rituals of blasphemy and obscenity which had been imposed on them. Anne Gilmour-Bryson has taken a complete category of depositions – those made by priests – to see if the nature of their testimony differs from that of the knights and serving brothers [26]. As she says, they could be expected to have at least minimal literacy, and this might have affected their perceptions of the order and of allegations against it. In practice, however, they seem to have had no more understanding of the accusations than other Templars, a finding which leads to the conclusion that they were as surprised as everybody else at the proceedings.

While the confessions are perhaps the most eye-catching of the evidence generated, the trial records can be used to elucidate other themes. Dale Streeter challenges the assumption that the reign of Philip the Fair saw a seismic shift in the balance of power between Church and State, pointing out that the king still needed papal co-operation, as can be seen by the creation in 1308 of a papal commission and diocesan tribunals [7]. The control and direction of such bodies were as much the result of patronage and compromises over appointments as they had ever been. Less studied are the inventories taken by officials at the time of the arrests. There were obvious financial reasons for them, but they also offer valuable information about economic activities, social relations and even liturgical practices in the early fourteenth century. Sometimes they offer an idea of the physical appearance of the

---

3 Emmanuel Le Roy Ladurie, *Montaillou: Cathars and Catholics in a French Village, 1294–1324*, trans. Barbara Bray (London, 1978) (originally 1975). See the criticisms of Leonard E. Boyle, 'Montaillou Revisited: *Mentalité* and Methodology', in *Pathways to Medieval Peasants*, ed. James A. Raftis (Toronto, 1981), pp. 119–40.

order's preceptories and can be valuable evidence when used in conjunction with archaeological investigation. Jochen Burgtorf's preliminary study of the French inventories demonstrates these possibilities, especially when used in comparative form [9]. In Aragon the inventories kept before the trial are little more than lists, but Sebastián Salvadó shows that they offer vivid detail after the arrests [15]. Some houses were lavishly equipped with valuable missals, psalters, chalices, crosses and reliquaries, among many other items. For Salvadó they are particularly interesting because of the image they offer of Templar devotion, especially its links with the Holy Land, but they also help in the task of assessing the wealth of the order in Aragon, which appears to have been considerably greater than in some other provinces of the order, such as England. The development of Peñíscola and its region, for example, described by Luis García-Guijarro Ramos [16], is matched by the lavishness and number of liturgical objects rapidly accumulated there.

The papers by Alain Provost and Paul Crawford show that others too found themselves the subject of legal oppression at this time, Guichard of Troyes because he had crossed the royal family [10], and Marguerite Porete because she had offended ecclesiastical sensibilities [11]. In both cases some of the same hands can be detected. The investigation into Guichard's activities in 1308–9 is proof of the contemporary climate of belief, especially in the workings of demonic forces in society. The condemnation of Marguerite Porete in 1310 shows that some of the masters at the university of Paris were evidently more willing to express an opinion on her position than they had been about the Templars' two years earlier. These cases emphasise why any overt defence of the Templars would have been a dangerous activity in contemporary Paris. The connection is the court of Philip the Fair, both in its addiction to the idea of diabolical conspiracy (later to reappear in the entirely imaginary 'lepers' plot' of 1321) and in its power to intimidate. In this context, Magdalena Satora's use of evidence from the trial as a means of understanding the extent and limits of the transmission of information is particularly pertinent, especially when examining the degree of control a powerful regime could exercise in the conditions prevailing in the early fourteenth century [13].

There is no doubt that the progenitors of the trial were the king of France and his counsellors, even though there are debates about their degree of relative responsibility. However, it may be significant for future research that 11 of the 28 papers in this volume examine events outside France, including Iberia, the British Isles, Cyprus, Italy, Flanders and Poland which, with the exception of Germany, covers almost every region in which the Templars had personnel and property. All large-scale institutions needed to establish a sound relationship with the local secular powers, whatever their theoretical exemptions and responsibilities towards Rome. In Portugal, Aragon, England, Cyprus and Sicily these relationships were severely tested by the circumstances which the trial created. Clive Porro reassesses the attitude of King Dinis in Portugal, showing that he had already been taking over Templar property before 1307, so that his conventional image as a staunch defender of the order needs considerable modification [14]. The trial enabled him to continue this process and, indeed, ultimately create the new order of Christ, but his attitude towards the Templars was not, in fact, directly linked with the proceedings demanded by the pope, which were never activated in Portugal. The result was a more localised order in keeping with the development of military orders in Iberia since the second half of the twelfth century. A similar trend can be discerned on the other side of the peninsula, where James II of Aragon was most concerned to secure the wedge of lands in northern Valencia which the Templars had built up over the previous decade [16]. In Luis García-Guijarro Ramos' interpretation of James II's motives, strategic considerations weighed most heavily, and this helps to explain the king's relatively tepid efforts against Templar castles in other parts of his lands. As in Portugal, the consequence was the emergence of a 'territorialised' military order, that of Montesa.

Neither Dinis nor James II were committed to Philip IV's programme, but both were obliged to operate in a world in which other pressures helped to determine their actions. This was equally true of Edward II of England and Amaury of Lusignan, governor of Cyprus. It is not conceivable that either would have arrested the Templars had they not received papal commands to do so, as it is apparent that neither believed in the accusations and that both found the Templars useful to their government. Edward II, however, could not afford to offend Clement V and Philip IV, because as Jeffrey Hamilton shows, he wanted their co-operation in bringing back Piers Gaveston, exiled from the kingdom in May 1308 [17]. Amaury of Lusignan, who had ousted his brother, King Henry II, in 1306, was beginning to lose the support he had initially enjoyed, and was desperate for papal confirmation. Peter Edbury's examination of the situation on the island demonstrates that Amaury's previous alliance with the Temple was of less importance to him than the need to shore up his own political position [20].

External circumstances were equally crucial in Ireland, Italy, Poland, and Flanders. In Ireland, although there was a substantial Templar settlement, one finds little appetite for pressing the charges, while in northern Italy, the procedure employed by Rinaldo da Concorezzo, archbishop of Ravenna, while correct, avoided the use of torture despite papal demands. The results, as Helen Nicholson and Elena Bellomo show, were negligible in comparison with the confessions of the afflicted Templars in the hands of the French government [18] [21]. Conditions in northern and central Italy were particularly unfavourable to the inquisitors, since many Templars disappeared, having had plenty of warning, and some were evidently abetted by local communes. As ever, political fragmentation hindered the application of general policies. As for Poland and the island of Sicily, there were no trials there at all, in the former case because the Templar establishment was quite slight and in the latter because of the estrangement of its rulers from the papacy. Maria Starnawska shows that Poland was not immune from papal command – the lands had to be transferred to the Hospitallers as set down in the papal bull *Ad providam* – but that, after 1244, no endowments had been made with the direct intention of supporting the Templars in the Holy Land, so inevitably local political and economic interests predominated [24]. Kristjan Toomaspoeg's study of southern Italy and Sicily again reflects local circumstances; even on the Angevin mainland the trial was a small-scale affair, despite the rulers' familial links to the French crown [22]. Flanders was a different case in that, as both Bernard Schotte and Filip Hooghe have found [4] [23], the wars with France impinged on all aspects of Flemish society, including the military orders. Nevertheless, even though there was conflict between the Templars and the authorities in Ypres in the early fourteenth century, it was not relevant to the trial. Templars from Flanders who confessed did so because they were enveloped in the French proceedings. As a means of enabling Clement V to take over the proceedings, the bull *Pastoralis praeeminentiae*, which in November 1307 extended the trial to other countries, was a failure.

The trial was much more prolonged than Philip the Fair and his advisers had envisaged. In some senses the settlement at Vienne, under which the Templar lands were transferred to the Hospital, shows that the French had accepted that, whatever their original goals, they were not about to achieve their own way. Inevitably, however, the actual mechanics of the transfer were likely to be painful. The Polish example is instructive; where the Hospitallers were already well established the take-over was relatively easy, but in places where other local interests were involved the whole procedure took much longer [24]. Simon Phillips describes the immense challenge this presented to an order already deeply involved in the difficult task of creating a new base at Rhodes [19]. The lands in England were eventually absorbed by the Hospital, but to achieve this end required negotiating skills, bribery, litigation and above all, persistence. The Hospitaller survey of its English properties of 1338 shows that this had still not been completed by this date. Even without deliberate obstruction the task was formidable, for the sheer size of the grant threw up innumerable logistical problems, while the escalating costs meant that any gain by the Hospital was essentially long term. However, as Theresa Vann demonstrates, the Hospitallers' needs on Rhodes were immediate, and they were evidently hindered by the reluctance of local priories to use revenues from Templar properties for payment to the central convent on the island [27].

John Walker's paper brings this collection to an appropriate conclusion [28]. The trial of the Templars is not a subject which is of interest exclusively to professional historians, for in the last twenty years it has attracted a much wider public, apparently not yet sated with stories of the Templars. There is an evident desire for simplification in a complicated world which makes 'conspiracy' an attractive portmanteau explanation. At the same time there is a pervasive public mistrust of the 'experts', whose knowledge in any field from medicine to dancing is set aside in favour of 'the real truth', assertively stated and bullishly promoted. Walker's piece shows that there is no evidence for any of it, but then it was never about the evidence in the first place.

PART I
Before the Trial

Chapter 1
Could Alleged Templar Malpractices Have Remained Undetected for Decades?

Alan Forey

In recent years credence has been given by some writers to a number of the accusations made against the Templars in the early fourteenth century, especially those relating to admission ceremonies: it has been maintained that denial of Christ, spitting on the cross and indecent kissing did occur, even if the Templars were not heretics.[1] If Templar testimonies are to be believed, malpractices had been taking place for a least half a century.[2] The arguments which have recently been advanced about Templar guilt may be questioned in various ways, but this paper will focus merely on the question whether malpractices could have remained sufficiently unknown for no action to be taken for that length of time.

Admittedly, during the trial a number of witnesses stated that the Templars had long been known for indecent kissing. Yet such reports had not usually been taken seriously: a Franciscan said that he and his family had joked about it when a kinsman was about to enter the Temple, and the Templar James of Troyes stated that he had heard of it before taking his vows, but added that he would not have entered the order if he had believed it.[3] The reaction suggests that the reports were no more than scurrilous rumours which were not thought to have any foundation;

---

1 Barbara Frale, *L'ultima battaglia dei Templari: Dal codice ombre d'obbedienza militare alla costruzione del processo per eresia* (Rome, 2001); eadem, *Il papato e il processo ai Templari: L'inedita assoluzione di Chinon alla luce della diplomatica pontificia* (Rome, 2003); eadem, 'The Chinon Chart: Papal Absolution to the Last Templar, Master Jacques de Molay', *Journal of Medieval History*, 30 (2004), 109–34; Alain Demurger, *Chevaliers du Christ: Les ordres religieux-militaires au moyen âge, XIe–XVIe siècle* (Paris, 2002), p. 223; idem, *Les Templiers: Une chevalerie chrétienne au moyen âge* (Paris, 2005), pp. 484–94; Arnaud de la Croix, *L'ordre du Temple et le reniement du Christ* (Paris, 2004); Jonathan Riley-Smith, 'Were the Templars Guilty?', in *The Medieval Crusade*, ed. Susan J. Ridyard (Woodbridge, 2004), pp. 107–24.

2 *PT*, vol. 2, p. 8; *UT*, vol. 2, pp. 64–5; *PUT*, vol. 2, p. 318 doc. 152; *EUT*, p. 326; Telesforo Bini, 'Dei Tempieri e del loro processo in Toscana', *Atti della Reale Accademia Lucchese di Scienze, Lettere ed Arti*, 13 (1845), 491; Jules Loiseleur, *La doctrine secrète des Templiers* (Paris, 1872), p. 202.

3 *PT*, vol. 1, pp. 257, 454; see also ibid., vol. 1, p.183; vol. 2, pp.139, 153, 223; Oxford, Bodleian Library, MS Bodley 454, fols 93, 94–94v, 157v; David Wilkins, ed., *Concilia magnae Britanniae et Hiberniae*, 4 vols (London, 1737), vol. 2, p. 360; *UT*, vol. 2,

and the ecclesiastical authorities, if they were aware of them, had presumably regarded them in this light. If the reports had been based on fact, it would also be surprising if this was the only matter which had become known. The evidence of non-Templar witnesses at the trial certainly does not suggest widespread awareness of other alleged abuses in the decades before 1307. Most non-Templars either stated that they knew nothing of the main accusations, or merely voiced suspicions or drew inferences, based usually on the secrecy of Templar chapters but also on other circumstances such as the distress apparently shown by some recruits after their reception.[4] More specific claims were few. Even if these claims were accepted, it would not be an indication of widespread knowledge of alleged abuses in the decades before the trial. In fact these specific assertions should not be accepted unquestioningly even to indicate that some precise knowledge existed long before the arrest of the Templars. They were all made several years after Philip IV had begun proceedings against the order, and some statements by outsiders related to reports circulating after proceedings had begun, while in some cases it is not clear when claims were first alleged to have been voiced. Almost all were made in the British Isles, which suggests that they reflect general attitudes towards the order rather than providing informed comment; in the Iberian Peninsula and Cyprus, where the Templars still had a military role and the order was not seen by some merely as a privileged and wealthy institution, almost no-one claimed any detailed knowledge of abuses.[5]

---

pp. 87, 382; *The Trial of the Templars in Cyprus: A Complete English Edition*, ed. and trans. Anne Gilmour-Bryson (Leiden, 1998), p. 415; *PUT*, vol. 2, p. 375 doc. 157.

4 For reports of distressed recruits, see MS Bodley 454, fols 96, 98v–99; Wilkins, *Concilia*, vol. 2, pp. 362–3; *PT*, vol. 1, pp.184, 454–5; *PUT*, vol. 2, p. 374 doc. 157; Antonio Benavides, *Memorias del rey D. Fernando IV de Castilla*, 2 vols (Madrid, 1860), vol. 2, p. 636; Fidel Fita y Colomé, *Actas inéditas de siete concilios españoles celebrados desde el año 1282 hasta el de 1314* (Madrid, 1882), p. 98.

5 For non-Templar witnesses, see MS Bodley 454, fols 59v–62v, 91v–100, 151–154, 157v–159 (incompletely edited in Wilkins, *Concilia*, vol. 2, pp. 348–9, 358–64, 378–80, 381–3); *Annales Londonienses*, in *Chronicles of the Reigns of Edward I and Edward II*, ed. William Stubbs, 2 vols (London, 1882–3), vol. 1, pp. 180–98; Barcelona, Archivo Capitular, codex 149A, fols 57v–59; codex 149B, fol. 6; *PT*, vol. 1, pp. 175–7, 182–7, 454–9, 642–8; *PUT*, vol. 2, pp. 372–6 doc. 157; *UT*, vol. 2, pp. 79–97, 152–65, 376–99; *Trial in Cyprus*, ed. Gilmour-Bryson, pp. 51–75, 405–41; Josep Maria Sans i Travé, 'L'inedito processo dei Templari in Castiglia (Medina del Campo, 27 aprile 1310)', in *Acri 1291: La fine della presenza degli ordini militari in Terra Santa e i nuovi orientamenti nel XIV secolo*, ed. Francesco Tommasi (Perugia, 1996), pp. 261–3; Benavides, *Memorias*, vol. 1, pp. 635–7; Fita y Colomé, *Actas inéditas*, pp. 95–8. The evidence of non-Templar witnesses is discussed by Anne Gilmour-Bryson, 'Testimony of Non-Templar Witnesses in Cyprus', in *MO*, 1, pp. 205–11, and 'The London Templar Trial Testimony: "Truth", Myth, or Fable', in *A World Explored: Essays in Honour of Laurie Gardiner*, ed. Anne Gilmour-Bryson (Melbourne, 1993), pp. 49–50, 52–6, although the latter article is based only on the testimonies published by Wilkins.

It is, of course, true that only on a few points could outsiders easily have gained first-hand knowledge of alleged abuses. A number of non-Templar priests testified during the trial that they had assisted at services conducted by Templar chaplains, and would therefore have known if the latter had omitted the words of consecration in the Mass. In fact they testified to the innocence of the order's chaplains on this point.[6] If this accusation had been generally true, it would have become widely known. But non-Templars were not present at chapters, where most of the abuses – including those which have featured in recent discussions – were alleged to have occurred. During the trial, stories were admittedly told of attempts to eavesdrop on Templar chapters, but these were always reported at second or third hand, and hardly carry conviction.[7]

It might, however, be suggested that it was almost inevitable that outsiders would have overheard comments made by Templars, as many non-Templars worked in the order's convents and lived in close proximity with brothers: one Templar stated during the trial that secular priests in the order's service ate with brothers and slept in the same dormitory.[8] Some outsiders were in the order's service in this way for many years,[9] and it is likely not only that they would have heard about any abuses but also that some would have spoken out. In fact a number of outsiders joined the order after serving it for a long period.[10]

Abuses could alternatively have become known because Templars themselves publicly denounced them. The impression given by many statements made during the trial is that brothers objected to the practices allegedly occurring at admission ceremonies, but did not speak out openly. Templar representatives addressing the papal commissioners in Paris argued, however, that this would not have happened they spoke of:

> the many noble and powerful men from various lands and countries – some of them of considerable age and many renowned in the world, and born of leading families – who, inspired by zeal for the orthodox faith, have made their profession in the order of the Temple, remaining in it until the end of their lives. If such men had known, seen or heard of anything dishonest in the order of the Temple, especially the so detestable insults and blasphemies of the name of

---

6 *UT*, vol. 2, pp. 380, 382, 383, 389; *Trial in Cyprus*, ed. Gilmour-Bryson, pp. 411, 414, 416, 425; Sans i Travé, 'Inedito processo', pp. 261–3; MS Bodley 454, fol. 62v; Wilkins, *Concilia*, vol. 2, p. 349.

7 MS Bodley 454, fols 92–92v, 95v–96, 98–98v; Wilkins, *Concilia*, vol. 2, pp. 359, 361, 362; *UT*, vol. 2, p. 80; *Annales Londonienses*, pp. 183–4.

8 *PT*, vol. 1, p. 145.

9 *UT*, vol. 2, pp. 378, 379, 381, 383; *Trial in Cyprus*, ed. Gilmour-Bryson, pp. 409, 410, 414, 416; Sans i Travé, 'Inedito processo', pp. 261–2; Fita y Colomé, *Actas inéditas*, pp. 95–6; Benavides, *Memorias*, vol. 1, p. 635.

10 *PT*, vol. 1, pp. 266, 275, 614; vol. 2, p. 125.

> Jesus Christ, they would have cried out against them and revealed everything to the whole world.[11]

If admission ceremonies had taken place in the way in which they were described by many brothers and if the latter's reaction was as related in many testimonies, it seems likely that many would in fact have spoken out, as the denial of Christ and spitting or trampling on the cross were certainly not trivial matters in any circumstances. In addition, recruits joining an order whose stated purpose was the defence of Christendom, could hardly have taken such procedures lightly, especially at a time when the Church was vigorously seeking out suspected heretics. Some Templar witnesses, however, claimed that they were too frightened to leave the order or to speak out.[12] But the Temple was not an enclosed order and it was not difficult to abscond, and the power which the Temple itself could exert over deserters was limited. When brothers did desert, it was usually necessary for the order to invoke the aid of ecclesiastical and especially secular authorities, as it was unable to take effective action itself.[13] This situation is exemplified by one apostate's comment that 'after he left, he was no less afraid of his father and family, who wanted to take him and put him back in the order, even though he was unwilling, than of the Templars themselves'.[14] It should also be remembered that in western Europe Templars commonly joined the order at the house nearest to their place of residence, and were in a position to turn for support to their families, some of which were of considerable local standing. Gerald of Causso did argue that he would not have been believed if he had spoken out, and that in any case he needed a livelihood.[15] Obviously for some, entry to the order was a means of providing a living and this could have dissuaded them from leaving, but this was not true of all, and if several had spoken out together they were likely to have been taken seriously, especially when heresy was a widespread problem; and an individual would commonly be believed by his own family. The comments made by Templars about not daring to leave or speak out were probably merely attempts to exonerate themselves for not revealing the abuses to which they had confessed, and do not reflect the reality of the recruits' situation.[16]

---

11 *PT*, vol. 1, pp. 202–3; cf. Francesco Tommasi, 'Interrogatorio di Templari a Cesena (1310)', in *Acri 1291*, pp. 289, 294–5, 297.

12 Such comments were, for example, frequently made by those interrogated at Clermont: *Le procès des Templiers d'Auvergne (1309–1311)*, ed. Roger Sève and Anne-Marie Chagny-Sève (Paris, 1986), passim.

13 Alan Forey, 'Desertions and Transfers from Military Orders (Twelfth to Early-Fourteenth Centuries)', *Traditio*, 60 (2005), 188–90.

14 *UT*, vol. 2, p. 46.

15 *PT*, vol. 1, p. 387.

16 The same can be said of the Templar who claimed that he had not spoken out because he did not want to lose the important status he had in the order, and did not wish

Of course, a number of Templars did leave the order. Some were expelled for lying at their admission ceremony and were restored to spouses, lords or creditors;[17] some transferred to other religious orders, either because they sought a different – and often stricter – way of life, or because of offences which they had committed in the Temple; and some merely apostatised and returned to the world.[18] There is no evidence to suggest that these readily spoke out about the alleged abuses in the decades before the trial.[19] Yet, particularly for deserters returning to the world, of whom there was a considerable number, there would have been good reason to do so. Apostasy was a serious offence, and from 1298 incurred automatic excommunication.[20] Deserters were hunted fugitives, pursued by secular and ecclesiastical authorities; and if they were caught they were subjected to a lengthy and heavy penance. There would therefore have been a strong incentive for them to expose alleged malpractices and in this way to justify desertion, and it is difficult to believe that, if the accusations against the Templars had been true, they would not have done so. If it is argued that they were forbidden to reveal what happened in chapters, it may be countered that by deserting they had already shown a readiness to break their vows.

Many Templars did claim, however, that, even though they had not left the order or spoken out publicly, they had confessed to priests about malpractices before the brothers' arrest; yet this seems not to have led to public knowledge of abuses. Over 40 per cent of those who admitted to major charges before the papal commissioners in Paris said that they had confessed before 1307, as did 18 of the 40 brothers who accepted the validity of some of the main accusations at Clermont in 1309. Less than a fifth of these confessions were said to have been made to Templar chaplains. Most were to outsiders, especially friars. If the testimony of these Templars is accepted, they would have represented only a portion of the confessions of this kind which were made, for there would no doubt have been others by Templars who had died in the decades up to 1307.

---

to be remembered as the first to bring about the destruction of the Temple: *PT*, vol. 2, pp. 290–1.

17 See, for example, *PT*, vol. 1, p. 605; vol. 2, p. 44; Joseph Delaville Le Roulx, 'Un nouveau manuscrit de la règle du Temple', *Annuaire-Bulletin de la Société de l'Histoire de France*, 26 (1889), 207 art. 45; *The Catalan Rule of the Templars: A Critical Edition and English Translation from Barcelona, Archivo de la Corona de Aragón, Cartas Reales, MS 3344*, ed. Judi Upton-Ward (Woodbridge, 2003), p. 78 art. 177.

18 On transfers and desertions, see Forey, 'Desertions and Transfers', 143–200.

19 The Templar John of Todi, himself an apostate, testified that he had encountered a number of other apostates, but they had never mentioned any errors in the order: Tommasi, 'Interrogatorio di Templari a Cesena', p. 292.

20 Two Franciscans in England reported comments allegedly made – not in confession – by a former Templar chaplain: according to one, he had spoken of four idols kept by the Templars in England, but the other mentioned only *capita*; and it is not clear when the remarks were supposed to have been made: *UT*, vol. 2, pp. 92–3.

There are, however, some questionable aspects of the claims made by Templars. Some said they had confessed more than once about Templar malpractices, and had been absolved and undergone penance on more than one occasion. In some instances this claim might be explained by participation in several admission ceremonies.[21] Yet in many instances testimonies provided no justification for repeated confessions, absolutions and penances. Several claimed to have confessed more than once about the alleged practices after they had apostatised. Gerard of Passagio asserted that although he had confessed to a papal legate almost immediately after leaving the order, he had confessed again within two months to the bishop of Trier.[22] James of Bregecuria said that after apostatising he had confessed first to the bishop of Amiens and a year later to the abbot of a monastery near Amiens.[23] Pons of Masualier, who was not an apostate but who said that he had been present at no admission ceremonies other than his own, claimed to have confessed about the practices perpetrated at such ceremonies first to a secular priest and later to a Franciscan, while Iterius of Rochefort, who said that he had not seen any other brother admitted, maintained that he had confessed for a second time four years after his first confession;[24] and several brothers interrogated at Clermont in 1309 said they had confessed about the alleged abuses more than once (*pluries*) or to several priests, even though they had been present at no receptions other than their own.[25] Furthermore, although many claimed to have confessed about the alleged practices almost immediately after being received into the order, some said that they had done so only years later. Iterius of Rochefort said that he had first confessed four years after entering the order and the apostate James of Bregecuria stated that he had taken action five years after becoming a Templar, while John of Cassanhis apparently waited eleven years before confessing.[26] This provides a further reason for questioning the accuracy of claims. Some also had a suspiciously precise memory of penances allegedly imposed many years earlier. Giles of Rotangi apparently remembered that 26 years earlier he had received a penance of fasting on bread and water for five Saturdays, and he also recalled the details of two further penances supposedly imposed for the same reason.[27] Dominic of Dijon stated that the penance imposed 50 years earlier was that he should wear a hair shirt for three years, but that this had been commuted after a year to fasting on bread and water on Fridays for seven years.[28] As Templars

21 See, for example, *PT*, vol. 1, pp. 466–8.

22 Ibid., vol. 1, pp. 219–20.

23 *UT*, vol. 2, p. 46.

24 *PT*, vol. 1, p. 612; *UT*, vol. 2, pp. 47–8.

25 *Procès d'Auvergne*, pp. 129–30, 159–60, 174–5, 191–2, 204–5.

26 *PUT*, vol. 2, p. 322 doc. 153.

27 *PT*, vol. 1, pp. 467–8.

28 Ibid., vol. 1, p. 633–4. Here I differ from Anne Gilmour-Bryson, 'The Templar Trials: Did the System Work?', *Medieval History Journal*, 3 (2000), 52, who accepts the statements of Iterius of Rochefort partly because of his detailed description of penances.

were apparently expected to go to confession three times a year,[29] and no doubt had a variety of penances imposed on them, it would be surprising if they had a precise recollection of penances undertaken several decades earlier. It is also to be noted that although Dominic of Dijon stated that the priest he first approached had said that he did not have the power to absolve for the relevant offences,[30] others claimed to have been absolved by clerics of any standing.[31]

Nor do the claims made by Templars on this matter receive support from clergy who had heard Templar confessions. During the trial, some remarked that the brothers whose confessions they had heard seemed to be good Christians, and none stated that Templars had confessed on matters of which the order stood accused.[32] Admittedly none of these comments was made by French clerics, but no priest in France appears to have volunteered information about unorthodox confessions.

It is also difficult to believe that, if confessions had been made in the manner stated, no action other than the imposition of individual penances would have been taken by confessors. Not only were confessions supposedly commonly made to friars; they were not infrequently said to have been made to bishops and the patriarch of Jerusalem. If the claims were true some individual clergymen would have heard more than one confession about Templar malpractices. Two Templars, for example, claimed to have confessed to the same *lector* of the Franciscans at Auxerre[33] – he was reportedly equally *stupefactus* on both occasions – and at least one patriarch of Jerusalem would have heard two or more confessions, as there were more alleged confessions than patriarchs in the relevant period.[34] And if similar confessions had been made by others who were dead by 1307, it is likely that many would have heard repeated confessions. It may, of course, be argued that confessions were confidential, but confessors could have spoken in general terms of what had been said to them, without identifying individuals: certainly, as has been mentioned, during the trial priests were willing to comment on the nature of confessions made by Templars. It has also been argued that confessors – although apparently expressing stupefaction – realised that Templars were not

---

29 *PT*, vol. 1, pp. 140, 398, 508; vol. 2, p. 230; *UT*, vol. 2, pp. 41, 49, 52; Tommasi, 'Interrogatorio di Templari a Cesena', p. 293.

30 *PT*, vol. 1, pp. 633–4; cf. ibid., vol. 1, pp. 579–80, 593; vol. 2, p. 131.

31 Ibid., vol. 1, pp. 210, 246, 347, 372, 517, 545, 573, 585, 612; vol. 2, p. 76.

32 *PUT*, vol. 2, pp. 374–5 doc. 157; Sans i Travé, 'Inedito processo', p. 262. Claims by non-Templar witnesses that brothers had confessed to priests about some of the main charges were made at second hand: *UT*, vol. 2, pp. 79, 81, 87, 89, 90; Wilkins, *Concilia*, vol. 2, p. 359; MS Bodley 454, fols 91v–92.

33 *PT*, vol. 1, pp. 339–40, 342–3.

34 *PUT*, vol. 2, p. 326 doc. 154; *UT*, vol. 2, p. 59; *Procès d'Auvergne*, pp. 143, 188; Frale, *Il papato e il processo*, p. 204. See also *PUT*, vol. 2, pp. 356, 358 doc. 156 for two alleged confessions to John, bishop of Le Puy.

heretics.[35] Yet if alleged confessions had been similar to the testimonies given during the trial, it is difficult to see how confessors could have been so sure that there was no heresy in the order; as has been noted, a denial of Christ made in any circumstances was scarcely a trivial matter. In a period when popular heresy was still regarded as a serious threat to the Church, it is difficult to believe that clerics in positions of authority would have taken no action.

It may be suggested that the alleged confessions about malpractices made before 1307 in fact provide a further instance of brothers' seeking to distance themselves from the abuses which they had admitted took place. Just as they claimed that they had denied Christ with their mouths but not their hearts, and had spat near, not on, the cross, and that they had committed these acts only because of threats and violence, so an alleged confession could show that they had repented of what they admitted had been done, and sought absolution. Of course, in some cases brothers may have been referring to confessions which had actually taken place, but the important issue is what had been confessed. If they had confessed in the way they claimed, it is difficult to believe that abuses could have remained hidden.

It might, of course be argued that the likelihood of abuses becoming known would have depended on their extent. While some have implied that they were widespread,[36] it has also been maintained that they existed in only a minority of commanderies in France, and were carried from there to Italy and the East.[37] Yet the latter argument has hardly been substantiated.[38] As so many confessed in France, it is difficult to understand the claim that abuses were practised in only a few houses. The criteria adopted for judging the validity of confessions are not clear: it is merely argued that certain themes – such as being spared illicit acts during admission ceremonies and going to confession about what had happened on these occasions – recur in a number of testimonies, and that some comments are 'so circumstantial that they could hardly have been invented'. It might, of course, be pointed out that – as has already been seen with regard to alleged confessions – themes could recur for a variety of reasons, and that to fabricate detailed evidence to convince an interrogator does not require a great deal of ingenuity. Yet, if some testimonies were to be accepted on these grounds, it would seem to follow that others which admit malpractices could also be true: it is difficult to draw a line between acceptable and unacceptable evidence. It would even have to be admitted that some of those who maintained their innocence in Cyprus could have been involved in abuses. In this context it has further been stressed how isolated many

---

35 Demurger, *Templiers*, p. 492. Several Templars claimed that they had been asked by confessors whether they had acted from the heart: *PT*, vol. 1, pp. 493, 498.

36 This position is adopted in the writings of Frale and Demurger.

37 Riley-Smith, 'Were the Templars Guilty?', p. 124. Gilmour-Bryson, 'The Templar Trials', p. 42, states that 'there may have been some untoward behaviour on the part of some of the members, especially in rural or isolated areas'; but she does not elaborate.

38 Some Templars did say that they thought that abuses were not universal, but their comments should not be unquestioningly accepted.

Templar commanderies were,[39] but it is also argued that abuses spread from one house to another. The isolation of Templar houses may in fact be questioned, for there was usually a considerable interchange of personnel between houses within a province; in any case, some of the testimonies which seem to be accepted relate to major convents, such as Paris and Toulouse.[40] In fact no attempt has been made to identify the houses where abuses supposedly occurred. Nor is it explained how the alleged practices came to be transferred from one house to another: is it to be presumed that an incoming brother – without any central ruling – persuaded his new colleagues to adopt usages which suggested heresy and apostasy? If evidence such as that about confessions is accepted, the numbers of Templars involved in abuses would in any case have been considerable. And even if abuses had been limited to certain houses, they were nevertheless likely to become sufficiently known to attract the attention of the ecclesiastical authorities.

To ask whether malpractices could have remained undetected represents of course only one strand in the discussion of the acceptability of claims that abuses did take place, and needs to be set alongside examinations of other aspects of the evidence, as those who have advanced such claims have given too little consideration to possible objections to their arguments.

[39] Riley-Smith, 'Were the Templars Guilty?', p. 123.

[40] *PT*, vol. 1, pp. 404, 589–90; Riley-Smith, 'Were the Templars Guilty?', pp. 118–19.

Chapter 2

The Election of the Templar Master Jacques de Molay

Anthony Luttrell

How and when the last Templar master Jacques de Molay was elected is a matter on which authoritative publications disagree, sometimes on the basis of evident or probable misinterpretations.[1] Marie Luise Bulst-Thiele in 1974 dated Molay's election to 1293,[2] as did Barbara Frale in 2001;[3] in 1994 Malcolm Barber gave 1292 or 1293;[4] in 1996 the present author pointed to a text, already in print, issued by Molay as master at Nicosia on 20 April 1292, and gave April 1292 as the election date;[5] 1292 has subsequently been accepted, for example by Alain Demurger[6] and Pierre-Vincent Claverie.[7] All may be wrong.

The Templar master Guillaume de Beaujeu died on 18 May 1291 at the fall of Acre. The Grand Commander Thibaud Gaudin sailed from Acre for Sidon with perhaps ten Templars and the 'holy relics'.[8] There must have been other Templars at Sidon, probably sufficient to provide the necessary 13 electors, and there, in

---

1 Advice on particular points was kindly provided by Jochen Burgtorf, Pierre-Vincent Claverie, Barbara Frale, Helen Nicholson and Francesco Tommasi.

2 Marie Luise Bulst-Thiele, *Sacrae domus militiae Templi Hierosolymitani magistri: Untersuchungen zur Geschichte des Templerordens 1118/9–1314* (Göttingen, 1974), p. 305.

3 Barbara Frale, *L'ultima battaglia dei Templari* (Rome, 2001), pp. 18, 22.

4 Malcolm Barber, *The New Knighthood: A History of the Order of the Temple* (Cambridge, 1994), pp. 288, 387 n. 22.

5 Anthony Luttrell, 'Gli Ospitalieri di San Giovanni di Gerusalemme dal continente alle isole', in *Acri 1291: La fine della presenza degli ordini militari in Terra Santa e i nuovi orientamenti nel XIV secolo*, ed. Francesco Tommasi (Perugia, 1996), p. 86 n. 56.

6 Alain Demurger, *Jacques de Molay: Le Crépuscule des Templiers* (Paris, 2002), pp. 96, 98, incorrectly stating, however, that the text had been 'totalement négligé' by historians.

7 Pierre-Vincent Claverie, *L'ordre du Temple en Terre Sainte et à Chypre au XIII Siècle*, 3 vols (Nicosia, 2005), vol. 1, pp. 151–7.

8 *The Fall of Acre: Excidii Acconis Gestorum Collectio*, ed. Robert B.C. Huygens (Turnhout, 2004), p. 91; the French version (cited in Claverie, *L'ordre du Temple*, vol. 1, p. 95), gives ten rather than five Templars. For Demurger, *Molay*, p. 92, the *sacrosanctis reliquiis* included the archives.

exceptional circumstances, Gaudin was elected master.[9] Gaudin is last documented as alive in a letter he issued on 8 September 1291.[10] The obituary book of the Templars at Rheims placed Gaudin's death on 16 April;[11] since he was alive in September 1291 he would, if the obituary were correct, have died on 16 April 1292, and Molay would have been elected between 16 and 20 April of that year. The Temple's magistral elections of 1250 and 1273 took more than three months and over seven weeks respectively,[12] but an election lasting two or three days was not impossible. At least two masters of the Hospital, whose elections followed a procedure very similar to that for Templar masters, were chosen rapidly; Déodat de Gozon was elected between 7 and 13 May 1346 and Pierre de Corneilhan was chosen on the day following his predecessor's death on 7 December 1353; Gozon acted as preceptor or commander of the one-day election in which he himself was chosen.[13] It is possible that Gaudin summoned a general chapter, perhaps for Easter which fell on 6 April 1292; that he died on 16 April, possibly during the chapter; and that Molay was elected by the chapter in the normal way.[14] However the notice from Rheims was possibly incorrect, since it would mean that within at most three days of his election Molay had his own magistral seal and used it to send detailed administrative instructions to the Templars in Aragon.[15]

Two relevant texts are testimonies given in 1311 by French Templars during their trial in Paris. Their evidence was given some 20 years after the event and they were testifying under torture or the threat of torture in extremely difficult circumstances. Yet these were important matters at which one of the two certainly, and the other very probably, had been present, and so they could have been well informed. Their remarks do not seem to have derived directly from any accusations against them; nor, apart from hostility to Molay, had they any obvious motive for any invention. If their evidence was in some ways unsatisfactory, it could have been that their memories of events two decades earlier were imprecise; or that

9 *... se fist maistre dou Temple par l'ehlaison des freres que il avoit o luy*: *Cronaca del Templare di Tiro (1243–1314)*, ed. Laura Minervini (Naples, 2000), p. 226. The acting ruler of the Teutonic order, Heinrich von Bolanden, was also killed at Acre and in another exceptional election the senior brothers chose as master Konrad von Feuchtwangen who was present there: Indrikis Sterns, 'The Teutonic Knights in the Crusader States', in *A History of the Crusades*, ed. Kenneth Setton, vol. 5 (Wisconsin, 1985), p. 377.

10 Alan Forey, 'Letters of the Last Two Templar Masters', *Nottingham Medieval Studies*, 65 (2001), 161. A papal letter of 23 January 1292 to the Templar master did not give his name: Claverie, *L'ordre du Temple*, vol. 3, pp. 594–5.

11 Demurger, *Molay*, pp. 98–9, checked the original.

12 Claverie, *L'ordre du Temple*, vol. 1, pp. 146–7, 149–50.

13 Anthony Luttrell, *The Town of Rhodes: 1306–1356* (Rhodes, 2003), pp. 12–13, 191.

14 As proposed by Jochen Burgtorf, who kindly communicated his views.

15 Cf. Demurger, *Molay*, pp. 98–9, 108–9, suggesting the possibility that the news of Gaudin's death might have reached Rheims on 16 April.

they failed to express themselves clearly; or that the scribes at the trial either did not understand the technicalities of Templar procedures or that they translated somewhat inaccurately into Latin the witnesses' vernacular, in both cases the *langue d'Oc*, which French-speaking scribes may well have misunderstood.

The Templar sergeant Jean Senaud spent five years at Sidon before 1291;[16] he became commander of La Fouilhouze in the Auvergne just south of Montferrand, and in 1311 he spoke, according to the Latin version of his testimony, as follows:

> *dixit se audivisse in civitate Nicosiensi, ab ore magni Magistri qui nunc est, quod ipse extirparet aliqua que erant in ordine sibi displicencia, ex quibus dubitabat quod finaliter male accideret ordini, et hoc fuit illo anno quo civitas Aconensis fuit perdita, et predicta dixit dictus Magister in capitulo generali, in quo erant circiter quadringinti fratres, inter quos erant dictus frater Durandus Lastic, Hugo de Salhens de Alvernia, et Berbo de Lur Bergundus, deffuncti.*[17]

Jean Senaud stated that he had been present in Nicosia at a 'general chapter' attended by about 400 brothers in the year in which Acre fell, that is in 1291, and that Molay there spoke of his intention to reform certain matters which could bring harm to the Temple; Senaud could have meant within a year of the fall of Acre, that is between May 1291 and May 1292. Such a chapter would possibly have involved those Templars present in the east rather than a full general chapter attended by western representatives. The Paris manuscript of the proceedings clearly did give *quadringinti* or 400,[18] and almost all scholars have accepted that reading; there may, however, have been an error for *quadrageni* or 40. The Templars' eastern manpower had been decimated early in 1291. Reinforcements may have hurried to Cyprus from the west, but mobilization and sea transport were slow, and the maintenance of brothers in the disadvantageous circumstances of Cyprus was costly. There is no other indication whatsoever that nearly 400 Templars had reached Cyprus in 1291 or early 1292; that seems highly unlikely. Indeed, a statute of the Hospitallers, who held a general chapter on Cyprus in October 1292, envisaged the permanent presence there of a mere 50 military brothers, 40 knights and 10 sergeants.[19] A Templar chapter at Paris did decide, apparently in 1297, to

---

16 *PT*, vol. 2, pp. 136–41. Senaud was also interrogated at Clermont in June 1309: Roger Sève and Anne-Marie Chagny-Sève, *Le Procès des Templiers d'Auvergne: 1310–1311* (Paris, 1986), pp. 72–3, 118–21, noting many contradictions between his two depositions.

17 *PT*, vol. 2, p. 139.

18 Paris, Bibliothèque Nationale de France, MS Lat. 11796, fol. 191v (apparently the rough copy), which the present author has checked; the fair copy done for the pope in the Archivio Vaticano (Arm. D. 206) is not accessible; Michelet used only the Paris manuscript, which apparently has never been collated with the Vatican version.

19 Text in Luttrell, 'Gli Ospitalieri', p. 80 n. 25.

send 300 brothers to Cyprus;[20] there were more than 120 at Limassol in about 1304,[21] and reportedly 118 on Cyprus in 1308.[22]

Molay would scarcely have announced a firm intention to reform the Temple before he had been elected.[23] Two English Templars spoke in 1310 of *observantie* passed in a *magno Capitulo Cypri* or *in Magno Conventu Cypri*, and they mentioned that when Molay and the Visitor General Hughes de Peyraud visited England, which was in 1293/4, they held chapters about their statutes: *tenuerunt capitula super observancijs suis*.[24] These would have been recent reforming statutes, promulgated at the 'great chapter' held on Cyprus at the latest before May 1293 by which date Molay was in the west[25] and presumably in 1291/2. It may be that Gaudin died between 8 September 1291 and the end of that year and that at a conventual chapter of some 40 Templars, which was not technically a general chapter, Molay was elected and then spoke of his reforming intentions. All of that could be consistent with Senaud's testimony, given that the Templars' definition of a chapter or general chapter was frequently ambiguous.[26]

Hughes de Faure from the diocese of Limoges was received as a Templar *miles* in about 1286 and spent 14 years in the east. He must have served on Cyprus, and in 1311 he recounted a suspiciously bizarre tale of necrophilia and a female head which he had heard from Jean de Tanis or Tannes, *bailli* of Limassol.[27] He could well have been present at Molay's election about which he testified, as recorded in the Latin form which may have been read back to him for confirmation since

---

20 *PUT*, vol. 2, pp. 334–5.

21 *PT*, vol. 1, p. 562.

22 *Chroniques d'Amadi et de Strambaldi*, ed. René de Mas-Latrie (Paris, 1891), p. 286. In November 1307 the pope mentioned a Templar *miles* at a 'chapter' on Cyprus with Molay and 200 or more brothers, about 100 of them *milites*: *Foedera, conventiones, litterae, etc.*, ed. Thomas Rymer et al., new edn., vol. 2, part 1 (London, 1818), pp. 16–17.

23 Frale, *L'ultima battaglia*, p. 19, writes of 'una serie di urgenti riforme'.

24 Oxford, Bodleian Library, MS 454, fols 64v–65v, published in *Concilia Magnae Britannicae et Hiberniae*, ed. David Wilkins, vol. 2 (London, 1737), pp. 350–51; new transcript and other data kindly provided by Helen Nicholson. Such new legislation is otherwise unknown and no post-1291 statutes are known. Demurger, *Molay*, pp.121, 363–5, gives general chapters at Nicosia, 1291; Montpellier, 1293; Paris, 1295 and 1307; and Arles, 1296. Claverie, *L'ordre du Temple*, vol. 1, pp. 137–41, omits Paris 1295 but adds a possible but unlikely chapter in Nicosia in 1306. Note a reference of March 1311 *in capitulo generali Parisius sunt vi anni vel circa*: *PT*, vol. 1, p. 628. Demurger, *Molay*, pp. 95–6, considers that Senaud's testimony indicates a 'general chapter' with 400 brothers, including Molay and western representatives, held at Nicosia in 1291, possibly in September or October.

25 Ibid., pp. 118, 313 n. 21.

26 Jonathan Riley-Smith, 'The Structures of the Orders of the Temple and the Hospital in c.1291', in *The Medieval Crusade*, ed. Susan Ridyard (Woodbridge, 2004), 136–41; Claverie, *L'ordre du Temple*, vol. 1, p. 137.

27 *PT*, vol. 2, pp. 220–24; cf. Claverie, *L'ordre du Temple*, vol. 1, pp. 349–51.

his testimony concluded with the remark that he understood Latin: *et intelligebat Latinum*:[28]

> *et dixit quod dictus Magister, cum esset discordia ultra mare in conventu eorum de creacione Magistri, et provinciales Lemovicinii et Alvergnie, qui faciebant majorem partem conventus, vellent habere in Magistrum fratrem Hugonem de Penrando, et minor pars dictum Magistrum, prefatus Magister juravit, coram Magistro Hospitalis qui tunc erat, et coram domino Odone de Grandi Sono milite, et pluribus aliis, quod ipse consentiret in dictum fratrem Hugonem, et quod ipse nolebat esse Magister. Et cum hoc major pars consensisset quod ipse fieret magnus preceptor, qui fieri consuevit post obitum Magistri dictus Magister, cum tractaretur postea quod dictus frater Hugo fieret magnus Magister, mandavit eis quod, ex quo facerent capam, id est ipsum magnum preceptorem, facerent capucium, id est est magnum Magistrum, quia vellent aut nollent ipse esset Magister, et sic per impressionem factus fuit.*[29]

Hughes de Faure claimed that there had been discord at Molay's election; that the brothers from Limousin and Auvergne, who – he stated – formed the 'greater part' of the 'convent', wanted Hughes de Peyraud or Pairaud, a leading Templar in the west; that Molay swore before the master of the Hospital and before Otton de Granson and 'several others' that he would accept Peyraud and did not himself wish to be master; that the majority accepted Molay as the *magnus preceptor* who was normally appointed when a master died; but that when it came to electing Peyraud, Molay declared that since he was *magnus preceptor* and whether the brothers liked it or not, he himself would be master; and so 'through pressure it was done'. The grand commander was a senior conventual officer, and it is conceivable that Molay secured that office after Gaudin's election left it vacant in May or June 1291. However, almost nothing is known about Molay's whereabouts or rank before his election,[30] and had he been at Acre when it was lost the fact would probably have received some mention. Faure's testimony itself clearly meant not that Molay was grand commander of the Temple but that he was the *magnus preceptor* who was chosen to govern the order *ad interim* on the death of a master. The rule established that when a master died the chapter was to choose a grand commander to govern the Temple until there was a new master; later

---

28 *PT*, vol. 2, p. 225.

29 Ibid., vol. 2, pp. 224–5.

30 Molay was in Acre circa 1285: *PT*, vol. 1, p. 418. Demurger, *Molay*, pp. 82, 280, has Molay in Paris with Hughes de Peyraud, 'then master in France', in 1285, following *The Trial of the Templars in Cyprus: A Complete English Edition*, ed. and trans. Anne Gilmour-Bryson (Leiden, 1998), p.140, but *UT*, p. 208, read *XV*, giving 1295, rather than *XXV*. Molay was in Paris in 1295 and Peyraud became master in France in 1292.

the convent was to name a commander of the election to supervise the complex electoral arrangements.[31]

Only a few brothers from the Limousin, which formed part of the extended Templar province of Auvergne, served on Cyprus.[32] However, those from the province as a whole were quite numerous and if, as seems likely, Molay was elected by only some 40 brothers, a Limousin-Auvergne group could have had some preponderance if not an overall majority.[33] It might have supported Hughes de Peyraud who was originally from their province, in opposition to a Burgundian mastership. Barber is sceptical, judging that Faure had a 'strong tendency to repeat gossip and embroider stories',[34] but his testimony cannot necessarily be dismissed and may have reflected a real situation; Frale and Claverie largely accept it,[35] while Demurger considers it unclear, problematic and in part improbable.[36]

The divisions were not necessarily straightforward. The Templars of the Auvergne province, roughly that is from south of the Loire, presumably spoke the *langue d'Oc* rather than French. Hughes de Peyraud apparently came from

---

31 *RT*, arts 198–223, clearly distinguishing the *grant comandeor qui tiegne leu de Maistre* from the *comandeor de l'eslection de Maistre*; cf. Claverie, *L'ordre du Temple*, vol. 1, pp. 145–50. Demurger, *Molay*, p.102, considers that Molay might have been marshal before Gaudin's death because he, supposedly, had the authority to insist on reforms at the supposed chapter of 1291; that seems unlikely. Frale, *L'ultima battaglia,* pp. 18–19, assumes, without evidence, that Molay was probably at Acre in 1291; curiously, however, that was never mentioned, as most probably it would have been, either by the chroniclers or even in the extensive proceedings and justifications of the later trial.

32 Claverie, *L'ordre du Temple*, vol. 1, pp. 153, 189–90; Jean-Marie Allard, 'Templar Mobility in the Diocese of Limoges according to the Order's Trial Records', in *International Mobility in the Military Orders (Twelfth to Fifteenth Centuries): Travelling on Christ's Business*, ed. Jochen Burgtorf and Helen Nicholson (Cardiff, 2006), pp. 130–41.

33 Claverie, *L'ordre du Temple*, vol. 1, pp. 153, 187–93, 203, in general, but with no direct evidence relating to 1291/2, assumes that there were 400 Templars at Nicosia in 1291. Demurger, *Molay*, pp. 102–3, rejects the possibility of a Limousin-Auvergne majority, but on the dubious assumption that 400 brothers were involved. Idem, 'Outre-Mer: Le passage des Templiers en Orient d'après les depositions du procès', in *Chemins d'Outre-Mer: Études sur la Méditerranée médiévale offertes à Michel Balard*, ed. Damien Coulon et al., vol. 1 (Paris, 2004), pp. 224–30, analysing trial depositions, found that, of 65 brothers recorded as in the east, 24 – or over a third – were from the Limoges-Auvergne area, including seven from the diocese of Limoges. During the trial there were French translations from the Latin, while in 1310 Templars from the *langue d'Oc* requested a separate meeting: Joan Verdegal, 'La tradicion traductora de la orden del Temple', in *Las órdenes militares: Realidad e imaginario*, ed. María Dolores Burdeus Pérez et al. (Valencia, 2000), p. 345.

34 Barber, *New Knighthood*, p. 187; Claverie, *L'ordre du Temple*, vol. 1, p. 155, notes that Faure's testimony was unusual in type and the only one of its kind.

35 Frale, *L'ultima battaglia*, pp. 17–23; Claverie, *L'ordre du Temple*, vol. 1, pp. 150–7.

36 Demurger, *Molay*, pp.101–6.

Peyraud in the Dauphiné and was not therefore born a French subject,[37] but in 1291 he was commander of Bure in Burgundy within the Templar province of France. He was a competent administrator who seems only once, in about 1279, to have been in the east.[38] His uncle Humbert de Peyraud had been a leading Templar in the west; Hughes de Peyraud came, but only after Molay's election, to be visitor in France and to represent a pro-French element within the order.[39] Had the French king had time to intervene in the election, which seems improbable, Peyraud might have been his candidate, while Molay would probably have appeared likely to be antagonistic to royal interests. Molay came from the Franche-Comté and was not a subject of the French crown, and his election came at a time of hostilities between the king and the nobility of the Franche-Comté.[40] Following his election, Molay's 'Burgundocracy' favoured Burgundian and also Catalan rather than French brothers, and in 1292 only one of his six senior officers was from northern France.[41] The reported 'discord' of 1291 may have concerned policies as well as personalities, with Molay rejecting Guillaume de Beaujeu's advocacy of ententes and truces with the Mamluks.[42] Molay's early career was apparently almost entirely a Levantine one during which he is not known ever to have held office, possibly precisely because he was opposed to Beaujeu's policies. The role of the Hospitaller master, Jean de Villiers, is unknown; he was prior of France when elected in 1285 and may have been a subject of the French crown. Villiers had served in Syria and had escaped from the siege at Acre; he probably knew Molay in Syria and perhaps shared his views on policy.[43] The attitude of King Henry of Cyprus is unknown.

How the decisive 'pressure' was exerted was not explained. The Temple's regulations for a magistral election involved a full chapter of provincial officers in the east and an electoral college of 13 controlled by the specially appointed commander of the election; preference was to be given to the choice of someone

---

37 Claverie, *L'ordre du Temple*, vol. 1, pp. 154–5; cf. Jean-Bernard de Vaivre, *La commanderie d'Épailly et sa chapelle templière durant la période médiévale* (Paris, 2005), pp. 22–6.

38 *PT*, vol. 2, p. 14; Frale, *L'ultima battaglia*, p. 18, says Peyraud was never in the east, while Claverie, *L'ordre du Temple*, vol. 1, p. 155, guesses that Peyraud was at Nicosia in 1291 and met Molay there, but that seems unlikely.

39 Barber, *New Knighthood*, p. 186, says, apparently wrongly, that Peyraud was visitor and the senior Templar in the west when Molay was elected.

40 Demurger, *Molay*, p.107.

41 Ibid., pp. 181–3; Claverie, *L'ordre du Temple*, vol. 1, pp. 153, 186–7.

42 Ibid., vol. 1, pp. 86–100.

43 Coincidentally, a revised statute concerning the election of the Hospitaller master and the role of the commander of the election was passed either in 1287 or in 1292, with much further discussion of the matter in 1295: Anthony Luttrell, 'The Hospitallers' Early Statutes', *Revue Mabillon*, 75 (2003), 18–19.

already present in the east.[44] In practice it was too lengthy and too expensive to wait for the arrival of representatives from western Europe, and anyone elected while in the west could take many months to arrive and might lack eastern experience. It was the 13 electors, not the majority of the chapter, who chose a master. It may be that Molay, having by his false oath secured the position of grand commander, was able to manipulate the choice of electors to secure a majority of the 13 to achieve his own election, perhaps by bullying or bribing them.

The role of Otton de Granson, another Burgundian from the Franche-Comté, may well have been important; he was a devoted representative of the English king and had commanded the English regiment at Acre in 1291. According to various versions of a debatable passage in the Armenian chronicle of Hethoum, Granson accompanied both the Templar and Hospitaller masters to Cilician Armenia; this journey has usually been dated to 1292.[45] Demurger concludes that the three went to Armenia in 1298 or 1299 rather than 1291/3,[46] but that seems impossible, since in 1298 and 1299 the Hospitaller master was in the west[47] and so was Granson.[48] A reference in the 'Templar of Tyre' shows that early in 1294 Granson was returning from a visit to the Armenian king which he made alone,[49] but that was at the time

44 *RT*, art. 216; when in 1296 the Hospital elected a master who was in the west a major crisis ensued: Jonathan Riley-Smith, *The Knights of St. John in Jerusalem and Cyprus c.1050–1310* (London, 1967), pp. 206–9, 298–302.

45 Hetoum, *La Flor des Estoires de la Terre d'Orient ou Flos Historiarum Terre Orientis*, in RHC, Doc arm, vol. 2, pp. 327, 330. Hetoum, *La Flor*, p. 327, said that Granson was invited to Armenia in 1291 when Hayton began his two-year rule, mentioning *et aliis* from Cyprus but not the masters. However, the badly damaged French version (ibid., p. 211) gave *et les maistres de l'ospital [... ... ...] homes de lour convent*. Under circa 1299 another passage (ibid., p. 330) wrote of a summons to Granson and the two masters and their brothers; that cannot have been in 1298/9 and so would have been earlier.

46 Demurger, *Molay*, pp.114–18; cf. Luttrell, 'Gli Ospitalieri', pp. 78, 86, but that requires considerable amendment. Christopher Tyerman, *England and the Crusades 1095–1588* (Chicago, 1988), pp. 237–8, considers that it was probably after May 1291 that Granson travelled to Jerusalem, but his sources indicate the journey without demonstrating the date.

47 Riley-Smith, *Knights*, pp. 206–8. *Chroniques d'Amadi*, p. 234, said that it was the master of the Temple and the grand commander, as lieutenant of the Hospitaller master (not the master himself), who were in Cyprus in November 1298.

48 Charles Kingsford, 'Sir Otho de Grandison, 1238?–1328', *Transactions of the Royal Historical Society*, 3rd ser., 3 (1909), 152–5; Esther Clifford, *A Knight of Great Renown: The Life and Times of Othon de Grandson* (Chicago, 1961), pp.158–73; George Cuttino, 'Bishop Langton's Mission for Edward I, 1296–1297', in *Studies in British History*, ed. Cornelis W. de Kiewiet (Iowa City, 1941), pp. 147–83 (photocopy most kindly provided by Paul Crawford).

49 Minervini, *Templare di Tiro*, p. 262.

of the Venetian-Genoese battle of 28 May 1294;[50] yet by mid-1293 Molay was in the west.[51] By December 1294 Granson too was somewhere in the west.[52] His visit to Armenia early in 1294 does not necessarily exclude the possibility that Granson and the two masters earlier attended a coronation there in 1292 or early 1293, since Hethoum abdicated several times; alternatively, the chronicle was itself confused.[53] There is nothing to show that Granson could not have been in Cyprus in either 1291 or 1292; he might therefore have influenced Molay's election.[54]

Molay may have owed Granson some kind of debt since at some point he and the convent granted Granson an annual pension of 2,000 *livres tournois* in consideration of the great services he had performed for them. Molay, who became close to Pope Boniface VIII,[55] could have made the grant in order to help the pope who owed Granson money;[56] in September 1295 Boniface gave Granson 4,000 silver marks, explicitly said to be for his expenses and losses at Acre in 1291, and in 1302 Boniface awarded him 3,000 silver marks for the same reason.[57] Molay's grant was made at Paris with the consent of his 'convent' and using the lead seal of the convent in 1295, 1296 or 1297,[58] and it was subsequently confirmed by

---

50 Georgius and Johannes Stella, *Annales Genuenses*, ed. Giovanna Petti Balbi, in *Rerum Italicarum Scriptores*, ns., vol. 17 part 2 (Bologna, 1975), p. 35; this date is now accepted, e.g. in Demurger, *Molay*, p. 117; Claverie, *L'ordre du Temple*, vol. 2, p. 244; Angus Stewart, *The Armenian Kingdom and the Mamluks: War and Diplomacy during the Reign of Het'um II: 1289–1307* (Leiden, 2001), p. 97, using Arabic and other sources.

51 Bulst-Thiele, *Sacrae domus*, pp. 305, 356–7; Forey, 'Letters', 155–6.

52 Georges Digard, *Philippe le Bel et le Saint-Siège de 1285 à 1304*, vol. 1 (Paris, 1936), p. 206 n. 2, citing a lost document from the Angevin archives in Naples showing that on 18 December 1294 Carlo II issued Granson a safe conduct for his arrival somewhere. Charles Kohler, 'Deux Projets de Croisade en Terre Sainte', *ROL*, 10 (1903/4), 419, wrongly states that Granson was in England in December 1293; amend Kingsford, 'Grandison', 150/151 n. 6; Luttrell 'Gli Ospitalieri', p. 86 n. 56; and others.

53 Cf. Stewart, *Armenian Kingdom*, pp. 94–8.

54 Frale, *L'ultima battaglia*, p. 22, suggests, unconvincingly, that Granson 'acted very probably on instructions from Philippe le Bel attempting to boycott the election of Jacques de Molay'.

55 Demurger, *Molay*, pp. 121, 129–30, 135–6.

56 As suggested in De Vaivre, *La commanderie d'Épailly*, p. 39 n. 183.

57 *Les registres de Boniface VIII: 1294–1303*, ed. Georges Digard et al., 4 vols (Paris, 1894–1939), nos 826, 830, 4490.

58 Text of 1308 in *Reg. Clem. V.*, no. 2938; this text recopied Molay's grant, giving the date as Paris, July 1277 *(septuagesimo septimo mense iulii)*, on Sunday after the feast of Saints Peter and Paul. However, the date in Clement V's register is really 1287 (*octuagesimo septimo*): Demurger, *Molay*, p. 314 n. 43. That Sunday fell on 6 July in 1287 but on 30 June (not July) in 1297, while it fell on 3 July in 1295 and 1 July in 1296: Bulst-Thiele, *Sacrae domus*, pp. 307 n. 57, 357, dating Molay's grant to 1295 or 1296. The Paris 'general chapter' was in 1295 according to Radulphus de Taverniaco: *PT*, vol. 1, pp. 627–8. Molay was apparently in Italy in August 1295: Bulst-Thiele, *Sacrae domus*, p. 357. He held

Clement V in 1308 and again in 1312.[59] Molay's text was included in Clement's confirmation with Molay's name but the registered version gave the date as 1287 and Demurger argues that the grant was made in that year, that is, before Molay became master;[60] that assumes that the scribe confused the master's name rather than the date, but the opposite would be more likely and more explicable, especially as Beaujeu is not known to have been outside Syria in 1287 and was at Acre in 1286/7.[61] Granson was not in Syria between 1272 and late 1290 or early 1291.

Apparently at least seven of the 24 Templar masters were appointed 'through the direct influence of secular rulers'.[62] The master of the Hospital reported that the pro-French Guillaume de Beaujeu was chosen in 1273 'out of reverence' for the king of France and for Robert of Artois, count of Flanders.[63] Beaujeu died on 18 May 1291 and Thibaud Gaudin, elected soon after, died on Cyprus between 8 September 1291 and 20 April 1292, possibly on 16 April 1292 but equally possibly before the end of 1291. It may have been that Molay was elected at a local chapter in or after September 1291 and subsequently held a general chapter at which reforms were enacted. No solution to the problem of the date fits all the evidence; hypothesis is unavoidable. Molay's whereabouts before and after the fall of Acre are unknown. He was apparently elected in an atmosphere of dissent and pressures, possibly at a local chapter of some 40 brothers. Probably there was no formal general chapter in 1291 followed by an election chapter in 1292, but rather a single chapter possibly held late in 1291 at which Molay was elected and at which he announced some intention to reform the order; the Cyprus chapter did, in fact, pass new statutes. These events may have reflected both a clash of personalities and disagreements over general policies. There seem also to have been confrontations

a chapter general at Arles on 15 August 1296 (Demurger, *Molay*, p. 339) and was apparently in Paris some time in 1295 or 1296 (*UT*, vol. 2, p. 208) and on 24 June 1297 (*PT*, vol. 1, pp. 474–5). These dates are uncertain, since they are based on trial testimony. However, at Paris on 14 July 1296 Granson gave the Temple 200 *livres* of rent at Salins in consideration of 'les acceptables et agreables bienfaiz aides et suffrages les quiey? relegieus hommes et mes chiers amis en dieu freres Jaques de Molai a ces temps Maistres de la saincte Ordre de la cheualerie dou Temple et si deu aua? et li freres de celle meismes Relegion ont fait a mes anccesseurs e a moi deca mer et de la mer en la sainte terre e ne cesse encore de faire': Lyon, Archives départementales du Rhône, 48 H Malte 2944 pièce 2. This does not confirm that Granson knew Molay in the 'holy land', though that seems probable. It does show Granson, and possibly Molay, in Paris on 14 July 1296, perhaps in connection with the grant from Molay which he possibly made on 1 July 1296. Maybe Granson was acquiring a lifetime annuity of 2,000 *livres* in return for a perpetual rent of 200 *livres* a year.

59 *Reg. Clem. V.*, nos 2938, 4404.

60 Demurger, *Molay*, pp. 121–3, 339, arguing that Boniface's act of 1297 confirmed an (unexplained) grant made by Beaujeu in 1287. Granson did not leave Italy for Acre until late 1290: Kingsford, 'Grandison', 138.

61 Bulst-Thiele, *Sacrae domus*, p. 281 n. 93.

62 Barber, *New Knighthood*, p. 186.

63 *CH*, vol. 3, no. 3507.

between French and non-French subjects, but exactly when and how Molay was chosen remains uncertain. Hughes de Faure in 1311 apparently felt aggrieved at his memory of Molay's anti-French election coup; Philip the Fair, who was already king when Molay was elected, probably shared that feeling.

Chapter 3

Institutional Dependency upon Secular and Ecclesiastical Patrons and the Foundations of the Trial of the Templars

Nicholas Morton

When the military orders were first founded they were only small-scale operations. The Templars were a band of pilgrim knights patrolling the roads to Jerusalem; the order of the Hospital was a *xenodocium* in the holy city and the Teutonic order began as a hospice sheltering under a ship's sail. Over time, however, as their reputations grew, these institutions were able to attract the patronage that would fuel their development into international religious orders. For the Templars this process began in part with the advocacy of Bernard of Clairvaux who drew public attention to the merits of their vocation.[1] The Teutonic Knights made a name for themselves during the Fifth Crusade.[2] From these beginnings these organisations attracted the praise of landowners from across Christendom who then endowed them with the properties that would eventually combine to form commanderies and consequently the financial backbone of such establishments. The papacy also offered its support: initially by granting license for these organisations to pursue their vocation and subsequently by conferring privileges, immunities and wealth. In these ways the military orders were built upon the goodwill of princes and the papacy. This pattern of growth is well known; however, this paper will look at this subject from a different angle and ask the question: what happened when this goodwill was lost? It will examine the consequences of alienating a secular or ecclesiastical benefactor and attempt to provide some context for the greatest expression of this issue: the trial of the Templars.

One of the main characteristics of the great military orders was their ability to focus the resources of their commanderies in western Christendom upon the Latin East. This concentration of men and materials enabled their commanders in the eastern Mediterranean to deploy a force that was considerably greater than their local landholdings alone could support. Despite this, although the advantages

1 Bernard of Clairvaux, *De laude novae militiae*, in *Sancti Bernardi Opera*, ed. Jean Leclercq and Henri Rochais, vol. 3 (Paris, 1963), pp. 213–39.

2 Marie-Luise Favreau-Lilie, 'L'Ordine Teutonico in Terrasanta (1198–1291)', in *L'Ordine Teutonico nel Mediterraneo*, ed. Hubert Houben (2004), p. 61. N. Morton, *The Teutonic Knights in the Holy Land, 1190–1291* (Woodbridge, 2009), pp. 31–42.

of this structure were felt in the Latin East, they were not without their price. With the bulk of an order's troops patrolling the frontiers, its commanderies in Christendom's heartlands were virtually unguarded – after all, the orders were not set up to fight Christians – and indeed documentation from the trial of the Templars demonstrates that the Templars generally retained few soldiers in the west and maintained no great stores of arms.[3] In this way, the Templars, Hospitallers and, in some regions the Teutonic Knights, were all dependent upon the goodwill and protection of local princes and rulers for the retention of their properties. This did not cause a problem for much of the twelfth and thirteenth centuries because the rulers of the Iberian Peninsula, Italy, France and the princes of Germany were generally conscious of the value of the military orders in the defence of Christendom; however, a number of exceptions will now be examined.

It is likely that the majority of disputes between the military orders and their secular and ecclesiastical overlords were relatively minor affairs, perhaps concerning issues such as finance or local jurisdiction. It is well known that brothers came to play an important role as advisors, bankers and agents for a number of rulers, and although such positions could bring benefits to an order they could also cause contention.[4] Helen Nicholson has shown, for example, that money was occasionally wrested from the Templars by the kings of France and England. One of the most famous incidents occurred when Edward, son of Henry III of England, seized money from the Templar compound in London in 1263.[5] During the first crusade of Louis IX, 30,000 *livres* were forcibly taken from the Templars to pay for the ransom of the king of France.[6] Political considerations could also exacerbate disputes, and in 1160 three Templars were ejected from France after they had surrendered three royal castles to Henry II of England.[7] There were also times when minor disagreements took place between an order and the papacy. In the 1260s the Templars resisted the papal demand that they remove their marshal, Stephen of Sissy, from his position.[8] These instances mark a handful of occasions where minor disputes and quarrels disturbed the relationship between patron and institution.

---

3 Malcolm Barber, *The Trial of the Templars*, 2nd edn (Cambridge, 2006), p. 69.

4 Helen Nicholson, *The Knights Templar: A New History* (Stroud, 2004), p. 161. For further details of financial concerns of this kind see Helen Nicholson, 'The Hospitallers in England and Relations with Rhodes in the Fourteenth Century', *Sacra Militia*, 2 (2002), 32.

5 Nicholson, *Knights Templar*, p. 161–3.

6 Jean de Joinville, *Vie de Saint Louis*, ed. Jacques Monfrin (Paris, 2002), pp. 366–70.

7 Helen Nicholson, *Templars, Hospitallers and Teutonic Knights: Images of the Military Orders, 1128–1291* (Leicester, 1993), p. 27.

8 *Les registres de Clément IV*, ed. Edouard Jordan, vol. 1 (Paris, 1893), no. 836; Nicholson, *Templars, Hospitallers and Teutonic Knights*, p. 20.

There were other cases when an order could decisively fall out of favour with a secular prince. At such times, any lands held by an order in that ruler's country could be endangered and its general position imperilled. In 1211, King Andrew II of Hungary permitted the Teutonic order to colonise and defend the region of Transylvania. The brothers established themselves there and built seven castles, coining the name 'Siebenbürgen' for their territory. Nevertheless, after Andrew's return from the Fifth Crusade, relations began to deteriorate as fears rose that the order had exceeded its mandate. In 1225, the king finally expelled the order from Hungary.[9] This episode demonstrates the intense reliance of an order on the goodwill of the local ruler and his court. A further example of serious antagonism between a ruler and a military order can be seen in the kingdom of Jerusalem. During the reign of King Amalric (1163–74), the Templars repeatedly provoked his wrath. The first instance took place in 1165 when the Templars surrendered a castle too swiftly – in Amalric's opinion – to besieging forces and were punished with the execution of 12 brothers. A second instance took place in 1173 when Templar brothers murdered an envoy from Assassin territory, who was under royal protection. The chronicler William of Tyre records that Amalric was furious and summoned his barons to discuss what should be done with this errant order. He then travelled to the Templar compound in Sidon in person to demand satisfaction.[10] A further case can be seen in the kingdom of Sicily where in 1239 Frederick II expressed a fear that if the properties belonging to the Templars and Hospitallers were allowed to grow unchecked they would swallow up the whole island.[11] These examples demonstrate that as a military order grew in power, it could be perceived as a threat by the local ruler, provoking reprisals.[12] This situation was only compounded by the fact that the major orders were all exempt from service to any authority except the pope, potentially heightening the level of threat felt by a local ruler. Indeed, in the aftermath of the abovementioned attack upon the Assassins' envoy, the Templars claimed that only the pope held the right to judge the perpetrator of this crime.

On most occasions rulers were able to curb or expel any overly-mighty military order, but there were instances when an institution developed such power that it could defy the authority of its secular master. In 1276, Hugh of Antioch-Lusignan, king of Cyprus, claimed the throne of Jerusalem and attempted to take up the

---

[9] Klaus Militzer, *Von Akkon zur Marienburg: Verfassung, Verwaltung und Sozialstruktur des Deutschen Ordens 1190–1309* (Marburg, 1999), p. 335. Nicholson has shown how a similar scenario occurred with the Templars and Hospitallers in Hungary in later years: Nicholson, *Templars, Hospitallers and Teutonic Knights*, p. 28.

[10] William of Tyre, *Chronicon*, ed. Robert B.C. Huygens (Turnhout, 1986), vol. 2, pp. 879, 954–7.

[11] Matthew Paris, *Chronica majora*, ed. Henry R. Luard, Rolls Series 57, vol. 3 (London, 1876), p. 556; Malcolm Barber, *The New Knighthood: A History of the Order of the Temple* (Cambridge, 1995), p. 238.

[12] Nicholson, *Templars, Hospitallers and Teutonic Knights*, p. 27.

reins of power. Nevertheless, he departed in wrath for Cyprus shortly afterwards, claiming that it was impossible to rule with the continual interference of the Templars. Some years later, he tried again to impose his authority on the mainland but was again resisted; he responded by confiscating Templar property on Cyprus.[13] The relationship between the king of Cyprus and the Templars deteriorated further after the fall of Acre, and in 1306 the order was involved in a coup against Henry II. Although this was ultimately unsuccessful it shows just how serious a threat could be posed by such an institution if it were allowed to reach a position of prominence.[14]

Friction could also occur between a monarch and the military orders on occasions when the ruler saw no further use for them. Initially, kings and princes generally granted such institutions property and wealth in the expectation that their benevolence would either support the work of Christianity or be repaid with local military assistance against the attacks of non-Christian enemies. If the ruler believed that these functions were not being performed, the need for the military orders evaporated. Accordingly, in 1287, King Alfonso III of Aragon threatened to confiscate Templar lands because he did not consider them to be contributing sufficient manpower to the defence of the kingdom.[15] In fourteenth-century Aragon, with the disappearance of the border with Islamic territory, similar questions were raised about the need for the Hospitallers.[16] These examples demonstrate that a military order was generally invited into a region for a specific military purpose. If this function was no longer required the position of the order could become precarious. Overall it can be seen that, from a ruler's perspective, institutions such as the Templars, Hospitallers and Teutonic Knights were a double-edged sword: on the one hand, they could provide high quality troops for local defence or support the wider needs of Christendom; on the other, they needed to be kept in check and prevented from assuming too much power.

The military orders' relationship with the papacy could similarly result in conflict. As religious organisations the military orders were – in theory – entirely subject to the governance of Rome. Their policy, their way of life and their very existence was dependent upon papal consent. The papacy was accustomed to direct the orders' actions and even to divert them from their customary roles. In

---

[13] *Les gestes des Chiprois*, in RHC, Doc arm, vol. 2, p. 783; *L'estoire de Eracles empereur et la conqueste de la Terre d'Outremer*, in RHC, Oc, vol. 2, p. 474. The date given in the *Gestes des Chiprois* is 1278, but Riley-Smith has shown that it was in fact 1276: Jonathan Riley-Smith, *The Feudal Nobility and the Kingdom of Jerusalem: 1174–1277* (London, 1973), p. 308.

[14] Peter W. Edbury, *The Kingdom of Cyprus and the Crusades, 1191–1374* (Cambridge, 1991), pp. 112–17, 121 note 76.

[15] Alan Forey, *The Military Orders: From the Twelfth to the Early Fourteenth Centuries* (London, 1992), p. 207.

[16] Anthony Luttrell, 'The Aragonese Crown and the Knights Hospitallers of Rhodes: 1291–1350', *English Historical Review*, 76 (1961), 1–19.

1288, when the throne of Antioch-Tripoli became contested between Lucy, sister of Bohemond VII, and the men of Tripoli, Pope Nicholas IV responded by ordering the three military orders to support Lucy.[17] The pontiff seems to have emphasised his commands at the same time by conferring the ability to excommunicate disobedient military orders upon the patriarch of Jerusalem.[18] Such severe punishments could be implemented by the papacy in return for disobedience, and this can be seen in 1237 with Pope Gregory IX's actions towards the Livonian order of the Swordbrothers. Before this time the Swordbrothers had repeatedly ignored papal instructions and those of papal legates.[19] Accordingly, after a decisive defeat at the hands of the pagans in Livonia, the order was dissolved by Gregory IX and the survivors were placed under the authority of the Teutonic Knights.[20] A further example of papal censure can be seen only two years later in Gregory IX's reprimands to the Teutonic Knights. The brothers were accused of siding with the excommunicated emperor, Frederick II, and plotting against the papacy. Gregory initially chastised the order in 1239 by stripping it of its considerable privileges.[21] The following year he demanded that the brothers submit to the authority of the Hospitallers.[22] In 1247, further sanctions were imposed upon both the Teutonic Knights and Hospitallers by Gregory's successor, Innocent IV, seemingly for their loyalty to Frederick.[23] The above examples demonstrate that both secular rulers and the papacy believed that they had the right to govern and direct the actions of the military orders. Princes felt that because they had donated their own land to such institutions, they had the right to influence their policies. The pontiff, as head of the Church, required complete obedience. Patrons of both kinds were prepared to enforce their claims with severe punishments.

Given that, in most instances, the military orders were highly dependent on the goodwill of secular rulers and were bound to serve the papacy, the need arose for such institutions to work to maintain cordial relations with these benefactors. This imperative, however, could be jeopardised at times when their sponsors were at war with one another. In 1229, the Templars, Hospitallers and Teutonic Knights were placed in an impossible position. Emperor Frederick II, on crusade in the

---

17 Alan Forey, 'The Military Orders and Holy War against Christians in the Thirteenth Century', *English Historical Review*, 104 (1989), 13.

18 *Les registres de Nicolas IV*, ed. Ernest Langlois (Paris, 1886–1905), vol. 1, no. 225; vol. 2, no. 6985.

19 Henry of Livonia, *Heinrichs Livländische Chronik*, ed. Leonid Arbusow and Albert Bauer, Monumenta Germaniae Historica, Scriptores Rerum Germanicarum, vol. 31 (Hanover, 1955), pp. 209–11.

20 Eric Christiansen, *The Northern Crusades* (London, 1997), pp. 102–3.

21 *Epistolae saeculi XIII e regestis Pontificum Romanorum selectae*, ed. Karl Rodenberg, Monumenta Germaniae Historica (Berlin, 1883), vol. 1, no. 749.

22 *CH*, vol. 2, no. 2247.

23 Innocent IV, *Littere 'secrete' d'Innocenzo IV*, in *Miscellanea Francescana*, ed. Giuseppe Abate, vol. 55 (Rome, 1955), no. 246.

Holy Land, had been excommunicated and was in conflict with Pope Gregory IX. This created a major dilemma for the masters of the military orders because their active support was demanded by both the pontiff and the emperor. On the one hand, Gregory sent commands through two friars to the Holy Land who instructed the Templars, Teutonic Knights and Hospitallers to defend themselves against the emperor.[24] Frederick, on the other hand, was present in the Levant with a large force, was prepared to act in the interests of the Latin East and was the secular overlord to many of these institutions' estates in western Christendom. In this situation, the military orders were divided by their loyalties to *imperium* and *sacerdotium.* Torn between two vital patrons, the orders were pressured to take sides and risk the anger of whichever benefactor they alienated. In the event – although all three tried to find a middle path between these obligations – Frederick believed the Templars and Hospitallers to have sided against him, so he confiscated their lands in Sicily and Apulia.[25] Gregory considered the Teutonic Knights to have become allies of the emperor, and he responded by stripping them of their independence and placing them under the authority of the Hospitallers.[26] The events of 1229 serve to demonstrate how the military orders' dependence upon their secular and ecclesiastical obligations could place them between Scylla and Charybdis during times when their patrons were at war. Such situations revealed an inherent weakness in the military orders that could cause significant damage.

Incidentally, a conflict between two important patrons did not always place the military orders in a conflict of interests, and there were occasions when such a situation could work to their advantage. According to Thomas Parker, during the civil war which gripped England between 1138 and 1153, the Templars benefited from the support of both the Empress Matilda and her enemy King Stephen, raising the possibility that both were competing for the order's assistance.[27] There was the potential in such situations for an order to provoke a bidding war with their support as the prize.

As a military order grew in power and influence, the political stance it assumed in a time of international conflict became more conspicuous and was therefore increasingly perilous. This can be seen in the case of the Teutonic Knights. To take the above example of the political crisis of 1229, it is notable that although the political stance adopted by the Teutonic Knights, Templars and Hospitallers is described in many letters and chronicles, the posture adopted by the smaller orders of St Thomas of Acre or St Lazarus is not even mentioned. Furthermore, although in 1229 the position and subsequent punishments of the powerful Teutonic order were described by contemporaries, 15 years previously, when the order had still

---

[24] *L'estoire de Eracles empereur*, RHC, p. 370.

[25] Matthew Paris, *Chronica majora*, vol. 3, pp. 154–5. Morton, *Teutonic Knights*, pp. 60–71.

[26] *CH*, vol. 2, no. 1944.

[27] Thomas W. Parker, *The Knights Templars in England* (Tucson, 1963), p. 15. I am indebted to Richard Napier for this idea.

been very small, its role in political affairs had barely been mentioned. Certainly, in the conflict which emerged over the throne of Germany between Philip of Swabia, Otto IV and Frederick of Hohenstaufen during the early thirteenth century, the Teutonic order's political stance is not mentioned, even though it was patronised by each of these claimants.[28] Accordingly, it can be seen that, in times of political crisis, obscurity could bring safety for a military order.

Despite the dangers of being caught between the crossed swords of *regnum* and *sacerdotium*, there was the potential that in a scenario where an order became estranged from one patron, another might act as protector. In 1224, when the Teutonic Knights' possession of their lands in Hungary was in jeopardy through their deteriorating relations with King Andrew II, they were able to turn to Pope Honorius III for support. Honorius responded by issuing letters which placed the order's lands under his direct protection.[29] Ironically – although well intentioned – it has been suggested that this only increased the king's concern that the order might attempt to annex Siebenbürgen, and so in 1225 he expelled the brothers from his country.[30] Consequently, although unsuccessful to the point of being counterproductive, the pope's intervention on this occasion still demonstrates the principle that, having alienated one patron, another might attempt to resolve the situation on behalf of the order in question. A further example can be found in 1231, after Frederick's seizure of Templar and Hospitaller properties in Sicily and Apulia. At this time, after the peace agreement between Frederick and Gregory IX, the papacy worked for many years to restore the orders' confiscated lands.[31] To take a fourteenth-century example, it is perhaps interesting to note that, at the start of the trial of the Templars, the order turned immediately for protection to the papacy, which was entirely in keeping with the policy of the military orders

---

[28] For Otto IV's gifts see *Tabulae Ordinis Theutonici: Ex tabularii regii Berolinensis codice potissimum*, ed. Ernst Strehlke (Toronto, 1975), no. 252; *Codex diplomaticus ordinis Sanctae Mariae Theutonicorum*, ed. Johann Heinrich Hennes (Mainz, 1845), no. 12; *Archieven der Ridderlijke Duitsche Orde: Balie van Utrecht*, ed. Jan Jacob de Geer van Oudegein, vol. 1 (Utrecht, 1871), no. 2. Philip of Swabia placed the order under his protection and seems to have made a number of further gifts but these are only mentioned in subsequent confirmation documents: *Codex diplomaticus ordinis Sanctae Mariae Theutonicorum*, no. 7. *Codex diplomaticus et epistolaris regni Bohemiae*, ed. Gustav Friedrich, vol. 2 (Prague, 1912), nos. 108, 165. Frederick of Hohenstaufen subsequently became a major patron of the order and granted them land property and privileges throughout his life. See also: Morton, *Teutonic Knights*, pp. 28–30.

[29] For a selection of the papal letters written to help regain the order's lands in Hungary see, *Regesta Honorii papae III*, ed. Pietro Pressutti, vol. 2 (Hildesheim and New York, 1978), nos 5531–2, 5702, 5832, 5833.

[30] *Tabulae Ordinis Theutonici*, nos 164–5. For the suggestion that the expulsion of the order from Hungary was linked to Honorius' protection of the order's lands, see William Urban, *The Teutonic Knights: A Military History* (London, 2003), p. 36.

[31] *Historia diplomatica Friderici Secundi*, ed. Jean L.A. Huillard-Bréholles, vol. 3 (Paris, 1852), p. 280.

in earlier decades. On this occasion, however, papal support was not forthcoming, although the Templars 'continued to place their faith in the efficacy of papal action on their behalf. At no time during the seven years which the trial lasted was this faith to be justified.'[32]

The above examples have explored the nature of the power dynamics which existed between the military orders and their patrons at times of crisis. It is clear that there were instances when such an institution could pose a threat to a ruler; however, this generally occurred in locations where that order concentrated its military resources. In all other areas, the order was highly dependent on the local ruler and this reliance did not diminish significantly as the order grew in power. Furthermore, it has been shown that the position of an order was only secure in a ruler's domains whilst the perceived need for that order persisted.

The trial of the Templars marks a culmination of many of the points discussed thus far. In the early twelfth century, the Templars had been described to the Christian world as a Maccabean order of warriors who defended the Latin East.[33] The order had risen to great prominence and enjoyed much patronage on the strength of this reputation. Despite this, with the fall of the Latin East, as success turned to failure, adulation turned to criticism.[34] In the eyes of many in the west, the Templars had failed Christianity and God, and some called their usefulness into question. Furthermore, the sheer size of the Templar institution made it vulnerable, whilst its concentration of military resources in the Eastern Mediterranean left its western properties unprotected. Although these factors were not themselves responsible for the trial of the Templars, they ensured that apologists for the continuation of the order had very few cards to play.

On 13 October 1307, the Templars were arrested throughout France and their lands were seized. Although the king of France's motives are difficult to define, he was determined to bring about their dissolution, and the brothers now had very few allies. As shown above, the papacy proved 'fully prepared to sacrifice the order for these greater objectives.'[35] It would seem likely that where previously the order had been a shining example of papal power and authority, by 1307 it had become a weak spot in the papacy's diplomatic defences. Indeed, this vulnerability turned the order into a flaw in the Church's armour and therefore a potential target for 'a frontal assault on papal authority.'[36] In the past, Gregory IX had fought hard to regain both the Templar lands confiscated by Frederick II and the Teutonic order's territories taken by the king of Hungary; however, during the trial of the Templars, this support was not forthcoming. Furthermore, just as the military orders had been pawns in the conflict between papacy and empire in 1229, so

32 Barber, *Trial*, p. 89.

33 *Papsturkunden für Templer und Johanniter*, ed. Rudolf Hiestand (Göttingen, 1972), no. 8.

34 Nicholson, *Templars, Hospitallers and Teutonic Knights*, pp. 125–128.

35 Barber, *Trial*, p. 89.

36 Sophia Menache, *Clement V* (Cambridge, 1998), p. 207.

too in 1307 did the Templars become the focus of a wider game between *regnum* and *sacerdotium*.[37] Consequently, bereft of papal support, the Templars were now faced with the direct aggression of one patron and the impotence of another. Of course, the order remained in favour with many rulers of other countries, such as Edward II of England; however, the tide had turned and it was not to be long before the order was disbanded in these countries also.

Nevertheless, this was not the first time that a military order had lost the support of both the papacy and a major secular patron simultaneously, and the position of the Teutonic Knights in the 1240s forms an interesting point of comparison. During this decade, the Teutonic order incurred the wrath of both Innocent IV and Frederick II. Since the 1220s, the order's loyalties had been in demand by the empire and the papacy, and the ongoing pressure of these claims had caused political rifts within the institution. In 1249, with the death of the master, Heinrich von Hohenlohe, the order became split on this issue between two candidates for the mastership: Wilhelm von Urenbach and Günther von Wüllersleben.[38] The papacy, infuriated by the knights' continually fluctuating loyalties, responded in 1249 by permitting papal legates to strip the order of its privileges and immunities across much of western Christendom.[39] The emperor reacted by seizing the brothers' properties in Apulia and Sicily at around the same time (seemingly the emperor's standard punishment for an erring order).[40] In these ways, bereft of the support of their major secular and ecclesiastical benefactors, the position of the Teutonic order in 1249 was similar to that of the Templars in 1307; the vulnerability of the order was revealed and they were unprotected.

Despite this, there were two major differences between this event and the trial of the Templars. Firstly, by 1249 the Teutonic Knights possessed two independent territories. This was a crucial factor because such autonomy partially freed the order from its dependency upon the papacy and the empire. Ownership of the Baltic regions of Prussia and Livonia meant that although the institution was still subject to the papacy and held lands in other rulers' countries, the fundamental survival of the order could only be threatened by a military invasion. With such strength the Teutonic Knights could respond to the censure of any patron in any region not merely with the complaints of a religious order, but with the wrath of an independent state. As a result, comparing the position of the Templars and Teutonic Knights, it would seem that, whereas in 1307 the future of the Templars fell into the hands of the papacy and the secular princes, in 1249, the Teutonic Knights, by holding independent territories, had taken their future into their own hands.

---

37 Barber, *Trial*, p. 89.

38 For this discussion see Militzer, *Von Akkon zur Marienburg*, pp. 73–4; Kurt Forstreuter, *Der Deutsche Orden am Mittelmeer* (Bonn, 1967), pp. 207–9.

39 *Les registres d'Innocent IV*, ed. Elie Berger, vol. 2 (Paris, 1887), nos 4711, 4747.

40 *Historia diplomatica regni Siciliae: Inde ab anno 1250 ad annum 1266*, ed. Bartolommeo Capasso (Naples, 1874), no. 19.

Although territorial independence was a distinct advantage, it did not guarantee an order's security from its local enemies, foreign invaders or even its Christian patrons. Passing over the fact that an order's autonomous lands could be destroyed by the invasion of non-Christians (e.g. the Hospitallers' loss of Rhodes to the Ottomans in 1522) or by rebellion (e.g. the Templars' loss of Cyprus in 1192) it is vital to recognise that it was still not immune from either the reprimands of the papacy or other Christian rulers. Although, as has been said, such patrons could only seriously endanger an autonomous *Ordenstaat* with an invasion, there were cases when either the pontiff or Christian princes were prepared to take the field against a military order. A good example of this can be seen with the Swordbrothers who, along with the local bishop, ruled the Baltic region of Livonia. In 1230, the papal legate, Baldwin of Aulne, was sent to Livonia to resolve the issues which had arisen over the succession to the bishopric of Riga. As part of these negotiations Baldwin instructed the order to return lands in Estonia which had been claimed by the king of Denmark. The order resisted these demands and, in response, Baldwin raised a force of knights in 1233 and invaded the Swordbrothers' lands to enforce his instructions.[41] Admittedly, Baldwin's force was decisively crushed, however, this episode still demonstrates the principle that territorial autonomy did not dissuade the papacy from imposing its punishments upon a rogue order. Furthermore, the Teutonic Knights in the fifteenth century fell prey to the invasions of Christian rulers who attacked their lands in Prussia. These factors emphasise that, although territorial autonomy could grant an order a greater degree of protection, it did not completely shield that institution from the wrath of the papacy or from secular princes. In short, this factor alone did not save the Teutonic order in the 1240s, just as in 1307 it did not assure their survival and that of the Hospitallers during the widespread criticism of the military orders.

As a result, we shall examine a second difference between the predicament of the Teutonic order in 1249 and that of the Templars in 1307. In the 1240s, the papacy, empire and Christendom as a whole were highly conscious of their need for the Teutonic order. With the destruction of Hungary and Poland in 1241 by the Mongols, the order's provinces of Prussia and Livonia became vital bulwarks in Christendom's eastern defences. Contemporaries fully expected a second Mongol invasion, and both the papacy and the empire could not afford to permanently weaken the order's ability to resist such an attack. The order was also a keystone in the defence of the Latin East that could not be removed. In these ways, although the policy of the Teutonic Knights infuriated both the papacy and the empire in 1249, and although the order was subjected to their censure, they could not afford to dissolve the institution or even to leave it permanently weakened. In the event, the lands confiscated by Frederick were returned within two years, and there is no evidence to prove that any of Innocent's legates implemented their powers to strip the order of its privileges.

---

41 Christiansen, *Northern Crusades*, pp. 102–3.

The position of the Templars, during the trial, was very different. By 1307, the Latin East had been lost and, although the eastern Mediterranean was in frequent need of reinforcement, many viewed the loss of Acre in 1291 as a judgment both upon Christianity as a whole and the defenders of the kingdom of Jerusalem in particular. The military orders were blamed for their alleged quarrels in the later thirteenth century, and accusations were lodged against them.[42] Goodwill decreased, as did, seemingly, the will to protect them.[43] All three of the orders were exposed to criticism at this time; however, the Teutonic Knights, fighting against the pagans in Prussia and Livonia, and the Hospitallers, establishing themselves on Rhodes, still had a part to play.[44] The Templars, by contrast, found themselves abandoned or under attack from their patrons and, without the advantage of independence, were ready to fall.

To conclude, the military orders were institutions that were fundamentally dependent upon the goodwill and patronage of secular and papal patrons. This key dependency helped lay the foundations for the trial because, just as a military order was built on such patronage, so too could it be destroyed when such support was withheld. Throughout the twelfth and thirteenth centuries there were flashpoints when the policies of an order came into conflict with those of its patrons. In virtually every case, it was the order which suffered. During the wars of Frederick II and the papacy the three most powerful orders became drawn into the wider ongoing conflict between *regnum* and *sacerdotium*. This in turn pressured all three of these institutions to take sides. By the time of the trial, the military orders were tremendously rich and influential but the foundations of their power were shaken. The goodwill of Christendom – expressed previously in gold, troops and patronage – had diminished. The patrons' need for the military orders had fallen, just as their awareness of their wealth and frailty had increased. The Hospitallers and Teutonic Knights, fortified in their autonomous realms and demonstrating a continuing role in the defence of Christendom, had evolved beyond a complete reliance upon patronage, but the Templars were still vulnerable. As a result, when the struggle between *regnum* and *sacerdotium* re-opened, the Templars found themselves exposed upon this political fault-line.

---

42 Forey, *Military Orders*, pp. 208–10.

43 Ibid., p. 241.

44 Ibid., p. 223.

Chapter 4
Fighting the King of France: Templars and Hospitallers in the Flemish Rebellion of 1302

Bernard Schotte

In Lissewege, a small village near the town of Bruges in Flanders, stands the statue of a warrior who fought against the French in the battle of the Golden Spurs on 11 July 1302. Willem van Saeftinghe was a lay brother in the Cistercian abbey in Lissewege. He responded to a call to arms from the Flemish rebels against the French occupiers in May–July 1302 and stole a horse from his abbey. He rushed to the battlefield in Courtrai where he exchanged his horse for a *goedendag* (a type of short club-like pike) and fought very valiantly, killing several French knights. In the thick of the battle, Willem van Saeftinghe struck down with one blow the warhorse of the French commander-in-chief, Count Robert of Artois, who was then slain by other warriors.[1] Willem's heroic deeds are mentioned in both contemporary chronicles and official documents. He was described by chroniclers as a very tall man who was as strong as an ox. One particular document, an account of 1300–1301, suggests that Willem may have been a former Templar.[2] Other contemporary sources, chronicles as well as city accounts, give clearer evidence of the involvement of Templars, and also of the Hospitallers, in the Flemish rebellion of 1302 against the French.

When, in 1297, the count of Flanders made a treaty with the English King Edward I, it resulted in an open war with the French King Philip IV (the Fair). On 20 August 1297, the Flemish army was defeated in a battle near the Flemish town of Veurne, and consequently the French occupied most of the towns and villages in Flanders. Their attempt to annex the county of Flanders, however, was thwarted

---

1 Lodewijk van Velthem, *Voortzetting van den Spiegel Historiael (1248–1316)*, ed. Herman Vanderlinden, Willem de Vreese and Paul De Keyser, vol. 2 (Brussels, 1931), pp. 323–4; Napoléon de Pauw, 'Guillaume de Saeftingen', *Biographie Nationale de Belgique*, vol. 21, pp. 963–6; *Annales Gandenses (Annals of Ghent)*, ed. Hilda Johnstone (Oxford, 1985), pp. 91–2.

2 Bruges, City Archives, 430, Potteriegasthuis, account 1300–1301; Bernard Schotte, 'De tempelier Willem van Saeftinghe (1300)', *Brugs Ommeland*, 50 (2010) (in preparation).

by a popular revolt led by the people of Bruges and the family of the imprisoned count of Flanders, Guy de Dampierre.[3]

The revolt started in Bruges, a large trading town near the coast of Flanders. On the first day of May 1302, insurgents of Bruges stormed a castle near the town that was occupied by a French garrison. Although the assailants suffered heavy losses they managed to conquer the castle. They massacred the French garrison and looted the castle. They also burned down a manor nearby belonging to the lord of Sijsele who was collaborating with the French.[4] These events are well documented by different contemporary chroniclers. They all give more or less the same account, with only one difference, namely that, according to some chroniclers, the raid was led by one or two popular leaders of Bruges, the weaver Pieter de Coninck and the butcher Jan Breidel, whilst others mention only a grandson of the count of Flanders, Willem van Jülich, as leader of the raid. Two chroniclers have left us a remarkable story and even mention the involvement of a Knight Templar, while none of the other chroniclers mention the Templars at all.

Gilles le Muisit (1272–1353) was the abbot of the abbey of St Martin in Tournai, a French town near the border with Flanders. He has been considered by historians as an excellent chronicler with a critical mind, who gained his information by interviewing eyewitnesses and using written sources.[5] According to Gilles le Muisit, the Bruges rebels conspired together with a knight called the 'lord of Boenhem' whom Gilles called a Templar, *miles de ordine Templariorum*. His account of these events is as follows:

> *millesimo ccc secundo, illi de Brugis, prima die mensis may, coeperunt rebellare de consilo cujusdam militis de ordine Templariorum, vocati dominus de Boinem, et, inter se habita deliberatione, concordaverunt ire ad domum de Male, ubi erant provisiones facte a domino de Sancto Paulo, ex parte regis, de victualibus et de vinis. Et ad certam diem coadunati, duce eorum et gubernatore Johanne dicto Breidel, qui erat carnifex, iverunt ad dictam domum et eam spoliaverunt, atque illos, qui ex parte regis ibi erant, necaverunt.* [6]
>
> On the first day of May 1302, the men of Bruges rose in revolt at the request of a knight of the order of the Temple, called the lord of Boenhem, and, after a discussion between themselves, they decided to go to the castle of Male, where supplies of food and wine were stocked by the lord of St Pol on behalf of the

3 Jan Frans Verbruggen and Kelly DeVries, *The Battle of the Golden Spurs (Courtrai, 11 July 1302): A Contribution to the History of Flanders' War of Liberation, 1297–1302*, trans. David Richard Ferguson (Woodbridge, 2002), pp. 11–26.

4 *Annales Gandenses*, p. 19.

5 Véronique Lambert, ed. *Chronicles of Flanders (1200–1500)* (Ghent, 1993), pp. 61–4.

6 Gilles Le Muisit, *Chronique et annales*, ed. Henri Lemaître (Paris, 1906), pp. 62–3.

> king. And having assembled on a certain day, they went with Jan Breidel the butcher as their leader to the said castle, and they plundered it, and slew those who were there on behalf of the king (of France).

If the French abbot were the only one mentioning this involvement of a Templar, we might wonder if his imagination was running wild. However, there is another French chronicler, also an inhabitant of the city of Tournai, whose account of the raid on the castle corroborates the story of the abbot of St Martin. Again, the central figure in this story is the lord of Boenhem who is described by the chronicler as a Templar. Although the chronicle dates from the mid-fourteenth century, the unknown author was a reliable writer who has left us accurate accounts of several events that took place during the Flemish revolt. He describes the start of the revolt as follows:

> *L'an mil IIIc II... jour de may se releva le quemuns de Bruges contre ceulx que le roy y avait ordonné, et fu par le conseil de Bonne, liquelz estoit templiers, et prinrent à seigneur Guillaumes de Jullers, et puis s'en alerent à Male et prinrent chiaulx qui y estoient de par le roy et leur firent copper les tiestes.*[7]

> On a day in May 1302, the common folk of Bruges revolted against the men whom the king (of France) had stationed there, and they did so on the advice of the [lord of] Boenhem, who was a Templar, and they chose Lord Willem van Jülich as their leader and went to Male, where they captured those who were there on behalf of the king (of France) and beheaded them all.

These two French chroniclers, writing as far as we know independently from each other, indicate that a Templar was in some way involved in the insurrection against the French from the beginning of the uprising when the castle of Male, occupied by a French garrison, was attacked on 1 May 1302 by the Bruges rebels. The rebels were under the command of several leaders, namely the butcher Jan Breidel and the weaver Pieter de Coninck from Bruges, the grandson of the count of Flanders, Willem van Jülich, who was considered by the insurgents in 1302 as their commander-in-chief, and the lord of Boenhem.

Brother Willem van Boenhem, knight, is mentioned in a document of 1297 as lord of Boenhem, a manor near the city of Damme and also not far from the castle of Male.[8] Although Gilles le Muisit and the unknown chronicler of Tournai call him a Templar, there is no evidence to support this statement. Yet he was certainly a member of a military order, as in 1297 and 1310 'Brother Willem van Boenhem' is mentioned in contemporary documents and on the inscription of his

---

7 *Chronique Artésienne (1295–1304) et Chronique Tournasienne (1296–1314)*, ed. Frantz Funck-Brentano (Paris, 1899), p. 39.

8 Maurits Coornaert, *Dudzele en Sint-Lenaart* (Dudzele, 1985), pp. 299–302 (with a copy of the charter dated 2 February 1297).

seal as a Knight Hospitaller.[9] It is possible that Gilles le Muisit and the chronicler from Tournai who describe the lord of Boenhem as a Templar could have meant a Knight Hospitaller, because it was common in Flanders to use the name 'Templars' to apply also to Hospitallers, sometimes making a clear distinction between 'White Templars' and 'Black Templars', in reference to the colour of their habits. Even centuries after the downfall of the Templar order, Flemish common folk and clerks still referred to the Knights Hospitaller as 'Templars'. Houses in Bruges belonging to the Knights Hospitaller are described in property documents dated 1346, 1392, 1416, 1429 and 1585 as properties belonging to the 'Templars'.[10] Even Knights Hospitaller themselves were referred to as 'Templars'. In a document of 1413 for example, Brother Richard Couse, commander of the Knights Hospitaller in Flanders, is called 'lord and commander of the Templars'.[11]

Willem van Boenhem, then, was a Knight Hospitaller. We know that the lord of Boenhem fought in the battle of the Golden Spurs on 11 July 1302 where the Flemish militias defeated a French army of knights. Lodewijk van Velthem, a parson and historian from Brabant, who, in 1316, wrote a detailed and excellent account of the battle, mentions Lord Willem van Boenhem several times. He describes him as one of the bravest knights of his time: Lord Willem van Boenhem was one of the leaders on the left flank, and he personally killed several Frenchmen. He was among a handful of Flemish knights who restored the line of battle after panic had broken out during the final charge of the French knights under the command of their leader, Count Robert of Artois, and his fighting spirit was an example to many. After the French mounted charges had been stopped, the lord of Boenhem was noted as ruthless, together with Bruges militias, in the pursuit of fleeing soldiers from Hainaut who had fought alongside the French.[12] In the chronicle, the author does not specify that the lord of Boenhem was a Hospitaller, but, as already noted, we know from other sources that Willem van Boenhem was a member of this military order. Willem van Boenhem had already fought the French five years earlier in 1297, at the beginning of the French occupation. He recaptured the town of Damme and chased the French away. As with the raid on the castle in Male, this

---

9 Leo Delfos, *Het avontuur van de Liebaards 1297–1302–1304: Geschiedenis van een Vlaamse opstand 'omme die defense van den lande'* (Tielt, 1952), p. 126; Germain Demay, *Inventaire des sceaux de la Flandre* (Paris, 1872–1873), p. 322; Filip Hooghe, Walter Verstraeten and Luc Rochtus, *Het kasteel van Bornhem*, vol. 1 (Puurs, 2007), pp. 146, 456.

10 Bruges, Archives of the Office of Public Relief, Dis Onze-Lieve-Vrouwekerk, Charters, 24 (1346); Bruges, Archives of the Office of Public Relief, Sint-Niklaasgasthuis, fol. 47 (1392); Bruges, State Archives, Onze-Lieve-Vrouwekerk, 725, fols 24, 26 (1416); Bruges, Archives of the Office of Public Relief, Dis Onze-Lieve-Vrouwekerk, 169, fol. 75 (1429); Bruges, City Archives, 198, Klerken van de Vierschaar, 880, fol. 274 (17 May 1585).

11 Bruges, City Archives, 299, Makelaars, Houses in the Zuidzandstraat (1413)

12 Van Velthem, *Voortzetting van den Spiegel Historiael*, vol. 2, pp. 319, 330, 336.

event took place not far from his manor. He was clearly on well-known territory during those two military actions. Some time after the battle of the Golden Spurs, he was appointed as captain in this area.[13]

On 11 July 1302, the Flemish militias won a battle, but the king of France was not yet beaten, and a month and a half later, Philip IV personally led a new army to confront the Flemish one more time. The lord of Boenhem is mentioned again as one of the leaders of the Flemish army but, as at the battle of the Golden Spurs, he is not explicitly described as a Knight Hospitaller.[14]

We have another source, however, this time a document from the city archives, that indicates that Hospitallers, as well as Templars, participated in this military campaign. As a new French army, 16,000 men strong and led by the king in person, headed towards Flanders, the town militias in Flanders also mobilised their troops. Ghent, Ypres and Bruges were among the cities which sent troops to the border. The city accounts of Bruges give us detailed information about the strength of the Bruges communal army that participated in this campaign to Douai in September–October 1302. The communal army of Bruges left the town on 30 August 1302. It was composed of guildsmen, crossbowmen and small groups of mercenaries and professional soldiers. The numerical strength of the bands of crossbowmen and soldiers from 30 guilds was between 1,480 and 2,200 men. The town of Bruges paid for the supply wagons and horses used by these townsmen and also for those used by other small groups of warriors. When it became clear that the rebellious town of Bruges was going to confront the armies of the king of France, the town spent a lot of money to win knights and professional warriors to fight for its cause. Although the main body of the army during the whole of the war consisted of guildsmen, the Flemish armies also had small groups of professional warriors in their ranks. In 1302, 1303 and 1304, for instance, small bands of English mercenaries and archers fought alongside the townsmen of Bruges in campaigns against the French and the Dutch.[15]

Among the Bruges communal army that took part in the expedition launched in September–October 1302, one month and a half after the battle of the Golden Spurs, there were also fighters from outside the town. They are mentioned in the city accounts and we sometimes even learn the names of their leaders. Among them were 10 knights of Zeeland and their entourage, some 220 to 325 men strong, a few crossbowmen from Germany, a dozen soldiers from the city of Aachen in Germany, a small group of Dutch soldiers and three bands of professional soldiers who wore blue, yellow or grey tunics. The town of Bruges also paid for the

[13] *De rekeningen van de stad Brugge (1280–1319)*, ed. Carlos Wyffels and A. Vandewalle, vol. 2 (1302–19) (Brussels, 1995), pp. 92, 890; Delfos, *Het avontuur van de Liebaards 1297–1302–1304*, p. 126.

[14] Van Velthem, *Voortzetting van de Spiegel Historiael*, vol. 2, p. 370.

[15] Jan Frans Verbruggen and Rolf Falter, *1302: Opstand in Vlaanderen* (Tielt, 2001), pp. 173–6; Jan Frans Verbruggen, *Vlaanderen na de Guldensporenslag* (Bruges, 1991), pp. 66–7, 146–7; *De rekeningen van de stad Brugge (1280–1319)*, vol. 2, pp. 94, 487.

wagons and four horses used by 'White Templars' (*Witten Templiers*) (see Figure 4.1) who were led by their captain, Wouter die Grote. Soldiers who wore white tunics with red crosses (*soudeniers metten witten frocken ende metten roeden crucen*) received an additional amount of money, as did – mentioned in the same list – soldiers with black tunics with white crosses (*soudeniers metten zwarten frocken ende metten witten crucen*). As the men in white tunics with red crosses were specifically identified as 'White Templars', it is most probable that those who were listed immediately before them, and who wore black tunics with white crosses, were the Flemish 'Black Templars', that is, the Hospitallers. Besides, the description of the tunics can in fact only refer to Hospitallers.

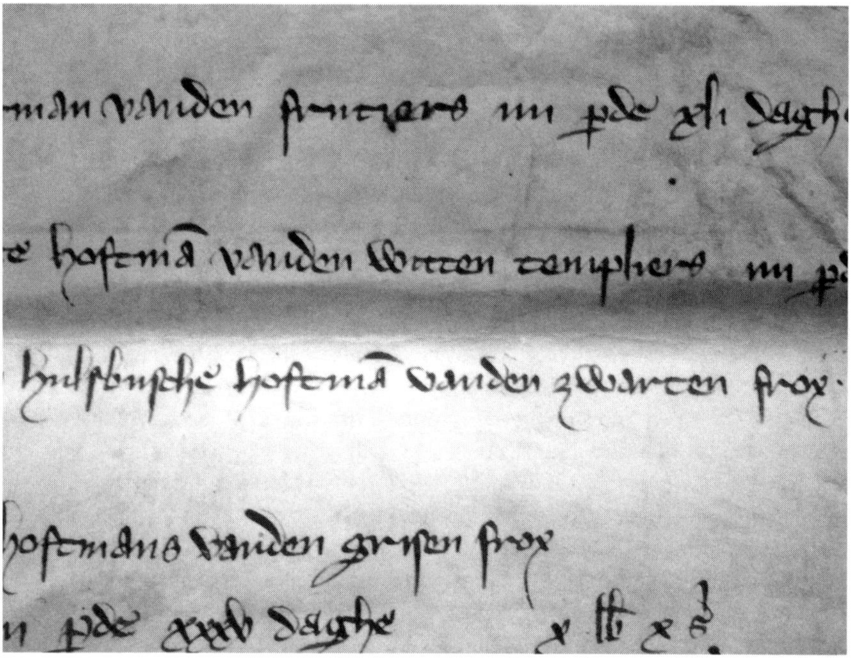

Fig. 4.1 Detail of the list of soldiers of the Bruges army who participated in the campaign to Douai in September-October 1302, mentioning 'White Templars' and 'black tunics' (Hospitallers)

Later, some of the soldiers who had participated in the expedition to Douai received further payments, among them once more soldiers with black tunics (*soudoiers as noirs cotes*) and soldiers with white tunics (*soudoiers as blankes cotes*). The captain of the soldiers with black tunics was a man called Hannekin vanden Hulsbusche (see Figure 4.1). He received money for the use of wagons and six horses.[16] We do not know anything else about the two men who led the 'White

16 *1302: Le compte communal de la ville de Bruges*, ed. Jules Colens (Bruges, 1886), pp. 163, 165–6; *De rekeningen van de stad Brugge*, vol. 2, pp. 97–9, 843–7, 891; *Inventaire*

Templars' and the men in black tunics with white crosses. Although there was an important family of knights called De/Die Grote, we have no evidence that Wouter die Grote was a member of this family. Besides, the family name De Grote (the Great) is very common in Flanders.

This city account shows that both Templars and Hospitallers participated in the military campaign of September–October 1302 against the French army. Both groups of soldiers were very small, probably not more than a handful. We can estimate, when we take into account the number of horses they needed to pull their wagons with supplies, that the Templars formed a band of 13 to 20 men, and the Hospitallers had some 20 to 30 men in arms.

We also know for how many days these Templars and Hospitallers marched with the Bruges communal army. The expedition lasted 41 days, from 31 August to 10 October 1302. The 'White Templars' served for 37 days in the Bruges army and the Hospitallers for 31 days.[17] The campaign did not result in an open battle. Although the French king had a greater army than the one that had been defeated at Courtrai on 11 July 1302, his army was less experienced, since the French had lost so many knights in the battle of the Golden Spurs, and he did not dare risk a frontal attack and engage in hand-to-hand combat with the Flemish army. For many years to come, no French army would again risk a frontal attack against a Flemish army of town militias. When, on 29 September, the Flemish army made some preparations to attack the French army near Douai, the French king and the leaders of the army decided to withdraw. They even let their camp fall into the hands of the Flemish troops. Some Flemish militias, amongst them the Bruges communal army, began to plunder the camp and went in pursuit of the retreating French army. There were some skirmishes with French warrior bands, before and after the French withdrew. One Flemish chronicler mentions the loss of 200 French knights and 100 French and Genoese foot-soldiers. The Flemish army looted the countryside and burned down a small town. They also killed some French soldiers. The army advanced towards the town of Tournai and started to plunder the outskirts of the town. On 9 October 1302, there was a battle before a gate of the town. The defenders were driven back into town and lost several men. But the Flemish assailants had no real intention of besieging the town, and went back to their camp.

On 9 October 1302, the Flemish leaders disbanded the army and everyone went home. The Bruges communal army was already home one day later, so we may assume that they were not involved in the attack on Tournai. The withdrawal of the French army, led by their king and in the face of their enemies, was seen as a disgrace by the French population. King Philip the Fair even felt the need to make a statement to explain this manoeuvre: the army had experienced (he claimed) a shortage of supplies, and the Flemish field army had taken up a very

des archives de la ville de Bruges: Inventaire des chartes, ed. Louis Gilliodts-Van Severen, vol. 1 (Bruges, 1871), pp. 84–90, 188 (*Dit es die coste van den waghene en van de perden die waren in die hervard te Duay*).

17 *De rekeningen van de stad Brugge*, vol. 2, p. 845.

good position which had been difficult to attack. The king, however, promised to launch a new offensive very soon. In reality the commanders of the French army feared a new debacle, as in the battle of the Golden Spurs, and also faced unrest in their own army. Violent clashes broke out between groups of soldiers; French town militias started to revolt, because they had not been paid as agreed, and looted the countryside around the French camp. As some French noblemen feared that these would make common cause with the rebellious Flemish townspeople, they decided to withdraw.[18]

Meanwhile, in the town of Bruges, the council was paying for all the costs incurred by the different knights and bands of warriors they had engaged. Some of them received expensive cloth, which was used to make tunics: for instance, the crossbowmen of the town received yellow and blue cloth. A band of knights, called the *Oostheren* ('Eastlords'), who had been sent as auxiliary troops by Jean de Namur, a son of the count of Flanders, were given white cloth with blue stripes. Willem van Jülich, one of the commanders during the battle of the Golden Spurs, and his knights received all kinds of cloths in July 1302.[19]

It is interesting that 'White Templars' and 'Black Templars' received similar gifts from the city council of Bruges. The city accounts of May 1302–February 1303 mention purchases of special white cloth for the 'White Templars' (*Witten Templiers*) which amounted to more than 30 pounds, a considerable sum of money, equalling the annual salary of a Bruges tax-collector. The 'Black Templars' (*Zwarten Templiers*) were given black cloth.[20] These payments of cloth indicate that Templars and Hospitallers had rendered military assistance in the same way as the town's crossbowmen, the Oostheren and the knights of Willem van Jülich, that this assistance was very much appreciated and that the town council wanted them to remain in their service.

Apparently the Templars and Hospitallers also participated in another military expedition in 1302 or 1303. Hidden in a Bruges city account, dated August (or maybe April?) 1302–31 May 1303, there is an account in a 'confiscation register' that sets out how much of the money confiscated from citizens who had supported the French king was used to pay for the wagons and horses used by a specific communal army of guildsmen and bands of professional soldiers. Among these soldiers were 'White Templars' (*Witte Tempeliers*) (see Figure 4.2), and also soldiers with black tunics (*Zwarte Frocken*).[21] Since this account is not precisely dated, it is not clear in which military expedition this army took part, but perhaps it was engaged in the offensive against the county of Hainaut in March 1303,

---

18 Van Velthem, *Voortzetting van de Spiegel Historiael*, pp. 368–91; Verbruggen and Falter, *1302: Opstand in Vlaanderen*, pp. 173–6.

19 *1302: Le compte communal de la ville de Bruges*, pp. 188–91. *De rekeningen van de stad Brugge*, pp. 803–4.

20 *1302: Le compte communal de la ville de Bruges*, pp. 189–90.

21 Bruges, City Archives, 271, Confiscation Registers, 1A (1302–1303), fols 227–229.

when the town of Lessines was looted and burned down. A Bruges army certainly took part in this campaign, although we know nothing about its strength and composition. It is also possible that the army mentioned in the 'confiscation register' can be identified with the first Bruges communal army that had left the city at the end of May 1302 to liberate several towns and villages and to assemble with the other Flemish troops in Courtrai. On 31 May, the first army left the city, and two weeks later a second army marched to Courtrai. Evidence survives only

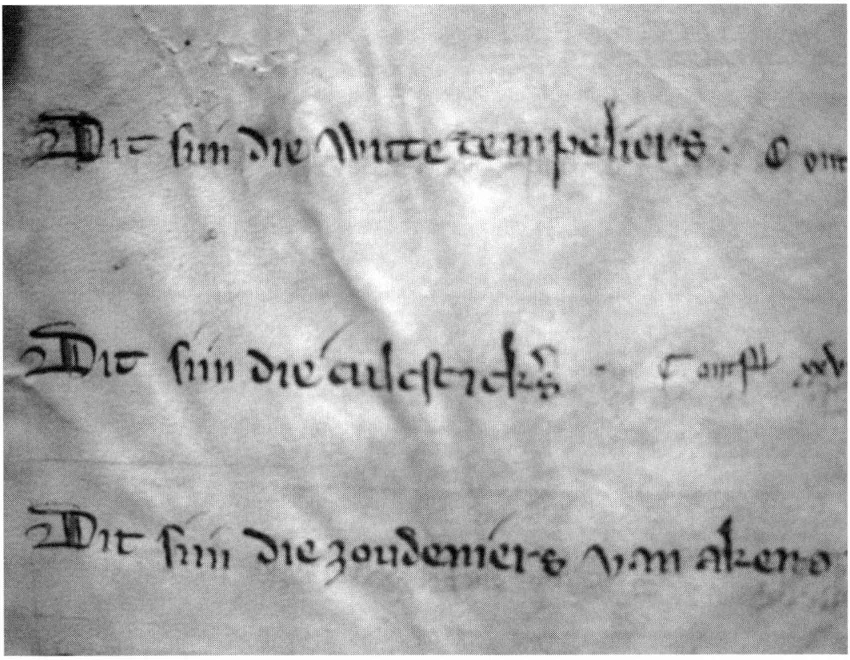

Fig. 4.2 Detail from the confiscation register, with the Bruges army that participated in an unknown military expedition in 1302 or 1303, mentioning, among other soldiers, 'White Templars'

for the strength and composition of this second army, and is lacking for the first army. The confiscation register may shed some light on this first army of Bruges guildsmen and other soldiers.[22]

In any case, these payments by the city of Bruges, alongside and similar to payments to military units involved in action against the French, indicate that Templars and Hospitallers were engaged in two military expeditions. Their engagement in the uprising went even further. Due to the imprisonment of the count, Guy de Dampierre, the county of Flanders was governed by Philip de

22 Bernard Schotte, 'Twee Brugse legers op de Groeningekouter', *Brugs Ommeland*, 43 (2003), 219–45.

Chieti, a son of the count. From 1303 to 1305 he was a zealous and strong leader of the Flemish in their battles with the French. One of his counsellors was a Knight Templar, Brother Pieter uten Sacke (see Figure 4.3), who was, together with Jan van Doornik and Sir Gillis die Clerc, mentioned as Philip de Chieti's counsellor in a document dated 14 May 1305.[23] How long the Templar had already been his advisor, we do not know. However, in 1303 (on 25 November), Brother Pieter uten Sacke and the aforementioned Jan van Doornik assisted the two exchequers of the county in their financial activities.[24] Thus, it is possible that the Templar Pieter uten Sacke was a close collaborator of Philip de Chieti during the whole of his administration (the count's son ruled over Flanders from May 1303 until July 1305). Philip de Chieti also received financial support from the Templars, as in 1306 he owed them a sum of money of no less than 1,400 pounds.[25] A few years later, in 1309, Sir Gillis die Clerc, who had been a counsellor of Philip de Chieti together with the Templar Pieter uten Sacke, was appointed as one of the three counsellors to rule the county during the absence of the new count, Robert

Fig. 4.3 Seal of Pieter uten Sacke, Templar brother and former commander of the order of the Temple in Flanders, 1304

de Bethune. The count was in France during that period, negotiating with the French king.[26] Clearly this handful of men were close collaborators of the rulers of Flanders.

---

23 *De rekeningen van de stad Brugge*, vol. 2, p. 712.

24 *Inventaire des archives de la ville de Bruges*, vol. 1, p. 191.

25 Demay, *Inventaire des sceaux de la Flandre*, p. 322.

26 *Annales Gandenses*, pp. 93–4.

Brother Pieter uten Sacke was a man with a great deal of influence. He came from a rich Bruges family and had been a member of the Templar order since at least 1272. He was commander of the order of the Temple in Flanders during the period of 1280–97, perhaps longer. Pieter uten Sacke always had a very good relationship with Count Guy de Dampierre, who was imprisoned by the French king at the time of the rebellion. The count even called the commander of the Flemish Templars his 'good friend' (*bon ami*).[27] In 1304, Pieter uten Sacke was no longer commander of the Knights Templar in Flanders, and had been succeeded by another member of an important Bruges family, Brother Jacop die Repere.[28] Nevertheless, it is noteworthy that an influential Knight Templar and a former commander of the Templars was a counsellor of the ruler of Flanders during the war against France.

All this evidence indicates that the 'White Templars' and the 'black' Hospitallers participated in the uprising. They were engaged in the military expedition to Douai and also in another unknown expedition in 1302 or 1303. The former commander of the Templars acted as an advisor to the ruler of the county. One Knight Hospitaller played a remarkable role: Lord Willem van Boenhem was a Hospitaller who fought in the battle of the Golden Spurs and in the campaign near Douai one month and a half later, and seems to have been involved in organising the revolt.

As Alan Forey has shown, it was not unknown for the military orders to be involved in holy war against Christians.[29] Given that in 1302 an anonymous French cleric was preaching that the French war against the Flemish was a holy war, perhaps the Templars and Hospitallers justified their part in the rebellion on similar grounds.[30] There certainly were 'holy war feelings' amongst the Flemish clergy, as the parson Lodewijk van Velthem observes in his book, written in 1316, that the victorious Flemish in the battle of the Golden Spurs were wading knee-deep in the blood of the fallen *Sarracins*: these thousands of Frenchmen killed on the battlefield brought their downfall on their own heads because 'they all acted against God and the orders of the pope'.[31] The Flemish Templars and Hospitallers may also have engaged themselves in the uprising of 1302 out of loyalty to the count of Flanders, the ruler of the county where they were living. There are, in the late thirteenth century, other examples of the involvement of these two military orders in local wars between Christians. Knights Templar fought at the battle of

---

27 Paul Rogghé, *De Orde van de Tempelridders en haar geschiedenis in het oude graafschap Vlaanderen* (Ghent, 1973), pp. 98–101.

28 Bruges, Archives of the Office of Public Relief, Hospitaal O.-L.-Vrouw ter Potterie, Charters, 154bis (1304); Bernard Schotte, 'Jacob die Repere, commandeur van de tempeliers van Vlaanderen in 1304', *Brugs Ommeland*, 50 (2010) (in preparation).

29 Alan Forey, 'The Military Orders and Holy War against Christians in the Thirteenth Century', *English Historical Review*, 104 (1989), 1–24.

30 Norman Housley, *The Avignon Papacy and the Crusade* (Oxford, 1986), p. 89.

31 Velthem, *Voortzetting van de Spiegel Historiael*, pp. 305, 320.

Falkirk in 1298, and some 30 years earlier a contingent of Hospitallers had fought alongside Charles of Anjou in Italy at the request of the pope.[32]

During the Flemish rebellion of 1302, there were also other warriors with religious nicknames on the pay-roll of the town of Bruges in 1302, for instance Brother Everard the Hermit with three squires, Brother Willem of Los, the *convers* (or lay-brother), and the Knight Hendrik of Cruninghe, 'the monk'.[33] The latter probably took part in the battle of the Golden Spurs.[34] Given his nickname, he may have belonged to a military order, but we have no other information about him other than that he had been engaged to fight for the town of Bruges. The same goes for the other two, who served in the army of the Flemish rebels in 1302.

Then there was the famous lay-brother Willem van Saeftinghe from a Cistercian abbey near Bruges, who fought so valiantly in the battle of the Golden Spurs. We may speculate whether he was the same Brother Willem van Saeftinghe who, in 1300, had collected money for the Templar order in Flanders, and who could have become a lay brother in a Cistercian abbey a few years later. He was obviously a man with a violent temper because, in 1308, he joined a rebellion of lay brothers in the Cistercian abbey in Lissewege, killed a monk and wounded the abbot severely – acts of aggression which resulted in his excommunication. Later on he joined the ranks of the Hospitallers to fight in the Holy Land.[35] If he had been a Templar in 1300, it is possible that his violent temper and rebellious attitude were the cause of conflict with his superiors, and that consequently he was expelled from the Templar order and had to seek a new life as a lay brother. Then, on 11 July 1302, he wrote his name in the history books. These are intriguing questions which bring us to another, even more important, question.

The Templars and the Hospitallers who fought alongside the Flemish rebels would have been very recognisable in plain view of their foe, as they wore white tunics with red crosses or black tunics with white crosses. When, in September 1302, the Templars confronted the French army which was led personally by the French King Philip the Fair near Douai, they openly defied the king who would cause their downfall a few years later. One may speculate whether their involvement in the war of the Flemish against the French, which caused so much distress to Philip IV, played a role in triggering the conflict between the king of France and the order of the Temple.

---

32 Helen Nicholson, *The Knights Templar* (Stroud, 2004), pp. 167, 169; Dominic Selwood, *Knights of the Cloister: Templars and Hospitallers in Central-Southern Occitania c.1100–c.1300* (Woodbridge, 1999), p. 45.

33 *De rekeningen van de stad Brugge*, vol. 2, pp. 82, 90, 801, 826, 887, 889.

34 Verbruggen and DeVries, *Battle of the Golden Spurs*, pp. 181.

35 Bruges, City Archives, 430, Potteriegasthuis, account 1300–1; *Annales Gandenses*, pp. 91–2; *Codex Dunensis, sive diplomatum et chartarum mediiaevi amplissima collectio*, ed. Joseph Kervyn de Lettenhove (Brussels, 1875), pp. 236–8, 241–3.

Chapter 5
The Monetary Fluctuations in Philip IV's Kingdom of France and Their Relevance to the Arrest of the Templars

Ignacio de la Torre

Upon Philip IV's accession to the French throne in 1285 the main French currency, the *gros tournois*, was exchanged for an equivalent of 3.95 grams of silver, very close to its original value of 4.05 in 1266.[1] In 1303, four years before the arrest of the Templars, every *gros* was exchanged for an equivalent of 1.35 grams of silver.[2] In essence, the value of silver had dramatically increased during that period. This inflation of the precious metal versus the currency, which was also felt in relation to many other goods of consumption, was aggravated due to the practice of debasing the coins, a practice very much employed by Philip IV's mints.[3] The economic and political implications of this monetary policy had a deep impact on Philip IV's kingdom, as I shall demonstrate in this paper.

Existing research has suggested that the financial tensions experienced during Philip IV's kingdom could have played a role in the arrest of the Templars. Malcolm Barber states that:

> In the late thirteenth century the price of precious metals had been consistently high, and any sustained attempt to maintain the value of money of account in

---

[1] Abbreviations: *LP* (and *l.p.*) = *livres parisis*; *LT* (and *l.t.*) = *livres tournois*. For the exchange rates between silver and the French currency, I have used Leon-Louis Borrelli de Serres, 'Les Variations monétaires sous Philippe le Bel et les sources de les histoires', *La gazette numismatique française* (1902), 382, and Jules Piquet, *Des banquiers au moyen âge: Les Templiers: Etude de leurs opérations financières* (Paris, 1939), pp. 156–69. Piquet expresses the exchange ratios as the number of *gros* that could buy one mark of silver (one mark being a unit of weight equivalent to 245 grams). From this I have calculated the implicit exchange ratios from the *gros* to grams of silver.

[2] Piquet, *Des banquiers*, pp. 156–69.

[3] Evidence survives of the production of eight out of the eleven royal mints for the period of 1301–10. From these data it can be shown that each of these eight mints issued coins to an equivalent of 3,488 kilograms of silver per year. This would make the annual issue around 40 tons of silver, equivalent to around 10 millions *gros* or 0.5 million *LT*. Furthermore, two mints produced golden coins at 1,207 kilograms a year each: Peter Spufford, *Dinero y moneda en la Europa medieval* (Barcelona, 1991), p. 533.

> relation to precious metals at the standard set under Louis IX in 1266 was bound to leave the king short of stocks of precious metals; the necessity of finding a new source of this may ultimately have resulted in the arrest of the Templars in 1307.[4]

It should also be considered that the treasurer of the Paris Temple acted as a royal official, receiving funds and paying cash on behalf of the king's treasure deposited at the Paris Temple. These services were compensated for by the king paying 600 *livres parisis* per year to the treasurer. [5] Marion Melville has judged that relationships such as this one created a sense of a 'state within the state', something that seriously disturbed Philip IV's plans to centralise the royal administration. [6]

Warfare, fiscal deficits and the scarcity of silver

King Louis IX, Philip IV's grandfather, had reorganised the country's finances in 1266. He established that every *livre parisi* (*LP*) should be equivalent to 80% of each *livre tournois* (*LT*). The *livre parisi* was a unit of measure which did not exist physically,[7] but was commonly used for the making of the royal budget – that is, it was 'money of account'. Each *livre parisi* contained twenty *sous*, which in turn comprised of twelve *deniers*, hence every pound contained twenty *gros*, or 240 *deniers*.[8]

Louis IX also ordered that silver should be melted into coins equivalent to the *sous*, so that every new coin, the *gros tournois*, was to contain 4.05 grams of silver of a total weight of 4.24; the rest of the coin was to contain billon (a mixed metal containing a predominance of base metal), and the king would keep the difference in silver (around 4.3%) as a right of *seigniorage*. This practice, known as 'debasing the coinage', was common in the middle ages as long as the proportion of metal extracted was kept at a low percentage; only an extraordinary circumstance could justify increasing it.[9] If such was the case, once the extraordinary situation, such as war, disappeared, the prince was expected to restore the usual content of silver to the issued coins.

---

4 Malcolm Barber, *The Trial of the Templars*, 2nd edn (Cambridge, 2006), p. 52.

5 *The Cambridge Economic History of Europe*, vol. 3 (Cambridge, 1963), p. 473.

6 Marion Melville, *La vida secreta de los Templarios* (Gerona, 1995), p. 296.

7 Jean Favier, *Philippe le Bel* (Paris, 1978), p. 144.

8 Jacques Heers, *L'Occident aux XIVe et XVe siècles* (Paris, 1994), p. 222.

9 Leon-Louis Borrelli de Serres, *Recherches sur divers services publics du XIII au XVII siécle*, vol. 2 (Paris 1895–1902), p. 505.

Philip IV's aggressive spending

Philip IV succeeded to the throne in 1285. The monetary situation of the kingdom was sound; every *gros* was traded for an equivalent of 3.95 grams of silver. However, Philip IV's increased expenditures soon put the fiscal balance into the negative, as by November 1286 the king owed the Templar order 101,845 *LP*.[10] If we take into account the fact that total ordinary revenues[11] of the kingdom that year stood at 604,941 *LP* (to reach this figure we must add up the revenues of the three accounting terms employed at that time by the royal administration: *Chandeleur* in February, *Ascension* by May/June and *Tous les Saintes* in November), the kingdom's debt load stood at a considerable 17% of one year's ordinary revenue, or more than 8,000 kilograms of silver. This debt was easily paid off, as by 1287 the kingdom was still generating more revenues than expenses, with a surplus of 74,368 *LP*.

After 1289, two factors drove the financial imbalances: the scarcity of silver and continuous warfare. Around 1290, the production of the Saxon silver mines started to decrease, which had a direct impact on the circulation of the metal throughout Europe and increased its relative price. [12] This appreciation was especially aggravated due to the fact that commercial activity kept increasing, which made currency even more necessary despite the scarcity of silver. On the other hand, Philip IV engaged in a very aggressive and expensive foreign policy: the war against Aragon cost around 1.5 million *LT*, and the war with England for Gascony, in the period of 1294–9, cost around 1.73 million *LT* according to some authors, [13] or 2–3 million, according to others.[14] This policy soon produced increased fiscal deficits, which can be studied from the accounting reports that the

---

[10] For the fiscal accounts of Philip the Fair's kingdom, I have used the editions in Comptes royaux (1285–1314), ed. Robert Fawtier and François Maillard, vol. 1: Comptes généraux (Paris, 1953); vol. 2: Comptes particuliers et comptes spéciaux ou extraordinaires (Paris, 1954); vol. 3: Introduction – Appendice – Supplément – Indices (Paris, 1956); and Léopold Delisle, Mémoire sur les opérations financiéres des templiers (Paris, 1889; repr. Geneva, 1975), pp. 118–32. On the consolidated accounts of the kingdom see Gerard Sivéry, Les Capétiens et l'argent au siècle de Saint Louis: Essai sur l'administration et les finances royales au XIIIe siècle (Paris, 1995), pp. 155–64.

[11] That is, excluding revenues accruing from coinage or real rights, which despite their magnitude were not consolidated in the royal budget developed in the Paris Temple; Sivéry suggests that total revenues could well double ordinary revenues. The consolidation of overall revenues would only occur by 1295, when the royal treasure was transferred from the Temple to the Louvre: Sivéry, *Les Capétiens*, p. 155.

[12] Piquet, *Des banquiers*, p. 162.

[13] Barber, *Trial*, p. 44.

[14] Favier, *Philippe le Bel*, p. 142.

Templar treasurer produced for the king three times a year, summarising revenues, expenses and the debtor-creditor balance between the king and the order.[15]

In the year ending November 1289, expenses were above revenues by more than 14%: revenues stood at 595,318 *LP*, with expenses at 681,528 *LP*, giving a total deficit of 86,210 *LP*. Such was the negative state of public finances in 1289 that Pope Nicholas IV allowed the king, in an extraordinary measure, to collect a tithe from Church revenues. This tithe, usually employed to finance the crusade, was to support Philip in his 'crusade' against Aragon. The tithe was also to include the order of Cîteaux, which was normally exempt from this levy, and its collection was assigned to the order of Temple.[16] Overall revenues accrued from the tithe stood at 152,000 *LP*, and consequently, the total revenues from the Church in France could be estimated at 10 times that amount, or 1,520,000 *LP*. During the whole of 1289, ordinary royal revenues stood at 595,318 *LP* and overall revenues probably close to twice that amount, or 1.2 million *LP*;[17] this means that the Church's revenues were higher than those of the crown. Any ambitious king who noticed that his revenues were below those of the Church would be severely tempted to try to appropriate some of that additional revenue, and it seems unlikely that Philip was immune to this sort of temptation.

The scarcity of silver and the persistent deficits could be reasons behind the arrest of the Lombards ordered by Philip IV in 1292. 1292 saw the deficit rise even higher, to 27,897 LP. Despite the debasement of the coin, fiscal deficits continued through the 1290s: in the year ending November 1290, the deficit stood at 56,450 LP – 6% of the total revenues – although in 1291 the treasury was able to collect more revenues than there were expenses, generating a surplus of 152,069 LP. The Lombards' goods were confiscated by royal agents,[18] and the Lombards were arrested and forced to 'purchase' French nationality; the resulting revenues could have totalled from 230,000 to 250,000 LT.[19] The financial situation failed to improve despite these arrests, as in February 1293 account expenses were still 46% higher than revenues, with a deficit of 132,310 LP. In that year, Philip IV was still using as financiers both the Templars[20] and the Florentine brothers Franzesi, known as Biche and Mouche.[21] Royal accounting was still undertaken at the

15 Sivéry, *Les Capétiens*, pp. 155–64.

16 Ibid., p. 168.

17 Ibid., p. 155.

18 Melville, *La vida secreta*, p. 307.

19 Favier, *Philippe le Bel*, p. 189.

20 Fawtier, *Comptes*, vol. 2 (Paris, 1954), entries 15000, 15016, 15090 and 15091.

21 *Pro mutuo facto Appariato de Sancto Felice, servienti armorum, pro se et sociis suis per Templum ad Omnes Sancto XCIIo: 236 l., et per Bichium, pro exercitu Hanonie, ut erat a tergo magnarum partium XCIIo: 1,160 l. Solvit per compotum magistri Johannis Prepositi, de dicto exercitu, anno XCIIo: 1,000 l. tur. nomine thesaurarii Tholose et nomine thesaurariii Templi: 300 l.t.:* Fawtier, *Comptes*, vol. 2, entry 14724.

Paris Temple, as we can deduce from the February 1293 budget which states *iste computus factus fuit per Templum*.[22]

We know that by February 1295, before the king's treasure was transferred from the Paris Temple to the Louvre palace, expenses again outpaced revenues by 5,485 *LP*, generating a total balance in favour of the Templar order of close to 28,854 LP, which is more than 2,000 kilograms of silver. Soon after this, Philip IV replaced the Templars as the main royal financiers, and began to use the Florentines Biche and Mouche exclusively. Part of the reason behind Biche's and Mouche's influence was their capacity to raise loans from Italian merchants: for instance, in 1294, they were able to raise the huge loan of 160,000 *LP*, or 43% of the ordinary royal revenues collected during 1292. Obviously this capacity to raise funds through loans could not be rivalled by the Templars, and the king would use this credit facility very often, as we can see from various accounting entries in 1292[23] and 1294.[24]

The military situation was so dire that the king convinced Biche and Mouche to provide a loan to the crown in order to pay a sum of 64,000 LP to the Holy Roman emperor, Adolf of Nassau, to make sure he would remain neutral towards France.[25] Despite the increased influence of Biche and Mouche, and despite the fact that the royal treasure had already been transferred to the Louvre, we know from the accounts of the French governors that the Temple continued to act as an agent of royal payments. [26]

---

[22] Ibid., vol. 1, entry 144.

[23] Ibid., vol. 2, accounts of 1292, for example, entry 14724 (see above, note 20).

[24] Ibid., vol. 1, accounts of 1294, for example (note the intervention of the Franzesi in the first document): (a) entry 8879: *Compotus bichi et moucheti guidi, valletorum domini regis, receptorum in senescallia tholosana et albiensi pro domino eustachio de bello marchesio, militis, senescallo tholosano et albiensi, de termino ascensionis domini, anno ejusdem mccxciii, usqe ad alliud sequens festum ascensionis domini, anno ejusdem mccxciiii*; (b) entry 7380: *Pro toto residuo summe 1000 l. mutuarum Regi a maiore et communia ville Pictavensis, reddito eisdem maiori et communie, ut patet per modum solutionis scriptum a tergo: 206 l. 8 s. 6 d.*; (c) entry 8879: *Consulibus Moysiaci, pro mutuo per eos facto incerte recordationis ... Regi Francorum, per ejus litteras: 1,000 l. tur. de mandato domini constabularii Francie et domini Petri Flote*; (d) entry 8986: *De mutuo de Navarra recuperatoo a certis nobilibus de Tholosa, quarum partes sunt in infine istius rotuli computate: 1289 l. 12 s. 4 d. Tur.*; and (e) entry 9961: *Consulibus de Vauro, de summa 2.000 l.t. que debebantur eis pro mutuo facto Regi, olim, pro via Gerone, que recepte fuerunt in solutum cum eorum publico instrumento a Guillelmo Petri Olerii in hiis que debebat pro ejus affranquimento: 12 l.t.*

[25] Heers, *L'Occident*, p. 246.

[26] As we can deduce from the following entry: *Expensa. Pro denariis reditis de mandato Regis domine Vierzoni, pro dote sua quam debebat percipere apud Templum, recuperandis super terra Virzionis: 1040 l.p.*: Fawtier, *Comptes*, vol. 1, entry 360.

Currency manipulation

As warfare continued and fiscal deficits persisted, Philip IV had no remedy but to use debasement of coinage as an alternative tool to meet his military expenditures.[27] Whereas at the accession of Philip IV to the throne every *livre parisi* was exchanged for an equivalent of 3.95 grams of silver, by January 1295 the exchange rate was 3.21.

During his last 19 years as king, Philip IV manipulated the currency on 22 occasions. Nine of them took place between 1295 and 1303, and six between 1304 and 1305.[28] It should be made clear that these decisions were not considered immoral at that time, as they were the prince's accepted right, and this right could be taken far if a special situation, such as war, justified it. Furthermore, in a context where the inflation of silver produced a severe scarcity of currency despite its need, due to the commercial revolution, the issue of coins with a lower content of silver was needed to maintain circulation. Finally, Philip IV's direct and indirect taxes were much less developed than those of other monarchs, such as the English kings. This made debasement of coinage a key source of income for the French king, who, from 1295 onwards, proceeded to devalue the coin at a rate not seen during the thirteenth century.[29]

Economic consequences of currency manipulation

In today's terms, Philip IV's financial policy was no different from printing money to pay for public deficit spending (as was widespread in the 1970s and 1980s). We know today that these measures bring inflation and currency depreciation to the country which employs them, but these effects were not known in the thirteenth century.

Another economic impact of these manipulations is what is known as Gresham's law, or the displacement of the strong currency by the weak one, in short, 'bad money drives out good'. In Philip IV's France, the persistent debasement of coinage would make people wary of taking their coins to royal mints, since the reissued coins would be handed back with a lower content of silver. They would rather take their silver abroad to exchange it for strong currencies. Finally, the issue of golden coins at a very attractive exchange rate in relation to the silver to facilitate its circulation produced a strong flow of export of silver and import of

---

[27] Even though the exact revenue derived from debasement and military expenses can be followed only after the transfer of the royal treasure to the Louvre in 1295/6, we know that this practice had been utilised earlier, since the issue of coins with a lower content of silver had the direct impact of a devaluation of the *LP* in relation to the price of silver, measured in marks of Troyes. One mark contained 245 grams, of which 218.1 were grams of silver.

[28] Borrelli de Serres, *Recherches*, vol. 2, p. 507.

[29] Spufford, *Dinero y moneda*, p. 387.

gold from Italy, to arbitrage the exchange rates in relation to the market rates. [30] All this led to a dramatic disappearance of silver in France. Such was the scarcity that a royal decree of 1301 forbade the transportation of gold or silver in order to avoid its export.[31]

A final economic consequence of such policies is that increased inflation damages creditors *vis-à-vis* debtors, as loans provided in a strong currency are paid back in a weaker one. Hence, traditional creditors such as the aristocracy and the Church found that these measures had a negative impact on their real income, but not even indebted classes gained from this perceived benefit, as high inflation increased their cost of living, causing social unrest. We see examples of both during Philip IV's reign. This alienated both upper and lower classes from the king.

Even though the consequences of these monetary fluctuations were not anticipated at the time, the king probably noticed that they had not occurred with this magnitude during the reign of Louis IX, when the currency had been sufficiently strong. Yet to go back to the purity of Louis IX's coins would have required a lot of silver, and silver was precisely what the king lacked at that time.

Financial crisis in times of war

England and France went to war in 1294. This conflict accelerated the financial problems incurred by the French monarch. In three years, as the use of debasement increased, the real value of the French currency depreciated by 15% in relation to the English silver sterling and the Florentine golden florin. Two years after the outbreak of war between France and England, the county of Flanders declared its independence from France, which severely constrained the French army and its finances. The crown's tendency to continue the fiscal imbalances through the issue of weak coin and through borrowing accelerated from 1296 on. In this year, loans (*mutua*) to the crown represented 7.5% of the total revenues.[32]

The desperate need for funds continued, and the debasement of coinage kept accelerating. The accounts between November 1296 and Christmas 1299 show that the kingdom obtained by *monnayage* (debasement of the coin and taxes associated with it) 1,419,238 LP (in November 1296, 81,149 LP; at Christmas 1298, 555,097 LP; in June 1299, 406,708 LP; and by Christmas 1299, 376,284 LP), and was more than able to finance war expenses of that same period totalling 1,066,266 LP. The impact of this coinage policy can be followed in the depreciation of the French currency in relation to silver, due to its lower content of the precious metal. In 1295, the *gros* was exchanged for an equivalent of 3.21 grams of silver, but by

30 Ibid., p. 239.

31 Piquet, *Des banquiers*, p. 186.

32 Loans (*mutua*) amounted to 41,329 *LP* and total revenues to 550,923 *LP*: Fawtier, *Comptes*, vol. 2, p. LVI.

October 1299 the exchange was made at 2.57 grams (by November 1297, the rate was 3.03, and by May 1298, 2.91).

Warfare intensified during 1302, as the city of Bruges also declared its independence from the French king, an example followed by other cities of Flanders. To offset this rebellion, Philip IV sent the French army to the north, but it was seriously defeated in the battle of Courtrai.[33] This disaster devastated French finances: the 15 months which followed this battle saw a depreciation of the currency by 37%, and new decrees were issued forbidding the export of gold and silver outside France and even ordering French officials and citizens to send their silver vessels (all of them in case of officials, half of them in the case of other citizens) to the mints in order to be melted into coins.[34]

As people tried to offset these prohibitions by concentrating their wealth in non-monetary assets in order to take them out of the country, a new decree from November 1303 forbade the export of any merchandise without previous royal permission.[35] This situation depreciated the value of the French currency, forcing the king to legally recognise the devaluation: on 22 August, new coins were issued with a content of silver of just one third of that of the coins issued by Louis IX in 1266.[36] To offset the fiscal imbalance, the king introduced new taxes of 20% on moveable property and 5% on real estate. As desperate measures to stabilise his finances, the king obtained from the new pope, Benedict XI, the concession of the crusade tithe[37] and ordered his royal treasure to be returned to the Temple, in order to use the Temple as a creditor again. At that time (1303–1304), the financial situation produced by the debasement of coinage was so dire and had made such a negative impact on the revenues of the main creditors (high clergy and nobility) that the bishops, in a *declaratio prelatorum*, stated their wish that the king should not proceed to further debasement of the coin without previous consent from the Church and the nobility.[38]

On the military front the king ordered a general levy of troops for 1302–1304 (a duty from which one could only be exempted by the payment of a duty: the Flanders subsidy)[39] and hired foreign mercenaries, mainly Genoese archers.[40] These efforts resulted in the naval victory of Mons-en-Puelle in August 1304, after which a peace agreement was signed with England and Flanders. Yet the victory

---

33 Adolphe Vuitry, *Le gouvernement royal et l'administration des finances sous Philippe le Bel et ses trois fils (1285–1328)* (Paris, 1880), pp. 37–8.

34 Piquet, *Des banquiers*, p. 165.

35 Ibid., p. 186.

36 Heers, *L'Occident,* p. 242.

37 Piquet, *Des banquiers*, p. 166.

38 Spufford, *Dinero y moneda*, p. 389.

39 Vuitry, *Le gouvernement*, p. 38.

40 Ibid., p. 42.

exacted a high price: the amphibious operation had involved 49 ships, at a total cost of 63,000 *LP*.[41]

Financial reorganisation: the arrest of the Jews

Having stabilised the military front, Philip IV decided to stabilise the financial and monetary situation. By this time, every *gros* was exchanged for just 1.3 grams of silver, compared to the 4 grams for which it had been traded during Louis IX's reign. In other words, the coins' purity had decreased from 94% to just 30%. Of course, to salvage French finances, new coins with a larger content of silver needed to be issued. The key problem was where to find that amount of silver.

A first decision was taken on 8 June 1306, by a decree that ordered that in three months from June every *gros* was to be reissued at an exchange rate of 3.96 grams of silver, and – to avoid the coexistence of strong and weak currencies – the coins issued in 1303, which had a very low content of silver (1.3 grams each), were devalued by law by two thirds. Probably to provision the mints with silver to put such a revaluation into effect, the Jews were arrested on 22 July and their goods confiscated on 23 August, [42] measures which could have raised between 140,000 and 2,000,000 *LP* for the kingdom.[43]

This revaluation, which in effect supposed a decrease of the value of silver of 70%, had some perverse effects, as debtors had to repay in the stronger currency debts which had been incurred in the weak currency, and it was soon evident that the prices of other consumer goods were not falling by that amount. Furthermore, many lease payments were to be made on the new strong currency, which impoverished the debtors' position. This situation was a key element in igniting a revolt in Paris against the king on 30 December, during which Philip IV took refuge in the Temple fortress.[44]

The fall of the Temple

Economically speaking, the coexistence between the new revalued coins and the older ones proved to be a cause of social unrest: an overall reissue of coins with the new high content of silver was needed. This situation brought the kingdom back into financial anarchy[45] with the disappearance of silver and new depreciations

---

41 Ibid., p. 48.

42 Piquet, *Des banquiers*, p. 167.

43 Stéphane Mechoulan, 'The Expulsion of the Jews from France in 1306: A Modern Fiscal Analysis', *Journal of European Economic History,* 33.3 (2004), 555–84.

44 Camille Piton, *Le Temple à Paris* (Paris, 1811), p. 36; Favier, *Philippe le Bel*, p. 166; Barber, *Trial*, p. 52.

45 Melville, *La vida secreta*, p. 307. Piquet, *Des banquiers*, p. 168.

of the currency.[46] Such was the distress and the perceived part that the currency played in it that, in a letter of 1307, Philip IV stated his aim of strengthening the currency to solve these ills;[47] this could show that the money extracted from the Jews had not been sufficient to provide stability. In my opinion, at this point the Temple's fate was sealed, as the Templar treasury was probably the only remaining source of silver able to provision royal mints in order to issue strong currency.

It should be remembered that the silver mines from Saxony had exhausted their reserves during the late thirteenth century and, if Philip IV had decided to use the fiscal surplus that his revenues would confer following the end of the war (around 500 kilograms of silver per annum), it would have taken France 222 years to accumulate such an amount of silver.

By way of comparison, when the Templars of Aragon were arrested in Miravet by King James II in 1308, a treasure of 70,000 sous of Barcelona (each one comprising 3.24 grams of silver, totalling 226 kilograms) was found in its tower, where it had been safeguarded by the provincial master after he had learned of the arrests in France;[48] in Cyprus, a treasure of 120,000 white besants (one besant comprising of 3.84 grams of silver, totalling 461 kilograms) was found when the Templars were arrested in Limassol,[49] and when King Edward II, in desperate need of funds, broke into the New Temple in September 1307, he found a treasure of 50,000 pounds sterling or 18,375 kilograms of silver.[50] Is it reasonable to assume that no treasure was found in the Temple of Paris when the Templars were arrested by surprise in October 1307, considering that the Paris Temple was a key financial centre of the order? In his testimony given at Poitiers in 1308, a Templar priest claimed that the grand master had returned to France with 150,000 golden florins – more than 600 kilograms of gold (or its equivalent in silver, i.e. 10 times that amount: 6,000 kilograms) and other monies (*quando magister venit de ultra mare, portavit secum centum et quinquaginta milia florenorum auri et decem somarios oneratos Turonum grossorum magister divisit, postquam fuit in Provincia*).[51]

Yet Philip IV found the desperately needed kilograms of silver to source his royal mints in order to bring the kingdom back from the financial chaos produced by the devaluations. In my opinion, the only plausible source was the Templar

---

46 Melville, *La vida secreta*, p. 307.

47 *Lettres inédites de Philippe le Bel*, ed. Adolphe Baudouin (Paris, 1886), vol. 4, p. 195, no. 177.

48 Josep Maria Sans i Travé, *El proces dels Templers catalans* (Lleida, 1991), p. 303.

49 Barber, *Trial*, p. 254.

50 This money belonged to Walter Langdon, bishop of Coventry and Lichfield, who was using the London Temple in London as a bank: *Chronica Walteri de Gyseburne*: *The Chronicle of Walter of Guisborough*, ed. Henry Rothwell, Camden Society 3rd series, 89 (1957), p. 383; Thomas Parker, *The Knights Templars in England* (Tucson, 1963), p. 60.

51 *UT*, vol. 2, pp. 37–8. Thanks to Anne Gilmour-Bryson for providing me with this testimony.

treasure. This may provide us with one of the reasons behind the arrest of the Templars. If I am right, many hunters of Templar treasures have wasted their time and money, as the famous Templar treasure was nowhere but at the king's mints, being melted into purer coins.

This paper has offered some monetary evidence which could point towards one of the reasons for the arrest of the Templars in the context of the arrest of the Lombards and that of the Jews. Of course, many other factors played a role in this event. Indeed, it is also possible that Philip IV believed the charges and then opportunistically profited from this sincere belief. In any case, let us end this paper with verses from the Divine Comedy in which Dante, in the early fourteenth century, already pointed towards currency manipulation as a factor which influenced the end of the Temple:

Italian	English
Maladetta sie tu, antica lupa, / che più che tutte l'altre bestie hai preda / per la tua fame sanza fine cupa![*]	Accursed mayst thou be, thou old she-wolf, / That more than all the other beasts hast prey, / Because of hunger infinitely hollow!
Veggiolo il novo Pilato si crudele, / che ciò nol sazia, ma sanza decreto / portar nel Tempio le cupide vele![†]	I see the modern Pilate so relentless, / This does not sate him, but without decretal / He to the Temple bears his sordid sails!
Lí si vedrà, il duol che sovra Senna / induce, falseggiando la moneta, / quel che morrà di colpo di contenna.[+]	There shall be seen the woe that on the Seine / He brings by falsifying of the coin, / Who by the blow of a wild boar shall die.

Notes

[*] Purgatorio, canto XX.
[†] Purgatorio, canto XX.
[+] Paradiso, canto XIX.

Appendix: The Temple as royal treasury

The main reason behind the decision to re-transfer the treasure to the Temple is found in the fact that the Temple had acted as a financier during the years in which the royal treasure had been held in its fortress; this is to say, when royal revenues were below expenses, the Temple acted as creditor of the balance, using the order's own money. In the dire situation of Philip IV's finances by 1303 it seems reasonable to assume that the king returned his treasure to the Temple in order to enjoy this credit facility. This move was followed by the employment of the Templar Visitor Hugues of Pairaud as royal official in charge of the collection of the war subsidy, except for the Languedoc region.[52] Finally, the Templar treasurer was again named as the king's representative in the exequer of Normandy, regaining his role as the king's treasurer (although supervised by three non-Templar vice-treasurers appointed by the king)[53] and as one of the 15 members of the camera compotorum.[54] These moves also produced changes in the accounting system, as again royal revenues and expenses were accounted for three times a year (February, August and November), instead of twice yearly (June and December) as practised by Italians. By September 1303, the king was already ordering some of his rents to be sent to his account in the Temple,[55] and in 1304 the use of the Temple as a centre of royal finances became widespread.[56]

---

[52] *Lettres inédites de Philippe IV*, p. 163, no. 148.

[53] Delisle, *Mémoire,* p. 58.

[54] Vuitry, *Le gouvernement*, p. 1.

[55] Claude de Vic, *Histoire générale du Languedoc*, 16 vols (Toulouse and Paris, 1868–1905), vol. 10, col. 417; Delisle, *Mémoire*, p. 56.

[56] Fawtier, *Comptes*, vol. 2, 'Compte de Hugues de Bouville des Joyaux du Roi (1304)', p. 539, from Rouen, Bibliothèque municipale, MS Leber 8670 (Menant VIII), fol. 31.

PART II
The Trial in France

Chapter 6
Terror, Torture and the Truth: The Testimonies of the Templars Revisited

Thomas Krämer

A confession had been since Roman antiquity the *regina probationum*. The confessions of the Templars represented the most important proof of their guilt during the trial. But since then these confessions have never ceased to be used in a surprisingly contradictory manner, either to condemn the order or to prove its innocence. Most medievalists, while acknowledging that most of the charges did not apply to the Templars, 'find it difficult to accept that an affair of such enormity rests upon total fabrication and they cannot bring themselves to reject entirely such a large body of confessions decorated, as they often are, with such apparently realistic detail'.[1] It cannot be the goal of this paper to answer the question of guilt or innocence; instead, this study will focus on the above-mentioned 'realistic details'. In other words: do these details really strengthen the credibility of the depositions or are they rather a product of the inquisitorial procedures?

For this contribution, the interrogations in the seneschalsy of Nîmes-Beaucaire were selected as source material. The depositions from Aigues-Mortes, Nîmes and Alès have not received the same attention as trial documents from other parts of Europe even though the text is one of the best-preserved sources for the interrogations in the French provinces. It allows us to follow in detail the chronological course of events.[2] Doing so, one can compare up to three testimonies of the same brother made under quite different conditions and their respective outcome.

The 66 interrogated brothers, who were arrested as everywhere in the kingdom of France on 13 October 1307, originated from commanderies in the Templar province of Provence, one of the richer provinces of the order.[3] They came from a

[1] For the trial in general see Malcolm Barber, *The Trial of the Templars*, 2nd edn (Cambridge, 2006); for the quote see ibid., p. 306; Alain Demurger, *Les Templiers: Une chevalerie chrétienne au moyen âge* (Paris, 2005).

[2] The only edition is Léon Ménard, *Histoire civile, ecclésiastique, et littéraire de la ville de Nismes avec des notes et les preuves, suivie de dissertations historiques & critiques sur les antiquités & de diverses observations sur son histoire naturelle*, vol. 1 (Paris, 1750), preuves, no. CXXXVI, pp. 166–219.

[3] For the history of this province see Damien Carraz, *L'ordre du Temple dans la basse vallée du Rhône (1124–1312): Ordres militaires, croisades et sociétés méridionales* (Lyon, 2005); Dominic Selwood, *Knights of the Cloister: Templars and Hospitallers in*

comparatively small number of houses which were all situated in the Languedoc. The vast majority resided in the important convents of St Gilles or Montpellier-Lunel and their dependent *membra.* A small group lived at Jalès or on possessions in the diocese of Le Puy.[4] The first interrogations, conducted by royal officials, took place between 8 and 16 November 1307. On 22 April 1308, the bishop, Bertrandus II of Nîmes, authenticated eight testimonies. The inquiries against the individual members of the Temple, as ordered by Clemens V in *Faciens misericordiam*, were held at a relatively late date between 24 June and 14 July 1310. In contrast to other trials, the inquisitor conducted an additional second inquiry in August 1311. The judgments were pronounced after more than five years of imprisonment, during November 1312.[5]

The most influential persons involved were certainly Odoardus de Malodumo, seneschal of Nîmes and Beaucaire, Bishop Bertrandus II of Nîmes and his inquisitor, Guillelmus de S. Laurencio, *rector* of the St. Thomas church in Durfont. Odoardus de Malodumo had military, administrative and diplomatic skills. He had served as an admiral in the French fleet, was commander of Calais and one of the ambassadors of Robert Bruce of Scotland to the papal court before he assumed control over one of the most important seneschalsies.[6] He accomplished the arrest of the Templars and conducted the first interrogations, but was replaced by his successor Bertrandus Jordanus de Insula before 8 November 1307.[7] Bertrandus de Languissel had studied in Italy before his long pontificate at Nîmes (1280–1324).[8] Unfortunately, nothing else is known about Guillelmus de S. Laurencio.

The protocols from the first interrogation in November 1307 are especially important because they were used as further evidence in the later episcopal inquisitions. The Templars were bound to their former depositions if they were to hope for their excommunication to be lifted and if they did not want to risk being

Central-Southern Occitania c.1100–c.1300 (Woodbridge, 1999). The latter should be used with caution. See also Alan Forey, *The Templars in the Corona de Aragón* (London, 1973), pp. 88–103.

4 Demurger, *Templiers*, p. 439. Carraz, *L'ordre*, pp. 524–30.

5 For the chronology of events see Alain Demurger, 'Encore le procès des templiers: A propos d'un ouvrage récent', *Revue Historique*, 97 (1991), 29; Carraz, *L'ordre*, pp. 524–33; Vincent Challet, 'Entre expansionnisme capétien et relents d'hérésie: Le procès des Templiers du Midi', in *Les ordres religieux militaires dans le Midi* (Toulouse, 2005), pp. 141–52.

6 Geoffrey Barrow, *Robert Bruce and the Community of the Realm of Scotland* (Edinburgh, 2005), p. 395.

7 The order to arrest the Templars was addressed to Odoardus de Malodumo, but in a report to the king about the arrest from 8 November, he is called only 'knight', while Bertrandus Jordanus de Insula is named as seneschal: Ménard, *Histoire*, p. 195.

8 Bernard Guillemain, 'Origines sociales, intellectuelles et ecclésiastiques des évêques de la province de Narbonne entre 1249 et 1317', in *Les évêques, les clercs et le roi (1250–1300)*, Cahier de Fanjeaux, 7 (Toulouse, 1972), p. 97.

sentenced as *relapsi*. It is therefore necessary to look at how, and the conditions under which, these protocols were written.

The interrogations in November 1307 were conducted under the auspices of Odoardus de Malodumo himself. He was joined by Petrus Johannis, *magister* Mattheus de Mancina, respectively royal advocate and procurator in the seneschalsy, Bartholomeus de Clusello, judge of Aigues-Mortes, the vicar and castellan of Aigues-Mortes and the vicar of Bagnols. In addition, G. de S. Justo, the seneschal's lieutenant, and a third jurist, Guillelmus de Romanis, acted as witnesses.[9] Although it is not possible to clarify their role precisely, it is evident that the brothers were confronted with the highest ranks of the royal administration. Furthermore, the presence of the advocate (Petrus Johannis), the judge (Bartholomeus) and the procurator (Mattheus) ensured the participation of experienced, able and high-ranking jurists. In contrast to this impressive assembly, only one notary attended the sessions: Poncius de Cauna, notary of the king's court at Nîmes, wrote the protocols at the request of the seneschal.[10] All but one were royal officials, so we cannot expect them to be neutral. On the contrary, as a royal advocate or procurator it was the duty of Petrus Johannis and Mattheus de Mancina to protect the king's interests.

On the last day of the interrogations, Odoardus de Malodumo called for two Dominicans from the convent at Nîmes. The inquisitors Deodatus Cathalani, prior of the convent, and Petrus Fabri, *lector* of the same house, authenticated the depositions of the Templars held at Aigues-Mortes and Nîmes itself.[11] On 22 April 1308, Bishop Bertrandus II of Nîmes confirmed in addition the testimonies of eight Templars from the commandery of St Gilles who had been interrogated at Nîmes on 16 November 1307. As Johannes Fried has pointed out, the authorisation by Philip IV to use torture moved in a legal grey zone.[12] The king and his advisers met these concerns by seeking the affirmation of the testimonies produced so far through inquisitors or high ecclesiastical dignitaries. Considering the witnesses of the above-mentioned confirmation, it is therefore likely that the bishop acted at the request of the new seneschal. Apart from Bertrandus Jordanus de Insula and his

---

9 Ménard, *Histoire*, p. 207.

10 Petrus Johannis was at the same time a member of the law faculty at the university of Montpellier. He had acted as lieutenant of the seneschal or the *judex major* since 1287. He probably knew Guillaume de Nogaret, who had also studied at Montpellier and was *judex major* of the seneschalsy of Nîmes in 1294. One of his successors was Guillaume de Plaisians (1300–1303): Jan Rogozinski, 'The Counsellors of the Seneschal of Beaucaire and Nimes, 1250–1350', *Speculum*, 33 (1969), 430–433; Joseph R. Strayer, *Les gens de justice du Languedoc sous Philippe le Bel* (Toulouse, 1970).

11 Ménard, *Histoire*, p. 205.

12 Johannes Fried, 'Wille, Freiwilligkeit und Geständnis um 1300: Zur Beurteilung des letzten Templergroßmeisters Jacques de Molay', *Historisches Jahrbuch*, 105 (1985), 397.

lieutenant, Mattheus de Mancina and Guillelmus de Romanis were also present.[13] Although Bertrandus II seems to have acted sometimes in quite an independent manner,[14] in the case of the Templars he did not actively intervene in the trial but gave way to the pressure of the royal administration.

This alone does not mean that the texts are necessarily corrupted. Nonetheless, the formation of the protocols we read today poses fundamental problems. Firstly, the translation of the Latin *interrogatorium* into vernacular questions by the inquisitor and the retranslation of the answers into Latin by the scribe could have caused interpretations or mistakes. By comparing two protocols from 1367 and 1381, Herbert Grundmann has proven that the older acted as a model for the younger document.[15] The results were astonishing similarities not only of the questions, but also of the answers, because the older document was used as a guide for the translation from the vernacular into Latin. The fact that the charges in Philip IV's order of arrest from 14 September 1307 are nearly identical with the depositions made in front of Odoardus de Malodumo further undermines their credibility. This phenomenon however is not limited to the testimonies of the Templars. In a number of protocols from other inquisitions there are conspicuous similarities between the *interrogatorium* and the answers.[16] In the case of the interrogations by the seneschal, these correspondences turned the charges as expressed by the king and his advisers into something like self-fulfilling prophecies. The only purpose of these protocols was to get the greatest possible number of usable testimonies.[17]

The second and third rounds of interrogations were recorded by Johannes del Roure, notary of Alès, who wrote under the auspices of the inquisitor Guillelmus de S. Laurencio. James Given has recently shown in detail how the inquisitors effectively used written records.[18] Their value as a source is controversial. Yet Emmanuel Le Roy Ladurie believed in his famous study on Montaillou in the pristine character of his source and denied the utilisation of torture.[19] The first

13 Ménard, *Histoire*, pp. 181–3.

14 Guillemain, *Origines*, p. 525.

15 Herbert Grundmann, 'Ketzerverhöre des Spätmittelalters als quellenkritisches Problem', *Deutsches Archiv für die Erforschung des Mittelalters*, 21 (1965), 537.

16 Thomas Scharff, 'Auf der Suche nach der "Wahrheit": Zur Befragung von verdächtigen Personen durch mittelalterliche Inquisitoren', in *Eid und Wahrheitssuche: Studien zu rechtlichen Befragungspraktiken in Mittelalter und früher Neuzeit*, ed. Stefan Esders and Thomas Scharff (Frankfurt a. M., 1999), p. 150.

17 Or, as the editors of the trial in the Auvergne expressed it: 'il fallait essentiellement obtenir des aveux, car la vérité recherchée était non la réalité des faits mais la conformité des dépositions avec les accusations': *Le procès des Templiers d'Auvergne*, ed. Roger Sève and Anne-Marie Chagny-Sève (Paris, 1986), p. 47.

18 James Given, *Inquisition and Medieval Society: Power, Discipline and Resistance in Languedoc* (Ithaca, NY, 1997), pp. 25–51.

19 Emmanuel Le Roy Ladurie, *Montaillou: Village occitan de 1294 à 1324* (Paris, 1991), pp. 16–17; following his views: Matthias Benad, *Domus und Religion in Montaillou:*

to express his doubts about the seemingly unaltered truth of the registers was Leonard E. Boyle.[20] Going one step further, Thomas Scharff recommended that the registers and protocols should only be used with great caution.[21] The editors of the trials have assessed the credibility of their respective sources quite differently. Anne Gilmour-Bryson was convinced that the testimony made in front of an inquisitor was 'one of the few small windows open to thought, behaviour, and action of ordinary persons at this time'.[22] For the editors of the trial at Clermont, the 'présentation uniforme des réponses ne permet absolument pas de distinguer les termes propres au templier interrogé de ceux du rédacteur du procès-verbal'.[23]

To ease the task of their colleagues, quite a number of inquisitors wrote manuals to provide counsel concerning the most effective methods and tactics. They reflect a deep-rooted mistrust towards every suspect. Because heretics were assumed to hide their errors, the task of uncovering them grew increasingly difficult.[24] Bernard Gui, inquisitor in Toulouse and author of a famous manual, recommended that, *non tamen expedit quod omnes interrogationes scribantur, set tantum ille que magis verisimiliter tangunt substantiam vel naturam facti et que magis videntur exprimere veritatem*.[25] The truth thus became what the interrogator thought to be the truth. The Dominican also suggested that the testimonies should all have the same length, so that nobody could claim that something was missing in the shorter versions. The ambition of the notaries to create similar-looking protocols thus explains to a certain extent the conformity of the testimonies. The least one can say about these registers and protocols is that they contain revised versions of testimonies and by no means a verbatim and neutral report, even more so because it took various steps until the final form of the protocols was achieved.[26] They

Katholische Kirche und Katharismus im Überlebenskampf der Familie des Pfarrers Petrus Clerici am Anfang des 14. Jahrhunderts (Tübingen, 1990), pp. 9–10.

20 Leonard E. Boyle, 'Montaillou Revisited: *Mentalité* and Methodology', in *Pathways to Medieval Peasants*, ed. James A. Raftis (Toronto, 1981), pp. 119–40.

21 Scharff, 'Suche', p. 150; idem, 'Seelenrettung und Machtinszenierung: Sinnkonstruktionen der Folter im kirchlichen Inquisitionsverfahren des Mittelalters', in *Das Quälen des Körpers: Eine historische Anthropologie der Folter*, ed. Peter Burschel, Götz Distelrath and Sven Lembke (Cologne, 2000), p. 154.

22 *The Trial of the Templars in Cyprus: A Complete English Edition*, ed. and trans. Anne Gilmour-Bryson (Leiden, 1998), p. 13.

23 Sève, *Le procès des Templiers d'Auvergne*, p. 53.

24 Scharff, 'Suche', 144; for the Franciscan David of Augsburg's complaint about the *moderni haeretici*, see *Der Tractat des David von Augsburg über die Waldesier*, ed. Wilhelm Preger, *Abhandlungen der historischen Classe der Königlich Bayerischen Akademie der Wissenschaften*, 14 (1878), 228.

25 Bernard Gui, *Manuel de l'inquisiteur*, ed. Guillaume Mollat, vol. 1 (Paris, 1964), p. 32.

26 These steps are, for example, known for Jacques Fournier's inquisition protocols: Le Roy Ladurie, *Montaillou*, p. 18. The protocols of the Templars also passed through several steps before they reached their final form: Ménard, *Histoire*, p. 173.

represent an aid of and for inquisitors to unmask supposed heretics that contained many more negative than exonerative details about a suspect and were therefore 'active instruments not only of knowledge but also of coercion'.[27]

Anke Krüger has demonstrated how the conduct of interrogation and the method of taking minutes influenced the outcome. She compared the depositions of brothers who had been admitted by the same receptor concerning this ceremony and the events around their reception. For instance, she took the 16 Templars admitted by Poncius de Brozeto, Templar master of the Provence from 1286 to 1296. While the descriptions of the reception ceremonies are quite similar, the statements about the illicit acts during or around the ritual differ considerably.[28] Only the responses from brothers who were interrogated in the same place, in this case Cahors, Carcassonne or Nîmes, show none of these variations. But compared with the testimonies from other inquiries, it seems as if Poncius de Brozeto conducted quite different ceremonies. Even the *illicita* that allegedly took place during two receptions in Montpellier were described in totally different ways.[29] For Anke Krüger there are thus only two possible explanations. On the one hand, the conduct of the inquiries itself favoured the emergence of quite similar testimonies. On the other hand, it is always the first witness of the day who to a large degree determined with his statements the further depositions. The best examples are the 29 brothers who denied every charge at Clermont: they were all interrogated on 7 June 1309.[30] But we also find similar incidents during the inquiries at Aigues-Mortes and Nîmes. The testimony of Bertrandus Arnaudi, the first witness to be interrogated on 8 November 1307, shaped the depositions of all subsequent brothers who were questioned that day.[31] Even more unequivocal were the testimonies of the 28 brothers who were questioned for a second time in 1311. According to the protocol, they all deposed exactly the same as the former

27 Given, *Inquisition*, p. 39.

28 Anke Krüger, 'Schuld oder Präjudizierung?', *Historisches Jahrbuch*, 117 (1997), 346–9. She is thereby able to refute the findings of Barbara Frale who does not take into consideration the circumstances of the single testimonies sufficiently, but (due to her computer-aided method) treats them more or less equally. Frale therefore cannot explain the sometimes quite substantial contradictions in the depositions of the same brother: Barbara Frale, *L'ultima battaglia dei Templari: Dal codice ombra d'obbedienza militare alla costruzione del processo per eresia* (Rome, 2001), pp. 169–207.

29 Krüger, 'Schuld', 352.

30 Sève, *Le procès des Templiers d'Auvergne*, pp. 52, 220–42.

31 Ménard, *Histoire*, pp. 197–8. For the subsequent three testimonies this is clear, for they are only repeating: *sponte & devote dixit et confessus fuit idem in omnibus & per omnia, in substantia & effectu, quod dictus frater Bertrandus Arnaudi supra*. All brothers came from the commandery Jalès in the diocese of Uzès. After them, four brothers from the house of St Gilles were interrogated. Their 'confessions' were styled the same way after the first testifying brother, Poncius Placuti, who was in fact making the same declarations as Bertrandus Arnaudi. According to Malcolm Barber, the same pattern can be found at Cahors and Carcassonne: Barber, *Trial*, p. 76.

preceptor of St Gilles, Bernardus de Selgues.[32] As a result we do not have a large number of detailed depositions but abbreviated statements that are based on a comparatively small number of extensive 'confessions'. This may reduce their importance for a historian but was sufficient for the aims of the royal administration and, apparently, of the inquisition.

If we pay closer attention to the procedure of the inquiries we find further instructive details. The order in which persons were interrogated did not come about by chance. The first Templar who was interrogated by Odoardus de Malodumo and his associates was the above-mentioned Bertrandus Arnaudi. He had joined the order at the important commandery of Richerenches where he was admitted by the commander Raimundus Chambarut. We are not told his age, but the fact that he had been received 30 years earlier suggests that the seneschal took one of the oldest brothers to obtain his first deposition.[33] Apparently the royal officials found it easier to get a 'confession' from an older than from a younger man. His testimony was used to incriminate the following brothers who were under pressure to justify, explain or devaluate it. The only interrogated priest brother was Raimundus Saguerii. On account of his education as a cleric and his post as a procurator of the commandery of Montpellier, he probably had at least some knowledge of customary as well as canonical law.[34] He was the last Templar questioned by the royal administration and was therefore, after dozens of 'confessions', put under the highest possible pressure. Unsurprisingly, his testimony paralleled that of the others.

Guillelmus de S. Laurencio used the same sequence of witnesses and thus followed the approach of the royal administration. The testimonies of two of the three brothers with whom the seneschal and the inquisitor started their respective interrogations were identical.[35] Bertrandus Arnaudi, like Petrus de Tholosa, denied in his first statement nearly every charge against the order and was therefore sent back to prison.[36] After an unknown period of time, the inquisitor interrogated him again. This time he admitted all the charges, *reversus ad cor suum, volens corrigere dictum suum & etiam emendare in melius, & puram et meram dicere veritatem*. The changes even included the time of reception. His receptor was still Raimundus Chambarut, but now he had entered the order no longer three decades, but only 14 or 15 years before, thus 1295 or 1296. We do not know why he altered his testimony in this seemingly innocuous detail, too, but we have a clear hint

32 Ménard, *Histoire*, pp. 210–15.

33 Ibid., pp. 173–6, 197.

34 Ibid., p. 204. The term *procurator* in this case probably does not mean 'lieutenant', as in other cases, but, rather, a person acting for the house in legal disputes with secular or ecclesiastical opponents.

35 The two brothers were Bertrandus Arnaudi and Petrus de Tholosa. The third, Johannes Tardini, was not interrogated by Odoardus de Malodumo.

36 He admitted that at his reception there were only members of the order present and that every novice was to swear to reveal nothing of the order's secrets: ibid., p. 173.

that he did not tell the truth in the second hearing. Raimundus Chambarut was commander of Richerenches between 1263 and 1280, which would confirm the first statement.[37]

For Alain Demurger, these altered statements after an interruption are a clear indication of the use of torture or at least intimidation.[38] The interrogations by Guillelmus de S. Laurencio corroborate this. Of the 32 Templars interrogated by the inquisitor during June and July 1310 only three 'confessed'. All others denied the charges. Even a brother whose earlier 'confession' from 1307 was read out to him rejected the accusations.[39] Two of them were questioned for a second time, while one was a renegade from the diocese of Poitiers. This Drohetus was also the only one who referred in detail to an earlier confession. Shortly after his reception he had confessed his errors to a related Franciscan from Paris. This mendicant had imposed a penance and recommended that he should leave the order, which he did.[40] What is striking is less what is said but rather who said it. It is the only testimony of Drohetus, for he was not interrogated by the seneschal, nor does he appear later in the trial. Such details have led some scholars to the assumption that there must be a grain of truth in stories like these. The testimony of the preceptor of another Languedocian house, Iterius de Rupe forti from Douzens, seems to prove this.[41] He deposed that he confessed two times and described the details of his penances. Although Anne Gilmour-Bryson admitted that the witnesses of the hearing in Poitiers in 1308 were carefully selected, she among others was ready to believe in the authenticity of this statement.[42] However, it was the same brother who declared that he had been tortured even after he had confessed because his custodians were not yet satisfied with his deposition.[43] He needed to convince them with a plausible story because custodians and inquisitors alike not only wanted to hear 'a guilty plea, but a specific statement that contained details that "none but the criminal could possibly know"'.[44]

Why the Templars were tortured seems therefore obvious. The aim of both the seneschal and the inquisitor was to obtain information. Peter Suedfeld has identified up to four additional aims: incrimination, indoctrination, intimidation and isolation.[45] These reasons apply in principle also to the trial of the Templars,

---

37 Carraz, *L'ordre*, p. 310.

38 Demurger, *Templiers*, p. 504. For further examples: Scharff, 'Seelenrettung', 156.

39 Ménard, *Histoire*, p. 183.

40 Ibid., pp. 176–7.

41 *UT*, vol. 2, pp. 47–8.

42 Anne Gilmour-Bryson, 'The Templar Trials: Did the System Work?', *The Medieval History Journal*, 3 (2000), 51–2. For a similar assessment: Frale, *L'ultima battaglia*, pp. 186–7.

43 *UT*, vol. 2, p. 48. Demurger, *Templiers*, p. 443.

44 Edward Peters, *Torture* (Oxford, 1985), p. 50.

45 Peter Suedfeld, 'Torture: A Brief Overview', in *Psychology and Torture*, ed. Peter Suedfeld (New York, 1990), p. 2.

albeit not to the same extent. Apparently the royal officials did not torture all brothers in 1307.[46] In fact, it was not necessary, because the brothers had already been incriminated and pressured by earlier depositions. In addition, they knew that some brothers were being tortured and that the only way to avoid the same treatment was to act as was expected of them. The inquisitors consciously exploited this fear. David of Augsburg even suggested that they should increase this fear to panic, since nothing could soften a heart like fear of death and hope of life.[47]

To ensure that the testimonies could not be contested for formal reasons, the seneschal and the inquisitor emphasised that all the witnesses testified *juratus super sancta Dei evangelia corporaliter tacta dicere & confiteri veritatem, sponte et devote*, or were *solutus omnibus vinculis & carcere liberatus*.[48] This ensured that nobody could claim that his confession had been made out of fear of violence or the product of coercion. Hypothetically it was sufficient to take the interrogated into another room and to unchain him in order to demarcate the preliminary proceedings, which could include torture, from the inquisition itself. By this means the voluntary nature of the testimony was legally provided.[49] The importance of this merely formal separation for the value of the 'confessions' became clear during the interrogations in 1310. Guillelmus de S. Laurencio dismissed the objection of one brother who claimed that his testimony had been the product of fear and torture, on the ground that the revocation was not plausible because his former statements compiled in the records were up to standard.[50]

The inquisitor also stressed that only some of the brothers had been tortured three weeks before his second round of interrogations.[51] For him it went without saying that this period was long enough (and more than legally demanded) to give the 'confessions' the required validity. While contemporaries could proceed from the assumption that the truth would finally be extorted from guilty suspects, modern historians cannot follow in their footsteps. Nobody today would assume

46 These brothers were Raimundus Corrigie, Guillelmus Penchenati and Marcho Bonetoni: Ménard, *Histoire*, pp. 185, 186, 194.

47 *David von Augsburg*, ed. Preger, 223: *Timor enim mortis et spes vite emolliunt cor quod vix aliter possit emolliri.*

48 For example, Petrus de Tholosa or Johannes Tardini, in front of Odoardus de Malodumo: Ménard, *Histoire*, pp. 198 and 171.

49 For the relevant canonical sources: Fried, 'Wille', 393–6.

50 Ménard, *Histoire*, p. 183. Poncius de Castello-Bono declared: *quod illam confessionem numquam fecerat, & si eam fecerat, eam fecerat sine memoria & metu tormentorum, ut dixit, & ideo eam revocabat, & in ea perseverare non volebat; ymo contenta in ea asseruit esse falsa, in quantum faciunt contra ordinem predictum; dicto domino G. de S. Laurencio hoc non credente, cum dictus frater Poncius, ut supra legitur, dictam confessionem fecerit sponte & devote, & dictam heresim abjuraverit in bona memoria existens, ut dictus dominus G. apparere dixit per acta suprascripte sue confessionis.*

51 Ibid., p. 215: *Et est sciendum quod quidam de predictis fratribus fuerunt questionati moderate, tres septimane & plus sunt elapsi, & ex tunc citra questionati non fuerunt.*

that the effects of torture and the fear of its reapplication have disappeared after a few days. The *sequelae* of torture and harsh imprisonment are undisputed among modern psychologists and can be found even after 40 years.[52] The most widespread disorders such as anxiety, obsessive compulsive symptoms, depression, paranoid ideation, anger-hostility, phobias etc. sometimes shine through in the protocols.[53] Petrus Chalendoni made his first testimony in front of Guillelmus de S. Laurencio *quasi trepidando ... quasi balbuciendo & verba intricate proferendo*, while Matheus de Bigorra was *titubando & quasi tremendo*.[54] These descriptions were inserted because inquisitors were obliged to pay attention to such reactions. According to the manuals they were signs of possible lies and not the result of probably traumatic experiences.[55]

According to the terms of the protocol, Petrus Calendoni and Matheus de Bigorra had not been tortured before they made their statements, but that does not necessarily mean that there was no torture. A notary did not need to note the recourse to torture because the suspect had not been tortured during the inquisition but only during the preliminary investigation; he only took minutes of the deposition.[56] The rare mentions of torture have led some historians to underestimate the importance and the frequency of its use.[57] However, a further factor becomes evident in their behaviour even if the Templars were not tortured. Beside torture, inquisitors had another very effective means at their disposal. One of the 'more novel aspects of the inquisitors' work was the use they made of imprisonment'.[58] It represented probably the most effective technique of interrogation, because it put the suspects under considerable mental and physical pressure. The stay in prison did not count

---

52 Thomas W. Miller, 'Long-Term Effects of Torture in Former Prisoners of War', in *Torture and Its Consequences. Current Treatment Approaches*, ed. Metin Başoğlu (Cambridge 1992), 109.

53 Sepp Graesser and Mechthild Wenk-Anhsohn, *Die Spuren von Folter: Eine Handreichung* (Berlin, 2000), pp. 64–79; Murat Paker et al., 'Psychological Effects of Torture: An Empirical Study of Tortured and Non-Tortured Non-Political Prisoners', in *Torture*, ed. Başoğlu, p. 77; Pia Moisander and Erik Edston, 'Torture and Its Sequel: A Comparison between Victims from Six Countries', *Forensic Science International*, 137 (2003), 136–7; Finn Somnier et al., 'Psychological Consequences of Torture: Current Knowledge and Evidence', in *Torture*, ed. Başoğlu, p. 66. These symptoms are described as typical for post-traumatic stress disorder, but it seems quite difficult to verify this more than 700 years later.

54 Ménard, *Histoire*, pp. 187 and 193.

55 Scharff, 'Suche', p. 155.

56 Fried, 'Wille', 395.

57 Scharff, 'Seelenrettung', pp. 154–7; for the Templars see, for example, Joseph Strayer, *The Reign of Philip the Fair* (Princeton, 1980), p. 291. Barbara Frale also misjudges the effects of torture and incarceration, as she is not aware of the progress of research into the inquisition since Henry Charles Lea: Frale, *L'ultima battaglia*, pp. 103–8.

58 James Given, 'The Inquisitors of Languedoc and the Medieval Technology of Power', *The American Historical Review*, 94 (1989), 343.

as torture, so the duration and the conditions were not bound by restrictions. And after fighting the Cathars for more than 70 years, the Languedocian inquisitors were especially experienced in dealing with incarceration.[59] Bernard Gui was convinced that a period of several years would make even the most recalcitrant suspect confess his errors.[60] If required, they could tighten the conditions by putting the prisoners in chains or by depriving them of food (or both).[61] Others recommended the supplementary application of lies and threats and their surveillance by informers.[62] A few weeks sufficed in most cases to persuade a prisoner to confess.[63] The average length of time between the detention of a suspect, his confession and absolution is given in the register of Jacques Fournier as 24 weeks.[64] At the time of their first deposition in front of the inquisitor, the Templars of Alès had spent nearly three years continuously in prison. Their second statement followed again one year later. Even if these men had been at the beginning of the trial comparable to the defenders of Acre or Ruad – and Alain Demurger stressed that they were not[65] – after all these years they could not be the same.

At the moment of their second interrogation these Templars had been in jail for nearly four years. Convinced that certain Templars had agreed in prison to deny the charges and how to answer the questions, Guillelmus de S. Laurencio had

---

59 Barber, *Trial*, p. 70.

60 Bernard Gui, *Manuel*, vol. 2, pp. 56–7. Over 40 per cent of those interrogated by Bernard Gui stayed in prison for some time before they confessed: Given, *Inquisition*, p. 57. In one case a suspect had stayed over 19 years in prison before he was sentenced: Charles Molinier, *L'inquisition dans le midi de la France au XIIIe et au XIVe siècle: Etude sur les sources de son histoire* (Paris, 1880), p. 99.

61 Bernard Gui, *Manuel*, vol. 1, pp. 182–3. These techniques were also part of the instructions of Bishop Guillaume of Paris for the inquisition in his diocese: Barber, *Trial*, p. 133. These were also adapted in the diocese of Nîmes: Ménard, *Histoire*, p. 167.

62 *David von Augsburg*, ed. Preger, 223: *Si autem recuset hoc facere, recludatur in carcere et incuciatur ei timor, quod testes contra ipsum habeantur, et si per testes convictus fuerit, nulla fiat ei misericordia, quin morti tradatur; et sustentetur tenui victu, quia timor talis humiliabit eum, et non permittatur aliquis accedere complicium suorum, ne roboret eum vel instruat quomodo calide respondeat et nullum prodat, nec alii accedant, nisi aliquando duo fideles et providi, qui caute quasi compacientes moneant qum, ut a morte se liberet et sincere confiteatur quod erravit et in quibus, et promittant ei, quod si hec fecerit, quod tunc possit evadere ne cremetur*. Guillelmus de S. Laurencio also used this tactic: after the Templar Johannes Tardini had rejected the charges, Guillelmus told him that he possessed his confession made in front of the episcopal judge and several witnesses. Either this interrogation, of which we have no other mention, is lost today or the inquisitor simply lied: Ménard, *Histoire*, p. 173.

63 Given, *Inquisition*, p. 57.

64 Ibid., p. 58.

65 Demurger, *Templiers*, p. 504.

ordered the recourse to torture because the accused stubbornly denied their guilt.[66] This seems to support at first sight the view that torture was needed to break the oaths of secrecy sworn by the Templars,[67] but only if we adopt the reasoning of the inquisitors and the royal administration. In southern France only those brothers who had already been tortured admitted to such agreements. Bertrandus Arnaudi conceded that he had made arrangements with other brothers captured in Alès, but only after an interruption in his second deposition.[68] Of the three persons Guillelmus Penchenati incriminated in his testimony, one was already dead, while the two still alive denied these agreements.[69]

The effects of incarceration help to explain the span of time between the interrogations in the early summer of 1310 and the second inquiry in August 1311. The inquisitor, unsatisfied with his first results, decided that it could be useful to give the Templars a little time for consideration. When the opening of the council of Vienne was approaching, he was obliged to produce results. The duration of the interrogations demonstrates that a serious investigation of individual deeds or beliefs, essential to prove the guilt of the single brother, was not Guillelmus de S. Laurencio's aim at that time. Instead, he played it safe: the use of torture ensured that in only one day 28 Templars confessed nearly everything. Even Odoardus de Malodumo interrogated at most 16 brothers per day. Interestingly, the fact that they all confessed nearly the same things means that all, knight brothers as well as servants, had attended the provincial chapter and seen the devil in the shape of a cat, the demons, the idol etc., whereas normally only the preceptors of the commanderies took part in provincial chapters.[70] Surprisingly, Raimundus Sagerii and Poncius Seguerii, who had certainly attended these meetings, denied such occurrences.[71]

---

66 Ibid., p. 209: *constet etiam michi per confessiones factas coram me per fratrem Betrandum Arnaudi & Petrum de Tholosa, & Drohetum, servientes templi, se & alios fratres templarios supradictos concordasse in carcere quod omnes illos errores quos confessi fuerunt coram aliis inquisitoribus, coram me negarent, quia eram competens judex: idcirco pronuncio predictum Raymundum Sagerii, presbiterum, qui coram me negavit illa que confessus fuerat coram aliis supradictis inquisitoribus, esse torquendum moderate; & nedum [!] ipsum Raymundum Sagerii, sed etiam omnes alios templarios qui negaverunt coram me illos errors quos confessi fuerant se dixissi & fecisse coram supradictis inquisitoribus, scilicet domino Odardo & predictis fratribus predicatoribus*; Bertandus Arnaudi and Petrus de Tholosa were interrogated twice by the inquisitor, with quite contradictory depositions.

67 Jonathan Riley-Smith, 'Were the Templars Guilty?', in *The Medieval Crusade*, ed. Susan J. Ridyard (Woodbridge, 2004), p. 115.

68 Ménard, *Histoire*, p. 175.

69 Ibid., pp. 213–14.

70 Demurger, *Templiers*, p. 150.

71 Ibid., pp. 211–12, 214.

The effects of torture and imprisonment become clear when one compares the number of the interrogated. In the 13 months of imprisonment three of the 32 Templars disappeared from the protocols. They are not listed among those Templars who tried to defend their order, and it is also improbable that they had been released or moved to another diocese. One has to assume that they had died in prison. It is significant that, as in the cases of Bertrandus Arnaudi and Petrus de Tholosa, two of these were in all likelihood tortured. The losses are even greater for the period between the interrogations of 1311 and the sentences pronounced in November 1312, by which time seven further brothers had disappeared. Altogether, more than 30 per cent of the brothers who were still alive in 1310 did not survive the period of the trial.

In the context of this study, the three depositions of Bernardus de Selgues, knight brother and former commander of St Gilles, are a particularly apt demonstration of what has been said. He was one of the highest-ranking Templar brothers interrogated in southern France. His three statements were not abbreviated, which argues for the importance the interrogators attached to them. His first deposition dates from 10 November 1307 and was thus over two weeks later than the 'confessions' of Jacques de Molay. He acknowledged the charges strictly according to the *interrogatorium* in the order of arrest from 14 September 1307. But there are two noteworthy details. Firstly, his receptor, with whom he had exchanged the three illicit kisses, had worn a rag around his hips during the ceremony. This is otherwise only found in the deposition of Bertrandus de Selva, a knight brother from Montpellier. Since he had been the first to be questioned on 10 November 1307, it can be assumed that his deposition acted as a model.[72] Secondly, Bernardus admitted the common use of non-consecrated hosts, yet he deposed to know nothing about the veneration of an idol or a head.[73]

On 24 June 1310, Bernardus was interrogated by Guillelmus de S. Laurencio for the first time. In contrast to his former deposition he denied every charge. The inquisitors asked him in detail about the receptions in which he had taken part, but they did not find much to condemn. This time, the new brothers had kissed their receptors only on the mouth and nowhere else.[74] The inquisitor showed a special interest in the chapters and the veneration of an idol. Bernardus de Selgues was questioned with painstaking accuracy about the existence of a golden, silver or metallic head, the veneration of a cat or a raven or the appearance of a woman. Having given a denial to every question, Bernardus insisted instead on the

---

[72] Ibid., p. 201.

[73] He himself knew nothing about that, but when he talked with a brother from Lombardy, this Templar thought that non-consecrated hosts were usual. The only other brother who was questioned about the use of hosts was the priest brother Raimundus Sagerii: ibid., pp. 202, 204.

[74] Ibid., p. 180: *dixit quod recipiens receptum in sua receptione osculabatur in ore & non alibi.*

righteousness of the order.[75] To assess this decision, it is necessary to remember the circumstances. At the moment of his deposition, Bernard de Selgues' incarceration had lasted for nearly 31 months, that is, longer than that of any suspect of Jacques Fournier.[76] The Templars at Alès knew about the 'confessions' of their leaders, which heightened the psychological pressure on them. In addition, all attempts to defend the order had by then come to an abrupt end through the burning of 54 brothers and the disappearance of Peter of Bologna.[77] Notwithstanding, Bernard de Selgues and 28 out of 32 brothers rejected every accusation.

More than a year later, Guillelmus de S. Laurencio summoned the Templars again. Bernardus de Selgues was the first witness who was interrogated after torture, and this time he expressed the desire to alter his former deposition. What follows is the exact copy of his first testimony made in front of the Seneschal Odoardus de Malodumo. Only upon express inquiry did he alter the standardised answers concerning incidents during several provincial chapters at Montpellier. Now he declared that he had seen someone holding a head during one chapter which, as usual, had taken place at night. The devil had suddenly appeared in the form of a cat and promised the assembled Templars good yields and worldly riches. Bernardus admitted that he himself and all the other brothers had venerated the head which answered questions. Moreover, demons in the shape of women had materialised during this ceremony.[78] After four years of imprisonment and the assignment of torture the inquisitor finally obtained the desired confession.

---

75 Ibid., p. 179: *Requisitus singillatim si ibi erat, vel asserebatur, vel adorabatur, seu venerabatur, aliquod ydolum, vel forma argentea, vel aurea, vel metallina, vel alia, capitis hominis? Dixit quod non. Item requisitus singillatim per intervalla si catus ibi vel alibi adorabatur, vel unquam vidit catum adorari vel etiam apparere inter fratres aliquos dicti ordinis, vel corvos seu corvum? Dixit quod non. Item si mulier seu mulieres in aliquo dictorum capitulorum vel in eis apparebant seu apparuerunt? Dixit quod non sciat ... Et petit idem qui loquitur quod redderetur sibi ecclesia qui injuste, ut dixit, sibi fuerat denegata, quia, ut dixit, ordo predictus bonus est.*

76 Given, *Inquisition*, p. 58. The longest proceedings lasted a little over two years.

77 For the details: Barber, *Trial*, pp. 178–82.

78 Ménard, *Histoire*, p. 211: *Item frater Bernardus de Selgues dixit & confessus fuit requisitus se fuisse in diversis seu multis capitulis provincialibus templariorum in villa Montis-pessulani, & quod vidit in uno dictorum capitulorum, quod de nocte more solito fuit factum, tenebatur unum caput sive testa, & quod tunc apparuit ibi dyabolus in figura seu specie cati, euntis circumquaque dictum caput, loquentis & dicentis dictis fratribus templariis ibi astantibus se daturum eis bonas messes, & divitias possessionum auri et argenti & aliorum bonorum temporalium. Item dixit & confessus fuit quod ipse & omnes alii fratres templarii qui ibi erant adorabant & adoraverunt ibi dictum capud seu testam. Item dixit & confessus fuit quod statim facta adoratione demons in figura seu specie mulierum apparuerunt ibidem, quibus quilibet fratrum assistentium volens accipere abutebatur; sed ipse, ut dixit, non fuit usus. Item dixit quod dictum caput et testa, ad requisitionem dicti magistri ibi presentis, dabat responsum de hiis de quibus requirebatur.*

Most of the inquisitors, like Guillelmus de S. Laurencio, were convinced that they were dealing with guilty heretics when they were interrogating the Templars. For reasons inherent to inquisitorial procedures, they tried to extract confessions whenever possible. They used an elaborate set of tactics for this purpose. Torture was only one means, perhaps not even the most effective, certainly not the most frequent. However, it was definitely used more often than is apparent from the sources. It was quite difficult for the Templars to alter their statements after their first depositions. If they did, their interrogators saw their doubts confirmed and rejected the revocation. In this respect the inquisitors were to a certain degree prisoners of their own logic. In combination with their methods they were able 'to create their own, tailor-made realities. Through their interrogation procedures, the inquisitors could make manifest the ideas, fears, and fantasies that had previously resided only in their own minds'.[79] A valid confession as a sign of real repentance represented additionally the *conditio sine qua non* for penitence. This was essential, because inquisitors conceived themselves more as theologians than jurists.[80] These two points combined meant that the Templars had to persuade the inquisitors of the sincerity of their statements not just with a story, but with convincing details.

One could pose the question of Anne Gilmour-Bryson again: Did the system work?[81] Yes, it did, but for the royal administration and against the Templars, because fear and torture were not a fault but an integral part of the system, and it was, as Bernard Gui had shown, only a matter of time before the expected 'confessions' would be extracted. Nevertheless it would be too simple and sweeping to conclude that there were no lies where torture was not used and vice versa. It has not been the goal of this article to prove the innocence of the order. To conclude this reassessment of the details of the 'confessions': they were necessary only to convince the inquisitor, and therefore cannot act as proof of these confessions' credibility.

---

79 Given, *Inquisitors*, p. 351.

80 Scharff, 'Seelenrettung', 163; Jean-Louis Biget, *Hérésie et inquisition dans le midi de la France* (Paris, 2007), p. 189.

81 Gilmour-Bryson, 'The Templar Trials', 41.

Chapter 7
The Templars Face the Inquisition: The Papal Commission and the Diocesan Tribunals in France, 1308–11

Dale R. Streeter

The sudden arrest of the Templars in France on 13 October 1307, their subsequent interrogation and trial, and the eventual dissolution of the order by Pope Clement V in 1311 make for one of the most captivating and controversial episodes in the long struggle between Church and State during the medieval period. The Templar affair also represents a transition from the haphazard method of investigating heresy developed in the thirteenth century, which responded primarily to local conditions, to a more formalized and ritualized process that would characterize the Inquisition during the remainder of the medieval period. This standardization of practice and theory became codified in texts and manuals and gave the inquisitorial process a reliability and uniformity that was conspicuously lacking in civil judicial procedure.

The central factor in the demise of the Templars was the ability of the French king, Philip IV (also known as Philip the Fair, for his handsome visage rather than for his sense of justice), to use the prelates and procedures of the Church itself to achieve his desired end – the suppression of the order and the seizure of its assets. By far the most effective of his strategies was the use of compliant bishops, appointed through royal influence and dependent on the king's patronage, to expedite and facilitate his plan and bring about the dissolution of the military order.

In August 1308, while residing at Poitiers in France, Pope Clement V promulgated the bull *Faciens misericoridiam,* which summarized his understanding of the charges against the military order of the Temple, whose suppression was sought by the French king.[1] In the preceding months, the pope had already accepted the necessity of a papal commission of inquiry to investigate the charges against the military order, and both the papal commission and diocesan inquiries were to begin the following year.[2] At this stage, the conditions under which the Templars had been held since their arrest on 13 October 1307 were dire indeed. Confessions

---

1 For Philip's motivations in desiring the downfall of the Templars, see Joseph Strayer, *The Reign of Philip the Fair* (Princeton, 1980), pp. 287–93.

2 Malcolm Barber, *The Trial of the Templars*, 2nd edn (Cambridge, 2006), p. 125.

to a litany of serious offences such as heresy, blasphemy and idolatry had been coerced, and if the brothers were to recant at a later date they faced the even more fearful prospect of being charged with contumacious heresy and its inevitable penalty – to be burned at the stake.

The crisis facing Clement was daunting. His desire to maintain some degree of ecclesiastical control over the evolving problem required steps in several directions: he called for a general council to meet at Vienne in two years' time; he also formulated plans for a papal commission to examine the statements of the leaders of the Templars and the charges against the order generally. He reserved for himself the disposition of the affair. For the bulk of the order's members under arrest in the French kingdom, diocesan tribunals were established to investigate and adjudicate the charges against the brothers.[3] The composition of those tribunals and the papal commission is the focus of attention here. Who were the men responsible for this task, and what loyalties were tested in the performance of their duties?

The matter of who sat on the diocesan tribunals and the papal commission became the key to the king's strategy to bring about the downfall of the military order, for without a record of legitimate judicial proceedings his charges would be perceived as mendacious and without merit. Despite his relationship with previous popes, Philip's reliance on the bishops' tribunals during the Templar affair underscored the continued relevance of the papacy in the fourteenth century, for without papal cooperation the king's desire to suppress the Templars could not be realized either in France or elsewhere.

Clement's position in this affair was ambiguous. To thwart the desires of the king was to invite intimidation and, perhaps, a repeat of the horror of Anagni, where his predecessor, Boniface VIII, had been humiliated and brutalized by this same Philip the Fair. Clement desperately wanted a solution that would at once deliver him from the influence of the implacable Philip and that would deal justly with the serious allegations against the Templars. Clement's composure was not improved by the implication made by one of the king's adherents, Gilles Aycelin, the archbishop of Narbonne, who reportedly whispered to the pope that 'when a prelate fails to stamp out error, it is as if he made himself guilty of it'.[4] Although Clement was deeply shocked at the confessions that were submitted and very likely believed the accusations to have merit, he also believed that it was a papal right and obligation to determine their validity and ought not to be the product of the exertions of the king's torturers.

The establishment of bishops' tribunals would thus bring the more orderly process of the Inquisition into play (although the Inquisition itself had only

[3] *Reg. Clem. V*, vol. 3, pp. 284–7, no. 3402; the full text of *Faciens misericordiam* can also be found in Roger Sève and Anne-Marie Chagny-Sève, *Le procès des Templiers d'Auvergne (1309–1311)* (Paris, 1986), pp. 93–7.

[4] Guillaume Mollat, *The Popes at Avignon, 1305–1378*, 9th edn, trans. Janet Love (London, 1963), p. 236.

a small part to play in this affair), with the proper presentation of accusations, the testimony of witnesses, cataloguing of property and the opportunity for the accused to present a defence – all of which would be recorded and establish the legality of the process.[5]

On 13 July 1308, the pope had stipulated that the diocesan tribunals appointed to examine the evidence against the Templars would consist of the ordinary or his official, two canons of the cathedral chapter, two Dominican friars, and two Franciscan friars. The friars were presumed to be familiar with the inquisitional process and therefore reliable and impartial participants.[6] The inclusion of secular religious would also provide a sense of balance and objectivity. Guillaume de Baufet, the bishop of Paris, had issued instructions in late 1308 about the procedure to be followed in his diocese that detailed the exacting steps to be taken to determine the validity of the charges. Each Templar was to be brought before the bishop or the inquisitor and 'to swear on the holy gospels to tell the pure and full truth concerning both themselves and others'.[7] Then a uniform set of questions would be asked of each brother: the time and place of his reception into the order, who had been present, and the manner of the reception. In addition, each brother was to reveal if any special or unusual activities had occurred and whether any witnesses could be called to verify the brother's testimony.[8] Those who refused to testify would be subject to a harsh regime of treatment beginning with reduced rations and culminating in threats of torture, but only to be used as a last resort to deal with the most intransigent. Conversely, those who willingly confessed to the various charges of heresy, blasphemy and sodomy and sought forgiveness were to be treated kindly and, though still held in custody, enjoy an easier mode of confinement.

These diocesan tribunals represent the first formalized example of the inquisitorial process by which qualified and capable men employed a standardized and regular method of investigation of charges.[9] The king's inquiries, in contrast, were noticeably lacking such formalized procedures. The object of the inquisition (and, by extension, these tribunals) in the eyes of the Church was 'to lead the accused along the path of penitence and reconciliation'.[10]

Such was the proclaimed aim of the diocesan tribunals and of Clement's desire to contain and control a serious problem for the Church and deflect an avenue of attack against it. Events leapt ahead of this plan, however, and the king's determination to realize his goal was not to be thwarted by procedural constraints.

---

5 *PUT*, vol. 1, p. 232; Sève and Chagny-Sève, *Procès des Templiers*, pp. 21–4.

6 *PUT*, 235; Barber, *Trial*, p. 124.

7 Barber, *Trial*, p. 133.

8 Ibid., p. 133, citing *Le livre de Guillaume Le Maire*, ed. Célestine Port, in *Mélanges historiques: Choix de documents*, vol. 2 (Paris, 1877), pp. 446–8.

9 Jean-Marie Vidal, *Bullaire de l'inquisition française au XIVe siècle et jusqu'à la fin du grand schisme* (Paris, 1913), pp. lxvi–lxix.

10 Barber, *Trial*, p. 134.

In fact, the king retained custody of the arrested Templars and employed the full range of coercion to obtain the desired confessions. The fear of additional torture seems to have been sufficient to bring all but the strongest wills into conformity with royal desires.

The papal commission and the diocesan tribunals provided Clement's best hope of asserting his plenary power over the Church, including his right of jurisdiction over the Templars, an exempt order, that is, subject to papal authority alone, and of the ordinary authority of his bishops to teach and defend the faith. Who sat on these inquisitorial boards was to be the most significant factor in the outcome of the proceedings. It is not a coincidence that for several years the king had been placing in important dioceses men whose loyalty could be counted on in any test of wills between king and pope. When the time came, many of these bishops had to choose whether to stand with their nominal superior, the pope, or with the source of their patronage, the king. Once installed, a bishop had a canonical claim to both the authority in his diocese and its income. He could be translated, if the pope chose to move him to another diocese, but the custom required promotion to a more prestigious or lucrative diocese rather than demotion to one less desirable. Thus, a bishop enjoyed a sense of immunity and stability in his status and revenue that few others shared.

Aubert Aycelin, bishop of Clermont, convened the first major diocesan tribunal in June 1309. During the five-day period from the 4th to the 10th of June, the commission interrogated 69 Templars, devoting the final day of the proceedings to hear those who denied the charges laid against the order.[11] Such a noticeable lack of enthusiasm for the king's cause is somewhat surprising for one who obviously benefited from the royal connection. Aubert was the nephew of one of the king's closest ecclesiastical advisors, Gilles Aycelin, archbishop of Narbonne, who was the bishop's uncle as well as his metropolitan, that is, his ecclesiastical superior.

Gilles Aycelin was totally the creature of the king. Gilles came from a noble family in the Auvergne. His older brother, Hughes de Billom, had been cardinal bishop of Ostia, and another brother, Jean, had also been bishop of Clermont from 1298 to 1301.[12] The family was one of those in which ecclesiastical careers were the chief form of advancement. Gilles spent the bulk of his career as a royal clerk under Philip IV. Although the term suggests a minor functionary, royal clerks served the king in a wide range of capacities, from quite modest to exalted. The term merely represents a category of employment by clerics in royal service.[13] In 1285, the first year of Philip's reign, Gilles was appointed provost in the cathedral

---

[11] Ibid., pp. 134–5.

[12] Konrad Eubel, *Hierarchia catholica medii aevi* (hereafter cited as *HCMA*) (Münster, 1898), vol. 1, p. 199.

[13] Ferdinand Lot and Robert Fawtier, *Institutions royals* (Paris, 1958), vol. 3, pp. 55–9.

church of Clermont and to a canonry at Narbonne about the same time.[14] Later, in 1288, the king sent him as a proctor to the papal court, and in 1290, Gilles was appointed archbishop of Narbonne, an important and wealthy archdiocese in the south of France (the episcopal income for the archdiocese of Narbonne was in excess of 30,000 florins per annum and among the highest in the kingdom).[15] Gilles' spectacular rise from obscurity to prominence is persuasive evidence of the value the king placed on Gilles' abilities and his loyalty. Aycelin did not remain long in his new diocese but appointed an episcopal vicar and returned to the French court where he became one of Philip the Fair's main agents, along with Pierre Flote and Gilles de Remini, both laymen, and Pierre Belleperche, a canon at Bruges and later bishop of Auxerre.[16] Gilles Aycelin was deeply involved in the affair of Bernard Saisset, bishop of Pamiers, which provoked, or served as the pretext to, the conflict between the Philip the Fair and Pope Boniface VIII. With such a strong connection to the king, it is not unlikely that the appointment of his nephew to the see at Clermont in 1307 was a patronage appointment to gratify Gilles Aycelin. It was also likely intended to help the king extend the reach of his power into areas traditionally outside Capetian control, such as the Midi.

Thus, the short shrift given to the Templar business by the newly appointed bishop of Clermont suggests a lack of attachment to the king's desires or, perhaps, represented a pro forma gesture in which the process itself mattered more than any specific result.

For some time, the king had been pressuring the pope to use his power of reservation and provision to appoint royal supporters to vacant episcopal sees. Once installed in their dioceses, these prelates would then be in a position to further royal interests from within the Church, while the king's lay advisors, such as Flote and later Guillaume Nogaret, worked from without. Between 1306 and 1309, Philip had managed to place a number of his clerks into important French dioceses. Certainly the most important was the appointment of Philip de Marigny as archbishop of Sens. Marigny was the brother of Philip IV's powerful financial advisor, Enguerrand de Marigny. Philip de Marigny had been bishop of Cambrai, an important and wealthy diocese in Flanders, since 1306 and was translated to the archdiocese of Sens in 1309 (the episcopal income for the diocese of Cambrai was 18,000 florins per annum and the same for the archdiocese of Sens, which, however, was a metropolitan see).[17] This was a crucial appointment because in this position Marigny was metropolitan of the province in which Paris lay, and he could influence any judicial proceedings that took place in his province. This proved to be the case on 11 May 1310, when, with the approval of a hastily summoned

---

14 *Gallia Christiana veteris editionis*, ed. Scevloe Sainte-Marthe (Paris, 1656), vol. 1, p. 592.

15 Hermann Hoberg, *Taxae pro communibus servitiis ex libris obligationum ab anno 1295 usque ad annum 1455 confectis* (Vatican City, 1949), p. 83.

16 *HCMA*, vol. 1, p. 122.

17 Hoberg, *Taxae pro communibus*, pp. 27, 110.

provincial council, he ordered 54 Templars who had recanted their confessions to be burned at the stake outside Paris as relapsed heretics. Marigny took this drastic step before the papal commission had concluded its investigation – indeed the purpose of the mass execution was to forestall any possibility that the imprisoned Templars would withdraw their coerced confessions or that the commission might reach a conclusion detrimental to the king's objective. Just a few days later, on 16 May 1310, nine more Templars were burned at Senlis.[18] These actions had their desired effect, and there were no additional recantations from the imprisoned brothers. Although the archbishop's action was preemptive, it was within his authority as the metropolitan of the ecclesiastical province of Sens.

From 1306 through 1308, Philip had been able to place other reliable clerks in valuable diocesan sees and establish a foundation for exerting effective royal control over the Templar affair. One of the clerks mentioned previously, Pierre de Belleperche, was appointed bishop of Auxerre in 1306. Belleperche was a native of the Bourbonnais and had studied law at the universities in Bologna and Toulouse. As a doctor of laws, his writings brought him to the attention of the king, and he entered royal service in 1296. He became a trusted advisor to the king, who could reasonably consider Belleperche a reliable supporter of his policies. Unfortunately for the king, Belleperche died in 1308. He was replaced by another royal clerk, Pierre de Grez, who at the time of his appointment to the see of Auxerre was precentor (the canon in the cathedral chapter responsible for the liturgical music) at Notre Dame in Paris. He, too, had excellent connections with the royal family. De Grez had earlier served the queen, Jeanne of Navarre, and, after her death in 1305, her eldest son Louis, the heir to the throne. Another indication of the close connection between the crown and de Grez is that his brother, Jean de Grez, was the marshal of France. Pierre held the diocese of Auxerre until his death in 1325. De Grez was typical of those bishops whom Philip placed in importance sees – trained in royal service and loyal to their benefactor.

Another significant appointment arranged by Philip for one of his clerks was the translation of Pierre de Levis to the see of Cambrai in 1309. This important diocese in the north of France had the substantial annual income of 18,000 florins and, consequently, would be reserved for the most reliable and efficient of the king's servants. De Levis had earlier been bishop of Maguelonne since 1306 and, in 1324, would again be translated to the diocese of Bayeux.[19] The provision of another of Philip's clerks, Raoul Grosparmi, to the important diocese of Orleans in 1308 is another example of those useful appointments that Philip used to strengthen his hold on the Gallican Church.[20] Grosparmi had served on the commission the

[18] Mollat, *Popes at Avignon*, p. 238; *Le dossier de l'affaire des Templiers*, ed. Georges Lizerand, 2nd edn (Paris, 1964), pp. 155–7.

[19] *Lettres communes de Jean XXII*, ed. Guillaume Mollat, 16 vols (Paris, 1906–47), nos 19215, 19218.

[20] *HCMA*, vol. 1, p. 120; *Registres du tresor des chartes*, ed. Robert Fawtier (Paris, 1958), vol. 1, pp. 520, 1028.

king had called to investigate the charges against Guichard, bishop of Troyes, in 1300.[21] Grosparmi's membership on that committee reflects the trust the king had in him and his reliability in supporting the king's interests. Over time, during a long reign (1285–1314), Philip IV had established 'effective control of the higher clergy' in France and adjacent areas.[22]

These prelates had to negotiate the fine line between loyalty to their royal patron and obedience to their ecclesiastical superiors and the plenary power of the pope. Often they found their obligations to the king distasteful (as, perhaps, did Aubert Aycelin of Clermont in 1309) and sought to avoid too partisan a stance. But political realities in the fourteenth century often trumped fine distinctions – the stakes were too high and miscalculation too costly.

The papal commission set up in 1309 to determine the truth of the allegations against the Templars was Clement's final attempt to gain control over Philip's assault on the order. The king had suggested the proposed membership to Clement, and the pontiff, for the most part, seems to have accepted his nominees.[23] The president of the commission was none other than Gilles Aycelin, the previously mentioned archbishop of Narbonne.[24] Oddly, in 1311, Gilles would be asked to exchange his archdiocese in the Midi with that of the pope's nephew, Bernard de Farges, who in 1306 had been made archbishop of Rouen, one of the most important and wealthiest of the northern dioceses, with an annual income of about 36,000 florins. Bernard, it seems, found the climate of northern France uncongenial.

Gilles's appointment to head the commission appeared to be a decisive step in fulfilling the king's desire to eliminate the Templars. Other prelates named to the papal commission included Guillaume Durant, bishop of Mende, a king's man and the nephew of the eponymous canonist; Guillaume Bonnet, bishop of Bayeux, also a king's man; and Reginald de la Porte, bishop of Limoges and later archbishop of Bourges before his promotion to cardinal in 1320. Also named to the commission were Matthew of Naples, a papal notary; Giovanni of Mantua, an auditor in the service of Cardinal Piero Colonna; Jean of Montlaur, the archdeacon of the diocese of Maguelonne; and Jean Agarvi, the provost of the cathedral chapter of Aix-en-Provence.[25] Because two of the non-episcopal members were curialists and the remaining two were capitular officials from southern French dioceses, these would

---

[21] Joseph Strayer, 'The Case of Bishop Guichard of Troyes', in *Charanis Studies: Essays in Honor of Peter Charanis*, ed. Angeliki E. Laiou-Thomadakis (New Brunswick, 1980), pp. 248–60.

[22] Barber, *Trial*, p. 137.

[23] Ibid., p. 138.

[24] *Reg. Clem. V*, no. 6775 (5 May 1311); Vincent Tabbagh, *Diocèse de Rouen* (Turnhout, 1998), vol. 2, p. 92; for the income of Rouen see Hoberg, *Taxae pro comunibus*, p. 103.

[25] Georges Lizerand, *Clément V et Philippe IV le Bel* (Paris, 1910), pp. 128–32, 139–50; Mollat, *The Popes at Avignon*, p. 237; Jean Dunbabin, *A Hound of God: Pierre de Palud and the Fourteenth-Century Church* (Oxford, 1991), p. 22.

be individuals who were more likely to be supportive of the papal position, and thus their appointment was an attempt to bring some balance to the commission. But it appears indisputable that the dominant members of the papal commission convened to judge the charges against the military order were cognizant of the king's desires in the matter.

The commission began its deliberations at the monastery of St Geneviève in Paris on 8 August 1309 and concluded its business on 5 June 1311. In the end, its conclusions were tainted by the inability to examine all of the accused Templars and witnesses to their alleged blasphemies. Malcolm Barber believes this was because the king was reluctant to allow testimony before the commission that he could not control and did not want evidence presented that did not support his case.[26] This assertion is informative on two levels: firstly, it suggests that the king was careful not to allow any facts into evidence that undermined or refuted his charges against the Templars. Why should this concern him except that he wanted the process to appear to be legitimate and yet still achieve his desired result? He could not suppress or disregard sworn testimony and still maintain judicial impartiality. The process of the tribunals and their findings formed an important record of his own administration, and Philip always wanted his actions to appear to be legitimate. One need only recall the efforts he went to in discrediting Boniface VIII, always seeking to place himself in the position of a concerned Christian monarch seeking reform. Secondly, another consequence of the king's actions was the implicit recognition of the jurisdiction of the papal commission over an exempt order of the Church and, by extension, of the plenary power of the pope to install such a commission and to act on its findings.

Perversely, the king's actions had undermined his own position by which he undertook the campaign against the Templars. His appeal to the masters of theology at the university of Paris in March 1308 had been based on the principle that as a Christian monarch he had the right and obligation to root out heresy and corruption in his own realm.[27] By accepting a papal commission and even filling its membership with his own supporters, the king recognized the overriding authority of the pope to administer the affairs of the Church and to adjudicate disputes and impose discipline within it.

The bishop of Paris, Guillaume de Baufet, issued detailed instructions late in 1308 on the proper conduct of the tribunal judging the Templars in his diocese.[28] Much of what was contained in his instructions would later appear in inquisitorial manuals written by the Dominican Friar Bernard Gui and the Cistercian Inquisitor Jacques Fournier, later Pope Benedict XII.[29] In its conclusion, Baufet's document maintains that the authority of the tribunal is an extension of three separate

---

26 Barber, *Trial*, pp. 139–40.

27 *CUP*, vol. 2, no. 664, p. 125.

28 *Le dossier*, ed. Lizerand, pp. 139–45; Barber, *Trial*, p. 133.

29 Bernard Gui, *The Inquisitor's Guide: A Medieval Manual on Heretics*, (trans. and ed.) Janet Shirley (Welwyn Garden City, 2006), pp. 29–32; *Le registre d'inquisition de*

jurisdictional entities: first, the power of the pope to appoint legatine authority in the Church; second, the inquisitorial power of the pope to purify the Church against heresy; and third, the ordinary power of every bishop to rule in his diocese and protect the Church and its members (*Item, de cibis et aliis agatur cum eis sicut cum illis de primo articulo, exceptis auditis per papam et inquisitorem et ordinarios, qui tute tenebuntur, donec aliud ordinetur*).[30]

The determination of the king to suppress the order of the Temple and charge its members with the crimes of heresy, blasphemy, sodomy and idolatry forced him to recognize the overriding authority of the Church and of the papacy in adjudicating the matter. To achieve his end, Philip had to accept the principle of exemption – the jurisdiction of the pope over the order – and cajole, coerce, and intimidate the pope and prelates of France to act. As a result, the inquisitional process within the Church was developed and refined to a high standard for the time, certainly in contrast to royal justice. The king needed compliant bishops to bring about his objective, a resource he had carefully cultivated over time.

Ironically, Pope Clement V, in submitting to the demands of the king and authorizing the establishment of a papal commission and diocesan tribunals, effectively asserted the right of the Church to control its own clerics and to establish an inquisitorial process that would be professional, impartial and just. By losing the initiative to the king, the pope won the point, for the king had recognized the overriding authority of the papacy to judge its own members.

The king's activities against the order of the Temple brought him neither profit nor approbation, particularly because proceedings against the Templars in other kingdoms produced no corroboration of his charges; nor did those investigations resort to the brutality and injustice of Philip's actions. Clement, too, has suffered in the historical record as a weak and vacillating pope who allowed a great injustice to take place because of his reluctance to resist the king's demands. Such judgments come easy from a great distance in time, but Philip was clearly a formidable individual: determined in his purpose, relentless in his methods and implacable in his hatred. In the end, both pope and king died in the same year, 1314 – cursed, it has been said, by the dying words of Jacques de Molay, the grand master of the Templars, as he was burned to death in Paris in March 1314 on the king's orders.

Jacques Fournier, évêque de Pamiers (1318–1325), ed. Jean Duvernoy, 3 vols (Toulouse, 1965).

30 *Le dossier*, ed. Lizerand, pp. 144–5.

Chapter 8
Three 'Traitors' of the Temple: Was Their Truth the Whole Truth?

David Bryson

On 27 November 1309, in the chapel of the bishop's palace alongside the cathedral of Notre Dame in Paris, Ponsard de Gisy, the preceptor of the Templar house of Payns (or Payens), stood before the papal commissioners. They asked him whether he wished to defend the order of the Temple, and Ponsard replied that the articles accusing the Templars of denying Christ, spitting on the cross and having license to have carnal relations with each other were false, and that the respective confessions had been made under torture and threat of death. Having said that, Ponsard handed the commissioners a note in his own handwriting, which read as follows: 'These are the traitors, those who have spoken falsely and disloyally against those of the order of the Temple: Guillaume Robert, the monk, who tortured them; Esquieu de Floyrac from Béziers, co-prior of Monfaucon; Bernard Pelet, the prior of Mas d'Agenais; and Gérard de Boyzol, a knight who came to Gisors'.[1] This article will address three questions: Who were these persons? What had they allegedly done or said that resulted in them being called 'traitors'? And what does this tell us about the guilt or innocence of the order of the Temple?

To take the identity of these four individuals first: Guillaume Robert, the monk who tortured them, has been identified as Guillaume de Paris, the grand inquisitor of France, the very person in charge of the Paris trial of 1307–08.[2] However, the family name of Guillaume de Paris was 'Imbert', while the aforementioned monk's family name was 'Robert'. A document of 5 February 1311 shows that, in fact, a monk named *Guilhem Robert* of the Benedictine priory of St Martin de Bergerac in Dordogne was granted royal letters of safeguard 'because of his exposure to great risks due to his involvement in the affair of the Templars'.[3]

---

1 *PT*, vol. 1, pp. 36–7: *Ces sont le treytour, li quel ont proposé fauseté et delauté contra este de la religion deu Temple: Guillalmes Roberts moynes, qui les mitoyet à geine, Esquius de Floyrac de Biterris, cumprior de Montfaucon, Bernardus Peleti, prieus de Maso de Genois, et Geraues de Boyzol cehalier, veneus à Gisors*. English translations are my own except where otherwise noted.

2 *UT*, vol. 1, p.311; see Alain Demurger, *Les Templiers: Une chevalerie chrétienne au moyen âge* (Paris, 2005), pp. 430–1.

3 *Registres du trésor des chartes*, ed. Robert Fawtier (Paris, 1958), p. 307, no. 1583: Paris, 15 February 1311.

The second person, Esquieu de Floyrac of Béziers, co-prior of Monfaucon, is notorious because of the stories about him recounted by later historians.[4] Esquieu's letter attributing various illicit actions to the Templars is dated months after the trials had commenced,[5] but what matters here is the precise identity of the 'Monfaucon' of which Esquieu was said to have been co-prior. Alain Demurger has proposed the Benedictine priory of Monfaucon in the canton of La Force, *arrondissement* of Bergerac, in Dordogne, and the Templar trial records confirm this identification. During the testimony of Gérard de Lavergne, the preceptor of Périgord and of the Templar house of Andrivaux near Périgueux, given at Cahors in October and November 1307, it was stated that, among the non-Templar witnesses present, there was one *Hugone Moretelli*, prior of Monfaucon in the diocese of Périgord.[6] This establishes the link between the priory of which Esquieu de Floyrac was said to have been the co-prior and the Templar trial.

There can be no doubt about the identity of the third person on Ponsard's list, Bernard Pelet, the prior of Mas d'Agenais. He was a councillor of the king of England (in the latter's capacity as duke of Aquitaine)[7] and had delivered a letter from King Philip IV of France concerning the accusations against the Templars to King Edward II of England. Edward's reply of 30 October 1307 was one of angry disbelief, but it appears that Bernard was not a traitor, his role having been no more than that of the bearer of the bad news: 'We have had set forth before us, our prelates, our barons, and others of our council, by Master Bernard Pelet, clerk, what he had to say about the detestable heresy of which your letters make mention; as these things seem unbelievable, we have ordered our seneschal of Agenais, where these rumours began, to appear in our presence'.[8]

Thus, we come to Ponsard de Gisy's fourth 'traitor', namely Gérard de Boyzol, a knight who came to Gisors. At least two historians[9] have identified him as Gérard de Lavergne, the preceptor of Andrivaux and of Périgord. No doubt the effect was electrifying when Gérard de Lavergne stood up before his inquisitors in the house

[4] These are too numerous to mention, but they appear to derive from the republication of Giovanni Villani, *Cronica*, vol. 2, in 1845, and also thereafter from Finke's publication, *PUT*, in 1907.

[5] *PUT*, vol. 2, pp. 83–5.

[6] *PUT*, vol. 2, pp. 317–21; see ibid., p. 321 note 1.

[7] Jean-Paul Trabut-Cussac, *L'administration Anglaise en Gascogne* (Geneva, 1972), p. 380.

[8] *Notices et extraits des manuscrits de la Bibliothèque impériale*, ed. Edgard Boutaric (Paris, 1861), 'Documents relatifs à l'histoire de Philippe le Bel', in vol. 20, no. XXIII, pp. 161–2. This English translation from the French is my own. See also Demurger, *Templiers*, p. 431; *Gascon Rolls 1307–1317, Preserved in the Public Record Office*, ed. Yves Renouard, under the supervision of Robert Fawtier (London, 1964), no. 661; and Margaret Wade Labarge, *Gascony: England's First Colony* (London, 1980), p. 105.

[9] Demurger, *Templiers*, p. 431; Gilette Ziegler, *Les Templiers* (Paris, 1973), p. 141, where he is also described as 'de Neyzol'.

of the bailiff of Cahors and said: 'I was in great fear of death, because I was told that I would lose my body, because I am he who first revealed the secrets of the order'.[10] At last, a Templar candidate for the label of 'traitor'!

Guillaume Robert's Benedictine priory of St Martin de Bergerac and Esquieu de Floyrac's Benedictine priory of Monfaucon were just 20 kilometres apart, and they formed the east-west base of a triangle at the apex of which was Gérard de Lavergne's Templar preceptory of Andrivaux, located 40 kilometres to the north in the valley of the river Isle, west of Périgueux. There is another link: in late 1304, Bertrand de Got, then archbishop of Bordeaux, but soon to become Pope Clement V, visited his dioceses of Agen and Périgueux, moving from Bernard Pelet's priory of Mas d'Agenais to visit Esquieu de Floyrac's priory of Monfaucon north of Fleix on the Dordogne, and then staying at Guillaume Robert's priory on the banks of the Caudeau stream just north of Bergerac.[11] Yet, was Gérard de Lavergne indeed also known as Gérard de Boyzol, and did he 'come to Gisors' as Ponsard de Gisy had stated? I will return to these questions. Meanwhile, the issue is who or what may have been the source of the 'false and disloyal' information mentioned in Ponsard's note.

To pursue this question, the focus of this investigation will now shift from Périgord to Quercy, a hundred kilometres farther inland, to the region of Cahors in the Lot, where Gérard de Lavergne was brought to trial. Not far to the north-east, in the wild rocky upland called the Causse, was the remote Templar house of Le Bastit, whose preceptor, from 1305 to 1307, had been Gérard de Causse.[12]

Between 1307 and 1311, Gérard de Causse testified four times during the trial in Paris.[13] At his fourth and final appearance on 12 January 1311, perhaps the most compelling of the entire trial, Gérard began by stating that he had been received into the order 12 or 13 years earlier (i.e. some time between 1296 and 1298) in the Temple of Cahors, in the presence of Raymond Robert, who was the preceptor of Le Bastit at that time.[14] According to Gérard, after his reception together with two others, some sergeants of the order locked the door, held up a cross and said (and here, as well as for the next quote, I translate Raymond Oursel's dramatised French version which conforms closely to Jules Michelet's edition of the text):

---

10 *PUT*, vol. 2, p. 318.

11 Archives départementales de la Gironde, Bordeaux, MS G. 264, *Visite de Clément V*, transcribed in *Archives historiques du département de la Gironde*, vol. 23 (Bordeaux, 1883). See also Anne Gilmour-Bryson, 'L'elezione di Bertrand de Got (Clemente V) e l'incontro a St. Jean d'Angély', *Rivista di Storia della Chiesa in Italia*, 53, n. 2 (1999), 429–34.

12 See Malcolm Barber, *The Trial of the Templars*, 2nd edn (Cambridge, 2006), pp. 65, 146–7; also 1st edn (Cambridge, 1978), pp. 253–7; Malcolm Barber and Keith Bate, eds, *The Templars: Selected Sources* (Manchester, 2002), pp. 256–7, 289–92.

13 21 October 1307 (*PT*, vol. 2, p. 290); 22 November 1309 (*PT*, vol. 1, p. 28); 22 February 1310 (*PT*, vol. 1, p. 81); 12 January 1311 (*PT*, vol. 1, pp. 379–94).

14 *PT*, vol. 1, p. 379.

> 'Renounce God!' We, stupefied and terrified, certainly refused. 'You must!' (And bared their swords.) Then, under the grip of terror, we who carried no arms renounced God. I did it by mouth and not by heart; the two others also, I believe. 'Spit on the cross', the sergeants then commanded us. As we refused, they said that they would grant us grace, on the condition that we would keep it to ourselves and not denounce them. Then, one of them told us that if we sensed any natural heat, we could always couple between ourselves; that would be better for the reputation of the order than to chase after women.[15]

Later in his testimony, Gérard stated:

> A month later, still completely affected, I went to find Monseigneur Sicard,[16] bishop of Cahors, at his château of Mercuès[17] and confessed these abominations to him; he was stupefied and gave me absolution; as penance, he ordered me to wear an iron vest over my shirt for a set period;[18] to fast on specified days on bread and water; to promise all the good I could do for the renunciation of my sins; and finally, to leave for overseas as soon as possible. All of that, I accomplished.[19]

Thus, Gérard vividly described what allegedly happened during the time when Raymond Robert was preceptor of Le Bastit.[20] Yet, who or what connects his testimony to Ponsard of Gisy's 'traitors'?

There are at least two such possible connections. Bishop Secard of Cahors need not directly have betrayed the secrecy of confession to have passed on the substance of Gérard de Causse's revelations to others, including Bertrand de Got, the archbishop of Bordeaux, and thus, potentially, to Ponsard's 'traitors'. Indeed, existing canon law supported the following view of the priest's correct conduct: 'If he needs sage advice, let him seek it cautiously without mentioning the person'.[21] Secondly, Gérard de Causse himself may have repeated his reception experiences to others, possibly during the time of his voyage overseas after 1298. Given this

---

15 *PT*, vol. 1, p. 386; see Raymond Oursel, *Le procès des Templiers* (Paris, 1955), p. 179.

16 Secard de Montaigu.

17 On the river Lot, a short distance west of Cahors.

18 One might expect the penitent to have been required to wear the iron vest under, not over, the shirt, but the word is 'over' in the text.

19 *PT*, vol. 1, p. 387; see Oursel, *Procès*, p. 180.

20 1277–1302; see Emile-G. Léonard, *Introduction au cartulaire manuscrit du Temple (1150–1317) constitué par le Marquis d'Albon et conservé à la Bibliothèque Nationale suivie d'un tableau des maison françaises du Temple et de leurs précepteurs* (Paris, 1930), pp. 177, 72.

21 Fourth Lateran Council, 1215, canon 21, cited in *Readings in Medieval History*, vol. 2, ed. Patrick J. Geary (Toronto, 2003), pp. 126–7.

time frame, 'overseas' probably meant Cyprus, but there is no record of a Gérard de Causse in the records of the Cypriot trial.[22] This is not surprising because Gérard had returned to Le Bastit as its preceptor by 1305, namely five or six years before the Cyprus trial took place.

In 1307, Gérard de Causse was already in Poitiers, in the presence of Clement V, together with the master of the Temple (Jacques de Molay), the visitor of France (Hugues de Peraud), and the Provincial Master Bernard de Larroque.[23] Why would Gérard de Causse, the preceptor of a very minor, very remote rural house, appear among these Templar notables? Indeed, one could make a case that it was not Gérard de Lavergne but, rather, Gérard de Causse who was Ponsard's 'Gérard de Boyzol, a knight who came to Gisors'. Gérard de Causse, already in Poitiers with the other notables in 1307 and later tried in Paris, was much more likely to have been held in the prison of Gisors[24] than Gérard de Lavergne, who was tried in Cahors. Furthermore, in his testimony, Gérard de Causse referred to Le Bastit as 'Basoez', and the names 'Basoez' and 'Boyzol' may be linguistic variants of the same place, Le Bastit.[25] Or, might there be another explanation?

If Gérard de Causse was indeed one of Ponsard's traitors, then Raymond Robert, who had been preceptor of Le Bastit for some twenty years before Gérard's reception (1296/8) at which he was present, and who subsequently continued as preceptor of Le Bastit for another five years (until 1302),[26] must be considered the primary suspect responsible for the illicit actions described in Gérard's testimony. It would be surprising if some word of the illicit acts mentioned by Gérard de Causse as having occurred during Raymond's twenty-five year term[27] as preceptor of Le Bastit had not leaked out. One possible source of such a leak, as a third connection, is particularly intriguing. Could Raymond Robert have been related to the monk Guillaume Robert, another one of Ponsard's 'traitors'? While 'Robert' is a common family name, there is one fact that lends support to this conjecture. In 1311, Guillaume Robert (as noted above) received a royal safeguard 'due to his involvement in the affair of the Templars'.[28] He later requested and received, by

---

22 *The Trial of the Templars in Cyprus: A Complete English Edition*, ed. and trans. Anne Gilmour-Bryson (Leiden, 1998).

23 *Reg. Clem. V*, no. 7183: 1 July 1311, confirming an act of 9 June 1307 at Poitiers. The 'Itinéraire de Clément V', in *Tables des registres*, ed. Robert Fawtier et al. (Paris, 1948), p. 2, shows Clement at Ligugé on 8, 9 June 1307; at Poitiers on 10 June 1307; and also at Poitiers on 9 June 1308.

24 On Templars held in Gisors to be tried in Paris see *PT*, vol. 1, p. 250.

25 *PT*, vol. 1, p. 379.

26 Léonard, *Introduction*, pp. 72, 77.

27 1277–1302; see Léonard, *Introduction*, pp. 77, 72.

28 *Registres du trésor des chartes*, p. 307, no. 1583: Paris, 15 February 1311.

1319, a transfer from his priory at Bergerac to the abbey of Figeac in the Lot, 30 kilometres south-east of Le Bastit.[29]

Is there any evidence of Raymond Robert's career before coming to Le Bastit as its preceptor in 1277? To consider this question, let us examine the following chronological progression of Templar preceptors in the same region, as listed by Emile-G. Léonard:

1. 1263, Raymond de Dumo (or del Boisso), preceptor, Peyriac-Minervois (Aude);
2. 1265–71, Raymond del Boisso, preceptor, La Chapelle-Livron (Tarn-et-Garonne);
3. 1272, Raymond del Boissono, preceptor, Cahors (Lot);
4. 1275–77, Raymond del Boysso, preceptor, Monclar-de-Quercy (Tarn-et-Garonne);
5. 1277, Raymond Rotberti (or Roberti), preceptor, Toulouse (Haut-Garonne);
6. 1277–1302, Raymond Rotberti (or Roberti), preceptor, Le Bastit (Lot).[30]

It would seem reasonable to make the assumption (as Léonard appears to have done) that the Templar preceptors 1–4 known as Raymond del Boisso (and variants) were one and the same person. Could it be that 5 and 6 were also the same person, namely Raymond del Boisso(no) (or Boysso), who had, after leaving his post as preceptor of Monclar-de-Quercy in 1277 to take up the position of preceptor of Toulouse and later of Le Bastit, for whatever reason begun to use the family name 'Robert' in lieu of the descriptive name 'del Boisso'? Unfortunately, there is no direct evidence to support such a conjecture. However, there is some circumstantial support in addition to the chronological sequence and geographical proximity of these appointments. For example, Raymond del Boisso was preceptor of the Templar house of La Chapelle-Livron for the six years between 1265 and 1271. Considering that Le Bastit was a dependency of La Chapelle-Livron,[31] del Boisso had, therefore, been in command of Le Bastit for that same period. More importantly, in his testimony, Gérard de Causse called Le Bastit 'Basoez', and Ponsard de Gisy seems to have called Gérard de Causse 'Geraues de Boyzol', that is 'Gérard of Le Bastit'. I have pointed out above that 'Basoez' and 'Boyzol' may have been linguistic variants of 'Bastit'. It may also be that 'Basoez' and 'Boyzol' were variants or confusions of 'Boisso' or 'Boysso'. Perhaps one day the mystery of whether Raymond del Boisso and Raymond Robert were, in fact, identical will be solved.

---

29 *Lettres communes de Jean XXII*, ed. Guillaume Mollat, 16 vols (Paris, 1906–47), no. 8784: 2 January 1319.

30 Léonard, *Introduction*, pp. 70–2, 77, 165.

31 Ibid., p. 70.

Raymond Robert is presumed to have died in 1302, the year in which he ceased to be preceptor of Le Bastit, and Guillaume de Jocono took over the post in that same year,[32] before being succeeded by Gérard de Causse in 1305.[33] In October 1307, Raymond Robert was recorded as 'deceased'.[34] Raymond del Boisso was described as 'deceased' at the Clermont trial of 1309.[35] Gérard de Causse, after his major testimony of 12 January 1311,[36] was never heard from again. One month later, Ponsard de Gisy was mentioned in a trial testimony as 'deceased',[37] and a month after that, Gérard de Lavergne was also described as 'deceased'.[38] The monk Guillaume Robert, it would appear, was still alive in 1319.[39]

As I have shown, the inquisitors and the papal commissioners attributed unusual importance to the testimony of a single person, Gérard de Causse, the last Templar preceptor of one remote and insignificant place, the house of Le Bastit in the Lot. The wrong practice so vividly described in his testimony points, if true, only to a particular and isolated instance of guilt.[40] As such, it is not, in my view, representative of the order in general. If unrepresentative, it points, therefore, less to the guilt of the order than to its fundamental innocence.

32 Ibid., p. 72.

33 Ibid., p. 72.

34 *PT*, vol. 2, p. 291.

35 *EUT*, p. 329.

36 *PT*, vol. 1, pp. 379–94.

37 *PT*, vol. 1, p. 521: 9 February 1311.

38 *PT*, vol. 2, p. 20: 9 March 1311.

39 *Lettres communes*, ed. Mollat, no. 8784.

40 On this see Jonathan Riley-Smith, 'Were the Templars Guilty?', in *The Medieval Crusade*, ed. Susan J. Ridyard (Woodbridge, 2004), pp. 123–4.

Chapter 9

The Trial Inventories of the Templars' Houses in France: Select Aspects[1]

Jochen Burgtorf

'Therefore, let it be known that I, Durand Sartoris, the aforementioned notary public, have made and written and presented this public document or inventory, since it could not be written or condensed onto one parchment, onto six parchments of the large kind, all joined and glued together'.[2] Thus reads the concluding statement of the inventory of Fos, a Templar house in southern France, written on 24 January 1308 by an official who was apparently overwhelmed by the extent of what he had just recorded. An integral part of the proceedings against the Templars, the making of the inventories of the order's movable and immovable goods, had begun in the domains of King Philip IV of France on 13 October 1307.[3] His relative, Charles II of Anjou, who ruled over Provence, followed suit three months later,[4] and the inventories compiled in the latter's territories are among the most detailed documents of the entire affair. Within a few years, inventories were made all over Christendom, from Aragón to Cyprus, and from England to Italy.[5] Moreover, when

1 Abbreviations: *CA* = Paris, B.N., n.a.l. 1–71 (*Collection d'Albon*).

2 *CA* 8, fol. 454: *Sciendum vero est quod ego, idem Durantus Sartoris, notarius publicus ut supra, hoc presens publicum instrumentum seu inventarium, cum in uno eodemque pergameno scribi seu capere non posset, feci et scripsi et in hanc publicam formam redegi in sex pergameni forme majoris, simul conjunctis et conglutinatis.*

3 Based on the king's orders of arrest issued on 14 September 1307: *Le dossier de l'affaire des Templiers*, ed. Georges Lizerand (Paris, 1923), pp. 16–29, containing the following instructions to the royal officials: *et tantost ils seront envoié en chascun lieu pour prendre les persones et saisir les biens et ordener de la garde; et se prendront garde que les vignes et les terres soient cultivées et semées convenablement et commentront la garde des biens a bonnes persones et riches du païs, ovec les mesnies qui seront trouvées es meisons, et eus presens il feront celui jour inventoire en cescun lieu de touz les moebles et les seeleront et iront si efforciement que li frere et leur mesnie ne puissent contrester, et auront serjans ovec eus pour eus fere obeir* (ibid., p. 24).

4 On 13 January 1308, Charles II wrote to his officials, instructing them to open an attached sealed letter on 24 January and execute its contents immediately: Damien Carraz, *L'ordre du Temple dans la basse vallée du Rhône (1124–1312): Ordres militaires, croisades et sociétés méridionales* (Lyon, 2005), p. 523.

5 Overviews of published inventories: Anne-Marie Legras and Jean-Loup Lemaître, 'La pratique liturgique des Templiers et des Hospitaliers de Saint-Jean de Jérusalem',

Pope Clement V, on 2 May 1312, transferred the Templars' possessions to the Hospitallers,[6] a new round of inventories had to be commissioned to ensure that what had been recorded at the beginning of the trial was still accounted for several years later.[7]

Thus far, historians have had rather limited use for these inventories, presumably because only a few of them have been edited. In 1858, Léopold Delisle published several trial inventories, among them that of Baugy, a house of the order in Normandy; the text was re-printed by Georges Lizerand in 1923 and has become the most frequently cited one.[8] The trial inventories of southern France received considerable attention in the 1880s: Antoine Du Bourg edited one of the Toulouse inventories;[9] Konrad Schottmüller offered a preliminary edition of the inventory of Limaye;[10] and Hans Prutz published 10 pages of inventories of the Templars' goods in Provence.[11] Yet, dozens of folios of extant archival material remained (and remain) unedited. Thus, in the early twentieth century, the French

---

in *L'Ecrit dans la société médievale: Textes en hommage à Lucie Fossier*, ed. Caroline Bourlet and Annie Dufour (Paris, 1991), pp. 77–137, here p. 100, notes 108–10; Alan Forey, 'Literacy and Learning in the Military Orders during the Twelfth and Thirteenth Centuries', in *MO*, 2, pp. 185–206, here pp. 196–7, note 64. The inventories on Cyprus are mentioned in the narrative sources: *Chroniques d'Amadi et de Strambaldi*, ed. René de Mas Latrie (Paris, 1891), vol. 1, p. 287. For the trial inventories in Italy see Elena Bellomo, *The Templar Order in North-West Italy (1142–c.1330)* (Leiden, 2008), pp. 208–14. Alan Forey, *The Fall of the Templars in the Crown of Aragon* (Aldershot, 2001), p. 117, et passim, describes the problems that officials encountered when attempting to inventory the order's goods.

6 Ferdinand Wilcke, *Geschichte des Ordens der Tempelherren*, 2nd edn (Halle, 1860), vol. 2, pp. 483–8. The papal bull about this transfer (*Ad providam*), referring to the Templars' goods at the time of the arrests in France, contains the following lists: *ipsam domum militiae Templi, caeterasque domus, ecclesias, capellas, oratoria, civitates, castra, villas, terras, grangias, et loca, possessiones, jurisdictiones, redditus atque jura, omniaque alia bona, immobilia et mobilia vel se moventis, cum omnibusque membris, juribus et pertinentiis suis, ultra et citra mare ac in universis et quibuslibet mundi partibus consistentia* (ibid., pp. 485–6).

7 Pope Gregory XI's pontifical inquest of 1373 could be viewed as an additional set of inventories of the Templars' (former) possessions; see Helen Nicholson, *The Knights Hospitaller* (Woodbridge, 2001), pp. 52–3.

8 Léopold Delisle, *Etudes sur la condition de la classe agricole et l'état de l'agriculture en Normandie au moyen âge* (Paris, 1851), appendix, pp. 721–3; *Le dossier*, ed. Lizerand, pp. 46–55. This inventory is cited, for example, by Alan Forey, *The Military Orders: From the Twelfth to the Early Fourteenth Centuries* (London, 1992), p. 151; Alain Demurger, *Vie et mort de l'ordre du Temple*, 3rd edn (Paris, 1993), pp. 192, 299–300; and Malcolm Barber, *The Trial of the Templars*, 2nd edn (Cambridge, 2006), pp. 68–9.

9 Antoine Du Bourg, *Histoire du grand-prieuré de Toulouse* (Toulouse, 1883), pp. xv–xvii.

10 *UT*, vol. 2, part 3, pp. 429–32.

11 *EUT*, pp. 335–45.

Marquis André d'Albon, impressed by Joseph Delaville Le Roulx's monumental publication of Hospitaller material,[12] collected Templar charters, trial records and inventories from all over Europe, particularly France. When he died in 1912, only in his mid-forties, he had published just one volume, but had assembled over 70 manuscript volumes of material. These are now in the Bibliothèque Nationale in Paris,[13] and they contain at least 30 transcriptions of trial inventories from France (primarily from the southern part of the country).

Since then, apart from the 1956 edition of the inventory of Sainte-Eulalie du Larzac which has recently been discussed by Jean Delmas,[14] the inventories have not really been the focus of scholarly investigation. To be fair, they have not been completely ignored either. Malcolm Barber has cited them as typical evidence for the Templars' extensive agricultural activities;[15] Anne-Marie Legras, Jean-Loup Lemaître and Alan Forey have interpreted the lists of books contained in some of the inventories;[16] and Dominic Selwood, Benoît Beaucage and Damien Carraz have utilized them as valuable sources for the Templars' local history.[17]

How is this to be explained? First of all, the inventories are scattered, and they do pose a number of lexical challenges.[18] Secondly, they are not nearly as 'juicy' as the trial's interrogations and confessions. Unless one has a pronounced interest in liturgical instruments, clothing, bedding, books, cooking utensils, tools, monies in various currencies, livestock, different sizes of wine bottles, food staples, as well as lists of rents, incomes, services due, types of buildings and so forth, the inventories make for monotonous reading – somewhat similar to the Hospitallers' lists of items that might be found in the inheritance of their deceased brothers.[19]

---

[12] *CH*.

[13] *CA*; see Henri Omont, 'Nouvelles acquisitions (1921–1923) du département des manuscrits', *Bibliothèque de l'Ecole des Chartes*, 85 (1924), 11–16; Emile-G. Léonard, *Introduction au cartulaire manuscrit du Temple (1150–1317) constitué par le Marquis d'Albon et conservé à la Bibliothèque Nationale suivie d'un tableau des maison françaises du Temple et de leurs précepteurs* (Paris, 1930).

[14] Arlette Higounet-Nadal, 'L'inventaire des biens de la commanderie du Temple de Sainte-Eulalie du Larzac en 1308', *Annales du Midi*, 68 (1956), 255–62; see Jean Delmas, 'L'inventaire des biens de la commanderie de Sainte-Eulalie du Larzac en 1308', in *La Commanderie: Institution des ordres militaires dans l'Occident médiéval*, ed. Anthony Luttrell and Léon Pressouyre (Paris, 2002), pp. 319–27.

[15] Barber, *Trial*, pp. 68–9.

[16] Legras and Lemaître, 'La pratique liturgique', pp. 77–137 (with an overview of the books contained in Templar inventories on pp. 121–6); Forey, 'Literacy', pp. 195–7.

[17] Dominic Selwood, *Knights of the Cloister: Templars and Hospitallers in Central-Southern Occitania 1100–1300* (Woodbridge, 1999), pp. 197–207; Benoît Beaucage, 'La fin des Templiers en Provence: L'exemple de la vignerie d'Aix', *Provence historique*, 49 (1999), 79–91; Carraz, *L'ordre du Temple*, pp. 329, 331, 526.

[18] Higounet-Nadal, 'L'inventaire des biens', 256.

[19] For example: *CH*, 2, no. 2213, *usances* 111–18; see Jochen Burgtorf, 'The Order of the Hospital's High Dignitaries and Their Claims on the Inheritance of Deceased Brethren:

Thirdly, and this is perhaps the main reason, the inventories cannot be used to prove the order's guilt. Alan Forey has pointed out that, while the 'absence of incriminating material evidence, such as idols and copies of secret statutes, is … in itself not a conclusive proof of innocence … [in order] to explain away the lack of idols and secret statutes in France, it would have to be assumed that, although they were not anticipating the arrests and seizures which took place in October 1307, the French Templars had already undertaken a very thorough destruction of all incriminating material in every part of the kingdom'.[20] To my knowledge, there is no evidence that the Templars undertook any such precautionary measures.

The absence of idols from the inventories must have been striking to those accusing the Templars.[21] So, of what use are the inventories for historians today? To answer this question, this article, which is merely a step toward a larger 'inventories' project, takes a look at the inventories of both major commanderies and minor houses in France, assembled in 13 different volumes of the Marquis d'Albon's abovementioned collection,[22] as well as those French inventories published to date.[23] This article will address three particular points: the procedure of compiling the inventories; their information about the physical appearance of the order's commanderies; and the assessment of the movables discovered *in situ*.

Regulations and Conflicts', in *Autour de la première croisade*, ed. Michel Balard (Paris, 1996), pp. 255–65.

[20] Forey, *Military Orders*, p. 231.

[21] Philip IV had specifically mentioned idols in his orders of arrest: *Le dossier*, ed. Lizerand, p. 18: *Dereliquit fontem aque vive, mutavitque gloriam suam in similitudinem vituli et ydolis immolat gens immunda*; see Helen Nicholson, *The Knights Templar: A New History* (Stroud, 2001), pp. 207–17, 242.

[22] *CA* 8, fols 42–172 (Arles, 1308), 371–406 (Arles, 1309), 422–56 (Fos, 1308); 9, fols 160–82 (Avignon, 1308), 199–203 (Limaye, 1308), 549–60 (Fonfrède, 1308); 10, fols 36–8 (Aix, 1308), 68–75 (Bayles, 1308), 380–90 (Rué/Ruou, 1308), 429–37 (Toulon, 1308); 11, fols 242–8 (Bisot, 1308), 249–63 (Grasse, 1308), 264–72 (Château Rigaud, 1308); 14, fols 178–90 (Jalès, 1312); 32, fols 526–37 (Toulouse, 1313), 539–45 (Toulouse, 1313), 546–48 (Toulouse, 1313), 549–58 (Toulouse, 1314); 33, fols 302–14 (Laramet, 1313), 359–62 (Larmont, 1313); 37, fols 348–52 (La-Lande-de-Parthenay, 1313); 38, fols 347–51 (Ancenis, 1313); 44, fols 304–17 (Moisy, 1324); 46, fols 77–84 (Sours, 1310); 49, fols 410–419 (Laonnais, 1319), 420–24; 58, fols 326–7 (Auvergne, 1313).

[23] Adolphe Tardif, 'Inventaire des ornements et vases sacrés de la chapelle de la commanderie de Joigny, au commencement du XIVe siècle', *Annales archéologiques*, 7, no. 2 (1847), 85–6 (Joigny, 1313); Delisle, *Etudes*, pp. 723–4 (Bretteville-le-Rabet, 1307), 725 (Voismer, 1307), 726–7 (Courval, 1307), 727–8 (Louvigny, 1307); *Le dossier*, ed. Lizerand, pp. 46–55 (Baugy, 1307); Higounet-Nadal, 'L'inventaire des biens', 255–62 (Sainte-Eulalie du Larzac, as well as Le Frayssinel, Gals, La Cavalerie, La Salvage, and Millau, 1308). Otherwise, the *CA* versions will be used because they are more complete than the partial editions of Du Bourg, Schottmüller and Prutz.

What do the texts reveal about the procedure of compiling the inventories? Several inventories from the south of France state that the orders to arrest the Templars and seize their goods were to be kept secret.[24] Yet, all the secrecy and the commissions' intentions to make their 'visit' a surprise notwithstanding, there were the occasional obstacles. In January 1308, when the royal officials came to Château Rigaud, they found that the Templar in charge of the place was not at home (*nullus ibidem erat Templarius*), that the house was locked (*domus eorum erat clausa*) and that the keys had to be retrieved from a certain layperson who happened to be the nephew of the absent Templar (*laycum, nepotem Templarii qui inibi residentiam faciebat*). Fortunately, said nephew came to open the house with his keys, and thus the officials were able to commence their work with only a minor delay.[25] Alain Demurger has identified at least one instance (at Toulon in January 1308) where the Templars were warned and fled;[26] the same may have happened at Château Rigaud as well as at other places for which no Templars are mentioned by name in the inventories.

If the sequence in which things are listed in the inventories mirrors the order in which the officials inspected the Templars' possessions – and some of the texts actually state, 'we went from this building to that building, and then on to the next building' – many inquests seem to have started in the commanderies' chapels.[27] At least with regard to the early inventories (1307–08), it is conceivable that the inspections started there because it was assumed that the brothers had committed their heretical, sexual and idol-worshipping crimes in their chapels: the commissioners may have expected to find incriminating evidence there. However, another, much more practical reason for starting in the chapels could have been that these were most likely to contain unique valuables, particularly relics; for example, relics pertaining to St Blaise, one of the 14 holy helpers, were found at both Avignon and Grasse.[28] Yet, there were numerous exceptions to the 'chapel first' rule. At Baugy in Normandy, the officials seem to have visited the fields and stables first; after that, they inspected the barns, the kitchen, the courtyard and only then the chapel, followed by the commander's chamber, the dormitory, the hostel and finally, the remainder of the main house and its cellar.[29] At Bisot, the commission did not start in the chapel either. In fact, its members must have come with an appetite, for the inventory begins with 'eleven hams of pork, nine small

---

[24] *CA* 8, fols 42 (Arles), 423 (Fos); 9, fol. 160 (Avignon); 11, fol. 265 (Château Rigaud).

[25] *CA* 11, fol. 265.

[26] Demurger, *Vie et mort*, p. 302.

[27] *CA* 8, fols 372 (Arles), 424 (Fos; chapel of the order's hospice); 9, fol. 199 (Limaye); 10, fol. 68 (Bayles); 14, fol. 178 (Jalès); 32, fol. 527 (Toulouse); 33, fol. 359 (Larmont); 38, fol. 347 (Ancenis); 46, fol. 81 (Sours); Tardif, 'Inventaire', 85 (Joigny); Higounet-Nadal, 'L'inventaire des biens', 258 (Sainte-Eulalie du Larzac).

[28] *CA* 9, fol. 164 (Avignon); 11, fols 251–2 (Grasse).

[29] *Le dossier*, ed. Lizerand, pp. 46–55.

cheeses, ten pork legs',[30] various other specified pieces of pork, as well as barrels of salted fish, wine and so forth. Thus, the *modus operandi* was apparently left to the officials conducting the inquests and compiling the inventories.

The inventories were expected to be completed the same day the arrests were made. However, the documents reveal that this was, at least in some cases, wishful thinking. At Château Rigaud, the commission took time out to re-seal two collections of charters.[31] In several places, the survey took days, or even weeks, because the actual holdings of the Templars could only be ascertained by summoning the order's tenants.[32] The time that was spent on compiling an inventory largely depended on the size of the commandery and the extent of its holdings. Also, the notaries were, at least in some locations, expected to produce triplicate copies of the inventories.[33] Moreover, the inventories of 1307–08 had to be revisited when the Hospitallers took over the Templars' possessions in 1312 and thereafter. To the Hospitallers, it must have seemed that even some of the immovables had grown legs. In early 1314, an inventory compiled on behalf of the Hospitallers in Auvergne spoke of the 'houses formerly of the Temple which are now in debate and question'.[34] Surprisingly, in some places, such as La-Lande-de-Parthenay in Poitou, the livestock (or, rather, some livestock) was still accounted for in 1313.[35] However, in the same year, when the Hospitallers wanted to take over the former Templar house of Sours in the diocese of Chartres and their representative asked the administrator about the livestock, the latter replied that he could, at present, not find the pertaining document, but that he would make a copy of it available as soon as he retrieved it.[36] The procedural information contained in

30 *CA* 11, fol. 243: *undecim baconos de porco, novem caseos parvos, decem cambos porcis*.

31 Ibid., fol. 271: *Item duo cartularia inquisitionem et quamplurime alie scripture que fuerunt per ipsos dominos cum diversi instruments congregate, in presence suprascriptorum hominum et in duobus linteaminibus ligmate ac etiam earum silligis sigillate et infra alique candele de cera que omnia in ipsa arqua reposita fuerunt et ipse dictis sigillis sigillate*.

32 The compilation of the exceptionally long Arles inventory began on 24 January 1308 (*CA* 8, fol. 42), additional instructions from the royal chancery followed on 1 February 1308 (ibid., fol. 83), and it appears that the inquests continued at least until mid-February (ibid., fol. 103).

33 *CA* 10, fol. 389 (Rué/Ruou): *De quibus omnibus et singulis predicti domini bajulus et judex ac eciam dictus Guillelmus Ardoyni pecierunt fieri per me notarium infra scriptum tria publica instrumenta unius et ejusdem tenoris*.

34 *CA* 58, fol. 326: *aucunes mesons jadis dou Temple qui estoyent en debat et en question*.

35 *CA* 37, fol. 352.

36 *CA* 46, fol. 84: *Preterea prefatus frater Johannes nomine dicti prioris interrogavit dictum majorem sub debito juramenti quot erant animalia bestie equi et kervagium in dicta domo et jus pertinentiis, qui per juramentum suum responsit quod hec sub certo precio habuerat et habebat, de quo et ipsis non recolebat ad presens super quibus erat et fuerat*

the trial inventories is extensive. Its further systematic analysis will significantly contribute to our understanding of what became of the Templars' possessions.

The trial inventories are excellent sources for the physical appearance of Templar commanderies in France. Some of them read like virtual tours of the places they describe.[37] For example, according to one of its inventories, the Templar house at Arles was situated between the Rhône river, a garden and two public roads.[38] The description of the house itself is even more detailed: there is, for example, a reference to a corridor (*coritorium*), as well as a detailed description of the various adjacent chambers and their contents,[39] and Damien Carraz has used the Arles inventory to re-create the hypothetical layout of this commandery.[40] At Bayles, the officials conducting the inquest took note of a bell tower with two bells and a little bell for use during the Eucharist before they entered the order's local chapel.[41] According to the inventory of Sours, there was a *domus feminarum* and a *camera mulierum* (i.e. a house and a chamber of the women);[42] these women probably worked for the house, perhaps as washer women, but whoever they may have been, they were apparently 'in residence'. The *grangia* of Larmont in the area of Toulouse featured a chapel as well as a *palacium*,[43] which suggests that *grangia* here has to be translated in the Cistercian sense as the 'maison affiliée' of a major house, and not in the agricultural sense, as a 'granary', because there would be no reason for a granary to have its own chapel and palace.[44]

The inventory of Aix lists the various buildings and open spaces of that commandery: the house itself, its chapel or church, the cemetery, the courtyard, the great hall and its chambers, the orchard, the oven, the stables, the hospice, the pastures, the mill and the adjacent land.[45] Probably the most detailed description of the premises of a Templar 'dépendance' can be found in the inventory of Jalès in

---

littera concordita quam adhuc non habebat nec per ipsum steterat, set quanto ipsam habebit de ipsa copiam eidem fratri vel alii nomine dicti domini prioris libenter dabit.

37 See Damien Carraz, 'Archéologie des commanderies de l'Hôpital et du Temple en France (1977–2007)', *Cahiers de recherches médiévales*, 15 (2008), 175–202, here 177, note 8.

38 *CA* 8, fol. 44: *domus confrontatur ab una parte Rodano, ab alia cuidam orto dicte domus et ab aliis duabus partibus viis publicis.*

39 Ibid.

40 Carraz, *L'ordre du Temple*, pp. 266–7.

41 *CA* 10, fol. 68: *Primo invenit duas campanas in campanili item unam campanulam parvam pro elevando corpore Christi.*

42 *CA* 46, fol. 83.

43 *CA* 33, fols 359, 361.

44 Jan Frederik Niermeyer, *Mediae latinitatis lexicon minus* (Leiden, 1984), p. 473.

45 *CA* 10, fols 37–8: *Item invenerunt in civitate Aquensis domum Templi cum sua capella seu ecclesia et cimiterio et cum curte aula et cameris suis et cum uno viridario et cum furno suo et stabulis ... unum hospicium ... quandam ferraginem ... aliam ferraginem ... unum molendinum ... quandam magnam terram.*

Ardèche, which lists a chapel with a cemetery, a house also referred to as 'palace', another house, a house for the oven, a small chamber, a house with a crypt that was the cellar and that served as a granary upstairs, two chambers adjacent to the latter, a great hall with a gate at the ground-floor level, another house nearby, a long house, a stable, another stable, a gate, a house in which they stored casks, two houses with upper rooms, a house for the pigs, a long house in which they kept straw and where one could find the threshing floor, a barn and another house.[46] Jalès is still an impressive site today: several of the buildings described in the inventory remain recognizable (including the chapel with the adjacent cemetery), and the Jalès inventory has been used by Robert Saint-Jean to establish the original layout of the commandery.[47] However, given the fact that many trial inventories remain unedited, one wonders whether archaeologists excavating Templar sites are fully aware of these invaluable primary sources. It would seem that these texts could serve as ideal starting points for archeological field work.[48]

We now turn to the assessment of the movables discovered *in situ*. Most of the inventories were compiled in the presence of several individuals. Apart from the fact that the commissions probably wanted to be numerically prepared to arrest all Templars they might encounter, there may have been another reason for bringing more people than just the local *bailli* and judge. Making an inventory involved the assessment of the value of what was found. In 1313, at Toulouse, the commission working on the inventory featured, among others, a Cistercian, a doctor of the laws, a clerk, a legal expert, a notary, someone referred to as 'master of the arts', a merchant, another clerk, and another notary.[49] This impressive panel of experts was, however, indicative of the round of inventories composed after the dissolution of the order, when the former Templar possessions were the subject of litigation between royal administrators, the Hospitallers, and various locals.

Some of the assessment of the value of the seized goods was straightforward, such as in the case of livestock, which was listed by species, number, age and physical condition, as well as with reference to meat or milk yield.[50] When there

---

46 *CA* 14, fols 178–9: *capella cum cimiterio ... domus vocata palacium ... quedam domus ... domus furni ... parva camera ... domus cum crota qua est cellarium et supra sunt graneria ... due camere juxta dicta graneria ... quedam aula cum portallo cum sotolo ... alia domus prope dictam aulam ... quedam domus longa ... quoddam stabulum ... aliud stabulum ... omnia ista sunt infra unam portam ... domus in qua sunt tines ... alia domus cum solerio ... alia domus cum solerio juxta dictam domum ... domus porcorum ... infra primam portam est quedam longa domus in qua palee reponuntur et ibi est area ... grangia ... quedam domus.*

47 Robert Saint-Jean, 'La commanderie de Jalès: Les bâtiments, XIIe–XVIIIe siècles', *Revue du Vivarais*, 91 (1987), 53–70, especially 54.

48 This has already been suggested by Marion Melville, 'Deux aspects de l'architecture des Templiers', *Archeologia*, 27 (1969), 20–7, here 24.

49 *CA* 32, fols 536–7.

50 *Le dossier*, ed. Lizerand, p. 46 (Baugy).

were various items of the same kind, but made from different materials, the most valuable ones were usually listed first; for example, at Baugy, the officials found 'in the chamber of the commander, three cups of solid silver, two big and one small; then, one little cup [made out] of onyx with a silver pedestal; then, two cups [made out] of onyx with a silver pedestal of lesser quality, and other insignificant cups [made out] of wood'.[51] The assessment of some of the items listed in the inventories is actually entertaining. At Sours, there were 'two covers lined with rabbit fur, old and worm-infested'.[52] At Arles, the officials recorded a 'ladder, consumed by fire'.[53] In the same house, they found 'nine vessels, both great and small, of which three were filled with wine, namely one with mediocre [wine], and two with lesser [i.e. presumably less than mediocre wine]'.[54] If the making of these inventories involved the actual tasting of beverages and foodstuffs, it is not surprising that some of them could not be completed in one day.

The inventories' descriptions of books are, at times, very detailed. For example, at Arles, the officials compiling the inventories found 'a cartulary in which there are seven written folio, and the second line of the first folio begins with the words "These are" and on the last folio the writing begins with' – and then the manuscript becomes unreadable.[55] This is not an exception. There are frequent references to various types of bindings, size, the opening words of the first page, the last words of the last page and the general quality of the books. Not surprisingly, there were many liturgical books, and especially the ones found at Arles have attracted scholarly attention (probably because of the considerable length of the Arles inventory).[56] While these liturgical books may not necessarily be evidence for 'literacy and learning' in the order (to cite the title of Alan Forey's respective article), they do suggest piety and orthodoxy. There was, however, also the occasional surprise in the commanderies' book collections. At Bayles, there was a 'beautiful book with the lives of the fathers and a collection of saints' lives and a breviary, all in one volume, as well as another large book of historical legends'.[57] At Arles, the officials found a book dealing with the interpretation of

---

51 Ibid., p. 50: *en la chambre au commandoour, iii henaps d'argent pleins, ii grans et i petit; item, i petit henapin de mardre a pié d'argent; item, ii henaps de mardre a pié d'argent mauvais, et autres menus henaps de bois.*

52 *CA* 46, fol. 83: *duo coopertoria fourrata de cuniculis que premisse sunt vetera et comesta vermibus.*

53 *CA* 8, fol. 46: *unam scalam igne consumptam.*

54 Ibid., fol. 59: *Item novem vasa tam parva quam magna quorum tria sunt plene vino scilicet unum de mediocribus et alias duo de minoribus.*

55 Ibid., fol. 46: *quoddam cartularium in quo erant septem folia scripta quod incipit in secunda linea in primo folio 'Hec sunt' et in ultimo folio scripto incipit ...*

56 Legras and Lemaître, 'La pratique liturgique', pp. 100–3, 121–2; Forey, 'Literacy', pp. 196–7.

57 *CA* 10, fol. 68: *Item unum pulcrum librum continentem vitam [sic] patrum seu sanctorum legendarium et breviarium in uno voluminem. Item unum alium librum magnum*

Hebrew names.[58] At Sours, the commission discovered *quedam hystoria de sancto Ludovico*,[59] which suggests that even before Joinville's famous biography, which, in 1308, was still being written, books about King Louis IX of France were in circulation in the order of the Temple.

One of the remarkable features of the trial inventories is that they were ambitious: everything was to be recorded, down to the little box containing a small quantity of saffron,[60] even items that, if offered for sale, would yield little or nothing. For such items, the documents often employ a negative scale: *nullius valoris* (of no value), *quasi nullius valoris* (of almost no value), *pauce valoris* or *parvi valoris* (of little value) and *modici valoris* (of small or reasonable value).[61] Interestingly enough, there is no positive scale, but there are certain items that, based on their description, must have impressed the officials. For example, at Toulouse, the commissioners recorded 'a cross, made from wood, coated with silver, and said to contain wood from the True Cross in two places, with jewels of various colours, namely a total of forty-five, both small and large'.[62] Another impressive cross reliquary was found at Sainte-Eulalie du Larzac.[63] The inventories feature various types of crosses, great and small, simple and ornate. At the same time, the inventories do not withhold a negative assessment when items are *devastati* (wasted), *consumpti* (destroyed) or *lacerati* (torn).[64] The mere notion that someone would spit, trample or urinate on the cross of Christ[65] must have been shocking to fourteenth-century Christians. It is noteworthy, then, that all the crosses listed in the inventories seem to have been found in an agreeable condition, and while this does not acquit the Templars, it must have been an inconvenient truth for the prosecution.

---

legendarium istoriarum; see Legras and Lemaître, 'La pratique liturgique', p. 122.

58 *CA* 8, fol. 378: *librum interpretationum nominum ebreorum*; see Legras and Lemaître, 'La pratique liturgique', p. 122.

59 *CA* 46, fol. 82.

60 *CA* 10, fol. 383 (Rué/Ruou): *in una picxide aliquantulum de safrano*.

61 *CA* 8, fol. 59 (Arles); 9, fol. 200 (Limaye); 14, fol. 181 (Jalès); 33, fol. 305 (Laramet).

62 *CA* 32, fol. 527: *Item quandam crucem in ligno deargentatam in qua dicebantur esse de ligno Sancte Crucis in duobus locis cum quibusdam lapidibus diversorum colorum usque ad summam quadraginta quinque lapidum inter parvas et magnas*; Du Bourg, *Histoire*, p. xvi; see Selwood, *Knights*, p. 202.

63 Higounet-Nadal, 'L'inventaire des biens', 258: *quandam crucem sanctam munitam lapidibus preciosis incastratam in auro et argento*; see Delmas, 'L'inventaire des biens', 322.

64 See for example *CA* 8, fols 45–6, 52–9, 61, 68–9, 72, 371 (Arles); 46, fols 82–3 (Sours).

65 The articles of accusation against the order use the verbs *spuere* (spit), *conculcare* (trample), and *mingere* (urinate) in the context of the Templars' alleged actions with regard to the cross: *PT*, vol. 1, p. 90; see Barber, *Trial*, p. 202.

To sum up, the inventories of the Templar trial deserve much more attention than they have received thus far. Procedurally, they have much to tell about the actual arrests and seizures. They provide an insight into the daily life and material culture of both major commanderies and minor houses, and they indicate the value or non-value that early fourteenth-century society ascribed to the order's various possessions. Moreover, the inventories are a gold mine for the prosopographer and an important textual aid for the medieval archaeologist. Historians have paid much attention to the trial testimonies which were, at least in part, obtained with the use of torture. Meanwhile, they have largely neglected the trial inventories. Yet, these inventories represent the CSI, the crime scene investigation, and, thus, should be considered an integral part of the trial. Perhaps they have been neglected because they do not support in any way the idea that the Templars were guilty of the charges brought against them. Yet, perhaps the inventories were never intended to support the trial but, rather, to assure that the order's possessions would find their way, undiminished, into new hands.[66] This transfer of the order's possessions, as the inventories show rather clearly, did not take place under the gaze of 'Baphomet' or some other idol. Rather, it was the *ymago Beate Marie supra altare* – the image of the Blessed Virgin Mary (mentioned in several inventories)[67] – that silently witnessed the fall of the Templars.

---

[66] See Malcolm Barber, *The New Knighthood: A History of the Order of the Temple* (Cambridge, 1994), p. 298; Nicholson, *Knights Templar*, p. 225. Philip IV's orders of arrest already contained very detailed instructions as to what was to be done with the Templars' possessions: *Le dossier*, ed. Lizerand, p. 24.

[67] *CA* 8, fol. 424 (Fos); 11, fol. 252 (Grasse); 32, fols 527, 547 (Toulouse); 33, fol. 360 (Larmont).

Chapter 10

On the Margins of the Templars' Trial: The Case of Bishop Guichard of Troyes

Alain Provost

Scholars often seek to account for the Templars' trial by 'genealogical' means, tracing the course of events which had begun one and a half centuries earlier in Champagne and the Holy Land. Here I would like to change this perspective, by studying a contemporary case which is less famous yet nevertheless well documented, the trial of Guichard, bishop of Troyes in Champagne, and attempting to define its relationship to the Templars' affair.[1] The trial of Guichard de Troyes[2] was one of a series of cases in the early fourteenth century in which politics and religion were intertwined.[3] At first sight, the case might seem to resemble an item in a modern gossip column, as it has many of the features of a court intrigue. However, I will propose that this case should be taken seriously: set in the heart of the *tournant démoniaque* identified by Alain Boureau as taking place in the years

---

[1] I would like to thank Helen Nicholson, Paul Crawford and Jochen Burgtorf for their invitation to the sessions devoted to the Templars at the International Medieval Congress in Leeds in July 2007 and for their assistance in the development of this paper. My participation in these sessions was largely helped by an award from the Malta Study Center at the Hill Museum & Manuscript Library in Collegeville, Minnesota, and I am also grateful to Theresa Vann for her support.

[2] The standard study remains the thesis of Abel Rigault, *Le procès de Guichard, évêque de Troyes, 1308–1313* (Paris, 1896). See also Alain Provost, 'Déposer, c'est faire croire? A propos du discours des témoins dans le procès de Guichard, évêque de Troyes (1308–1314)', in *La preuve en justice de l'Antiquité à nos jours*, ed. Bruno Lemesle (Rennes, 2003), pp. 95–118; idem, 'La procédure, la norme et l'institution: Le cas de Guichard, évêque de Troyes (1308–1314)', in *Les procès politiques (XIVe–XVIIe siècle)*, ed. Yves-Marie Bercé (Rome, 2007), pp. 83–103. See: Alain Provost, *Domus Diaboli. Un évêque en procès au temps de Philippe le Bel* (Paris, 2010)

[3] Recent research has shown that alongside the better-known cases it is also necessary to consider the many trials of bishops which are recorded in ecclesiastical documents from the beginning of the thirteenth century. See, for example, Julien Théry, 'Faide nobiliaire et justice inquisitoire de la papauté à Sienne au temps des Neuf: Les *recollectiones* d'une enquête de Benoît XII contre l'évêque Donosdeo de'Malavolti (ASV, Collectoriae 61A et 404A)', in *Als die Welt in die Akten kam: Prozessschriftgut im europäischen Mittelalter*, ed. Susanne Lepsius and Thomas Wetzstein (Frankfurt, 2008), pp. 275–345.

1280–1330,[4] it could well provide a way into the 'mysteries of state' (Ernst H. Kantorowicz) of the France of Philip the Fair.[5]

The trial of Bishop Guichard was a complex, many-layered case whose development can be traced from the summer of 1308.[6] By an act of 9 August 1308, Pope Clement V commissioned the archbishop of Sens to proceed with an investigation against the bishop of Troyes in Champagne. Guichard was suspected of 'enormous crimes and sacrileges' (*enormia et nephanda*):[7] firstly, that a few years earlier, in 1305, he had caused by enchantment the death of the queen of France, Jeanne de Navarre, and also that he had tried to poison the brother and the elder son of the king, Charles de Valois and Louis de Navarre – the future Louis X. To these crimes, which injured the divine majesty and the royal majesty, was added the charge that he had previously caused, also by means of poison, the death of Queen Jeanne's mother, Blanche d'Artois. Following the pontifical mandate of August 1308, an investigation took place during which nearly 300 witnesses were questioned in Paris, Troyes and Provins between October 1308 and December 1309. The investigation was carried out by the ecclesiastical commissioners that the pope had appointed: the archbishop of Sens, that is, the bishop of Troyes's metropolitan – Etienne Bécart in the initial phase – and two of his suffragans, the bishop of Orléans and the bishop of Auxerre. However, this procedure came to a halt; no judgement was reached, and its result resembled a compromise. We next find Guichard in Avignon with the pope. He was neither deposed nor degraded; he was transferred to a peripheral episcopal see, that of the Church of Bosnia,[8] which he certainly did not occupy, for it was in Champagne that the former bishop of Troyes died in January 1317.[9]

Before promotion to the episcopacy in 1298, Guichard had been a monk of the abbey of Montier-la-Celle, close to Troyes, prior of St-Ayoul de Provins – a significant priory dependent on Montier-la-Celle – and then abbot of this same abbey. His career path, characterised by its local dimension, can be understood to

---

4 Alain Boureau, *Satan hérétique: Naissance de la démonologie dans l'Occident médiéval (1280–1330)* (Paris, 2004).

5 On the reign of Philip IV see Jean Favier, *Philippe le Bel* (Paris, 1978); Joseph R. Strayer, *The Reign of of Philip the Fair* (Princeton, 1980), pp. 300–13 (for the trial of the bishop of Troyes). See also now Elisabeth Lalou, *Itinéraire de Philippe IV le Bel (1285–1314)* (Paris, 2007).

6 Around a dozen documents on the case are preserved at Paris, in the Archives Nationales, in the 'layettes du trésor des chartes des rois de France', at shelf marks J 438A and J 438B (continuous numbering from J 438, no. 1, to J 438, no. 12).

7 Poitiers, 9 août 1308: Paris, A.N., J 438, no. 3 bis; Rigault, *Le procès de Guichard*, pp. 269–70 (pièces justificatives, no. 12: mandement d'enquête de Clément V contre Guichard).

8 Djakovo, now in Croatia. For the transfer see *Reg. Clem. V*, nos 10192, 10302; Rigault, *Le procès de Guichard*, pp. 223–5.

9 See Rigault, *Le procès de Guichard*, pp. 225–6.

have resulted from the support of two queens, Blanche d'Artois and her daughter Jeanne, heiress of Champagne and Navarre, who married the heir to the throne of France – Philip IV, the Fair – in August 1284. Ascending the throne in 1285, Philip the Fair thus exerted control over the administration of the county of Champagne, which adjoined the eastern border of his kingdom, and so he could have had need of local connections.[10] Moreover, the charges formulated against Guichard inform us that when he was disgraced he was expelled from the king's council: *ex causa de consilio regio ejectus fuerat et expulsus*.[11] His career had thus led him very close to the heart of power. It could be suggested that this was a case of a wasted career: this cleric could have been an invaluable servant of the monarchy in the context of the process of integrating the Champagne area into the Capetian state. All this was combined with the rivalries and alliances within Jeanne de Navarre's entourage, where Simon Festu, archdeacon of Vendôme and later bishop of Meaux, and Noffo Dei, a Florentine merchant active in the fairs of Champagne and hanged in 1313 for an unknown crime, appear to have been Guichard's principal adversaries – if we take this agonistic view of the case.

Lastly, Guichard's career took place between Provins and Troyes: we should not ignore the proximity of the Champagne fairs, which at that time were still significant financial centres. Certain testimonies emphasised the relations that Guichard would have maintained with a certain number of Italian merchants who attended the fairs.[12] Although it is not possible to consider the financial dimension as the key to the affair, it nonetheless should not be neglected, in particular because it was the flight (around 1300) of a canon guilty of fraud named Jean de Calais, for which the bishop was held responsible, which was given as the fundamental underlying cause of the bishop's disgrace.[13]

---

[10] See Olivier Guyotjeannin, 'L'intégration des grandes acquisitions territoriales de la royauté capétienne (XIIIe–début XIVe siècle)', in *Fragen der politischen Integration im mittelalterlichen Europa*, ed. Werner Maleczek (Ostfildern, 2005), pp. 211–39.

[11] Paris, A.N., J 438, no. 6 (cf. nos 3 and 7), art. 2; Rigault, *Le procès de Guichard*, pp. 275–8 (pièces justificatives, no. 14: premiers articles contre l'évêque de Troyes relatifs aux accusations d'envoûtement et d'empoisonnement, séance du 8 octobre 1308).

[12] See, for example, the deposition of Nicolaus de Castro Forti: *dicens quod a tempore quo dictus nunc episcopus erat prior dicti prioratus Sancti Aygulphi, ipse qui loquitur vidit pluries et frequenter plures lombardos mercatores et feneratores in dictis nundinis conversantes cum dicto tunc priore, et extunc communiter dicebatur quod ipsi tenebant pecuniam a dicto tunc priore, quam pro dicto priore in dictis nundinis ad usuras mutuabant*; Paris, A.N., J 438, no. 6, fol. 31.

[13] Paris, A.N., J 438, no. 8, art. 1; Rigault, *Le procès de Guichard*, pp. 270–5 (pièces justificatives, no. 13: articles contre l'évêque de Troyes proposés par le bailli de Sens aux commissaires apostoliques, août-octobre 1308): *Primo quod dictus episcopus causam odii contraxit contra recordationis inclite dominam Johannam, reginam Francie, domini nostri regis conjugem et consortem, tempore quo dicta domina regina vivebat, ex eo quod ipsa domina regina, exequtrix testamenti domine regine Navarre, matris sue, exegit juste ab ipso episcopo ea quibus episcopus tenebatur dicte domine regine Navarre, eo quod falso*

The origin of the investigatory procedures against the bishop of Troyes relied on the word of a hermit who assisted Guichard's intrigues in his hermitage and was his accomplice in his evil spells. Fleeing the bishop, this hermit took refuge in Sens, in order to confess his sins. Then he repeated the content of his confession to the bailiff of Sens, Guillaume de Hangest. The bailiff took up the case and referred it to the king; from whence we come to Clement V's mandate to investigate. Such, in any case, is the reconstruction of events suggested by a reading of the trial documents. These reveal a small group of crucial witnesses, protagonists, even accessories to Guichard's clandestine intrigues: the hermit already mentioned, as well as, among others, a female soothsayer, a midwife, and even the bishop's chamberlain. The depositions of these first witnesses comprised structured, precise, developed accounts which seriously implicated Guichard in intrigue, in particular evoking the practices of enchantment and the manufacture of poison, and with them the manipulation of the supernatural. These depositions were decisive in the course of the proceedings: they laid the foundation of Guichard's *diffamatio*, after which the investigation would follow its logical course.[14] Subsequently other charges were set out in the shape of new lists of *articuli*, many of which were rather banal – the practice of usury and simony and keeping a concubine; these charges were easily produced and conform to those which were drawn up in comparable cases. In all, they draw a portrait of a bad pastor, scandalous and corrupt, proud and greedy, bad tempered and violent – to some extent, word for word, the reverse image of the holy bishop.[15] Some of the charges – stereotyped, yet effective – aimed to reveal retrospectively the indications of Guichard's supposedly demonic nature throughout the course of his life, even going back to the time of his birth – since central to this set of accusations was the claim that Guichard was the son of an incubus.

Diabolic manifestations, enchantments and poison, treason towards the royal family, competition in the field of power and financial stakes: this combination of elements may appear suspicious. Chronicles and literary works carry an echo of the trial. As a whole, these texts are favourable towards the bishop and substantiate the picture of a miscarriage of justice, of a veritable plot against an innocent man, of jealous revenge against a 'parvenu' who wanted to impress the powerful. The trial

ac proditiose, corruptusque pecunia, deliberaverat Johannem de Calesio, qui quamplura bona maliciose subtraxerat dicte domine Navarre regine viroque suo quondam, quod totum ad ipsam dominam reginam Navarre pertinere debebat post mortem mariti sui predicti, et quem Johannem dictus episcopus in custodia receperat ad instanciam ipsius domine regine Navarre et ad securitatem debiti supradicti.

14 Depositions of the hermit Regnaud de Langres, the soothsayer Margueronne de Bellevillette, the midwife Perrote de Pouy, the bishop's chamberlain Lorin de la Chambre and of four other witnesses: Paris, A.N., J 438, no. 6, fols 1–7.

15 For the ideal holy bishop, as described in the canonisation process, see André Vauchez, *La sainteté en Occident aux derniers siècles du moyen âge d'après les procès de canonisation et les documents hagiographiques* (Rome, 1988).

documents allow us to reflect on the conditions under which the testimonies were produced. Among the dozens of witnesses questioned were, firstly, members of the clergy of the diocese of Troyes, in particular the members of the cathedral chapter and monks of the abbey of Montier-la-Celle, who could have been in conflict with Guichard as abbot, then as bishop.[16] Reading the depositions, it appears difficult to argue that the whole trial was faked. On the other hand, this does not exclude the possibility that certain testimonies – although not all – were distorted, particularly in the initial phase of the trial. At issue here is a certain 'false hermit' in the chronicle of Jean de Saint-Victor; other chroniclers also refer to false witnesses.[17] Hence the foundations of the procedural edifice are problematic, for coercion had undoubtedly been used at the beginning of the investigation. One can, then, accept the idea that the royal power used the trial as a tool and incorporated it into its preexistent strategies. Evidence of this includes the production of a forgery intended to compromise the bishop, which ends with these words: 'Put this letter on the fire when you have read it'.[18]

Having stated this, I wish to show that it is possible to go beyond analogies and speak of real convergences, even of connections and interactions, between the trial of the bishop of Troyes and two other trials of much greater breadth: the posthumous trial of Pope Boniface VIII and the trial of the Templars. We should also remember the trial of Bernard Saisset, bishop of Pamiers, who was accused by the king of high treason in 1302 and not pardoned until 1308. I will analyse the similarities between certain characteristics of these trials and then concentrate on how they fit into the general context of relations between the king of France and Pope Clement V.

The parallels between these various trials have long been established: Jules Michelet, in a famous passage, asserted: 'the first years of the fourteenth century

---

16 In particular, seven members of the cathedral chapter including the dean, Henri de la Noue; three monks of Montier-la-Celle and the abbot Hulric; eight priors of priories subordinate to Montier-la-Celle, including Etienne, prior of St-Ayoul de Provins; and Jean Faucille, treasurer of the same priory. See Paris, A.N., J 438, nos 6 and 7.

17 On the echo of the trial in chronicles and literary works, see *Grandes chroniques de France*, ed. Jules Viard (Paris, 1934), pp. 263–4 (1308) and 293–4 (1313); *Chronique de Guillaume de Nangis et de ses continuateurs*, ed. Hercule Géraud (Paris, 1843), pp. 369 (1308), 400 (1313), 433 (1316); *Continuatio Chronici Girardi de Fracheto*, in *Recueil des Historiens des Gaules et de la France* (henceforth cited as *RHGF*), vol. 21, ed. Joseph-Daniel Guigniaut and Natalis de Wailly (Paris, 1865), pp. 31 (1308) and 40 (1313); *Excerpta e memoriali historiarum Johannis a Sancto Victore*, in *RHGF*, vol. 21, ed. Joseph-Daniel Guigniaut and Natalis de Wailly (Paris, 1865), pp. 644 (1305), 652 (1308), 655 (1310); *La chronique métrique attribuée à Geffroy de Paris*, ed. Armel Diverres (Paris, 1956), p. 148; *Le Roman de Renart le Contrefait*, ed. Gaston Raynaud and Henri Lemaître (Paris, 1914), vol. 2, pp. 89–90.

18 Paris, A.N., J 206, no. 4; Rigault, *Le procès de Guichard*, p. 28.

are just one long trial'.[19] But it should also be noted that, well before Michelet, these trials had often been copied and included in compilations, in particular in seventeenth-century scholarly collections.[20] It is also necessary to consider the initial archival classification of these trial documents, in the French king's *layettes du trésor des chartes*, a classification that continues to influence our work because in a sense it pre-defined the objects of our study. This proximity between the various trials was a result of the involvement of the same men, the use of comparable sets of charges and similar modes of operation.

Around the centre of power there were networks where men, ideas, techniques and methods circulated. The commission charged to inquire into the case of the bishop of Troyes was initially made up of the archbishop of Sens, Etienne Bécart; the bishop of Orléans, Raoul Grosparmi; and the bishop of Auxerre, Pierre de Grès. Raoul is known to have been the cousin of Alips of Mons, second wife of Enguerran de Marigny, while Pierre was the brother of the marshal of France, Jean de Grès; he also was a relative of Marigny.[21] It is also known that Etienne Bécart was present at the Louvre when Guillaume de Nogaret in March 1303 and Guillaume de Plaisians in June of the same year formally read out the charges formulated against Boniface VIII.[22] Although these facts are not necessarily conclusive, they convey the structures of bureaucracy and the career paths of the men of government. It is more significant to note that Etienne Bécart's successor to the archiepiscopal see of Sens in April 1309 was Philippe de Marigny whose role in the trial of the Templars is well known.[23] His name was not explicitly

---

19 Jules Michelet, *Histoire de France*, vol. 3 (Philippe le Bel-Charles V) (repr. St-Marguerite sur Mer, 2008), p. 141.

20 Jacques Chiffoleau, 'Le crime de majesté, la politique et l'extraordinaire: Note sur les collections érudites de procès de lèse-majesté du XVIIe siècle français et sur leurs exemples médiévaux', in *Les procès politiques (XIVe–XVIIe siècle)*, ed. Yves-Marie Bercé (Rome, 2007), pp. 577–662. See also Jacques Chiffoleau, 'Dire l'indicible: Remarques sur la catégorie du *nefandum* du XIIe au XVe siècle', *Annales (Economies, Sociétés, Civilisations)*, 45.2 (1990), 289–324, and idem, '"Ecclesia de occultis non iudicat"? L'Eglise, le secret, l'occulte du XIIe au XVe siècle', *Micrologus*, 14 (2006), *Il Segreto*, pp. 359–481.

21 Jean Favier has remarked that the church of Auxerre was one of those where Marigny bestowed beneficies: *Un conseiller de Philippe le Bel: Enguerran de Marigny* (Paris, 1963), pp. 30–32.

22 Etienne Bécart was one of the five French archbishops, with the chancellor of the university of Paris, who were addressees of the Colonnas' indictment of the government of Boniface VIII (1297): see Jean Coste, *Boniface VIII en procès: Articles d'accusation et dépositions des témoins (1303–1311): Edition critique, introductions et notes* (Rome, 1995), pp. 51–2.

23 Etienne Bécart died in March 1309, having retired a month previously from the investigation against the bishop of Troyes. On Philippe de Marigny's role in the trial of the Templars, see Malcolm Barber, *The Trial of the Templars* (Cambridge, 1978; 2nd edn, Cambridge, 2006), ch. 6 (The End of Resistance), passim, and Alain Demurger, *Les Templiers: Une chevalerie chrétienne au moyen âge* (Paris, 2005), pp. 463, 481.

mentioned in Guichard's trial, but his appointment indicated that this trial took place within the royal power's sphere of control. In particular, it is impossible to be unaware of the intervention of Guillaume de Nogaret, keeper of the king's seal since November 1307. One of the documents of the bishop of Troyes's trial is addressed to him (a draft of the charges); another is doubtless in his hand (charges suggested against Guichard by the bailiff of Sens).[24] The ideas and the methods of Nogaret were thus also at work here, which is suggested by an examination of the charges formulated during these trials; Rigault was certainly not mistaken in seeing the keeper of the seal's hand in them.

In the case of Bishop Guichard, as in that of the Templars or that of Pope Boniface VIII, it is striking that, contrary to what has sometimes been claimed, there is a logic and coherence to the charges. They meet strategic and tactical requirements; the existence of outlines and drafts demonstrates that they were assembled in a dynamic process, which forbids us to view their production as a formless accumulation. It is as if the charges were drawn from a catalogue of accusations, organised around the themes of keeping company with the devil and sexual scandal, and aiming to discredit and demonise the opponent. One example will suffice here, related to the question of the sacraments and particularly to the eucharist. In the accusations against the Templars appears the charge that the formula of dedication was omitted at the time of the mass – depriving the sacrament of its effectiveness since the unconsecrated host is not the body of Christ. Among the charges outlined but not retained against the bishop of Troyes a form of eucharistic profanation appeared: Guichard was suspected of preserving the host in his mouth and later spitting it out.[25] In addition to offering evidence of the process of developing and redrafting accusations, this charge belongs to a particular context, between the development of sacramental theology and the charges of the same type then being formulated against the Jews.

Finally, concerning the methods and modes of operation, a few words on the publicising of the trials will suffice. According to Jean de Saint-Victor, on Sunday, 6 October 1308, a meeting of common people and clerks was held in the king's garden. The chronicler linked this assembly to the imprisonment of the bishop of Troyes. It is therefore probable that the same method, using this type of meeting, was used to disseminate information about Guichard, as had been done for the Templars and Boniface, demonstrating a certain aptitude for influencing public

---

[24] Paris, A.N., J 438, no. 9 (the draft) and no. 8 (the bailiff of Sens's charges). I am very grateful to Sébastien Nadiras for this information. On Nogaret's methods, see Nadiras's thesis from the Ecole nationale des chartes: 'Guillaume de Nogaret et la pratique du pouvoir', available online from http://theses.enc.sorbonne.fr/document117.html. I had previously underestimated the importance of the intervention of the keeper of the seal (see the works cited in note 1).

[25] *Item, qu'il est bougres et mescreans en la foy, quar, quant il chantoit la messe, il tenoit le cors Nostre Seigneur en sa bouche sanz user et gitoit jus*, Paris, A.N., J 438, no. 4, art. VII.

opinion.[26] This said, it is an examination of the chronology which best reveals the connections between the various trials.[27]

The decisive and documented phase of the trial of Guichard of Troyes took place between 1308 and 1314.[28] The fact that the start of Guichard's trial occurred in 1308 is not insignificant. Philip the Fair had put pressure on Pope Clement V in autumn 1305, at the beginning of the latter's pontificate, but it seems that this pressure was increased in the first months of the year 1308 (in particular with the questions addressed to the theologians of the university of Paris – the response to these is dated 25 March 1308 – and the meeting of the estates of the kingdom in Tours, 5–15 May 1308), reaching its apex in the confrontation between the king of France and the pope in Poitiers in the spring and summer of 1308.

Philip the Fair arrived at Poitiers on 26 May 1308 with his entourage and his army. He left about 25 July, leaving his advisers – Aycelin, Nogaret and Plaisians – on the spot to continue the negotiations. Within this timeframe, the two speeches made in consistory on 29 May and then on 14 June 1308 by Guillaume de Plaisians express with great clarity the offensive that Clement V had suffered. The pope was firmly advised to settle the affair of the Temple ('Act then, act. Otherwise, we will have to speak to you in a different language'),[29] otherwise the secular power would take action ('If then the right hand, i.e. the ecclesiastical arm, fails to defend this sacred body [Plaisians had just affirmed that we are "one body with Christ"], won't the left arm, i.e. temporal justice, rise to its defence?').[30] The terms contained in the charges which were suggested at the same time – between August and October 1308 – by the bailiff of Sens against Guichard de Troyes (of which the surviving copy is most probably, as we have pointed out, in Nogaret's hand) are very similar: having taken counsel, the king noted the crimes committed by the bishop against the divine majesty and the royal majesty, and against the Catholic faith; he affirmed

[26] Jean de Saint-Victor, in *RHGF*, vol. 21, p. 652. For these assemblies and their typology see Elisabeth Lalou, 'Les assemblées générales sous Philippe le Bel', in *Recherches sur les états généraux et les états provinciaux de la France médiévale*, Actes du 110e congrès national des sociétés savantes, Montpellier, 1985 (Paris, 1986), pp. 7–29.

[27] See Barber, *Trial*; Demurger, *Les Templiers*; and *Le dossier de l'affaire des Templiers*, ed. Georges Lizerand, (Paris, 1923; repr. 1964). See also the reconsideration of the trial proposed by Julien Théry, in his article in the *Dictionnaire des ordres militaires au moyen âge*, ed. Nicole Bériou and Philippe Josserand, (Paris, 2009), pp. 743–51.

[28] Guichard's successor in the see of Troyes, Jean d'Auxois, was appointed on 14 March 1314; it should be remembered that Jacques de Molay was executed on 11 or 18 March 1314.

[29] Speech of 29 May 1308, in the account of Jean Bourgogne, representative of Jaime II of Aragon at the papal court: Barber, *Trial*, 2nd edn, p. 107; printed in *PUT*, vol. 2, pp. 141–7. French translation in Charles-Victor Langlois, 'L'affaire des Templiers', *Journal des savants* (1908), 417–35, here 429.

[30] Speech of 14 June 1308: *Si igitur dextera, brachium scilicet ecclesiasticum, deficiat in deffensione corporis hujus sacri, nonne brachium sinistrum, scilicet justicia temporalis, ad deffensionem assurget?* Cf. *Le dossier*, ed. Lizerand, pp. 132–3.

that it would be a dangerous precedent if these crimes were to remain unpunished, and declared that, if necessary, he would render justice himself, to preserve the honour of the Church and to avoid such danger and abomination.[31]

The decisions taken by Clement V at the end of the confrontation, in August 1308, also allow us to put the launch of the investigation against the bishop of Troyes into significant perspective. There were three decisions. Firstly, through the bull *Faciens misericordiam*, dated 12 August 1308,[32] a double investigation was instituted in the Templars' trial, against the order and against its members. Then, also on 12 August, the bull *Regnans in coelis* convened a general council for 1 October 1310. Lastly, it was at the same time that Clement V agreed to the opening of an investigation into the case of his predecessor Boniface, to look into the charges brought against the latter. The pope announced that he would deal with this business after his installation in Avignon where he arrived in March 1309; after sending out a summons on 13 September of this same year, the posthumous trial of Boniface VIII opened on 16 March 1310.

Clement V's command to open the investigation against the bishop of Troyes was dated 9 August 1308: it seems difficult to believe that this was only a coincidence. In brief, August 1308 was the decisive moment for two trials, that of the Temple and that of Boniface VIII, to which was added the case of Guichard de Troyes as an additional element of pressure from the king and his agents. Everything indicates that in the closely fought game that unfolded at Poitiers in the spring and summer of 1308, Clement V had ended up accepting a form of compromise with Philip the Fair: while conceding certain points, he strove to preserve some means of action in order to preserve the pontifical function. This is a well-established picture, but one that is confirmed by examining Bishop Guichard's trial.

The dossier of evidence can be completed by a reference to later interactions between these trials. The pontifical commission of Paris which investigated the Templars, chaired by Gilles Aycelin, archbishop of Narbonne, sat between August 1309 and June 1311 at the abbey of St-Geneviève. It was at the same place that during the year 1309 the commissioners charged with hearing the witnesses in the investigation relating to Guichard de Troyes had assembled. Of course, one would like to know more about the interactions which could have occurred despite the intervals and discontinuities in the two procedures,[33] but it is only possible

---

31 Paris, A.N., J 438, no. 8, art. XXVII: *Nec etiam ipse dominus rex honeste posset obmitere quominus in ecclesie defectum, quod absit, debitum suum exsolveret in predictis ad servandum honorem ecclesie et ad vitanda hec pericula ac scandala*. Cf. Rigault, *Le procès de Guichard*, pp. 274–5 (pièces justificatives, no. 13).

32 But perhaps antedated. The numerous bulls were dated 'en bloc' on 12 August, a date before Clement V finally left Poitiers, 19 August 1308. See *Les registres de Clément V: Tables*, ed. Yvonne Lanhers, Cyrille Vogel, Robert Fawtier and Guillaume Mollat (Paris, 1948–57).

33 For Guichard's trial, the first mention of the Abbey of St-Geneviève was on 13 February 1309; the investigation halted between May and October 1309, and the bishop

to note that these men who knew each other crossed each other's paths in these circumstances.

The question of the timing of the trials suggests a last series of observations. In the summer of 1310, at an interval of several weeks, Philip the Fair addressed two letters of similar content to Clement V: the king expressed his astonishment at the time necessary to hear the witnesses in the investigation into the reputation of Boniface VIII. Tardily, on 23 August 1310, Clement V replied: he declared that he was working day and night on outstanding matters and noted 'that trials against *magnas personas* generally have sad and dangerous results, as recent examples have shown'[34] – Jean Coste saw here an allusion to the lawsuits against Bernard Saisset and Guichard de Troyes.[35] In particular, it can hardly be missed that the timing of the bishop of Troyes's trial could almost be superimposed on the trial of the former pope. Indeed, on 18 July 1310, Clement V addressed a letter to the investigating prelates calling for the results of the investigation and the bishop to be sent to him, to which the reply came that the investigation was not finished; the pope had to repeat his request on 9 February 1311. In both cases, that of Boniface VIII and that of Guichard de Troyes, while the fate of the order of the Temple remained undecided, it was undoubtedly the prospect of the opening of the general council which dictated the timing of the trial. The council of Vienne opened in October 1311 and was concluded on 6 May 1312. There is no evidence to prove that the bishop of Troyes's case was directly evoked at the time of the council, but it is likely that it was important for the pope to have this file to hand. It was well before October 1311 – between the last days of March and the first days of April of the same year – that the notaries carried out the drafting of the documents recording the prelate's trial.[36]

Let us risk some words of conclusion. Going beyond the analogies of form between these various cases, it is possible to suggest a structural convergence between them. Although the charges produced against the bishop of Troyes draw a demonic portrait of him, the truth of this portrait is of little importance. In this case as in others, the main purpose of the charges was to delimit borders, categories and norms. They designate enemies. They express a vision of the world in which the order and the unity of the body of Christendom and the body of the kingdom are threatened by subversion. But all this was not restricted to the ideological level.

---

appeared for the last time on 13 December 1309; Paris, A.N., J 438, no. 7, fols 2 and 8v. For the Templars: *PT*, vol. 1, pp. 14–15.

[34] Cited from the commentary of Coste, *Boniface VIII*, p. 596. The content of the king's letters is included in Clement V's reply: Paris, A.N., J 490, no. 777; Bernard Barbiche, *Les actes pontificaux originaux des archives nationales de Paris*, vol. 3 (1305–1415) (Citta'del Vaticano, 1982), no. 2409; Pierre Dupuy, *Histoire du différend d'entre le pape Boniface VIII et Philippes le Bel roy de France* (Paris, 1655), pp. 292–5 (see Coste, *Boniface VIII*, p. 595, n. 2).

[35] Coste, *Boniface VIII*, p. 596.

[36] Paris, A.N., J 438, no. 7, fol. 8 v.

These devices and discourses relied on procedural forms. The investigation gave justification to the king to act, in particular when it was a question of magical practices, progressively denounced as diabolical. The definition of the crime was the key which made royal intervention possible. The 'great trials'of the time of Philip the Fair, because they expressed threats which worked against the royal majesty and the divine majesty, gave access to very concrete devices by which obedience and sovereignty were established or reinforced. These formed nothing more than an exclusively vertical and abstract bond, but, through the procedure of testimony, an articulation of the various registers concerned with social control and the discipline of speech and behaviours, the 'great trials' are characteristic of a stage in the ongoing construction of what one could be tempted to name the hegemonic state.[37]

[37] This is taken from Mario Sbriccoli's work on the emergence of 'penal hegemony'. See Mario Sbriccoli, 'Justice négociée, justice hégémonique: L'émergence du pénal public dans les villes italiennes des XIIIe et XIVe siècles', in *Pratiques sociales et politiques judiciaires dans les villes de l'Occident à la fin du Moyen Age*, ed. Jacques Chiffoleau, Claude Gauvard and Andrea Zorzi (Rome, 2007), pp. 389–421.

Chapter 11

The Involvement of the University of Paris in the Trials of Marguerite Porete and of the Templars, 1308–10[1]

Paul F. Crawford

Near dawn on Friday the thirteenth, October 1307, agents of King Philip the Fair of France suddenly arrested the members of the order of the Temple in France. Virtually every member in the kingdom was taken, including the master, Jacques de Molay, who was visiting the west in order to discuss plans for a new crusade. Torture and other pressures were immediately applied to the unfortunate Templars. A couple of weeks later, on 25 and 26 October, they had been cowed enough to be displayed in public to the 'religious and secular masters, bachelors and scholars of the school at Paris', as a notarized document attesting to the display put it.[2] Names of many of the members of the university were recorded (fortunately for twenty-first-century historians).

A storm of controversy followed the arrests. Outside France, especially in England and Aragon, there was widespread disbelief in the French government's charges. The pope, Clement V, immediately attempted to intervene on the Templars' behalf, despite Philip's claim to have been acting on the pope's behalf (he was not). The French government found itself in a somewhat defensive position, needing support for its actions. One of the first places it sought that support was in the faculty of the University of Paris. Sometime between December 1307 and February 1308, the government sent a list of seven leading questions to members of the theology faculty, asking for their approval of the government's actions. In particular, the government sought to have the theologians' support for the idea that a secular prince could act independently of the Church against erring clerics if the issue was serious enough, especially since, in the government's view, the Templars' confessions (forced or otherwise) nullified any supposed exemption from secular interference, and since (said the government) the Templars were not really an exempt clerical order at all, but merely a college of knights.[3]

---

1 Thanks are due to a great many people who commented constructively on this paper, but especially to William J. Courtenay, William Chester Jordan and John van Engen.

2 *PUT*, vol. 2, no. 149, pp. 307–9, for 25 October only.

3 *Le dossier de l'affaire des Templiers*, ed. Georges Lizerand (Paris, 1923), pp. 56–63.

On 25 March 1308, 14 of the theology masters replied. They were cautious in their tone, but on the core issue of whether the government's actions were warranted, they were rather uncompromising: no secular prince, they said, had the right to act against heretics without the Church's express approval, and even if the danger were so great that the prince felt required to act before he could obtain that approval, he was obliged to turn the miscreants over to Church custody as swiftly as possible (something Philip had clearly not done). Furthermore, the masters said firmly, the mere fact that the Templars were knights did nothing to prevent them from comprising an order of exempt religious, and since they had made their profession to the Church, the Church alone could judge them.[4] In other words, the government was sharply rebuffed. Sharply – and probably unexpectedly, since five years earlier, in 1303, the government had been quite successful in enlisting at least the tacit support of the university members in its campaign against Pope Boniface VIII.

I have compared the events of 1308 with those of 1303 elsewhere,[5] so will not repeat that comparison here, except to note that the differing outcomes appear to have been due to a variety of reasons, not least of which was the fact that university members seem to have viewed Philip's contest with Boniface as 'someone else's fight', a conflict not really impinging on their interests. The secular clergy had a particular reason to be unenthusiastic about defending Boniface in 1303, as he had taken the part of the mendicant regulars against the seculars in the 1290s, and bitterness still lingered over this.[6]

I have also examined the composition of the group of 14 masters involved in the 1308 response elsewhere, with significant results.[7] They included (in alphabetical order):

- Alexander of Alexandria, also called Alexander Bonnino and Alexander Lombard, a member of the Franciscans;[8]
- Alexander Fassitelli of Sant'Elpidio, a member of the Augustinian hermits;[9]
- Gaut[h]ier (Walter) of Gamaches, sometimes called 'of Cluny', about whom little is known (he was a member of the Cluniac, and thus a

4 *Le dossier*, ed. Lizerand, pp. 62–71.

5 Paul F. Crawford, 'The University of Paris and the Trial of the Templars', in *MO*, 3, pp. 115–22; and a number of conference papers (see below, notes 29–30).

6 For accounts of this conflict, see Decima L. Douie, *The Conflict between the Seculars and the Mendicants at the University of Paris in the Thirteenth Century* (Blackfriars, 1954), and Michel-Marie Dufeil, *Guillaume de Saint-Amour et la polémique universitaire parisienne 1250–59* (Paris, 1972).

7 See above, note 5.

8 Palémon Glorieux, *Répertoire des maitres en théologie de Paris au XIIIe siècle,* vol. 2, (Paris, 1933), § 340, pp. 199–202.

9 Glorieux, *Répertoire*, vol. 2, § 408, pp. 319–20.

Benedictine);[10]

- Gérard of Bologna, prior-general of the Carmelites since 1289;[11]
- Gérard of St Victor, the first Victorine regent master of theology at Paris;[12]
- Henry, called 'the German', a member of the Augustinian hermits;[13]
- Hervé Nédellec (Hervaeus Natalis), a Dominican;[14]
- Jacques of Thérines, a Cistercian (clerical exemption generally was a major preoccupation of Jacques of Thérines throughout his life, as was the probable innocence of the Templars);[15]
- John of Mt St Eloi, a member of the abbey of Mt St Eloi, a group of canons regular of St Augustine;[16]
- Laurence of Poulengy, sometimes called 'of Dreux,' prior-general of Val-des-Écoliers, another group of Augustinian canons;[17]
- Peter of St Omer, a canon of the cathedral of Notre Dame in Paris, who had been chancellor of the university between 1296 and 1301;[18]
- Raoul (Ralph) of Hotot, a secular master;[19]
- Romeus of Brugaria, a Catalan Dominican;[20]
- William Alexander, like Peter of St Omer a secular canon of the cathedral of Notre Dame in Paris, but unlike Peter, relatively minor.[21]

---

10 Ibid., vol. 2, § 374, p. 271.

11 Ibid., vol. 2, § 420, pp. 336–7.

12 Ibid., vol. 2, § 222, p. 449. Glorieux believed that Gérard was a secular master, as the Victorine chair had at first, in the thirteenth century, been held by a secular cleric, but in fact Glorieux was mistaken. Gérard of St Victor was from the abbey of St Victor, and was the first regular cleric to hold the chair.

13 Glorieux, *Répertoire*, vol. 2, §406, p. 317. Evidently Henry 'of Friemar, the Elder'.

14 Ibid., vol. 1, § 64, pp. 199–206.

15 Ibid., vol. 2, § 367, pp. 261–2; William Chester Jordan, *Unceasing Strife, Unending Fear: Jacques de Thérines and the Freedom of the Church in the Age of the Last Capetians* (Princeton, 2005); see especially chapters 2 ('The Pope in Avignon and the Crisis of the Templars') and 3 ('The Exemption Controversy at the Council of Vienne'), pp. 18–55.

16 Glorieux, *Répertoire*, vol. 2, § 393, p. 288.

17 Ibid., vol. 2, § 383, p. 280.

18 Ibid., vol. 1, § 204, pp. 404–5; he continued writing scholarly works until at least 1309.

19 Ibid., vol. 1, § 225, pp. 453–6. It appears that this master ought not to be confused with Ralph Brito, as has often been done.

20 Ibid., vol. 1, § 62, p. 196. Glorieux indicates that this is the same person as Romeus Ortiz, but this appears not to be the case: Ortiz was a Franciscan (not Dominican) provincial at about the same time.

21 Ibid., vol. 1, § 224, p. 452.

Six of these 14 masters, or almost 43 %, were members of exempt mendicant orders: a Franciscan, a Carmelite, two Augustinian hermits and two Dominicans.[22] Five more, almost 36 %, were members of exempt or partially-exempt religious orders: two Augustinian canons, a Cistercian, a Victorine, and a Cluniac Benedictine.[23] Only three, or about 21 %, were clearly secular clergy, and two of those were minor figures: William Alexander and Ralph of Hotot.[24] Of these three clearly secular clergy, two were canons of the cathedral chapter at Notre Dame in Paris, or so it seems. One of them, Peter of St Omer, clearly was. Another, William Alexander, certainly was later and probably was at the time.

The cathedral chapter of Notre Dame was generally strongly royal; most of its members were there because of royal appointments. But there are qualifiers in the case of Peter of St Omer, who had been chancellor from 1296 to 1301. There are some reasons to speculate that Peter of St Omer was neither a strong royal supporter nor as hostile to exempt orders as some of his colleagues. For one thing, he had not set his name to a document produced in 1303 when the Notre Dame cathedral chapter witnessed the public retraction of Martin of Rippa's opposition to Philip the Fair's letters of adhesion against Boniface VIII, thereby missing an opportunity to show his public support for the royal position. Many other significant canons' names are found in this document, but not Peter's.[25] There could have been many reasons for this omission, but in context it looks suggestive, especially when one compares his behavior to that of his important colleagues Simon of Guiberville and John of Gand.[26] There is also a curious detail about the disposal of his goods after his death: he bequeathed several manuscripts of the works of St Thomas Aquinas, a Dominican, to the university, something which suggests that, although he was a secular cleric, he might not have been entirely opposed to the exempt mendicants, and therefore might have been a little bit sympathetic toward the exempt Templars as well. If this speculation is accurate, then it would help explain why Peter of St Omer, though a canon of Notre Dame, is found among those refusing to condemn the Templars in 1308.[27]

There are also qualifiers for William Alexander, who was a little known secular canon who had either received additional benefices and appointments within the chapter from Clement V on 7 November 1308, or else had actually been appointed

22 Alexander Bonnino (Lombard) of Alexandria, Gérard of Bologna, Hervaeus Natalis and Romeus of Brugeria.

23 John of Mt St Eloi, Alexander Fassitelli of Sant'Elpidio, Henry of Friemar ('the Elder' or 'the German'), Jacques of Thérines, Gérard of St Victor, Walter of Gamaches and Laurence of Poulengy (or 'of Dreux') of Val-des-Ecoliers.

24 William Alexander and Ralph of Hotot.

25 *CUP*, vol. 2, no. 635, 8 July 1303. He may have been dead by 1310.

26 See below, notes 64–6.

27 Palémon Glorieux, 'Notices sur quelques théologiens de Paris de la fin du XIIIe siècle', *Archives d'histoire doctrinale et littéraire du moyen âge,* 3 (1928), 224.

to the chapter then.[28] Was he, like Gérard of St Victor, being rewarded for taking the risk of supporting exemption and the Templars a few months earlier?[29] The evidence does not indicate this clearly, but the suggestion – the possibility at least – is there.

From a study of the profile of this group, and from a more detailed examination of several of its members, including Jacques of Thérines, Gérard of St Victor and Romeus of Brugaria,[30] I have concluded that membership in exempt or partially exempt orders was a significant factor in motivating many of them to resist the government's attempt to gain legitimacy for its arrests of the Templars (though there were also, clearly, other factors at work as well, and concern for exemption was not the only explanation for their actions).[31]

But not all the members of the theology faculty in 1308 were part of this group who opposed the government and defended exemption and the Templars. Some remained silent. Why? To help answer that question, let us turn from the composition of the group of 14 masters who handled the inquiry over the Templars in 1308, to the composition of the group of 21 masters who handled the inquiry into the heresy accusations against Marguerite Porete two years later, in 1310. Similarities, or differences, between these two groups of masters may shed light

28 *CUP*, vol. 2, no. 672.

29 *CUP*, vol. 2, no. 675; I discussed this issue at length in my paper '*Quid pro quo?* Gérard of St Victor and the Trial of the Templars', given at the 4th International Conference of the London Centre for the Study of the Crusades, the Military Religious Orders and the Latin East, London, 11 September 2005.

30 For Gérard, see above, note 29. For Jacques of Thérines, see a brief discussion in Crawford, 'The University of Paris and the Trial of the Templars', p. 120, and a discussion in considerably more depth in idem, 'Jacques de Thérines, the University of Paris, and the Trial of the Templars', given at the 6th Conference of the Society for the Study of the Crusades and the Latin East, Istanbul, 26 August 2004, and in 'The University of Paris and the Trial of the Templars', given at the 39th International Medieval Congress, Kalamazoo, Michigan, 6 May 2004. I discussed Romeus de Brugaria at length in 'Agent of the King? Romeus de Brugaria and the Templars', given at the 41st International Medieval Congress, Kalamazoo, Michigan, 4 May 2006.

31 Helen Nicholson has shown that during the depositions in Ireland and England, the friars in particular were almost unrelentingly hostile in their testimony about the Templars (and see Helen Nicholson, 'The Trial of the Templars in Ireland', pp. 225–35). This contrasts sharply with the apparent sympathy shown to them by friars and other religious at the university of Paris, but it can probably be explained by the fact that inside the university, and in the context of the French government's persecution of the Templars, the mendicants and other exempt religious found that their philosophical, theological and legal situations gave them much in common with the military orders, whereas outside the university, the mendicants and military orders were competitors for donations and other resources. It may also be explained, as Nicholson notes in 'The Trial of the Templars in Ireland', pp. 225–35, by the fact that the friars had problems of their own and found the Templars' troubles to be useful distractions.

on the reasons why some of the university's masters were willing to oppose the government in the matter of the Templars, while others were not.

Marguerite Porete was a woman from northern France, probably from Hainault, who produced a book called the *Mirror of Simple Souls*.[32] In it she advanced a mystical, semi-gnostic theology, separating the Church into a 'greater' and a 'lesser' Church, with the lesser Church being closely associated with the visible, earthly, sometimes-worldly church of the early fourteenth century, and the greater Church being associated with those privileged few who understood her arcane ideas and went beyond what she saw as the feeble and even futile efforts of the lesser Church. The book contained subtle and not-so-subtle taunts for the sophisticated and complex Biblical exegesis of the scholastics, including statements to the effect that Marguerite's spiritual understanding was too advanced for mere scholars to apprehend. She particularly despised literal exegesis of the Bible, such as that espoused by her contemporary, the theologian Nicolas of Lyra.[33]

The book quickly attracted ecclesiastical attention, and was condemned and publicly burned in her presence some time between 1296 and 1306 by Bishop Guy II of Cambrai.[34] Marguerite was warned to desist from propagating her ideas. She did not desist, however. In defiance of the bishop, Marguerite continued to advance her views, and even sent copies of the *Mirror* to theologians, seeking their approval despite the fact that once the book had been publicly condemned by a bishop, there was little chance of gaining a reversal of the verdict, and continuing to argue on its behalf was a rather dangerous undertaking.

Surprisingly, Marguerite managed to get three theologians to issue supportive statements for at least some of her book. Their approval was inserted into the prefaces of subsequent copies.[35] Two of these theologians are now unknown except for their names and orders: a Franciscan, John of Quaregnon, and a Cistercian, Dom Franco of Villers.[36] The third was not only identified by name, but was a very

---

32 See, generally, Margaret Porette, *The Mirror of Simple Souls*, trans. Edmund Colledge, J.C. Marler and Judith Grant, with a foreword by Kent Emery (Notre Dame, IN, 1999); Marguerite Porete, *The Mirror of Simple Souls*, trans. and intro. Ellen Babinsky (New York, 1993).

33 See Colledge et al., in *Mirror*, pp. ix, lv–lvi. Marguerite also made derogatory remarks about secular clergy and about William of Nogaret (which might explain why he had papers relating to her trial amongst his own effects when he died). The discussion above is a superficial account of her arguments, but it is not the purpose of this paper to engage Marguerite's ideas in detail; for a discussion for them, see *Mirror*, trans. Colledge et al.; Paul Verdeyen, 'Le procès d'inquisition contre Marguerite Porete et Guiard de Cressonessart (1309–1310)', *Revue d'histoire ecclésiastique*, 81 (1986), 47–94; *Mirror*, trans. Ellen Babinsky; Robert Lerner, *The Heresy of the Free Spirit in the Later Middle Ages* (Berkeley, 1972).

34 *Mirror*, trans. Colledge et al., p. xxxviii.

35 Ibid., p. xl, and Appendix I.

36 *Mirror*, trans. Babinsky, p. 22; Lerner, *Heresy of the Free Spirit*, p. 72. See Verdeyen, 'Le procès', pp. 86–7, for transcriptions of texts mentioning these three theologians.

big name indeed: Godfrey of Fontaines, whose qualified approbation must have proven embarrassing to subsequent critics of the *Mirror*.[37]

Having achieved this coup, Margaret then presented the amended and reinforced *Mirror* to the bishop of Châlons, apparently hoping to get the bishop of Cambrai's condemnation cancelled, an attempt which Edmund Colledge rightly describes as 'rash or ill-advised'.[38] Predictably, the bishop of Châlons sent her into the custody of the inquisitor of Haut-Lorraine, who brought her to Philip of Marigny, brother of the royal advisor Enguerrand of Marigny, apparently bishop of Cambrai as of 1306 and then archbishop of Sens in 1309. By late 1308 Marguerite had apparently been arrested in Paris by the inquisitor-general of France, William Humbert of Paris.[39] A long inquiry followed, during which Marguerite defied her inquisitors repeatedly and refused to cooperate with them.

We may skip over most of the details of this inquiry for the sake of brevity, and also because they are not very relevant here. Suffice it to say that the inquisitor-general eventually asked the theologians of the University of Paris to pass judgment on a number of propositions extracted from Marguerite's *Mirror*. On 11 April 1310,[40] a group of 21 theology masters responded to the inquisitor's request, finding that these propositions did indeed contain heresy.[41] Marguerite continued her refusal to cooperate or to renounce her work, however, and so, on 1 June 1310, she was burnt at the stake.

The trial of Marguerite Porete has significant differences from the trial of the Templars. Marguerite was not accused by the government directly, but rather by the offices of the Church, nor did her trial have the political implications of the trial of the Templars.[42] In fact, inasmuch as the French government was involved in the trial of Marguerite Porete, it seems to have been so because it was anxious

---

37 Emery, in *Mirror*, trans. Colledge et al., pp. x–xi.

38 *Mirror*, trans. Colledge et al., p. xlii.

39 Robert Lerner, 'An "Angel of Philadelphia" in the Reign of Philip the Fair: The Case of Guiard of Cressonessart', in *Order and Innovation in the Middle Ages: Essays in Honor of Joseph Strayer*, ed. William Chester Jordan, Bruce McNab and Teofilo Ruiz (Princeton, 1976), p. 346.

40 Many sources, including recent secondary sources, give the date of the verdict of the theologians on Marguerite Porete as 11 April 1309, but this is erroneous. See *Mirror*, trans. Babinsky, pp. 56–7, n. 83, citing Robert Lerner's correction. Lerner, in 'Angel', p. 346 and n. 12, notes that some of the confusion arose when Henry Charles Lea misdated one of the documents.

41 Paris, Archives Nationales, layette J. 428, 15a, as transcribed in Verdeyen, 'Le procès', pp. 50–1; see also *CUP*, vol. 2, no. 681, p. 143. The meeting was convened by Inquisitor-General William Humbert of Paris at the church of the Mathurins, which was the administrative center of the University of Paris. The site was also used, for example, for a meeting of the university in which special protections were issued to the scholars of the abbey of St Victor in 1309 (*CUP*, vol. 2, no. 675, p. 138).

42 Neither *Mirror*, trans. Colledge et al., nor Verdeyen, 'Le procès', demonstrate a very good grasp of what was going on in the trial of the Templars, and need to be corrected

to demonstrate its support for orthodoxy and for the Church – more Catholic, as it were, than the popes it had been attacking so relentlessly for the previous 15 years or so. It may also have been anxious to reassure the members of the mendicant orders, who clearly took a dim view of the government's persecution of the exempt Templars, that it was not in fact their enemy. Paul Verdeyen notes that Marguerite and her supporters were suspected, rightly or wrongly, of being involved in the beguine and beghard movement, which many (though not all) mendicants opposed, and suggests that the government may have hoped that if it could be seen as sharing that opposition, the mendicants might generally become more favorable to the royal cause.[43]

To the theologians of Paris, then, taking a position on the trial of Marguerite Porete did not carry the political risks which taking a position on the trial of the Templars carried. This was a 'merely' theological matter. So we might expect to find more masters willing to involve themselves in Marguerite Porete's case than in the Templar case – and indeed, the group of masters involved with Marguerite Porete was exactly 50 % larger than the group involved with the Templar trial: 21 members instead of 14.

So far, matters seem to be as one might expect. One might expect, too, to find that there was a higher ratio of secular masters compared to regular masters, and that high-profile administrators were more willing to be involved in the trial of Marguerite Porete than the explosively dangerous trial of the Templars. Let us examine these 21 masters to determine if these assumptions are borne out. Here are their names and affiliations (in alphabetical order), along with other relevant data; some will be familiar from the above list of masters involved in the Templar trial:

- Alexander Fassitelli of Sant'Elpidio, an Augustinian hermit who had been a participant in the response to the government's inquiry regarding the Templars in 1308;[44]
- Berengar of Landore, a Dominican;[45]
- Gérard of Bologna, the Carmelite prior-general (participant in the 1308 Templar response);[46]

---

by more recent accounts by historians of the military orders, especially by that given in Malcolm Barber, *The Trial of the Templars*, 2nd edn (Cambridge, 2006).

43 Verdeyen, 'Le procès', p. 85; *Mirror*, trans. Babinsky, p. 24. Verdeyen, p. 47, actually calls her a beguine, but this seems unproven from the other sources, and there is no general agreement on this point. Not all mendicants were hostile to the beguines; for a discussion of their attitudes, see John van Engen, *Sisters and Brothers of the Common Life: The Devotio Moderna and the World of the Later Middle Ages* (Philadelphia, 2008).

44 Glorieux, *Répertoire*, vol. 2, § 340, pp. 199–202.

45 Ibid., vol. 1, § 65, pp. 207–9.

46 Ibid., vol. 2, § 420, pp. 336–7.

- Gérard of St Victor, a Victorine, participant in 1308;[47]
- Gregory of Lucca, an Augustinian hermit;[48]
- Henry the German, also an Augustinian hermit and a participant in 1308;[49]
- Jacques of Ascoli, a Franciscan;[50]
- Jacques of Dijon, a Cistercian;[51]
- Jacques of Thérines, also a Cistercian (and a participant in 1308);[52]
- John of Clairmarais, apparently a secular master, of whom almost nothing is known;[53]

---

47 Ibid., vol. 1, § 222, p. 449 (as noted above, Glorieux was mistaken in believing that Gérard of St Victor was a secular master).

48 Ibid., vol. 2, § 407, p. 318.

49 Michael Buchberger, Josef Höfer and Karl Rahner, *Lexikon für Theologie und Kirche*, 2nd edn, vol. 5 (Freiburg, 1957–67), col. 188 (and note the difference between Henry the Elder and Henry the Younger, which is not immediately apparent); Glorieux, *Répertoire*, vol. 2, § 406, p. 317, is outdated.

50 Glorieux, *Répertoire*, vol. 2, § 348, pp. 236–7.

51 There is no Glorieux entry for Jacques of Dijon, and little information about him, other than his Cistercian affiliation. Denifle and Chatelain identified him with Jacques Fournier, but this is incorrect: see Robert Lerner, 'A Note on the University Career of Jacques Fornier, O. Cist., Later Pope Benedict XII', *Analecta cisterciensia*, 30 (1974), 66–9 (but note that Lerner, p. 68 n. 10, in turn misidentifies the 'Jacobus Cisterciensis' of *PUT*, vol. 2, pp. 309–13, as Jacques Dijon when in fact he is yet another Jacques, namely Jacques of Thérines).

52 Glorieux, *Répertoire*, vol. 2, § 367, pp. 261–2, and see note 14, above.

53 There is also no Glorieux entry for John of Clairmarais; he seems to have been entirely overlooked. Denifle and Chatelain, in the *Index personarum* to *CUP*, vol. 3, classified him speculatively as '[Ord. Min.] ', but their only justification for this obvious guesswork seems to be that he appears in the list of masters in the condemnation of 11 April 1310 (Verdeyen, 'Le procès', pp. 50–1, citing Archives Nationales, layette J. 428, 15a) along with the Franciscans Nicolas of Lyra and Jacques d'Ascoli, but that alone is no justification for a classification, as members of the Cistercian order, for example, are strewn randomly about in the list, and are not contiguous to each other. John of Clairmarais does not appear in Wadding's *Annales minorum* (Luke Wadding and José Maria Ribeiro da Fonseca, *Annales Minorum seu trium ordinum a S. Francisco institutorum*, various imprints and reprints), nor in Giovanni Giacinto Sbaraglia's *Supplementum et castigatio ad scriptores trium ordinem S. Francesci a Waddingo* (Rome, 1908–36), nor in Stefano Rinaldi's 'Supplemento bibliografico al Waddingo e allo Sbaraglia', in *Miscellanea Francescana*, 26 (1926), 81–95 and 133–8, which strongly suggests he was not, in fact, Franciscan. Nor does he appear in the *Cartulaire de l'église Notre-Dame de Paris*, ed. Benjamin Guérard, 4 vols, (Paris, 1850), which strongly suggests that he was not a canon of Notre Dame either. Nor is he mentioned in the documents dealing with the trial of Guiard of Cressonessart, concurrent to that of Marguerite Porete (see Appendices I–III, in Lerner, 'Angel', pp. 359–64). On the basis of these non-appearances, and lacking any further trace of this individual, I have tentatively concluded that John of Clairmarais, like John of Pouilly (except in fame and importance), was a secular cleric, but unaffiliated with the cathedral chapter of Notre Dame.

- John of Gand (or Ghent), a secular canon of Notre Dame;[54]
- John of Mt St Eloi, an Augustinian canon and participant in 1308;[55]
- John of Pouilly, also a secular canon, though not of Notre Dame, and a noted public detractor of the Templars;[56]
- Laurence of Poulengy, prior of the Augustinian canons of Val-des-Ecoliers and a participant in the 1308 Templar inquiry;[57]
- Nicholas of Lyra, a Franciscan and a well-known and prestigious theologian;[58]
- Peter of St Denis, a Benedictine member of the royal abbey of St Denis;[59]
- Ralph of Hotot, a very minor secular master (and a participant in the 1308 Templar inquiry);[60]
- Roger of Roseto, another very minor secular master;[61]
- Simon of Guiberville, called Simon the Dean, a secular canon of Notre Dame, and chancellor of the university from c.1301 to 10 December 1309;[62]
- Thomas of Bailly, a well-known secular canon of Notre Dame;[63]
- William Alexander, yet another minor secular canon of Notre Dame, and the only one such to take part in both consultations of 1308 and 1310.[64]

In sum: the list contains seven exempt mendicants (the Carmelite Gérard of Bologna, the Dominican Berengar of Landore, the Augustinian Hermits Alexander Fassitelli of Sant'Elpidio, Henry the German (the Elder) of Friemar and Gregory

If he were in fact a Franciscan, the figures given below would change somewhat, but not significantly enough to alter the conclusions I have drawn from them.

54 Glorieux, *Répertoire*, vol. 1, § 218, p. 446.

55 Ibid., vol. 2, § 393, p. 288.

56 Ibid., vol. 1, § 223, pp. 450–452, and see a brief discussion of his attitude towards the Templars in Crawford, 'The University of Paris and the Trial of the Templars', p. 121. Interestingly, John of Pouilly was a student of Godfrey of Fontaines, whose opinion had been solicited by Marguerite: see Noël Valois, 'Deux nouveaux témoignages sur le procès des Templiers', *Comptes rendus des séances de l'Académie des Inscriptions et Belles-Lettres* (Paris, 1910), p. 230.

57 Glorieux, *Répertoire*, vol. 2, § 383, p. 280.

58 Ibid., vol. 2, § 345, pp. 215–31.

59 Ibid., vol. 1, § 221, p. 448.

60 Ibid., vol. 1, § 225, pp. 453–6, again noting that he apparently ought not to be confused with Ralph Brito.

61 Ibid., vol. 1, § 220, p. 447.

62 Ibid., vol. 1, § 212, p. 440; for his chancellorship, see *CUP*, vol. 2, pp. 136–7, no. 673, dated 10 December 1308 but corrected by Denifle to 1309.

63 Glorieux, *Répertoire*, vol. 1, § 214, pp. 442–3; he would succeed Francisco of Carraciolo as chancellor, beginning some time in 1309 or 1310 and ending 31 May 1316.

64 Ibid., vol. 1, § 224, p. 452.

of Lucca; and the Franciscans Nicholas of Lyra and Jacques of Ascoli) – a trifle over 33 %, which is almost 10 % lower than the percentage of exempt mendicants involved in the trial of the Templars. It also contains six other members of exempt or partially exempt orders (a little over 28 %, making this group somewhat more than 7 % smaller than its counterpart in the Templar inquiry): the Benedictine Peter of St Denis, the Victorine Gérard of St Victor, the Cistercians Jacques of Thérìnes and Jacques of Ascoli, the Augustinian canon and prior of Val-des-Écoliers, Laurence of Poulengy/Dreux, and another Augustinian canon, John of Mt St Eloi. Of these, the Benedictine Peter of St Omer belonged to the royal abbey of St Denis, a foundation especially close to the French crown, but nonetheless exempt.

The group's secular membership, moreover, is in fact much larger than it had been in the case of the trial of the Templars. There are apparently eight secular members, an almost three-fold increase: Simon of Guiberville, Thomas of Bailly, William Alexander, John of Gand, John of Pouilly, Ralph of Hotot, apparently John of Clairmarais and Roger of Roseto – about 38 %, or an almost 17 % increase over their share of the composition of the group consulted about the Templar trial.

This raises the question of why so many more secular masters were willing to participate in the inquiry into Marguerite of Porete than were willing to participate in the Templar inquiry. The question becomes even more intriguing when we look further at these eight secular members. Of these eight, four were members of the important cathedral chapter of Notre Dame: Simon of Guiberville (dean and ex-chancellor), Thomas of Bailly (future chancellor), John of Gand and William Alexander (a member at least since November 1308, and possibly before).[65]

All the evidence we have indicates that every one of these four men, who we find participating in the relatively uncontroversial condemnation of Marguerite Porete in 1310, *could* also have participated in the university's response to the questions about the Templars in 1308. They were all theology masters through the entire time, and as far as the sources indicate, were present in Paris.[66]

But only one of them did take part in the Templar inquiry 1308: William Alexander (and even that assumes that he was a canon of Notre Dame even before Clement V awarded him benefices within the chapter in November 1308, which is not clear). The other three canons of Notre Dame were discreetly silent in 1308. It is difficult to escape the conclusion that this was because they did not wish

---

65 Unlike the former chancellor Peter of St Omer, Simon of Guiberville and John of Gand were both present at Martin of Rippa's retraction in July 1303. For more on Peter, see above, p. 132.

66 Even – or perhaps *especially* – if they were not in Paris, their absence would raise the question of why they were gone: were they deliberately evading the issue? The language in the 1307 document suggests that some of them might have, in making the excuse that some members had been away and that their absence had delayed the collective reply. This might have been in itself convenient for some of the members.

to become involved in the matter of the Templars. This may have been because of the danger of opposing a powerful royal benefactor who was so nearby that he may have been able to keep an eye on them from his bedroom window, or perhaps because they really were supporters of royal policy (for example, Simon of Guiberville and John of Gand had both appeared in 1303 as witnesses to the retraction that Martin of Rippa had been forced to make regarding the matter of adherence to Philip's attacks on Boniface VIII, thus witnessing his submission to royal pressure).[67] Or it may have been because as members of the powerful, secular chapter of Notre Dame, they actively disliked exempt orders like the Templars, and had no wish to lend a hand in their defence. Or all of these reasons at once, which is perhaps more likely.

This impression is strengthened by examination of at least one of the other four seculars: John of Pouilly.[68] John held multiple canonries across northern France: St Gery, St Quentin, and St Symphorien de Reims (and if the 'John of Pouilly' mentioned in a document of 1362 is the same person, then he was still collecting canonries into his eighties!).[69] He had become a master in 1306, so he was very

67 *CUP*, vol. 2, no. 635; note again that Peter of St Omer was *not* a witness to Martin of Rippa's retraction, which might indicate that he had a distaste for the proceedings and for the king's position. It must be acknowledged, however, that it is possible that he was simply ill or otherwise occupied that day, though it would seem unwise to be 'otherwise occupied' when the royal eye is on one.

68 For an overview of John of Pouilly, see, inter al., *The Medieval Theologians*, ed. Gillian R. Evans (Oxford, 2001), pp. 236–7, and Noël Valois, 'Jean de Pouilli, théologien', *Histoire littéraire de la France*, 34 (1914), 220–81. See also Ludwig Hödl, 'The *Quodlibeta* of John of Pouilly', in *Theological Quodlibeta in the Middle Ages: The Fourteenth Century*, ed. Christopher Schabel (Leiden, 2007), pp. 199–229 (which appeared too recently to be fully integrated into this article).

John of Pouilly's views and actions during his career bring the intellectual and ecclesiastical issues involved in the trial of the Templars into sharp focus. Research over a period of several years into the University of Paris's involvement with the Templars has convinced me that a more complete study of John's writings and actions will be necessary to achieve a fuller understanding of how and why theologians reacted as they did to the trial of the Templars, of what the issues were and of why some masters and prelates took one side, and others the other. Such a study will have to wait for another time, however. In the meantime, some discussion of John of Pouilly, the Templars, exemption and the rights of church vs. monarchy, may be found in William Courtenay, 'Learned Opinion and Royal Justice: The Role of the Paris Masters of Theology during the Reign of Philip the Fair', in *Law and the Illicit in Medieval Europe,* ed. Ruth Mazzo Karras, Joel Kaye and E. Ann Matter (Philadelphia, 2008), pp. 278–9 (which appeared while this article was being prepared for publication). See also Valois, 'Deux nouveaux témoignages', pp. 230–38.

69 *CUP*, vol. 3, no. 1264, dated 1362. Valois says it is 'impossible' that he was the Jean of Pouilly mentioned in a document of 1344 (Valois, 'Jean de Pouilli, théologien', p. 257 n. 5), but there seems no reason to dismiss out of hand the idea that he might have lived to 1344, or even 1362. The minimum age for a master's degree, which he received in 1306, was 30, which would make him 86 in 1362. If this were the case he would have had

much available in 1308. If he had wanted to join the 14 masters who defended exemption, he would have, just as he would join the less controversial evaluation of Marguerite Porete's *Mirror* two years later. But he did not do so in 1308. His views on the Templars were no secret: in fact, he hated them, and wrote widely against them, from the time of the arrests (1307 and 1308) to the council of Vienne (1311 and 1312).[70] His views on exempt clergy generally were no secret either: he had a similarly violent dislike for mendicants and participated in that conflict somewhat earlier;[71] in his *quodlibets* (themes for academic disputation) in 1312 and again in 1314, he would attack the validity of the papal license granted to mendicants to hear confessions.[72] (The secular master Thomas of Bailly also addressed this issue in several of his *quodlibets*, underlining the importance it held for seculars and religious alike in the early fourteenth century.[73]) John of Pouilly's challenge resulted in an investigation of *him,* and in 1321 three of his propositions were condemned as heresy by Pope John XXII. Unlike Marguerite of Porete, however, John of Pouilly submitted and withdrew the controversial statements.

There is yet another interesting detail to be found by comparing the list of masters involved in evaluating Marguerite Porete in 1310 with those returning an opinion on the Templars in 1308, and that is in the case of Peter of St Denis. Peter was a Benedictine, so he was at least theoretically a member of the regular clergy. In addition, the abbey of St Denis enjoyed a considerable degree of exemption as a royal abbey.[74] Peter had been a master for even longer than John of Pouilly (perhaps since 1303), and like John was almost certainly available to join the

---

to have survived a couple of bouts of plague in the meantime, but even so, it hardly seems impossible that he might still have been alive in 1362. John claimed to have heard Albertus Magnus and Thomas Aquinas, which would indeed suggest considerable longevity (if it were true), but Ludwig Hödl questions this claim, which is made in *Quodlibet* I, q. 5 (see Hödl, '*Quodlibeta* of John of Pouilly', p. 199, n. 3). Hödl does think, however, that John died c. 1328.

70 John may have been the author of a rather lengthy document (*Le dossier*, ed. Lizerand, pp. 70–83, and *PUT*, vol. 2, pp. 101–7) arguing against the Templars and possibly dating from around 1310 (see Barber, *Trial*, pp. 171–4, and Valois, 'Deux nouveaux témoignages', pp. 230–8. John was also part of a group of 22 masters who dealt with the question of the Templars in 1312, around the time of Vienne, according to his unpublished fifth *quodlibet*, discussed in Valois, 'Deux nouveaux témoignages'.

71 Valois, 'Deux nouveaux témoignages', p. 230.

72 *Medieval Theologians*, ed. Evans, p. 236.

73 See Palémon Glorieux, *Thomas de Bailly: Quodlibets* (Paris, 1960), esp. IV:14, pp. 324–35.

74 On the issue of St Denis and exemption, see Robert F. Berkhofer, *Day of Reckoning: Power and Accountability in Medieval France* (Philadelphia, 2004), pp. 40, 45–6, 60–1; St Denis received confirmation of its exempt status from Pope Alexander II in 1065 and King Philip I in 1068 (pp. 46, 60). See also William Chester Jordan, *A Tale of Two Monasteries: Westminster and Saint-Denis in the Thirteenth Century* (Princeton, 2009). I am grateful to William Chester Jordan for his generous assistance on this point.

group of masters defending exemption and the Templars in 1308. But like John of Pouilly and most of the canons of Notre Dame, he did not. This was probably for similar reasons which can be deduced from his background. Peter of St Denis was a member of a very royal establishment, the abbey of St Denis, from which the *Grandes Chroniques de France* were produced; one of its abbots (Suger) had even served as regent of France during the Second Crusade in the 1140s.

One raindrop hardly makes a storm, nor does one bit of suggestive evidence make a case. But many raindrops together do tend to get things awfully wet – and likewise, an accumulation of suggestions, all pointing in the same direction, begins to look like a good case. In summary: if one compares the composition of the group of masters who delivered an expert opinion on the status of the Templars in 1308 with the group which delivered an expert opinion on the orthodoxy of Marguerite Porete in 1310, one finds a very interesting anomaly. There were a number of masters from the latter group in 1310 who could have joined the former group in 1308, but did not. There seems a clear reason why they did not. Those masters who could have helped the Templars, but did not, were almost all secular canons, most of them from the cathedral chapter of Notre Dame, and their interests lay with the king and against the exempt clergy, such as the mendicants … and the Templars. Some of them appear to have actively disliked the Templars.

This places the university's involvement in the trial of the Templars in 1308 squarely in the context of the much larger, long-ranging conflict between mendicants and seculars in the thirteenth and early fourteenth centuries, and it highlights the strains caused by conflicting loyalties to king and pope. Neither shocking nor unreasonable, perhaps, but certainly intriguing.

Appendix: Masters of the University of Paris involved in the trials of the Templars and of Marguerite Porete

Name	Templar trial	Porete trial
Alexander of Alexandria, Franciscan	X	
Alexander Fassitelli of Sant'Elpidio, Augustinian hermit	X	X
Berengar of Landore, Dominican		X
Gautier (Walter) of Gamaches, Cluniac Benedictine	X	
Gérard of Bologna, Carmelite	X	X
Gérard of St Victor, Victorine	X	X
Gregory of Lucca, Augustinian hermit		X
Henry of Friemar the Elder, Augustinian hermit	X	X
Hervé Nédellec (Hervaeus Natalis), Dominican	X	
Jacques of Ascoli, Franciscan		X
Jacques of Dijon, Cistercian		X
Jacques of Thérines, Cistercian	X	X
John of Clairmarais, secular (?)		X
John of Gand (Ghent), secular		X
John of Mt St Eloi, Augustinian canon regular	X	X
John of Pouilly, secular		X
Laurence of Poulengy, Augustinian canon regular	X	X
Nicholas of Lyra, Franciscan		X
Peter of St Denis, St Denis Benedictine		X
Peter of St Omer, canon of Notre Dame	X	
Raoul (Ralph) of Hotot, secular	X	X
Roger of Roseto, secular		X
Romeus of Brugaria, Dominican	X	
Simon of Guiberville, secular		X
Thomas of Bailly, secular		X
William Alexander, secular	X	X

Chapter 12
The Trial Depositions as Evidence of Kinship Influences in the Order of the Temple

Jochen G. Schenk

Historians interested in the social and economic developments of local Templar communities tend to agree that in most parts of Catholic Europe these communities were deeply rooted in society and recruited most of their personnel from local families.[1] In fact, the toponyms functioning as Templars' surnames recorded in charter documents make it relatively easy to pinpoint the regions and localities from which individual Templar communities drew their personal support. Only rarely, however, do the same sources indicate any personal relationships between the brothers, which caused Alan Forey, for one, to conclude that it was extremely difficult to trace family ties in the order back more than two generations.[2] Questions regarding the significance of personal relationships for the social composition of Templar communities and the importance of these relationships for understanding the inert social dynamics of the order are, therefore, very difficult to answer. And yet, they are worth asking and contemplating, because the way we answer them inevitably affects our understanding of the order's standing in society and functionality as a whole.

1 See e.g. Elena Bellomo, *The Templar Order in North-West Italy (1142–c.1330)* (Leiden, Boston, 2008), pp. 128–47; Damien Carraz, *L'ordre du Temple dans la basse vallée du Rhône (1124–1312): Ordres militaires, croisades et sociétés méridionales* (Lyon, 2005), pp. 291–307; Michel Miguet, *Templiers et Hospitaliers en Normandie* (Paris, 1995), pp. 130–7; idem, 'Le personnel des commanderies du Temple et d'Hôpital en Normandie', in *La commanderie: Institution des ordres militaires dans l'Occident médiéval*, ed. Anthony Luttrell and Léon Pressouyre (Paris, 2002), pp. 93–105, here p. 95; Laure Verdon, *La terre et les hommes en Roussillon aux XIIe aux XIIIe siècles. Structures seigneuriales, rente et société d'après les sources templières* (Aix-en-Provence, 2001), pp. 25–7; Valerie Alanièce and François Gilet, *Les Templiers et leurs commanderies: L'exemple d'Avalleur en Champagne* (Langres 1995), pp. 164–84; *Cartulaires des Templiers de Douzens*, ed. Pierre Gérard and Élisabeth Magnou (Paris, 1965), p. xxxiii. See also Malcolm Barber, *The New Knighthood* (Cambridge, 1994), p. 261, and Alain Demurger, *Les Templiers: Une chevalerie chrétienne au moyen âge* (Paris, 2005), pp. 132–4.

2 Alan Forey, *The Templars in the Corona de Aragón* (London, 1973), p. 53.

One way towards a better, more detailed knowledge of the Templars' personal inter-relations is to scrutinize more closely what they themselves had to say about the matter of family relations when they were asked to testify regarding the abominable charges brought against them in the trial. The result will add little to the debate of whether or not the charges brought against the Templars were indeed justified.[3] What it hopefully will do, however, is contribute to a better understanding of the social composition of Templar communities and the circumstances and channels which potentially would have facilitated modes of misconduct or unorthodoxy to survive and flourish in the Temple.

When François Juste Marie Raynouard published his *Monumens historiques relatifs à la condamnation des chevaliers du Temple* in 1813, he included in the appendix a short list of 65 Templars who had received their own relatives into the order, based on the depositions before the papal commission. The list, although one of a kind, has never attracted much attention; nor did Raynouard himself make much use of it in his further investigations into the reasons for the order's demise.[4] Since the publication of Raynouard's study, a number of Templar depositions from other parts of Europe have come to light, and many of them include evidence of family relationships.[5] So far I have collected the names of

---

[3] There is still a broad consensus among historians that the trial of the Templars was politically motivated and unjust. One recent voice in the dark is Jonathan Riley-Smith, 'Were the Templars Guilty?', in *The Medieval Crusade*, ed. Susan J. Ridyard (Woodbridge, 2004), pp. 107–24.

[4] François J.M. Raynouard, *Monumens historiques, relatifs à la condamnation des chevaliers du Temple, et à l'abolition de leur ordre* (Paris, 1813), pp. 221–2.

[5] Most of the evidence in this paper I was able to draw from the Paris depositions, but other depositions have also been taken into consideration, notably those from Aragon (*EUT*, pp. 346–55); Auvergne (*Le procès des Templiers d'Auvergne (1309–1311): Edition de l'interrogatoire de juin 1309*, ed. Roger Sève and Anne-Marie Chagny-Sève (Paris, 1986); for Clermont see also *EUT*, pp. 327–34); Bigorre (*EUT*, pp. 324–5); Bayeux (*EUT*, p. 325); Caen (*PUT*, vol. 2, pp. 313–16); Cahors (*EUT*, p. 326, *PUT*, vol. 2, pp. 316–21); Carcassonne (*PUT*, vol. 2, pp. 321–4); Chinon (*PUT*, vol. 2, pp. 324–9); Cyprus (*The Trial of the Templars in Cyprus: A Complete English Edition*, ed. and trans. Anne Gilmour-Bryson (Leiden, 1998), and *UT*, vol. 2, pp. 143–400); England (*UT*, vol. 2, pp. 75–100; *Concilia Magnae Britannie et Hibernie*, ed. David Wilkins, 4 vols. (London, 1737), vol. 2, pp. 328–401); Lerida (*PUT*, vol. 2, pp. 364–78); the papal states (*UT*, vol. 2, pp. 403–19; *The Trial of the Templars in the Papal States and the Abruzzi*, ed. Anne Gilmour-Bryson (Vatican City, 1982)); Poitiers (*UT*, vol. 2, pp. 9–71; *PUT*, vol. 2, pp. 329–42); Navarre (*PUT*, vol. 2, pp. 378–9); and Tuscany (Jules Loiseleur, *La doctrine secrète des Templiers: Etude suivie du texte inédit de l'enquête contre les Templiers de Toscane et de la chronologie des documents relatifs à la suppression du Temple* (Paris, 1872), pp. 172–212). Most depositions contain only very little personal information, or none at all. In the case of Cyprus this surprises little since here the Templar community was almost entirely made up of foreigners. In other cases it may have been that the scribes ultimately suppressed the deponents' personal information as unnecessary or irrelevant.

137 inter-related Templars who lived during the final 50 years of the order's existence. To these perhaps another 25 can be added, whose inter-relationship is very likely but not explicitly explained in the depositions. This is a remarkably high number, bearing in mind that the Templars arrested in 1307 were never explicitly questioned about their family relations in the order and that it excludes most of the many more Templars with common surnames whose relations to one another are still unaccounted for.[6] Instead they were asked to reveal the details and circumstances of their own reception, as well as of any other reception in which they had participated or of which they had any general knowledge. It was in this context that family relations between Templars surfaced in the testimonies. It is therefore hardly surprising that almost all accounts of blood relations between individual Templars relate to reception ceremonies at which some or all of the relatives in question had been present. This can lead to the misconception that ties of kinship between Templars played a more crucial role in the recruitment of new brothers than they actually did. It would be more accurate to say that accounts of receptions provided the Templars with the only opportunity to include information about the order's internal social dynamics in the depositions, which they may even have done unintentionally. On the other hand, the evidence of family ties between Templars, as recorded in the depositions, is substantial enough for us to assume that they may have had an influence on the constellation and consistency of individual Templar communities, and even of the order as a whole.

Of the 137 Templars with family connections in the order, 45 were related as brothers (*fratres carnales* or *consanguinei germani*).[7] Four Templars were cousins of one of the others,[8] whereas six more were related to one of the others as either brothers or cousins (meaning that the depositions merely indicate that they shared the same uncle).[9] In five cases involving 12 Templars, the relationship between two brothers was that of father and son.[10] Fourteen other Templars were simply

6 It does include, however, in a category labelled 'eventual additions', Templars with common surnames, and usually with same first names, who operated in the same region and often held similar or same offices (e.g. John/John de Turno, *PT*, vol. 1, pp. 595–6, 597; Peter/Peter de Coderc, *Auvergne*, ed. Sève and Chagny-Sève, p. 167; *UT*, vol. 1, pp. 277; *UT*, vol. 2, p. 48; *PT*, vol. 1, p. 614; Lambert/Lambert de Cormellis, *PT*, vol. 1, pp. 439–40, vol. 2, pp. 4–6; but also Johannes/Henricus de Anisiaco, *PT*, vol. 1, pp. 137, 348, vol. 2, pp. 366–7; Guido/Guillelmus de Preyssac, *PT*, vol. 2, p. 123).

7 *PT*, vol. 1, pp. 205–6, 234, 265, 435, 505, 564, 568, 599; vol. 2, pp. 13, 22, 50, 100, 151–2, 184–5, 212, 331, 368, 370; *UT*, vol. 2, p. 198; *EUT*, p. 326; *Papal States*, ed. Gilmour-Bryson p. 22; Loiseleur, *La doctrine*, p. 184.

8 *PT*, vol. 1, p. 241; vol. 2, p. 97.

9 *PT*, vol. 1, pp. 406–8; vol. 2, pp. 84, 230.

10 *PT*, vol. 1, p. 234, and vol. 2, p. 225 (John de Sancto Hilario, brother of Peter Reginald, must be identical with John de las Chaussandas. It is therefore very likely that he also was the father of Guy de las Chaussadas, Peter Reginald's nephew); vol. 2, pp. 151–2; *UT*, vol. 2, p. 14, *EUT*, p. 326; Raynouard, *Monumens*, p. 222

remembered as being related to – or a kinsman of – one of the others.[11] Seventy-seven Templars, and this constitutes 57 per cent of all cases, were related to one or two of the others as either uncle or nephew, which suggests that most had joined the order before they had the time or opportunity to establish families of their own.[12]

Reception ceremonies are the context in which most family ties between Templars were recorded. On four occasions the depositions relate that multiple members of the same family were received into the order at the same time. The knight Adam de Valencourt entered the order in Paris in 1296 together with his *frater carnalis*,[13] whereas the priest Guillaume and his *frater carnalis* Anricus were received together at Lanville in 1303.[14] The *agricola* Peter was received together with his brother John somewhere in Picardy.[15] And the priest Peter Mathei and his nephew John Mathei, who became a Templar sergeant, were both received on the same day in 1290 at Nanteuil.[16] Most numerous are those examples in which Templar priests, knights or sergeants were apparently passive witnesses to the reception of a relative. I have counted 33 such cases, involving 63 Templars.[17] The knight Humbert de Sancto Jorio, for example, witnessed the reception of his nephew Peter de Toluo at Neuville in 1302 and of his nephew Aymon de Clermont, also at Neuville, in 1303;[18] Guillaume Charnier, a Templar sergeant from Auvergne, witnessed the reception of his nephew Hugh Charnier at St Pourçain in Auvergne in 1280.[19] And 22 years later, in 1302, Hugh, Durand senior and Humbert Charnier were present when another relative, Durand junior Charnier, entered the order at Celles in Auvergne.[20]

More insightful are those cases in which individual Templars instigated or actively participated in the reception of relatives. In my sample these cases amount

---

11 *PT*, vol. 1, pp. 13, 79, 138, 265–6, 505; *Auvergne*, ed. Sève and Chagny-Sève p. 258. In the case of the English Templar brothers William of Grafton senior and William of Grafton junior a close family relationship, albeit not explicitly stated, seems very likely: Wilkins, *Concilia*, vol. 2, pp. 356, 366.

12 *PT*, vol. 1, pp. 225, 265, 406–8, 468, 485, 506–7, 562, 575, 604–5, 611, 630; vol. 2, pp. 23–4, 27, 31–2, 45, 84, 93, 94, 103, 123, 134, 143, 157, 182–3, 230, 235, 265–6, 323, 343, 362, 390, 394; *PUT*, vol. 2, pp. 75, 330–1; Raynouard, *Monumens*, p. 221; *UT*, vol. 2, p. 211, n. 2.

13 *PT*, vol. 1, p. 599.

14 *PT*, vol. 1, p. 568.

15 *PT*, vol. 2, p. 331.

16 *PT*, vol. 2, p. 84.

17 *PT*, vol. 1, pp. 64, 205–6, 265, 368–9, 435, 501, 506–7, 575, 611, 630; vol. 2, pp. 21–2, 23–4, 45, 77, 93–4, 96–7, 100, 105, 123, 134, 138, 143, 151–2, 182–5, 225, 235, 241, 265–6, 394, 407–8; Raynouard, *Monumens*, pp. 221, 222.

18 *PT*, vol. 1, pp. 407, 408.

19 *PT*, vol. 2, p. 143.

20 *PT*, vol. 2, p. 241.

to 15, involving 29 Templars.[21] The pattern was usually such that one relative received another – a process that was sometimes witnessed by one or more of the recipient's other Templar relatives. On 29 October 1309, Humbert Blanc, the last grand preceptor of Auvergne, testified in London that four or five years earlier he had personally received his nephew Perceval de Sancto Albino into the order.[22] Hugh de Pairaud told the inquisitors in November 1307 that 44 years earlier he had been received by his uncle Humbert de Pairaud.[23] He himself had presided over receptions in the presence of his nephew Hugh de Chalon, who in turn recalled having received new brothers in the presence of his nephew, the Templar sergeant Peter de Modies.[24] The Templar priest Robert de Sancto Justo received his cousin Baldwin de Sancto Justo into the order when he was preceptor of the baillie of Sommereux.[25] In 1306, Baldwin in turn presided over the reception of his nephew John de Sancto Justo at La Forest in the diocese of Ambroise.[26] The knight Reynard de Bort, from Limousin, recalled that he had been received by his uncle Franco de Bort, in 1275, and in the presence of his father Roger de Bort, Franco's brother.[27] The knight Garin de Granvillier presided over the reception of his nephew Robert and, in 1298, in his function as master of the baillie of Ponthieu, ordered the reception of John de Baal at Beaulieu, a reception at which his nephew Robert was present as a witness.[28]

Elsewhere I have already voiced my suspicion that a number of Templars (and I was then concerned with Templars of non-noble stock) had been received into the order because a relative in the order had actively lobbied for them to be accepted; at least this is what the expression 'receiving someone *de mandato*' of a relative seemed to imply.[29] Those Templars with the authority to make such requests were usually middle and high-ranking officers in the order, although not all were necessarily knights. Thomas de Boncourt, a serving brother from the diocese of Ambroise, for example, remembered that he had been received in the Templar chapel of Sour in the diocese of Chartres by the priest Peter de Maysonseles and *de mandato* of his uncle Ralph de Boncourt, who was the preceptor of Chartres at

---

21 *PT*, vol. 1, pp. 13, 241, 243, 465, 485, 595–6; vol. 2, pp. 27, 97, 152, 230, 323, 362; *UT*, vol. 2, pp. 14, 198, 211.

22 *Auvergne*, ed. Sève and Chagny-Sève, p. 251; *Trial in Cyprus*, ed. Gilmour-Bryson, p. 144; Wilkins, *Concilia*, vol. 2, pp. 337–8.

23 *PT*, vol. 2, p. 362.

24 *PT*, vol. 2, pp. 266, 343.

25 *PT*, vol. 1, p. 241.

26 *PT*, vol. 1, p. 243.

27 *PT*, vol. 2, pp. 151–2

28 *PT*, vol. 2, p. 44.

29 Jochen Schenk, 'Aspects of Non-Noble Family Involvement in the Order of the Temple', *The Military Orders*, vol. 4: *On Land and by Sea*, ed. Judi Upton-Ward (Aldershot, 2008), pp. 155–61.

the time.[30] Guillaume d'Erree, who entered the order at Aynes in the diocese of Le Mans as a young boy in c. 1259, remembered being received *de mandato* of his relative, Hugh Guiscard, the master of Aquitaine. The reception was presided over by the preceptor of Aynes, Peter Armenart, and among those who witnessed it was the preceptor's own brother, John Armenart.[31]

Due to the nature of the evidence, the kinship networks in the order that one can reconstruct from such snapshot accounts are not extensive. Forty-three of the 54 Templar family units that I have been able to discern from the depositions consisted of only two people. Some examples that fit the pattern of this most elemental form of family unit – for example the reception of Guillaume d'Erree on the order of his relative Hugh Guiscard or that of Hugh de Pairaud by his uncle Humbert – can be traced to the 1250s and 1260s.[32] They show that the existence of small family groups within the order was not a phenomenon of the order's final years, a claim that can be further substantiated with evidence from Templar cartularies.[33] But the depositions sometimes provide evidence of more complex networks of family relationships in the order. The last preceptor of Ponthieu, Baldwin de Sancto Justo, for example, had at least two relatives in the order: his cousin Robert de Sancto Justo, who had received him at Sommereux, and his nephew John de Sancto Justo, whom he eventually received at La Forest.[34] The last preceptor of the baillie of Châlons-sur-Marne, Humbert de Sancto Jorio, witnessed the reception of his nephew Peter de Toluo at Neuville in c. 1304 and of his nephew Aymo de Clermont, also at Neuville, the following year.[35] The depositions contain evidence of at least five more family groups of three.[36] To these must be added the group of relatives that centred on Garin de Granvillier and which counted between three and five heads: Garin himself, his nephews Robert and Eudes, and Clemens and John Roche de Granvillier, who were said to have been of one *parentela*.[37] Another group that should be added is that of Templars related to Pons de Masualier. A Templar sergeant from Limousin, Pons had been received into the order in c. 1281, in the chapel of Mas Deu de Lombertz, and in the presence of his uncle Aymeric

30 *PT*, vol. 2, p. 485.

31 *PT*, vol. 2, p. 13.

32 *PT*, vol. 2, pp. 13, 361–2.

33 The many Templar charters predating the period of roughly 50 years covered by the depositions in fact often allow for the establishment of wide-reaching and close-knit family networks in the Temple. Jochen Schenk, *Templar Families. Landowning Families and the Order of the Temple in France, c. 1120–c.1307* (Cambridge, forthcoming).

34 *PT*, vol. 1, pp. 241, 243.

35 *PT*, vol. 1, pp. 407–8.

36 Bort: *PT*, vol. 2, pp. 151–2; Sancto Benedicto: *PT*, vol. 2, pp. 93, 96–7; Merlot, Podio, Bergerius: *PT*, vol. 1, p. 265; Rougepere, Divione, Wala: *PT*, vol. 1, pp. 632–4; vol. 2, pp. 368–9; Mathei: *PT*, vol. 2, p. 84.

37 *PT*, vol. 2, pp. 44, 77–9, 323, 353, 390.

Masualier.[38] Fifteen years later Aymeric, in his function as preceptor of Mas Deu de Lombertz, received another nephew (also with the name of Aymeric) in the same chapel. Present at this reception was Bosco Masualier, who may have been another family member.[39] The Templar Bertrand de Tecayo had three sons who followed his example and joined the order.[40] The kinship group that centred on Humbert and Hugh of Pairaud, who were uncle and nephew, counted six members. Apart from the knights Humbert and Hugh these included two nephews of Hugh de Pairaud, namely the knight Hugh de Chalon and a certain Peter, as well as Hugh de Chalon's nephew Peter de Modies and a certain Franco de Milli, who was a 'kinsman' of Peter de Modies.[41] One family from Auvergne, whose members went by the surname of Charnier, may have sent as many as seven members into the Temple in the late thirteenth and early fourteenth centuries; they certainly sent four. All of them were serving brothers, and at least three had remarkable careers in the order. One, William Charnier, was at one time *hostarius* of Pope Nicholas III and the preceptor of St Giustini and St Girolamo in Perugia. He later took over the function of preceptor and *magister* of the patrimony of St Peter in Tuscia and as such received Bernard Charnier from the diocese of Clermont, who was very likely a relative of his, into the order in 1282.[42] By 1289 William had returned to his native Auvergne, where he ended his career as preceptor of Le Chambon.[43] His nephew Hugh Charnier, whom William had once witnessed being received at Le Chambon,[44] served for a while at Tortosa, but eventually returned to Auvergne, where he took over the commandery of St Pourçain.[45] Two other relatives, an uncle and nephew, who both went by the name Durand Charnier, were attached to the commandery of Celles in Auvergne. Durand the Elder functioned at one point as preceptor of Celles; and it was also at Celles that he witnessed the reception of his nephew into the order.[46] Another possible kinsman, Robert Charnier, also served

---

38 *PT*, vol. 1, p. 611.

39 *PT*, vol. 1, p. 611; vol. 2, p. 230.

40 *EUT*, p. 326

41 *PT*, vol. 2, pp. 265–6, 343, 361–2; *PUT*, vol. 2, p. 75.

42 Amédée Trudon des Ormes, 'Maisons du Temple en Orient et en France', *ROL*, 7 (1899), 223–74, 504–89, 549–50; *Auvergne*, ed. Sève and Chagny-Sève, pp. 42, 225; *EUT*, p. 333.

43 *PT*, vol. 2, p. 137; *Auvergne*, ed. Sève and Chagny-Sève, pp. 180, 225; *Papal States*, ed. Gilmour-Bryson, pp. 202–3, 206, 221; Francesco Tommasi, 'L'ordine dei Templari a Perugia', *Bollettino della deputazione di storia patria per l'Umbria*, 78 (1981), 5–79, 12, 17 and no. 7, 51; Marie Luise Bulst-Thiele, 'Templer in königlichen und päpstlichen Diensten', in *Festschrift Percy Ernst Schramm*, ed. Peter Classen and Peter Scheibert (Wiesbaden, 1964), vol. 1, pp. 289–308, here pp. 303–4.

44 *PT*, vol. 2, p. 143; *Auvergne*, ed. Sève and Chagny-Sève, pp. 143–4.

45 *PT*, vol. 2, pp. 141, 143–5; *Auvergne*, ed. Sève and Chagny-Sève, pp. 106, 143–6; *EUT*, p. 330; Trudon des Ormes, 'Maisons', 549, 554.

46 *Auvergne*, ed. Sève and Chagny-Sève, p. 135; *PT*, vol. 2, pp. 138, 242.

the order in Auvergne. Since he managed to escape in 1307, however, we only know very little of him.[47]

Not only did members of these family groups – Hugh and Humbert of Pairaud, for example, or William Charnier – often have remarkable careers in the order; the careers of Templars from the same families were often also remarkably similar, with relatives holding similar offices or fulfilling similar functions in the same communities.[48]

The Templar depositions provide snapshots of the social composition of Templar commanderies and smaller communities during the last half-century of the order's existence. They also suggest that networks of friends and kinsmen were commonplace in the Temple and that in particular in the last decades of the order's existence these networks could influence the social composition and constellation of Templar communities considerably. Of course, ties of kinship and friendship influenced the social setting of any religious community (Bernard of Clairvaux allegedly had entered Cîteaux along with around 30 of his friends and relatives).[49] In the light of the charges brought against the order, however, which implied that modes of misconduct had been common among Templars from particular areas or regions,[50] the assumption that a nepotistic culture could have infested the order from top to bottom is worth taking seriously and investigating further. Whether or not the charges which were brought against the Templars were indeed justified still remains doubtful, and the mere fact that familial ties existed in the order does little to lift these doubts. The least that can be said is that by the end of the thirteenth century many Templar communities hosted multiple family units of Templar brothers who had received one another into the order and witnessed and supported each other's claims and actions. And from this evidence one can suspect that family involvement in the order of the Temple was commonplace, and its influence upon the order's overall conduct and inner discipline may well have been considerable.

---

47 *Auvergne*, ed. Sève and Chagny-Sève, p. 280.

48 See Schenk, 'Aspects', pp. 155–61.

49 Pierre Aubé, *Saint Bernard de Clairvaux* (Paris, 2003), p. 57.

50 As has recently been argued in Riley-Smith, 'Were the Templars Guilty?'.

names	family members total	eventual additions	brothers	brothers or cousins	uncle-nephew	father-son	cousins	"relatives"	possible relatives	reference
Johannes de Sancto Hilario (Johannes de las Chaussadas); Guido de las Chaussadas; Petrus Reginaldi	4		2		2	2				*PT*, vol. 1, p. 234; vol. 2, p. 225+K2
Balduinus de Sancto Justo; Johannes de Santo Justo; Robertus de Santo Justo (Robertus de Pantaleone)	3				2		2			*PT*, vol. 1, pp. 241, 243, 465–6, 468; M.-L. Bulst-Thiele, *Sacrae domus militiae Templi* (Göttingen, 1974), pp. 363–4; A. Trudon des Ormes, *Étude sur les possessions de l'ordre du Temple en Picardie* (Amiens, 1892), pp. 28–9, 39
Humbertus de Sancto Jorio; Aymon de Claromonte; Petrus de Tolio	3			2	3					*PT*, vol. 1, pp. 406–8
Thomas de Boncourt; Radulphus de Bonecourt	2				2					*PT*, vol. 1, p. 485
Adam de Benovalle; Galterus de Liencourt	2							2		*PT*, vol. 1, p. 501

names	family members total	eventual additions	brothers	brothers or cousins	uncle-nephew	father-son	cousins	"relatives"	possible relatives	reference
Johannes le Verjus; Jacobus le Verjus	2		2							*PT*, vol. 1, p. 505
Radulphus de Buris; Johannes de Rumpreyo	2				2					*PT*, vol. 1, pp. 506–7
Bartholomeus Merlotis; Humbertus de Podio; Guillelmus Bergerius	3		2		2			2		*PT*, vol. 1, p. 265
Franco de Bort; Rogerius de Bort; Renardus de Bort	3		2		2	2				*PT*, vol. 2, pp. 151–2
Helias Raynaudi; Hugo Raynaudi	2		2							*PT*, vol. 2, pp. 21–2
Petrus Theobaldi; Arnaudus	2				2					*PT*, vol. 2, pp. 21–2
Johannes de Sancto Benedicto; Petrus de Sancto Benedicto; Guillelmus de Sancto Benedicto	3				2		2			*PT*, vol. 2, pp. 93, 96–7
Stephanus de Ambasia; Andreas de Monte Laudato	2				2					*PT*, vol. 2, p. 103
Guillelmus Charnerii; Hugo Charnerii; Durandus Charnerii (I); Durandus Charnerii (II); [Robert Charnerii; Humbert Charnerii; Bernard Charnerii]	4	3			2			2	3	*PT*, vol. 2, pp. 130, 138, 143, 241; Trudon des Ormes, 'Maisons', 549, 554
Johannes Armenart; Petrus Armenart	2		2							*PT*, vol. 2, p. 13
Guillelmus d'Eree; Hugo Gisardi	2							2		*PT*, vol. 2, p. 13

names	family members total	eventual additions	brothers	brothers or cousins	uncle-nephew	father-son	cousins	"relatives"	possible relatives	reference
Petrus Agate; Philippus	2				2					*PT*, vol. 2, p. 27
Robertus de Grandi Villari; Garinus de Grandi Vilarii; Johannes Rocherii de Grandi Villarii; Clemens de Grande Villarii; Odo de Grandi Villari; [Radulphus de Grandevillarii]	5	1			3			2	1	*PT*, vol. 2, pp. 44, 77–9, 323, 353, 390
Petrus de Lenhi (I); Petrus de Lenhi (II)	2				2					*PT*, vol. 2, pp. 45, 76
Guillelmus Aymerici (I); Guillelmus Aymerici (II)	2				2					*PT*, vol. 2, p. 123
Guido de Preyssac; Guillelmo de Preyssac		2							2	*PT*, vol. 2, p. 123
Franco de Montinhaco; Peter de Montinhaco	2				2					*PT*, vol. 2, p. 134
Johannes de Montealto; N.N.	2					2				*UT*, vol. 2, p. 14 (Poitou)
Hugucio de Vercellis; Antonius	2				2					*PT*, vol. 1, p. 562
Richardus de Monte Claro; Johannes de Monte Claro	2		2							*PT*, vol. 1, p. 564
Guilelmus; Anricus	2		2							*PT*, vol. 1, p. 568
Adam de Cercellis; Petrus de Cercellis	2				2					*PT*, vol. 1, p. 575

names	family members total	eventual additions	brothers	brothers or cousins	uncle-nephew	father-son	cousins	"relatives"	possible relatives	reference
Johannes de Turno (I); Johannes de Turno (II)		2							2	*PT*, vol. 1, pp. 595–7
Adam de Valencourt	2		2							*PT*, vol. 1, p. 599
Aymericus de las Gorsolas; P. Raynandi (perhaps also linked to St Hilario network)	2				2					*PT*, vol. 1, pp. 604–5
Aymericus Masualier (I); Aymericus de Masualier (II); Poncius de Masualier; [Bosco de Masualier]	3	1		2	3				1	*PT*, vol. 1, p. 611; vol. 2, p. 230
Baudoynus; Martinus	2				2					*PT*, vol. 2, p. 94
Johannes de Ruans; Johannes de Ruivans	2				2					*PT*, vol. 2, p. 94
Gerardus de Bonart; Hugo de Bonart	2		2							*PT*, vol. 2, p. 100
Hugo de Cabilone; Petrus de Modies; Humbertus de Paraudo; Hugo de Paraudo (Penrado); Petrus; Falco de Milli	6				5			2		*PT*, vol. 2, pp. 265–6, 343, 361–2; *PUT*, vol. 2, p. 75
Guillelmus de Vollenis; Bono de Vollenis	2				2					*PT*, vol. 1, p. 630
Guilhemus Talheboys; Guilelmus Talheboys	2				2					*PT*, vol. 2, pp. 182–3

names	family members total	eventual additions	brothers	brothers or cousins	uncle-nephew	father-son	cousins	"relatives"	possible relatives	reference
Guilhelmus de Plexeyo; Stephanus de Plexeyo	2		2							*PT*, vol. 2, pp. 184–5
Arnaudus de Aurifolio; Arnaudus de Breion	2				2					*PT*, vol. 2, p.190
Helias Cotati; Johannes Costati	2		2							*PT*, vol. 2, p. 212
Guillelmus Juyto; Peter	2				2					*PT*, vol. 2, p. 235
Ricardus Stephani; Raimundus Stephani		2							2	*PT*, vol. 2, p. 259
Egidius de Vilert; Remundus de Vilert		2							2	*PT*, vol. 2, pp. 492, 496 (Elne)
Nicolaus de Moncuccho; Iacobus de Monte Cucco	2		2							Gilmour-Bryson, *Papal States*, 22; *UT*, vol. 2, p. 198
Ademarus de Peyrucza; N.N.	2				2					*PT*, vol. 2, 157
Humbertus Blancus; Percevallus de Sancto Albino	2				2					Sève, *Auvergne*, p. 251; *UT*, vol. 2, pp. 153, 166, 211, 357
Petrus de Coderc (I); Petrus de Coderc (II)		2							2	Sève, *Auvergne*, p. 167; *UT*, vol. 1, p. 277; vol. 2, p. 48; *PT*, vol. 1, p. 614

names	family members total	eventual additions	brothers	brothers or cousins	uncle-nephew	father-son	cousins	"relatives"	possible relatives	reference
W. de Grafton junior; W. de Grafton senior; Richard de Grafton; Johannes de Grafton	2	2						2	2	Sève, *Auvergne*, p. 258; Wilkins, *Concilia*, vol. 2, pp. 342–3, 346, 353–4, 356, 366
Petrus; Johannes	2		2							*PT*, vol. 2, p. 331
Radulphus de Gisi; Baldoinus	2		2							*PT*, vol. 2, p. 370
Reginaldus de Toisiaco; Lambertus de Toisy	2				2					*PT*, vol. 2, p. 394
Robertus de Torteville; Henricus de Torteville		2							2	*PT*, vol. 2, p. 398
Guillelmus Rougepere; Dominicus de Divione; Wala	3		2			2				*PT*, vol. 1, pp. 632–4; vol. 2, pp. 368–9
Johannes de Anisiaco; Henricus de Anisiaco		2							2	*PT*, vol. 1, pp. 137, 348; vol. 2, pp. 366–7
Lambertus de Cormellis (I); Lambertus de Cormellis (II)		2							2	*PT*, vol. 1, pp. 439–40; vol. 2, pp. 4–6
Petrus Mathei (I); Petrus Mathei (II); Johannes Mathei	3			2	3					*PT*, vol. 2, p. 84
Guaufredus Guilhon; Guillelmus Guilhon	2		2							*PT*, vol. 2, p. 50

names	family members total	eventual additions	brothers	brothers or cousins	uncle-nephew	father-son	cousins	"relatives"	possible relatives	reference
Raynaldus de Tecayo; Petrus de Tecayo; Bertrandus de Tecayo; Johannes	4		3			4				*EUT*, p. 326
Jacobus de Castillione; N.N.	2				2					*PUT*, vol. 2, pp. 330–331
N.N.; N.N.	2					2				Raynouard, *Monumens*, p. 222
Martinus de Monte Trichardi; Balduinus de Monte Trichardi	2				2					*PT*, vol. 2, pp. 52, 88–90, 94, 107
Johannes de Annonia; Radulphus de Annonia	2		2							*PT*, vol. 1, p. 435
Huguetto de Buris; Guillelmus de Buris	2		2							*PT*, vol. 1, pp. 205–6
Petrus de Madic; N.N.	2				2					Raynouard, *Monumens*, p. 221
Petrus de Grumenil; Albertus de Grumenil	2				2					*PT*, vol. 2, pp. 23–4
Bartholo de Florentina; Johannes	2	2							2	Loiseleur, *La doctrine*, p. 184
TOTAL	**137**	**25**	**41**	**6**	**77**	**14**	**4**	**14**	**25**	
TOTAL (incl. possible members)	**162**									

Chapter 13

The Social Reception of the Templar Trial in Early Fourteenth-Century France: The Transmission of Information

Magdalena Satora

For some decades, the Templar affair has caused discussion of the propaganda of Philip the Fair's court and its influence on French society. Studies already exist concerning the techniques used and the efficiency of the actions pursued by Philip the Fair's advisors.[1] From texts written during and after the fall of the Templar order, the attitudes of French commentators has also been studied.[2] In this article, I would like to focus on a few elements concerning this question and analyse them from a specific point of view. I have decided to study some of the means used to spread information concerning the Templars' trial (not only those used by the king but also those used by the pope and his representatives) and their effectiveness, through comparison with reactions and written commentaries from the different levels of French society.

Both the unexpected arrest of the French Templars in October 1307 and the trial of the order that ended with its dissolution five years later were commented on by numerous observers in France and in many other countries of western Europe. For the first time, a powerful institution dependant only on the pope was the target of an attack by a lay authority. This attack led the 200-year-old Templar order to its downfall. One of the most important elements of this political action against the order was the propaganda that was spread throughout French society. The political aim of the propaganda was to create a picture of general support for the royal actions against the Templars and therefore to incite Pope Clement V to re-open

---

1 Malcolm Barber, 'Propaganda in the Middle Ages: The Charges Against the Templars', *Nottingham Medieval Studies*, 17 (1973), 42–57; Sophia Menache, 'Contemporary Attitudes Concerning the Templars' Affair: Propaganda's Fiasco?', *Journal of Medieval History*, 8 (1982), 135–47; Barbara Frale, *L'ultima battaglia dei Templari: Dal codice ombra d'obbedienza militare alla construzione del processo per eresia* (Rome, 2001), pp. 298–9.

2 Ansgar Konrad Wildermann, *Die Beurteilung des Templerprozesses bis zum 17. Jahrhundert* (Freiburg, 1971), pp. 26–70; Helen Nicholson, *Love, War and the Grail: Templars, Hospitallers and Teutonic Knights in Medieval Epic and Romance 1150–1500* (Leiden, 2000), passim.

a papal inquiry against the order, which he had suspended at the beginning of 1308. This particular method, already used by the French court during the conflict between Philip the Fair and Pope Boniface VIII in the years 1302–03, was based on differences in the roles of different social groups of the French population.[3] For this specific reason, the content and the means of propaganda used and transmitted to the French population were themselves very diverse. I will focus here more precisely on the information intended to influence the maximum number of people possible from different social strata of French society.

The first official announcement concerning the royal actions towards the French Templars was proclaimed two days after the members of the order had been arrested, on 15 October 1307. On that day, a public meeting was organized in the royal gardens in Paris. According to a chronicle, the clerics were first to speak (apparently, members of the Franciscan order). After that, court officials gave their reasons for their actions against the members of the Templar order, including the list of accusations of heresy directed against the Templars.[4]

According to a letter from the French grand inquisitor and the king's confessor, Guillaume de Paris, to the other French inquisitors, the official version of the reasons for the Templars' arrest (which was detailed with great precision) should have been disseminated by the members of the mendicant orders.[5] The only details concerning the Paris gathering mentioned in the chronicles are the speeches of Philip the Fair's advisors. The fact that members of the mendicant orders publicly presented the reasons for the royal actions was never mentioned.

At the beginning of 1308, Clement V suspended the proceedings against the Templars just two months after they had begun. In response, Philip the Fair started a propaganda campaign asserting the correctness of the royal actions against the order and attacking the pope for restraining them. One of the campaign's main elements was to summon an assembly at Tours. The convocation letters were sent all over the kingdom between 22 and 29 March. The gathering was set to begin three weeks after Easter, on 5 May 1308. The letters had to be transmitted by the members of the territorial administration: *baillis* and seneschals.[6] Prelates and nobles were personally summoned.[7] The letters sent to townsmen had to reach every single village that had a marketplace.[8] Analysis of the documents

---

3 For the propaganda methods used in that campaign, see Sophia Menache, 'A Propaganda Campaign in the Reign of Philip the Fair: 1302–1303', *French History*, 4 (1990), 450–2.

4 *Continuatio chronici Guillelmi de Nangiaco*, in *Recueil des historiens des Gaules et de la France* (hereafter cited as *RHGF*), vol. 20, p. 596; *Excerpta e memoriali historiarum Johannis a Sancto Victore*, in *RHGF*, vol. 21, p. 649.

5 *PUT*, vol. 2, no. 29, pp. 44–6.

6 *Documents relatifs aux états généraux et assemblés réunis sous Philippe le Bel*, ed. Georges Picot (Paris, 1901) (hereafter cited as Picot), no. 661, pp. 491–2.

7 Ibid., nos 658–9, pp. 488–90.

8 Ibid., no. 862, p. 606.

concerning the meeting in Tours led to the conclusion that the means used to forward information in the French kingdom was very efficient. If one compares the dates that the summons was sent by the Paris royal chancery and by the *baillis* and seneschals with the dates that the responses were written, a certain regularity can be noticed. For instance, using the dates on the town and village procurations, we can conclude that there was a maximum ten-day period in which all letters were written.[9] This means that the royal letters generally arrived everywhere with no significant delays.

On a side note, the royal territorial administration had already proven its efficiency at the beginning of the Templar case. The arrest order was sent by Philip the Fair's court through the *baillis* and the seneschals in the middle of September 1307, one month before the intended date of arrest. The information concerning the effective arrest date was most likely not transmitted in written form, but orally. According to the current sources, the arrest was a surprise to the members of the order. The proof of this is that very few members of the order actually managed to escape arrest,[10] indicating that the royal arrest order was kept secret. This shows the efficiency of the royal administration, as well as the members of the administration's attitude towards the Templars' case, which was not favourable enough to warn the Templars of impending danger.

The summons to the assembly at Tours in 1308 sent to the lower clergy by the *baillis* and the seneschals was then transmitted to the bishops, who in turn forwarded the summons to their dioceses. The dates of the clergy's letters and procurations differ significantly from each other. There is not the same regularity as was observed earlier in the activities of the royal territorial administration. This may have been caused by the imperfection of the information-spreading system among the clergy, or a negative attitude towards participation in the assembly among at least part of the group.[11] The content of some of the clerics' letters also reveals certain mistakes in the transmission of information. For instance, some of the clerics (mainly from the diocese of Narbonne) thought that the gathering was to take place in Poitiers.[12]

Strong support for the royal action was only explicitly detailed in the letters of the prelates who were close collaborators of Philip the Fair. An example of this is the letters written by the archbishop of Rouen, in which he expressed the disgust that both he and the bishops of his diocese felt after receiving information on the horrible crimes that the Templars had committed.[13] Another example is the bishop of Bourges, Gilles de Rome (a doctor of theology of the university of Paris), whose letter very clearly showed his support for the royal action by writing on the

9 Ibid., nos 818–1075, pp. 588–719.

10 *PUT*, vol. 2, no. 50, pp. 74–5; Malcolm Barber, *The Trial of the Templars* (Cambridge, 1978), p. 46; 2nd edn (Cambridge, 2006), pp. 60–1.

11 Picot, nos 666–780, pp. 497–568.

12 For instance, ibid., no. 668, pp. 498–9; no. 729, p. 537; no. 731, pp. 538–9.

13 Ibid., no. 749, pp. 548–9.

obligation to defend the Church's honour, as well as the obligation of spreading the faith.[14] The Templars' crimes were described only very slightly in the other letters. In most of the letters, the 'Templars' affair' was only briefly mentioned, without presenting any opinion on the subject.[15] The clerics would mention the importance of following royal and sometimes papal duties as the reason for their participation in the assembly of Tours.[16]

Some of the clerics (mainly abbots and some bishops) decided not to personally attend the gathering in Tours. The main excuses were health reasons and 'important affairs' needing to be attended to.[17] The case of Bertrand de Languissel, the bishop of Nîmes, in the archdiocese of Narbonne, is well known. Before making any decision about sending a representative to the Tours gathering, he personally interrogated Templars who were imprisoned in his town. There is a high probability that he carried out these interrogations because of his lack of confidence in the information coming from the royal court.[18]

The difference in the attitude of some prelates close to the court and the other clerics can also be proven by the information about the proceedings of the council of Vienne in 1311–1312, during which Clement V decided to dissolve the Templar order. According to the information related by ambassadors of the king of Aragon, James II, and by a few chronicles, only a few French archbishops and bishops who were the closest collaborators of Philip the Fair wanted to condemn the members of the order directly without giving them a chance to defend themselves. Their attitude was the same as that of the French king. Most of the participants of the council, including the French, had contrasting opinions on this matter.[19]

Most of the nobles decided not to personally attend the gathering in Tours.[20] Their particular attitude could either be interpreted as a rejection of the king's position on the Templars' case or as their reluctance towards the general assembly. The letters addressed to that particular group of French society, as opposed to the ones addressed to the other groups, did not have any description of the Templars'

---

14 Ibid, no. 690, pp. 511–12.

15 For instance, ibid., no. 669, pp. 499–500; no. 672, p. 501; no. 673, pp. 501–2; no. 681, pp. 505–6.

16 For instance, ibid., no. 667, p. 498; no. 687, pp. 509–10; no. 691, pp. 513–14; no. 693, pp. 515–16.

17 For instance, ibid., nos. 700–701, pp. 521–2; no. 703, pp. 522–3; no. 707, pp. 524–5; no. 709, pp. 525–6.

18 Ibid., no. 734, p. 540; Vincent Challet, 'Entre expansionnisme capétien et relents d'hérésie: Le procès des Templiers du Midi', *Cahiers de Fanjeaux*, 41 (2006), 144–5.

19 *Secunda vita Clementis V auctore Ptoleameo Lucensi ordinis Praedicatorum*, in *Vitae Paparum Avenionensum*, ed. Etienne Baluze, new edn by Guillaume Mollat (Paris, 1914–27) (hereafter cited as *Vitae*), vol. 1, p. 42; *PUT*, vol. 2, no. 128, p. 251; *Dokumenty soborów powszechnych: Tekst grecki, łaciński, polski,* vol. 2, ed. and trans. Arkadiusz Baron and Henryk Pietras (Kraków, 2003) (hereafter cited as *Dokumenty*), p. 478.

20 Picot, nos 781–817, pp. 569–88.

crimes. They merely vaguely mentioned the Templars' 'disgusting errors'. The king only insisted on the fact that the nobles had obligations of allegiance.[21] This leads us to suspect that the royal court did not seem to expect such an ideological commitment from the nobles.

We know too that the Templars' wealth was seized by the king after their arrest and in turn administered by the royal administration and some nobles. In August 1308, Clement V ordered that the administration of the order's wealth was to be taken over by his representatives. According to bulls written during the period from 1308 to 1310, that specific order was not followed.[22] This leads us to suspect that in this case the nobles followed the same policy as the king.

The social group most anxious to take part in the assembly of Tours were the townsmen. According to some procurations, the people of the towns and villages where the representatives were elected by their communities were very interested in this case. This is revealed in the descriptions of public meetings and the lists of their participants.[23] From nearly all the texts available, we know that these representatives went to Tours 'to listen and to transmit royal decisions and orders'.[24] The authors very rarely mention the reason why the meeting was called. Also, in some procurations, requests from communities addressed to the king concerning, for instance, hospital requests, can be found.[25] We can be led to believe that, for that social group, the assembly of Tours was only an element of their political collaboration with the king, which was developing rapidly at the beginning of the fourteenth century.[26]

In 1311, at the same time as the beginning of the council of Vienne, Philip the Fair summoned the representatives of every level of French society to assemble for the second time. This assembly took place in Lyons. Unfortunately, as there are at present no documents available about this meeting, one cannot analyse social attitudes towards it.

Information and opinions concerning the Templars' case were disseminated not only by the royal court but also by the ecclesiastical hierarchy. The most important pieces of information addressed to the largest part of the population were the papal bulls. Each event of the trial was described, along with the pope's attitude towards it. The pope ordered the bulls to be translated into French and recited at every solemn mass, along with written copies to be attached to church doors and displayed in public squares.[27] As no comments survive on these actions

---

21 Ibid., no. 659, pp. 489–90.

22 *Reg. Clem. V*, vol. 4, no. 5011, pp. 433–5.

23 For instance, Picot, no. 817, p. 588; no. 820, pp. 589–90.

24 For instance, ibid., no. 821, p. 590; nos. 875–6, pp. 612–13.

25 Ibid., no. 949, p. 647.

26 Sophia Menache, 'The Templar Order: A Failed Ideal?', *The Catholic Historical Review*, 79 (1993), 16.

27 *Livre de Guillaume le Maire*, ed. Célestine Port, in *Mélanges historiques: Choix de documents*, vol. 2 (Paris, 1874), pp. 240–1; *Dokumenty*, p. 500.

or the contents of these bulls, one can suspect that they were not very important to French observers.

Another example of the transmission of information by the ecclesiastical hierarchy was the fact that the papal commission, which started its investigations on 8 August 1309, summoned everybody who wanted to defend the Templars' cause to Paris. A letter was sent to the arrested Templars and the whole of French society by the intermediary of the ecclesiastical hierarchy.[28] During the next three months, nobody came to Paris. On November 26, Philip the Fair ordered the *baillis* and the seneschals to help members of the order to come to Paris.[29] Only after that was the summons respected, and a few hundred Templars came to Paris. It is possible that either the first summons never reached the arrested Templars or that royal officers prevented the arrested Templars from going to Paris. The fact that nobody outside the order responded to the commission's call must be underlined. This could be an indication of the attitude of French society towards the Templars.

Next to the oral and written information transmitted by royal representatives and members of the ecclesiastical hierarchy, members of every group of French society had the opportunity to view the arrest of the Templars and the executions of some members of the order. In 1310, a few dozen Templars were burnt because they had changed their earlier testimony. Fifty-four members of the order were executed in the suburbs of Paris. According to chronicles, crowds of people witnessed this. [30] Similarly, there was the event in March 1314 when the grand master, Jacques de Molay, was burnt in Paris.[31] It seems that these events had the most influence on observers. In almost all the French chronicles written in the first decades of the fourteenth century describing the Templars' case, these specific events are mentioned.[32] However, this was quite different with regard to

[28] *PT*, vol. 1, pp. 47–50.

[29] Ibid., pp. 50–52.

[30] *Continuatio chronici Guillelmi de Nangiaco*, pp. 600–1; *Excerpta e memoriali historiarum Johannis a Sancto Victore*, p. 655.

[31] *Continuatio chronici Guillelmi de Nangiaco*, p. 609; *Chronique rimée attribuée à Geffroi de Paris*, in *RHGF*, vol. 22, p. 145.

[32] *Continuatio chronici Guillelmi de Nangiaco*, pp. 595–609; *Excerpta e memoriali historiarum Johannis a Sancto Victore*, pp. 649–58; *Anonymum S. Martialis chronicon ad annum MCCCXX continuatum*, in *RHGF*, vol. 21, pp. 812–13; Bernard Gui, *E floribus chronicorum, seu catalogo Romanorum pontificum, necnon e chronico regum Francorum*, in *RHGF*, vol. 21 pp. 717–23; *Chronicon Girardi de Fracheto et anonyma ejusdem operis continuatio*, in *RHGF*, vol. 21, pp. 29–40; *Extraits d'une chronique anonyme française, finissant en 1308*, in *RHGF*, vol. 21, p. 137; *Chronicon Guilleumi Scoti,* in *RHGF*, vol. 21, pp. 205; *Extraits d'une chronique anonyme intitulée 'Anciennes chroniques de Flandre'*, in *RHGF*, vol. 22, pp. 398–9; *Chronique rimée attribuée à Geffroi de Paris*, pp.122–45; *E chronici Rotomagensis continuatione*, in *RHGF*, vol. 23, pp. 347–8; Gilles le Muisit, *Chronique et annales*, ed. Henri Lemaître (Paris, 1906), pp. 78–82; *Sexta vita Clementis V auctore Amalrico Augerii de Biterris priore Sanctae Mariae de Aspirano in dioecesi Elnensi*, in *Vitae*, vol. 1, pp. 93–104; *Les grandes chroniques de France*, ed. Jules Viard,

the activities of the apostolic see, especially at the council in Vienne. Although information about them was given to French society many times in the papal bulls, only very few comments on the council exist, which most likely originated from people around the papacy.[33]

The authors of chronicles and literary works disagreed on the role of Philip the Fair and Clement V in the Templars' case.[34] It seems that they rarely discussed the truth of the accusations. Most of the chroniclers simply repeated the most important accusations. Some of the commentators mentioned nothing about the accusations, but their writing on the fall of the order focused on the main elements of the popular image of the Templars that existed at the end of the thirteenth and beginning of the fourteenth century. For instance, the anonymous author of a satirical poem, *Le Roman de Renart le Contrefait*, wrote on the tremendous wealth of the Templars and on the pride of their brothers.[35] These accusations were often associated with the Templar order at the end of the thirteenth and the beginning of the fourteenth century, but never used by the French court against the Templars.[36] Numerous authors who wrote during the trial and the few decades after it used the Templars' case and the negative image of the order to show subjects often different from the official version of the case. Guillaume de Monlauzun, the French canonist, thought that secret meetings were the main reason for the order's collapse.[37] Gilles de Rome used the Templars as an example during the discussion on the evils of privileges of exemption, which took place during the council of Vienne.[38] This means that the majority of the authors attached importance only

---

vol. 8 (Paris, 1934), pp. 272–95. For a more detailed analysis of French chronicles and other texts written during the trial and in the years that followed, see Wildermann, *Die Beurteilung*, pp. 26–70.

33 *Continuatio chronici Guillelmi de Nangiaco*, pp. 595–609; *Excerpta e memoriali historiarum Johannis a Sancto Victore*, pp. 649–58; *E floribus chronicorum*, pp. 717–23.

34 For the opinions about the role of Philip the Fair and Clement V in the Templars' case in western European chronicles, see Menache, 'Contemporary Attitudes', 137–8.

35 *Le Roman de Renart le Contrefait*, ed. Gaston Raynaud and Henri Lemaître (Paris 1914), p. 53.

36 See Joshua Prawer, 'Military Orders and Crusader Politics in the Second Half of the XIIIth Century', in *Die Geistlichen Ritterorden Europas*, ed. Josef Fleckenstein and Manfred Hellmann (Sigmaringen, 1980), pp. 217–29; Alan Forey, *The Military Orders: From the Twelfth to the Early Fourteenth Centuries* (Basingstoke and London, 1992), pp. 205–13; Helen Nicholson, 'Jacquemart Gièlèe's Renart le Nouvel: The Image of the Military Orders on the Eve of the Loss of Acre', in *Monastic Studies I: The Continuity of Tradition*, ed. Judith Loades (Bangor, 1990), pp. 182–9; eadem, *Templars, Hospitallers and Teutonic Knights: Images of the Military Orders, 1128–1291* (Leicester, 1993); Menache, 'The Templar Order', 9–10.

37 Louis Viollet, *Guillaume de Monlauzun*, in *Histoire littéraire de la France*, 35 (1921), pp. 469–70.

38 Félix Lajard, *Gilles de Rome,* in *Histoire littéraire de la France*, 30 (1888), pp. 545–6.

to the facts concerning the dissolution of the order and not to the essence of the accusations against them.

According to Helen Nicholson, who has studied the image of the military orders in medieval romance and epic, the writers' interest in the Templars as a military order did not decrease even though less important roles were attributed to the Templars following the dissolution of the order.[39] This indicates that the negative image of the Templars put forth in the propaganda of the French court did not persist in the authors' minds.

These short reflections on a few elements of the Templars' trial and the information disseminated during the case shows us some typical aspects of the methods used to transmit information through French society. One can state that the means of transmitting information throughout the French kingdom used by Philip the Fair and his advisors was very efficient. In most of the available sources analysed above concerning the reactions of members of different social levels to events linked to the proceedings against the Templars, we find the reflections of decisions and royal orders present in documents and official discourse. We see the efficacy of methods utilized by the royal court even better when we compare them with the transmission of information by the ecclesiastical hierarchy (for example, the convocation letters of the Assembly of Tours).

By studying the extant commentaries written during and after the end of the trial, we can also see that for members of the different groups of French society, information concerning the king and his decisions were much more important than information concerning the pope and the clergy. This could be an indication of the strong position of Philip the Fair in his kingdom as opposed to the Church's weak one. On the other hand, we can note that the information disseminated by the royal officers was not as frequent as information concerning the events that the observers could attend (for example, executions). The latter influenced the commentators much more than information transmitted in other ways.

Taking into consideration all that we have said until now, we can finally note that the efficacy of methods of transmitting information utilized by Philip the Fair and his advisors during the trial of the Templars did not affect all elements of official messages. In most of the commentaries, we do not find references to information concerning the crimes of the Templars or the reasons for royal actions, although these were the principal elements of royal propaganda. We may suspect that this information influenced the authors of commentaries far less than information concerning royal orders and decisions. This can be considered as a failure of propaganda.

39 Nicholson, *Love, War and the Grail*, pp. 189–90.

PART III
The Trial in the Iberian Peninsula

Chapter 14
Reassessing the Dissolution of the Templars: King Dinis and Their Suppression in Portugal

Clive Porro

It has been generally assumed that the suppression of the Templars in Portugal rode on the coat-tails of the dissolution process in Castile and León and the Aragonese diplomatic initiative at Avignon as King Dinis sought, vainly, to retain the order of the Temple. The scarcity of records concerning the activities of Dinis' envoys at the papal court and the absence of any trace of a papal commission in Portugal has left our understanding of the suppression of the Templars in Portugal, almost literally, as a footnote in history, and led to the rather simplistic notion of Dinis as an obdurate defender of the Temple, whose acquiescence in a new military order was only as the better alternative to unification with the Hospitallers.[1] This paper offers a somewhat different perspective and suggests that the Portuguese crown had a very clear view about its relationship with the Templars, that it had the legal means to impose that view at home and that, through its diplomatic efforts, it was active in asserting it at the papal curia.

The trial of the Templars in Portugal was meant to conform to the arrangements ordered by Clement V in the summer of 1308. The pope's various decrees of August 1308, which gave form to the process to be adopted in each metropolitan province, were addressed, among others, to the Portuguese primate, the archbishop of Braga. As elsewhere, a commission designated by the pope and led by the archbishop was to examine the order on the basis of the articles of accusation accompanying the bull *Faciens misericordiam*.[2] The archbishop of Braga and the bishop of Porto were named as the administrators of Templar property in Portugal.[3] Finally the

---

[1] This view is summarised in José Valente, 'The New Frontier: The Role of the Knights Templar in the Establishment of Portugal as an Independent Kingdom', *Mediterranean Studies*, 7 (1998), 49–50.

[2] *Reg. Clem. V*, Year 3, docs 3400 and 3401, pp. 281–4.

[3] Ibid., Year 3, doc. 3515 at p. 315; also printed in *Monumenta Portugaliae Vaticana*: *Súplicas dos pontificados dos Papas de Avinhão Clemente VII e Bento XIII e do Papa de Roma Bonifácio IX,* ed. António Domingues de Sousa Costa, vol. 2 (Braga, 1970), p. XXI (hereafter cited as *MPV*).

bull *Regnans in coelis* summoned both King Dinis and several of his prelates to the council to be held at Vienne to pronounce on the fate of the order.[4]

Nor did matters rest there. Like certain other rulers, Dinis was pressed by the pope in December 1308 to ensure that the results of the torture and confession of the brothers were remitted to the holy see.[5] Similar exhortations were issued on 27 June 1311.[6] There is no doubt, therefore, that the process which the papacy had established to determine the fate of the Templars was intended to apply equally to Portugal.

Arrests and confiscations

There is only circumstantial evidence to suggest that arrests were carried out in accordance with papal strictures. Several of the witnesses questioned as part of a royal inquiry in 1314 alleged that Dinis placed his own castellan in charge of Templar fortresses to provide the brothers with rations and lock them in at night. It seems likely that the events described related to the period between 1307 and 1312.[7]

There is also a curious letter from Fernando IV of Castile addressed to Gonzalo Perez, master of the order of Alcántara, dated 13 February 1312. It describes how he had Fr Vasco Fernandes, the Portuguese provincial Templar master, arrested and his possessions seized, including 50,000 *livres tournois* which had been lent to

---

4 Arquivo Nacional da Torre do Tombo (hereafter cited as ANTT), Gaveta VII, maço 5, doc. 5; published in a slightly deficient form in *As Gavetas da Torre do Tombo*, vol. 2 (Lisbon, 1962), pp. 439–45. A sixteenth-century copy was included in Biblioteca Nacional de Lisboa, Fundo Geral, Dr Pedro Alvares Seco, *Livro das Escrituras da Ordem de Cristo* (hereafter cited as *Escrituras*), cod. 735, fols xi–xvi.

5 *Callidi serpentis* dated 30 December 1308, ANTT, Bulas, Maço 2, doc. 12, summarised in *Quadro Elementar das Relações Políticas e diplomáticas de Portugal com as diversas potências do mundo*, ed. Visconde de Santarém (Manuel Francisco de Barros e Sousa de Mesquita de Macedo Leitão e Carvalhosa), vol. 9 (Paris and Lisbon, 1864), p. 298. A sixteenth-century copy was included in *Escrituras*, cod. 735, fols xvi–xviii. The bulls were also addressed to Fernando IV and Jaume II, among others. See Aurora Javierre Mur, 'Aportación al estudio del proceso contra el Temple en Castilla', *Revista de Archivos, Bibliotecas y Museos*, 69 (1961), doc. X, 64, and Antonio Benavides, *Memorias de Fernando IV de Castilla*, vol. 2 (Madrid, 1860), doc. 420, pp. 626–8.

6 *Reg. Clem. V*, Year 6, doc. 7525, at pp. 438–9.

7 The original rolls of evidence survive in two separate fragments as ANTT, Gaveta VII, maço 2, doc. 4, and ANTT, Gaveta VII, maço 18, doc. 2. Sixteenth-century copies are transcribed in ANTT, Leitura Nova, Livro de Reis ii, fols lvii^{v}–lxv (hereafter cited as Reis) and ANTT, Leitura Nova, Livro dos Mestrados, fols cviii–cl (hereafter cited as Mestrados).

Gonzalo Perez by the Templar and was now forfeited.[8] Fr Vasco's arrest in Castile may have followed an attempt to flee Portugal along with some of his men. Royal documents dating from 1317 and 1319 imply that at least some brothers had been displaced from Portugal and imprisoned in Castile.[9]

It also seems that most of the Templar possessions in Portugal came into the crown's hands. On 30 September 1318, the master, Fr Vasco, and two other former Templars publicly averred that the title to most of their estates had been given into the custody of either Dinis or his wife, Queen Isabel.[10]

As elsewhere, it was the crown which arranged for the cost of keeping the Templars to be met from the confiscated estates. When, on 20 November 1319, the newly installed master of the order of Christ, Fr Gil Martins, gave Dinis quittance of the revenues covering the period prior to the creation of the new order, it was in recognition of, among other things, the cost he incurred in providing for the former Templars.[11] The obligation to pay the remaining pensions however did not transfer to the order of Christ. Instead, it seems it was the Hospitallers in Aragon and Catalonia who were required to bear the cost of these pensions, worth two *tournois* a day, to former Portuguese Templars.[12] Exchanges between Jaume II and the archbishop of Tarragona and other clerics reveal how, in spite of a reluctant and obstructive prior of the Hospitallers, the pope enforced the payment of these pensions to five Portuguese former Templars, the cost of which was eventually assigned to the revenues of the convent of Gardeny.[13]

---

8 Benavides, *Memorias*, vol. 2, doc. DLXVII, pp. 828–9. Henrique de Gama Barros, *História da Administração Pública em Portugal no séculos XII a XV*, vol. 2 (Lisbon, 1945), p. 235, n. 1.

9 The first reference is found in the appeal by the Ifante Afonso against the papal grant of Tomar to Cardinal Bertrand of Monte Favecio, ANTT, Gaveta VII, maço 11, doc. 1, transcribed in Mestrados, fols cxxxviii– cxliii,. and printed in *MPV*, pp. viii–xviii. The second is in the document restoring the estates expropriated from the Templars in 1309–10 to the order of Christ, *Escrituras*, cod. 736, fols cclx–cclxi[v], and printed in Fr Francisco Brandão, *Monarquia Lusitana*, 3rd edn, vol. 6 (Lisbon, 1980), pp. 291–2.

10 ANTT, Gaveta VII, maço 16, doc. 2 and Mestrados, fols. xxii[v]–xxviii and li[v]–lxxvi, printed in part in *MPV*, pp. li–lii.

11 ANTT, Gaveta VII, maço 2, doc. 6, printed in *Monumenta Henricina*, ed. António Dias Dinis, vol. 1 (Coimbra, 1960), doc. 68, p. 129 and in part in *MPV*, p. xlvi.

12 Alan Forey, *The Fall of the Templars in the Crown of Aragon* (Aldershot, 2001), p. 227.

13 I am very grateful to Dr Alan Forey for supplying me with his research notes and commentary on this.

Episcopal inquiries

The most striking feature of the dissolution process in Portugal, however, is the absence of any trial. It has been assumed that the part played by João de Solhães, the bishop of Lisbon, particularly in presiding over a hearing at Orense in Galicia (probably in 1310), before which 28 Templars and six other witnesses appeared, was the Portuguese element of a wider inquiry in Spain.[14] In fact, the bishop's role simply reflected the diocesan arrangements in place in western Iberia since 1199 when Innocent III had settled the dispute over the ecclesiastical jurisdictions of the restored metropolitan archbishoprics of Braga and Compostela. Braga retained authority over its Galician suffragans, including Orense. Compostela received authority over most of the ancient Lusitanian province including Lisbon.[15] This arrangement was a Visigothic relic, and Clement V quickly recognised the difficulties overlapping ecclesiastical and political jurisdictions posed in giving effect to his instructions concerning these two Templar provinces.

Therefore, as part of the series of bulls issued on 12 August 1308, he made exceptional provision for the commissioners appointed to the province of Braga to inquire into the conduct of the Templars and administer their properties within the whole of Portugal, including those dioceses which were suffragans of Compostela.[16] A similar arrangement applied in Castile and León. Consequently among the commissioners appointed in the Compostela province was one of its suffragans, the bishop of Lisbon, whose activities in Castile and León were therefore limited only to the trial of the Templars in those kingdoms.[17]

However it would be equally wrong to assume that the Templars were left unmolested in Portugal, protected by a staunchly supportive crown. In the summer of 1307 Dinis had set in train legal proceedings against the Templars with the aim of removing two major portions of territory from their control. On 18 August, a royal court composed of leading clerics heard a dispute between the crown and the

---

14 A misconception propounded by Pedro Rodríguez de Campomanes, *Dissertaciones historicas del orden y cavalleria de los Templarios* (Madrid, 1747), p. 105; perpetuated by François Raynouard, *Monumens historiques relatifs à la condemnation des chevaliers du Temple et à l'abolition de leur ordre* (Paris, 1813), pp. 314–15 and 264–7, and accepted by later historians including Malcolm Barber, *The Trial of the Templars*, 2nd edn (Cambridge, 2006), p. 240 and n. 98.

15 José Mattoso, *Identificação de um País: Ensaios sobre as origens de Portugal 1096–1325*, vol. 2 (Lisbon, 1985), pp. 184–6; *Bulário Português Inocêncio III (1198–1216)*, ed. Avelino de Jesus da Costa and Maria Alegria F. Marques (Coimbra, 1989), pp. 64–74, 82–95, 103–5 and nos 44–5, 49–52, 56 and 61; Armando Luís de Carvalho Homem and Maria Helena da Cruz Coelho, *Nova História de Portugal*, ed. Joel Serrão and António Henrique Rodrigo de Oliveira Marques, *Portugal em Definição de Fronteiras* (Lisbon, 1995), p. 227.

16 *Reg. Clem. V*, Year 3, docs 3532 and 3533 at pp. 319–20; also printed in *MPV*, pp. xxii–xxiii.

17 See note 2 above.

order of the Temple, concerning its possession of the towns of Soure and of Idanha a Velha and their districts. The royal procurator, Domingo Martins, claimed that Soure and its dependencies (Ega, Pombal and Redinha) were wrongly held by the Temple. He argued that these properties belonged to the crown by right and that the Templars had misappropriated them from the king. The order had possessed them for a time, but only by royal consent and because of the service they rendered the crown.[18]

The master, Fr Vasco Fernandes, challenged unsuccessfully the competence of the court to exercise any such jurisdiction over his order and then requested a nine-month period of grace in which to consult the grand master and obtain various documents to support his defence, prompted perhaps by Jacques de Molay's expected visit to Portugal.[19] In June 1308, when the order's representative failed to appear, the court awarded possession of these properties to the crown by default.[20]

In June 1309, Domingos Martins again appeared before the court and requested that the crown be judged in full possession of the properties, since a year and a day had elapsed from the time when the order was pronounced in default, and it had not yet appeared to defend itself. Ninety days later, in accordance with law and custom, he asked leave of the court to submit evidence of royal rights to these estates. This took the form of a dossier of oral evidence gathered from local witnesses during the preceding few months. The judges accepted this evidence and, on 27 November 1309, they ruled definitively in favour of the crown.[21] On 19 January 1310, Idanha a Velha, Segura, Rosmaninhal, Proença and Salvaterra were similarly declared royal property.[22]

Thus, relatively swiftly, almost painlessly, and with the minimum of resistance from the order itself, already overwhelmed by events elsewhere, King Dinis established his title to around 15 per cent of the value of the Templars' property in Portugal. But more than that, he had established the jurisdiction of his court to deal with such territorial claims, and he had laid down an extremely important precedent.

---

18 ANTT, Gaveta XII, maço 1, doc. 7 transcribed in Reis ii, fols. iii[v]–vi and ANTT, Gaveta XII, maço 7, doc. 19, transcribed in Reis, ii, fols xix[v]–xxi. Both have been printed in Fernando Félix Lopes, 'Das actividades políticas e religiosas de D. Fr. Estêvão, bispo que foi de Porto e de Lisboa', *Lusitana Sacra*, 6 (1962–3), docs 2 and 3, pp. 80–87.

19 *PUT*, vol. 2, doc. 24, p. 37.

20 ANTT, Gaveta XII, maço 7, doc. 19.

21 ANTT, Gaveta XII, maço 1, doc. 7.

22 ANTT, Gaveta XIII, maço 4, doc. 7 transcribed in Reis ii, fols vi–viii, and printed in Alfredo Pimenta, *Alguns documentos para a historia de Idanha a Velha* (Lisbon, 1940), doc. 9, pp. 63–7.

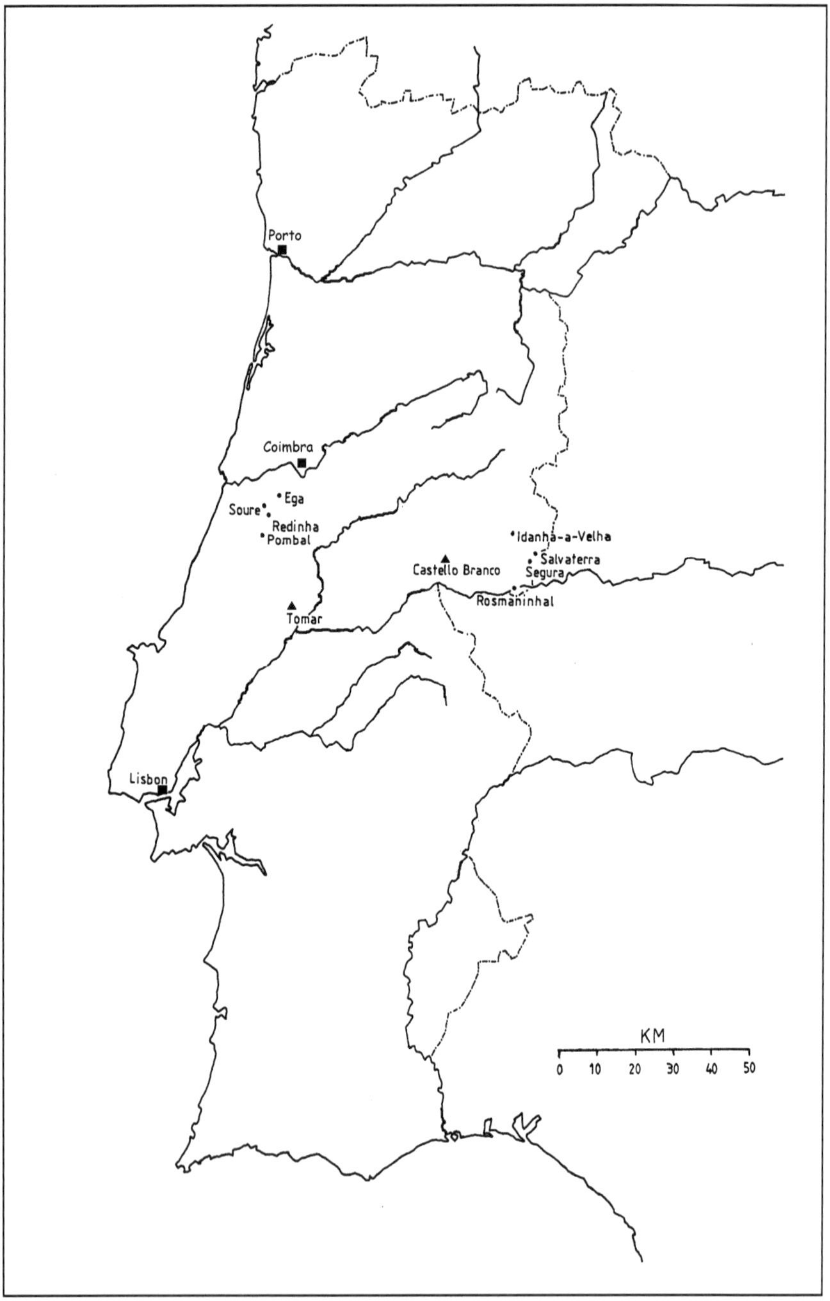

Fig. 14.1 The commendas of Soure and Idanha and their districts, 1307

If domestically Dinis pursued a distinct policy against the Templars, when dealing with the papacy he chose to make common cause with his fellow Iberian kings. Consequently, in the period between the summoning of the council of Vienne and its actual meeting, the Iberian rulers formed a united diplomatic front. On 21 January 1310, Fernando IV of Castile wrote to Dinis committing himself to act with the Portuguese king on matters concerning the lands of the Temple, should the order be dissolved.[23] The agreement was guaranteed by a fine of 30,000 silver marks to be paid in the event of non-compliance by either of the parties. On 14 April, Dinis duly replied in identical terms.[24]

Jaume II of Aragon was not initially a signatory to this 'pact', but a clause in the agreement allowed for his admission. He joined in 1311. In his letter of 17 August of that year, Jaume II assured Fernando IV that he had already despatched his ambassadors to the curia with instructions to act jointly with the Castilian and Portuguese envoys.[25] On 12 July 1312, in the immediate aftermath of the papal decisions concerning the Templars, Jaume II wrote to Dinis proposing that information obtained from the curia should be exchanged.[26]

Like Jaume II, Dinis was continuously and effectively represented at the papal curia in the period between the council of Vienne in 1311 and the eventual creation of the order of Christ in 1319. As early as April 1310, the Franciscan Fr Estêvão, one of the judges in the Soure and Idanha case and by now bishop of Porto, was already at Avignon, although the reason for his mission is not clear.[27] The Portuguese episcopal contingent to the council of Vienne was led by the archbishop of Braga.[28] Initially at least, Martinho de Oliveira acted in a dual capacity as the representative of both Dinis and Fernando IV to Vienne. Informed of this fact by the Castilian king, Jaume II replied on 17 August 1311 expressing the view that it was wiser to have lay men rather than clerics acting on the kings' behalf in this matter. He seems to have exerted some influence. Writing to him on 23 October 1311, just days after the start of the council, Jaume II's envoys reported the archbishop of Braga as saying that he was representing the crown pending the arrival of a royal knight.[29]

The Portuguese envoys went on to act effectively with their Aragonese counterparts in defending the rights of the Iberian monarchs over the Templars' possessions. Reporting to Jaume II on 17 March 1312, his ambassadors recalled

---

[23] ANTT, Gaveta VII, maço 4, doc. 9, printed in Brandão, *Monarquia Lusitana*, pp. 109–10.

[24] ANTT, Cabido da sé de Coimbra, 2a Incorporação, maço 43, doc. 1745, printed in *MPV*, p. xxxiii.

[25] Barros, *Administração Pública*, p. 328 and n. 2; Jaime Villanueva, *Viage literario a las iglesias de España*, vol. 5 (Madrid, 1806), doc. 5, pp. 206–7.

[26] Villanueva, *Viage*, doc. 8, pp. 225–6.

[27] *MPV*, pp. xxxi–xxxii.

[28] *Reg. Clem. V*, Year 3, doc. 3629, p. 394.

[29] Villanueva, *Viage*, doc. V, pp. 206–7. *PUT*, vol. 2, doc. 126, p. 239.

how, worried about the implications of the full-day meeting which the pope had had with Enguerrand de Marigny, Philip IV's chamberlain and principal actor in this affair, they and the Portuguese envoys actively sought to counter any potential problems. First they met with all the Iberian prelates to convey their concerns over the defence of royal rights. They then went on to speak with the cardinals, warning them that it would be difficult to apply any papal judgment which disregarded the well-known position of the Iberian kings. On 11 March they also attended a consistory where they made the case to the pope that any decisions about the fate of the Templar property should only be made with their respective kings' consent. This was followed by further meetings with the pope and the cardinals.[30]

In a further letter of 15 April 1312 the Aragonese envoys explained how, although the pope and Philip IV favoured the transfer of the Templars' property to the Hospitallers, they and their Portuguese colleagues remained firm in their opposition to the idea of a merger.[31] Certainly the terms of the bull *Ad providam* of May 1312 are a testament to the persuasive powers of the Portuguese and Aragonese envoys. They had achieved partial success and prevented the transfer of the Templar properties in Portugal, Castile, Aragon and Mallorca to the Hospitallers. Now they had to convince Clement V that this exemption should be made permanent in a way that would be acceptable to all concerned.

Figure 14.2: Portuguese diplomatic representation at the papal curia, 1310–19

year	**envoys**	**cause**
1310	Fr Estêvão, bishop of Porto	unknown
1311–12	archbishop of Braga, bishop of Porto, bishop of Coimbra, bishop of Tuy	council of Vienne
1313	Fr Estêvão, bishop of Lisbon	fate of Templars after suppression
1314–16	João Lourenço and Vicente Annes	fate of the Templars and other matters
1317–18	Manoel Pessanha and Vicente Annes	separation of the order of Santiago from León and Ifante Afonso's discord
1318–19	João Lourenço and Pero Pires	creation of new order endowed with Templar properties

The sustained Portuguese diplomatic initiative at the papal court in the years after 1312 was underpinned by the accumulation of evidence at home to support the crown's own interpretation of the limited and subordinate nature of Templar

30 *PUT*, vol. 2, doc. 139, pp. 280–285.

31 Ibid., doc. 145, pp. 295–6.

lordship. The most crucial piece was the outcome from a set of inquiries carried out in the Templar estates at Soure, Tomar, Castello Branco, Nisa and Montalvão in March and April 1314.[32] These investigations established five main findings: that the Templars asked the king for the material means to fight the Moors when they first came to Portugal; that these grants were conditional on the continuation of the war against Islam; that the crown retained jurisdiction over those lands; that the order and the master of the province were subject to royal supervision; and that the Templars owed and paid military service to the crown. Other evidence included the production, on 5 June 1313, of a notarised copy of the conditional grant made by King Afonso Henriques to the Templars in September 1169 of a third of all the territory which they conquered and populated beyond the Tagus for as long as he was at war with the Moors.[33] A further inquiry was undertaken on 15 November of 1314 at Tomar where witnesses were required to reply to 44 articles about the allegiance, homage and vassalage which the Templars owed to the kings of Portugal, from the time of Count Henry of Portugal until its suppression.[34]

However, at the curia, the Iberian 'pact' was beginning to unravel. On 6 April 1313, as negotiations with Clement V reached an impasse, Jaume II's ambassadors were advising him, among other things, to form a united front with the Portuguese and Castilian kings.[35] Clement V's death a year later brought negotiations to a standstill.[36] The return of Jaume II's envoys to Avignon following the election of John XXII led to a resumption of negotiations which were concluded successfully, on 10 June 1317, with the creation of the new order of Montesa.[37] Despite Dinis' hitherto equally effective diplomacy, he failed to settle in 1317. The reasons for this were largely domestic.

At home Dinis was facing increasing political distractions. His heir, the Ifante Afonso, was growing ever more restless, fearful that the king might name the royal bastard, Afonso Sanches, heir presumptive. The northern nobility was, in its turn, frustrated by increasing royal centralisation. This discontent erupted

---

32 See note 7 above.

33 ANTT, Gaveta VII, maço 13, doc. 6, printed in Abiah Elisabeth Reuter, *Chancelarias Medievais Portuguesas: Documentos da Chancelaria do Afonso Henriques*, vol. 1 (Coimbra, 1938), doc. 213, pp. 317–19; *Documentos Medievais Portugueses*, ed. Ruy Pinto de Azevedo, vol. 1, pt 1 (Lisbon, 1958), doc. 295, pp. 384–5.

34 The original document has not survived but its existence has been recorded: José Anastácio de Figueiredo, *Nova História da Militar Ordem de Malta e dos Senhores Grão-Priores della em Portugal*, vol. 1 (Lisbon, 1830), pp. 14–15; also mentioned in Rodrigo da Cunha, *Historia da Igreja de Lisboa*, vol. 1, pt. 2 (Lisbon, 1642), p. 234.

35 *PUT*, vol. 2, doc. 117, pp. 221–3; Forey, *The Fall of the Templars*, p. 168.

36 Forey, *The Fall of the Templars*, pp. 166–70.

37 However, the order was not properly established until 22 July 1319. See ibid., pp. 178–83.

into open rebellion in 1319 with the Ifante demanding that Dinis hand over the administration of justice to him.[38]

This deteriorating political situation also embroiled one of his chief agents in the Templar affair at the very point that negotiations over their estates were poised to resume with the new pope. The Franciscan Friar Fr Estêvão Migueis had risen through royal judicial service to high ecclesiastical office. Already the royal confessor, in February 1310 he was rewarded with the bishopric of Porto. In 1311, he was a member of the Portuguese delegation to the council of Vienne, and in 1313 he was again at Avignon defending the Portuguese position with regard to the fate of the Templar properties and where he was advanced to the diocese of Lisbon.[39] Sometime in 1316, Fr Estêvão fell out with the King. In a manifesto complaining about the actions of the Ifante Afonso, dated 1 July 1320, Dinis recalled how, ever since he had punished two of Fr Estêvão's nephews for the murder of a Lisbon citizen in the course of an argument, he became estranged from the king and sought to do his interests harm including at the papal court.[40] Dinis also alleged that, when the see of Braga fell vacant in 1313, he had asked the pope to give the archbishopric to Fr Estêvão. Instead Fr Estêvão used the 40,000 *libras*, which he had been given to negotiate the fate of the Templar estates with the papacy, to obtain the bishopric of Lisbon for himself and that of Porto for his nephew.[41] Dinis blamed his lack of success with Clement V, at least in retrospect, on Fr Estêvão's private ambitions.

The king sought the papacy's help in his attempts to bring his son into line. Early in 1317, armed with 4,000 florins, his envoys were instructed among other things to secure papal support against the queen, his heir, the Ifante Afonso and Fr Estêvão. On 10 June 1317, the very day he established the order of Montesa, John XXII also issued a set of bulls which admonished the troublemakers on pain of excommunication. These were of limited effect, and on 21 March 1318 John XXII wrote again advising the queen and the ifante to banish those sowing discord between them and the king, sign a peace accord and thus avoid the looming danger of war. The pope also threatened the bishop of Lisbon with severe penalties and assured Dinis that he was prepared to act against Fr Estêvão if he

[38] For an account of the rebellion see José Mattoso, 'A Guerra Civil de 1319–1324', in *Portugal Medieval: Novas Interpretações* (Lisbon, 1985), pp. 293–308; Fernando Félix Lopes, 'Santa Isabel de Portugal: A larga contenda entre el rei D Dinis e seu Filho D Afonso', *Colectânea de Estudos*, 4 (1953).

[39] Fr Estêvão was at the curia on 27 October that year where Clement V addressed a bull to him, as bishop of Lisbon, concerning a loan of 6,000 florins for his new bishopric: *MPV*, p. xxxvii.

[40] Lopes, 'Fr. Estêvão', 64–5.

[41] ANTT, Gaveta XIII, maço 11, doc. 12, published in Lopes, 'Fr. Estêvão', 88, printed in part in *MPV*, p. xxxvi.

received appropriately framed accusations.[42] Eventually forced to leave Portugal, Fr Estêvão was translated to the see of Cuenca in 1322.[43]

Yet if Dinis' difficulties at home distracted him, and John XXII, from decisions about the Templar properties in Portugal in the summer of 1317, it is also the case that neither the pope, nor the king, were yet close enough in their positions to secure a mutually acceptable settlement. As early as 1308, Jaume II was already willing to entertain the possibility that the Templar property in Aragon would not revert to the crown. By September 1311, he was instructing his envoys to the council of Vienne on proposals which were to form the basis of the eventual outcome decreed by John XXII in 1317.[44] Dinis however had shown no such capacity for compromise.

In December 1317, for example, the crown's position was reasserted in an appeal against the grant of the castle and town of Tomar to Cardinal Bertrand of Monte Favecio the previous July. It was argued that the papal grant was null and void mainly because Tomar was part of the Templar estates in Portugal and so could not be alienated to a person other than the king, because those lands had belonged originally to the crown and were held by the Templars on condition of service against the infidel.[45]

It was not until 14 August 1318 that Dinis finally provided instructions to his ambassadors to negotiate a final settlement over the fate of the Templar properties. Even so, on 30 September 1318 at an assembly presided over by the bishop of Lisbon, the royal procurator, Domingo Pais, claimed many of the royal property grants to the Templars were defective. The aim of such an act was clearly to bolster the continuing claim of reversionary right by casting doubt on documents which may have suggested the opposite.[46] Nonetheless, six months later, on 14 March 1319, John XXII's bull *Ad ea ex quibus* founded the new order of Christ endowed with all the property of the former order of the Temple as well as with the royal fortress of Castro Marim in the Algarve as its convent.[47]

So what conclusions can we draw from this Portuguese perspective on the suppression of the Templars? First, Dinis's legal challenge to important Templar lordships in August 1307, before any other authority had moved against the order, suggests that Philip IV's own actions later the same year were no accident. The Templars' vulnerability must have been more obvious than may previously have been thought the case.

---

42 See Lopes, 'Santa Isabel', 13–15 and 27–30.

43 Lopes, 'Fr. Estêvão', 70–1.

44 Forey, *The Fall of the Templars*, pp. 156–8.

45 See note 9 above.

46 See note 10 above.

47 ANTT, Gaveta VII, maço 5, doc. 2, printed in *Monumenta Henricina*, doc. 61, pp. 97–110; cf. a coeval Portuguese translation in ANTT, Gaveta VII, maço 8, doc. 5, and Mestrados, fol. cxx[v], published in ibid., doc. 62, pp. 110–19.

Second, the action taken by Dinis against the Templars at home was in marked contrast to the French approach. His chosen legal weapon was the tried and tested inquiry process which he had successfully employed against seigneurial interests. Dinis secured judgments in Portuguese law which justified his resumption of Soure and Idanha on the grounds that the Temple no longer performed its crusading functions. In this way, unlike Philip IV, he kept the matter in a strictly secular sphere.

Third, the assumption that the Iberian diplomatic initiatives with regard to the fate of the Templar properties were driven largely by the Aragonese needs some rebalancing. The evidence that exists illustrates how the Portuguese envoys played at least as important a role as their counterparts from Aragon.

Fourth, despite his alliances with the other Iberian rulers and their effective intervention with the papacy following the suppression of the Templars, Dinis' line remained more inflexible than that of the other Iberian kings. As a result and despite events which could easily have derailed his negotiations and undermined his resolve, his unique success in gaining a new order with its Templar inheritance intact, if short of the reversion he had sought, vindicated the tenacity with which he pursued his objective.

Fifth and finally, the action taken by the Portuguese crown against the Templars in the summer of 1307 has received virtually no attention from historians, although it was potentially a very grave attack on the status of the order. The legal basis on which Dinis challenged the order's continued enjoyment of estates which it had held since its arrival in Portugal in the twelfth century carried serious implications for the Templars. It is arguable that, if Philip IV had not precipitated the final crisis when he did, Dinis may well have extended his legal challenge to other Templar estates. On this interpretation of events, therefore, Dinis emerges not as the protector of the Templars but as one of their earliest and most dangerous adversaries.

Chapter 15

Icons, Crosses and the Liturgical Objects of Templar Chapels in the Crown of Aragon

Sebastián Salvadó

A 1304 inventory of the Templar chapel of Orrios describes its contents in the following manner: *primerament I vestiment dominical e otro ferial e II libros e I missal, el huno domincal e el otro santoral e I libro misto santoral e dominical e I caliz d'estano e II campanas e II cruces e una capa oficiadera, I acelde, II sobrepellices, I enssensero.*[1] If an art-historical inquiry were carried out on such a list of objects, scholars would be hard pressed to understand fully the nature and scope of items used in the Templars' daily liturgical celebrations. As this example illustrates, the inventories produced by Templars in the crown of Aragon in their chapels tended to be short, concise, and often verbatim repetitions of the previous year's list.[2] Surviving examples from the chapel of the commandery of Xivert between 1302 and 1305 further exemplify this point. From a total of 11 inventories, historian Maria Vilar Bonet transcribes only those of 3 March 1302 and 22 June 1304, noting that the rest are copies of these two.[3] To judge from this conciseness and lack of detailed descriptions, these lists served the primary function of keeping a tally on the items present in chapels and were not created to meet any strict financial inquiry on the value of the chapel goods.

As a consequence of the turmoil following the 1307 accusations, the inventories carried out on Templar chapels ordered by King Jaume II of Aragon (1291–1327) provide a striking point of comparison.[4] Suddenly, inventories and lists burst with details affording a more informed reassessment of not only what was owned by Templars, but of how these objects reflected Templar religious ideals and tastes. Books are now often described by their function, language, incipit and finit, colour and types of cloth and by their bindings.[5] Liturgical objects are likewise described

1 Maria Vilar Bonet, *Els béns del Temple a la Corona d'Aragó en suprimir-se l'orde (1300–1319)* (Barcelona, 2000), appendix 8, p. 119.

2 Ibid., appendices 2, 4, 6, 8, 10.

3 Ibid., appendices 4, 10.

4 J. Ernesto Martínez Ferrando, 'La Cámara Real en el reinado de Jaime II (1291–1327): Relaciones de entradas y salidas de objetos artísticos', *Anales y Boletín de los Museos de Arte de Barcelona,* 11 (1953–4), 1–230; cf. Alan Forey, *The Fall of the Templars in the Crown of Aragon* (Aldershot, 2001).

5 Martínez, 'La Cámara', doc. 32.

in minute detail: *unum calicem argenti deauratum intus et extra cum sua panna deaurata, et est in medio dicte panne una crux cum una manu que facit signum crucis, et dictus calix stat in uno stygo nigro, qui aderebatur fuisse forrat vel forrato livido.* [6] As enticing as this level of description is, unfortunately very few inventories of this vivid nature have survived. Twenty-one chapel inventories have been located dating to the period before King Philip IV of France's accusations, while those inventories and lists of chapel objects made for Jaume II number 23. (see appendix at the end of this paper). Of these latter, only eight identify which commandery the objects originate from, and the thoroughness of their contents is varied. The remaining lists merely ascribe their contents as having belonged to the Templars and give no mention of geographic origin. Notwithstanding the limited number of extant inventories created under Jaume II, these lists attest to well over 300 liturgical objects belonging to the Templars in the crown of Aragon.[7] This great number of objects provides an exceptional opportunity to recreate and investigate the devotional spaces of Templar commanderies.

These inventories have drawn the attention of a number of scholars in the past,[8] notably for the information they provide of vernacular language and for the literary culture and level of education they display.[9] Among the latest to transcribe these inventories, Maria Vilar Bonet is the only scholar to give an overview of the different chapel objects and their respective function within the liturgy.[10] Notwithstanding the valuable synopsis of items included, these lists have not been studied for what they can tell the historian about Templar religious devotion. Upon a first reading, what springs forth from these pages is the utter sumptuousness of Templar chapels. These spaces were not stoic embodiments of monastic restraint as their brothers, the Cistercians, extolled, rather Templar chapels were so full of colour, ornament and opulence that they rivalled the most extravagant of Benedictine monasteries.[11]

---

6 Ibid., doc. 90, p. 121.

7 This number only takes into account items present in inventories where the commandery is stated and does not include the many lists of objects subsequently created by Jaume II which would undoubtedly greatly increase this figure.

8 Jaime Villanueva, *Viage literario a las iglesias de España* (Madrid, 1803–52), vol. 5, pp. 200–202; Jordi Rubió, Ramon d'Alós and Francisco Martorell, 'Inventaris inèndits de l'Orde del Temple a Catalunya', *Anuari de l'Institut d'Estudis Catalans*, 1 (1907), 358–407; Antoni Rubió y Lluch, *Documents per l'historia de la cultura catalana mig-eval* (Barcelona, 1908–21), 2 vols; Joaquím Miret y Sans, 'Inventaris de les cases del Temple de la Corona d'Aragó en 1289', *Boletín de la Real Academia de Buenas Letras de Barcelona*, 42 (1911), 61–75; Francisco Martorell y Trabal, 'Inventari dels bens de la cambra reyal en temps de Jaume II (1323)', *Anuari de l'Institut d'Estudis Catalans*, 4 (1911–12), 553–67.

9 Cf. Alan Forey, 'Literacy and Learning in the Military Orders during the Twelfth and Thirteenth Centuries', *MO*, 2, pp. 185–206.

10 Vilar Bonet, *Els béns,* pp. 95–110. This book is a printing of her 1950 dissertation.

11 Conrad Rudolph provides a good overview of such discrepancies between religious orders; cf. Conrad Rudolph, *The 'Things of Greater Importance': Bernard of Clairvaux's*

Through a reading of the detailed descriptions and lengthy lists of objects one is privy to the mesmerizing effect of glittering crosses, intensely colourful vestments and opulent reliquaries that embellished the Templars' daily services of mass and the offices. In the following pages, I examine these inventories to foreground the often overlooked importance Templars ascribed to their liturgical celebrations. The analysis of these sources results in a portrait of the active and conscious agency Templars exercised in the manner and level of solemnity with which their divine liturgy was adorned and performed.

Fig. 15.1 Peñíscola, chapel

Through the comparison of the inventories produced before the 1307 accusations to those created in their aftermath, the chapel of Peñíscola immediately stands out (see Figure 15.1).[12] The inventories clearly record a rapid and large amalgamation of wealth there. In its 1302 inventory, the quantity of liturgical items present is comparable to those found in Corbins, which had a considerably longer period of occupation than Peñíscola.[13] At this time, Peñíscola held approximately 60 items. This is comparable to those items held at Xivert, but a rather large quantity when compared to inventories from nearby Ares, Camañas and Orrios.[14] However, two inventories from 1307, just five years later, witness a rapid growth of the number of liturgical objects amassed at Peñíscola.[15] One pronounced area of growth is the quantity of books held. Compared to 1302, which noted an already enviable number of ten books to officiate the liturgy, the 1307 inventory testifies to 30 books. Among those added are three extra missals, five responsories, two psalters and two customaries. Surprisingly, this very large quantity of liturgical books approaches the number a small monastery would need, especially in the number of missals and responsories owned. Notwithstanding this already rapid increase, by 1311 an inventory was created which attests to the truly opulent level of lavishness the chapel of Peñíscola had reached.[16]

The sheer abundance of liturgical objects in the chapel of Peñíscola outnumbers the extant sources we have from the chapels of Corbins, Miravet, Montsó, and

Apologia and the Medieval Attitude Toward Art (Philadelphia, 1990).

12 Vilar Bonet, *Els béns*, appendices 4, 16–17; Martínez, 'La Cámara', doc. 32.

13 Vilar Bonet, *Els béns*, appendices 2, 4.

14 Ibid., appendices 4, 6, 8.

15 Ibid., appendices 16–17.

16 Martínez, 'La Cámara', doc. 32.

Xivert.[17] This has very great implications for whoever was using these objects, as usually only one chaplain officiated over the liturgy at Templar houses, and as has been argued by Josep Sans i Travé, there were many times when Templars simply had to go on without one.[18] The liturgical vestments alone number well over 20 pieces, and this was not a disorderly amalgamation of goods that we would expect if the Templars were simply amassing vestments from various chapels. On the contrary, the collection exhibits a careful organization, geared towards the enrichment of the liturgical season. The seven chasubles at Peñíscola offer a wonderful glimpse into the colours Templars saw during the liturgical year. There were chasubles of purple for Advent and Lent, gold or white for Christmas, green used from the end of Epiphany to Septuagesima and from the end of Pentecost to Advent, and red for holy week and Pentecost. Of the four dalmatics present, two are in black, i.e., the last colour necessary for requiems and Good Friday. The most impressive dress was reserved for Advent and Lent, both penitential periods. For these periods the priest of Peñíscola officiated mass with a chasuble, maniple and stole of gold threads and purple silk with decorations in the form of pine cones and eagles. The dalmatic completed the set, made of gold cloth, with the pine cone and eagle decorations embroidered in purple silk.[19] In conjunction with the priest's colour-coding of liturgical seasons there were the varied frontals, or *antependia,* which adorned the priest's altar.[20] The altar, the most sacred liturgical implement responsible for supporting the Bible, bread and wine, was sumptuously adorned to reflect the liturgical tides of the year. When considering the variety of vestments and altar dressings together, the liturgical rites the Templars witnessed were impregnated with rich and vivid colours that worked to augment the experience of the passing liturgical seasons.

In addition to these items which allow a recreation of the lush visual image ever present before the Templars, the Peñíscola inventories describe two objects which connote very precise liturgical actions. One item is described as *un mig ciri*

---

17 There is no way to compare Peñíscola fully to Miravet and Montsó as no complete inventories survive from these latter commanderies. What survives is fragmentary or only mentions select objects, cf. Vilar, *Els bens,* appendices 50–53; Martínez, *Cámara Real*, doc. 48; Rubió y Lluch, *Documents*, 1, doc. XLVIII.

18 Robert Burns, *The Crusader Kingdom of Valencia: Reconstruction on a Thirteenth-Century Frontier* (Cambridge, 1967), vol. 1, pp. 57–8; Josep Sans i Travé, 'L'Orde del Temple als Països Catalans: La seva introducció i organització (segles XII–XIV)', in *Actes de les Primeres Jornades sobre els Ordes Religioso-Militars als Països Catalans (segles XII–XIX)* (Tarragona, 1994), p. 27. I am currently working on a study which focuses on these issues and specifically the liturgical rites of the Templars in the crown of Aragon: Sebastián Salvadó, 'Templar Liturgy and Devotion in the Crown of Aragon', forthcoming.

19 *Et aliam dalmaticam panni auri cum operibus similibus pinyes et aquilis, que est serici violati*, cf. Martínez, 'La Cámara', doc. 32, p. 40.

20 E.g., *unum frontale altaris cum operibus auri et textum cum serico rubeo, viridi et livido, et flocatum cum flochs serici diversorum colorum; unum apparatum frontalis flocatum cum serico diversorum colorum*, cf. Martínez, 'La Cámara', doc. 32, pp. 40–41.

de Corpus Christi.[21] This half-used candle vividly evokes the solemn procession Templars enacted on the feast of Corpus Christi. Another item, described as follows, *un missale cohopertum cum postibus, cohopertis panno lino in quo est unum corporale in quo sunt prose et antifone notate*, presents a completely different liturgical moment.[22] Of note about this missal is the inclusion of the corporal that accompanied it. The corporal is a piece of white linen which exists in two sizes, a larger one to be laid over the altar, and another, which, if it fitted inside the missal as the one noted here, is of a smaller dimension and was used to cover the mouth of a chalice. This missal with its corporal elicits the image of the elaborate protocol both to handle and clean it. Because of this item's direct contact with the body and blood of Christ, this was the most sacred cloth of the liturgy. When in use it could only be handled by the priest. Before being washed it had to be thrice rinsed by the priest before it could be touched by somebody else. Its presence in the missal and its description in the inventory allow a rare glimpse of the private liturgical rites normally carried out by Templar priests in preparation for mass.

While what has been said above appears to relegate the Templars to a passive role in relation to the officiating priest, brothers had other ways of partaking in the liturgical rite. One altarpiece from Peñíscola demonstrates the way in which they literally inserted their order into the rites and placed themselves alongside biblical saints. The altarpiece is described as follows: *quator pecias frontalis argenti cum figuris apostolorum, cum signis de carts [sic] et Templi in capitibus, et sunt ibi tres aquili argenti cum quibus anuntur*.[23] This four-piece silver altarpiece depicted the cross of the Knights Templar above the 12 apostles. Through the commissioning of such an altarpiece and the insertion of the Templar insignia onto the physical space of the altar, the Templars as an order both participated in the biblical narrative and gained a privileged proximity to the intercession of the apostles.[24] This impulse to inscribe the order within the fabric of liturgical celebration is mirrored in a set of silver lamps adorned with enamel shields of the Knights Templar, namely those of the provincial master (Berengar de Cardona) and the commander of Peñíscola (Arnauld de Banyuls).[25] The desire both to partake in the liturgy and to be inscribed into the actual implements of its celebration is further reflected in the luxurious books Templars owned, such as Berengar de Cardona's lavish copy of the Genesis, Miravet's Berenguer of San Just's two-volume Bible and an edition

---

[21] Vilar Bonet, *Els béns*, appendix 4, p. 117.

[22] Martínez, 'La Cámara', doc. 32, p. 39.

[23] Ibid., doc. 32, p. 42; cf. doc. 77.

[24] Cf. Hans Belting, *Likeness and Presence: A History of the Image Before the Era of Art*, trans. Edmund Jephcott (Chicago, 1994), pp. 297–310.

[25] Martínez, 'La Cámara', doc. 32, p. 42, *duas lanteas argenti cum catenis esmaltatis cum signis Templi, et fratris Berengarii de Cardona et fratris Arnaldi de Banyuls*. For a description of these seals, see Alan Forey, *The Templars in the Corona de Aragón* (London, 1973), pp. 453–4.

of the Apocalypse from Montsó that could have belonged to Berengar de Bellvís.[26] However interesting these observations are for the art Templars commissioned and liturgical books they purchased, these activities are in line with normal medieval devotional practices.[27]

What sets the liturgical spaces of the Templars in the crown of Aragon apart from their contemporaries are not these insertions of insignia into altarpieces, lamps and other objects, but rather the relics they owned and the way they were represented to the devout brothers inside their chapels. Like their counterparts in the Latin East, the Templars who occupied these chapels demonstrated a pronounced veneration of the True Cross.[28] Multiple crosses with fragments of the *lignum Domini* appear in the inventories, and a total of four smaller, specifically *lignum Domini* reliquary crosses are recorded in the extant sources. Listed in an inventory which does not state their commandery of origin, these crosses are remarkable due to their taking the form of the four-armed Byzantine *lignum Domini* relic.[29] An example which recalls the Templar reliquary crosses of Acre and Astorga is described as *quandam crucem cum folio argenti superaurato et cum IIII brachiis in qua sunt reliquie, et quedam crux parva ligno Domini, et ymago crucifixi, et viginti sex perle, et sex lapides virides, et quidam pes argenti superaurati dicte crucis* (see Figure 15.2).[30] This contrasts with the typical altar cross accounted for in various inventories, which took the traditional Latin form yet held a piece of the True Cross within. The most opulent of these four-armed crosses is described as:

> *quandam croetam argenti subtilem, que pertitur, queque deaurata est, in cuius parte quadam fermata est quadam parva crux cum quatuor brachiis, et videtur quod in ea fuerit de ligno Domini, et in alia parte dicte crucis est quadam media crux fixa, et ista medi crux cohopertur cum alia in qua est una pecia de ligno Domini; est eciam intus cruce preditam quadam modica croeta rotunditatis unius denarii, et in una parte dicte crucis que pertitur est quidam cruxifixus, et ex alia parte in medio crucis est ymago Virginis gloriose [te]nentis filium suum in brachio, et in quolibet quatuor brachiorum dicte crucis medie sunt singule imagines, medie quatuor evanglistorum, et eciam in dicta cruce quadam pecia*

---

26 Rubió et al., 'Inventaris', doc. IX; Vilar, *Els bens*, appendix 51; Rubió y Lluch, *Documents*, vol. 1, doc. XLVIII; Rubió y Lluch, *Documents*, 1, doc. CXXXIV, reports on a two-volume *Moralia in Job* book that does not specify the commandery of origin.

27 Belting, *Likeness*, pp. 195–207, 330–48.

28 Alan Murray, '"Mighty Against the Enemies of Christ": The Relic of the True Cross in the Armies of the Kingdom of Jerusalem', in *The Crusades and their Sources*, ed. John France and William Zajac (Ashgate, 1998), pp. 217–38.

29 Martínez, 'La Cámara', docs 53, 130.

30 Ibid., doc. 53, p. 76; Jaroslav Folda, *Crusader Art in the Holy Land: From the Third Crusade to the Fall of Acre, 1187–1291* (New York, 2005), pp. 141–2; for an image of the Templar reliquary cross of the Museo Diocesano de Astorga; cf. Juan Atienza, *Guia de la España Templaria* (Barcelona, 1985), p. 174.

reliquie nigre grossitudinis unius favete. In medio autem dite cruces fecimus poni de ligno Domini.[31]

What is being described in this text is an extremely sumptuous triple *lignum Domini* reliquary cross. The multiplicity of True-Cross relics gleaming from every gilded surface, paired with the multiple enclosed inner reliquary which itself hides another relic, is an object whose explicit intention is to induce true stupor and wonder on its beholder. The value this cross held for contemporaries is highlighted when it appears as a gift from Jaume II to his son Joan, archbishop of Toledo, ten years later in 1323.[32] The configuration of the *lignum Domini* reliquaries in such opulent and distinct forms consciously recalled both their Byzantine tradition and the rediscovery of the True Cross through the Latin conquest of the Holy Land. Although the popularity of the four-armed shape spread within Europe as a result of Venice's large acquisition of Byzantine *spolia,* its distinctive shape continued to signify throughout the thirteenth, fourteenth and later centuries a vivid association with the Holy Land.[33]

Fig. 15.2 Four-armed *lignum Domini* reliquary cross

These *lignum Domini* reliquaries are not the only items Templars owned and displayed within their chapels which consciously evoked such distinct ties to the Holy Land. Described as a Venetian work within the inventory, a set of gilded silver *tabulae* open up to reveal on one side the figure of Christ and the

31 Martínez, 'La Cámara', doc. 130. Document 53, an earlier mention of this reliquary, gives a description which is slightly more difficult to understand.

32 Ibid., doc. 130.

33 Folda, *Crusader Art,* pp. 141–2. In addition, figures 355, 356, 403 illustrate the four-armed cross depicted on the obverse of Crusader icons.

12 apostles above other figures. These figures are described as being covered by crystal and are bordered by a total of 24 pearls and precious stones. The other *tabula* depicts an image of the Virgin Mary holding Christ in her arms, and she is likewise surrounded by the 12 apostles. Her image is decorated on its borders, as on the other side, with pearls and stones.[34] However she is not described as being covered by crystal, and this is crucial for identifying what type of artwork is being described. Throughout the inventories and lists of objects in Jaume II's registers, items are consistently described by the particular artistic technique employed. Niello and enamel applications are described in multiple entries.[35] It is unlikely that, had the *tabula* been fashioned with enamel medallions, it would not have been described as such, or if the entire image had been made of enamel – as was the case with the Limoges enamel images – it would not also have been described as such.[36] Yet in this instance the entry specifically notes that Christ and the other *figure sunt cohoperte cristallo*. The only objects that could fit this description are the Byzantine-made micro-mosaic icons. Through this technique, figures in icons are created from hundreds of minute glass *tesserae*, giving the effect of a glimmering composition with a shimmering crystalline surface. The fact that the description of the opening *tabulae* makes this object a diptych reinforces this deduction, since micro-mosaic diptychs were overwhelmingly created as items of personal devotion, with small physical dimensions.[37] What is described, therefore, is a Byzantine diptych which a Venetian craftsman enriched with lavish jewelled decorations, as was the custom with the Byzantine *spolia* circulating among the European nobility.[38]

The presence of such icons in Templar chapels foregrounds the direct relationship the order tried to create and maintain with the Holy Land. Templar ties to the east are not merely eloquent ruminations to be read in St Bernard's *De laude novae militiae*; rather, this longing for the east actively expressed itself in the choice of objects Templars selected to venerate in their liturgy. The item

---

34 Martínez, 'La Cámara', doc. 53, p. 76: *quasdam tabulas operis Venecie cohopertas folio argenti deaurato, intus quas tabulas in altera parte est figura Domini Ihesu Christi et figura duodecim apostolorum, ultra alias figures que sunt in ipsa parte, et dicte figure sunt cohoperte cristallo, et sunt in eadem parte viginti IIII inter perlas et lapides, et in alia parte est ymago beate Marie tenentis filium in brachio, et sunt ibi figure duodecim apostolorum et totidem lapides et perle sive nacres, sicut in alia parte.*

35 Martínez, 'La Cámara', docs 27, 32, 39, 41, 90, 94.

36 Vilar Bonet, *Els béns*, appendix 2.

37 Cf. Arne Effenberger, 'Images of Personal Devotion: Miniature Mosaic and Steatite Icons', in *Byzantium: Faith and Power (1261–1557)*, ed. Helen Evans (New York, 2004), pp. 209–14.

38 Cf. Maria Georgopoulou, 'Venice and the Byzantine Sphere', in *Byzantium*, ed. Evans, pp. 489–514. A good introduction to this practice, albeit with related materials, is discussed in Frauke Steenbock's, *Der kirchliche Prachteinband im frühen Mittelalter: Von den Anfängen bis zum Beginn der Gotik* (Berlin, 1965).

that is most strikingly absent from the inventories and lists of Templar objects is the figure of the *Sedes Sapientiae*. This statue was the staple of every small church to large cathedral throughout Europe and also very present in the crown of Aragon.[39] As Jochen Burgtorf's contribution in the present volume notes, these statues were also widespread within French Templar chapels.[40] However, the Arago-Catalan inventories are mysteriously silent regarding their presence. Even those inventories taken previous to the 1307 accusations do not record any instances of them. Rather, only *lignum Domini* crosses, reliquaries and icons are listed. This is not a mistake or oversight of the inventories, but another expression of the Templars' careful control over the liturgical image they created. As Jaroslav Folda's work on the Latin East shows, *Sedes Sapientiae* are almost completely absent from devotional spaces there as well.[41] The Iberian audience's perception of icons as intimately related to Jerusalem and the crusader states is exemplified by Cantiga IX in Alfonso X's *Cantigas de Santa María*. Here a pilgrim is depicted purchasing an icon of Our Lady of Saidnaiya in an icon workshop in Jerusalem.[42] Templars in Aragon-Catalonia understood the connotations such iconography held. Lastly, as if to confirm their unambiguous familiarity with Byzantine religious iconography and practice, a jasper pendant icon with an incised image of Christ is found listed in Jaume II's registry (see Figure 15.3).[43] These intaglio pieces were elite objects of personal devotion, and were deeply entrenched in Byzantine devotional traditions. When considered as a group, the Veneto-Byzantine diptych, the four-armed reliquary crosses, and the intaglio pendant icon demonstrate the strong identification Templars had with the Holy Land. Possession of these objects highlighted both their direct and privileged relationship to the Latin East as well as foregrounding their particular and, I venture to say, more authentically eastern taste. Possessing these items was not a simple matter of chance, but on the contrary a very calculated choice which carried for the owner an understanding of

---

39 Cf. Ilene Forsyth, *The Throne of Wisdom: Wood Sculptures of the Madonna in Romanesque France* (Princeton, 1972); José Sánchez Pérez, *El culto mariano en España* (Madrid, 1943).

40 Jochen Burgtorf, 'The Trial Inventories of the Templars' Houses in France: Select Aspects' (see above, in this volume).

41 Nowhere in the two volumes of Folda's monograph on the art of the Latin East does he discuss the production of *Sedes Sapientiae* statues by crusaders. His closing meditations on crusader art prove instructive, Folda, *Crusader Art,* pp. 511–27; idem, *The Art of the Crusaders in the Holy Land, 1098–1187* (New York, 1995).

42 Afonso X, o Sabio, *Cantigas de Santa Maria*, ed. Walter Mettmann (Coimbra, 1959–72), vol. 1, Cantiga IX; Benjamin Kedar, 'Convergences of Oriental, Christian, Muslim, and Frankish Worshippers: The Case of Saydnaya', in *De Sion exibit lex et verbum domini de Hierusalem: Essays on Medieval Law, Liturgy, and Literature in Honour of Amnon Linder*, ed. Yitzhak Hen (Turnhout, 2001), pp. 59–69.

43 Martínez, 'La Cámara', doc. 134, p. 195, *item I jaspi en figura de Ihesu Xrist encastat en argent penjat en I cadeneta.*

Fig. 15.3 Intaglio pendant icon

the religious meanings and connotations conveyed by such an iconographically distinct object.[44]

Lastly, this discussion would not be complete without touching on the extensive list of other types of relics the Templars of Peñíscola owned.[45] The concentration of relics tied to the Holy Land is clearly immediately palpable. Of the 30 objects listed which note a specific relic or relics, five pieces of the *lignum Domini* appear in addition to a piece of cloth from Christ's tunic and a *lapidem de Iherusalem de reliquiis*. A crystal ampulla with relics echoes the appearance of two ampullae with oil from the shrine of Saidnaiya listed on another entry.[46] Of the large number of saints' relics, seven do not specify to whom they belong, while the following are those named in the Peñíscola chapel inventory: two relics of *Sancta Margarita,* and one relic of each of the following female saints, *Sancta Barbera, Sancta Euphania, Sancta Maria Magdalena, Sancta Stienne.* Of the male saints, the following are listed: two relics of *Sancto Blasio martire*, and one relic for each of the following saints, *Sancti Benvenyat de Pisa, Sancto Bartholomeo apostolo, Sancto Nicholao confessore, De camisia sancti Staphani, Sancto Panasio, Sancte Luche.*[47] Besides

[44] For a general and revealing discussion of French interaction with relics from the Holy Land; cf. David Jacoby, 'Society, Culture, and the Arts in Crusader Acre', in *France and the Holy Land: Frankish Culture at the End of the Crusades*, ed. Daniel Weiss and Lisa Mahoney (Baltimore, 2004), pp. 97–137.

[45] Martínez, 'La Cámara', doc. 32.

[46] Ibid., doc. 106, p. 146, *unam capciam veterem de vorio in qua est una burçia de sindone et unam ampuletam cum modico olei de cerdenay;unum conservatorium de corio in quo est de oleo de çardenay.*

[47] Martínez, 'La Cámara', doc. 32.

the almost equal number of female and male saints, the majority of these saints are directly tied to the Bible or possess strong roots in the Holy Land and the early Church. Without delving into the possible meaning each of these saints may have held for the Templars, the concentration of such a hoard of early saints inadvertently foregrounds the lack of other local saints. Throughout the Arago-Catalan crown, saints such as St Eulalia, St Vincent, St George or the omni-present Virgin Mary were widely popular.[48] The absence of local saints further helps to characterize and shape our understanding of the Templars' liturgical experience.[49] Through its collection of eastern saints, the Peñíscola chapel continuously bade its congregation to keep their prayers and thoughts on the Holy Land. The physical presence of these relics in Peñíscola guaranteed that Templars would hold additional devotional masses for them and elevate their feast days to especially solemn celebrations.

From the foregoing discussion, a rich portrait of the Templars' devotional practices and character begins to form. Forever pilgrims to Jerusalem and far from the recently lost Holy Land, Templars in Peñíscola and other commanderies of the crown of Aragon would work to recreate the spiritual homeland of their order. As the highly lavish and elite devotional objects demonstrate, no expenses were spared on the liturgical vestments and other accoutrements of the divine celebration. Although such lavish items would most probably belong to the provincial masters and commanders, it does not deprive them of the power they exerted over Templar religious habits, for these high officials were in charge of overseeing the chaplains and fully contributed to the type of furnishings in their chapels. Through their own devotional practice, one should not negate the very real possibility of their influencing the type of religious outlooks and customs of the brothers under their control. Through the many contacts Templars had directly with the east or brothers who were stationed there, these devotional objects resonated with their experiences of these holy sites. As in the numerous chapels of the Holy Land, Templars in the crown of Aragon contemplated the divine word not while staring at Christ sitting on Mary's lap through its *Sedes Sapientiae* representation, but rather they gazed at the relic of the True Cross next to icons of Christ painted by St Luke himself.[50] Through the sheer opulence of wealth exhibited in these inventories a vivid image resurfaces. It is an image which portrays the Templars of the crown of Aragon in their most solemn celebrations and intimate moments incessantly contemplating the divine word with the physical representation of the Holy Land right before their very eyes.

---

48 Burns, *Crusader Kingdom*, pp. 73–101.

49 For those Templars in Majorca an altarpiece of St Bernard further helped emphasize the origin of their order and the ideals it had; see Sebastián Salvadó, 'Interpreting the Altarpiece of Saint Bernard: Templar Liturgy and Conquest in Thirteenth-Century Majorca,' *Iconographica: Rivista di iconografia medievale e moderna*, 5 (2006), 48–63.

50 The iconographic prototype of the Virgin Mary with Christ was believed to have been originally painted by St Luke; cf. Belting, *Likeness*, pp. 57–62.

Appendix
Inventories and lists containing Templar liturgical items (overview)

Templar property and commandery specified (in chronological order)

Ares, c.1300, *Ares*, ACA, reg. *Templariorum*, fol. 121 (Rubió et al, 'Inventaris', doc. I (a))

Peñíscola, c.1300, *Peñíscola*, ACA, reg. *Templariorum*, fol. 60 (Rubió et al., 'Inventaris', doc. I (b))

Corbins, 1 May 1300, *Corbins*, ACA, CRD de Jaume II, box 93, no. 552 (Vilar, *Els bens*, Appendix 2; cf. Miret y Sans, 'Inventaris', pp. 70–71)

Xivert, February 1302, *Xivert*, ACA, CRD de Jaume II, box 8, no. 1741 *unpublished*; Vilar, *Els bens*, appendix 10)

Xivert, March 1302, *Xivert,* ACA, CRD de Jaume II, box 8, no. 1742 (*unpublished*; Vilar, *Els bens*, appendix 10)

Peñíscola, Xivert, Ares, 3 March 1302, *Peñíscola, Xivert*, *Ares,* ACA, CRD de Jaume II, box 8, no. 1733 (Vilar, *Els bens*, appendix 4)

Peñíscola, Xivert, Ares, 1302, *Peñíscola, Xivert, Ares,* ACA, CRD de Jaume II, box 8, nos 1738, 1743, 1746 (*unpublished*; cf. Vilar, *Els bens*, appendix 4, f. n. 1)

Peñíscola, Xivert, Ares, 1304, *Peñíscola, Xivert, Ares,* ACA, CRD de Jaume II, box 10, no. 2022 (*unpublished*; cf. Vilar, *Els bens,* appendix 4, f. n. 1)

Camanes, 22 March 1304, *Camanes,* ACA, CRD de Jaume II, box 10, no. 2019 (Vilar, *Els bens,* appendix 6)

Orrios, 22 March 1304, *Orrios,* ACA, CRD de Jaume II, box 10, no. 2019 (Vilar, *Els bens,* appendix 8)

Xivert, 22 June 1304, *Xivert,* ACA, CRD de Jaume II, box 10, no. 2011 (Vilar, *Els bens,* appendix 10)

Peñíscola, Xivert, Ares, 1305, *Peñíscola, Xivert, Ares,* ACA, CRD de Jaume II, box 11, no. 2373 (*unpublished*; cf. Vilar, *Els bens,* appendix 4, f. n. 1)

Xivert, March 1305, *Xivert,* ACA, CRD de Jaume II, box 11, no. 2371 (*unpublished*; Vilar, *Els bens,* appendix 10)

Xivert, May 1307, *Xivert,* ACA, CRD de Jaume II, box 14, no. 2856 (*unpublished*; Vilar, *Els bens,* appendix 10)

Peñíscola, 23 May 1307, *Peñíscola,* ACA, CRD de Jaume II, box 10, no. 2019 (Vilar, *Els bens,* appendix 16)

Peñíscola, 1307, *Peñíscola,* ACA, CRD de Jaume II, box 14, no. 2846 (Vilar, *Els bens,* appendix 17)

Peñíscola, *without date*, *Peñíscola,* ACA, CRD de Jaume II, box 88, no. 60 (*unpublished*; cf. Vilar, *Els bens,* appendix 17)

Peñíscola, *without date*, *Peñíscola,* ACA, CRD de Jaume II, box 93, no. 650 (*unpublished*; cf. Vilar, *Els bens,* appendix 17)
Peñíscola, *without date*, *Peñíscola,* ACA, CRD de Jaume II, box 93, no. 658 (*unpublished*; cf. Vilar, *Els bens,* appendix 17)
Miravet, 17 December 1308, *Miravet,* ACA, CRD de Jaume II, box 88, no. 124 (Vilar, *Els bens,* appendix 50; cf. Rubió et al., 'Inventaris', doc. II)
Epila, 18 December 1308, *Items from Miravet,* ACA, reg. *Templariorum,* fol. 183v (Vilar, *Els bens,* appendix 51; cf. Rubió et al., 'Inventaris', doc. III)
Saragossa, 23 December 1308, ACA, *Items from Miravet,* ACA, reg. *Templariorum,* fol. 184 (Vilar, *Els bens,* appendix 52)
Saragossa, 25 December 1308, ACA, *Items from Miravet*, ACA, reg. *Templariorum*, fol. 184v (Vilar, *Els bens,* appendix 53)
Valencia, 22 April 1311, *Items from Peñíscola*, ACA, reg. 272, fol. 84 (Martínez, *Cámara Real*, doc. 32; cf. Rubió et al., 'Inventaris', doc. IV)
Lleida, 5 March 1312–13, *Items from Montsó*, ACA, reg. 273, fol. 246v (Martínez, *Cámara Real*, doc. 48; cf. Rubió et al., 'Inventaris', doc. V)
Prats, 2 July 1313, *Apocalypsis from Montsó*, ACA, reg. 274, fol. 21 (Rubió y Lluch, *Documents*, vol. 1, doc. XLVIII)
Barcelona, 18 August 1319, *Items from Peñíscola*, ACA, reg. 281, fol. 167 (Martínez, *Cámara Real*, doc. 106; cf. Rubió et al., 'Inventaris', doc. XVI)

Templar property, unspecified commandery (in chronological order)

Daroca, 24 October 1308, *Templar books,* ACA, reg. *Templariorum,* fol. 158 (Villanueva, *Viage,* vol. 5, doc. II)
Barcelona, 1 October 1313, *Templar objects,* ACA, reg. 274, fol. 90 (Martínez, *Cámara Real,* doc. 53; cf. Rubió et al., 'Inventaris', doc. VII)
Lleida, 5 September 1314, *Templar books,* ACA, reg. 275, fol. 61 (Rubió et al., 'Inventaris', doc. VIII)
Barcelona, 5 January 1315, *Objects for Montserrat image,* ACA, reg. 277, fol. 29v (Martínez, *Cámara Real,* doc. 77; cf.Vilar, *Els bens,* appendix doc. 68)
Barcelona, 30 December 1315, *Genesis book belonging to Berengar de Cardona,* ACA, reg. 277, fol. 19v (Rubió et al., 'Inventaris', doc. IX)
Tarragona, 24 April 1316, *Objects for Montserrat image,* ACA, reg. 300, fol. 108 (Martínez, *Cámara Real* doc. 80; cf.Vilar, *Els bens,* appendix doc. 71)
Lleida, 8 October 1316, *Three Templar books,* ACA, reg. 278, fol. 4v (Rubió et al., 'Inventaris', doc. XI)
Tortosa, 7 May 1318, *Distribution of objects,* ACA, reg. 279, fol. 185 (Martínez, *Cámara Real*, doc. 87; cf.Vilar, *Els bens,* appendix doc. 73)
Tortosa, 25 May 1318, *Distribution of objects,* ACA, reg. 279, fol. 204v (Martínez, *Cámara Real*, doc. 88; cf.Vilar, *Els bens,* appendix doc. 74)
Barcelona, 22 August 1318, *Distribution of objects,* ACA, reg. 279, fol. 290v (Martínez, *Cámara Real*, doc. 90; cf.Vilar, *Els bens,* appendix doc. 75)

Barcelona, 25 August 1318, *Distribution of objects,* ACA, reg. 279, fol. 293v (Martínez, *Cámara Real,* doc. 91; cf.Vilar, *Els bens,* appendix doc. 76)
Barcelona, 8 May 1319, *Templar privileges and documents,* ACA, reg. 281, fol. 116 (Vilar, *Els bens,* appendix 77)
Barcelona, 13 August 1322, *Distribution of objects,* ACA, reg. 283, fol. 195 (Martínez, *Cámara Real*, doc. 120; cf. Rubió et al., 'Inventaris', doc. XVII)
Barcelona, 18 July 1323, *Templar objects owned by Jaume II,* Archivo del Real Patrimonio, Libro II de Albaranes de Felipe de Boyl, fol. 87v (Martínez, *Cámara Real*, doc. 134; cf. Martorell, '*Inventari dels bens*')
Valencia, 19 January 1347, *Templar two-volume Moralia in Job book,* ACA, reg. 1310, fol. 138 (Rubió y Lluch, *Documents,* vol. 1, doc. CXXXIV)

Templar property identified by scholarship, not stated in source (in chronological order)

Santes Creus, 11 March 1315–16, ACA, reg. 277, fol. 104 (Martínez, *Cámara Real,* doc. 78; cf. Rubió et al., 'Inventaris', doc. X)
Barcelona, 24 November 1318, ACA, reg. 281, fol. 33 (Martínez, *Cámara Real*, doc. 95; cf. Rubió y Lluch, *Documents,* vol. 2, doc. XXXVIII)
Barcelona, 13 December 1318, ACA, reg. 281, fol. 44v (Martínez, *Cámara Real*, doc. 100; cf. Rubió et al., 'Inventaris', doc. XIV)
Barcelona, 18 August 1319, ACA, reg. 281, fol. 166v (Martínez, *Cámara Real,* doc. 105)
Barcelona, 1 February 1322–23, ACA, reg. 283, fol. 286 (Martínez, *Cámara Real*, doc. 125; cf. Rubió y Lluch, *Documents,* vol. 2, doc. XLV)
Barcelona, 4 March 1322–23, ACA, reg. 284, fol. 13 (Martínez, *Cámara Real*, doc. 126; cf. Rubió y Lluch, *Documents,* vol. 2, doc. XLVI)
Barcelona, 16 April 1323, ACA, reg. 284, fol. 32 (Martínez, *Cámara Real,* doc. 129; cf. Rubió y Lluch, *Documents,* vol. 2, doc. XLVII)
Barcelona, 23 April 1323, ACA, reg. 284, fol. 35 (Martínez, *Cámara Real,* doc. 130)
Barcelona, 1 March 1323–24, ACA reg. 284, fol. 154 (Martínez, *Cámara Real*, doc. 137; cf. Rubió y Lluch, *Documents,* vol. 2, doc. XLIX)
Valencia, 20 February 1318, ACA, reg. 279, fol. 118v (Rubió y Lluch, *Documents,* vol. 2, doc. XXXV)
Barcelona, 27 July 1326, ACA, reg. 285, fol. 237v (Martínez, *Cámara Real*, doc. 141; cf. Rubió et al., 'Inventaris', doc. XVIII)
Barcelona, 30 December 1326, ACA, reg. 286, fol. 76 (Martínez, *Cámara Real,* doc. 142; cf. Rubió y Lluch, *Documents,* vol. 2, doc. LV)

Possible Templar property (in chronological order)

Valencia, 26 November 1317, ACA, reg. 279, fol. 71 (Martínez, *Cámara Real,* doc. 85; cf. Rubió y Lluch, *Documents,* vol. 2, doc. XXXIII)
Barcelona, 11 November 1318, ACA, reg. 281, fol. 30 (Martínez, *Cámara Real,* doc. 93; cf. Rubió y Lluch, *Documents,* vol. 2, doc. XXXIX)
Barcelona, 15 November 1318, ACA, reg. 281, fol. 31 (Martínez, *Cámara Real,* doc. 94; cf. Rubió y Lluch, *Documents,* vol. 2, doc. XXXVII)
Barcelona, 27 November 1318, ACA, reg. 281, fol. 35 (Martínez, *Cámara Real,* doc. 96; cf. Rubió et al., 'Inventaris', doc. XII)
Barcelona, 13 December 1318, ACA, reg. 281, fol. 43v (Martínez, *Cámara Real,* doc. 98; cf. Rubió et al., 'Inventaris', doc. XV)
Barcelona, 13 December 1318, ACA, reg. 281, fol. 44 (Martínez, *Cámara Real,* doc. 99; cf. Rubió et al., 'Inventaris', doc. XIII)
Barcelona, 6 August 1319, ACA, reg. 281, fol. 157v (Martínez, *Cámara Real*, doc. 104; cf. Rubió y Lluch, *Documents*, vol. 2, doc. XL)
Barcelona, 26 August 1319, ACA, reg. 281, fol. 171 (Martínez, *Cámara Real*, doc. 105)
Tarragona, 23 December, 1319, ACA, reg. 281, fol. 122 (Martínez, *CámaraReal*, doc. 110; cf. Rubió y Lluch, *Documents*, vol. 2, doc. XLI)
Barcelona, 18 October 1322, ACA, reg. 283, fol. 232v (Martínez, *Cámara Real*, doc. 122; cf. Rubió y Lluch, *Documents*, vol. 2, doc. XLIV)
Barcelona, 5 October 1323, ACA, reg. 284, fol. 97v (Martínez, *Cámara Real*, doc. 136; cf. Rubió y Lluch, *Documents*, vol. 2, doc. XLVIII)
Barcelona, 13 July 1326, ACA, reg. 285, fol. 217 (Martínez, *Cámara Real*, doc. 140; cf. Rubió y Lluch, *Documents*, vol. 2, doc. LIV)
Barcelona, 28 November 1325, ACA, reg. 285, fol. 115v (Rubió y Lluch, *Documents*, vol. 2, doc. LI)

Chapter 16

The Extinction of the Order of the Temple in the Kingdom of Valencia and Early Montesa, 1307–30: A Case of Transition from Universalist to Territorialized Military Orders[1]

Luis García-Guijarro Ramos

The arrest and trial of the Templars between 1307 and 1312, and the canonical extinction of the order at the council of Vienne in March 1312 were among the highly significant turning points in the history of Latin Christendom, and they were also one of the most relevant series of events which marked the end of the period that historians have labelled as the central middle ages. The various episodes which epitomized that historical watershed held great significance and touched on all aspects of Latin societies at the time. Some of them, and most clearly those related to the order of the Temple, showed the triumph of territorial monarchies over universal powers, namely the Church of Rome, whose highest dignitary, the pope, had been abused at Anagni only a few years earlier by the compelling strength of the French King Philip IV.[2] The Temple and Montesa, its successor in the kingdom of Valencia, were both military orders but of a different nature. The first was linked

---

[1] This article is part of the research project 'The Conduct of Warfare: Approaches and Perspectives, c.950–c.1350' granted by the Spanish Ministry of Education and Science (HUM2007–64897/HIST).

[2] The literature on the conflict between king and pope is almost endless. The monographs on both figures deal at length with it: Joseph R. Strayer, *The Reign of Philip the Fair* (Princeton, 1980); Jean Favier, *Philippe le Bel*, 2nd edn (Paris, 1998); Thomas S.R. Boase, *Boniface VIII* (London, 1933). Extracts of different historians' writings on the subject appear in *Philip the Fair and Boniface VIII: State vs. Papacy*, ed. Charles T. Wood (New York, 1967). The doctrinal points of the controversy are dealt with by Jean Rivière, *Le problème de l'église et de l'état au temps de Philippe le Bel: Étude de théologie positive* (Louvain and Paris, 1926). A recent summary of the conflict has been given by Alessandro Barbero, 'Bonifacio VIII e la casa di Francia', in *Bonifacio VIII: Atti del XXXIX Convegno storico internazionale, Todi, 13–16 ottobre 2002* (Spoleto, 2003), 273–327.

to the universalist ambitions of the papacy, the second to the more limited though more realistic objectives of the king of Aragon, Jaime II.

The fate of the Templars also touched deeply on the territorial balance of power within privileged groups of western Europe, due to the great weight of Templar possessions in that wide area and to the rivalries which arose at the prospect of their control in the future, following the conciliar decision at Vienne. Some weeks after the suppression of the order on 22 March 1312, Pope Clement V assigned the Templar holdings to the Hospitallers, with one exception: the Iberian Peninsula.[3] In two of its political entities, Valencia within the crown of Aragon and Portugal, a stark novelty was introduced by the strenuous diplomatic efforts of King Dinis of Portugal and, above all, King Jaime II of Aragon: the order of Christ in the western kingdom and the order of Montesa in the kingdom of Valencia were established by Pope John XXII between 1317 and 1319.[4] Both of them took hold of the Templar patrimony in those regions, but were also given lands and strongholds which had formerly belonged to other institutions or to the king.[5]

The most distinctive trait of these new foundations emerged from the fact that they were monarchical orders to an extent that previous great Iberian military-religious establishments, such as Calatrava, Santiago, Alcántara in Castile and Leon or Avis in Portugal, were not. The latter were founded in the second half of the twelfth century, at a time when the monarchical powers did not yet have the strength or the commitment to fully promote and sustain such endeavours. The case was entirely different at the time of Jaime II (1291–1327), one of the great kings of the medieval crown of Aragon, who deserves a modern study to update the important work made more than 50 years ago by Jesús Ernesto Martínez Ferrando.[6] The order of Montesa was a product of the diplomatic efforts of Jaime II's envoys at Avignon, who first delayed a Church decision on the Templar territories in the

---

3 Bull *Ad providam* of 2 May 1312: *Reg. Clem. V*, vol. 7, doc. 7885, pp. 65–8; *PUT*, vol. 2, doc. 147, p. 302.

4 Order of Montesa: Bull *Pia matris ecclesie* of 10 June 1317, Archivo de la Corona de Aragón (hereafter cited as ACA), Cancillería Real (CR), 'Collectanea', Coleción de Bulas, doc. 390; transcription in Josep de Villarroya, *Real Maestrazgo de Montesa: Tratado de todos los derechos, bienes y pertenencias del patrimonio y maestrazgo de la Real y Militar Orden de Santa María de Montesa y San Jorge de Alfama* (Valencia, 1787), vol. 2, doc. 1, pp. 1–11, and in Vicente Ferrán y Salvador, *El castillo de Montesa: Historia y descripción del mismo, precedida de un bosquejo histórico de la Orden Militar de Santa María de Montesa y San Jorge de Alfama* (Valencia, 1926), doc. 1, pp. 143–8. Order of Christ: Bull *Ad ea ex quibus* of 14 March 1319; transcription in *Monumenta Henricina*, vol. 1 (Coimbra, 1960), doc. 61, pp. 97–110.

5 Enric Guinot Rodríguez, 'La fundación de la Orden Militar de Santa María de Montesa', *Saitabi*, 35 (1985), 73–86; Luis García-Guijarro Ramos, 'Los orígenes de la Orden de Montesa', in *Las Órdenes Militares en el Mediterráneo Occidental (siglos XIII–XVIII)* (Madrid, 1989), pp. 69–83.

6 Jesús Ernesto Martínez Ferrando, *Jaime II de Aragón: Su vida familiar*, 2 vols (Barcelona, 1948); idem, *Jaume II o el seny català* (Barcelona, 1956).

crown of Aragon, and then managed to get a ruling highly favourable to Jaime II's wishes.[7] For this reason, the first topic to be touched on when dealing with early Montesa is the attitude of the Aragonese king in the years between 1307 and 1317 (or better, 1319, when the papal foundation decrees of 10 June 1307 were put into effect). The understanding of pre-Montesa provides the clue to the early years of the institution, those between its effective establishment on 22 July 1319 at the royal palace in Barcelona, and the general chapter that the order held at San Mateo in northern Valencia on 25 May 1330 which fixed the administration of Montesa's lands in commanderies and a *tabula magistri*.[8] As almost always happens in history, the origins help to explain the fully developed subject.

It is quite surprising that modern historiography which has studied the fate of the Temple in the crown of Aragon after 1307 or the order of Montesa alone has not highlighted the key aspect on which the subsequent history of this new institution was built. What seems to be apparently a straightforward question is in fact a rather complex issue: why did Jaime II, at the city of Valencia on 1 December 1307, deliver instructions to arrest the Templars of that kingdom and forbid their vassals to assist them in any way, and on the next day extend those measures to Aragon and Catalonia?[9] Part of the problem lies in the fact that there is no explicit documentary answer to it, as Alan Forey, who knows the contents of the archive of the crown of Aragon better than most Spanish historians and who has made a recent thorough study of the fall of Templars in eastern Iberia, can attest.[10] That silence can be of no surprise to historians, who know that sources hide and distort the deep meaning of events as much as they illuminate them.

It has been repeatedly stated that the Aragonese monarchs had ceased to give their full favour to the Templars since the time of King Pedro II (1196–1213), alarmed as they were by the wide privileges assigned to the order by Ramón Berenguer IV in 1143 in response to the Temple's renunciation of their rights

---

7 A minute study of the negotiations has been done by Alan Forey, *The Fall of the Templars in the Crown of Aragon* (Aldershot, 2001), pp. 156–78. John XXII referred explicitly in the bull *Pia matris ecclesie* to the complex discussions that had taken place over years at the papal court in Avignon: *post longam et diutinam altercationem super hoc habitam*, see above, note 4.

8 The ceremony that took place in Barcelona on 22 July 1319 has been described by Hipólito de Samper, *Montesa ilustrada: Origen, fundación, principios*, vol. 1 (Valencia, 1669), pp. 59–60, and by Villarroya, *Real Maestrazgo de Montesa*, vol. 1, pp. 29–30. For the general chapter of 25 May 1330: Archivo Histórico Nacional (hereafter cited as AHN), Sección de Órdenes Militares (SOM), Pergaminos (Perg.), Montesa, Particulares (P) 918 and P 919; transcription in Villarroya, *Real Maestrazgo de Montesa*, vol. 2, pp. 140–51, and in Ferrán y Salvador, *El castillo de Montesa*, doc. 12, pp. 168–72.

9 Forey, *The Fall of the Templars*, p. 7.

10 See above, note 7, for the full reference.

under Alfonso the Battler's testamentary clauses.[11] The shrinking of donations was clearly perceived in the grants of lands to the Temple after the conquest of the Muslim kingdom of Valencia in the central decades of the thirteenth century.[12] But the argument that there was a loss of enthusiasm for the Templars has no force when dealing with the policy of Jaime II towards the order in that kingdom at the turn of the fourteenth century. There might have been tensions between the crown and the Aragonese Templars, as Alan Forey suggests, but it is highly doubtful that these determined the king's attitude and policy towards them in the autumn and early winter of 1307.[13] The territorial accretion of the Temple in the kingdom of Valencia in the years 1294 and 1303 clearly contradicts that assumption.[14]

In 1291, at the time when Jaime abandoned Sicily to succeed his brother Alfonso III as king of Aragon and Valencia and count of Barcelona, the Temple had just three commanderies in Valencia: possessions in the city and its surroundings, including the bailiwick of Moncada, houses and *alquerías* in Burriana, and the castle of Chivert. This stronghold was at that moment the only territory under Templar control in the most northerly regions of the kingdom; it had grown eastwards by incorporating Pulpis in 1277, after a dispute with the order of Calatrava which had held the area for some decades (see Figure 16.1 for this northern section). That total number of three convents had modestly risen to four by the autumn of 1307, but the real sense of that apparently moderate increase cannot be fully perceived without taking into account that the area controlled by the Templars in the kingdom had more than doubled in the interim; that is the relevance of the appearance of a new commander at Peñíscola (see Figure 16.2).[15]

---

[11] Alan Forey, *The Templars in the Corona de Aragón* (London, 1973), p. 31; idem, *The Fall of the Templars*, p. xii. The final accord between Ramón Berenguer IV and the Temple signed at Gerona on 27 November 1143 was transcribed in Próspero de Bofarull y Mascaró, *Colección de documentos inéditos del Archivo General de la Corona de Aragón*, vol. 4 (Barcelona, 1849), doc. 43, pp. 93–9.

[12] Forey, *The Templars in the Corona de Aragón*, p. 35.

[13] Forey, *The Fall of the Templars*, pp. xii–xiii.

[14] A detailed study of this expansion in Luis García-Guijarro Ramos, 'The Growth of the Order of the Temple in the Northern Area of the Kingdom of Valencia at the Close of the Thirteenth Century: A Puzzling Development?', in *Knighthoods of Christ: Essays on the History of the Crusades and the Knights Templar Presented to Malcolm Barber*, ed. Norman Housley (Aldershot, 2007), pp. 165–81. A different interpretation of the same events in Alan Forey, 'A Templar Lordship in Northern Valencia', in *Ordines Militares: Colloquia Turonensia*, 14 (2007), *Die Ritterorden als Träger der Herrschaft*, pp. 59–68.

[15] Alan Forey (in *The Fall of the Templars*, p. 121) has stated that the Templars possessed three commanderies in Valencia at the time of their arrest. In the list of officials included in his *The Templars in the Corona de Aragón*, he referred to four: p. 427 (Burriana), p. 429 (Chivert), p. 439 (Peñíscola) and p. 443 (Valencia). This is the correct number. The city of Valencia included its suburban possessions, mainly the rich bailiwick of Moncada; Peñíscola probably also administered the late acquisitions of Ares, Las Cuevas and Culla. That means that the seaside castle may have controlled a huge hinterland that reached

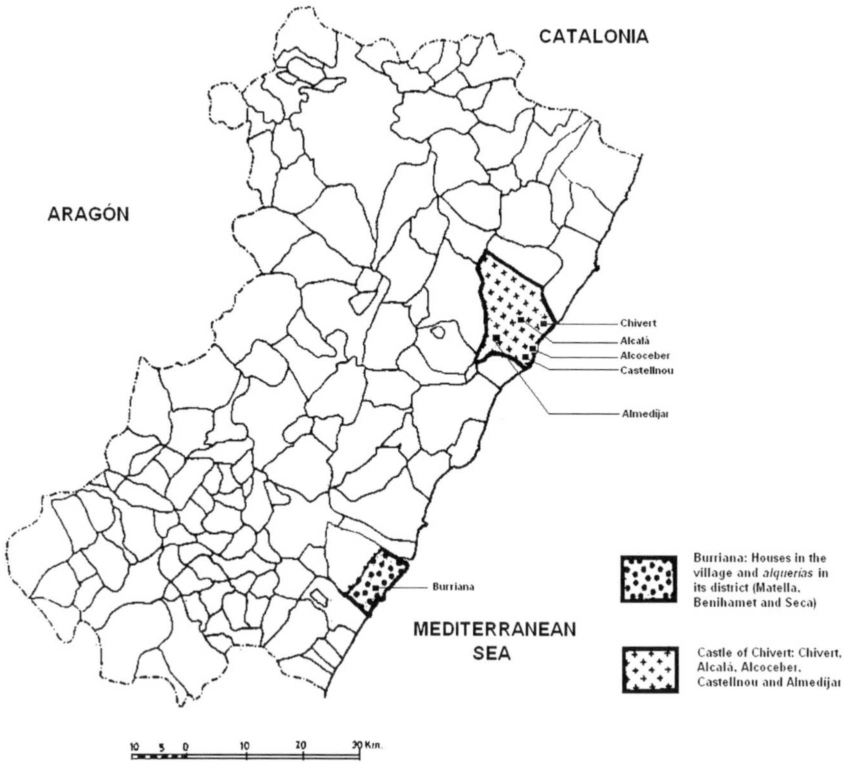

Fig. 16.1 Templar districts and possessions in the northern part of the kingdom of Valencia, c.1250

up to the borders with Aragon. There were interventions of the provincial master in the inland strongholds in the period 1294–1307, which attest that the order had not assigned a final administrative status to each of these new units before the final crisis of 1307. Ares, Las Cuevas and Culla only became separate districts under the Montesians: AHN, SOM, Perg., Montesa, P 918 and P 919. To assess the Templar territorial strength by the number of commanderies is misleading. Not all of them had the same extension and strategic importance. By the autumn of 1307 Peñíscola was most probably a macro-commandery in size and geopolitical status. It cannot thus be put on the same level as Chivert or Burriana.

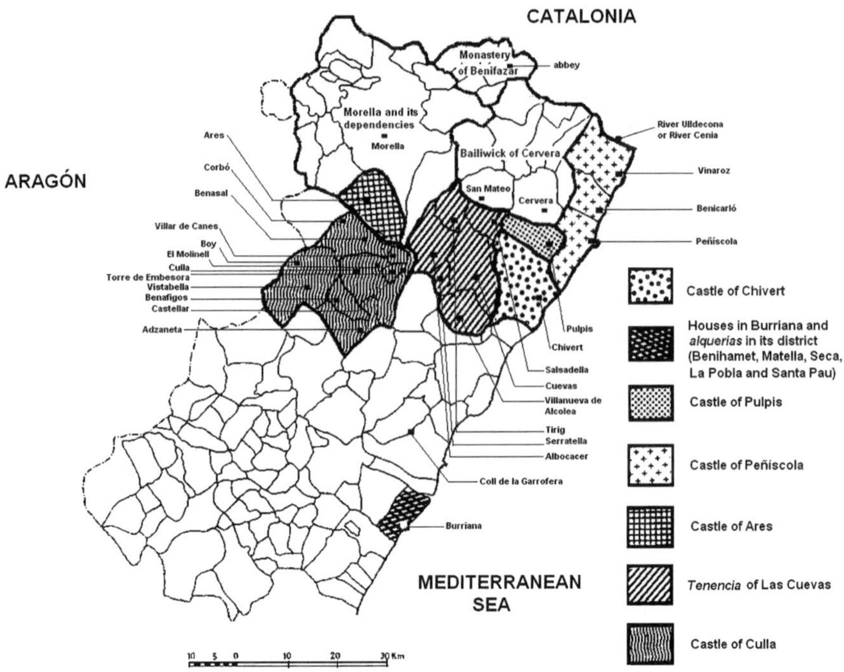

Fig. 16.2 Templar districts and possessions in the northern part of the kingdom of Valencia, 1303-07

The king was a key figure in that enlargement. The growth was precisely concentrated on the northern parts where previously the domains of the Temple had been scarce. As a result of these additions, Templar territory formed from then on a continuous belt that ran from the frontier between the kingdoms of Aragon and Valencia in the west to the Mediterranean Sea in the east. That strip of land isolated the most northerly Valencian outposts, specifically the district of Morella, the Cistercian monastery of Benifasar and the Hospitaller bailiwick of Cervera, from the rest of the kingdom. The strength of the order of the Temple in the south of Aragon (commanderies of Villel, Cantavieja and Castellote) and along the lower Ebro valley (Ascó, Miravet and Horta) gave an even greater value to the switch of power in northern Valencia that began to take place from 1294 onwards.

The monarchy did not just tolerate these momentous changes; it promoted them. In 1294, Jaime II urged the exchange of the city of Tortosa, which had been in Templar hands, first partly and then almost entirely, since its conquest in 1148, for the castles of Peñíscola and Ares and for the *Tenencia* of Las Cuevas. He planned this territorial reshuffling with outmost care. The seaside stronghold of Peñíscola had been in royal hands from the time when Jaime I occupied it peacefully in 1233. The other two areas had belonged permanently or intermittently to the

Alagón family since they were taken from the Muslims in 1232 and 1233. The king's direct control of these regions was a preliminary step to any interchange with the Temple. The *Tenencia* was hastily bought by the crown in July 1293 to make the accord feasible; a few days earlier the king had got hold of Ares as a result of an exchange of places with the noble Artal de Alagón.[16] All these new Templar possessions formed a wide strip of land which extended from the inner sierras to the sea. The control of Tortosa, which lay by the river Ebro near the sea and thus had paramount commercial importance, must have been important for the king. He must also have been well aware that as a result of that swap of territories he was strengthening the position of the Temple in a geostrategic area vital for the monarchy: the point where Aragon, Catalonia and Valencia had common boundaries. Had Jaime II entertained any kind of reluctance towards the Templars, he would never have favoured this kind of project in spite of his great interest for the city at the mouth of the Ebro.

This lack of ill-feeling was shown nine years later, when the king not only approved the transmission of the castle of Culla to the Temple, but acted as guarantor for the seller, the noble Guillermo IV of Anglesola. The price of the transaction was 500,000 *solidi*. The order was ready to pay such an exorbitant price for the last piece of a long strip of territory which would give it control over northern Valencia. As a participant in the transaction, Jaime II showed that he did not oppose the acquisition; he seemed to have favoured it in an active way. So, less than five years before the arrest of the brothers, the Aragonese king was ready to allow the Templars the control of crucial districts in the crown of Aragon and to grant the order an immense power over them.[17] Consequently, there are no reasons to suppose that the rapid action of the king on 1 December 1307, only a month and a half after the brilliant coup executed by Philip IV, was prompted by any deep suspicion or hostility towards the order, nor by any sort of greed over its possessions, as Malcolm Barber indicates.[18]

Alan Forey has pointed out several times in his exhaustive study of the detention of the Valencian Templars in December 1307 and the siege of those Templar strongholds in Aragon and Catalonia which resisted, in some cases for even as long as 19 months, that the king was doing an unpleasant job about which he was

---

16 Alan Forey thinks otherwise: 'The king had admittedly acquired Ares and Las Cuevas … but it cannot be taken for granted that in doing this he was acting in accord with Templar wishes relating to a future exchange', 'A Templar Lordship', p. 59. Nonetheless, it is a happy coincidence that two of the territories exchanged in 1294 had been purchased by Jaime II in the previous year.

17 Alan Forey agrees on this point: 'The order was in fact given exceptional exemptions and powers in its new territories', ibid., p. 64.

18 'James II may therefore have decided that if he delayed too long he would lose the opportunity of gaining any tangible benefits for himself from the affair ... He was developing an eye for Templar property', Malcolm Barber, *The Trial of the Templars*, 2nd edn (Cambridge, 2006), p. 231.

not fully convinced, and that he had no alternative but to comply with external forces, and mainly with Pope Clement V, who had already ordered him to arrest the brothers in the bull *Pastoralis preeminentie*, issued on 22 November 1307.[19] Alan Forey has also forcibly argued that Jaime II's actions of early December had nothing to do with the papal decree, which only reached the king after mid-January 1308; rather, they might have been prompted by letters of the king of France and others assuring him that many French Templars had confessed.[20] That is at least what Jaime II told the pope in a letter of 4 December, which was a neat and correct explanation of events in Valencia since 1 December devised to please Clement V, but which did not necessarily show the king's worries and intentions.[21] In my opinion, the news from France could have moved to action a ruler with weaker or no attachments to the Templars. As I have tried to put forward, that was not the case with Jaime II. In consequence, the basic question, why at that time and at that place the Aragonese king decided the arrest, remains unanswered.

The date and the city where the royal order was issued might offer a tentative response to the problem posed by a reluctant king apparently acting not in complete accordance with his thoughts and feelings. On 1 December 1307, papal commands had not yet arrived at the Aragonese court, but the letters from France must have made Jaime II realize that the Templars were doomed and that their arrest was only a question of time, whether he himself believed that the confessions reflected the Templars' behaviour or not. He must have also thought that he should not delay action if he were to keep control over the various Templar estates in the crown of Aragon, and prevent not only an unwanted papal decision over them but mainly the intervention of local nobles who might have wished to benefit from the situation. The fact that the king and the royal entourage were staying in Valencia at the time might not have been the accidental sojourn of an itinerant court, but a deliberate temporal residence in an area of potential problems. Jaime II might have wished to direct policies from Valencia itself, near the zone which would be most affected by the changes to come. As I have pointed out, that area was located at the northern part of the kingdom of Valencia; only a few years earlier it had become a solid strip of Templar territory accepted or even encouraged by the monarch himself. The guilt or innocence of the brothers must not have been at stake at that precise moment. It is most likely that Jaime II acted quickly to ensure that a strategic region on which much of the communications between Catalonia, Aragon and the centre and south of the kingdom of Valencia depended, and consequently a considerable amount of the political control over his dominions, was in his hands at that critical moment.

---

19 Forey, *The Fall of the Templars*, pp. 9, 39–40. Transcription of the bull in Jaime Villanueva, *Viage literario a las Iglesias de España*, vol. 19 (Madrid, 1851), doc. 48, pp. 317–19.

20 Forey, *The Fall of the Templars*, p. 6.

21 ACA, CR, Registros (hereafter Reg.) 291, fols 24v–25.

The monarch's decrees of 1 and 2 December 1307 were to affect all Templars in the crown of Aragon. It was symptomatic of the king's approach that he did not worry immediately about neighbouring Aragonese or Catalan Templar territories which immediately prepared for resistance (for instance, at Villel, Cantavieja, Castellote or Miravet). Jaime II must have been thinking about the belt of Templar lands that cut off Valencia from other domains of the crown. The brothers had suspicions in relation to their own security and had started to prepare their castles for defence, probably against nobles who might be tempted to intervene. This at least was what the provincial master told Jaime II when questioned in early November 1307 about the preventive measures.[22] In any case, the king's swift movement took the Valencian Templars, and the provincial master Jimeno de Lenda who was in the city as well, completely by surprise and made sure that in less than a month royal officials took charge of the strongholds of the order in the kingdom. Possessions and *fratres* in the city of Valencia, Burriana and Chivert passed under the control of crown delegates between 2 and 7 December. The most impressive of the fortifications, the castle of Peñíscola, surrendered without much of a fight on 12 December. Finally, the strongpoint of Ares and the *Tenencia* of Las Cuevas submitted to the king by 26 December.[23]

The fact that a peripheral city, Valencia, and not more central ones, Tarragona for instance, the metropolitan see where an ecclesiastical council on the guilt or innocence of the brothers took place in November 1312, became the place to decide the policy towards the Templars, was probably related to the key Valencian territories that were at issue. If such were the case, 'decisive action' was being taken in the region where the interests of the Aragonese monarchy might have been seriously at risk as a result of events which had originated elsewhere.[24] The king did not hesitate on the question at that time or later on, as Alan Forey implies.[25] He deliberately avoided causing much damage to property or to the brothers; he aimed at subduing the Templars while creating as little havoc as

---

22 Forey, *The Fall of the Templars*, p. 2.

23 Ibid., p. 11.

24 Alan Forey suggests that 'the measures which he [the king] took lacked the required decisiveness and careful planning' and that 'greater success might have been achieved at the end of 1307 [in Aragón and Catalonia] if Jaime II had taken more decisive action', ibid., pp. 7 and 18. Forey has in mind the precious time given to the Templars to organize resistance in some Aragonese and Catalan castles, but he does not seem to consider that not all Templar areas had the same importance for the crown at that precise time. Jaime II concentrated on his first priority, the northern part of the kingdom of Valencia, to deal later with isolated cases of resistance. He probably never contemplated swift comprehensive action, as had Philip IV in October 1307 or the English king, Edward II, on 10 January 1308, because his main aim presumably was to prevent any territorial erosion of his power rather than to proceed against the Templars.

25 'A doubting mind was hardly conducive to strong and vigorous action', ibid., p. 40.

possible. Jaime II's attitude was probably very different from that of Philip IV: he was not primarily interested in the Templar affair, and he might not have been convinced by the charges brought against them, but he was fully aware of the serious territorial consequences of those developments for the crown. That is why attention was focused on Valencia at the start. The court remained there until the objective of the control of the commanderies in the kingdom was fulfilled. From January 1308 onwards the fierce resistance of some Templar strongholds in Aragon and Catalonia drove Jaime II's attention elsewhere.

The Valencian possessions of the Temple, as well as all those in Aragon and Catalonia after the last centre of resistance, Monzón, capitulated on 1 June 1309, were provisionally administered by the king until a final agreement with the pope could be reached. These negotiations have been thoroughly studied by Alan Forey and began in earnest once the council of Vienne opened its sessions in the autumn of 1311.[26] Jaime II had instructed his ambassadors shortly before this.[27] The set of propositions which he then outlined remained basically unaltered in the lengthy process of talks at Avignon, which was further delayed by Clement V's death in April 1314 and the protracted election of his successor John XXII which took place in August 1316. Royal envoys came and went, proposals varied in their details but there was always a point which Jaime II maintained firmly: the Templar patrimony should not be handed to the Hospital. The reason was obvious: that order would then become one of the biggest powers in the Aragonese realms. The Valencian Templar belt would be increased by the bailiwick of Cervera and by the Templar and Hospitaller commanderies of southern Aragon and Catalonia.

Jaime II was conscious of the weight that the Hospitaller solution carried at Avignon. In a renewed set of instructions issued on 5 January 1313, he consented to the transfer of Templar lands to the Hospitallers providing that 17 former Templar strongholds passed to the king along with the necessary revenues for their upkeep.[28] The list is highly revealing: 11 were in southern Aragon, the lower Ebro valley and northern Valencia. In this last region the monarch had chosen the key posts of Chivert, Culla, Ares and Peñíscola; as has been pointed out, the last three castles had passed into the order of the Temple's control during his reign. The northern Valencian strongholds amounted to almost a quarter of those over which the king required total control due to their strategic importance. This is a clear testimony of the relevance that Jaime II gave at that moment, and also undoubtedly in December 1307, to the old Templar territorial belt between Valencia, Aragón and Catalonia.

Apart from the king's totally unfeasible idea of leasing Templar strongholds and lands from the pope, Jaime II's most cherished option was to grant the landed patrimony of the Temple to a branch of the order of Calatrava which would be

[26] See above, note 7.

[27] ACA, CR, Reg. 336, fols 72, 73–76v (6 September 1311) and fols 76v–78v (27 September 1311); Forey, *The Fall of the Templars*, pp. 156–8.

[28] ACA, CR, Reg. 336, fol. 172v; Forey, *The Fall of the Templars*, p. 165.

autonomous from the Castilian master. At some point of the negotiations the monarch offered his castle of Montesa in southern Valencia as the main headquarters for the new institution. The stronghold was referred to as being on the Muslim frontier, which was not quite true, but served the propaganda purposes of the king at a time when military orders were still strictly associated with the fight against the Saracens. Jaime II's plans clearly showed his desire to establish a territorial order linked to the Cistercians but independent from Castilian supervision. The final papal decision of 10 June 1317 was a modified form of this proposition. The order of Montesa would be connected to the Cistercians of Clairvaux via the Catalan abbey of Santes Creus or its Valencian daughter Valldigna, but its ties to Calatrava, which was linked to the Cistercian house of Morimond, would be formal and tenuous. The Hospital would be compensated with Templar holdings in Aragon and Catalonia, for which the castellan of Amposta, the highest Hospitaller dignitary in the crown of Aragon, or other high officials of the order would pay homage to the king.[29] That strengthening of Hospitaller power in Aragon and Catalonia did not seem to matter to Jaime II; the order would be bound to him and his successors by oath. The future proved him right: Anthony Luttrell has argued that in the mid-fourteenth century the Hospital in the crown of Aragon was 'almost a national order'.[30]

The king had thus succeeded in carrying out, with few alterations, his propositions on the basic points at issue since 1 December 1307: a dangerous concentration of power in northern Valencia had been avoided. Moreover, a new order, which was under royal control at the beginning and continued to be so in the future, had emerged. The universalism of the Temple had given way to the 'Aragonesism', or rather to the monarchism of Montesa.

Early Montesa cannot be understood without this background. Jaime II had been shrewd enough to tackle and take advantage of a situation that he had not promoted nor could have foreseen. However, in spite of total royal backing, the beginnings of Montesa were far from easy. Regardless of papal sanction in June 1317, the very existence of the new order was at stake due to the utter reluctance of the Castilian Calatravan master towards a project in which he rightly saw few advantages. In 1318, Jaime II played with several alternatives which even included the abandonment of his previous stern refusal of Hospitaller control of the Templar lands in Valencia. This change of mind was most likely on condition

---

[29] Bull *Ad fructus uberes* of 10 June 1317: ACA, CR, 'Collectanea', Colección de Bulas, doc. 391 = AHN, SOM, Perg., Montesa, inserted in P 692. The Hospitaller homage to the king was offered by the castellan of Amposta, Martín Pérez de Oros, on 22 November 1317 in Valencia: *flexis genibus positis coram ipso sacrosanctis quatuor evengeliis et cruce domini prestitit [castellanum] sacramentum et homagium fecit eidem domino Regi secundum formam iamdicti papalis rescripti*, ibid., P 692.

[30] Anthony Luttrell, 'La Corona de Aragón y las Órdenes Militares durante el Siglo XIV', in *VIII Congreso de Historia de la Corona de Aragón*, vol. 2.2 (Valencia, 1970), p. 73.

that the castellan of Amposta should explicitly do homage to the king for these lands, as had previously happened in relation to the Templar estates in Aragon and Catalonia. The king's proposal did certainly have a price of 100,000 pounds, a sum which may have seemed excessive to the master Foulques de Villaret, but which in fact was only four times greater than the amount that the Temple had paid in 1303 just for the castle of Culla.[31] Fifteen years had passed and the order of St. John could have been under economic strains at a period which involved such a deep change. However, this single element may provide the basis for an interesting comparison of finances between these two orders at an interval which involved such a deep change at that time. Different types of integration into the Hospitaller structure were contemplated at several moments later on in 1318, but the various projects were never put into practice.

Jaime II even contemplated an exchange of the crown's rights over Sardinia and Corsica in return for the Templar lands in Aragon, Catalonia and Valencia.[32] This last option shows that the future of the suppressed order's patrimony was also deeply related to the Mediterranean policy of the monarchy. The sea had become the only available 'frontier' for the crown of Aragon once land expansion into southern Islamic lands had been blocked by the Castilian control of Murcia. The king's interest in Nasrid ports such as Almería was related to this policy rather than to a conquest of the kingdom of Granada, which was a strictly Castilian affair.[33]

The difficulties of the year 1318 dissipated, and the original plan of 1317 was finally put into effect on 22 July 1319. The hard times experienced by any new foundation marked the first decade of Montesa in spite of constant royal favour. The growth of patrimony and members had been piecemeal and more or less harmonious in the old Hispanic orders. Montesa showed a paradox which marked its first moments: a rich patrimony formed by the old Templar and Hospitaller commanderies in the kingdom of Valencia contrasted with the lack of brothers and the slow growth of recruits.[34] One of the reasons put forward by Jaime II on 18 February 1318 for agreeing to the Hospitaller control of Templar domains in Valencia was precisely the difficulty in finding adherents to the recently established order who were not Castilian Calatravans; these brothers were totally unsuitable for the task because 'they would put his [Jaime II's] kingdom in great danger and the king would not accept them in any of the cases'.[35] On 22 July 1319, 11 *fratres* were received in the new institution. Eight months later, at a time when the order had taken possession of most of its lands from the royal officials who

---

31 The negotiations between the three parties, king, Hospitallers and pope, are described in detail in Forey, *The Fall of the Templars*, pp. 180–182.

32 Ibid., p. 181.

33 Templar rents which were then controlled by the king were used to finance the campaign against Almeria in 1309: ibid., p. 140.

34 The Hospitallers kept Torrente and the possessions they had in the city of Valencia and its immediate surroundings.

35 ACA, CR, Reg. 337, fols 283v–284; Forey, *The Fall of the Templars*, p. 180.

had administered them, and their inhabitants had sworn homage to Montesa, the number of brothers had gone up to only 14. This scarcity of professed members did not allow a quick development of the system of commanderies along the lines that had existed in Templar and Hospitaller times.[36] The process took 10 years. At the general chapter held at San Mateo on 25 May 1330, which assigned commanderies and established a *tabula magistri*, the total number of brothers had risen to about 60. The rough estimates of Aragonese Templars in 1307 made by Alan Forey set the number of brothers for the entire crown of Aragon as 200, and an average of about six *fratres* for each convent.[37] According to this guess, there would have been around 30 Templars at that time in the kingdom of Valencia; a similar or even slightly higher number of Hospitaller brothers should be added to that figure. This rough assessment of manpower of the so-called international military orders in Valencia shows by comparison the slight potential of recruits for the order of Montesa in its initial stages. Only by the end of the 1320s did Montesa probably attain the number of *fratres* that the Temple and the Hospital had kept in Valencia in the early years of the fourteenth century. The king's favour did not assure a great initial flow of professed members at a time when the enthusiasm for the military orders had subsided. Doubts of success might have given wings to several projects of amalgamation with the Hospital.

It was precisely the scarcity of members which prevented the order from providing manpower for the conquest of Sardinia in 1323–24. Nonetheless, the rents of Montesa were sparingly devoted to that purpose by the master and by the inhabitants of the places controlled by the institution: *congruum peccuniarium subsidium impenderunt*. The king thanked the brothers for their help and granted them on 26 February 1324, even before the Pisans had finally been subdued, free commerce with Sardinia and Corsica. In that charter, Jaime II was very explicit when he expressed that the order existed because he had worked strenuously for its foundation: *domum predictam montesie, que intercessionibus et operibus nostris erecta extitit et dotata, sub speciali favore gerimus et habemus*.[38] The financial help for this Mediterranean monarchical project was the first outward instance of the profound unity between the monarchy and Montesa. This link with the crown was the most relevant feature of a new order which sprang out of the ruins of the Temple but differed from it in so many respects.

---

36 For the number of brothers and the slow formation of commanderies in the first decade of the order of Montesa see Luis García-Guijarro Ramos, 'The Development of a System of Commanderies in the Early Years of the Order of Montesa, 1319–1330', in *La Commanderie: Institution des ordres militaires dans l'Occident medieval*, ed. Anthony Luttrell and Léon Pressouyre (Paris, 2002), pp. 57–73.

37 Forey, *The Fall of the Templars*, p. 17.

38 AHN, SOM, Perg., Montesa, Reales (R) 301, R 302 and R 303.

PART IV
The Trial in the British Isles

Chapter 17
King Edward II of England and the Templars

Jeffrey S. Hamilton

On Friday 13 October 1307 the Knights Templar were arrested throughout France in dawn raids ordered by King Philip IV the Fair. No similar activity took place in England. Although the Templars had been established in England since the reign of Henry I, they were not as deeply insinuated into the finances of the crown there as was the case in France, and not, therefore, so tempting a target. Moreover, the Templars appear to have retained a positive image in England even after the fall of Acre in 1291. The recently deceased king of England, Edward I, had been a comrade in arms with Templar knights during his own sojourn to the Holy Land following the failure of Louis IX's crusade to Tunis in 1270, and he corresponded with Jacques de Molay, master of the order, by way of the master of the Temple in England, William de la More, as late as 1304.[1] Nevertheless, it is remarkable that Edward II resisted the pressure to follow the lead of the French for some considerable time to come.[2] It is more remarkable still when one considers that Edward, not yet crowned, had been on the throne for a mere three months at the time and that he was betrothed to Isabelle, daughter of Philip IV. Although in the end he would gradually facilitate the suppression of the order in England, Edward II clearly disbelieved the charges against the Templars. Bowing to the inevitable, he ultimately profited from the situation both financially and politically, but taken in its entirety, his conduct throughout the trial of the English Templars reflects well on a much maligned king.

---

1 Michael Prestwich, *Edward I* (Berkeley, 1988), pp. 66–85; *CCR 1302–1307*, p. 208. See also Christopher Tyerman, *England and the Crusades, 1095–1588* (Chicago, 1988), pp. 230–40; Simon Lloyd, *English Society and the Crusade* (London, 1988), pp. 232–43. The following abbreviations are used here: *CCR* = *Calendar of the Close Rolls 1272–1485*, 45 vols (London, 1903–27); *CPR* = *Calendar of the Patent Rolls 1232–1509*, 59 vols (London, 1891–1916); *Foedera* = *Foedera, conventiones, literae et cujuscunque generis acta publica*, ed. Thomas Rymer et al., new edn, 4 vols in 7 (London, 1816–69).

2 Thomas W. Parker, *The Knights Templars in England* (Tucson, 1963), p. 92, suggests that 'adhering to his initial conviction but briefly, Edward in short order turned against the Templars', but this is a very superficial reading of the events. Evelyn Lord, *The Knights Templar in Britain* (Harlow, 2002) pp. 191–9, is more circumspect but raises the question of Edward's alleged homosexuality in accounting for the king's reticence, perhaps following Alain Demurger, *Vie et mort de l'ordre du Temple* (Paris, 1985), p. 341.

Philip the Fair very quickly apprised Edward of the guilt of the Templars, dispatching his trusted clerk, Master Bernard Pelet, to England to recount the charges.[3] As Malcolm Barber has noted, it would have been easy for Edward II to 'have seized the opportunity to score an easy success',[4] and yet he did not. Rather, on 30 October, Edward wrote to the king of France expressing his incredulity at the charges and announcing his intention to summon William de Dene, seneschal of Agen, to provide context to these 'rumours', which had apparently originated in Guienne.[5] Edward wrote to Dene on 26 November, summoning him into the king's presence to provide his testimony at Boulogne at Christmas.[6] This cannot have been seen by Philip IV as anything less than provocative. By localizing the charges against the Templars in Gascony, Edward may well have been making a not particularly oblique reference to the earlier case of Bishop Bernard Saisset of Pamiers, in which the French king had demonstrated his willingness to raise the twin specters of heresy and outrageous sin at the expense of the institutional Church.[7] Moreover, as Boulogne was to be the site of Edward's impending marriage to Isabelle of France – a marriage that Edward was at least rumored to be reconsidering in the fall of 1307 – linking these separate threads of policy constituted an affront to Philip IV that was palpable.[8]

Soon after writing to Dene, on 4 December 1307 at Reading, Edward addressed letters to the kings of Portugal, Castile, Sicily and Aragon, warning them against giving credence to the accusations being circulated about the Templars.[9] Four days later, Edward publicly rejected the charges against the Templars by writing to the pope himself stating that it was impossible to believe these outrageous charges.[10] On 20 December 1307, however, having received the bull *Pastoralis praeeminentiae* from Clement V, in which the pope authorized the arrest of the Templars on his

---

3 *Foedera*, vol. 2.1, p. 10.

4 Malcolm Barber, *The Trial of the Templars*, 2nd edn (Cambridge, 2006), p. 217.

5 *Foedera*, vol. 2.1, p. 10. The failure of Philip's initial propaganda campaign has been discussed by Sophia Menache, 'Contemporary Attitudes Concerning the Templars' Affair: Propaganda's Fiasco?' *Journal of Medieval History*, 8 (1982), 135–47; Malcolm Barber, 'Propaganda in the Middle Ages: The Charges Against the Templars', *Nottingham Medieval Studies*, 17 (1973), 42–57.

6 *Foedera*, vol. 2.1, p. 17.

7 For recent discussions of the Saisset case, and its implications for our understanding of Philip IV and the trial of the Templars, see James Given, 'Chasing Phantoms: Philip IV and the Fantastic', in *Heresy and the Persecuting Society in the Middle Ages*, ed. Michael Frassetto (Leiden, 2006), pp. 274–7; Sophia Menache, 'A Propaganda Campaign in the Reign of Philip the Fair, 1302–03', *French History*, 4 (1990), 427–54.

8 Elizabeth A.R. Brown, 'The Political Repercussions of Family Ties in the Early Fourteenth Century: the Marriage of Edward II of England and Isabelle of France', *Speculum*, 63 (1988), 573–95.

9 *Foedera*, vol. 2.1, p. 19.

10 Ibid., vol. 2.1, p. 20.

own behalf, Edward felt constrained to comply. Edward's response to the pope (dated 26 December) is a model of both humility and brevity: a greeting followed by two paragraphs, each paragraph comprised of a single terse sentence.[11] The king duly sent orders to the sheriffs to prepare for the unannounced arrest of the Templars throughout England, Scotland, Ireland and Wales, to take place on 8 January 1308.[12] In fact, the arrests were delayed for a couple of days, but seem to have been managed with little resistance or difficulty. Approximately 150 Templars were arrested in England (only 15 of whom were knights), a significant proportion of the order.[13] But they were maintained under very easy terms of confinement; a liberal allowance of 4*d.* per day was assigned to each, and the king specifically ordered the sheriffs 'not to place them in hard and vile prison'.[14] The master of the order in England, William de la More, was held at Canterbury, where he was provided with an allowance of 2*s.* per day, as well as the company of two brothers who were to receive a daily allowance of 6*d.* each. The three were given freedom to walk outside the city without supervision.[15] Further, from 27 May until 28 November 1308, de la More was freed on the request of Antony Bek, bishop of Durham and titular patriarch of Jerusalem.[16] Bek had been a close friend and ally of Edward II during the later years of the reign of Edward I, and one can perhaps discern the hand of the young king behind this intervention on the Templars' behalf.[17] The master was further comforted on 28 June when six Templar manors valued in excess of £100 per annum were assigned to him for provision of himself and his companions, who by now numbered 10.[18]

Shortly after the arrest of the Templars in England, Edward II sailed to France on 22 January 1308 for his wedding to Isabelle which took place three days later.

---

11 Ibid., vol. 2.1, p. 24.

12 Ibid., vol. 2.1, pp. 18–20, 23; *CCR 1307–1313*, pp. 48–9.

13 Clarence Perkins, 'The Knights Templars in the British Isles', *English Historical Review*, 25 (1910), 224, suggests that at the time of their arrest, there were only 144 Templars in Britain, including no more than 20 knights and 16 priests. See also idem, 'The Wealth of the Knights Templars in England and the Disposition of It after their Dissolution', *American Historical Review*, 15 (1910), 255.

14 *CCR 1307–1313*, p. 14. A renewal of the order to provide 4*d.* per day along with an order to repair the coverings of the New Temple was issued on 14 December 1308: *CCR 1307–1313*, p. 90.

15 Clarence Perkins, 'The Trial of the Knights Templars in England', *English Historical Review*, 24 (1909), 433. The king also licensed de la More, on 15 December 1307, to appoint Michael de Baskerville and Peter de Oteryngham as his attorneys in diverse matters concerning the order for a term of one year: *CPR 1307–1313*, p. 28.

16 *CCR 1307–1313*, p. 35. The writ to the sheriff of Kent states that Bek has mainperned More, with the king's consent.

17 For Edward II's regard for Bek, see Hilda Johnstone, *Edward of Carnarvon* (Manchester, 1946), p. 102.

18 Perkins, 'Trial of the Knights Templars', 433.

He was several days late, making his future father-in-law wait in Boulogne, and the wedding was preceded by contentious negotiations about a number of issues, but most of all the English tenure of Aquitaine.[19] The matter of the Templars was certainly discussed. Philip was accompanied to Boulogne by Enguerran de Floyran, who had initially denounced the order to Philip, while on the other side, Edward's envoy Thomas Cobham was prepared to respond to the charge that the English king had not been obedient to the king of France in the matter of the Templars.[20]

Whatever the exact nature of his conversations with Philip IV in Boulogne, having returned from France, and the Templars now having been arrested, Edward showed a concern to ascertain the extent of the Templar holdings in England – as he had been directed by the pope – but little concern to facilitate a hasty trial, let alone conviction, of the knights.[21] Clarence Perkins long ago argued that the treatment of the Templars in England changed for the worse in the autumn of 1308, when on 28 November Edward II ordered the rearrest of William de la More and all other Templars throughout the realm. Perkins' explanation for this reversal of policy is that Clement V had placed increased pressure on Edward to proceed with the suppression of the order in the bull *Faciens misericordiam* of 12 August, which described the confessions of the French Templars, and thus reaffirmed the original charges leveled against the order.[22] But *Faciens misericordiam* must be placed into a specifically English context. Edward's return from France in early 1308 had not been greeted with universal rejoicing. Political and financial issues dating back to the reign of Edward I, coupled with his favouritism towards Piers Gaveston and a perceived neglect of the young queen, led to growing tensions between the king and his magnates. The coronation itself was delayed, and rumours abounded that Philip IV was involved in plots against the favourite on his daughter's behalf. Under increasing pressure, on 18 May 1308, Edward had agreed to Gaveston's exile. Edward immediately wrote to both Clement V and Philip IV seeking their support in engineering the recall of Gaveston.[23] Towards that end,

---

19 Brown, 'Political Repercussions of Family Ties', 585–6; *Gascon Register A*, ed. George P. Cuttino, 2 vols (London, 1975), vol. 2, no. 78, pp. 365–73.

20 *Gascon Register A*, vol. 2, no. 78, p. 368. The possessions of the Templars in Gascony was also the subject of a subsequent petition from John Hastings, seneschal of Gascony, to Pope Clement V, leading the pope to write to Philip IV on 9 November 1310: ibid., pp. 223–6. The goods of the Templars continued to be a contentious issue in 1311, when Hastings issued a report on the state of Gascony: ibid., pp. 691–2.

21 Edward ordered the treasurer and barons of the exchequer to undertake this on 4 March 1309. *Foedera*, vol. 2.1, p. 70; *CCR 1307–1313*, p. 94. Inventories of these confiscated lands survive as The National Archives (TNA): Public Record Office (PRO) E 142/10–19, 89–118.

22 Perkins, 'Trial of the Knights Templars', 433.

23 For the causes of Gaveston's second exile and Edward II's response to it, see Jeffrey S. Hamilton, *Piers Gaveston, earl of Cornwall 1307–1312: Politics and Patronage*

on 16 June, the English king made a grant of the town and castle of Blanquefort to Bertrand de Got, nephew and namesake of the pope. Valued at £300 sterling (1,500 *livres chipotois*) per annum, this grant was made 'on account of the love we bear towards the most holy father in Christ, the supreme pontiff Clement'.[24] The placation of the pope would continue into the next year: in January 1309, several hundred pounds were spent on jewels for Clement himself, while in May of that year, the right of justice in Budos was conceded to Raymond-Guillaume de Budos, another nephew of the pope.[25] Edward also made political concessions to the pope, such as freeing the bishops of Glasgow and St Andrews, both of whom had languished in captivity since June 1306.[26] The entirety of Edward's policy throughout the second year of the reign – towards the pope, towards the king of France and towards the English nobility – was centered on obtaining Gaveston's return from exile in Ireland. In England this policy was remarked upon by the anonymous author of the *Vita Edwardi Secundi*, who said that the king 'bent one after another to his will, with gifts, promises and blandishments'.[27] These gifts and promises very likely included the lands and/or the wealth of the Templars,[28] and so on several different levels Edward's policy towards the order was more and more directed towards their ultimate suppression. Clement V's response to Edward's pleas for assistance was embodied in the previously mentioned papal bull *Faciens misericordiam*, but this, significantly, was followed on the next day by further letters exhorting the king and his barons to seek concord, and announcing the dispatch of papal negotiators, including Gaveston's nephew Betrand de Caillau, to achieve this goal.[29] The timing of these two letters, as well as their import, seems more than coincidentally linked, as does Edward's consequent behavior regarding the Templars. Edward's gifts to the pope and his relatives are best seen as part of the same initiative that led him to adhere ever more closely to the letter, if not necessarily the spirit, of papal directives concerning the Templars. His policy

---

in the Reign of Edward II (Detroit, 1988), pp. 48–57, 67–74.

[24] *Foedera*, vol. 2.1, p. 51.

[25] Ibid., vol. 2.1, pp. 72–3, 82.

[26] Ibid., vol. 2.1, pp. 53, 65; *CPR 1307–1313*, p. 94.

[27] *Vita Edwardi Secundi: The Life of Edward the Second*, ed. and trans. Wendy R. Childs (Oxford, 2005), p. 15..

[28] The king had immediately ordered inventories of the movables on Templar estates as well as estimates of annual income. Schedules of the accounts rendered by royal keepers on the confiscated lands survive as TNA: PRO E 358/18–20. As early as March 1308 the king began to present clerks to Templar churches, e.g. John Mahen of Norton to Cardynton in the diocese of Hereford, *CPR 1307–1313*, p. 57. At about the same time he ordered the wool stockpiled in various Templar estates delivered to the Ballardi of Lucca to pay royal debts. More importantly, the crown treated the Templar estates as escheats that could be alienated and distributed as patronage: *CCR 1313–1317*, pp. 255–6, 263; *CCR 1333–1336*, p. 638.

[29] TNA: PRO E 101/373/24 m. 2.

of 'gifts, promises and blandishments', bore fruit by the spring of 1309, when Clement V lifted the pending sentence of excommunication against Gaveston, clearing the way for the favorite's return.[30] But how did it affect the trial of the Templars?

On 13 September 1309, safe conducts were issued for the papal inquisitors – the abbot of Lagny and Master Sicard de Vaur, a canon of Narbonne – who were to join the bishop of Orléans along with the archbishops of Canterbury and York and the bishops of Durham, Lincoln, Chester and London as a board of inquiry.[31] Edward II's continuing doubts about the trial are indicated by his insistence that every session of this initial inquisition be attended by the bishop of London, Ralph Baldock, a trusted royal administrator of long experience.[32] Next day, nearly two years after the initial arrests in France and 20 months after their arrest in England, Edward ordered the sheriffs throughout England to bring the knights in their custody from their various counties to York, Lincoln and London respectively in order to appear before the inquisitors.[33] Interestingly, three months later, on 14 December 1309, the king issued another writ to the sheriffs containing an 'order to arrest all Templars wandering about … as the king understands that divers Templars are wandering about in secular habit, committing apostasy'.[34] Similar indications that the Templars were not being kept under close guard would continue to recur in the months and years ahead, suggesting royal indifference at the very least.[35]

The initial round of questioning in October and November 1309 proved very unsatisfactory to the papal inquisitors. Not only would none of the English Templars confess, but the inquisitors were also unable to convince seven recent initiates to abjure their oaths and leave the order. With no meaningful eyewitness testimony, confessions were essential. Torture was the obvious answer, but English common law and English popular sentiment were both against this. On 9 December 1309, the southern provincial council meeting at Lambeth petitioned the king on the inquisitors' behalf to allow the application of procedures consistent with ecclesiastical law. Edward consented, but only grudgingly and somewhat equivocally, allowing them to 'act and proceed against the Templars as related to their office although nothing should be done against our crown or the state of our kingdom'. A month later, on 15 January 1310, Edward II had to reiterate his assent.[36] Subsequently, on 29 January 1310, a second round of inquisitions was

---

30 *Registrum Simonis de Gandavo, Diocesis Saresbiriensis, 1297–1315*, ed. Cyril Thomas Flower and Michael C.B. Dawes (Oxford, 1934), vol. 1, pp. 314–16.

31 *CPR 1307–1313*, p. 190.

32 *CCR 1307–1313*, p. 230.

33 Ibid., pp. 175–76; *Foedera*, vol. 2.1, p. 94.

34 *Foedera,* vol. 2.1, p. 100; *CCR 1307–1313*, p. 189.

35 *Foedera*, vol. 2.1, p. 125 (4 January 1311).

36 *Councils and Synods with other Documents Relating to the English Church*, vol. 2, part 2, 1265–1313, ed. Frederick M. Powicke and Christopher R. Cheney (Oxford, 1964), pp. 1267–9.

undertaken. Ten days later, on 8 February, William de Dene was assigned by the king to oversee the work of torture.[37] This is, of course, the same seneschal of Agen to whom Edward had turned in his doubt of the initial charges more than two years earlier and is suggestive of his continuing doubts. The king also issued an order to subject the Templars to solitary confinement, along with a reiteration of his assent to the use of ecclesiastical practice (i.e., torture).[38] It is interesting to note that Edward's order to confine the Templars separately on 1 March 1310 was followed on the 12th with a letter to the sheriff of York suggesting the continuing ease of the Templars' confinement:

> Order to keep the Templars in his charge in such custody that he can answer for them at the king's order, as the king understands that he permits the Templars whom he lately ordered the sheriffs of Northumberland, Cumberland, Westmorland, Lancaster, Nottingham, Derby, Salop and Stafford to send to York castle to be guarded there by the said sheriff to wander about in contempt of the king's order.[39]

Despite the king's expressed displeasure, one wonders if another message was being conveyed to the sheriff by word of mouth, especially as the king wrote yet again some 10 months later, on 4 January 1311, once more voicing his surprise at learning that the sheriff 'permits [the Templars] to wander about, contrary to [the king's] orders'.[40]

Regardless of the strictness of their confinement, however, there were still no confessions forthcoming. Separate inquisitions in York (where the question of torture was debated by the northern provincial council, but seems never to have been approved or employed) and Lincoln in April and May 1310 proved no more successful than the earlier sessions. The inquisitors expressed their frustration in a letter to the archbishop of Canterbury in June 1310, blaming their failure on a lack of qualified torturers. They also suggested more drastic measures including, significantly, the removal of the prisoners from the custody of royal officials; a diet of bread and water (on alternating days); a public propaganda campaign to include the reading of the French Templars' confessions in order to sway popular sentiment; and perhaps most hopefully, the transfer of the English Templars to Ponthieu, where the methods of the inquisition might be applied more rigorously and more fruitfully.[41] Edward's indifference, if not outright opposition, to these proposals led to a further letter to the king from Clement V on 6 August 1310, complaining of the king's lack of zeal and the general obstruction of the process in England. Edward's response was symbolically to wash his hands of the whole

---

37 *CPR 1307–1313*, p. 209.

38 *Foedera*, vol. 2.1, p. 104; *CCR 1307–1313*, p. 196.

39 *CCR 1307–1313*, p. 206.

40 *Foedera*, vol. 2.1, p. 125; *CCR 1307–1313*, p. 295.

41 Perkins, 'Trial of the Knights Templars', 437–8.

affair by transferring the Templars into the keeping of the sheriffs of London. The conditions of the imprisoned Templars probably deteriorated at this point – autumn 1310 rather than autumn 1308 as argued by Perkins – and especially in the following spring, when the mayor and aldermen of London were ordered to provide the sheriffs with further gates for the custody of the Templars, many more having recently been sent from Lincoln to London to be examined by the inquisitors.[42]

The king having failed to respond favorably to a second request from the pope to relocate the inquisition to Ponthieu in December 1310,[43] another round of hearings was held in London in March and April of 1311, in which the prisoners who had previously been held in Lincoln were interrogated with the same unsatisfactory result. On Monday 5 July 1311, as the trial wound to a conclusion, the master of the order in England, William de la More, appeared before John Langton, bishop of Chichester, at the church of All Hallows Barking.[44] He declined the opportunity to offer a defense for the order, none being necessary as they were guilty of no crimes, as evident from the lack of confessions extracted after more than three years in custody.

Remarkably, in June and July 1311, during a fifth session of hearings in London, three English Templars finally confessed. The first of these three, Stephen de Stapelbrigg, had only been arrested on 10 June 1311, after having spent the previous three and a half years at large. On 23 June, he confessed to many of the charges against the Templars including denial of Christ and spitting on the cross. Thomas Totti of Thoroldsby also confessed that the Templars renounced Christ. Finally, on 1 July, John de Stoke, a Templar chaplain, after initial denials, admitted that the Templars renounced Christ.[45] The trial of the Templars in England was at an end. All that remained was the disposition of their persons and properties.

Following the trial, the Templars were informed that if they admitted not their guilt, but rather their inability to prove their innocence, and would submit to the provincial councils, they would be received back into the Church. Most seem to have followed this procedure and were then dispersed among monastic communities throughout England, still retaining their allowances of 4*d.* per day. Only the provincial master of the order, William de la More, and the preceptor of Auvergne, Imbert Blanke, remained imprisoned. More died in the Tower on 20 December 1312, after which his daily allowance of 2*s.* was transferred to

42 *CCR 1307–1313*, pp. 290, 291–92, 308. As late as 1322 Simon Corp, former mayor of London, was still seeking compensation for the expenses associated with the imprisonment of the Templars: *CCR 1318–1323*, p. 414.

43 *Reg. Clem. V*, vol. 5, no. 6670, pp. 84–6.

44 David Wilkins, *Concilia Magnae Britanniae et Hiberniae* (London, 1737), vol. 2, p. 390.

45 *CCR 1307–1313*, pp. 316–17; Wilkins, *Concilia*, pp. 345–6, 351, 356–7, 367, 383–8.

Blanke.[46] On 6 April 1313, Edward ordered that Imbert Blanke be transferred from the custody of the sheriffs of London to that of the archbishop of Canterbury, 'to ordain concerning him according to ecclesiastical law',[47] but the outcome of this transfer is unknown as Blanke disappears from the records after February 1314. Alan Forey has examined the process by which the former Templars – including even Stapelbrigg, Totty and Stoke – were absolved and assigned to religious houses throughout the kingdom.[48] The process seems to have moved very quickly in the southern province and only a bit less so in the northern. Forey detects little pattern to the assignment of the former Templars, aside for the avoidance of convents of friars. In terms of the severity of their penance, Forey detects an interesting pattern indicating that this was based on the longevity of their service in the order rather than their testimony at trial or any admissions of guilt. Most appear to have accepted their new circumstances fairly readily, and the greatest difficulties tended to be occasioned by financial considerations relating to their continued maintenance. This brings us to the question of the disposition of the Templar lands in England.

The conveyance of the Templar lands proved more complicated than the dispersal of the persons of the Templars, in part at least because the king once again took an active, and somewhat contrariant, role. On 1 August 1312, Edward II issued an order to the prior of the Hospital of St John of Jerusalem prohibiting him from proceeding further in the assignment of the goods of the Templars prior to the next parliament.[49] On 28 November, he issued orders to various keepers of Templar lands and holders of office to deliver the Templar lands to Albert de Nigro Castro (Schwarzburg), grand preceptor of the Hospital of St. John of Jerusalem, in accordance with the pope's decision at the council of Vienne, but 'saving the right of the king and his subjects according to the force and effect of his protest'.[50] Interestingly, the king seems to have anticipated trouble, as the sheriffs were ordered to execute these orders should the keepers themselves be remiss, and 'to protect the above persons whilst executing their commission'.[51] It would appear, moreover, that the king kept all of the moveable goods, particularly animals, on Templar lands for himself.[52] Even more importantly, he also kept all of the Templars' deeds, charters and rolls until August 1324, thereby preventing the Hospitallers from quickly enforcing their rights and taking seisin of Templar

46 *CCR 1307–1313*, p. 533.

47 Ibid., p. 523.

48 Alan J. Forey, 'Ex-Templars in England,' *Journal of Ecclesiastical History*, 53 (2002), 18–37.

49 *CCR 1307–1313*, p. 544.

50 *CPR 1313–1317*, p. 52.

51 *CCR 1313–1317*, pp. 29–30. A pair of notarial instruments enrolled in ibid., pp. 88–9, record Albert of Schwarzburg's request for delivery.

52 *CPR 1313–1317*, p. 44, where orders to that effect are given to Richard Squier, keeper of the Templar lands in Kent.

lands.[53] The statute transferring the Templar lands to the Hospitallers was only obtained on 26 March 1324 by the astute application of bribery not only to the king, but also the Despensers, by the prior, Thomas Larcher.[54] But even in the early years of the reign of Edward III, the Hospitallers were struggling to enforce their rights to former Templar lands universally and were heavily burdened with debt. This situation was eventually reversed by the efforts of Brother Leonard of Tibertis, who arrived in England in August 1327, and was appointed prior at the urging of Edward III in 1330.[55] By this point, virtually all of the former Templars had passed from the scene with little if any notice, leaving only their name on their former estates.

In conclusion, the trial and suppression of the Templars in England was far from cataclysmic, and much of the explanation for this lies with Edward II. Initially, and arguably finally, unconvinced of the charges against the order, the English king delayed, obstructed and mitigated the process in England at every turn. The Templars were suppressed in the end, but were hardly purged. Edward II profited greatly from the suppression of the order, holding onto Templar lands and goods long after the pope had awarded them to the Hospitallers. Nevertheless, it is important in the English case to separate the trial and treatment of the Templars themselves from the economic consequences of their suppression. In England, the latter was not the cause of the former, as it clearly appears to have been in France, but merely its consequence.

---

53 TNA: PRO E 40/1469 records a grant of 28 June 1324 of the messuage of the 'New Temple' in London by Larcher to the younger Despenser. See Perkins, 'Wealth of the Knights Templars', 259. This obstruction was particularly evident in the case of the New Temple in London: Parker, *Knights Templars in England*, p. 101 n. 124.

54 Perkins, 'Wealth of the Knights Templars', 260–261. See also Mark Buck, *Politics, Finance, and the Church in the Reign of Edward II: Walter Stapeldon, Treasurer of England* (Cambridge, 1983), p. 145.

55 Clarence Perkins, 'The Knights Hospitallers in England after the Fall of the Order of the Temple,' *English Historical Review*, 45 (1930), 285–9.

Chapter 18

The Trial of the Templars in Ireland

Helen J. Nicholson

Scholars of the trial of the Templars have tended to overlook Ireland. The trial was considered in two articles published early in the twentieth century by Anglo-Irish scholars, an M.Phil. thesis from University College Dublin in the 1980s, and a Ph.D. thesis from Evanston, Illinois, in the early twenty-first century. In addition, the inventories of the Templars' lands, taken when the brothers were arrested early in February 1308, were published in the 1960s.[1] The trial in Britain has not received much more attention from scholars, but it is surprising (although gratifying) that conspiracy theorists have not spent more time considering the trial in Ireland.

I suspect that this is largely because the natives of Great Britain now tend to overlook Ireland. However, in the middle ages, communications between the two islands were perceived to be much closer: the historian Paul Dryburgh has recently written of 'a historical tradition in which Ireland acts as a refuge for those fleeing persecution in England'.[2] To the seagoing peoples who inhabited its shores, the Irish Sea was not a barrier but a thoroughfare which could be travelled relatively easily in good weather. Possibly the most obvious evidence of this today is the large number of churches in south Wales dedicated to St Bride (the Irish saint St Bridget of Kildare) and the large numbers of people in Ireland surnamed 'Walsh'.[3]

---

1 Herbert Wood, 'The Templars in Ireland', *Proceedings of the Royal Irish Academy*, C 25 (1906–7), 363–75; M.H. MacInerny, 'The Templars in Ireland', *The Irish Ecclesiastical Review*, 5th series 11 (1913), 225–45; Martin Messinger, 'The Trial of the Knights Templar in Ireland', unpublished M.Phil. thesis, University College Dublin, 1988; Maeve B. Callan, '"No Such Art in This Land": Heresy and Witchcraft in Ireland, 1310–1360', unpublished Ph.D. thesis, Northwestern University, Evanston, IL (2002). I am very grateful to Dr Callan for permission to cite her thesis. For the inventories of Templar properties in Ireland, see: Gearóid MacNiocaill, 'Documents Relating to the Suppression of the Templars in Ireland', *Analecta Hibernica*, 24 (1967), pp. 183–226. For the manuscript evidence, see Oxford, Bodleian Library, MS Bodley 454, fols 134r–155 (summarised in *Concilia Magnae Britanniae et Hiberniae*, ed. David Wilkins, vol. 2 (London, 1737), which is hereafter cited as Wilkins), pp. 373–80.

2 Paul Dryburgh, 'The Last Refuge of a Scoundrel? Edward II and Ireland, 1321–7', in *The Reign of Edward II: New Perspectives*, ed. Gwilym Dodd and Anthony Musson (Woodbridge, 2006), pp. 119–39, here p. 119.

3 There are churches dedicated to St Bridget at St Brides in Pembrokeshire, St Brides Major, St Brides Minor and St Brides super Ely in the Vale of Glamorgan, St Brides Wentloog

Even those scholars of medieval England who habitually ignore the smaller island a few miles away to the west will be familiar with at least one famous episode involving Ireland, when a prominent figure in English politics went to Ireland or was sent to Ireland to escape trouble. For example, William de Braose, to escape the anger of King John, fled to Ireland in 1208–10, while Piers Gaveston was sent to govern Ireland in 1308 because King Edward II's nobles wanted him exiled.[4] For although the kings of England since John had claimed the title of 'lord of Ireland', in fact the English government in Ireland was not under close royal control. Kings of England generally left their representatives in Ireland to get on with the job of government without royal interference. While the native Irish continued their traditional conflicts, and carried on conflict with the Cymro-Norman and Anglo-Norman incomers as foreigners from over the sea, those same incomers regarded themselves as separate from the native Welsh, English and Anglo-Normans beyond the sea. By the early fourteenth century the descendents of those who had come to Ireland from Britain in the twelfth and thirteenth centuries regarded themselves as belonging to Ireland, not to Britain. So it is no surprise that the trial of the Templars in Ireland was somewhat different from that in Britain, in its procedures, its record, and its conclusion.

King Edward II of England sent instructions on 20 December 1307 to John Wogan, his justiciar in Ireland, to arrest the Templars, make an inventory of their possessions, and keep the Templars in custody but not in harsh prison until such time as he should order otherwise. The writ reached the justiciar on 25 January 1308, and the Templars were arrested on 3 February 1308.[5] The trial, however, did not begin for another two years. The *inquisitores pravitatis heretice* sent by Pope Clement V to conduct the trial in England, Scotland and Ireland were Deodatus, abbot of Lagny in the diocese of Paris, and Sicard de Lavaur, canon of Narbonne,

---

near Newport/ Casnewydd, St Brides Netherwent and Skenfrith in Monmouthshire. For 'Walsh', see Francis Xavier Martin, 'Introduction: Medieval Ireland', in *A New History of Ireland*, vol. 2: *Medieval Ireland, 1169–1534*, ed. Art Cosgrave (Oxford, 1987), p. lii.

4 Sidney Painter, *The Reign of King John* (Baltimore, 1949), pp. 238–50; Wilfred Lewis Warren, *King John* (London, 1961), pp. 186–7; Seán Duffy, 'John and Ireland: The Origin of England's Irish Problem', in *King John: New Interpretations*, ed. Stephen D. Church (Woodbridge, 1999), pp. 221–45; Jeffrey S. Hamilton, *Piers Gaveston, Earl of Cornwall 1307–1312: Politics and Patronage in the Reign of Edward II* (Detroit, 1988), pp. 50–66.

5 Wood, 'Templars in Ireland', 346–48; Messinger, 'The Trial of the Knights Templar in Ireland', pp. 16–17; *Foedera, conventiones, literae et cuiusque generis acta publica inter reges Angliae et alios quos in imperatores, reges, pontifices, principes vel communitates*, ed. Thomas Rymer, revised by Robert Sanderson, Adam Clarke and Frederick Holbrooke, vol. 2, part 1, 1307–27 (London, 1818), p. 23; *Calendar of the Justiciary Rolls, or Proceedings in the Court of the Justiciar of Ireland, I to VII years of Edward II*, ed. Herbert Wood and Albert E. Langman, revised by Margaret C. Griffith (Dublin, 1956), pp. 23–4.

papal chaplain and judge, who arrived in England in mid-September 1309.[6] They did not proceed to Ireland themselves but appointed judges-delegate: *Thomas [de Chaddesworth], decanus Dubliniensis, Bindum de Bandinell., Sancti Pauli, Florenc. dyocesis ac Johannem Balla, Clonfertensis, ecclesiarum canonicos*, who received a royal safe-conduct on 29 September 1309.[7] Thomas of Chaddesworth or Chedworth also acted as deputy of the absentee archbishop-elect of Dublin, collector of the papal tax of one-tenth of ecclesiastical incomes, and as lieutenant of the treasurer of Ireland. In addition, he was the leading light in the prosecution of Philip de Braybrooke, canon of Holy Trinity, who on 4 September 1310 was found guilty by the archbishop-elect of Dublin of being a relapsed heretic, and sentenced to do penance.[8] I have not been able to discover anything about the other two investigators in Ireland; one had presumably accompanied the two inquisitors from the pope, while the other was a local man. The archbishop of Dublin was not involved in the trial in Ireland as there was no archbishop of Dublin at the time: Richard de Haverings, who was appointed by the pope in 1307, was never consecrated and resigned from the appointment in 1311. Instead, Walter Calf, bishop of Kildare, appointed commissioners as required.[9]

The Irish interrogations were based on a short list of around 88 charges against the Templars that was used in episcopal inquiries, such as those in the British Isles and in Aragon.[10] Whereas the list of charges used in England had an error so that the English Templars were not asked whether they held chapter meetings at night,

---

6 Messinger, 'The Trial of the Knights Templar in Ireland', p. 17; *Foedera*, vol. 2.1, p. 88; MS Bod. 454, fol. 1r (Wilkins, p. 329).

7 Quoted by MacInerny, 'Templars in Ireland', 245; Wood, 'Templars in Ireland', 351; Messinger, 'The Trial of the Knights Templar in Ireland', p. 17; *Foedera*, vol. 2.1, p. 93; *Calendar of the Patent Rolls Preserved in the Public Record Office, Prepared under the Superintendance of the Deputy Keeper of the Rolls, Edward II* (hereafter cited as *CPR*) *AD 1307–1313* (London, 1894), p. 192.

8 'The Memoranda Roll of the Irish Exchequer for 3 Edward II', 2 vols, ed. David Victor Craig, unpublished Ph.D. thesis, University of Dublin, 1984, vol. 2: text and appendices, pp. 9, 337, 385, 414, nos 34, 1021, 1214, 1268 (my thanks to the librarian of Trinity College, Dublin, for permission to cite this thesis); Callan, '"No Such Art"', pp. 56, 100–136, 427–8. Callan describes Philip de Braybrooke's sentence as 'quite lenient': he was sentenced to a year under custody in All Hallows Priory, Dublin, with fasting on Wednesdays and Fridays (ibid., p. 100).

9 MS Bod. 454, fol. 150r; *A New History of Ireland*, vol. 9: *Maps, Genealogies, Lists: A Companion to Irish History, II*, ed. Theodore William Moody, Francis Xavier Martin and Francis John Byrne (Oxford, 1984), p. 314.

10 The short list of charges appears in MS Bod. 454, fols 7r–8v, and was printed by Wilkins, pp. 331–3. A longer list, comprising some 127 charges, was used in France by the papal commissioners, in the papal states, and in Brindisi: see *UT*, vol. 2, pp. 119–24. For use of these different versions of the charges, see *The Trial of the Templars in Cyprus: A Complete English Edition*, ed. and trans. Anne Gilmour-Bryson (Leiden, 1998), p. 9 and note 37; Alan Forey, *The Fall of the Templars in the Crown of Aragon* (Aldershot, 2001),

the list used in Ireland was correct; the Templars in Ireland replied that they did not. Rather than grouping the charges under subheadings as was done in England, the inquisitors asked the brothers to answer each charge individually, which meant that the records of the proceedings were rather lengthy. Proceedings began on 6 February 1310 and ended on 6 June.[11] On 14 July 1310, King Edward II granted safe-conduct through Ireland to the three judges-delegate in Ireland, who were presumably on their way back to England.[12]

Not all the Templars in Ireland during 1308–11 were actually interrogated. Nineteen Templars were paid an allowance by the royal exchequer in 1308:[13] Henry Danet, master in Ireland; Thomas de Lyndeseye, his *socius* (associate or aide); William de Warenne; Stephen de Stapelbrugge, his *socius*; Thomas de Rathenny; Robert de Porbryg; Hugh de Broghton; John de Faucresham; Henry Mautravers; Richard de Bostelesham; Henry de Aslakeby, Ralph de Bradley; Richard de Oppledene; John le Romeyn; Walter le Lung; Henry de la Ford; Michael de Sutton; Walter de Jonesby; William de Balygaueran.

Only 14 Templars were interrogated by the inquisitors in Ireland:[14] Richard de Bustleham (previously spelt 'Bostelesham'), Henry de Aslackby (Aslakeby), Robert de Pourbrigge (Porbryg), Henry Danet, Henry Mautravers, John Romayn (le Romeyn), Hugh de Broghem (Broghton), Ralph de Bradley, Adam de Langeport, Richard de Upleadon (Oppledene), Walter de Choneby, John de Faversham (Faucresham), William de Kilros, chaplain, and Henry de la Ford.

Two persons in the first list have different surnames in the second: Walter de Jonesby was also called Walter de Choneby, while William de Balygaueran was also known as William de Kilros. One Templar who was interrogated, Adam de Langeport, did not receive a pension from the Irish exchequer; no reason is given for this omission. Six Templars who received pensions from the Irish exchequer were not interrogated: Thomas de Lyndeseye; William de Warenne; Stephen de Stapelbrugge or Stapelbrigg; Thomas de Rathenny; Walter le Long; Michael de Sutton. Of these, I have no information about Thomas de Rathenny or Michael de Sutton; probably they died before interrogation. In addition, Peter de Malvern and Thomas le Palmer were mentioned in the sheriffs' inventories of the Templars' Irish lands, taken when the Templars were arrested in February 1308, but did not

pp. 79, 106–107 note 30; Alan Forey, 'The Charitable Activities of the Templars', *Viator*, 34 (2003), 114.

11 MS Bod. 454, fols 134r–155, omit the year when events took place. The first date given is on fol. 143r, where it is noted that the date of Brother Richard de Burthesham's first testimony was 6 February; the last date is 6 June, on fol. 155. Herbert Wood judged that this must have been 1310: Wood, 'The Templars in Ireland', 354.

12 *CPR 1307–1313*, p. 267.

13 *Irish Exchequer Payments, 1270–1446*, ed. Philomena Connolly (Dublin, 1998), p. 204.

14 MS Bod. 454, fols 135v, 155 (Wilkins, p. 380 only).

receive an allowance and were not interrogated; presumably they died shortly after the arrests.[15]

The other Templars who received allowances but were not interrogated require more attention. William de Warenne was commander of the Temple in Ireland from 1302 to early 1308.[16] At the time of the Templars' arrest in Ireland, he was commander of Clonoulty.[17] Even though Warenne was still alive in 1312,[18] he was not interrogated with the other Irish Templars in spring 1310. Brother William de Warenne was related to Edmund le Botiller, who was lieutenant justiciar of Ireland in 1304–05, 1312–14 and 1315–18, and earl of Carrick from 1315, although details of the relationship are not known.[19] This relationship to Edmund le Botiller may explain why he was exempted from the humiliation of being interrogated as an alleged heretic. The friars who gave evidence against the Templars in Ireland were particularly hostile toward Warenne;[20] this antagonism may have arisen from the fact that he had been excused from giving evidence during the trial of his order. William de Warenne was not the only leading figure in the English province who was excused from the interrogation: William de la More, grand commander of England, was also apparently spared the initial cross-examination.

Thomas de Lindsey was an English fugitive in Ireland, who was not interrogated in Ireland; on his return to England in 1312, he submitted to the Church and was assigned penance.[21] There is no explanation given as to why he was not interrogated in Ireland, although the royal justiciar in Ireland knew he was there because the exchequer was paying him a pension. I suggest that, because he was an outsider, the inquisitors in Ireland considered that it was not their responsibility to interrogate him. That said, they did not send him back to England to face interrogation.

Stephen de Stapelbrugge, recorded in Ireland at Michaelmas 1308 as *socius* of the former commander of Ireland, Brother William de Warenne,[22] was almost

---

15 MacNiocaill, 'Documents', 199, 202, 207.

16 See Wood, 'The Templars in Ireland', 333; *Calendar of the Justiciary Rolls or Proceedings in the Court of the Justiciar of Ireland Preserved in the Public Record Office of Ireland: Edward I, Part 2, XXXIII to XXXV Years*, ed. James Mills, under the direction of the master of the rolls in Ireland (London, 1914), pp. 291, 292, 334, 357.

17 MacNiocaill, 'Documents', 205.

18 *Irish Exchequer Payments*, p. 217.

19 Wood, 'Templars in Ireland', 333; *Calendar of the Justiciary Rolls: I to VII years of Edward II*, p. 36.

20 MS Bod. 454, fols 151r, 153r, 153v (Wilkins, p. 378 only).

21 *Irish Exchequer Payments*, p. 204; London, The National Archives of the UK: Public Record Office (hereafter cited as TNA:PRO) E101/235/13; MacNiocaill, 'Documents', 198, 222; Alan Forey, 'Ex-Templars in England', *Journal of Ecclesiastical History*, 53 (2002), 18–37, here 36.

22 *Irish Exchequer Payments, 1270–1446*, p. 204 (maintenance payments for Templars 3 Feb–29 Sept. 1308); on p. 209 (Michaelmas 1308–14 April 1309) he is not named; for the Latin, see TNA:PRO E101/235/13.

certainly the same as the Stephen de Stapelbrugge (now Stalbridge, Dorset),[23] who was reported as a fugitive by the Templars in England in 1309–10. He had been commander of Lydley in Shropshire, but departed before he could be arrested.[24] Stephen de Stapelbrugge was arrested on 10 June 1311 in Wiltshire, England, and was transferred under guard to London, where he was interrogated on 23 June 1311 and confessed to denying Christ on his reception into the order of the Temple and spitting next to the cross. On 27 June, he abjured all heresies and was formally admitted back into the Church. He was sent to a monastery to do penance.[25] Possibly he had not been interrogated in Ireland with the other Irish Templars because, like Thomas de Lindsey, he was an outsider.

Given that Thomas de Lindsey was definitely and Stephen de Stapelbrugge was probably a Templar fugitive from England, it is possible that the otherwise unknown Walter le Lung who was in Ireland in 1308 but who was not interrogated, was the 'Walter le Rebel' reported missing by the archbishop of York.[26] It is interesting that the England government in Dublin was prepared to pay the fugitives from England an allowance, but that the inquisitors did not interrogate them. If they did report these fugitives' whereabouts to the inquisitors in England, this was not recorded by the latter.

The Templars in Ireland were interrogated three times. In the course of the first set of interrogations several brothers amended their testimonies, but except for the grand commander, Henry Danet, none said anything that indicated that the Templars were heretics, although some did appear ill-informed or confused over the order's procedures regarding confession and penance.[27] When Brother William de Kilros, the only chaplain of the order in Ireland, was interrogated a fourth time, he made statements that could be interpreted to confirm some of the charges against the order, but in fact proved nothing.[28] He also complained that

---

23 Spelt 'Staplebrige' in Domesday Book: *Domesday Book*, ed. Ann Williams and Geoffrey H. Martin (London and New York, 2003), p. 1403.

24 MS Bod. 454, fol. 96v (Wilkins omits).

25 *Calendar of the Close Rolls Preserved in the Public Record Office, Edward II, AD 1307–1313* (London, 1892), pp. 316–17; Alan Forey, 'Desertions and Transfers from Military Orders (Twelfth to Early-Fourteenth Centuries)', *Traditio*, 60 (2005), 189 and n. 261; Forey, 'Ex-Templars', 18, 35; 'confessed' MS Bod. 454, fol. 160r–v (Wilkins, pp. 383–4).

26 *Irish Exchequer Payments*, p. 204; *The Register of William Greenfield, Lord Archbishop of York, 1306–1315*, ed. William Brown and Alexander Hamilton Thompson, part four, Surtees Society, 152 (London, 1938), p. 337.

27 The testimonies have been briefly analysed by Messinger, 'Trial of the Knights Templar in Ireland', pp. 25–43, and analysed in detail by Callan, '"No Such Art"', pp. 57–84.

28 MS Bod. 454, fol. 150r (Wilkins, p. 377, with some differences): *dicit quod quando magnus magister audit confessionem fratris alicuius dicti ordinis precepit fratri capellano eum absolvere a peccatis suis, quamvis capellanus confessionem fratrum non audivit.* If this was true, it would indicate sloppy procedures within the order but error of ignorance

priests in the order of the Temple could not be promoted above the level they held when they entered the order.[29]

I have recently considered Henry Danet's testimony in detail elsewhere.[30] He had arrived in Ireland only a few days before the arrest of the Templars there, and although he accused his fellow Templars in the east of heretical actions, he denied all wrongdoing himself. The American scholar Clarence Perkins judged that Henry Danet's 'contradictory statements must have been the result of torture',[31] but in fact there is no definite evidence that torture was used against the Templars in Ireland.[32] However, Brother Henry was in a vulnerable position. He had replaced a grand commander in Ireland who was not being interrogated. He was an outsider, from England, with no knowledge of Ireland, the Irish or the Anglo-Irish, neither of which groups had much love of the English. According to two of the friars who gave evidence against him, he had been a close associate of the grand master of the order (who had confessed in France to heretical practices) and had been given the command of Ireland for life as a reward for his services.[33] His testimony could have been intended to satisfy his interrogators while leaving himself apparently innocent. But as in Michaelmas term 1312 Henry Danet was released on bail,[34] it seems that the royal justiciar or his government were not worried about Henry Danet's alleged heresy.

The majority of the outside witnesses against the Templars in Ireland were friars. Irish-born friars had a past record of opposition to the English king, and in fact in 1315 many Irish Franciscans would support the Scottish Edward Bruce's invasion of Ireland, while within the mendicant orders in Ireland there were severe tensions between Irish and Anglo-Irish brothers, sometimes resulting in open violence.[35] The Templars in Ireland were either drawn from the Anglo-Irish

---

rather than heresy. *Item dicit quod quidem frater dicti ordinis moram trahens apud Killofan cuius nomen ignorat fuerat sodomititus & positus erat in firmaria apud Killofan & ibidem moriebatur*. The brother is not named, and it is not explained why he should have died.

29 MS Bod. 454, fol. 149v (Wilkins, p. 377).

30 Helen J. Nicholson, 'The Testimony of Brother Henry Danet and the Trial of the Templars in Ireland', in *In Laudem Hierosolymitani: Studies in Crusades and Medieval Culture in Honour of Benjamin Z. Kedar*, ed. Iris Shagrir, Ronnie Ellenblum and Jonathan Riley-Smith (Aldershot, 2007), pp. 411–23.

31 Perkins, 'Trial of the Knights Templars in England', 445.

32 The contemporary record of the Kilkenny witchcraft trial of 1324 states that one of the lay witnesses, a servant, was repeatedly flogged to force a confession: Anne Neary, 'The Origins and Character of the Kilkenny Witchcraft Case of 1324', *Proceedings of the Royal Irish Academy*, C 83 (1983), 337 and note 28. Nothing similar was recorded for the Templar trial.

33 MS Bod. 454, fols 151v, 153r–v (Wilkins, pp. 378–9, omits rest).

34 Callan, '"No Such Art"', p. 55 n. 133, citing Philomena Connolly's then forthcoming edition of the justiciary roll for 6–7 Edward II.

35 Niav Gallagher, 'Two Nations, One Order: The Franciscans in Medieval Ireland', *History Ireland*, 12.2 (2004), 16–20; John Watt, *The Church in Medieval Ireland* (Dublin,

and Cymro-Irish populations or had come directly from England;[36] none bore Irish names. It would be tempting to blame racial tensions for the friars' hostility towards the Templars in Ireland, but for the fact that none of the friars in Ireland who gave evidence against the Templars had Irish names. Their surnames either implied English or Welsh origin, or originated from the area around Dublin. Hence these hostile testimonies must have been inspired by other factors.

In the British Isles the mendicant orders were closely connected with the Templars. The order of the Temple had very few priests in the British Isles,[37] and it is clear from the trial testimonies that the mendicants performed priestly functions for the Templars.[38] That being the case, they should have known about the Templars' alleged heretical practices and taken action; yet they had done nothing until King Philip IV of France acted against the order in autumn 1307. Therefore the mendicants themselves would have been under suspicion for not reporting heresy. In addition, the Franciscan order was already under suspicion of heresy because of the extremism of the spirituals,[39] while the Dominicans in England were experiencing problems of discipline and procedure.[40] Bringing accusations against the Templars would distract attention from the friars' own internal problems. That said, the accusations comprised only unsupported anecdotes and repeated assertions that the Templars were guilty and that this had caused scandal in the Church and peril to souls.

Of 44 witnesses against the Templars in Ireland, very few had any other involvement with the Templars. Richard Balybyn, former minister of the order of Preachers in Ireland, was present during the interrogations of the Irish Templars

1972), pp. 64, 78–80.

36 Helen J. Nicholson, 'International Mobility versus the Needs of the Realm: The Templars and Hospitallers in the British Isles in the Thirteenth and Fourteenth Centuries', in *International Mobility in the Military Orders (Twelfth to Fifteenth Centuries): Travelling on Christ's Business*, ed. Jochen Burgtorf and Helen J. Nicholson (Cardiff, 2006), pp. 87–101.

37 William de Kilros was the only Templar priest in Ireland in 1308, of the 14 Templars interrogated. In England, Brothers Ralph of Barton, Thomas of Burton, William of Warwick, John of Stoke, John of Waddon, William of Winchester, Ralph of Evesham and Ralph of Ruston were priests (MS Bod. 454, fols 13r–v, 36r, 49v, 54r, 106v, 110v, 111r, 126v; Wilkins, pp. 335, 342, 345, 366, 372: two other 'presbyters' on p. 372 are mistranscriptions) while the priest Roger of Stowe (MS Bod. 454, fol. 32r; Wilkins, p. 342) had recently left the order; a total of 108 brothers were interrogated.

38 See MS Bod. 454, fols 91v, 92r–v, 94v, 96r, 97r–v, 151r, 153r–v (Wilkins, pp. 359, 378, 379; omits the rest).

39 Malcolm Lambert, *Medieval Heresy*, 3rd edn (Oxford, 2002), pp. 208–26; David Burr, *The Spiritual Franciscans: From Protest to Persecution in the Century after Saint Francis* (Philadelphia, 2001), pp. 67–158.

40 Andrew George Little, 'A Record of the English Dominicans, 1314', *English Historical Review*, 5 (1890), 107–12, and 6 (1891), 752–3.

and also gave evidence against them.[41] Roger de Eton, guardian of the Friars Minor of Dublin, was another witness of the interrogations of the Irish Templars, as well as giving evidence against the order.[42]

Philip de Slane, lector of the order of preachers in Dublin, who was present during the interrogations of the Templars, also acted as a special royal messenger, going to Munster in 1315–16 at the time of Edward Bruce's invasion of Ireland 'to bring various messages and orders of the king to the magnates there and explain them verbally'. In 1317, he went as a messenger to King Edward II from the king's council in Ireland; in 1318, he was again carrying out the king's business, and in November 1318, he was sent to the papal court by the council of Ireland on business relating to the king. By Easter 1318, he was a member of the king's council in Ireland; in 1321, Pope John XXII made him bishop of Cork, on the king's request.[43] Another official present during the interrogations was Master Philip of Herdele, officer of the court of Archdeacon Matthew of Bela. On 17 November 1309, he received custody of the Templars' former houses of their manor at Kilsarn, Co. Louth. However (according to Master Philip) the previous custodian, Stephen Gernoun, was unwilling to surrender it, and defended himself in the manor *vi et armis*, 'in clear contempt of the lord king's mandate and no small and grave damage to the aforesaid master Philip'. Stephen denied the accusation, stating that he had surrendered the houses as soon as he received instructions to do so, and demanded a formal inquiry; so the sheriff of Louth was ordered to bring him to Dublin for an investigation to be made.[44]

Master William de Hothum, chancellor of the Irish exchequer, was one of the guarantors for Henry Danet when the latter was released on bail. He was keeper of the office of treasurer of Ireland from 1313 to 1314, and chancellor of the Irish exchequer in 1312–17.[45] Brother Hugo le Luminour of the Friars Minor of Dublin,

---

41 *Irish Exchequer Payments*, pp. 171, 189; he is Richard de Balibin in *Calendar of Documents Relating to Ireland, Preserved in Her Majesty's Public Record Office*, ed. Henry S. Sweetman et al., 5 vols (London, 1875–86) (hereafter cited as *CDRI*), vol. 5, p. 166, no. 577, and p. 52.

42 For his death in 1315, see: BL Cotton MS Vespasian B. XI, fol. 131, printed in 'Manuscripts of Irish Interest in the British Museum', ed. Robin Flower, *Analecta Hibernica*, 2 (1931), 335; Callan, '"No Such Art"', p. 25, n. 5.

43 *CDRI*, pp. 245, 253, 257, 267, 295, 307; Urban Flanagan, 'Papal Provisions in Ireland, 1305–78', *Historical Studies*, 3, ed. James Hogan (London and Cork, 1961), pp. 92–103, at p. 100. For further information see Margaret Murphy, 'Slane, Philip (*d.* 1327)', *Oxford Dictionary of National Biography* (hereafter cited as *ODNB*), http://www.oxforddnb.com/view/article/25712.

44 'Memoranda Roll of the Irish Exchequer for 3 Edward II', ed. Craig, vol. 2, pp. 92, 352, nos 193, 1064.

45 Roy Martin Haines, 'Hotham, William of (*c.*1255–1298)', *ODNB*, http://www.oxforddnb.com/view/article/13857; *Irish Exchequer Payments*, p. 222; James F. Lydon, 'The Enrolled Account of Alexander Bicknor, Treasurer of Ireland, 1308–14', *Analecta Hibernica*, 30 (1982), 7–46, here 19 and note 8; Callan, '"No Such Art"', p. 55, n. 133.

a witness against the Templars, clearly had some interest in the Holy Land. In 1323–24, he accompanied his fellow Franciscan Friar Symon Simeonis on a journey to the Holy Land, and died on the journey.[46]

None of this information gives any additional insight as to why the friars in Ireland were so hostile towards the Templars, while hardly anyone else was prepared to come forward to say anything against the order. The fact that so few of these friars have left any trace in the records except for their brief appearance before the inquisitors suggests that the majority were nonentities who were pressurised by their superiors into making some sort of statement, or possibly that they hoped to win favour or advancement by testifying against the order. As well as these religious men, four laymen gave evidence. Two merchants (Robert of Hereford and Michelm of Bras) spoke against the Templars, based (they claimed) on what they had seen of the order in Cyprus.[47] A former servant of the Templars who had been on Cyprus, Thomas of Broghton, had some favourable and some unfavourable things to say about the order.[48] None of this evidence was corroborated by other witnesses.

The trial of the Templars in Ireland was rather different from that elsewhere. Any Templar who was a visitor, rather than a regular member of a commandery in Ireland, was not cross-examined. There is no evidence that the Templars were required to abjure all heresies. There is no record of the Irish Templars being sent to monasteries to do penance, as was done in England. They remained in prison until Michaelmas term 1312, when Henry Danet was released on bail.[49] The Irish historian Herbert Wood surmised that the other Templars in Ireland were released shortly afterwards. He did not discover where they went after this, although a regular pension was paid to them.[50]

Overall, it appears that the papal inquisitors attempted to investigate the Templars in Ireland with all due rigour, but that their efforts were not entirely successful. The commander of Ireland up to the day before the arrests was not interrogated; the man who had become commander on the day before the arrests made allegations against his brothers in Europe and in the east, but said nothing that the inquisitors could use against the order in Ireland. A number of friars gave evidence against the Templars, which amounted to little more than a statement of general dislike. The inquisitors did send some information to their colleagues in England which was included in the summary of the trial proceedings in the British

46 See Marios Costambeys, 'Symon Simeonis (*fl.* 1322–1324)', *ODNB*, http://www.oxforddnb.com/view/article/25562.

47 MS A, fols 153v–154r (Wilkins, pp. 379–80).

48 MS A, fol. 153v (Wilkins, p. 379).

49 Callan, '"No Such Art"', p. 55, n. 133.

50 Wood, 'Templars in Ireland', 357–9. The pension was still being paid, at a quarter of the original rate, when the responsibility for paying it passed to the Hospitallers on 7 April 1314: Callan, '"No Such Art"', p. 55.

Isles submitted to the papal commission preparing for the council of Vienne.[51] But overall, the fact that the Templar commander in Ireland was released on bail in 1311, with no evidence that he had to abjure heresies or perform penance, indicates that there was a distinct lack of enthusiasm for the trial among the Anglo-Irish administration, and no general conviction that the order was guilty as charged.

[51] Malcolm Barber, *The Trial of the Templars*, 2nd edn (Cambridge, 2006), pp. 260–61, 353, n. 11; MS Bod. 454, fols 91r, 91v (Wilkins, p. 358); Archivio Segreto Vaticano, *Armarium XXXV*, 147, fols 1v, 3v, 4v, 5r, 6r, 9v, 12r (published as: *Deminutio laboris examinantium processus contra ordinem templi in Anglia, quasi per modum rubricarum*, in *UT*, vol. 2, pp. 78–102: here pp. 79, 84, 86, 89, 95, 101).

Chapter 19

The Hospitallers' Acquisition of the Templar Lands in England[1]

Simon Phillips

The difficulties that the Hospitallers in England had in acquiring the Templars' possessions are as well known as the story of the Templars' dissolution on 22 March 1312 itself.[2] What more is there to say? Firstly, there is room for clarification of when the Hospitallers gained control of the Templars' property in England, which will be discussed in the first part of this paper. Secondly, it is profitable to

---

[1] I would like to thank Dr Nicholas Coureas, Professor Michael Hicks and Professor Christopher Schabel for reading and commenting on this paper. Abbreviations used in this paper are as follows: BL = British Library; *CCR* = *Calendar of Close Rolls Preserved in the Public Record Office*, 1288–1509, 45 vols (London, 1904–63); *CPL* = *Calendar of the Entries in the Papal Registers Relating to Great Britain and Ireland: Papal Letters, 1198–1492*, 15 vols (London, 1893–1960); *CPR* = *Calendar of Patent Rolls Preserved in the Public Record Office, 1281–1509*, 47 vols (London, 1893–1916); *Foedera*, Hague = *Foedera, conventiones, literae*, *et cujuscunque generis acta publica inter reges Angliae et alios quosvis imperatores, reges, pontifices, principes, vel communitates, ab ineunte saeculo duodecimo, viz. ab anno 1101. ad nostra usque tempora, habita aut tractate*, 3rd edn, ed. Thomas Rymer, 10 vols (Hague, 1739–45); *Foedera*, London = *Foedera, conventions, literæ, et cujuscunque generis acta publica, inter reges Angliæ, et alios quosvis Imperatores, Regis, Pontifices, Principes, vel communitates, ab ineunte sæculo duodecimo, viz. ab anno 1101, ad nostra usque tempora, habita aut tractata*, 2nd edn, ed. Thomas Rymer, 20 vols (London, 1727–35); TNA:PRO = The National Archives, Public Record Office, Kew; *VCH* = *The Victoria History of the Counties of England* (London, 1899–); 1338 Report = *The Knights Hospitaller in England: Being the Report of Prior Philip de Thame to the Grand Master Elyan de Villanova for AD 1338*, ed. Lambert B. Larking, Camden Society, 65 (London, 1857).

[2] Amongst others, see Malcolm Barber, *The Trial of the Templars* (Cambridge, 1978; 2nd edn, 2006); Malcolm Barber, *The New Knighthood: A History of the Order of the Temple* (Cambridge, 1994); Alan Forey, *The Military Orders: From the Twelfth to the Early Fourteenth Centuries* (Basingstoke, 1992); Alan Forey, *The Fall of the Templars in the Crown of Aragon* (Aldershot, 2001); *The Trial of the Templars in the Papal State and the Abruzzi*, ed. Anne Gilmour-Bryson (Vatican City, 1982); *The Trial of the Templars in Cyprus: A Complete English Edition*, ed. and trans. Anne Gilmour-Bryson (Leiden, 1998); Anthony Luttrell, 'The Military Orders 1312–1798', in *The Oxford Illustrated History of the Crusades*, ed. Jonathan Riley-Smith (Oxford, 1995), 326–64; Helen Nicholson, *The Knights Hospitaller* (Woodbridge, 2001).

highlight a few examples of attempted acquisitions, in order to understand better the process of acquisition. Finally, in conclusion, consideration will be given to what determined the success or failure of an acquisition bid.

On 2 May 1312, at the council of Vienne, Pope Clement V assigned the Templars' properties to the Hospitallers, with the exception of those in the Iberian Peninsula. The papacy wasted no time in putting this proclamation into action, as four days later papal letters were sent to the clergy all over England, Scotland and Ireland, informing them of the decision and ordering them to defend Hospitaller rights.[3] William Tothale, the head of the English priory (which included Hospitaller lands in Wales and Scotland), also acted swiftly, too swiftly it appears for King Edward II's liking, for on 1 August he was ordered not to proceed with assigning the goods of the Templars to the Hospitallers before the next parliament.[4] This brought a halt to the transfer until the following year, but in the meantime, claims to the ex-Templar lands or compensation for the loss of them continued to be made by lessees of the Templars, descendants of the original grantors of the lands, and those to whom the king had granted lands after the Templar arrests.[5]

Chronology of acquisition

When did the English Hospitaller priory gain possession of the Templars' lands? We are lucky to have Prior Thame's 1338 report, which is divided into separate sections for Hospitaller possessions and former Templar goods, with a summary of those Templar goods not in Hospitaller hands.

Fig.19.1 Templar lands not under Hospitaller control in 1338[6]

Place(s)	Possession(s)	County	Value (marks)	Holder
Strood	manor	Kent	75	countess of Pembroke
Denney	manor	Cambs.	100	countess of Pembroke
Hurst & Newsam	manors	Yorks.	180	countess of Pembroke
Faxfleet with Cave	manors	Yorks.	150	Sir Ralph Neville
York	watermills	Yorks.	20	Edward III

3 *CPL 1305–1342*, p. 95.

4 *CCR 1307–1313*, p. 544.

5 For example, see TNA:PRO SC 8/40/1979; SC 8/60/2963; SC 8/152/7568; SC 8/219/10943.

6 1338 Report, pp. 212–13.

Place(s)	Possession(s)	County	Value (marks)	Holder
Carleton	manor	Lincs.	20	Hugh Despenser
Normanton	manor	Yorks.?	15	Lord Roos
Lydley	manor	Salop.	100	earl of Arundel
Penkerne	manor	Glamorgan	30	earl of Gloucester
Guiting & Bradewell	manors	Glos./Oxon.	200	Pancio de Controno
Bisham	manor	Berks.	100	earl of Salisbury
Bulstrode	manor	Bucks.	75	abbess of Burnham
Saddlescombe	manor	Sussex	100	earl of Warenne

The 1338 report indicates that the Hospitallers had gained possession of the majority of Templar goods by that year, some 75 per cent (£2,280) of the total value of the Templars' possessions in Britain. Detailed inspection of the survey, along with the use of both published and unpublished state sources, also gives an indication of when particular properties came into Hospitaller hands (see Figure 19.2). Although we can rarely pin this down to a particular year, we can at least know under which prior these goods came into Hospitaller possession. The results indicate that the bulk of the Templar goods were acquired under Prior Archer.

Out of 46 references to ex-Templar possessions, where priors are named or dates given, one, possibly two, can be accredited to Prior Tothale (1297–1315), three to Prior Pavely (1315–19), six to Prior Tibertis (1331–34), and one, possibly two, to Prior Thame (1335–54). Thirty-three fall within Archer's administration (1319–30). Previously Archer has been seen as granting away property. It now appears, however, that this policy was necessary in order to gain the majority of Templar possessions. It was a policy that Archer's predecessor Richard Pavely and successor Prior Tibertis also found necessary to follow.[7] Archer deserves some credit for the acquisition of the Templar properties. It was, after all, during his office that the 1324 statute was passed, by which the English parliament acknowledged the Hospitallers' right to the Templar lands in the realm. Nevertheless, we must remember that he was prior in name only from about April 1328 until his death in late August 1330, by which time Tibertis was in effect prior.[8]

7 TNA:PRO E 40/4877; *CPR 1343–1345*, p. 247.

8 *CCR 1327–1330*, pp. 359, 365, 379; *CCR 1330–1333*, p. 152; *CPR 1327–1330*, p. 552.

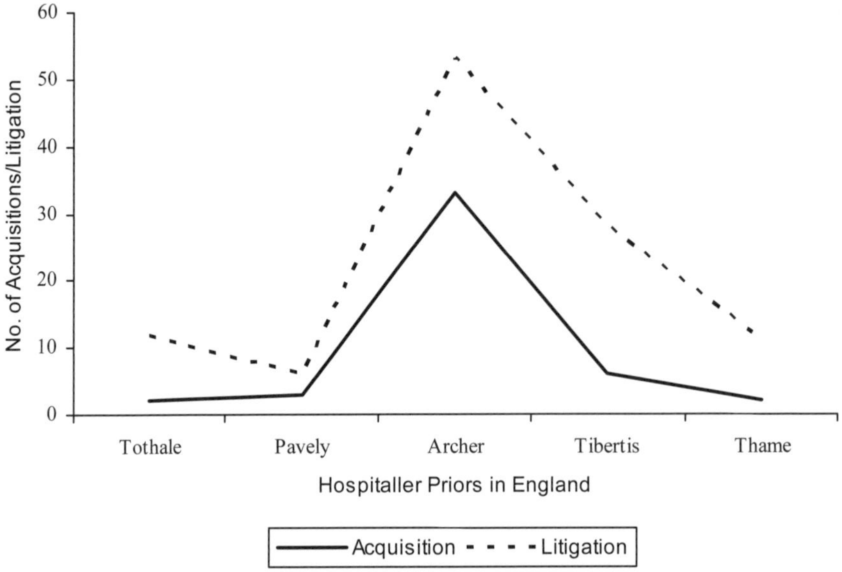

Fig. 19.2 Acquisition and litigation concerning the former Templar properties, 1312–54. 1338 Report, passim; TNA:PRO, various documents; various printed state rolls.

Attempts at acquisition: failures and successes

Nowhere in Europe was the transfer of Templar goods a smooth process. In the Iberian Peninsula, as Alan Forey has pointed out, crown opposition meant that, despite acquisition of the Templars' rights in Aragon and Catalonia, the Hospitallers lost out heavily to the newly created regional military orders, such as the order of Montesa.[9] In France, a settlement was reached with the crown in 1318, though as Malcolm Barber has observed, full seisin was not achieved until much later.[10] In both cases, the right to Templar lands came at a cost, and even then a smooth transfer was not assured.[11] In England, the agreement of the crown to the transfer, in principle, was achieved quickly. On 25 November 1313, representatives of the Hospitaller grand master pleaded with Edward II at Westminster for the Templars' goods to be transferred in accordance with the papal decision at Vienne. Three days later, the king gave his mandate for the Hospitallers to acquire the Templars' goods, orders were despatched to the keepers to deliver them and sheriffs were to ensure that the transfer did indeed take place, should the keepers of the lands fail

[9] Forey, *The Military Orders*, p. 229.

[10] Barber, *The New Knighthood*, p. 308.

[11] Forey, *The Military Orders*, p. 230.

to do their duty. Accordingly, on 5 December, the Hospitaller representatives gave the king quittance for the Templar lands in his dominions.[12] Edward II appears to have surrendered most of what he held personally the following year; at least, the keepers' accounts cease after 1314, and from February of that year the Hospitallers were ordered to pay pensions to ex-Templars.[13] However, the condition that the transfer would not be to the prejudice of the king or his subjects caused legal nightmares for the Hospitallers in the following decades. Luckily for us, the surviving records of these cases give us an insight into the process of acquisition, or loss, of Templar property.[14] A few examples follow as illustration of this.

Failure with Faxfleet, Temple Newsam and Temple Hurst

Faxfleet, as one of the Templars' most valuable preceptories, was destined to be disputed. The keeper's accounts for 1308 valued it at £290, confirming that this was a significant property.[15] Once the Templars had been arrested, the descendants of the original donors, and those who had been granted the Templars' properties, challenged the papal decision to allocate Templar goods to the Hospitallers. One such case, dating from about 1312 to 1313, concerns Joan Comyn of Buchan (Aberdeenshire), sister of William Latimer.[16] William had evidently held the manor at some time after the arrest of the Templars, but had granted it to Joan in compensation for the loss of her lands in Scotland during the war (June 1310 to June 1313). She had heard that Faxfleet was to be taken from her (presumably to be given to the Hospitallers) and requested that it remain under her control for a term of four to five years. Edward II granted that Joan could hold Faxfleet, on condition that the appropriate annual rent was paid, that it would be returned in the same condition that it was granted, and on security that was to be deposited at the exchequer. Thus the Hospitallers, who are not mentioned in the document, were eclipsed before even gaining control of the property. Similar claims were being made at this time in Yorkshire at the Hospitallers' expense. For example, a Margery Frendraught, to whom the king granted 100 marks yearly, again because of the loss of her lands in Scotland, was given custody of the manor of Wetherby in 1312.[17] The Hospitallers acquired Wetherby during Prior Archer's office and held on to it until the Reformation, but they were not so fortunate with Faxfleet.[18] The fate of Faxfleet was still in the balance in the early 1320s, as indicated by a

12 TNA:PRO E 30/1368; *CCR 1313–1318*, pp. 88–9; *CPR 1313–1317*, p. 52; *CCR 1313–1318*, pp. 29–30; TNA:PRO E 41/193; TNA:PRO E 135/1/25.

13 TNA:PRO E 358/18, 19, 20; *CCR 1313–1318*, p. 39.

14 TNA:PRO E 358/18–21; *CPL 1305–1342*, p. 198.

15 TNA:PRO SC 6/1077/19; *VCH Yorkshire*, vol. 3 (1974), pp. 256–60.

16 TNA:PRO SC 8/97/4835.

17 TNA:PRO SC 8/331/15642; *CPR 1307–1313*, p. 440.

18 1338 Report, p. 137; BL Cotton Claudius E VI, fols 175–175v, 235–235v.

document concerning the associated manor of Cave, in which a petition could not be answered because it concerned the tenements of the Templars.[19] However, it appears that Faxfleet was one of the manors ceded to the crown in 1324, in return for parliamentary assent to the granting of the Templar possessions to the Hospitallers. Faxfleet was still in the king's hands in 1327, and according to the 1338 report, Sir Ralph Neville held it with Cave by gift of the king.[20]

Further information on Faxfleet is available in the documents relating to another Yorkshire preceptory, Temple Newsam. As with Faxfleet, Temple Newsam was one of the richer Templar preceptories, valued at £174 in 1308.[21] It was leased out to Nicholas Segrave, who held the manor until his death in 1322, when it reverted to the king.[22] Although the 1324 parliament at Westminster granted the Hospitallers all the Templar lands in the realm, it is unlikely that they physically came into possession of Temple Newsam. Within six months of the statute (on 19 August 1324), Prior Archer, with the consent of the provincial chapter, granted the manor to the king and his heirs, along with the manors of Temple Hurst, Faxfleet, Denney and Strood.[23] The following day, the sheriff of York was ordered to take Temple Newsam into the king's hands, and in 1338 the king leased both Temple Newsam and Temple Hurst to the countess of Pembroke.[24] The Hospitallers did not give up hope of regaining these manors, as is indicated when Prior Hales tried, unsuccessfully, to gain possession from Philip Darcy in 1379, claiming that Darcy had a false deed of possession.[25] This dispute with the Darcy family was still ongoing in the early years of the fifteenth century, evident from John Darcy's petition to the 1402 parliament concerning the manors of Temple Hurst and Temple Newsam, asking if the dispute might be determined in parliament, since he feared a trial by inquest would go against him.[26] The Hospitallers lost this dispute, and both manors were still in Darcy family hands in the 1470s, though the churches within these manors remained Hospitaller possessions.[27]

19 TNA:PRO SC 8/144/7197.

20 TNA:PRO SC 6/1077/20; 1338 Report, p. 212.

21 *VCH Yorkshire*, vol. 3, pp. 256–60.

22 TNA:PRO SC 8/309/15450; TNA:PRO E 142/30.

23 *CPR 1377–1381*, p. 444.

24 *Calendar of Fine Rolls Preserved in the Public Record Office, 1272–1509*, 22 vols (London, 1911–62), *1319–1327*, pp. 296–7; 1338 Report, p. 212.

25 TNA:PRO SC 8/116/5776; TNA:PRO SC 8/19/925; *CCR 1377–1381*, pp. 187–8, 444; *CPR 1377–1381*, p. 444.

26 TNA:PRO SC 8/22/1089.

27 TNA:PRO E 210/4110, E 326/5246, E 326/5247, E 326/5249, E 326/5251.

Success with New Temple, London

Although the Hospitallers failed to acquire some significant Templar possessions, by 1338 they had gained control of the bulk of their goods, including New Temple, London. It is through the example of New Temple that the process by which the Hospitallers achieved this success will be illustrated. After the suppression of the Templars, Edward II granted New Temple to Aymer de Valence, earl of Pembroke,[28] but the latter surrendered it to Thomas, earl of Lancaster, in October 1314.[29] Following Lancaster's execution in 1322, the manor reverted to the crown, and was reallocated to Valence in the same year, but in 1324 it was back in the king's hands, after Valence had died without an heir.[30] Following the parliamentary statute of March 1324, Prior Archer, with the consent of the provincial chapter at London, granted New Temple to Hugh Despenser the Younger on 28 June, retaining the right of access to New Temple Church.[31] After the fall of the Despensers, the manor again reverted to the king, who entrusted it to William Langford until Edward III granted the whole manor to the Hospitallers in June 1338.[32]

The Victoria County History of London informs us of much of what we know about New Temple, but not everything. It mentions only in passing William Langford, but a closer inspection of the state records, both those printed and those in The National Archives, indicates that he may have been influential in securing New Temple for the Hospitallers and further reveals the process by which successful acquisition was achieved. The first mention we have of Langford, in connection with the Hospitallers, is on 21 June 1326, when he jointly acknowledged a debt with Prior Archer, work normally associated with one of the prior's attorneys.[33] Langford, however, was not simply in the service of the prior. Significantly, he was a crown employee, as is apparent from a reference to him in 1328 as the king's keeper of the ex-Templar manor of Bisham.[34] From this point on, Langford became more involved with the Hospitallers, granting land to them in West Smithfield on 20 June 1329 to fund a wax light in Clerkenwell Church, and on 8 June the following year Prior Archer confirmed a demise of Dinsley manor to Langford for life.[35] Then, in March 1331, Prior Tibertis confirmed a demise for life to Langford of £25 rent paid for the manor of Sutton and reversion of the manor on the current tenant's death.[36] Langford is also mentioned in a writ dated 4 January 1335, in which King Edward III ordered his escheator to remove his hands from

28 *VCH London*, vol. 1, pp. 485–91.

29 TNA:PRO DL 10/216; *CPR 1313–1317*, p. 184.

30 *Foedera*, London, vol. 2.1, p. 480.

31 TNA:PRO E 40/1469.

32 *VCH London*, vol. 1, pp. 485–91.

33 *CCR 1323–1327*, p. 571.

34 TNA:PRO SC 8/310/15468; *CCR 1327–1330*, p. 291.

35 *CPR 1327–1330*, 401; TNA:PRO C 143/207/29; *CPR 1327–1330*, p. 531.

36 *CPR 1330–1334*, p. 88.

the Hospitallers' lands.[37] Also in 1335, Langford granted property in the suburbs of London to the Hospitallers, and in March of the following year the Hospitallers demised Wydmore (Bucks.) and Shipley (Surrey) manors to Langford and John Pultney, mayor of London, for Langford's life.[38] Finally, on 20 March 1336, licence was given for alienation by ('Brother') William Langford to the prior of land in the suburbs of London, to find a chaplain to celebrate divine service daily in St John the Baptist's church for the souls of Langford and his ancestors.[39] These examples clearly show an ongoing relationship between Langford and the Hospitallers for at least 12 years before they gained total control of New Temple manor. It may be that Langford directed his piety towards the Hospitallers or he may even have been admitted to the order in some way, but what is clear is that there were land dealings between them. One suspects that Langford's position as a crown administrator of Templar lands influenced the Hospitallers' decision to favour him, in order to gain *his* favour.

The importance of having his assistance became apparent before the year was out. After a petition by the prior to parliament, claiming that Hugh Despenser the Younger had gained the manor by force and duress, and the following enquiry, in which William Langford gave evidence, on 1 September 1336, Hugh Despenser (d. 1349), son of Hugh Despenser the Younger, was dispossessed of houses at New Temple. Langford, as the keeper of the Temple, had the job of ensuring the dispossession was carried out, with the assistance of Alderman John Oxford.[40] It comes as no surprise, then, that in November 1336 the Hospitallers agreed to Langford having a more convenient pension agreement, and that this and other privileges were confirmed in December, at which point Langford was described as 'chief servitor of the order'.[41] The pattern of patronage continued into the following year, Langford granting land in West Smithfield to the Hospitallers in July 1337, in order to increase the lights in the church and to sustain two chaplains to celebrate divine service.[42] Then came the acquisition of the rest of New Temple. This was by no means certain and was endangered by the findings of crown officials on 18 May 1338, still investigating the Despenser case, who could uncover no evidence of force or duress, only that in 1327 Despenser held the manor by enfeoffment of the prior, which was in accord with the 1324 lease.[43] Hugh Despenser, son of Hugh Despenser the Younger, had some of his father's lands restored to him in 1337 and was clearly vying for more. Nevertheless, on 18 June 1338, the Hospitallers paid £100 towards Edward III's campaign in France, and in return they gained control

37 TNA:PRO SC 8/81/4023B.

38 TNA:PRO C 143/235/20; *CPR 1334–1338*, p. 226.

39 *CPR 1334–1338*, p. 239.

40 *CPR 1334–1338*, p. 314.

41 *CCR 1333–1337*, pp. 708–10; *CPR 1334–1338*, pp. 351–2.

42 TNA:PRO C 143/242/8; *CPR 1334–1338*, p. 467.

43 *CCR 1337–1339*, p. 417; TNA:PRO E 40/1469.

of New Temple.[44] Langford was the official who went to the king's treasurer on 10 July and gained acquittal for the prior of the amount paid for New Temple.[45] The importance of his role to the Hospitallers in this acquisition was acknowledged the following year (on 18 July 1339) in a confirmation of a grant for life of land without the bar of West Smithfield, adjoining the prior's great garden of Clerkenwell, as well as other lands in London. The stated reason for this grant was that it was for his services in obtaining the manor of New Temple for only £100.[46]

What can we learn from the above examples about how the Hospitallers failed, or succeeded, to acquire the Templars' possessions? Firstly, powerful lords gave the Hospitallers stiff competition when it came to the more desirable of the Templars' possessions. For example, as early as 1313 John de Warenne, earl of Surrey, petitioned Edward II (successfully) for the right to farm Saddlescombe and other Templar lands and still held Saddlescombe in 1338.[47] Furthermore, it is no coincidence that Aymer de Valence, one of the lords present at Westminster in November 1313 when the Hospitallers pleaded for the Templars' goods, was granted a considerable number of Templar possessions.[48] Nevertheless, it appears that the Hospitallers eventually gained most of the lands, including some of those still out of their possession in 1338. Even those Templar possessions that did not go to the Hospitallers were used to found other religious houses. For example, William Montacute, earl of Salisbury, used Bisham to found a house of Augustinian canons in 1337, Ralph Neville had allocated Denney to Franciscan nuns by 1342, and Thomas Holland, duke of Surrey (d.1400), used his ex-Templar properties to endow Mount Grace priory.[49] It is also possible that Templar property was leased out by the Hospitallers in the short term to clear debts. Of those holding lands in 1338, Valence, the Controno family and the Despensers had lent money to the English Hospitaller prior. Furthermore, others who are mentioned in land dealings, such as John Pultney (mayor of London 1334, 1337) and John Oxford (sheriff of London, 1324; alderman of London, 1336; mayor of London, 1342), lent money to the prior throughout the 1320s and 1330s.[50] Other properties were

---

44 *CPR 1338–1340*, p. 99; Anthony Tuck, *Crown and Nobility: England 1272–1461*, 2nd edn (Oxford, 1999), p. 99.

45 *CPR 1338–1340*, p. 108.

46 *CPR 1338–1340*, pp. 303–4.

47 TNA:PRO SC 8/152/7568; C 143/107/10; 1338 Report, p. 213.

48 *Foedera*, Hague, 1745, vol. 2.1, pp. 54–5.

49 Simon Phillips, 'The Recycling of Monastic Wealth in Medieval Southern England, 1300–1530', *Southern History: A Review of the History of Southern England*, 22 (2000), 48.

50 For Valence see *CCR 1318–1323*, p. 705; *CCR 1323–1327*, p. 191; For the Controno family see *CCR 1323–1327*, pp. 564, 634; *CCR 1327–1330*, pp. 103, 109; *CCR 1330–1333*, p. 133, 156, 554; for the Despensers see *CCR 1323–1327*, pp.490–1; For John Pultney see TNA:PRO E 40/1629, E 40/2464; *CPR 1334–1338*, p. 226; For John Oxford see TNA:PRO E 326/1974; *CPR 1334–1338*, p. 314; TNA:PRO E 326/1976.

leased out to honour grants made by the crown, for example, Strood manor to the earl of Pembroke, which Prior Thame confirmed to the countess for her lifetime in January 1338.[51] Successful acquisition of the Templars' goods required the assistance of crown officials, Langford, Pultney, Oxford and countless others, as the 1338 report clearly shows.[52] Anyone who has looked at the Hospitaller lease books for the 1530s will notice a similar increase in leases to crown officials, though in the latter case, this was aimed at retaining their possessions, rather than acquiring others.

---

51 *CPR 1334–1338*, p. 571.

52 For example, see 1338 Report, pp. 205–9.

PART V
The Trial in Other Countries

Chapter 20
The Arrest of the Templars in Cyprus

Peter W. Edbury

At the beginning of June 1308, the Templars who were living on Cyprus were placed under arrest. Modern scholarly descriptions of this episode all rely heavily on just one narrative source, the so-called *Chronique d'Amadi*.[1] This is an anonymous work which provides what I believe is by far the most detailed account of the arrest of members of the order anywhere in Latin Christendom, and so, before turning to the events themselves, some explanation of its nature and provenance is called for.

Amadi, as it is usually referred to for sake of convenience, is written in Italian and survives in a single manuscript dating from the mid-sixteenth century. This manuscript belonged to a Venetian bibliophile named Francesco Amadi – hence the name – and is now in the Marciana Library. It comprises a compilation spanning the history of the crusades and Lusignan rule in Cyprus from the First Crusade to the year 1442. Almost all the material in the sections covering the period before the middle of the first decade of the fourteenth century can be readily identified as having been drawn from extant sources: the Old French translation of William of Tyre and its continuations,[2] a version of the *Annales de Terre Sainte*,[3] Philip of Novara's account of the civil war between the Ibelins and the adherents of Frederick II (1220s–1242), and the narrative conventionally, if misleadingly, attributed to the

[1] 'La Chronique d'Amadi', in *Chroniques d'Amadi et de Strambaldi*, ed. René de Mas Latrie, 2 vols (Paris, 1891–93; repr. Nicosia, 1999), vol. 1, pp. 280, 283–91. For modern accounts, George Hill, *A History of Cyprus*, 4 vols (Cambridge, 1940–52), vol. 2, pp. 232–6; Peter W. Edbury, *The Kingdom of Cyprus and the Crusades, 1191–1374* (Cambridge, 1991), p. 121; Nicholas Coureas, *The Latin Church in Cyprus, 1195–1312* (Aldershot, 1997), pp. 139–40; Pierre-Vincent Claverie, *L'ordre du Temple en Terre Sainte et à Chypre au XIIIe siècle*, 3 vols (Nicosia, 2005), vol. 2, pp. 273–8; Malcolm Barber, *The Trial of the Templars*, 2nd edn (Cambridge, 2006), pp. 252–4.

[2] The *Amadi* compiler used the 'Colbert-Fontainebleau' version of the Old French Continuation of William of Tyre, which is to be found in only two of the 45 surviving manuscripts of that work. This is the main text edited in RHC Oc 2.

[3] Scattered through the material drawn from the 'Annales de Terre Sainte' are a few entries of Cypriot interest not found in the earlier versions. Two French texts of the *Annales de Terre Sainte* have long been known (Reinhold Röhricht and Gaston Raynaud, eds, *AOL*, 2 (1884), documents, pp. 427–61). For a third French text, see 'A New Text of the Annales de Terre Sainte', ed. Peter W. Edbury, in *In Laudem Hierosolymitani: Studies in Crusades and Medieval Culture in Honour of Benjamin Z. Kedar*, ed. Iris Shagrir, Ronnie Ellenblum and Jonathan Riley-Smith, (Aldershot, 2007), pp. 145–61.

'Templar of Tyre'.[4] All these earlier narratives were written in French, and so *Amadi* represents a translation into Italian.

When we come to the early fourteenth century, we find that *Amadi* has a detailed narrative of the events surrounding the period in which the lord of Tyre, Amaury of Lusignan, held power. In 1306, Amaury, the brother and heir-presumptive of the ill and incompetent King Henry II of Cyprus, assumed control of the kingdom. Henry was suspended from office in a *coup d'état* which at least initially commanded wide support. Amaury held power until 1310 when he was assassinated. The king then returned to power, and a number of his brother's adherents were imprisoned, never to regain their liberty. The events of the years 1306–10 occupy 150 pages in the published edition of *Amadi*. By comparison, the section dealing with the years 1218–42, the material drawn from Philip of Novara's well-known account of the civil war in Cyprus, fills only 80 pages, whilst the thirty-five-year reign of King Hugh IV (1324–59) is dismissed in a mere eight pages. There can be no doubt that the 1306–10 narrative, which was evidently written by a partisan of King Henry, was composed within a few years of the events themselves and, like the earlier materials, was originally written in French. But in this instance the French version has not survived. Besides giving a detailed description of the politics of the period, it contains an invaluable account of the start of the Hospitaller conquest of Rhodes,[5] as well as of the arrest of the Templars. *Amadi*, however, makes no mention of the formal interrogation of the Templars arrested in Cyprus or of the non-Templar witnesses who were called to give evidence, and for these the historian must consult the records preserved in the papal archives.[6]

There are, however, important questions relating to the *Chronique d'Amadi* that have not been sufficiently addressed. Did the translator also assemble the compilation, or did the work previously exist in its entirety in French? An answer to that question might help decide further questions about the relationship of *Amadi* to two other important narratives for medieval Cypriot history: those by Leontios

[4] Philip of Novara's history is edited as Filippo da Novara, *Guerra di Federico II in Oriente (1223–1242)*, ed. and trans. Silvio Melani (Naples, 1994). The *Amadi* compiler evidently used a text of Philip of Novara's narrative that differed at certain points from the extant French version, and the apparatus to Melani's edition indicates points at which the texts diverge. For the 'Templar of Tyre', see *Cronaca del Templare di Tiro (1243–1314)*, ed. and trans. Laura Minervini (Naples, 2000); English translation: *The 'Templar of Tyre': Part III of the 'Deeds of the Cypriots'*, trans. Paul Crawford (Aldershot, 2003). Whereas *Amadi* contains a full translation of Philip's text, the material from the 'Templar of Tyre' is often summarized, and, as there appears to be little or no use of the latter for the period from 1242, where Philip ends, to the late 1260s, it is quite possible that the compiler was not working from a text such as the *Gestes des Chiprois* in which Philip of Novara and the 'Templar of Tyre' are juxtaposed, but knew of them separately.

[5] 'Chronique d'Amadi', pp. 254–9.

[6] For the trial of the Templars in Cyprus see *UT*, vol. 2, pp. 147–400; *The Trial of the Templars in Cyprus: A Complete English Edition*, ed. and trans. Anne Gilmour-Bryson (Leiden, 1998); Barber, *Trial*, pp. 254–8.

Makhairas and Florio Bustron. Bustron was working in the sixteenth century;[7] the Italian of his *Historia overo Commentarii de Cipro* is far more literary than *Amadi*'s and the content more sophisticated; whereas we can certainly rule out the possibility that *Amadi* derived his material from Bustron, it is not clear whether Bustron utilized *Amadi*'s Italian text or a putative lost French original. The relationship of *Amadi* and Leontios Makhairas's Greek-language *Recital Concerning the Sweet Land of Cyprus* is even more problematic. There is no doubt that their narratives from the second half of the fourteenth century onwards are textually related. But precisely how awaits elucidation, as does the question of how much of the work that goes under his name was actually originated by Leontios. Then again there is the problem of precisely when and where the *Amadi* compiler was at work…[8] But rather than pursue these matters, we should return to our story.

As is well known, King Philip IV had ordered the arrest of the Templars in France on 13 October 1307, and on 22 November Pope Clement V, in what is generally seen as an attempt to wrest the initiative away from Philip, issued the bull *Pastoralis praeeminentiae* in which he instructed the European monarchs to arrest the Templars within their respective kingdoms and take control of their lands in the name of the papacy. In this letter the kings were informed that the pope had himself heard from a Templar knight that, at his reception into the order in Cyprus which had taken place in the presence of the master, Jacques de Molay, and 200 brothers, half of whom had been of knightly rank, he had been obliged to deny Christ.[9] Presumably, however, as a result of the closing of the sea routes to the east with the onset of winter, *Pastoralis praeeminentiae* did not arrive in Cyprus until the following May.

By then Amaury of Tyre had been in power for two years. According to *Amadi*, the popularity of his rule among the nobility was now beginning to show the first signs of crumbling, although our author also insists that, since his seizure of power, the Templars had consistently given him their backing. Thus *Amadi* records Jacques de Molay loaning Amaury 50,000 bezants in 1306 at the beginning of his

---

[7] Florio Bustrone, 'Historia overo Commentarii de Cipro', ed. René de Mas Latrie as 'Chronique de l'île de Chypre', *Collection de documents inédits sur l'histoire de France: Mélanges historiques*, 5 (1886), pp. 1–531 (repr. Nicosia, 1998).

[8] Gilles Grivaud believes that *Amadi* was composed around the middle of the sixteenth century and has offered the hypothesis that the author may have been a Cypriot nobleman named Hector Podocataro. From the evidence he adduces, it seems likely that the Podocataro family owned a copy of *Amadi*, but beyond that it is difficult to go: Gilles Grivaud, 'Ο πνευματικός βίος και η γραμματολογία κατά την περίοδο της Φραγκοκρατίας', in *Ιστορία της Κύπρου*, ed. Theodore Papadopoulos, vol. 5 (Nicosia, 1996), pp. 881, 1147–53.

[9] Pierre Dupuy, *Traittez concernant l'histoire de France: Sçavoir la condemnation des Templiers avec quelques actes* (Paris, 1654; repr. Paris, 1978), fols 189r–190v (for the version sent to the future King Robert of Naples); *Foedera, conventiones, litterae et acta publica*, ed. Thomas Rymer et al., new edn, 4 vols in 7 parts (London, 1816–69), vol. 2.1, cols 16–17 (for the version sent to Edward II of England).

rule, and the author notes that Jacques then helped in negotiations to determine the financial provision needed to support the now suspended King Henry. By the early months of 1308 relations between Amaury and his brother had reached a new low, and we hear of the marshal of the Temple, Aymon (or Ayme) d'Oiselay, taking an active part in Amaury's efforts to separate Henry from those nobles, knights and servants who had remained loyal to him and to force the king to designate Amaury as governor of Cyprus for life.[10]

In the late spring of 1307, in a bid to shore up his support by gaining papal endorsement for his rule and counter allegations he feared were being made to the pope by envoys from King Henry, Amaury had sent Het'um, lord of Gorhigos, who was both a member of the Cilician Armenian royal family and a canon of the Cypriot Praemonstratensian monastery at Bellapaïs near Kerynia, to the papal *curia*. Protracted negotiations, however, failed to persuade Pope Clement to give Amaury the backing for which he had hoped. Het'um returned in May 1308 to report his lack of success and brought with him the papal instructions for the arrest of the Templars.[11]

It is at this point that the *Amadi* narrative comes to the fore. But before embarking on a detailed account of the circumstances of the arrest in late May and early June 1308, the author provides a close paraphrase of a passage to be found in the narrative by the 'Templar of Tyre' summarizing events in France from the arrest of the Templars there until the suppression of the order five years later. In this section, he repeats this earlier author's scepticism about the validity of the charges and the Templar guilt.[12] The 'Templar of Tyre', however, has nothing of what follows.[13]

According to *Amadi*, on 12 May, Amaury, in execution of the papal mandate, sent Balian of Ibelin, prince of Galilee and one of his most prominent supporters, to the Templar headquarters at Limassol. The message was that the Templars should surrender their arms and horses and accept confinement in the archbishop's house at Nicosia. Clearly the authorities were reluctant to use force and were hoping that a peaceful surrender could be effected. The senior Templar officer in Cyprus was the marshal, Aymon d'Oiselay,[14] and he attempted to negotiate, offering to allow himself and the other members of the order in Cyprus to be held under guard on one of their rural estates while refusing to relinquish control of either their arms or their treasure. But if the Templars imagined that Amaury would be satisfied with a pretence of taking them into custody, they were mistaken. On 19 May, Amaury

---

10 'Chronique d'Amadi', pp. 248, 251, 260–61, 262, 266.

11 Edbury, *Kingdom of Cyprus*, pp. 118–21.

12 'Chronique d'Amadi', pp. 280–82; cf. *Cronaca del Templare di Tiro*, pp. 340–43.

13 The unique manuscript of the 'Templar of Tyre' is mutilated at the end, breaking off just four paragraphs further on in the middle of a description of the events that date to 1309. Florio Bustron (pp. 164–70) provides a parallel and self-evidently derivative account.

14 *Amadi* normally gives his name as 'Heme d'Ussellet' or similar.

issued orders that no-one was to receive a salary from the Templars or to pay a salary on behalf of the order, and anyone who had received payment from the order should keep it and be quit of any further obligation. At the same time he sent a canon of Nicosia cathedral named Baldwin to the Templars at Limassol with the message that they should come at his command and submit themselves to the judgment of the Church; if they refused he would come and arrest them by force, and any who resisted would be killed. This time they replied that they would submit in four months time, in other words in September, and in the meantime the lord of Tyre should send a galley to the pope for further instructions which they would then obey.[15]

Amaury then sent a canon of Limassol cathedral named Andrea Tartaro,[16] who encountered Aymon d'Oiselay and the Templar turcopolier[17] at the village of Nissou which lay on the main road south from Nicosia. It was there that on 24 May talks were held with a group consisting of Aimery of Lusignan, who was the constable of Cyprus and Amaury's younger brother, Balian of Galilee, Baldwin the canon of Nicosia and Raymond Viscount, the owner of Nissou. After lengthy discussions Aimery and Balian returned to Nicosia to get Amaury to agree to the deal they had negotiated. The upshot was that on 27 May the Templars arrived in Nicosia under a promise of safe conduct. Amaury summoned a large assembly of knights and clergy, and a notary read a statement on behalf of the Templars in which they made an orthodox profession of faith. Baldwin the canon then translated it into French for the benefit of the people and made a statement to the effect that the Templars were good Christians who believed what they had professed; he added that they had in the past shown themselves ready to die in defence of the Christian religion and that they had fought alongside the kings of Jerusalem and the crusaders from the west against the Muslims, mentioning in particular the events at Safed. (Safed had fallen as long ago as 1266, and the Templars in the garrison, who seem to have been tricked into believing that they were surrendering on terms, preferred to die rather than be forced into apostasy.[18]) Then the senior Templar officers who were present, the marshal, the commander of Cyprus, the draper and the treasurer,[19]

---

15 'Chronique d'Amadi', pp. 283–5.

16 *Amadi* states that Andrea was a canon of Famagusta, but documents of the period show that he was a canon of Limassol. *Notai genovesi in oltremare atti roggati a Cipro da Lamberto di Sambuceto*, ed. Romeo Pavoni (Genoa, 1987), no. 158 (1302); *Notai genovesi in oltremare atti roggati a Cipro*, ed. Michel Balard (Genoa, 1984), pp. 312–13 (nos 25–7) (1309).

17 Bartholomew of Gordo: see *Trial in Cyprus*, ed. Gilmour-Bryson, pp. 118–19 and n. 241.

18 The memory of this incident was subsequently recalled by two of the lay witnesses who participated in the Templar trial in Cyprus: *Trial in Cyprus*, ed. Gilmour-Bryson, pp. 71, 422–3.

19 The commander of Cyprus, Raimbaud de Caromb, had been arrested in France. The man referred to here was James of 'Doumanin' or 'Doymalin' who appears to have

together with a brother knight from each *langue* and two Templar sergeants swore their adherence to these statements both on their own behalf and on behalf of all the other members of the order in Cyprus. These were said by *Amadi* to total 83 knights and 35 sergeants. But while all this was happening, Amaury had secretly ordered a force comprising knights, other mounted men, infantry and marines to move from Famagusta to occupy Limassol. The following day (28 May), Amaury again convened an assembly of clergy, knights and burgesses and had the papal letters read out, specifying that he should confine the Templars and take possession of their treasure and movable goods because, on the basis of the examination of the Templars that the king of France had already made within his own kingdom, they had been found to be heretics.[20]

On 29 May, Amaury ordered the viscount of Nicosia to take a force of knights, together with the Hospitaller prior and members of the Franciscan and Dominican orders who were presumably needed as witnesses to what would ensue, to make an inventory and seal everything in the Templar house in Nicosia including the silver and gold vessels and the treasure. There was, so we are told, not much there because the Templars had had most of their valuables secretly taken to their Limassol headquarters. Although *Amadi* does not say so explicitly, it would seem that this act was in contravention of the agreement that had been hammered out at Nissou. Aymon d'Oiselay was very upset and immediately returned with his whole company to Limassol, leaving only the commander of Cyprus and another knight and three sergeants who followed shortly afterwards.[21] The viscount and his companions made a thorough inventory of the contents of the Templar church in Nicosia, which they then closed, even going to the trouble of removing the bell rope so that the bell could not be rung. Amaury ordered similar inventories to be made at the Templar houses in Paphos and Famagusta and in all their rural estates.[22]

The closing of the Templar church in Nicosia led King Henry to reprove the men of religion who had consented to it; although he was suspended from power, he ordered that it be re-opened, on the grounds that there was an endowment there that stipulated that two chaplains should say mass for his ancestor and namesake, King Henry I.[23] We thus have the paradoxical situation in which Amaury, who had enjoyed the support of the Templars, was acting against them, while the king, whose relations with the order had been poor for much of his reign, was apparently making

---

been acting in his absence; the draper was John of 'Villa' or 'Vilaers': Claverie, *L'ordre du Temple*, vol. 2, p. 254; *Trial in Cyprus*, ed. Gilmour-Bryson, pp. 117, 139 and nn. 238, 343.

20 Clearly a description of *Pastoralis praeeminentiae*: 'Chronique d'Amadi', pp. 285–7.

21 The knight is named as 'Piero Cadel', but in the trial documents Peter 'Cadelli' is described as a sergeant: *Trial in Cyprus*, ed. Gilmour-Bryson, pp. 140, 367.

22 'Chronique d'Amadi', pp. 287–8.

23 Although *Amadi* does not say so here, he had previously (p. 202, s.a. 1253) reported that Henry I was buried in the Templar church.

a gesture of support.[24] It should be added that the Templar church in Nicosia would seem to have been a substantial building: it was there in 1324 that Henry II's body was laid in state before his burial at the Franciscan church.[25]

Amaury now ordered what would appear to have been a general mobilization of his armed forces. At the same time the Templars armed themselves, but the Cypriot captains managed to avoid a full-scale engagement and instead succeeded in laying siege to the Templar headquarters in Limassol. They demanded that the Templars surrender their horses and arms, and, after a brief show of resistance, they capitulated on 1 June. The Cypriot captains thereupon gained entry to the building and took possession of their goods, making a full inventory of the considerable store of arms and equipment they found there. These were removed to the royal house at Limassol along with the foodstuffs that were surplus to the Templars' immediate requirements. In the treasury they found valuables with an estimated value of 120,000 white bezants together with 1,500 marks worth of silver plate. This was all inventoried and placed under seal, and a guard was set.[26] It was believed that the majority of the Templar wealth had been hidden secretly, although subsequent enquiries yielded nothing. So in Cyprus at least, stories of hidden Templar treasure started to circulate almost at once.[27]

The Templars themselves were divided into two groups. Half of them with the marshal, Aymon d'Oiselay, were sent to the Templar estate at Khirokitia; the other half, with the Templar commander of Cyprus, to another Templar property not far away at Yermasoyia. There they were well supplied with food and kept under guard. The treasure was moved to Nicosia; the horses and other beasts of burden, the supplies and furniture were all sold; the arms were taken to the royal armouries at Famagusta, and slaves belonging to the order were put to work on the fortifications at Famagusta, a major building project that was in progress at the time.[28]

Amadi concludes his account by recording that word later reached Amaury that the marshal and commander had written to friends in Genoa and were plotting to have ships brought secretly to Cyprus so that they could make their escape. Accordingly he ordered that the high-ranking officials, namely the marshal, the commander, the draper, treasurer and the commander of Apulia, should all be taken to the royal village of Lefkara and kept there under guard.[29]

---

24 'Chronique d'Amadi', p. 288.

25 'Chronique d'Amadi', p. 402. See Gilles Grivaud and Christopher Schabel, 'La ville de Nicosie', in *L'art gothique en Chypre*, ed. Jean-Bernard de Vaivre and Philippe Plagnieux (Paris, 2006), p. 107.

26 'Chronique d'Amadi', pp. 288–90. The degree of detail given in the text suggests that the original author would have had access to the inventories compiled at the time.

27 'Chronique d'Amadi', p. 290.

28 'Chronique d'Amadi', pp. 290–291. For the fortifications at Famagusta, see *Reg. Clem. V*, no. 2736; 'Chronique d'Amadi', pp. 326–7.

29 'Chronique d'Amadi', p. 291.

That is not quite the end of the Templars so far as *Amadi* is concerned. The narrative makes no mention of the Templar process in Cyprus, but it does record that on 7 November 1312 the papal legate assembled the clergy and leading laity in Nicosia cathedral and read out letters from the pope announcing that all the Templars' possessions were to pass to the Hospitallers.[30] *Amadi* records two other incidents involving the Templars that may come as something of a surprise. It might be imagined that Amaury's firm stance in securing their arrest and sequestrating their possessions would have left little room for further goodwill and co-operation between his regime and the order. However, in 1310, following Amaury's murder, the knights who were working for the restoration of the king evidently feared that the Templars held at Khirokitia would be recruited by their opponents, who were now led by Amaury's brother, Aimery of Lusignan, in what could well have developed into an armed struggle. Then, in 1311, Aymon d'Oiselay was named as a leading member of a group of erstwhile supporters of Amaury who were plotting to seize the kingdom in the name of Amaury's son, Hugh, who was then in Cilician Armenia. The plot was nipped in the bud, but it would seem that it was that episode rather than his position as a leading officer in the order that resulted in his incarceration in Kerynia castle where he died in 1316. *Amadi* asserts that many Templars died at Kerynia, although other evidence indicates that at least some of those arrested in Cyprus were allowed back to their places of origin and treated with leniency.[31]

As most of the senior officers who had not been rounded up in France at the time of the arrests there were in Cyprus, these events were significant. Many of the members of the order on the island should probably be regarded as being on active service. Certainly, as Alan Forey has shown, there was a much higher proportion of Templars in Cyprus who had been in the order for less than 10 years than is true of those arrested in the west, and we have to assume that these men were indeed younger.[32] Their numbers were substantial – 83 knights and 35 sergeants according to *Amadi* of whom 42 knights, 2 priests and 32 sergeants gave testimonies which survive in the trial documents[33] – and the quantity of arms and armour found in the headquarters at Limassol was appreciable. All this suggests that they could have been well able to defend themselves in the event of a military showdown, especially as it would seem that many of them were together in Limassol and not scattered around their estates. There is no hint in our sources that news had reached Cyprus of the arrests in France before Het'um arrived with the papal letters in May

30 'Chronique d'Amadi', p. 395.

31 'Chronique d'Amadi', pp. 360, 392, 398. For Templars repatriated from Cyprus, see Alan Forey, *The Fall of the Templars in the Crown of Aragon* (Aldershot, 2001), pp. 216, 243 n. 53; Peter W. Edbury, 'The Suppression of the Templars in Cyprus', *St John Historical Society Proceedings* (2003), 37–8 (for a French Templar, William of 'Valdreys' or 'Vadres', who reappeared in Burgundy in the 1330s).

32 Alan Forey, 'Towards a Profile of the Templars in the Early Fourteenth Century', in *MO*, 1, pp. 198–200.

33 *Trial in Cyprus*, ed. Gilmour-Bryson, p. 31.

1308, and so there is no way of knowing if either the government or the members of the order had made any contingency plans. It was of course conceivable that Amaury would choose to defy papal instructions rather than proceed against his own political allies at a time when his authority was beginning to be challenged by elements within the Frankish elite in Cyprus. As Helen Nicholson has pointed out, had 'the ruler of Cyprus supported the order, it would have been difficult for the pope to dissolve it'.[34]

But the ruler of Cyprus chose not to support the order. Maybe Amaury realized he could escape repaying the loan he had received in 1306; maybe he hoped to get his hands on Templar property; maybe he was glad to be rid of what was, after all, a substantial force of armed men on Cypriot soil not under his control, but it seems to me that there are two other, far more important reasons than these. Firstly, for Amaury to defy both the pope and the king of France was to invite intervention that could lead to the end of Lusignan rule in Cyprus altogether. As it was, the Angevin kings of Naples claimed the Lusignans' other royal title, that of king of Jerusalem, and in making this claim they could count on the support of both the king of France and the pope. What is more, the idea seems to have had currency in some circles in the west that the French king could acquire the rather tenuous Brienne claim to the Cypriot crown – this dated from a disputed succession in the 1260s – and use it to endow a junior member of the French royal family with the throne. What all this meant was that in the event of a French-led crusade to the east, the king of Cyprus would have good reason to feel apprehensive. In August 1308, the pope indeed proclaimed just such a crusade to begin the following year.[35] Quite possibly Het'um, on his return to Cyprus the previous May, had been able to tell Amaury that talk of a crusade was already in the air at the papal court. So reluctance to antagonize the papacy and fear of a French-led crusade, combined with signs that his rule was becoming unpopular, may have been sufficient to convince Amaury that he had no choice but to fall in with the papal mandates. Amaury's letter to the pope reporting that he had indeed carried out the instructions to arrest the Templars – a letter which incidentally corroborates many of the details recorded by *Amadi* – has survived, as has another letter which shows Pope Clement forwarding Amaury's missive to Philip the Fair. The surviving copy of Amaury's letter lacks the date, but the fact that it had reached the pope, who was then at Lusignan in Poitou, by 20 August 1308 shows that it must have been dispatched almost immediately after the arrests were effected.[36] It would thus seem that Amaury was making a virtue out of necessity and using the arrests to ingratiate himself with the pope.

The second principal reason is that, although the Templars had supported Amaury's rule, they were not integrated into Cypriot society. The trial documents

34 Helen Nicholson, *The Knights Templar: A New History* (Stroud, 2001), p. 228.

35 Edbury, *Kingdom of Cyprus*, pp. 107, 123.

36 *Vitae Paparum Avenionensium*, ed. Etienne Baluze, new edn by Guillaume Mollat, 4 vols (Paris, 1914–27), vol. 3, pp. 84–6; cf. Claverie, *L'ordre du Temple*, vol. 3, p. 618, no. 715.

show that some individual Templars had been received into the order in the Latin East, but it appears that these men were invariably from western Europe, and that the Templars did not recruit from among the members of the Frankish nobility. So there were no prominent families who might want to come to the defence of the order because their relatives were Templar brothers.[37] Although it is true that none of the lay witnesses called to testify in the Templar process in Cyprus were prepared to corroborate the charges levelled against them, positive support was clearly lacking. Indeed, the Ibelin family, which at this time was by the far the most prominent noble house in Cyprus, had, back in the 1270s, been attempting to hijack part of the Templar tradition. According to the version of the *Lignages d'Outremer* which was assembled at that time in Ibelin circles, Barisan, the founder of the house in the early twelfth century, had been given the castle of Ibelin because of his work in escorting pilgrims from Jaffa to Jerusalem.[38] The tradition of ill-feeling between the Templars and the Cypriot monarchy which extended back at least to the 1270s would also have affected the stance taken by the nobility, as would the criticisms of the order the nobles would have found embedded in literary works such as the Old French translation of William of Tyre's celebrated history.[39] Amaury of Lusignan and his associates who had seized power in 1306 counted the Templars among their political allies; they evidently did not count them among their friends.

---

[37] According to *Amadi* (p. 267) the Templar marshal, Aymon d'Oiselay, was the cousin of the prominent Cypriot nobleman, Rupin of Montfort. Rupin was among the first of the nobles to oppose Amaury, and in the summer of 1307 Aymon intervened to release him from confinement, whereupon Amaury banished him to internal exile on his mother's estate at Lapithos. The genealogy of the Montfort family is well known; if indeed the two men were related, their kinship cannot have been close. Aymon was himself a Burgundian: Claverie, *L'ordre du Temple*, vol. 1, p. 111. Rupin was named as one of the partisans of Henry II against whom Aymon was said to be plotting in 1311: 'Chronique d'Amadi', p. 392.

[38] *Lignages d'outremer*, ed. Marie-Adélaïde Nielen (Paris, 2003), p. 60, cf. pp. 22–3. For the circumstances of the grant of Ibelin in 1144, see Peter W. Edbury, *John of Ibelin and the Kingdom of Jerusalem* (Woodbridge, 1997), pp. 4–5.

[39] Claverie, *L'ordre du Temple*, vol. 1, pp. 86–97; vol. 2, pp. 242–71; Peter W. Edbury, 'The Old French William of Tyre and the Origins of the Templars', in *Knighthoods of Christ: Essays on the History of the Crusades and the Knights Templar presented to Malcolm Barber*, ed. Norman Housley (Aldershot, 2007), pp. 151–64; idem, 'The Old French William of Tyre, the Templars and the Assassin Envoy', in *The Hospitallers, the Mediterranean and Europe: Festschrift for Anthony Luttrell*, ed. Karl Borchardt, Nikolas Jaspert and Helen J. Nicholson (Aldershot, 2007), pp. 25–37.

Chapter 21
Rinaldo da Concorezzo, Archbishop of Ravenna, and the Trial of the Templars in Northern Italy

Elena Bellomo

At the beginning of the fourteenth century northern Italy was going through a delicate political period marked by manifold conflicts and the rise of the first *signorie*. The military orders, which had a solid footing in the area thanks to a wide network of houses and significant connections with aristocracy and lay and ecclesiastical institutions, were also more or less affected by political upheavals. This situation would already make an analysis of the trial of the Templars in this area an interesting case for study. However, it was the role played in this inquiry by a leading contemporary figure, Rinaldo, archbishop of Ravenna, that most significantly marked the development of the trial in northern Italy and gave it its distinguishing features. This article aims to investigate Rinaldo's action in the trial, taking into account his personal background and the complex political situation of northern Italy in this period.

Pope Clement V entrusted the inquiry into the Temple to the inquisition and to ecclesiastical commissions which were given responsibility for investigating the order and its local dignitaries, covering wide areas. These commissions were appointed by the papal bull *Faciens misericordiam* in August 1308. In northern and part of central Italy the committee as designated by the pope included Rinaldo da Concorezzo, archbishop of Ravenna, Lotterio della Tosa, bishop of Florence, Giovanni, archbishop of Pisa, and Rainerio de Casoli, bishop of Cremona. At the same time the pope also charged episcopal commissions with examining the individual Templars of each diocese, who were to be ultimately judged in provincial councils.[1]

---

[1] I would like to thank Renzo Caravita, who sent me his publications on Rinaldo da Concorezzo, for his kindness and interest in my work. Abbreviations: Caravita 1 = Renzo Caravita, *Rinaldo da Concorrezzo, arcivescovo di Ravenna (1303–1321) al tempo di Dante* (Florence, 1964). Caravita 2 = Renzo Caravita, 'Rinaldo da Concorrezzo: Arcivescovo di Ravenna (1303–1321), canonico di Laon, non di Lodi', *Archivio Storico Lodigiano*, 2nd series, 12 (1964), 27–48. Caravita 3 = Renzo Caravita, 'Rinaldo da Concorezzo, l'arcivescovo di Ravenna (1303–1321) "che nel processo ai Templari fu giudice libero ed umano"', in *Tutti gli uomini del cardinale*: *Atti del convegno internazionale del 10 maggio 2003, Pozzuolo*

This article will outline the role played by Rinaldo da Concorezzo in the inquiry into the Temple in northern Italy, both in his capacity as papally appointed *inquisitor contra singulares personas et ordinem militie Templi Jerosolimitani* and as archbishop of Ravenna. His action during the trial resulted in the absolution of the Templars who were tried and in an important assumption that the use of torture was wrong, an assumption which diverged greatly from contemporary practice. Rinaldo's favourable attitude toward the Templars resembled the positive inclination then current among some northern Italian lay and Church institutions toward the military order but, conversely, contradicted the resentment felt in some places which had probably resulted from the Templars' involvement in local political struggles. Rinaldo's actions will be examined here taking into account this complex background.

Before the trial

Before his appointment to the papal commission, Rinaldo had already had a long and brilliant career; his involvement in the trial of the Templars would be just one of its final episodes. Rinaldo da Concorezzo descended from a notable Milanese lineage which sided with the local Guelph faction led by the Torriani family.[2] He studied law, probably in Bologna, between 1280 and 1286, when he is attested to as *iuris peritus* for the first time.[3] This undertaking was in perfect accordance with the family tradition, since several members of the da Concorezzo had already been well-known jurisprudents and had acted for the commune of Milan as ambassadors and legal consultants.[4] In 1286, in his capacity as *iuris peritus*, Rinaldo started teaching law in Lodi[5] and later joined the entourage of Pietro Peregrosso (d.1295),

Martesana (Pozzuolo Martesana, 2004), pp. 81–119. *Reg. Clem. V*, vol. 3, docs 3584–5, pp. 363–6; Gerolamo Rossi, *Historiarum Ravennatum libri decem* (Venice, 1590), vol. 6, p. 512; *Carte in appendice ai monumenti ravennati del conte Marco Fantuzzi*, ed. Antonio Tarlazzi, 2 vols (Ravenna, 1875), vol. 1, part 2, doc. 315, p. 475; Caravita 1, appendix, doc. 35, pp. 266–9; Malcom Barber, *The Trial of the Templars*, 2nd edn (Cambridge, 2006), pp. 125–6, 217–58; Francesco Tommasi, 'Interrogatorio dei Templari a Cesena (1310)', in *Acri 1291: La fine della presenza degli ordini militari in Terra Santa e i nuovi orientamenti del XIV secolo*, ed. Francesco Tommasi (Perugia, 1996), pp. 276–9; Alan Forey, *The Fall of the Templars in the Crown of Aragon* (Aldershot, 2001), pp. 75–114.

2 Caravita 1, pp. 3–10; Paolo Grillo, *Milano in età comunale (1183–1276): Istituzioni, società, economia* (Spoleto, 2001), pp. 50–53, 165–6, 412–13.

3 Caravita 1, pp. 11–12; Mauro Sarti and Mauro Fattorini, *De claris archigymnasii Bononiensium professoribus, a saec. XI usque ad saec XIV*, 2 vols (Bologna, 1888–96), vol. 2, p. 67. In 1295, Rinaldo is attested to as master of law: *Carte*, vol. 1, part 2, doc. 273, p. 41.

4 See above, note 2.

5 See above, note 3, and Caravita 2, pp. 28–9.

cardinal deacon of San Giorgio al Velabro.[6] Rinaldo followed Pietro to Rome and on his missions to France, where Rinaldo also became a canon regular of the church of Laon.[7] After Pietro's death, Rinaldo entered the service of Cardinal Benedetto Caetani, nephew of pope Boniface VIII. In September 1295 the pope granted Rinaldo the revenues of some churches in the diocese of Laon and archdiocese of Milan. In this document he is also referred to as subdeacon and papal chaplain, *domesticus commensalis* of the apostolic see and chaplain of Cardinal Caetani.[8] The following year Boniface VIII asked some Milanese prelates to grant the first available benefice to Giovanni da Concorezzo, a relative of Rinaldo, who had been examined *de literatura* by a papally appointed commission also including Rinaldo himself.[9] These deeds show that, thanks to the patronage of Boniface's nephew and the pope himself, Rinaldo had attained a good position in papal circles.

In 1296, Boniface appointed Rinaldo bishop of Vicenza. Here his nomination led to a dispute, due to the fact that the cathedral chapter, probably under the influence of the local commune, had already elected another bishop, Giacomo de' Bissari. In the end the latter gave up his office and Rinaldo was consecrated bishop in 1298. Unfortunately we do not know if he ever took possession of this see in person. In fact, after the confirmation of his appointment, Rinaldo remained in Rome in order to deal with a quarrel between the church of Vicenza and the local commune, which had to be examined at the papal curia.[10]

Still in 1298, probably by virtue of his previous experience beyond the Alps with Cardinal Peregrosso, Rinaldo was appointed as papal nuncio in France by

---

6 For Cardinal Peregrosso, see Claudio M. Tartari, 'Profilo biografico di Pietro Peregrosso', in *Il cardinale Pietro Peregrosso e la fondazione francescana di Pozzuolo Martesana: 1295–1995* (Pozzuolo Martesana, 1996), pp. 41–60. Rinaldo is mentioned in Peregrosso's last will: Enzo Pini, 'Il testamento "disperso" di Pietro Peregrosso', ibid., pp. 61–72; 'Edizione del testamento di Pietro Peregrosso', ed. Enzo Pini, ibid., pp. 173–205 (the mention of Rinaldo is on p. 182. See also pp. 200, 204); Caravita 3, pp. 87–8; Agostino Paravicini Bagliani, *I testamenti dei cardinali del Duecento* (Rome, 1980), pp. 56–8, 271–5.

7 For the period spent by Concorezzo in Peregrosso's entourage, see Caravita 3, pp. 87–8, 95–6. Concorezzo's appointment in Laon has been often misunderstood, and it has been erroneously stated that he had been canon regular in Lodi. Caravita 2, pp. 34–40.

8 *Carte*, vol. 1, part 2, doc. 273, pp. 415–16. For Benedetto Caetani, cardinal deacon of Santi Cosma e Damiano, see Daniel Waley, 'Caetani, Benedetto', in *Dizionario Biografico degli Italiani*, vol. 16 (Rome, 1973), pp. 125–6.

9 Caravita 1, appendix, doc. 1, p. 207; Caravita 2, pp. 42–4.

10 *Regesta pontificum Romanorum ab anno p. Ch. n. 1198 ad annum 1304*, ed. August Potthast, 2 vols (Berlin, 1874–5), vol. 2, nos 24408, 24410, 24509, 24697, 25011; *Les registres de Boniface VIII*, ed. Georges Digard et al., 4 vols (Paris, 1884–1939), vol. 1, doc. 1382, col. 502; doc. 1387, col. 503; doc. 1412, cols 511–12; doc. 1854, col. 702; doc. 2066, col. 795; vol. 2, doc. 2611, col. 145–6; vol. 3, docs 3934–5, col. 9; Giovanni Mantese, *Memorie storiche della Chiesa vicentina*, 5 vols (Vicenza, 1952–82), vol. 2, *Dal Mille al Milletrecento*, pp. 316–25; Caravita 1, pp. 23–5; Caravita 3, p. 92.

Boniface VIII. Rinaldo's task was both financial and political. He was in charge of an extraordinary collection of funds from the French clergy and the request for a loan from the king of France. He was also instructed to have the papal arbitration of the dispute between the kings of France and England over Gascony approved by both sovereigns and to publish it. Finally, Rinaldo was charged with taking custody of the king of Scotland, John Balliol, who had rebelled against Edward I of England. By 1300, Rinaldo had successfully carried out most of his tasks (only the issue of the loan from Philip IV was still unsettled), and, probably tired of the delicate diplomatic work done in France, asked the pope's permission to go back to Italy.[11] Conversely, Boniface sent him, along with the bishops of Amiens and Auxerre, to Charles of Anjou, the brother of the king of France, with the task of persuading him to come to Italy and pacify Romagna and Sicily.[12] Charles, who was allowed by the pope to marry Catherine of Courtenay, the heiress to the Byzantine throne, agreed to this and, in the summer of 1301, was designated rector of Romagna. In reality he completely neglected his duties there, and Rinaldo, chosen as his vicar *in spiritualibus*, had to take upon himself the difficult task of governing the province alone.[13] At that time Romagna was politically deeply divided: communes and newly established *signorie* constantly challenged the pope's control over the area, ecclesiastical properties and rights were often trespassed and the struggle between Guelphs and Ghibellines raged in many cities. Rinaldo tried to act as a mediator amongst the several factions, and the positive results of his zealous work are confirmed by his appointment as vicar general *in temporalibus* in 1302.[14]

The following year was a turning point in Rinaldo's career: his patron, Boniface VIII, died while the bishop was still at the papal court in Perugia, and later Rinaldo was elected archbishop of Ravenna. Pope Benedict XI confirmed his appointment, also settling a dispute with another elected archbishop, Leonardo Fieschi, probably supported by some bishops suffragan. On this occasion the pope stated that 'by long experience he knew Rinaldo's praiseworthy merits'. He also

---

11 *Regesta pontificum Romanorum*, vol. 2, nos 24727–9, 24766, 24934; *Les registres de Boniface VIII*, vol. 2, doc. 3545, col. 680; doc. 3554, cols 686–7; doc. 3682, cols 761–2; *Carte*, vol. 1, part 2, doc. 295, pp. 450–51. This mission is described in Caravita 1, pp. 25–32.

12 *Regesta pontificum Romanorum*, vol. 2, nos 24936, 24972, 24982; *Les registres de Boniface VIII*, vol. 2, docs 2886–7, cols 315–18, doc. 2994, col. 380, doc. 3651, col. 742; Caravita 1, pp. 33–4.

13 Mantese, *Memorie*, p. 323; Caravita 1, pp. 38–40.

14 *Regesta pontificum Romanorum*, vol. 2, no. 25130, 25154; *Les registres de Boniface VIII*, vol. 3, doc. 4668, col. 481; doc. 4911, col. 591; docs 5006–7, cols 644–5; Caravita 1, pp. 40–42; Caravita 3, p. 94. For a picture of Romagna in this period, see John Larner, *The Lords of Romagna* (London, 1962); Augusto Vasina, 'L'area emiliana e romagnola', in *Storia d'Italia*, ed. Giuseppe Galasso, 24 vols (Turin, 1979–1995), vol. 7, *Comuni e Signorie dell'Italia nordorientale e centrale: Emilia-Romagna, Toscana*, pp. 511–26; Giuliano Milani, *L'esclusione dal comune: Conflitti e bandi politici a Bologna e in altre città italiane dal XII al XIV secolo* (Rome, 2003), pp. 205–413.

added that Rinaldo was educated and respectable, prudent *in spiritualibus* and cautious *in temporalibus*.[15]

Rinaldo da Concorezzo was still in Perugia when Benedict died, and also spent the papal vacancy period there until the election of Clement V.[16] He eventually went to Ravenna and immediately started dealing with the financial, administrative and religious problems of that archbishopric, showing clear awareness of the primacy of the metropolitan bishop and the inviolability of Church rights.[17]

The trial

In 1308, when the trial of the Templars started in most of northern Italy, Rinaldo was the perfect candidate to take part in the inquiry. Two popes had held him in the highest esteem. He occupied a very prestigious post and had already proved to be a skilled diplomat and a strenuous defender of the Church's prerogatives.

As we have seen, Rinaldo also knew the protagonists behind the trial in person. He had met Philip IV during the mission to France and was at the papal curia when Clement V became pope. He also had had continual contacts with the papal circles during the pontificates of Boniface VIII and Benedict XI and, therefore, it cannot be ruled out that he had also made the acquaintance of those Templars who were members of the papal entourage during those periods, namely the Templar masters of central and northern Italy and papal chamberlains Uguccione da Vercelli[18] and Giacomo da Montecucco,[19] the papal porter and Templar master of Sicily Albertino di Canelli,[20] and the proctor general Pietro da Bologna.[21]

There is no evidence mentioning any contacts between the Templars and Rinaldo in the archbishopric of Ravenna before the beginning of the trial. Even though there was no Templar house in Ravenna itself, the surviving primary sources show that the order had a solid footing in the archbishopric ruled by Rinaldo. The Templar houses formed a widespread network in the area, had a sizeable patrimony and were capable of continually and efficiently producing resources.[22] The order

---

15 *Regesta pontificum Romanorum*, vol. 2, nos 25302–3; *Le registre de Benoît XI*, ed. Charles Grandjean (Paris, 1905), doc. 48, col. 57; Caravita 1, pp. 46–8.

16 Caravita 1, pp. 51–2.

17 Ibid., pp. 53–6.

18 Elena Bellomo, *The Templar Order in North-West Italy. 1142–c. 1330* (Leiden-Boston, 2008), pp. 103–5.

19 Ibid., pp. 105–6, 204–8.

20 Ibid., pp. 102, 117, 137–8, 198, 200.

21 Ibid., pp. 100–101, 197–9, 206–7.

22 Ezio Trota, 'L'ordine dei cavalieri templari a Modena e l'ospitale del ponte di S. Ambrogio', *Atti e Memorie della Deputazione di Storia Patria per le Province Modenesi*, 11th series, 6 (1984), pp. 29–55; Cristina Dondi, '*Missale Vetus ad usum templariorum*: L'ordine dei cavalieri templari in area modenese nei secoli XII–XIV', *Aevum*, 68 (1994),

also enjoyed positive relations with lay and ecclesiastical authorities and local society in general. Moreover, Bologna and Piacenza, the two most important houses in northern Italy, which had often hosted Templar provincial chapters, were in dioceses governed by a suffragan and an exempt bishop respectively who had multiple links with the archiepiscopal see of Ravenna.[23]

Before *Faciens misericordiam* was issued, most of the northern Italian Templars were still living in the order's houses. Economic transactions made in this period prove that some of them were still carrying out their normal lifestyle.[24] Only for Piedmont is there evidence that, after the papal bull *Pastoralis praeeminentie* was issued in November 1307 and sent to Amadeus V of Savoy, some Templars actively tried to avoid capture.[25] In the summer of 1308, local inquisitors started arresting the Templars and seizing Templar possessions.[26] The inquisitorial province of Lombardy, which included the whole of northern Italy, was divided into a 'lower' and an 'upper' district and was under the control of Dominican inquisitors, whereas Romagna was under the Franciscans.[27] Their task was often far from easy: in at least one case, a Templar preceptor, and maybe some other brothers, tried to avoid arrest, and 25 armed men were necessary to apprehend

pp. 339–66; Cristina Dondi, 'Manoscritti liturgici dei templari e degli ospitalieri: Le nuove prospettive aperte dal sacramentario templare di Modena (Biblioteca capitolare O.II.13)', in *I Templari, la guerra, la santità*, ed. Simonetta Cerrini (Rimini, 2000), pp. 92–131; Roberto Greci, 'Prime presenze gerosolimitane nell'Emilia occidentale e nella bassa Lombardia', in *Riviera di Levante tra Emilia e Toscana: Un crocevia per l'ordine di San Giovanni, Atti del Convegno, Genova-Chiavari-Rapallo, 9–12 settembre 1999*, ed. Josepha Costa Restagno (Genoa, 2001), pp. 413–14; Bellomo, *The Templar Order*, pp. 114–17, 262–76, 312–13, 325–6, 330–31, 346.

23 Caravita 1, pp. 42–3; Bellomo, *The Templar Order*, pp. 116–17, 262–9.

24 Milan, Archivio di Stato, Fondo Religione, Miscellanea Materiale Restaurato, cartella 5, 6 April 1308; Alessandro Colombo, 'I Gerosolimitani e i Templari a Milano e la via della Commenda', *Archivio Storico Lombardo*, 3rd series, 53 (1926), doc. 8, p. 220; Turin, Archivio di Stato, Materie politiche per rapporto all'interno, Ordini Cavallereschi, Ordine dei Templari, mazzo I, no. 5; Bellomo, *The Templar Order*, pp. 182–3.

25 Turin, Archivio di Stato, Materie politiche per rapporto all'interno, Ordini Cavallereschi, Ordine dei Templari, mazzo I, no. 6; Caravita 1, appendix, doc. 34, pp. 265–6; Bellomo, *The Templar Order*, pp. 183, 332–3.

26 Caravita 1, pp. 115–16; Bellomo, *The Templar Order*, pp. 182, 227, 336. In some areas the confiscation, the arrests and the administration of the Templar properties were conducted by civil officials designated by the pope. *Carte*, vol. 1, part 2, doc. 336, pp. 539–42; Bellomo, *The Templar Order*, pp. 186–7, 227.

27 Gerolamo Biscaro, 'Inquisitori ed eretici lombardi (1292–1318)', *Miscellanea Storica Italiana*, 3rd series, 29 (1922), p. 450, note 1; Mariano D'Alatri, *Eretici e inquisitori in Italia*, 2 vols (Rome, 1986–87), vol. 1, pp. 117–20, 127–34; Mariano D'Alatri, *L'inquisizione francescana nell'Italia centrale nel secolo XIII* (Rome, 1954), pp. 17, 346; Tommasi, 'Interrogatorio', pp. 274–6.

them.[28] The inquisitor Filippo de Cumis who was in charge of the Templar houses of the Pavia area encountered very significant difficulties in his duty and even 'risked his life', or so he claimed, in the execution of his work.[29] Local lessees did not cooperate with him and often did not pay the rents, and some produce of the Templar houses was also stolen by 'people who rebelled against the inquisitor and did not obey him'. Filippo's account of experiencing hostility is significantly confirmed by the fact that a notary who came to Tortona in order to draw up some deeds concerning the Templar possessions had been beaten and had to stay there for 18 days before he recovered completely.[30]

The reason for this animosity was not necessarily a sympathetic attitude toward the Templars or the belief that they were innocent of the charges against them. Most probably many people were just trying to take advantage of the situation either by seizing Templar property or simply by stealing the harvest. For his part, the inquisitor attempted both to encourage the retrieval of the order's possessions and also to recover them directly, increasing local opposition to his work.[31]

Moreover, the inquisitors found that some Templar houses and their possessions in southern Lombardy, Emilia and Romagna were already abandoned, plundered or even completely devastated.[32] It is possible that the Templars themselves despoiled some houses before leaving them, while the acts of vandalism encountered were most probably connected to the struggle between Guelphs and Ghibellines that was raging in the region. These episodes took place in the Piacenza area in particular, where the local Templars, members of Guelph families, seemed to have sided with this faction.[33] Some of them were to pay personally for that choice: in 1308, the Templar master Giacomo Fontana, member of a lineage that had strong links with the Guelph leader Alberto Scotti, was robbed and beaten, and his house in Cabriolo was looted and burnt down.[34] After the end of the trial, in 1314, his relative Raimondo, preceptor of the house of Piacenza, was killed by men sent by the Ghibelline leader Vergiuso Landi.[35]

However, it is also worth remembering that other Templar detainees were strongly supported by both civil and ecclesiastical authorities. Giacomo, preceptor of the house of Tortona, was explicitly protected by the local commune.[36] The

---

28 *Carte*, vol. 1, part 2, doc. 350, pp. 579–80.

29 Ibid., doc. 339, p. 546.

30 Ibid., doc. 340, pp. 550–52; doc. 350, pp. 577–8, 580, 583–4.

31 See, for instance, *Carte*, vol. 1, part 2, doc. 353, pp. 589–91.

32 See, for instance, ibid., doc. 318, pp. 486–7; Bellomo, *The Templar Order*, pp. 183, 187–9.

33 Bellomo, *The Templar Order*, pp. 176–7, 203, 268–75.

34 *Carte*, vol. 1, part 2, doc. 332, pp. 523, 530.

35 Guarino, *Chronicon Placentinum ab anno MCCLXXXIX ad annum MCCCXIII*, in *Chronica tria Placentina a Johanne Codagnello, ab anonymo et a Guerino conscripta*, ed. Bernardo Pallastrelli (Parma, 1859), p. 382.

36 *Carte*, vol. 1, part 2, doc. 340, p. 551.

communes of Tortona and Pavia also asked for the release of the detained brothers *pro fideiussione*. The podestà, the captain of the *popolo*, the count and the bishop of Pavia also wrote some letters about the administration of the Templar property.[37] This obviously increased the problems that the inquisitors were facing, compelling them to meet frequently and to keep in constant touch with the pope to seek his advice.[38]

The commission which included Rinaldo da Concorezzo only started work in September 1309, more than one year after its appointment.[39] This inaction was probably due to the illness and death of Lotterio della Tosa (1309), bishop of Florence,[40] and the ongoing political crisis in Ferrara where the dispute for the succession to Azzo d'Este degenerated into open warfare also involving Venice and the pope. At this critical juncture Rinaldo da Concorezzo gave financial support to the papal legates sent to Ferrara and then went to that city in order to give them his guidance. They later recognized that his presence and prestige were immensely helpful on that occasion.[41] In September of that year, the commissioners in the Templars' trial met in Bologna.[42] From there they informed the bishops suffragan that the commission had been established, published the bulls on the inquiry, and nominated some vicars who had to replace the inquisitors and administer the Templar possessions.[43]

In 1309, Giovanni da Pisa was appointed nuncio for Tuscany, Lombardy, Dalmatia and Istria, but in reality he later focused his activity on Tuscany alone.[44] Rainerio de Casoli, bishop of Cremona, took part only in the first meeting in 1309; after that, there is no further mention of him in the documents concerning the trial. He met strong opposition to his election in Cremona and, probably because of

---

[37] Ibid., doc. 350, p. 583.

[38] Ibid., doc. 331, pp. 526–8; Bellomo, *The Templar Order*, pp. 189–90. For the *consilia* between inquisitors, see *Carte*, vol. 1, part 2, doc. 340, p. 552; doc. 350, p. 583; Marina Benedetti, 'Le parole e le opere di frate Lanfranco (1292–1305)', in *Le scritture e le opere degli inquisitori, Quaderni di Storia Religiosa*, 9 (2002), pp. 131–3.

[39] For the appointment of this commission, see *Carte*, vol. 1, part 2, doc. 314–15, pp. 474–9.

[40] *Hierarchia catholica medii et recentioris aevi*, ed., Konrad Eubel et al., 9 vols (Münster, 1913–78; repr. Padua, 1960–2002), vol. 1, p. 250.

[41] Giovanni Soranzo, *La guerra tra Venezia e la Santa Sede per il dominio di Ferrara. 1308–1313* (Città di Castello, 1905), pp. 114–76; Anna Laura Trombetti Budriesi, 'La signoria estense dalle origini ai primi del Trecento: forme di potere e strutture economico-sociali', in *Storia di Ferrara*, 7 vols (Ferrara, 1987–94), vol. 5, *Il Basso Medioevo. XII–XIV*, pp. 179–81; Caravita 1, pp. 56–7.

[42] The Templars of this house had good treatment thanks to Rinaldo. *Carte*, vol. 1, part 2, doc. 326, pp. 506–7.

[43] *Carte*, vol. 1, part. 2, docs 320–22, pp. 488–96; Caravita 1, pp. 120–21.

[44] Caravita 1, p. 118.

this situation, was not able to fulfil his duties as commissioner.[45] Between 1309 and 1311 Rinaldo was denoted as *inquisitor* for Lombardy, Tuscany, the march of Treviso and Istria[46] and, as the evidence from the archiepiscopal archive in Ravenna proves, he was the only person to whom the vicars working in the whole of northern Italy actually referred. Thus Rinaldo had to face the very complex and delicate situation described in the inquisitors' accounts by himself.[47]

In his capacity as papal commissioner, Rinaldo was entrusted with the investigation into the Temple and its local dignitaries covering a wide area. Thus he received at least three copies of *Faciens misericordiam*, each instructing his action in a certain area. In the copy regarding his mandate in Lombardy, the pope stated that he had already sent *certas personas* to this area in order to proceed against the local provincial master. This measure was probably taken due to the fact that the master of Lombardy, Giacomo da Montecucco, had recently escaped from prison in Poitiers, and the pope had put a price on his head and launched an investigation into his flight.[48]

Rinaldo was not only a papal commissioner, but also the leading figure in the diocesan commission which was to try the Templars in Emilia and Romagna; in 1309, along with the exempt bishop of Rimini, he conducted the investigation into two Templars in Cesena. The bishops of Cesena and Montefeltro and an inquisitor, probably Vincenzo da Bologna, were also present.[49] The commission examined the Templars using both the list of questions for the investigation into members of the order and the one on the order in general. Their answers are in a single transcript of interrogation. This seems to be an extraordinary procedure, justified by the fact that Rinaldo was also a papally appointed commissioner and probably targeted to conclude the proceedings as soon as possible just as the pope insisted.[50] At the same time we will emphasize that Rinaldo's intention always seemed to be to conclude the trial quickly, and this has been also interpreted as a way to reach a speedy absolution of the individual Templars.

---

[45] Carlo Fedele Savio, *Gli antichi vescovi d'Italia dalle origini al 1300 descritti per regioni. Lombardia*, 2 vols (Florence-Bergamo, 1913–32), vol. 2, part 2, pp. 144–5; Franco Tantardini, 'I Templari a Cremona e i vescovi Siccardo e Rainerio', *Bollettino Storico Cremonese*, new series, 6 (1999), p. 285.

[46] *Carte*, vol. 1, part. 2, doc. 320, p. 488; doc. 321, p. 490; docs 359–60, pp. 600–601.

[47] The charters on the trial of the Templars kept in the archiepiscopal archive in Ravenna are described in Caravita 1, passim, and Renzo Caravita, 'Nuovi documenti sull'ordine del Tempio dall'Archivio Arcivescovile di Ravenna', *Sacra Militia*, 3 (2002), pp. 225–78.

[48] *PUT*, vol. 2, doc. 39, pp. 59–60; doc. 74, p. 114; Bellomo *The Templar Order*, pp. 204–5.

[49] Tommasi, 'Interrogatorio', pp. 274–9.

[50] Ibid., pp. 281–2.

The members of the military order examined in Cesena were the sergeant Andrea da Siena and the priest Giovanni da Todi. Their depositions are the only complete surviving evidence of the Templars' examinations in northern Italy and, therefore, are very noteworthy. Both Giovanni and Andrea defended the order and its members, only admitting to minor errors of behaviour. Giovanni blamed the arrogance of the order as its major fault. However, he did not exclude the possibility that in France the Templars might perform completely different practices, since this had been stated by the pope himself. Andrea also agreed with that and did not want to question the pope's decisions and authority, but he emphasized that the use of torture had played a decisive role in those Templars' admissions of guilt. Andrea himself had abandoned wearing the Templar habit after being informed of the persecution and murder of his fellow brothers.[51] It is likely that most of the Templars examined in northern Italy made similar statements to those of Giovanni and Andrea. As we shall see, the arguments they put forth probably had a certain impact on Rinaldo, especially as regards the effects of torture.

According to the procedure set in the papal bulls, provincial councils had to be assembled in order to examine the results of local inquiries and the inquisitors were allowed to take part in these meetings. A first council, chaired by Rinaldo da Concorezzo, took place in Ravenna in January 1311. It was attended by the exempt bishops, the suffragans and the inquisitors of Emilia and Romagna.[52] Unfortunately, no evidence from this council has survived. The question of the Templars was in all likelihood thoroughly discussed, but the participants were not able to reach a satisfactory resolution.[53] Rinaldo thus convened another council in Bologna in order to sort out the issue once and for all.[54] At this meeting, he also requested the presence of the Templars who had been tried, in order to re-examine them. Here they would have also heard the final verdict.[55]

The second council was postponed and relocated to Ravenna probably because of the arrival in Italy of Henry VII. Later sources state that Rinaldo met the emperor but no contemporary evidence confirms this meeting ever occurred. As Renzo Caravita hypothesizes, the archbishop probably moved the council to Ravenna because the Guelph city of Bologna could have been one of the targets of the imperial army. The second council began by examining the results of the

---

51 Ibid., pp. 287–98.

52 A first provincial meeting was probably held at the end of 1309. Nothing is known about it: Caravita 1, pp. 124–5.

53 Caravita 1, pp. 140–41; Renzo Caravita, 'Il primo dei due concili provinciali ravennati sui Templari', in *Atti del XVII Convegno di Ricerche Templari* (Latina, 2000), pp. 81–9. For a list of the bishops who probably attended this assize, see Caravita 1, pp. 139–40.

54 *Carte*, vol. 1, part 2, doc. 359, pp. 600–601; Caravita 1, pp. 141–2. For the preparatory synods for this second council, see ibid., pp. 142–5.

55 Caravita 1, appendix 1, doc. 47, pp. 294–6; Caravita, 'Il primo dei due concili', pp. 90–91.

diocesan inquiries into the Templars. Then the Templars themselves were heard. The only surviving evidence of their statements is a summary of the depositions made by seven brothers from Piacenza, five from Bologna and one from Faenza. They answered the questions appended to *Faciens misericordiam*, confuting all the charges and the accusations levelled against them by some witnesses.[56]

Since the council seemed to be turning in favour of the members of the military order, the Dominican inquisitors attending the meeting reacted by stating that a protracted examination of the Templars, which should include the use of torture, was necessary. Rinaldo then asked the participants whether the investigation had been impartially carried out, to which the council agreed unanimously. Rinaldo then asked if the bishops and clerics present thought that it was necessary to carry out further investigations and use torture. Only the two Dominican inquisitors replied that it was essential. The Franciscan inquisitor sided with the rest of the council.[57] Rinaldo finally asked whether the pope's opinion on the issue was to be sought either right away or at the council of Vienne.[58] The council would not be held until much later, and Renzo Caravita correctly emphasizes that this question was oriented to further assist the Templars and bring the proceedings against them to a conclusion as soon as possible.[59] The council decided that the pope's opinion could be solicited at Vienne. At the end of the meeting Rinaldo and the prelates present in Ravenna approved a declaration that had no precedent; it stated that 'those who confess for fear of torture shall be considered innocent if they subsequently withdraw their confessions, as shall those not having the courage to retract for fear of torture and further punishment'.[60] The council also suggested that only if a majority of the Templars were guilty should the possessions of the order be confiscated, and that the sinful members of the Temple would have to perform penance in the order itself.

The prelates finally decided that the Templars tried in Ravenna could not simply be acquitted. They should be subject to a public compurgation. This was an oath by which a person charged with heresy or other crimes, who had not confessed and whose guilt had not been supported by evidence, could regain his or her reputation. The oath had to be corroborated by a certain number of witnesses called *testes compurgantes*. After the end of the council, Rinaldo determined the procedure of the compurgation. Usually, this oath had to be made within a year of the court order, but in this case Rinaldo asked that it be made within 40 days, emphasizing that this was a totally voluntary procedure. This is a clear sign that,

---

56 Rossi, *Historiarum*, pp. 525sqq.; Caravita 3, p. 103.

57 For the relationship between Rinaldo and the Franciscan order, see Caravita 3, pp. 95–7.

58 For this council see Ewald Müller, *Das Konzil von Vienne, 1311–1312: Seine Quellen und seine Geschichte* (Münster i. W., 1934); Barber, *The Trial*, pp. 259sqq.; Sophia Menache, *Clement V* (Cambridge, 1998), pp. 235–40, 279sqq.

59 Caravita 1, p. 149.

60 Rossi, *Historiarum*, p. 526.

after the outcome of the council, Rinaldo considered the Templars to have already been definitively acquitted. Each Templar had to find seven *testes compurgantes*, both clergy and laymen. They could not be members of the Temple, since the whole of the order had been put on trial.[61] A quick examination of the surviving lists of the *testes compurgantes* for three Piacenza Templars (12 people for each member of the order) clearly confirms their connection with the Fontana family and their Guelph entourage, several local ecclesiastical institutions, including the Hospital, and important figures such as Rogerio Caccia, probably a Templar's relative who is identifiable as the master of law and chaplain of Boniface VIII of the same name.[62]

Clement V subsequently insisted that the commissioners for northern and central Italy use torture in order to obtain truthful confessions.[63] The archbishop of Pisa complied with these papal instructions.[64] Conversely Rinaldo did not proceed any further against the Templars, conforming his action to the decisions of the provincial council of Ravenna rather than the pope's desires. He then took part in the council of Vienne. Here it became apparent that his behaviour had damaged his position. Even though Rinaldo was called to officially inaugurate the works of the council, he was not seated next to the pope as was the custom for an archbishop of Ravenna during general meetings. He was excluded from the examination of the trial transcripts and later was not asked to supervise the transfer of the Templar patrimony to the Hospital in his archdiocese.[65]

In conclusion, we have to ascertain why he acted so differently from the archbishop of Pisa. In all likelihood both his personal acquaintance with Philip IV and his commitment to the moral regeneration of the clergy made him suspicious about the accusations against the Templars. Rinaldo knew perfectly well of the king

61 Caravita 1, appendix, doc. 49, pp. 299–301; Renzo Caravita, 'La "purgazione" nel processo inquisitorio: Il caso dei Templari processati a Ravenna', in *Atti del XV Convegno di Ricerche Templari* (Latina, 1998), pp. 11–16.

62 *Carte*, vol. 1, part 2, docs 289–90, pp. 441–6; Caravita 1, appendix, doc. 49, pp. 301–7; Caravita, '"La purgazione"', pp. 19–20; Bellomo, *The Templar Order*, pp. 135, 194–5, 273.

63 *Reg. Clem. V*, vol. 6, docs 7527–8, p. 439; *Carte*, vol. 1, part. 2, doc. 628, pp. 628–9. Renzo Caravita hypothesizes that Dominican inquisitors immediately informed the pope of the results of the Ravenna council. Papal reaction was actually prompt and resolute. The council closed on 21 June, and Clement V wrote to Rinaldo asking for a new inquiry on 27 June. On that occasion the pope also informed the commissioners for northern and central Italy that master Pietro *iudex de Urbe*, *canonicus Veronensis* and *scriptor pape*, had been appointed as their new collaborator. It is apparent that his task was to control the commission and conform the results of its work to papal expectations. Renzo Caravita, *L'Arcivescovo di Ravenna Rinaldo da Concorezzo e il processo ai Templari* (Ravenna, 2008), pp. 50–51.

64 Telesforo Bini, 'Dei Tempieri e del loro processo in Toscana', *Atti della Reale Accademia Lucchese di Scienze, Lettere ed Arti*, 15 (1845), doc. 9, pp. 469–506.

65 Müller, *Das Konzil*, pp. 666, 675; Caravita 1, pp. 159–60; Caravita 3, pp. 105–6.

of France's financial problems and his ambitions, and he probably recognized that the trial was part of a wider hegemonic plan. Moreover, before the beginning of the inquiry Rinaldo had acted very resolutely and severely in correcting any abuses by and immorality of the clergy in his jurisdiction, but the Templars had never been involved in any of his inquests.[66] The direct examination of two Templars in Cesena probably convinced him even more of the Templars' innocence and made him realize the real role of torture in any trial. Moreover, Rinaldo possibly knew in person at least one Templar dignitary who confessed in France and then retracted his statements trying in vain to defend the order: Pietro da Bologna. It is worth remembering that after escaping from prison in Paris, Pietro went back to Bologna where he died in 1329. He was buried in the grounds of the local Templar house and, ironically, according to some sources, his epitaph highly praised the qualities of this *relapsus*.[67] This further confirms that Rinaldo was not an isolated supporter of the Temple. The general scepticism about the order's guilt was actually widespread in this part of Italy. Not only all the prelates who took part in the second council of Ravenna, but also the Franciscan inquisitor who was present at the Cesena inquiry eventually believed that the Templars should be acquitted. The fact that some Emilian Templars probably sided with the Guelph faction just as the da Concorezzo family did in Milan may have further strengthened Rinaldo's decision to protect them.

Unfortunately, we do not know how the inquiry was carried out in the other ecclesiastical provinces of northern Italy, but, for instance, in Ivrea the master of the local Templar house was well received at the episcopal curia in 1311, probably after being tried at a diocesan council.[68] In any case, Rinaldo was a *doctor legum*, and the inquiry he had overseen had actually been fair. It was conducted according to papal instructions and contemporary practice, with the only exception being the rejection of torture as an instrument of the trial. The issue of the Templars had been discussed at two councils. The results of local investigations had been closely examined. Not only were the Templars heard but also some witnesses who testified against them. A public compurgation closed the proceedings against the members of the military order. Following the procedures set by the pope, the council held in Bologna returned a verdict on the single members of the order. However, it also suggested guidelines for a verdict over the Temple as a whole which tallied with the results of the local inquiry. This further shows that not only Rinaldo but all the prelates present at the council thought that the outcome of their work did not merely have a local significance.[69]

Rinaldo's firm belief that the inquiry he had overseen was procedurally correct and fair is above all emphasized by his refusal to carry it on using torture. This

---

66 Caravita 1, pp. 87–94.

67 See Bellomo, *The Templar Order*, pp. 206–7.

68 Ivrea, Archivio Storico della Diocesi di Ivrea, Protocollo VIII.3.310/320, fols 6v, 10r–v; Bellomo, *The Templar Order*, pp. 196, 206, 282.

69 Caravita, *L'Arcivescovo di Ravenna*, pp. 52–3.

decision clearly opposed papal orders and was even more significant since Rinaldo was not only a prelate influenced by his personal knowledge of his own archdiocese but a skilled diplomat with international experience and long familiarity with papal circles. Therefore, one of the features of Rinaldo's personality that becomes particularly apparent, thanks to his involvement in the trial, is his independence of thought. In the end this proved to be detrimental to his career but paved the way for the recognition of a judicial principle of great worth: the rejection of torture as a means of finding out the truth.

Chapter 22
The Templars and Their Trial in Sicily

Kristjan Toomaspoeg

Southern Italy offers us an interesting local example of the abolition of the order of the Temple, because, as a consequence of the insurrection of the Sicilian Vespers in 1282, the region was divided into two kingdoms: the Aragonese island and the mainland, ruled by the Angevin dynasty.[1] So one could expect in this instance two different attitudes towards the trial, as the Aragonese had no special reason to attack the Templars, whereas the Angevin dynasty was closely tied to French politics, as was also the case in this matter. Thus the case of the two kingdoms of Sicily illustrates many different aspects of the trial. I would like to use this opportunity to present a very short summary of this argument, which is not well known to English-speaking scholars.[2]

The Templars

First, I will consider the importance of the Templars in southern Italian society. As can be seen (Figure 22.1), the landholdings of the order here were much less abundant than those of the Hospitallers[3] or even of the Teutonic Knights,[4] and this lack of fortune had some very precise reasons.[5] Most importantly, at the

---

[1] Denis Mack Smith, *The Medieval Sicily* (New York, 1969); Illuminato Peri, *Uomini, città e campagne in Sicilia dall'XI al XIII secolo* (Rome and Bari, 1978); idem, *La Sicilia dopo il vespro: Uomini città e campagne, 1282–1376* (Rome and Bari, 1981).

[2] On this topic, see *UT*, vol. 1, pp. 408–12, vol. 2, pp. 105–40; Giovanni Guerrieri, *I Cavalieri Templari nel Regno di Sicilia* (Trani, 1909); Litterio Villari, *Templari in Sicilia* (Latina, 1993); Cristian Guzzo, *Templari in Sicilia: La storia e le sue fonti tra Federico II e Roberto d'Angiò* (Genoa, 2003); Kristjan Toomaspoeg, *Templari e Ospitalieri nella Sicilia Medievale* (Bari, 2003).

[3] Toomaspoeg, *Templari*; Mariarosaria Salerno, *Gli ospedalieri di San Giovanni di Gerusalemme nel Mezzogiorno d'Italia (secc. XII–XV)* (Bari, 2001).

[4] Kristjan Toomaspoeg, *Les Teutoniques en Sicile (1197–1492)* (Rome, 2003); *L'Ordine Teutonico nel Mediterraneo: Atti del Convegno internazionale di studio Torre Alemanna (Cerignola)-Mesagne-Lecce, 16–18 ottobre 2003*, ed. Hubert Houben (Galatina, 2004).

[5] See, for example, Hans Prutz, *Die Geistlichen Ritterorden: Ihre Stellung zur kirchlichen, politischen, gesellschaftlichen und wirtschaftlichen Entwicklung des Mittelalters* (Berlin, 1908), p. 332.

beginning of the Templars' presence in Italy, in 1130, Roger II of Sicily was allied to the antipope Anacletus II, who crowned him as first king of Sicily, and remained until 1140 an enemy of Anacletus's rival, Pope Innocent II.[6] In territories such as Tuscany that were under the papal authority of Innocent, a supporter of Bernard of Clairvaux, the Templars and the Cistercians expanded their territories quite spectacularly during this period,[7] but in Sicily, their alliance to Innocent represented a considerable drawback, so that until 1150 there was no public support for the Templars, and the order acquired only some small land holdings through private donations.[8]

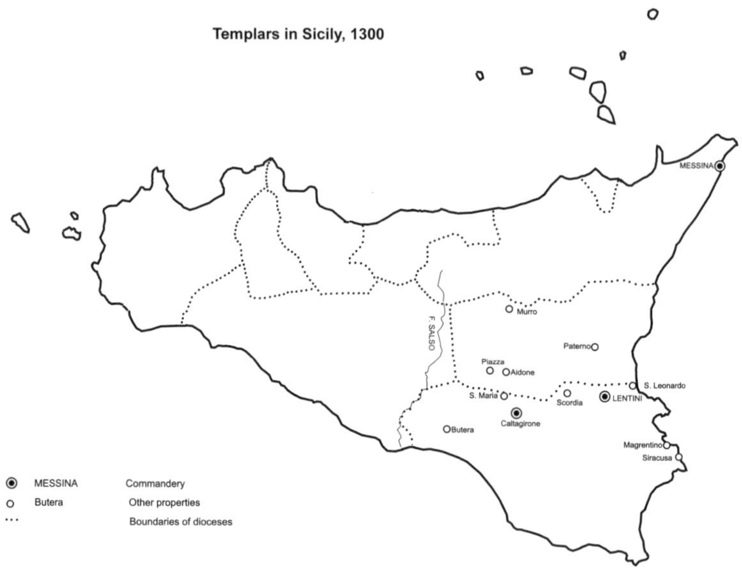

Fig. 22.1 Templars in Sicily, 1300

---

[6] Erich Caspar, *Roger II (1101–1154) und die Gründung der normannisch-sicilischen Monarchie* (Innsbruck, 1904); Hubert Houben, *Roger II. von Sizilien: Herrscher zwischen Orient und Okzident* (Darmstadt, 1997).

[7] Cf. Fulvio Bramato, *Storia dell'Ordine dei Templari in Italia: Le fondazioni* (Rome, 1991).

[8] Kristjan Toomaspoeg, 'L'insediamento dei grandi ordini militari cavallereschi in Sicilia, 1145–1220', in *La presenza dei cavalieri di San Giovanni in Sicilia: Convegno internazionale, Palermo, Palazzo dei Normanni, 17 giugno 2000 – Messina, Palazzo Zanca, 18 giugno 2000* (Rome, 2001), pp. 41–51; idem, 'Le patrimoine des grands ordres militaires en Sicile, 1145–1492', *Mélanges de l'École française de Rome, Moyen Âge*, 113.1 (2001), 313–41.

Fig. 22.2 Commanderies of the military orders in southern Italy, 1300

The king's court gave no important privileges and no relevant donations to the Temple until 1187 when, after Hattin and the fall of Jerusalem, the religious orders of the Holy Land received a lot of support in the kingdom, from the Norman nobility but also from Emperor Henry VI, crowned king of Sicily in 1194, and his wife Constance of Hauteville, and many of them created important settlements in southern Italy.[9] Yet the properties of the Temple on the island and the mainland remained still relatively small and in many cases insignificant.

[9] Geneviève Bresc-Bautier, 'Les possessions des églises de Terre Sainte en Italie du Sud (Pouille, Calabre, Sicile)', in *Roberto il Guiscardo e il suo tempo: Relazioni e comunicazioni nelle prime Giornate normanno-sveve (Bari, maggio 1973)* (Rome, 1975), pp. 13–39.

The real settlement of the Temple in southern Italy took place some years later, between 1208 and 1213. At this time, the young King Frederick II was declared to be of age to rule independently but remained in fact still a child. His court was controlled by a powerful nobleman of Norman origin, Paganus of Parisio, who was close to the Templars but also to the Hospitallers and Teutonic Knights.[10] Thanks to his influence, the Templars received many new properties in the kingdom: such a huge quantity that, afterwards, Frederick II, who considered the first part of his reign as a period of waste and dissipation of the royal domain, did not renew some of the donations to the Temple, because the donors had given to the order territories which were subject to the king's authority.[11]

After 1213, the Temple had properties in the whole eastern, i.e. Adriatic half of the kingdom, which we can divide into two parts (see Figure 22.2). On the one hand there were the order's houses, sometimes with hospitals and churches, in the big crusade ports at the final or supplementary stage of the so-called *Via Francigena*, such as Messina, Bari, Brindisi, Barletta and Trani.[12] These houses were evidently important because of their role in the traffic to the Holy Land, especially during the reigns of Charles I and Charles II of Anjou.[13] On the other hand, there were the big landholdings of the Temple which gave economic support not only to the urban and suburban houses inside the kingdom but also to the Templar houses in the Holy Land. These properties were especially notable in two areas: the coast of the Apulian region, between Manfredonia and Brindisi, and the central part of eastern Sicily, between the towns of Aidone, Caltagirone and Lentini.[14] The administration of this patrimony was based on two preceptories: Barletta and Messina. Both of them were created at the end of the twelfth century, but it seems that Barletta had always been more important than Messina, and on some occasions the Templar preceptor of Barletta was considered the chief of the order in the whole kingdom of Sicily.[15]

---

10 Carlo Alberto Garufi, 'Per la storia dei secoli XI e XII: Miscellanea diplomatica. Parte IV, I de Parisio e i de Ocra nei contadi di Paternò e di Butera', *Archivio storico per la Sicilia orientale*, 10 (1913), 345–73.

11 Villari, *Templari*, pp. 29–30.

12 Cf. Hubert Houben, 'Templari e Teutonici nel Mezzogiorno normanno-svevo', in *Il Mezzogiorno normanno-svevo e le Crociate: Atti delle quattordicesime giornate normanno-sveve. Bari, 17–20 ottobre 2000*, ed. Giosuè Musca (Bari, 2002), pp. 251–88.

13 Kristjan Toomaspoeg, 'Le ravitaillement de la Terre Sainte: L'exemple des possessions des ordres militaires dans le royaume de Sicile au XIIIe siècle', in *L'Expansion occidentale (XIe–XVe siècles): Formes et conséquences, XXXIIIe Congrès de la Société des Historiens Médiévistes de l'Enseignement Supérieur Public (Madrid, Casa de Velázquez, 23–26 mai 2002)* (Paris, 2003), pp. 143–58.

14 Alceste Roccella, *I templari e gli spedalieri in Piazza Armerina* (Piazza Armerina, 1878); Villari, *Templari*, pp. 15–18.

15 For the historical background, see Anthony Luttrell, 'Templari e Ospitalieri in Italia', in *La chiesa di San Bevignate a Perugia,* ed. Mario Roncetti, Pietro Scarpellini and

In the middle of the thirteenth century, there were some important changes in the Templar administration on the island of Sicily. In 1259, the Templar Master Thomas Bérard, who was obviously conscious of the weakness of the order's settlements in Messina, sold to the Dominicans some important properties near the city,[16] an action which stands alongside other modifications of the Templar patrimony in Italy made by Bérard, for example in Rome at the same year,[17] and which aimed to strengthen the order's properties in some areas and to abolish them in those regions where there was no possibility of growth. Even the headquarters of the Templars in Sicily were no longer at Messina but at Lentini on the eastern coast of the island.[18]

The political history of the Temple in the kingdom of Sicily is not well known because it remains overshadowed by two major topics: the order's history in the Holy Land and the relations between the Temple and the king and emperor, Frederick II.[19] As already stated, the Templar settlements in southern Italy had only acquired importance at the beginning of Frederick's rule. According to the older historiography, after his crusade and his first excommunication Frederick repressed the Templars of the kingdom and took away some of their properties. In reality, the consequences of the conflict between imperial authority and the Temple were not so drastic in southern Italy. Frederick was a very pragmatic ruler who aimed to maintain an internal peace in the kingdom and not to provoke new conflicts. Nevertheless the Templars did lose some of their properties under Frederick's rule, mostly because the king did not confirm some previous concessions made in his name. For example, in 1210, William of Orleans, the commander of the Temple in Sicily, received from a noble of Norman origin, Malgerius of Altavilla, the fief of Partenico.[20] This fief was part of the king's domain, and Malgerius could hold it only as a vassal of Frederick II, so that the donation to the Templars, confirmed by Paganus of Parisio in the king's name, was, if not illegal, at least damaging to

---

Francesco Tommasi (Perugia, 1987), pp. 19–26, and in Anthony Luttrell, *The Hospitallers of Rhodes and Their Mediterranean World* (Aldershot, 1992), article I.

16 October 1259: Vladimír J. Koudelka, 'Pergamene del convento domenicano di Messina (1218–1397)', *Archivum Fratrum Praedicatorum*, 44 (1974), no. 26, pp. 83–4.

17 Giulio Silvestrelli, 'Le chiese e i feudi dell'Ordine dei Templari e dell'Ordine di San Giovanni di Gerusalemme nella regione romana', *Rendiconti della Reale Accademia dei Lincei*, V, 26 (1917), 490–520.

18 Cf. Toomaspoeg, *Templari*, no. 164, p. 183.

19 James M. Powell, 'Crusading by Royal Command: Monarchy and Crusade in the Kingdom of Sicily (1187–1230)', in *Potere, società e popolo tra età normanna ed età sveva: Atti delle quinte giornate normanno-sveve* (Bari, 1983), pp. 135–8; Hartwig Cleve, 'Kaiser Friedrich II. und die Ritterorden', *Deutsches Archiv*, 49 (1993), 39–73.

20 June 1210: *Acta imperii inedita saeculi XIII et XIV: Urkunden und Briefe zur Geschichte des Kaiserreichs und des Königreichs Sizilien*, ed. Eduard Winkelmann (Innsbruck, 1880; repr. Aalen, 1964), vol. 1, no. 106, p. 93; Regesta Imperii, vol. 5.1, ed. Johann Friedrich Böhmer and Julius Ficker (Innsbruck, 1881–1901), no. 630, p. 168; Giuseppina Pecorella, *I Templari nei manoscritti di Antonino Amico* (Palermo, 1921).

the interests of the state. This and some other concessions were not confirmed by Frederick when he came of age to rule.[21]

There was other damage to Templar properties during the repression against some cities of eastern Sicily carried out by Frederick II,[22] and later, after Frederick's death in 1250, under the rule of his sons Conrad and Manfred. In these times there were cases of usurpation, especially in the region of Messina where an heir of the Parisio family, Jordanus of Pavia, attempted to revoke some donations made by Paganus to the Templars:[23] this explains the weakness of the Templar patrimony in Messina in the second half of the thirteenth century.

In 1265, when Charles I of Anjou took power in Sicily, a most glorious period began in the history of the Temple in the kingdom. The court of the new king was crowded with Templars and Hospitallers from Provence and from the kingdom of France, who exercised important functions in the administration of the kingdom: for example, Jacques de Taxy and Philippe d'Egly, Hospitaller commanders, were royal officers, and Guillaume de Beaujeu, a relative of King Charles, was at first commander of the Temple in the kingdom and then master of the whole order.[24] The first chiefs of the royal treasury were Templars, Arnulfus and Martanus; another Templar, Goffredus, was for some time head of the royal administration in Abruzzo. The Templars and Hospitallers did not exercise their functions only at the head of the kingdom but also in more specific fields, for example, the administration of the silver mines in Calabria, and in warfare.[25]

In 1274, when Charles I ordered a new lighthouse built in Brindisi, this work had to be supervised by one Templar, one Hospitaller and one Teutonic Knight, because, as the king explained, the military orders were the first to be interested in

21 Villari, *Templari*, pp. 26–27, 30.

22 The most recent research on this topic is by Daniela Santoro, *Federico II e la varietà delle dinamiche cittadine siciliane: Alcuni esempi, in Federico II nel Regno di Sicilia: Realtà locali e aspirazioni universali, Atti del Convegno (Barletta, 19–20 ottobre 2007)*, ed. Hubert Houben and Georg Vogeler, Quaderni del Centro di Studi Normanno-Svevi, 2 (Bari, 2008), pp. 123–47.

23 *I registri della cancelleria angioina ricostruiti da Riccardo Filangieri con la collaborazione degli archivisti napoletani*, vol. 12, 1273–76, ed. Riccardo Filangieri (Naples, 1959), pp. 280–82.

24 Damien Carraz, *L'ordre du Temple dans la basse vallée du Rhône (1124–1312): Ordres militaires, croisades et sociétés méridionales* (Lyon, 2005), pp. 447–62.

25 Cf. Toomaspoeg, 'Le ravitaillement', pp. 149–50.

the sea traffic in the central and eastern Mediterranean:[26] as is well known, Roger of Flor acquired his maritime knowledge from the Templars of Brindisi.[27]

The Angevin chancery also gives us some information about huge amounts of wheat, barley, beans and, sometimes, horses and money sent by the military orders to their houses in the Holy Land[28] and, later, the evacuation of Acre passed through the ports of the kingdom of Sicily, especially Barletta, where for some time the Teutonic Knights and Templars also kept their archives.

After the Sicilian Vespers of 1282 and the division of southern Italy into two independent kingdoms, there were some important changes in the life of the local Templars. The so-called War of the Vespers between the two kingdoms of Sicily and the papal excommunication of the island[29] resulted in a diminution of the importance of the Templar province of Messina, in Sicily, and the growth in prestige of the mainland *preceptoria* of Barletta. On the island, the Templar house in Messina, damaged by the attacks against the city by the Angevin army, fell quickly into complete ruin and, in a letter of December 1305, Nicolaus, bishop of Malta, who had visited the Templar church of St Marc of Messina, asked all people to help the Templars to repair the church.[30] At the same time, the few Templars still present on the island, in their new headquarters at Lentini, still enjoyed a good position in the local administration, for example, as agents of the royal treasury,[31] and it seems were sometimes seen as a link between the Roman Church and the royal court of Sicily. On the mainland, the landholdings of the Temple remained untouched by the war, and their economy and their activities as officers of the royal court suffered only small limitations as a result of the end of the Angevin dynasty's ambitions in the eastern Mediterranean, so that the crusade hospitals held by Templars in cities such as Barletta, Brindisi or Trani now held less importance than the order's big landholdings or fiefs in Apulia.

---

26 Georges Yver, *Le commerce et les marchands dans l'Italie méridionale au XIIIe & au XIVe siècle* (Paris, 1903), p. 165; see also Guzzo, *Templari*, p. 54; Kristjan Toomaspoeg, 'Carrefour de la Méditerranée et arrière-pays de la Croisade: Les ordres religieux militaires et la mer au Royaume de Sicile', in *Les actes du 130e congrès des sociétés historiques et scientifiques*, ed. Michel Balard (Paris, 2009), pp. 103–10.

27 Alain Demurger, *Vie et mort de l'ordre du Temple* (Paris, 1993), pp. 216–19.

28 Cf. Toomaspoeg, 'Le ravitaillement', pp. 149–53.

29 Steven Runciman, *The Sicilian Vespers* (Cambridge, 1958).

30 Kristjan Toomaspoeg, 'La fine dei Templari in Sicilia (1305–1327)', in *Religiones Militares: Contributi alla storia degli Ordini religioso-militari nel Medioevo*, ed. Anthony Luttrell and Francesco Tommasi, Biblioteca di 'Militia Sacra', 2 (Città di Castello, 2008), pp. 155–70.

31 For example, Gerardus de Finoleriis, on 17 June 1304: Stefano Borgia, *Difesa del dominio temporale della Sede Apostolica nelle due Sicilie in risposta alle scritture pubblicate in contrario* (Rome, 1791), app. 14; Toomaspoeg, *Templari*, no. 165, pp. 183–4.

The trial

In 1307, the news of the arrest of the Templars in France was a surprise to southern Italian public opinion and to both of the royal administrations, especially because there had been no previous negotiations about this matter, for example, between the Angevins of Naples and the French court. On the mainland, at the time of the French arrest of the Templars, King Charles II was at the papal court in Avignon. For some time he held a passive attitude but, once Pope Clement ordered the arrest in his letter *Pastoralis praeeminentiae*, Charles immediately ordered his son Robert, duke of Calabria, to arrest the Templars of the kingdom and to confiscate their properties.[32] A document from March 1308 tells us that seven Templars had been arrested in various parts of Apulia and were now imprisoned at the castle of Barletta, where they remained for more than two years without being interrogated. The royal court was interested in this matter only insofar as it concerned the administration of the confiscated Templar properties.[33]

In May 1309, Robert became the new king of Sicily, and the pope sent to the kingdom his inquisitor William of Saint Marcel to induce the local authorities to proceed against the order. In April 1310, the first trial was held in Lucera. On this occasion, six Templars, not the same as those held in Barletta, were interrogated and absolved of all charges.[34] The largest and most important trial of the Templars was held in Brindisi, at the church of Santa Maria del Casale, in May and June 1310, by a commission of papal and local ecclesiastics, including the archbishop of Brindisi, Bartholomeus, Arnolf Bataylle, Berengarius of Olargiis and James of Carapelle. Two Templars were interrogated, but we do not know the final judgment of the trial.[35]

As sources for both trials, in Lucera and Barletta, there survive six records of the interrogations and a list of 127 charges, *Super inquisitione facienda contra Ordinem militie Templi*,[36] so that it is possible to have an idea of the charges against the Templars of Sicily. The principal accusation, confirmed by the interrogated Templars – it is not known whether they were tortured or not, but it does not appear that they were – was to have repudiated Christ during the ceremony of reception into the order at the houses of Torremaggiore and Barletta. Some Templars said also that they had been forced to profane a cross or a crucifix during the ceremony. Finally, two Templars told about some episodes of veneration of a cat. At the same

---

32 Guerrieri, *I Cavalieri*, p. 59.

33 Ibid., pp. 60, 100–101, *Syllabus membranarum ad Regiae Siclae archivum pertinentium, 2, A Caroli II ad Roberti regnum*, ed. Antonio de Aprea (Naples, 1832–45), vol. 2.2, p. 204.

34 Guzzo, *Templari*, pp. 90–92.

35 'Inquisitio contra Templarios facta in civitate Brundusiensi', in *UT*, vol. 2, pp. 105–40.

36 Ibid.

time, it seems that nobody was accused of sodomy or other forbidden behaviour.[37] It is also possible to suppose that the defence strategy was based on the idea that single Templars were not guilty of what they had done during the ceremony of reception, because they had only obeyed their superiors and followed an existing ritual.

The case of the mainland kingdom is unique because, on the one hand, the action of the local authorities against the Templars was relatively fast and resolute, but on the other hand, the two trials revealed little interest from the authorities and had no significant results. Most of all, there was a lack of testimonies against the Templars, and obviously the local ecclesiastical, administrative and communal authorities had no reasons to persecute the order. At the same time, the number of Templars arrested was not very significant, and most probably none of them was executed. So, one could sum up the trial of the Temple in the mainland kingdom as noisy, but insignificant.

The island

At this time, the island of Sicily was ruled by James and Frederick of Aragon and belonged to a completely different political context.[38] It has been argued that the Templars of Aragon were persecuted only because their castles presented a direct danger to the interests of the king's court.[39] In Sicily, there were only few Templars and no significant fortifications of the order, so that the royal court never did intervene in the trial, and all action against the Templars was supposed to be carried out by the local ecclesiastical authorities, who traditionally had a good relationship with the order. The papal authority had very little opportunity to intervene in Sicilian affairs, even after the excommunication of the island was revoked.

All we know about the destiny of the Sicilian Templars results from the sources concerning the passing of the Templar properties into the hands of the Hospitallers, determined by the papal letter *Ad providam Christi* in May 1312. In the mainland kingdom, the Hospitallers did not have any great difficulty in obtaining the former Templar possessions, with a few exceptions: some of the biggest land properties in Torremaggiore and Serritella were usurped by the local noblemen, and some others were kept under the administration of the king's court.[40] All in all, when we compare the list of the former Templar possessions to the list of Hospitaller

---

37 Cf. Guzzo, *Templari*, pp. 90–91.

38 Cf. Henri Bresc, *Un monde méditerranéen: Économie et société en Sicile. 1300–1450* (Palermo and Rome, 1986).

39 Malcolm Barber, *The Trial of the Templars* (Cambridge, 1978; 2nd edn, Cambridge, 2006); I use the Italian edition, *Processo ai Templari: Una questione politica* (Genova, 1998), pp. 254–62.

40 Guerrieri, *I Cavalieri*, no. 6, pp. 118–20.

possessions at the end of the fourteenth century, it is possible to deduce that the Hospitallers had received approximately 75 per cent of the Templar properties.

On the island, the case was a little different: on the one hand, it is true that the Hospitallers were very influential at the king's court, and their prior, Sancho of Aragon, was a half-brother of King Frederick (and also of the king of Aragon, James II),[41] but on the other hand, the king had lost a lot of his influence to the local noblemen who helped him to fight against the Angevins, and he did not rule the whole territory of the kingdom.[42] So, the Hospitallers had to fight for many years to affirm, at least partially, their rights to the former Templar possessions. This process of *recuperatio* began in 1315 and lasted until the middle of the fourteenth century. It seems that the properties of the Temple had meanwhile not been officially expropriated but simply usurped, by private persons and by the royal court, and that the whole trial of the Temple had been shrouded in silence.

The Hospitallers found most of their difficulties in the central part of eastern Sicily where the Templars had concentrated the biggest and richest part of their properties. For example, only in 1326 did the new prior of the Hospitallers, Rodrigo Sanchez de Vergas, achieve success in a lawsuit against the knight Rosso Rosso, one of the most powerful men in the kingdom, who had usurped a large fief, called 'de Templo', in Scordia, but the fief still remained under the control of Rosso who just had to pay a very reduced and symbolic rent to the Hospitallers.[43] At the same time, the big Templar estate of Murro remained in the king's domain and was later given as a fief to the families of Moncada and Valguarnerio.[44]

Other important Templar properties were located in a region between the cities of Caltagirone, Piazza Armerina and Aidone and were in the same way threatened by usurpers. The process by which those possessions became Hospitaller property is interesting because only by this means can we find some information about the destiny of the former Templars.

One morning in June 1327, a Hospitaller commander called James of Calatafimi woke up and said to his fellow knights that he had dreamed that there was a holy knight buried near Caltagiorne, in the church of Santa Maria del Tempio. With a

---

41 Anthony Luttrell, 'The Aragonese Crown and the Knights Hospitallers of Rhodes', *English Historical Review*, 76 (1961), 1–19, and in Anthony Luttrell, *The Hospitallers in Cyprus, Rhodes, Greece and the West 1291–1440* (London, 1978), article XI, pp. 6, 11–15; idem, 'La Corona de Aragón y las Órdenes Militares durante el Siglo XIV', in *VIII Congreso de Historia de la Corona de Aragón*, 2 (Valencia, 1970), pp. 67–77, and in idem, *Hospitallers in Cyprus*, article XII, pp. 71, 77; Toomaspoeg, *Templari*, pp. 83–84.

42 Cf. Peri, *La Sicilia dopo il vespro.*

43 Carlo Marullo di Condojanni, *La Sicilia ed il Sovrano Ordine Militare di Malta* (Messina, 1953), no. 82, p. 112.

44 *I capibrevi di Giovanni Luca Barberi ora per la prima volta pubblicati da Giuseppe Silvestri*, ed. Giuseppe Silvestri (Palermo, 1879–90), vol. 1, p. 80; Giovan Luca Barberi, *Il 'Magnum Capibrevium' dei feudi maggiori*, ed. Giovanna Stalteri Ragusa (Palermo, 1993), vol. 2, pp. 664–9.

lot of noise, in a big procession, the Hospitallers went to the church and indeed found a tombstone and the remains of a knight called Gerlandus of Alamanna, a former Templar, who had remained to serve his church until his death.[45] The holiness of the remains was confirmed by many miracles which were experienced by the persons who approached them, and the body of Gerlandus was eventually transported to the cathedral of Caltagiorne. Declared as blessed (but never a saint), Gerlandus continued for many years to work miracles: his speciality was children's illnesses, and so his case gives valuable evidence of the history of paediatrics. The discovery of his remains gave the Hospitallers a good basis for affirming their rights to Santa Maria del Tempio, and this case shows how former Templars could continue their life without being threatened by the local authorities.

The history of the Templars and their trial in the two kingdoms of Sicily is unique. In the mainland kingdom, the court of Charles II and Robert was able to show to its allies, Pope Clement and King Philip of France, its desire to judge and suppress the order of Temple. In fact, only a few Templars were arrested and, it seems, all of them were released after a short and unwilling trial. On the island, there was never a trial of the Templars, and the members of the order sometimes continued their former life, sometimes became Hospitallers and sometimes left the religious life.

The reasons for this unwillingness to accuse and repress the Templars are to be found in the popularity of the Temple in southern Italian society. In some regions of Europe, the fall of Acre had a negative impact on the reputation of the military orders, but in southern Italy the exact opposite happened: the local population now became more interested in the Templars, Hospitallers and Teutonic Knights, and aimed to help them to get back to the Holy Land. The letter of the bishop of Malta from 1305, mentioned above, is a good example of this renewed interest in the Templars, and it is credible that the local Church hierarchies were not indifferent towards the destiny of the order which they knew very well.

The other reason was that the Templars were rich and influential in both kingdoms, but not at the same level as in France or Aragon or even in Tuscany. They were never seen as a menace to the interests of the local or central authorities, and there were no legends about their treasures or illegal financial activities. During the trial on the mainland, the charges against the Templars appeared artificial and dictated by the papal inquisitors without any real link to the local context. In Sicily, in 1327, a former Templar, Gerlandus of Alamanna, was presented as an example of a blessed man and miracle maker. Thus, the order of the Temple ended its existence in southern Italy in the best possible way, without great suffering and without shame.

---

[45] Ottavio Cajetani, *Vitae Sanctorum Siculorum*, vol. 1 (Palermo, 1657), p. 234; Henri Bresc and Jacques Rovinski, 'Les miracles du Bienheureux Gerland de Caltagirone (1327)', *Cahiers du Centre des études médiévales de Nice* (1984), 25–37; Villari, *Templari*, pp. 18–22.

Chapter 23

The Trial of the Templars in the County of Flanders (1307–12)[1]

Filip Hooghe

The aim of this study is to examine the circumstances before, during and after the arrest and dissolution of the Templars in the county of Flanders in the period of 1307–14. It focuses on the Templars in one of the order's major settlements in Flanders, the commandery of Ypres, with occasional reference to other Flemish towns, although my research on these other locations is still at an early stage. The fate of the Templars in the county of Flanders cannot be separated from the events of the preceding years. The Franco-Flemish War (1297–1304) was one of the most constant preoccupations of King Philip IV of France. It is noted elsewhere in this volume that a possible motivation for the Templars' arrest was the need to relieve King Philip IV's acute financial problems; one cause of these problems was the king's attempt to extend his power over Flanders.[2]

One of the conditions the king set for his support of the nomination of Cardinal Bertrand de Got as pope was that he should be allowed to collect the tithes in France for five years to continue the war in Flanders. Shortly after the new pope's coronation, Philip IV asked Clement V for a discussion about the situation in the Holy Land and about peace between France, England and *les Flandres*.[3] At the beginning of May 1307, Philip IV arrived in Poitiers where the pope was already; in his entourage was Robert of Béthune, count of Flanders.[4] Negotiations between

1 Special thanks to Dr Helen Nicholson, Jan Hosten, Gilbert Jansseune and Bernard Schotte. Abbreviations: *ADNL* = Archives départementales du Nord, Lille; *AG* = *Annals of Ghent*, ed. Hilda Johnstone (Oxford, 1985); *AGN* = *Algemene Geschiedenis der Nederlanden*, 15 vols, ed. Dirk Peter Blok et al. (Haarlem, 1977–83); *CDI* = *Corpus documentorum inquisitionis haereticae pravitatis Neerlandicae*, ed. Paul Frédéricq, 5 vols (Ghent, 1889–1906); *PT* = Jules Michelet, *Procès des Templiers*, 2 vols (Paris, 1841–51); OGVFS = Oorkonden van de graven van Vlaanderen, Fonds de St-Genois; *SAG* = The State Archive of Ghent.

2 Malcolm Barber, *The Trial of the Templars*, 2nd edn (Cambridge, 2006), pp. 42–5.

3 Karl Josef von Hefele et al., *Histoire des conciles d'après les documents originaux*, 11 vols (Paris, 1907–52), vol. 6, pp. 502–5.

4 Von Hefele, *Histoire des conciles*, vol. 6, part 1, p. 505.

Count Robert of Béthune and the French king at Poitiers in May and June 1307 resulted in a peace treaty.[5]

The Templars in Flanders

Although there seems to be a general consensus among modern historians that the Templars were not guilty as charged,[6] the accusation of abuse of power and corruption in defence of their rights and privileges seems to have had some basis in Flanders.[7] In 1284, two sisters (*sereurs*) were murdered on a Templar estate at Izenberge, near Veurne.[8] There is no certainty whether they were religious women or not but, as it was the Templars' estate, the obvious inference is that they were associated with the order of the Temple. The presence of women as lay religious or associate members in the order of the Temple in Flanders was not unusual: for example, one Adelisa was also living in the order's house at Ghent.[9] Two suspects were captured: one was dragged to the city of Veurne and hanged instantly, while the other, Staessin le Heistere, was thrown into prison. Since he was a tenant of the Templars of Izenberge, he appealed to Brother Pieter uten Sacke, master of the Temple in Flanders,[10] who at that time was residing at the court of the count of Flanders, Guy of Dampierre. The count, who referred to the master as his *bon ami*

---

5 Frantz Funck-Brentano, *Les origines de la Guerre de cent ans: Philippe le Bel en Flandre* (Paris, 1897), pp. 514–16; Isidore L.A. Diegerick, *Inventaire analytique et chronologique des chartes et documents appartenant aux archives de la ville d'Ypres*, 1 (Bruges, 1853), pp. 204–5, no. 252; Maurice Vandermaesen, 'Vlaanderen en Henegouwen onder het Huis van Dampierre 1244–1384', in *AGN*, vol. 2 (Haarlem, 1982), p. 415.

6 Malcolm Barber, 'The Trial of the Templars Revisited', in *MO*, 2, pp. 329–31, 342.

7 Michel Nuyttens, *Krijgers voor God: De orde van de tempeliers in de Lage Landen (1120 – 1312)* (Leuven, 2007), p. 189.

8 *SAG*, OGVFS, no. 1399.

9 Alan Forey, 'Women and the Military Orders in the Twelfth and Thirteenth Centuries', in *Hospitaller Women in the Middle Ages*, ed. Anthony Luttrell and Helen Nicholson (Aldershot, 2006), pp. 45–6; Francesco Tommasi, 'Men and Women of the Hospitaller, Templar and Teutonic Orders: Twelfth to Fourteenth Centuries', in ibid., pp. 80–81; Helen Nicholson, *The Knights Templar: A New History* (Stroud, 2001), pp. 130–32; For Adelisa, see 'Documents relatifs aux croisades', in *Le Chevalier au Cygne et Godefroid de Bouillon*, ed. Baron Frédéric A. F. T. de Reiffenberg, 3 vols (Brussels, 1846–1854), vol. 1, p. 429, no. 9.

10 The commander of the Temple in Flanders is called *preceptor Flandria, magister Templi in Flandria, commandeur* or even *custos beneficia Templariorum in Flandria*. He was under the supervision of the *preceptor in Francia*. Cf. Paul Rogghé, *De Orde van de Tempelridders en haar geschiedenis in het oude graafschap Vlaanderen* (Ghent, 1973), pp. 91–5. To distinguish him from the rest of the commanders of the several commanderies of Flanders, we will call him 'master of the Temple in Flanders'.

Pieron dou Sac,[11] pardoned the murderer and allowed his release.[12] Since 1157, a Templar, usually the Flemish master himself, had resided permanently at the comital court, not only as collector of feudal dues, but also as personal advisor and moneylender to the Flemish count.[13]

In 1322, Henri, son of Staes, of Izenberge testified in an inquiry into a dispute over the Hospitallers' jurisdiction at Izenberge. He related that one Brother Gilles, son of Marote, had been the victim of a theft in the parish of Izenberge. His brother by blood, Jaquemes, went to see the commander of the Temple and lodged a complaint against a certain Clai Willem who was *mannant* in *le singnorie dou temple de Rerof*, an otherwise unknown Flemish house of the Templars at Izenberge. The commander of the Temple wanted to prosecute, but his jurisdiction conflicted with that of William, lord of Leisele, who wanted Clai Willem to be released. However, when the commander returned from a meeting with Lord William, he gave judgment against this lord's wishes and condemned the suspect. Lord William protested and was himself sentenced to a fine of 60 *solidi*.[14]

Another example of the Templars' exploitation of their privileges in Flanders was given in 1322 by Lammin, son of Hanessen, of Izenberge, who related that the Templars had had the right to pass judgment over their *hostes*. He had seen with his own eyes how four persons were charged with trespass (Dutch: *huissoekinghe*) and were summoned several times but, as they came under the jurisdiction of the commander of the Temple, no judgment resulted.[15]

The run-up to the arrest of the Templars at Ypres

In the late thirteenth and at the beginning of the fourteenth century, several serious conflicts arose between the city council of Ypres and the Templars. In 1280, the weavers and fullers living in the Templar quarter of the city joined the *Cockerulle*, a revolt of artisans of the cloth industry against the patricians of Ypres.[16] On 11

---

11 Jan Hosten, *De tempeliers: De tempelorde tijdens de kruistochten en in de Lage Landen* (Amsterdam, 2006), p. 250.

12 *SAG*, OGVFS, no. 1399.

13 Mina Martens, *L'administration du domaine ducal en Brabant au Moyen Âge (1250–1406)* (Brussels, 1954), p. 62, note 3; Rik Opsommer, *'Omme dat leengoed es thoochste dinc van der weerelt': Het leenrecht in Vlaanderen in de 14de en 15de eeuw* (Brussels, 1995), vol. 2, p. 615; Myriam Vander Stichele, 'De Hospitaalbroeders van St.-Jan van Jeruzalem in de balije en commanderij Vlaanderen tot 1550: Een prosopografische benadering', unpublished dissertation, Catholic University of Leuven (1982), p. 213.

14 *SAG*, OGVFS, no. 1399.

15 Ibid.

16 Marc Boone, 'Social Conflicts in the Cloth Industry of Ypres (Late 13th–Early 14th Centuries): The Cockerulle Reconsidered', in *Ypres and the Medieval Cloth Industry in Flanders: Archaeological and Historical Contributions, Papers of the International*

October 1281, a new dispute arose, because the Templars' *hospites* had to pay for the damages caused by the *Cockerulle*.[17]

The aldermen of Ypres taxed the Templars' lands to pay the royal taxes, which ran counter to the Templars' privileges. In December 1296, Philip IV reassured the Templars that he would respect all their privileges and liberties.[18] Nevertheless, at the end of 1302, Ypres forced the Templars' *hospites* to contribute towards the costs of the construction of new fortifications, but the residents of the Temple protested against this, and they asked the count of Namur to issue an edict without prejudice so that this payment would not create a precedent.[19] In 1304, Ypres had to pay the commander of the Temple of Ypres a heritable annuity of 46 *solidi* for property expropriated for the new fortifications on the east side of the *Verde rue*.[20] The *nouvelles fourtreches* had divided the *Upstal* where the commandery of the Temple was situated.[21]

Symposium 'A good Yarn! Archaeological and Historical Research into the Medieval Cloth Industry of Flanders', Ypres 29–30.11.1996, ed. Marc Dewilde, Anton Ervynck and Alexis Wielemans, Archeologie in Vlaanderen, Monografie 2 (Asse and Zellik, 1998), pp. 147–52; Filip Hooghe, 'De Cokerulle (1280–1285): Een conflict tussen Ieper en zijn hinterland over de lakennijverheid', *Handelingen van het Genootschap voor Geschiedenis*, 143 (2006), 425–39.

17 *Recueil de documents relatifs à l'histoire de l'industrie drapière en Flandre*, ed. Georges Espinas, Henri Pirenne and Henri-E. De Sagher, vol. 3 (Brussels, 1920), p. 686, no. 851; pp. 697–8, no. 862; Hooghe, 'De Cokerulle', p. 439; Michel Nuyttens, 'De Tempeliers te Ieper', *Iepers Kwartier*, 9 (1973), 24–5.

18 Diegerick, *Inventaire*, vol. 1, pp. 145–7, nos 172–4; Theo Luykx, *Het grafelijk geslacht Dampierre en zijn strijd tegen Filips de Schone* (Leuven, 1952), p. 138; Vandermaesen, 'Vlaanderen en Henegouwen', pp. 406–7.

19 Diegerick, *Inventaire*, vol. 1, pp. 177–8, no. 224; Warnkönig and Gheldolf, *Histoire de la Flandre*, vol. 5, pp. 6–97.

20 *Comptes de la ville d'Ypres de 1267 à 1329*, ed. Guillaume Des Marez and Emile De Sagher, vol. 1 (Brussels, 1909), p. 157.

21 *Comptes*, vol. 1, p. 152.

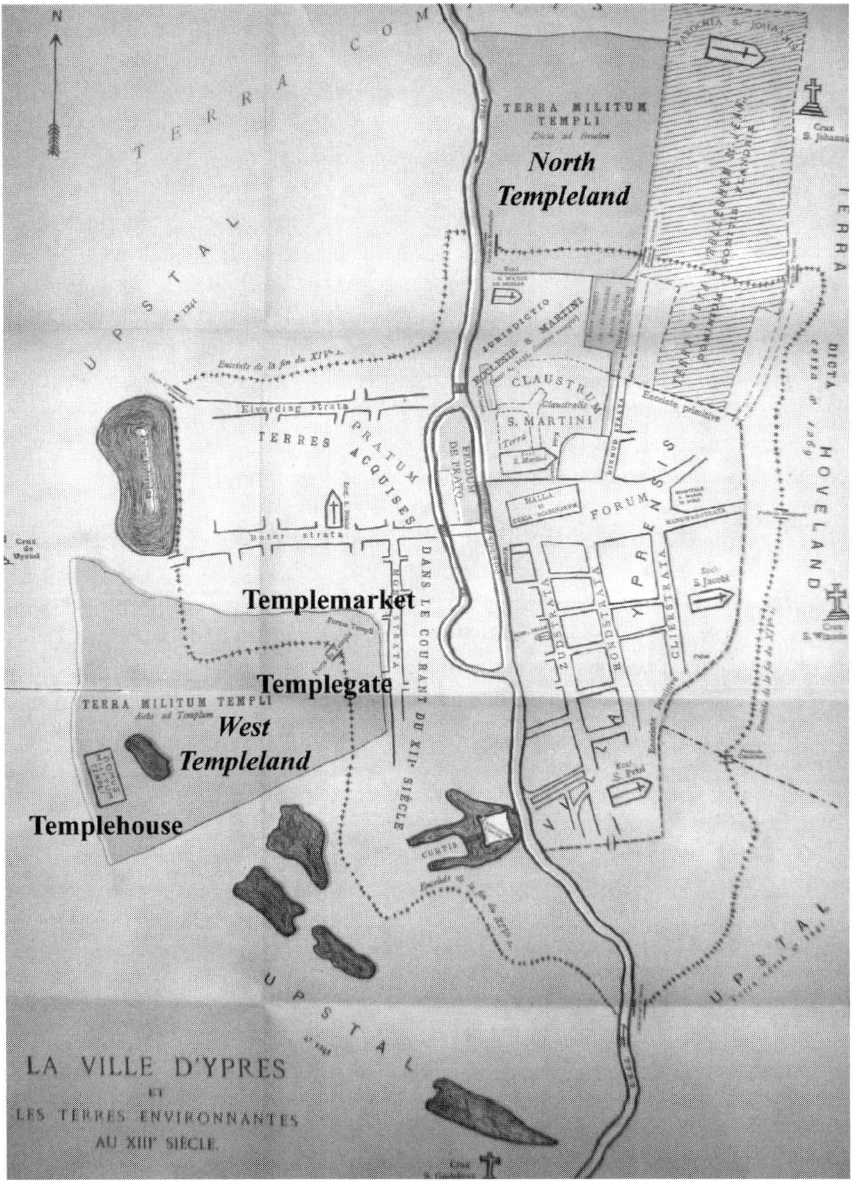

Fig. 23.1 The Templars' lands in Ypres at the end of the thirteenth century. Cf. Guillaume des Marez, *Étude sur la propriété foncière dans les villes du moyen-âge et spécialement en Flandre* (Recueil de travaux, Université de Gand, Faculté de philosophie et de lettres, vol. 20) (Ghent, 1898).

An agreement of 1289 stipulated that as long as the aldermen of Ypres were unable to repay a loan of 1,000 *livres*, they should pay Pieter uten Sacke, master of the Temple in Flanders, 100 *livres* a year for his lifetime. On Pieter's death, the aldermen of Ypres would have to repay the whole sum of 1,000 *livres* to the Templars.[22] In 1305, the master of the Temple in Flanders was paid 200 *livres*, the equivalent of two years' annuity as agreed in 1289.[23] Most likely, the turbulent political situation at the end of 1303 and in 1304 prevented the aldermen from paying the first 100 *livres*. On 29 November 1303, the eve of St Andrew, a bloody revolt took place at Ypres when some leaders of the cloth guilds murdered nine members of the magistracy of the city together with another 14 patricians and weavers. Several revolts of the craftsmen followed until 21 July 1304.[24]

As the war caused many expenses to the city, the councillors of Ypres, in 1305, demanded that the count force the Templars' *hospites* to contribute to the costs and expenses of the war, but the delegates from the Templars' estates begged him to compel the city of Ypres to maintain the old customs.[25] On 21 May 1306, Count Robert of Béthune ordered the Templars of Ypres to pay a contribution of 4,000 *livres* towards the costs of protecting the city of Ypres and the Templars' estates during the war against France. This sum was to be levied not by the magistrate of Ypres, but by the commander of the Temple.[26] On 27 June 1306, Count Robert reconsidered his decision and stated that the Templars should instead pay only seven years of excise dues to the city of Ypres,[27] thus demonstrating the Templars' favoured relationship with the count. In the months before the Templars' arrest in 1307, relations between the Templars and the city of Ypres deteriorated so badly that the aldermen even inserted in their book of laws a prohibition against giving money to the Templars to say prayers, on pain of a fine of £50.[28]

---

22 Jean-Jacques Lambin, 'Les Templiers d' Ypres', *Messager des Sciences et des Arts de la Belgique ou Nouvelles Archives Historique, Littéraire et Scientifique*, 2 (1834), p. 198; Nuyttens, *Krijgers voor God*, p. 146.

23 *Por le rente hiritable avoec les 100 lb. par an le maistre dou Temple: 200 lb. 19 s. 11 d. 1 obole*: cf. *Comptes*, vol. 1, p. 179.

24 Leo Delfos, *Het avontuur van de Liebaards 1297–1302–1304: Geschiedenis van een Vlaamse opstand 'Omne die defense van den lande'* (Tielt, 1952), pp. 282–3; Funck-Brentano, *Philippe le Bel*, pp. 446–8; Els Matthys, 'Onlusten te Ieper in 1303 en 1304: De rol van een interne stedelijke opstand in het democratiseringsproces van een grote Vlaamse industriestad', unpublished Master's thesis, Catholic University of Leuven (1999), pp. 120–46.

25 Michel Nuyttens, *De Tempelorde in Vlaanderen van 1128 tot 1307* (Leuven, 1971), p. 227; Warnkönig and Gheldolf, *Histoire de la Flandre*, vol. 5, pp. 96–8.

26 *ADNL*, B 1359, no. 43009; Diegerick, *Inventaire*, vol. 1, p. 201, no. 247; Hosten, *De tempeliers*, p. 216; Nuyttens, *Krijgers voor God*, p. 147; *SAG*, OGVFS, no. 588; Warnkönig and Gheldolf, *Histoire de la Flandre*, vol. 5, p. 98.

27 Diegerick, *Inventaire*, vol. 1, p. 202, no. 248.

28 Lambin, 'Les Templiers d' Ypres', p. 199.

The arrests in the county of Flanders

On 14 September 1307, King Philip IV of France sent sealed letters to his officials throughout his kingdom with orders to make preparations for the arrest of the Templars in France. He dispatched Reinout of Péquigny, *vidame* of Amiens, to Flanders.[29] On 11 October 1307, in the house of Pieter Van den Zoldere, citizen of Ypres, the papal notary William of Beauvais, clerk of the diocese of Thérouanne, drew up a deed containing a copy of four documents, formulated on the request of *vidame* Reinout of Péquigny, and in the presence of witnesses, namely Gerald of Pinchon, knight, Master Pieter of Renenghes, canon of the chapter of the church of St Martin in Ypres, and John, clerk of the *vidame*.[30]

The first document in this notarial deed was Philip IV's command, drawn up at Pontoise on 20 September 1307 and addressed to the clerical and secular authorities of his kingdom of France, in which he ordered them to obey Reinout of Péquigny, *vidame* of Amiens, John of Varennes, knight, and the *bailli* (bailiff) of Amiens.[31] The second document was Philip IV's instruction of 14 September 1307, in which he revealed the alleged heresies and horrible practices of the Templars, and in which he charged the above-mentioned three persons with arresting all the members of the order of the Temple, delivering them to the inquisition and confiscating all their belongings.[32] The royal officials of Amiens were to seize all the Templars they found in the jurisdiction of the *bailliage* (bailiwick) of Amiens.[33]

The bailiff of Amiens was the king's local official who also had supervision over Flanders. In the years preceding the Franco-Flemish War (1287–96), the bailiff of Amiens had been interfering with increasing frequency in matters concerning the count of Flanders's jurisdiction. The king even ordered his bailiff of Amiens to supervise the sessions of the court at Ghent, while the provost of St-Quentin was ordered to attend the sessions of the count's court. This was not to the liking of Count Guy of Dampierre.[34]

The third document was the order of the papal inquisitor, Friar Preacher William of Paris, drawn up at Pontoise on 22 September 1307, addressed to the inquisitors

---

29 Barber, *Trial*, p. 59; Fernand Vanhemelryck and Daniël Peetermans, *Marginalen in de geschiedenis: Over beulen, joden, hoeren, zigeuners en andere zondebokken* (Leuven, 2004), p. 98; Rogghé, *De Orde van de Tempelridders*, p. 148.

30 *CDI*, vol. 2, pp. 52–9; Lieven K. Cumps, *De tempeliers in Vlaanderen* (Tielt, 1976), p. 115; Rogghé, *De Orde van de Tempelridders*, p. 148.

31 *CDI*, vol. 2, pp. 52 and 54; Pierre Dupuy, *Histoire de l'ordre militaire des Templiers ou chevaliers du temple de Jérusalem, depuis son établissement jusqu'à sa décadence et sa suppression* (Brussels, 1751), p. 195.

32 *CDI*, vol. 2, pp. 52–6; Dupuy, *Histoire de l'ordre militaire des Templiers*, pp. 196–9; *ADNL*, B 1458, no. 4590.

33 Dupuy, *Histoire de l'ordre militaire des Templiers*, p. 196.

34 Jan Frans Verbruggen and Rolf Falter, *1302: Opstand in Vlaanderen* (Tielt, 2001), pp. 56–7, 60.

of Toulouse and Carcassonne and to all the other priors, subpriors and *lecteurs* of the order of the Preachers in the kingdom of France, in which he revealed the alleged heresies and horrible practices of the Templars. Since the papal inquisition could not take action everywhere at the same time, William of Paris ordered the friars of his order to act on his behalf in interrogating the arrested Templars and to inform the Minorites and the other regular clergy about the course of the affair in order to prevent any scandal arising among them or among the common people. The Templars' confessions were to be sent without delay in writing, under seal, to the king and to the inquisitor.[35] The fourth document was an instruction drawn up in French by William of Paris about how the appointed inquisitors and the secular authorities were to deal with the arrested Templars and their confiscated properties.[36] These four documents were probably also sent to other Flemish city magistrates at Bruges and Ghent.[37]

The arrests at Ypres seem to have passed unnoticed. According to the Annals of Ypres, the arrests were executed by French royal troops, but apparently these officials were not able to do their work properly.[38] It seems that nothing changed, as the city of Ypres still had to pay the master of the Temple in Flanders the annuity of 1289 of 100 *livres parisis*.[39] It also seems that Count Robert of Béthune did not fully comply with the French king's orders to arrest the Templars.[40] On 13 November 1307, Philip IV commanded Count Robert to hand over all the Templars living in the county of Flanders to the lord of Péquigny, *vidame* of Amiens, his delegate in Flanders. This indicates either that the Flemish Templars had not been arrested by mid-November or that, if their arrest had taken place, they had not been handed over to the French king.[41] Nevertheless, Count Robert of Béthune must have submitted to the papal bull *Pastoralis praeeminentiae* of 22 November 1307, in which all the princes were summoned to arrest the Templars in their territories and to confiscate their goods.[42]

Some cruel scenes occurred in the parts of Flanders that had been put under the French king's control as a result of the treaty of Athis-sur-Orge (1305). In the suburbs of Arras, a gang of soldiers of the city assaulted the Templar commandery

35 *CDI*, vol. 2, pp. 53 and 56–7; Dupuy, *Histoire de l'ordre militaire des Templiers*, pp. 199–201.

36 *CDI*, vol. 2, pp. 53 and 57–9; Dupuy, *Histoire de l'ordre militaire des Templiers*, pp. 196, 201–3.

37 Rogghé, *De Orde van de Tempelridders*, p. 148.

38 Lambin, 'Les Templiers d'Ypres', p. 198.

39 *Comptes*, vol. 1, pp. 215, 239, 264.

40 Lambin, 'Les Templiers d'Ypres', p. 198.

41 Cumps, *De tempeliers in Vlaanderen*, pp. 115–16 and notes 284 and 288; Rogghé, *De Orde van de Tempelridders*, p. 148.

42 Cumps, *De tempeliers in Vlaanderen*, p. 117.

of Arras and strangled half of the brothers. The others were arrested and locked up in Arras.[43]

In the western regions of the county of Flanders, adjacent to the French border, some French officials raided the Templars' lands and carried off their belongings. It is interesting to note that the family of the castellans of St Omer, which had played a significant role in the establishment of the order of the Temple, its acquisition of possessions in Flanders and in the crusades during almost one and a half centuries, also played an important role in the confiscation of many of the Templars' possessions in 1307.[44] The castellan of St Omer occupied fiefs at Estaires, Steenbecque, Morbecque, Nordpeene, Nieppe, Steenwerck, Rubrouck and Renescure; he also had some vassals at Nieverlet, near St Omer, who had previously paid their dues to the Temple, and some dues from fiefs at Berquin that were previously owned by the Temple.[45] In a list of confiscations dated c.1320, there is some evidence that the castellan of St Omer took over the feudal dues from the Templars' estates in the castellany of Cassel, although he had no jurisdiction in this region which was under the authority of the count of Flanders.[46] The castellan gave the feudal dues from the fiefs at Eecke that had previously belonged to the Temple to a certain Lord Philip of Ypres.[47] Moreover, Lord Franchois of Haveskerke took over many of the Templars' estates in the castellany of Cassel, for example in the forest of Nieppe, Neuf-Berquin and Vieu-Berquin, Steenbecque, Lederzeele, Estaires, Morbecque and Renescure.[48]

The trial of the Templars in Flanders

On 25 March 1308, King Philip IV summoned a meeting of the estates-general at Tours.[49] On the following day, he wrote to Count Robert of Béthune from Melun, informing him of the Templars' errors, which were so horrible that every Catholic and in particular the prelates of the Church were obliged to destroy them.[50] He asked the count, by virtue of the loyalty he owed as a vassal to his lord, to join

---

43 Rogghé, *De Orde van de Tempelridders*, p. 148.

44 Hosten, *De tempeliers*, pp. 237–46; Rogghé, 'Oste de Saint Omer: Vlaams Tempelier uit de XIIe eeuw', pp. 245–59.

45 *ADNL*, B 1294, no. 5374[5], fols 3v, 4r.

46 *ADNL*, B 1294, no. 5374[5], fols 1r, 8v.

47 Ibid., fol. 4r.

48 *Che sont li fief que Franchoys de Haveskerke conquoist as templiers*; cf. *ADNL*, B 1294, no. 5374[5], fol. 2v.

49 Cumps, *De tempeliers in Vlaanderen*, p. 117; Marion Melville, *La vie des Templiers* (Paris, 1951), pp. 256–7; Barber, *Trial*, pp. 101–4; *Le dossier de l'affaire des Templiers*, ed. Georges Lizerand (Paris, 1923), pp. 102–7 at p. 103, note 1.

50 *ADNL*, B 1458, no. 4606; Dupuy, *Histoire de l'ordre militaire des Templiers*, p. 234 and note 1; *CDI*, vol. 2, pp. 51–2.

him within three weeks after Easter at Tours, or send an attorney or attorneys to represent him, to discuss what should be done, because they would have to address the Holy See in this matter soon.[51] The bailiffs were ordered to expedite matters as quickly as possible; the bailiff of Amiens responded promptly, on 7 April 1308.[52]

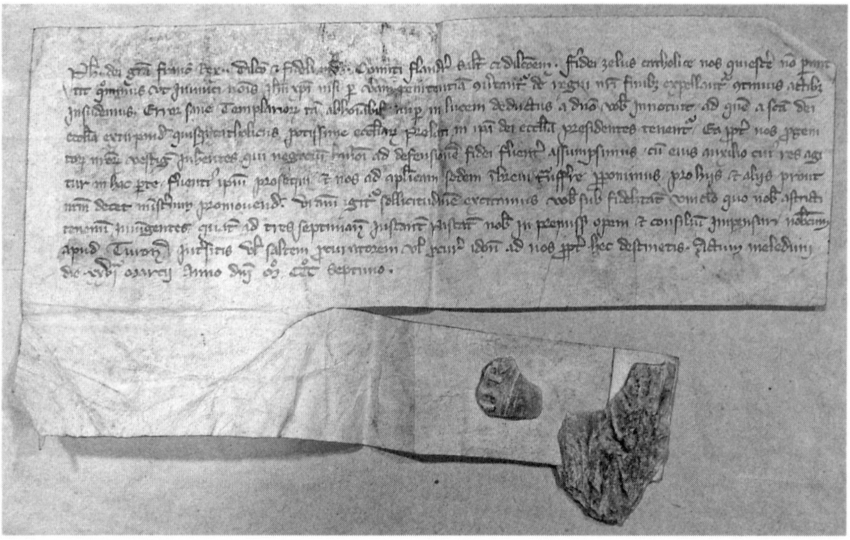

Fig. 23.2 King Philip IV's letter of 26 March 1308 to Count Robert of Béthune

The Flemish communities were also summoned to send their representatives to Tours.[53] In the city accounts of Bruges for the year 2 February 1308–1 February 1309, a messenger was paid six *livres* and six *solidi* by the city for his journey from the king to the city 'because of the Templars' between 13 and 16 April 1308.[54] This must have been the messenger carrying King Philip IV's summons to the aldermen of Bruges to join the estates-general at Tours.

The meeting at Tours took place between 15 May and 8 June 1308. Many nobles were absent. Count Robert of Béthune was represented by his eldest son Louis I of Nevers and by Livinus of the chapter of St Veerle at Ghent. Curiously enough, it was Louis I of Nevers who fulminated most against the Templars.[55] Eventually, in the months of April and May 1308, Robert of Béthune, count of Flanders, and his

[51] *CDI*, vol. 2, p. 52; Barber, *Trial*, pp. 101–104.

[52] Barber, *Trial*, p. 103.

[53] Rogghé, *De Orde van de Tempelridders*, p. 149.

[54] *De rekeningen van de stad Brugge, Tweede deel, eerste stuk 1302–1306, Tweede stuk 1306–1319*, ed. Carlos Wyffels and André Vandewalle (Brussels, 1965–71), p. 1145.

[55] Rogghé, *De Orde van de Tempelridders*, p. 149 and note 1285.

eldest son Louis, count of Nevers and Rethel, were among the 26 nobles of France who authorised action against the Templars in their domains.[56] In July 1308, some months after the meeting at Tours, Pope Clement V and King Philip IV agreed to continue the trial against the Templars through two commissions, one diocesan and one pontifical, whose reports would be presented at the Church council of Vienne in November 1310. Nothing is yet known about the functioning of the diocesan commission in Flanders.

Some studies mention that Pieter uten Sacke died under mysterious circumstances on 27 April 1309. [57] He had already been replaced as master of the Temple in Flanders by Goswin of Bruges.[58] One year after his death, the aldermen of Bruges informed Count Robert that, if he thought it necessary, he could investigate the death, which indicates that the case was certainly serious enough for an investigation.[59] There is no evidence to prove that this person was the former master or a Templar, but the city accounts of Ypres provide some indirect evidence. The city of Ypres had continued to pay Pieter uten Sacke the annuity of 100 *livres*, following the agreement of 1289, but in the city's accounts for 8 November 1309, after the record of the payment of 100 *livres* of heritable annuity to the master of the Temple in Flanders, there is a note that the city could buy this heritable annuity from the Temple for 1,000 *livres*.[60] This suggests that the Templar Pieter uten Sacke had died in that year.

On 12 May 1309, Philip IV ordered the *vidame* of Amiens and the other curators or superintendents responsible for the houses of the Temple in Flanders to pay certain sums of money which the Templars of Flanders had owed to the citizens of Ypres at the time of their arrest. The citizens of Ypres, as creditors of the Templars, had obtained this order from the French king to settle their claims against the possessions of the Temple.[61]

The pontifical commission of France began its work on 8 August 1309, comprising the archbishop of Narbonne and three bishops, who summoned all the Templars in the kingdom to Paris to testify. It was nevertheless several months before the witnesses arrived, as only in February 1310 did King Philip IV allow the imprisoned Templars to travel to Paris. In that month, around 75 Templars from the north of France arrived in the French capital, coming from the dioceses of Thérouanne, Tournai, Cambrai, Arras, Liege and Utrecht. Among them was

---

56 Dupuy, *Histoire de l'ordre militaire des Templiers*, pp. 234–5.

57 Rogghé, *De Orde van de Tempelridders*, pp. 100–101; Jules de Saint-Genois, *Inventaire analytique des chartes des comtes de Flandre, avant l'avènement des princes de la maison de Bourgogne* (Ghent, 1843–1846), pp. 349–50, no. 1214, note 1.

58 Nuyttens, *Krijgers voor God*, pp. 175–6.

59 *SAG*, OGVFS, no. 1214.

60 *Comptes*, vol. 1, p. 304.

61 Warnkönig and Gheldolf, *Histoire de la Flandre*, vol. 5, pp. 99, 446–7.

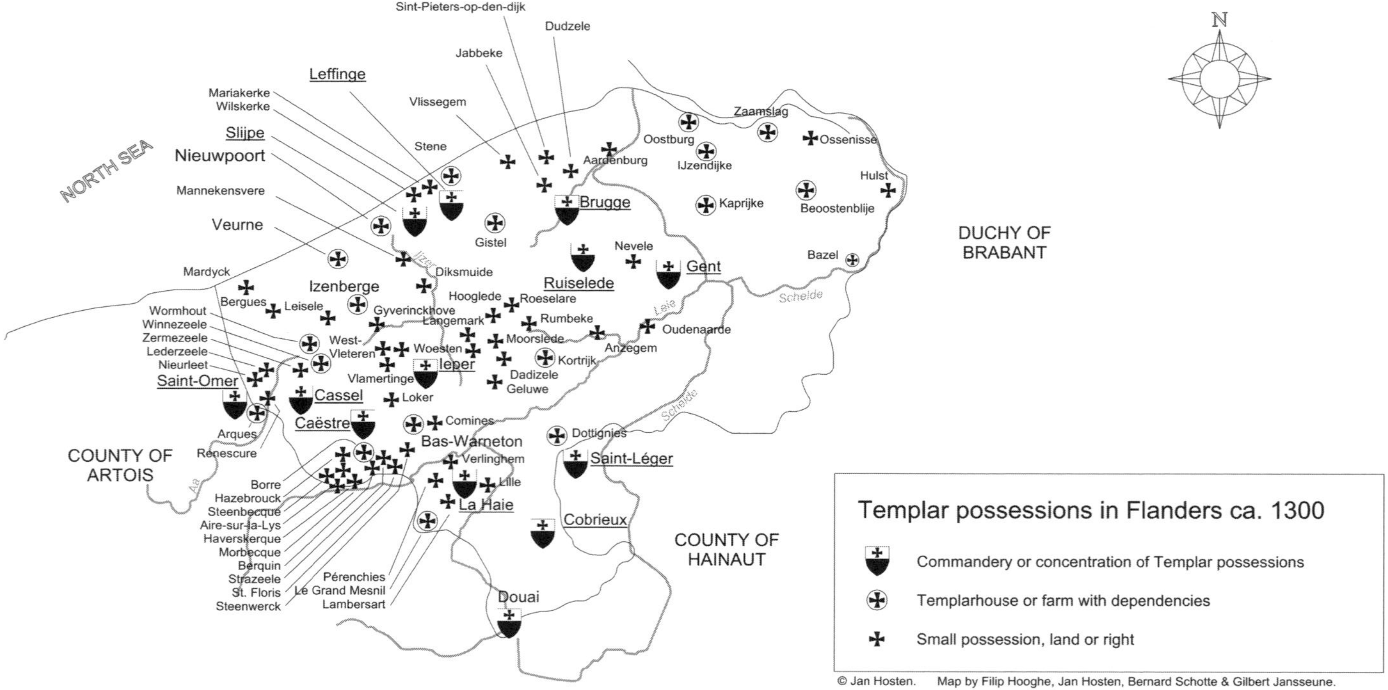

Fig. 23.3 The Templars' possessions in the county of Flanders at the beginning of the fourteenth century. Based on the research of Filip Hooghe, Jan Hosten, Bernard Schotte and Gilbert Jansseune. Copyright Jan Hosten

Gonsoynus de Brugis, Goswin of Bruges, master of Flanders.[62] These Templars stayed in several houses in Paris: 12 in the abbey of St Magloire in Paris and seven in the house of Johannes de Chaminio in the district of Porta Bauderii, including one Lambertus *Flamengi*, 'the Fleming'. Others were lodged in the house of Colart of Evreis or of Evreux, *en la maison de Leurage*, in the house of Gossin of Brabant in the *Grande Rue St-Jacques*, and elsewhere.[63]

The Flemish Templars appeared before the commissioners over several days in the months of February, March and April 1310. Almost all the Templars were *servientes*, sergeants, or chaplains. When asked if they wanted to appoint procurators to defend the order, they refused, preferring to defend the order in person. On 9 and 17 February 1310, a sergeant brother, Bernart of Caestre from the diocese of Thérouanne, was interrogated with other Templars who all stated that they wanted to defend the order personally. Afterwards he was imprisoned in an abbey in Paris together with 12 other Templars, some of whom were from Flanders, and, on 2 April 1310, some commissioners came to interrogate them there; they all made the same reply as before. Bernart thus was one of the obdurate Templars who refused to confess to the allegations and be reconciled to the Church. He remained in prison: in October and December 1310, and, in May 1311, he was in Beauvais with approximately the same fellow prisoners as in the abbey in Paris; in April 1312, he was in Asnières-sur-Oise, under the guard of royal officials.[64]

Eleven Templars who were imprisoned in the house of Colart of Evreux produced a written statement in which they vigorously defended their order. They protested not only against the allegations, declaring their Catholic faith, but also against the way they were treated, namely kept in chains and for long periods without bread or water. They ended their statement by requesting that they be allowed to consult eight of their fellow Templars, including *frere Gossein commandeur de Flandres*, in order to prepare their defence.[65]

---

62 Rogghé, *De Orde van de Tempelridders*, pp. pp. 149–51; *PT*, vol. 1, pp. 40–41, 60, 63–6, 69, 97–8, 103, 107, 114, 471; for Goswin see pp. 64, 107, 114. Those from the diocese of Tournai were: Goswin of Bruges, commander of Flanders, Symon lo Reppe, Gossin of Ghent, Joannes Versinara, Nicolas Versequi, Jacobus Candebur, Helinus of Templemars, Joannes de Biersi, P. Capon, Enricus de Ardenbort, Philippus de Marino, Joannes de Brueria, Jacobus Cadeleta, Robertus and Lambertus Flamingi, and probably also Joannes de Furno, Joannes de Slijpe and Gobertus de Malle; from the diocese of Thérouanne: Arnulf Brem, Bernard of Caestre, Joannes de Campaneis, Arnulf Arbia and Philip of Menin; five Templars came from Liege: Hendrik of Brabant, Gerard and John de Geneffe, Jean de Osqueriis and Jean de Nivelles; from the diocese of Utrecht: chaplain Egidius de Perbone. Philippe de Douai came from the diocese of Arras and some others, including two priests, came from the diocese of Cambrai (Rogghé, *De Orde van de Tempelridders*, 149–50).

63 *PT*, vol. 1, pp. 131, 136, 140, 145, 147, 148; Rogghé, *De Orde van de Tempelridders*, pp. 149–150, 158; Cumps, *De tempeliers in Vlaanderen*, p. 119.

64 *PT*, vol. 1, pp. 60, 74, 131; Vander Stichele, *De Hospitaalbroeders*, p. 28.

65 *PT*, vol. 1, pp. 145–6; Rogghé, *De Orde van de Tempelridders*, pp. 150–51.

Only occasionally do the records mention a Templar who had been reconciled, which meant that the individual had acknowledged the allegations made against him and the order. Among those who stubbornly refused to do this we find six brothers from Flanders:[66] Hélin de Templemars, Bernard de Caestre, Enricus de Ardenbourg, Jacques Candebur, Pierre Capons and Jean de Varsenaere. After the burning at the stake of 54 Templars because they had withdrawn their earlier confessions, the pontifical commissioners, on 30 May 1310, postponed their investigation until 17 October. On 5 June 1311, the commission ended its work without any conclusion.[67]

On 23 July 1311, Robert, archbishop of Reims, sent a letter to the bishop of Soissons about a new provincial council at Senlis to convict the Templars. The dioceses of Flanders (Thérouanne and Tournai) belonged to the ecclesiastical province of Reims. As papal and diocesan inquisitor, Robert had sentenced several Templars at the provincial council held by himself and his suffragans, but some of the Templars refused obstinately to admit their guilt, so that the case could not yet be concluded. Therefore the archbishop would hold a new council on Thursday after Ascension Day (19 August) at Senlis to settle the matter of these heretical Templars. The bishop of Senlis was put in charge of summoning this council. On 1 October 1311, a general council would be held, at which the archbishop would be able to submit all the evidence.[68]

In fact, the general council at Vienne did not reach a conclusion on the Templars' affair but, on 22 March 1312, Pope Clement V decided in his papal bull *Vox in excelso* to dissolve the order of the Temple.[69] On 2 May 1312, in his bull *Ad providam*, he decreed that he had decided after careful consideration that all the Templars' confiscated possessions, which belonged to the Holy See, should be transferred to the Hospital of St John of Jerusalem. All who kept such properties in their possession should transfer them to the Hospitallers within the month, on pain of excommunication and other punishments.[70] Yet the transfer of the possessions of the Temple to the Hospitallers did not proceed smoothly outside France, including the county of Flanders.[71]

The aftermath

The fate of the Flemish Templars who defended the Temple in Paris is unknown. The sole exception is Bernard of Caestre, probably a dignitary of the Templars'

---

66 *PT*, vol. 1, p. 131; Rogghé, *De Orde van de Tempelridders*, pp. 150–51.

67 Barber, *Trial*, pp. 182, 200–201.

68 *CDI*, vol. 2, pp. 65–66, no. 40.

69 Nicholson, *Knights Templar*, p. 221.

70 *CDI*, vol. 2, pp. 67–70, no. 41.

71 Jean Favier, *Un conseiller de Philippe le Bel: Enguerran de Marigny* (Paris, 1963), pp. 147–8.

house at Eecke, who was admitted to the order of the Hospitallers. He became commander in this order at Caestre and even entered the service of the Flemish count. Perhaps other Flemish Templars joined the Hospitallers and survived the drama of the Templars in this way. Those Templars who had confessed received absolution and were reconciled to the Church; those who showed no remorse received ecclesiastical punishments, while others lived off alms or a small pension, or perhaps joined other monasteries, or rejoined the secular world and even married.[72]

At the end of 1316, the Hospitallers complained that there were still some Templars living in the county of Flanders who were not yet reconciled to the Church of Rome.[73] It seems the situation in 1316 in the county of Flanders still was not as the pope and the king of France wished it to be. A certain Brother *Mille dou Sac* or Mille uten Zacke and several other Templars were on the loose in the county. The Knights Hospitaller asked the count to deal with this problem and to stop hindering their brothers from observing the orders of the Church of Rome.[74] Military orders such as the Hospitallers often lacked the means to apprehend fugitive Templars, and therefore it was necessary to invoke the aid of secular rulers and their officials, such as the count of Flanders and his bailiffs.[75]

---

[72] Rogghé, *De Orde van de Tempelridders*, pp. 151–2; Cumps, *De tempeliers in Vlaanderen*, pp. 119–20; Hosten, *De tempeliers*, p. 251; Barber, *Trial*, pp. 278–81; Elisabeth Lalou, 'Templerprozeß', *Lexikon des Mittelalters*, vol. 8 (1997), col. 538.

[73] Von Hefele, *Histoire des conciles*, vol. 6, part 1, p. 508, note 1.

[74] *ADNL*, B 1458, no. 5135; Vander Stichele, *De Hospitaalbroeders*, pp. 23–4.

[75] Alan J. Forey, 'Desertions and Transfers from Military Orders (Twelfth to Early-Fourteenth Centuries)', *Traditio*, 60 (2005), 188–90.

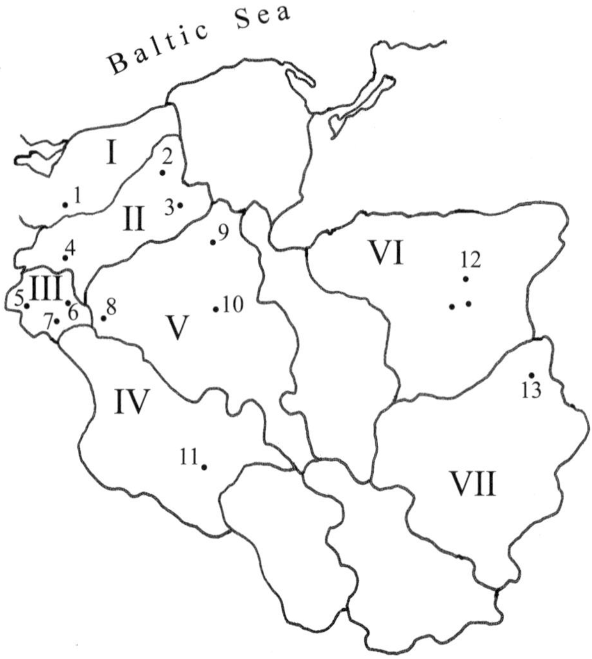

Key

Duchies or provinces

I = Western Pomerania
II = New March
III = Region of Lubusz
IV = Upper Silesia
V = Great Poland
VI = Mazovia
VII = Region of Sandomierz

Centres of the order

1 = Rurka (Rörchen)
2 = Czaplinek (Tempelburg)
3 = Wałcz (Deutsch Krone)
4 = Chwarszczany (Quartzen)
5 = Leśnica (Lietzen)
6 – Sulęcin (Zielenzig)
7 = Szydłów (Schidlo)
8 = Wielka Wieś
9 = Grzybowo, Studzieniec, Milossovo
10 = Gniezno (Gnesen)
11 = Mała Oleśnica (Klein Öls)
12 = Orzechowo, Dręszew Skuszew
13 = Łuków

Figure 24.1 Centres of the Knights Templar in the Polish Lands

Chapter 24
The Commanderies of the Templars in the Polish Lands and Their History after the End of the Order

Maria Starnawska

The Knights Templar operated in the Polish lands for less than 90 years and created only a few commanderies, dispersed over this area. This territory was far removed from the centres of religious and cultural life of medieval Europe. Although the Templars did not play a significant role in the religious life of the Polish lands, it is worth tracing their activity in this peripheral area of Europe as well as the fate of the houses of this order after its suppression. In fact, the history of the Templar commanderies in the Polish lands reflects the transformations of the crusade idea in a peripheral area in the period when the crusade movement was dying down.

The Knights Templar settled in the Polish lands relatively late, when the crusade movement in the Holy Land was nearing its end. Despite the peripheral situation of their country, a few Polish dukes and magnates had gone on pilgrimages to the Holy Land or taken part in crusades as early as the second half of the twelfth century. As a result of those pilgrimages, in the 1160s, the Knights Hospitaller of St John and canons of the Holy Sepulchre were brought from the Holy Land to Poland where they developed with much success until the end of the middle ages.[1] In the second half of the twelfth century, those orders also settled in other countries of central Europe. This shows that they were brought there on the initiative not only of the pilgrims from central Europe, but also of the authorities of the orders.[2]

---

1 Mikołaj Gładysz, *Zapomniani krzyżowcy: Polska wobec ruchu krucjatowego w XII–XIII wieku* (Warsaw, 2002), pp. 45–69, 98–117, 139–43; Maria Starnawska, *Między Jerozolimą a Łukowem: Zakony krzyżowe na ziemiach polskich w średniowieczu* (Warsaw, 1999), pp. 26, 73–4, 157–38; Zbigniew Piłat, *Fundator i fundacja klasztoru bożogrobców w Miechowie*, in *Bożogrobcy w Polsce: Praca zbiorowa* (Miechów and Warsaw, 1999), pp. 13–35; Ryszard Kiersnowski, *Jaksa i jego monety, Społeczeństwo Polski średniowiecznej*, vol. 5 (Warsaw, 1992), pp. 153–60; Jerzy Rajman, 'Pielgrzym i fundator: Fundacje kościelne i pochodzenie księcia Jaksy', *Nasza Przeszłość*, 82 (1994), 5–10, 27–33.

2 Gerhard Knoll, *Zur Entstehung und Geschichte der Johanniterkommende Werben im 13. Jahrhundert* (Berlin, 1971), pp. 21–3; Tore Nyberg, 'Zur Rolle der Johanniter in Skandinavien', in *Die Rolle der Ritterorden in der mittelalterlichen Kultur*, ed. Zenon Hubert Nowak (Toruń, 1985), pp. 130–31; Ivan Hlaváček, 'Zwei Miszellen zur Geschichte

At that time, the Knights Templar did not strive after gaining possessions there. Their expansion in the Polish lands in the second half of the twelfth century was also hampered by the Polish dukes' links to Emperor Frederick Barbarossa. The Templars were attached to the pope and the duke of Saxony, Henry the Lion, who was in conflict with the emperor. Yet, the arrival of the Knights Templar in Poland and Bohemia in the second quarter of the thirteenth century shows that this order found gaining possessions in central Europe profitable and useful.[3]

In the thirteenth century, when the Knights Templar were coming to the Polish lands, Poland was divided into several duchies, governed by the dukes of the Piast dynasty or some other families (as in Pomerania). As a result of the political disintegration of the country, the main factor that integrated the Polish lands was their subjection to the ecclesiastical metropolis of Gniezno. The development of the network of Templar houses in the Polish lands was not the result of a consistent foundation process, but of the initiatives of individual dukes who agreed with their policies. This impeded the rise of a uniform network of commanderies. The Templars had to compete in the Polish lands with about ten earlier established houses of the Knights Hospitaller of St John[4] and five houses of the canons of the

---

der Ritterorden in den bömischen Ländern', in ibid., p. 207; Arthur Breycha-Vauthier de Baillamont, 'Das Grosspriorat von Böhmen-Österreich', in *Der Johanniter-Orden, der Malteser-Orden, der ritterliche Orden des hl. Johannes von Spital zu Jerusalem: Seine Aufgabe, seine Geschichte*, ed. Adam Wienand et al. (Cologne, 1970), p. 352; Michael Skopal, 'Založeni komendy johanitů na Malé Straně: Přispěvek k otázce přichodu řádu do Čech', *Pražský Sbornik Historický*, 26 (1993), 29–35; Karl Borchardt, 'Military Orders in East Central Europe: The First Hundred Years', in *Autour de la première croisade: Actes du Colloque de la Society for the Study of the Crusades and the Latin East* (Clermont-Ferrand, 22–25 juin 1995), ed. Michel Balard (Paris, 1996), pp. 247–9; Libor Jan, 'Die Johanniter in Böhmen: Bild des Lebens', in *Vergangenheit und Gegenwart der Ritterorden: Die Rezeption der Idee und die Wirklichkeit*, ed. Zenon Hubert Nowak and Roman Czaja (Toruń, 2001), pp. 183–6; Anthony Luttrell, 'The Hospitallers Province of Alamania to 1428', in *Ritterorden und Region: Politische, soziale und wirtschaftliche Verbindungen im Mittelalter*, ed. Zenon Hubert Nowak (Toruń, 1995), p. 23.

3 Karl Borchardt, 'The Templars in Central Europe', in *The Crusades and the Militar y Orders: Expanding the Frontiers of Medieval Latin Christianity*, ed. Zsolt Hunyadi and Jósef Laszlovszky (Budapest, 2001), pp. 234–6.

4 Maria Starnawska, 'Crusade Orders on Polish Lands during the Middle Ages: Adaptation in a Peripheral Environment', *Quaestiones Medii Aevi Novae*, 2 (1997), 137; eadem, *Między Jerozolimą a Łukowem*, pp. 26–54; Edward Rymar, 'Kolińska komturia na tle dawnych dziejów joannitów', *Stargardia*, 3 (2003), 49–63; Franciszek Dąbrowski, 'Geneza i początek działanośći komandorii joannitów w Zagośći', *Między Wisłą a Pilicą. Studia i Materiały Historyczne*, 3 (2003), 11–44; Dariusz Wybranowski, 'Przyczynek do genezy i rozwoju komandorii joannitów w Sławnie do połowy XIII w.', *Zeszyty Naukowe Uniwersytetu Szczecińskiego*, no. 170, *Szczecińskie Studia Historyczne*, no. 9 (1995), pp. 99–115; Hermann Hoogeweg, *Die Stifter und Klöster der Provinz Pommern*, vol. 2 (Stettin, 1925), pp. 869–75, 891–2; Robert Heś, *Joannici na Śląsku w średniowieczu* (Kraków, 2007), pp. 57–69; Roman Stelmach, 'Zachowane dokumenty do dziejów komendy

Holy Sepulchre.[5] This competition also impeded the development of a network of Templar commanderies.

The initiative of the Templar authorities who wanted to gain possessions in this region of Europe must have coincided with the needs of the founders of their houses, since from the second quarter of the thirteenth century until the beginning of the fourteenth century they gained 13 land endowments, and in the early fourteenth century six commanderies were established.[6] Thus it is worth considering to what extent the tasks fulfilled by the Templar commanderies in the Polish lands were connected to the activity of this entire order in defence of the Holy Land, and to what extent they resulted from local needs.

Around 1225, the Knights Templar received their first landed property in the Polish lands: three villages from the duke of Great Poland, Ladislaus, son of Odo. The order received further endowments at regular intervals of several years until about 1257. Later the Templars gained only one grant: lands around Czaplinek in Great Poland, from Duke Przemysł II in about 1290.[7]

As regards their location, the Templars' possessions may be divided into three groups. Most of them lay in the borderland between Great Poland, the region of Lubusz and western Pomerania. There, the Templars held eight possessions

joannitów w Tyńcu nad Ślężą', *Sobótka*, 56 (2001), 331–3; idem, 'Komenda joannitów w Strzegomiu w świetle zachowanych dokumentów', *Rocznik Świdnicki*, 30 (2002), 57–63; Tadeusz Wojciech Lange, 'Joannici na Pomorzu Gdańskim: Stan badań, interpretacje, próba syntezy', *Zapiski Historyczne*, 9 (1994), 9–19; Krystyna Gancarczyk, 'W kwestii początków zakonu joannitów na Śląsku', *Sobótka*, 40 (1985), 191–201; Kazimierz Dola, 'Zakon joannitów na Śląsku do połowy XIV w.', *Studia Teologiczne Śląska Opolskiego*, 3 (1973), 46–4, 82–3, 85; Joanna Banik, 'Komenda joannitów w Łosiowie (1238–1810)', in *Prace uczestników seminarium doktoranckiego 5* (Opole, 2003), pp. 21–28.

5 Starnawska, 'Crusade Orders', pp. 139; eadem, *Między Jerozolimą a Łukowem*, pp. 74–93; Piłat, *Fundator i fundacja*, pp. 23–43; Mieczysław Tobiasz, 'Bożogrobcy w Miechowie (w 800-lecie sprowadzenia zakonu do Polski)', *Nasza Przeszłość*, 17 (1973), 8–12, 47, 49–50, 52–4; Zbigniew Pęckowski, *Miechów: Studium z dziejów miasta i ziemi miechowskiej do roku 1914* (Kraków 1967), pp. 80–81, 373–7, 467–70; Franciszek Sikora, 'Najstarsze dokumenty i dzieje klasztoru bożogrobców w Gnieźnie', *Studia Źródłoznawcze*, 19 (1971), 47–50; Kazimierz Dola, 'Szpitale średniowieczne Śląska', *Rocznik Teologiczny Śląska Opolskiego*, 1 (1968), 277.

6 Starnawska, 'Crusade Orders', 138–9; eadem, *Między Jerozolimą a Łukowem*, pp. 55–68.

7 *Urkunden und Regesten zur Geschichte des Templerordens im Bereich des Bistums Cammin und der Kirchenprovinz Gnesen*, ed. Winfried Irgang (Cologne and Vienna, 1987), nos 1, 41, 64; Mateusz Goliński, 'Uposażenie i organizacja zakonu templariuszy w Polsce do 1241 roku', *Kwartalnik Historyczny*, 98 (1991), 3–20; Piotr Hope, 'Kwestia sprowadzenia templariuszy do Polski: Rozwój uposażenia zakonu w Wielkopolsce', *Poznański Rocznik Archiwalno-Historyczny*, 1(1993), 25–7; Walter Kuhn, 'Ritterorden als Grenzhüter des Abendlandes gegen das östliche Heidentum', *Ostdeutsche Wissenschaft*, 6 (1959), 42–9.

granted to them between 1229 and 1290.[8] Only one of these, around Szydłów, donated by Silesian dukes before 1241, was soon lost by the order under unknown circumstances.[9] Other possessions, divided between five commanderies, belonged to the Templars until the suppression of their order. Another group consisted of estates in the borderland of Mazovia[10] and the duchy of Sandomierz, granted in the second and third quarters of the thirteenth century.[11] They belonged to the order for a short time, and nothing more is known about the circumstances of their loss. No actual commanderies had arisen within their bounds.

In the second quarter of the thirteenth century, the Templars also received some possessions in the centre of Great Poland and Silesia. Those in Great Poland they soon lost, probably because the order did not find a good field for its activities there. A good example of a failed foundation of a Templar house in the centre of Great Poland was the hospital in Gniezno, given to them in 1232 by Duke Ladislaus, son of Odo, which in 1243 was entrusted to the canons of the Holy Sepulchre. Although the Templars sporadically happened to run hospitals in Europe, theirs was above all a chivalric order, and they did not generally engage in

8 *Urkunden und Regesten*, nos 4, 5, 6, 11, 12, 14, 27, 32, 38, 64; Helmut Lüpke, 'Die Wüstungen Grossdorf und Giemeln im Lande Sterneberg', *Die Neumark: Mitteilungen des Vereins für Geschichte der Neumark*, 9 (1932), 53–70; idem, 'Das Land Tempelburg: Eine historisch-geographische Untersuchung', *Baltische Studien*, 35 (1933), 42–5, 86; Goliński, 'Uposażenie', 3–10, 12–14, 15–16; Józef Spors, 'Początki i stan posiadania templariuszy w ziemi kostrzyńskiej w latach 1232–1261', *Studia i Materiały do Dziejów Wielkopolski i Pomorza*, 16 (1987), fasc. 2, pp. 111–28; Edward Rymar, 'Powstanie i stan posiadania pomorskich komend templariuszy w Chwarszczanach i Myśliborzu w XIII wieku', *Przegląd Zachodniopomorski*, 31 (1987), 193–200; idem, 'Komandoria chwarszczańska templariuszy i joannitów (1232–1540)', *Nadwarciański Rocznik Historyczno-Archiwalny*, 9 (2002), 11–25; Anzelm Weiss, *Organizacja diecezji lubuskiej w średniowieczu* (Lublin, 1977), pp. 210–11; Benedykt Zientara, *Henryk Brodaty i jego czasy* (Warsaw, 1975), pp. 223, 226, 278–9; Zygmunt Boras, Ryszard Walczak and Andrzej Wędzki, *Historia powiatu wałeckiego* (Poznań, 1961), p. 27; Hope, 'Kwestia sprowadzenia', 28–40; idem, 'Curia Militiae Templi in Liceniz: Z dziejów templariuszy na zaodrzańskim obszarze diecezji lubuskiej', *Poznański Rocznik Historyczno-Archiwalny*, 2/3 (1994–5), 11–18; Hoogeweg, *Die Stifter und Klöster*, pp. 857–66; Walter Kuhn, 'Kirchliche Siedlung und Grenzschutz 1200–1250 (am Beispiel des mittleren Oderraums)', *Ostdeutsche Wissenschaft*, 9 (1962), 35, 42–3.

9 *Urkunden und Regesten*, no. 23; Kuhn, 'Kirchliche Siedlung', 44; Helmut Lüpke, 'Untersuchungen über den sagenhaft überlieferten oder fälschlich vermuteten Besitz der Tempelherren in Deutschland', *Jahrbuch für Brandenburgische Kirchengeschichte*, 31 (1936), 83–6; Goliński, 'Uposażenie', 15–16.

10 *Urkunden und Regesten*, nos 19, 37; Goliński, 'Uposażenie', 15–16.

11 *Urkunden und Regesten*, no. 41; Kuhn, 'Ritterorden', 42–9; idem, 'Kirchliche Siedlung', 44.

hospital services.[12] Thus, the transference of this hospital to the Templars had been an abortive idea.[13] On the other hand, the commandery at Mała Oleśnica, situated in the centre of Silesia and given to the Templars by Duke Henry the Bearded in 1227, belonged to the order until its suppression.[14]

The majority of the Templars' landed properties in the Polish lands was given to them by the dukes of various provinces, and only two possessions were given by lesser magnates.[15] Most of these were large estates, but they were usually in a poor state of cultivation, frequently thinly populated and forested. It was the order that brought settlers and founded villages there. Even if it owned a town, the seats of the commanderies were situated in the countryside. For example, the town of Sulęcin, granted to the Templars in 1244, was subject to the commandery in the village of Wielka Wieś or Chwarszczany.[16] At the time of its suppression, the order had six commanderies, one in Silesia, and five in the region of Lubusz, the New March, and Pomerania (all of them subject to a German prior). Towards the end of the thirteenth century, those commanderies started to form a separate group with a prior residing at Leśnica, Chwarszczany and Mała Oleśnica.[17]

In view of the late arrival of the Templars and their competition with the Knights Hospitaller and canons of the Holy Sepulchre, the fact that their six commanderies had arisen and persisted in the area of the metropolis of Gniezno until the suppression of the order can be considered a great success for them. This was certainly the result of their skilful adaptation to this peripheral environment. Their authorities wanted to gain possessions in central Europe so that the revenues coming from there would help in financing their activities in the Holy Land and in the recruitment of new brothers or crusaders. Their intentions may have coincided

---

12 Jacques Juillet, *Commanderies sur le chemin de Rocamadour* (Saint-Yrieux-La-Perche, 1975), p. 33; Jean Fardet, *Les Maisons-Dieu sur les chemins de Saint Jacques de Compostella (avec une étude particulière d'Armorique)* (Nantes, 1965), pp. 87, 179; Lelja Dobronić, *Viteški redovi: Templari i Ivanovci u Hrvatskoj* (Zagreb, 1984), pp. 59; Borchardt, 'The Templars', p. 238.

13 *Urkunden und Regesten*, no. 6; *Kodeks dyplomatyczny Wielkopolski*, ed. Ignacy Zakrzewski, vol. 1 (Poznań, 1977), no. 238; Goliński, 'Uposażenie', 3–4; Sikora, 'Najstarsze dokumenty', 55–6; Tobiasz, 'Bożogrobcy w Miechowie', 52–3; Hope, 'Kwestia sprowadzenia', 28–9.

14 *Urkunden und Regesten*, no. 3; *Vita sanctae Hedwigis*, ed. Aleksander Semkowicz, in *Monumenta Poloniae Historica*, vol. 4 (Lwów, 1884), p. 545; Goliński, 'Uposażenie', 11–13; Hope, 'Kwestia sprowadzenia', 16–22; Kurt Eistert, 'Der Ritterorden der Tempelherren in Schlesien', *Archiv für schlesische Kirchengeschichte*, 14 (1956), 2–21; Zientara, *Henryk Brodaty*, p. 207; Edmund Burzyński, 'Templariusze na Śląsku: Komandoria w Oleśnicy Małej', *Słupskie Studia Historyczne*, 13 (2007), 157–72.

15 Sulęcin (Zielenzig): *Urkunden und Regesten*, no. 27; Wałcz (Deutsch Krone): *Urkunden und Regesten*, no. 32.

16 *Urkunden und Regesten*, nos 27, 28, 63; Kuhn, 'Kirchliche Siedlung', 42–43; Weiss, *Organizacja diecezji lubuskiej*, p. 211.

17 Borchardt, 'The Templars', p. 238; *Urkunden und Regesten*, nos 65, 70, 81.

with those of Ladislaus, duke of Great Poland, who granted to the Templars their earliest property in the Polish lands and probably took part in the Fifth Crusade.[18] Some other benefactors of the order also justified their grants by stating that their intention was to help the defence of the Holy Land. This shows that the representatives of the top social élite in the Polish lands in the thirteenth century regarded the financial support of the crusades to the Holy Land as their duty. However, in the course of the thirteenth century, the crusade idea and the desire to support the crusaders in the Holy Land were in decline, as was also evident in the Polish lands. The last Polish document corroborating an intention to support the activities of the Templars in the Holy Land dates from 1244.[19] Later the donations granted to them were not justified in this way. Thus, the wish to give financial support to the fight against the Muslims in the Holy Land was not the only reason for endowing this order in the Polish lands.

The Templars' possessions in the Polish lands probably did not bring them the expected profits. Though the estates were large, their management required considerable outlay. We do not know how soon they started to bring in revenues, or whether the brothers who administered them conscientiously transferred the surplus of their income to the central authorities of the order or retained it for themselves. We do know that, in the high middle ages, the Knights Hospitaller in Silesia neglected this duty and consumed the income themselves.[20] The Templars might have acted in a similar way, though we have no information to this effect. The order was also entitled to collect money for the crusades, but we do not know whether it availed itself of this right,[21] nor do we have any information as to the participation of the Templars from the area of the metropolis of Gniezno in the conflict in the Holy Land. The staff of their houses in the Polish lands was small: there were usually only three or four brothers in a commandery.[22] Thus, we may infer that there were probably few volunteers willing to enter the order in this area.

The main task of the Templars, that is, helping the defence of the Holy Land, was not their only form of activity in the Polish lands. The local commanderies took up other tasks that resulted from the needs of the local community. The most

---

[18] Wincenty Swoboda, 'Księżna kaliska Bułgarką? Przyczynek do rozbioru krytycznego Annalium Długosza', *Studia i Materiały do Dziejów Wielkopolski i Pomorza*, 13 (1980), 61–78; for the contrary view, see: Gładysz, *Zapomniani krzyżowcy*, pp. 158–68.

[19] *Urkunden und Regesten*, nos 4, 6, 7, 11, 12, 19, 29.

[20] Dola, 'Zakon joannitów', 78; Maria Starnawska, 'Der Johanniterorden und Schlesien im Mittelalter', *Würzburger medizinhistorische Mitteilungen*, 22 (2003), 410.

[21] Marion Melville, *Dzieje templariuszy* (Warsaw, 1991), pp. 157–8.

[22] Goliński, 'Uposażenie', 19–20; idem, 'Templariusze a bitwa pod Legnicą: Próba rewizji poglądów', *Kwartalnik Historyczny*, 98.3 (1991), 10; Maria Starnawska, 'Notizie sulla composizione e sulla struttura del ordine del Tempio in Polonia', in *I Templari: Mito e storia*, ed. Giovanni Minnucci and Francesco Sardi (Siena, 1989), pp. 147–50.

natural of them, befitting a chivalric order that resided far from the Holy Land, was fighting against the pagans. The Polish dukes had conducted the fight against their pagan neighbours, Pruthenians and Sudovians, organized on the model of the crusades, since the middle of the twelfth century.[23] Therefore, as early as the second half of the twelfth century, some dukes tried to enlist the Knights Hospitaller and canons of the Holy Sepulchre in the conflict,[24] and, additionally, in the second quarter of the thirteenth century, the order of Calatrava and the order of the Knights of Christ,[25] especially created for that purpose, as well as the Teutonic Knights. Only the latter saw some possible advantage in taking part in the

[23] Starnawska, *Między Jerozolimą a Łukowem*, pp. 182–8; eadem, 'Military Orders and the Beginning of Crusade in Prussia', in *The Crusades and the Military Orders*, ed. Hunyadi and Laszlovszky, pp. 418–19; Krzysztof Benyskiewicz, 'Rycerstwo polskie wobec pogan i pogaństwa w XI–XIII wieku', in *Rycerstwo Europy środkowo-wchodniej wobec idei krucjat*, ed. Wojciech Peltz and Jarosław Dudek (Zielona Góra, 2002), pp. 28–34; Gładysz, 'Wyprawa jaćwińska Kazimierza Sprawiedliwego w relacji mistrza Wincentego: Przyczynek do recepcji haseł krucjatowych XII-wiecznej Polsce', in ibid., pp. 99–167; Krystyna Zielińska-Melkowska, *Polskie wyprawy krzyżowe do Prus w II połowie XII i w pierwszej połowie XIII wieku na tle idei krucjatowej*, in ibid., pp. 69–89; Gładysz, *Zapomniani krzyżowcy*, pp. 70–97; 126–30; Roman Grodecki, 'Polska wobec idei wypraw krzyżowych', *Przegląd Współczesny*, 7 (1923), pp. 109–14; Jan Powierski, *Stosunki polsko-pruskie do 1230 r. ze szczególnym uwzględnieniem roli Pomorza Gdańskiego* (Toruń, 1968), pp. 106–15, 125–62.

[24] Starnawska, 'Military Orders', pp. 419–20; eadem, *Między Jerozolimą a Łukowem*, pp. 189–94; Zenon Hubert Nowak, 'Der Anteil der Ritterorden in der preussischen Mission (mit Ausnahme des Deutschen Ordens)', in *Die Rolle der Ritterorden in der Christianisierung und Kolonisierung des Ostseegebietes*, ed. Zenon Hubert Nowak (Toruń, 1983), pp. 79–91; Lange, 'Joannici na Pomorzu Gdańskim', 11.

[25] Starnawska, 'Military Orders', pp. 420–22; Jerzy Hauziński, 'O kalatrawensach nad Bałtykiem raz jeszcze', in *Memoriae amici et magistri: Studia historyczne poświęcone pamięci Prof. Wacława Korty (1919–1999)*, ed. Marek Derwich, Wojciech Mrozowicz and Rościsław Żerelik (Wrocław, 2001), pp. 79–87; Romuald Frydrychowicz, 'Der Ritterorden von Calatrava in Tymau bei Mewe', *Altpreussische Monatschrift*, 17 (1890), 315–20; Zenon Hubert Nowak, 'Milites Christi de Prussia: Der Orden zu Dobrin und seine Stellung in der preussischen Mission', in *Die geistlichen Ritterorden Europas*, ed. Josef Fleckenstein and Manfred Hellmann (Sigmaringen, 1980), pp. 339–52; Wanda Polkowska-Markowska, 'Dzieje Zakonu Dobrzyńskiego', *Roczniki Historyczne*, 2 (1926), 145–210; Kuhn, 'Ritterorden', 26–7, 38–42; Powierski, *Stosunki polsko-pruskie*, pp. 167–8; idem, *Prusowie, Mazowsze i sprowadzenie Krzyżaków do Polski*, vol. 1 (Malbork, 1996), pp. 12–17; Tadeusz Manteuffel, *Papiestwo i cystersi ze szczególnym uwzględnieniem ich roli w Polsce na przełomie XII i XIII w.* (Warsaw, 1955), pp. 97–106; Gerard Labuda, 'O nadaniu biskupa Chrystiana dla dobrzyńców roku 1228', *Roczniki Humanistyczne*, 20.2 (1972), 43–9; Klemens Bruski, *Ziemie nad dolną Wierzycą od XIII do początku XV wieku* (Gdańsk 1997), pp. 44–6; Francis Gutton, *L'ordre de Calatrava* (1955), pp. 229–30; Edward Rymar, 'Ze studiów nad genealogią książąt Pomorza Gdańskiego w pierwszej połowie XIII wieku: Daty zgonów', *Zapiski Historyczne*, 42 (1977), 19.

crusade to Pruthenia (Prussia) and from 1230 on conducted a systematic conquest, eventually creating their own state.[26] The granting to the Templars of possessions in Mazovia[27] and the duchy of Sandomierz in strategically important places during the fight against the Sudovians shows that the duke of Mazovia, Boleslaus I, and of the duchy of Sandomierz, Boleslaus the Chaste, intended to enlist the Templars' assistance in this action. They did not succeed in their attempts, however, since the Templars were unwilling to take up a crusading role outside the Holy Land. The crusade organized by Boleslaus the Chaste did not materialize since the Teutonic Knights, alarmed by the possibility of finding rivals, intervened in this matter with the pope.[28]

The Templars found the best conditions for their development in the borderland between Great Poland and Pomerania. In the thirteenth century, this area was the object of rivalry between the dukes of Great Poland, Silesia and western Pomerania.[29] The extent of their rule was in constant flux. In the middle of the thirteenth century, the march of Brandenburg also joined this rivalry. In 1250, the margraves bought the region of Lubusz, and subsequently wrenched successive areas from Great Poland and Pomerania and created from them the so-called New March. Towards the end of the thirteenth century Brandenburg gained a dominant position in this region.[30]

This area was thinly populated, and the rulers who vied for this territory were willing to grant property to the order there, so as to manifest their sovereignty. Each of the rulers who struggled with one another probably expected that the knights of the order thus endowed would defend the borderlands of his duchy. Probably for this reason the seats of the Templar commanderies were situated among marshes or between lakes that provided a natural defence. Initially, the order took advantage

26 Marian Biskup, Roman Czaja, Wiesław Długokęcki, Marian Dygo, Sławomir Jóźwiak, Andrzej Radzimiński and Janusz Tandecki, *Państwo zakonu krzyżackiego w Prusach: Władza i społeczeństwo* (Warsaw, 2008), pp. 64–72.

27 *Urkunden und Regesten*, no. 19; Goliński, 'Uposażenie', 15–16; Starnawska, *Między Jerozolimą a Łukowem*, pp. 198–9.

28 *Urkunden und Regesten*, no. 41; *Vetera monumenta Poloniae et Lithuaniae*, ed. Augustinus Theiner, vol. 1 (Rome 1860), nos 119, 126, 139, 142, 145; *Preussisches Urkundenbuch*, vol. 1.2 (Königsberg, 1882), no. 28; Starnawska, 'Crusade Orders', 129–30; Kuhn, 'Ritterorden', 42–51; Jadwiga Karwasińska, 'Sąsiedztwo kujawsko-krzyżackie 1235–1343', in eadem, *Kujawy i Mazowsze: Wybór pism* (Warsaw, 1997), pp. 55–77; Władysław Abraham, *Powstanie organizacyi Kościoła łacińskiego na Rusi*, vol. 1 (Lwów, 1904), pp. 156–62; Jan Powierski, 'Sprawa Prus i Jaćwięży w polityce Zakonu Krzyżackiego i książąt polskich po ugodzie wrocławskiej z 4 sierpnia 1257 roku', *Komunikaty Mazursko-Warmińskie*, 23 (1979), 255–63.

29 Zientara, *Henryk Brodaty*, pp. 151–62, 214–31, 277–80, 314–15; Spors, 'Początki i stan posiadania', 111–20; Rymar, 'Komandoria chwarszczańska', 11–18.

30 Kazimierz Walachowicz, *Geneza i ustrój polityczny Nowej Marchii do początków XIV wieku* (Warsaw and Poznań, 1980), passim; Kuhn, 'Kirchliche Siedlung', 14, 36; Spors, 'Początki i stan posiadania', 121–6; Rymar, 'Komandoria chwarszczańska', 19–25.

of this situation skilfully, accepting grants from all the competing dukes, while retaining its neutrality. The lack of traces of any deliberate fortifications of those sites shows that it avoided serious engagements in those conflicts.[31]

However, the year 1261 (or 1262) saw a confrontation with the Brandenburg margraves who became a dominant political power in the region. They seized from the Templars a part of their possessions around Chwarszczany.[32] After this, the order recognized the margraves as the most important power in the region and consistently supported them, counting on the resulting profits. A good example of this support was the subjection of the commandery at Czaplinek to the margraves' power after the donor of this estate, Przemysł II, then king of Poland, was murdered at the margraves' instigation in 1296.[33] The order's ties with the Brandenburg margraves were strengthened by the influx of knightly families from Brandenburg to the Lubusz region and to the New March, whose descendants joined the order.[34] These families found an important basis in the vast estates, partly cultivated before Brandenburg took over this area.[35] Their prestige rose when their descendants acquired the rank of Templar commanders. Due to their cooperation with the margraves and Brandenburg knights coming to the New March, the Templar commanderies could run their estates in peace. Consequently, the order became integrated into the local environment.

The way of life of the Knights Templar who administered monastic estates became similar to that of their lay kinsmen. The small dimensions of the chapels preserved in the commanderies of Rurka and Leśnica show that the knights of the order did not attach too much weight to religious life and pastoral work among the local population. In the second half of the thirteenth century, only the chapel at Chwarszczany, initially also small, was expanded. This was done more for the sake of prestige, since the prior of the Templars in the Polish lands was then resident in that commandery. A building that bears actual testimony to the activities of the brothers is a huge stone granary in the commandery at Leśnica. The erection

---

31 Zbigniew Radacki, *Średniowieczne zamki Pomorza Zachodniego* (Warsaw, 1976), pp. 111–21, 123, 253–5; Błażej Skaziński, 'Sztuka w kręgu zakonu templariuszy', in *Templariusze: Historia i mit, Katalog wystawy*, ed. Sławomir Majoch (Toruń, 2004), pp. 34–6; Przemysław Kołosowski, 'Stan badań archeologicznych nad siedzibami templariuszy na ziemiach polskich', ibid., pp. 52–69.

32 *Urkunden und Regesten*, no. 48; Edward Rymar, 'Datacja układu templariuszy z margrabiami brandenburskimi w sprawie komandorii chwarszczańskiej i myśliborskiej (31 I 1262)', *Nadwarciański Rocznik Historyczno-Archiwalny*, 8 (2001), 311–15; idem, 'Komandoria chwarszczańska', 19–25.

33 Walachowicz, *Geneza i ustrój polityczny*, p. 43.

34 Starnawska, 'Notizie', pp. 149–50.

35 Zbigniew Wielgosz, 'Rola rycerstwa w brandenburskiej ekspansji na wschód', in *Europa-Słowiańszczyza-Polska: Studia ku uczczeniu Profesora Kazimierza Tymienieckiego* (Poznań, 1870), pp. 115–26; Antoni Czacharowski, *Społeczne i polityczne siły w walce o Nową Marchię 1319–1373* (Toruń, 1958), pp. 54–92.

of such a structure in the thirteenth century testifies to the importance that the Templars attached to agriculture.[36] Due to those transformations, the Templar commanderies in the metropolitan area of Gniezno developed with much success, but the brothers grew more and more linked to the local environment, and their ties with the order as a whole slackened.

The activity of the Templar commanderies came to an end with the suppression of the order. Its causes had no connection with its activity in the metropolis of Gniezno metropolis, since the pope's decision to transfer the Templars' estates to the Knights Hospitaller concerned the order as a whole. In Silesia and Pomerania, this transfer was effected without any obstacles. The Knights Hospitaller owned Mała Oleśnica as early as 1314 and Rurka before 1329.[37] In both these provinces the Hospitallers had held their own commanderies even earlier.[38] Thus, the Knights Hospitaller found it easy to see to the implementation of the pope's decision.

However, in the region of Lubusz and the New March where the Knights Hospitaller had no houses at the beginning of the fourteenth century, the Templars' commanderies suffered a different fate. The margraves tried to seize their possessions without fearing the opposition of the Hospitallers. However, the German prior of this order claimed a right to these estates. Negotiations were concluded with the agreement of Cremmen in 1318, according to which the Hospitallers were to take over the Templars' commanderies with the exception of estates around Sulęcin. In defiance of this agreement the margraves also seized the commandery at Czaplinek. The Templars' possessions in the New March were not fully regained by the Hospitallers until 1345–47. They retained the commanderies previously established by the Templars at Leśnica, Czaplinek and Chwarszczany in the same localities. The commandery at Wielka Wieś was subjected to the new commandery at Łagów, and in 1373 the seat of the commandery was moved from Rurka to Swobnica.[39]

---

36 Jarosław Jarzewicz, *Gotycka architektura Nowej Marchii: Budownictwo sakralne w okresie Askańczyków i Wittelsbachów* (Poznań, 2000), pp. 215–45; Radacki, *Średniowieczne zamki*, pp. 114, 121; Hope, 'Curia Militiae Templi', 33; Kołosowski, 'Stan badań', pp. 52–3, 64–5; Lothar Lambacher, 'Die pauperes commilitones Christi templique Salomonis in der Mark Brandenburg', *Sprawozdania Poznańskiego Towarzystwa Naukowego: Wydział Nauk o Sztuce*, 108 (1991), 72–3, 83.

37 *Urkunden und Regesten*, no. 85; *Pommersches Urkundenbuch*, vol. 7, ed. Hans Frederichs and Erich Sandow (Cologne and Graz, 1958), no. 4512; Eistert, 'Der Ritterorden', 21.

38 Starnawska, 'Der Johanniterorden und Schlesien', 405–15; eadem, *Między Jerozolimą a Łukowem*, pp. 29–31, 35–7, 249–82; Dola, 'Zakon', 81–6; Hoogeweg, *Die Stifter und Klöster*, pp. 869–95.

39 *Codex diplomaticus Brandenburgensis*, Part A, vol. 19, ed. Adolph Friedrich Riedel (Berlin, 1860), pp. 128–9, 196–7, 131–2; Julius Pflugk-Harttungk, *Die Anfänge der Johanniterorden in Deutschland, besonders in der Mark Brandenburg und in Mecklenburg* (Berlin, 1899), pp. 66–8; idem, *Der Johanniter und der Deutsche Orden im Kampfe*

The previous Templar commanderies taken over by the Knights Hospitaller played a different role in Silesia than in Brandenburg-Pomerania. In Silesia, the Hospitallers had formed a strong order even before taking over the commandery of Mała Oleśnica and engaged mainly in pastoral work in towns. Most of their commanderies were situated in towns, near parish churches, and their members were mainly priests from burgher families.[40] The commandery at Mała Oleśnica adjusted itself to this pattern. It retained its seat in the countryside, but on its territories a sanctuary was erected – with many relics, probably assembled by the Templars. In 1385, eight priests resided in the commandery permanently and held services for the pilgrims. The previous commandery of knights became similar to the priests' monasteries of other orders. The only trace of its crusade origin was the title of commander, used by its superior, as well as the presence of some relics brought from the Holy Land, for example, that of the Holy Innocents.[41]

On the other hand, in the region of Brandenburg-Pomerania, the incorporation of the Templars' five rich commanderies caused serious transformations in the Hospitaller order. Until the takeover of the Templars' possessions, the Hospitallers' activities in Pomerania (as well as in Silesia) consisted mainly of administering the urban parishes (at Stargard near Szczecin and at Sławno).[42] After the takeover, the number of commanderies in this region grew to seven. This group of communities started striving for independence from the German priory. In 1382, the German prior agreed to the creation of the Brandenburg bailiwick, subordinated to him and encompassing the Hospitallers' commanderies in Brandenburg and Pomerania.[43] The *baili* resided at Chwarszczany or Łagów, and after 1428 at the castle bought for this purpose at Słońsk.[44] Another important consequence of the incorporation of the Templars' commanderies was the adoption of their model in the whole of the bailiwick. After 1351, the commandery attached to the urban parish church at Sławno was closed down. The seat of the commandery was moved from Stargard to the little township of Suchań situated in this commandery.[45]

Ludwigs des Bayern mit der Kurie (Leipzig, 1900), pp. 50, 236–9; Hoogeweg, *Die Stifter und Klöster*, pp. 895–6, 898; Rymar, 'Komandoria chwarszczańska', 25–8.

40 Starnawska, 'Der Johanniterorden und Schlesien', 412–14.

41 The State Central Archive of the Czech Republic, Řád Maltézský-Listiny, nos 825, 827, 831, 886; *Codex diplomaticus Silesiae*, vol. 16, ed. Colmar Grünhagen and Conrad Wutke (Breslau, 1892), no. 2708; Dola, 'Zakon', 75.

42 Hoogeweg, *Die Stifter und Klöster*, pp. 882, 892.

43 *Codex diplomaticus Brandenburgensis*, Part B, vol. 3, ed. Adolph Friedrich Riedel (Berlin, 1846), pp. 84–7; Hans Prutz, *Die geistlichen Ritterorden* (Berlin, 1908), p. 313.

44 *Codex diplomaticus Brandenburgensis*, Part A, vol. 19, pp. 148–9; Pflugk-Harttungk, *Die Anfänge*, pp. 19–25, 102; Radacki, *Średniowieczne zamki*, p. 154.

45 *Pommersches Urkundenbuch*, vol. 6, ed. Otto Heinemann (Stettin, 1907), nos 3785, 3977; Hoogeweg, *Die Stifter und Klöster*, pp. 874–5, 882, 892.

Just as under the Templars, the majority of the brothers came from the knightly families who had settled in Pomerania or the New March.[46] At the seats of the commanderies, castles were erected similar to those in the estates of the Hospitallers' lay kinsmen (for example, at Swobnica, Gorgast, Drahim, Mahliny and Suchań).[47] The Hospitallers' commanders, just like their lay cousins, frequently stayed in the entourages of the dukes of Pomerania and margraves of Brandenburg as their courtiers, advisers or diplomats.[48] Their way of life started to resemble that of their lay kinsmen. Due to this evolution, the Hospitaller order and individual brothers played an important role in the political life of Pomerania and the New March. At the same time, their connection to the rest of their religious order became weaker. It was reduced to paying 324 guldens of annual contribution to the grand master for the defence of the island of Rhodes against the Turks.[49] The Brandenburg bailiwick became transformed into a semi-secular chivalric fraternity that ensured the endowment of the descendants of illustrious families with landed property.

The Templars of the metropolitan area of Gniezno did not play a significant role in the region or in the defence of the Holy Land. However, the model of their commanderies that had arisen in the borderlands of Great Poland and Pomerania turned out to be attractive for the Knights Hospitaller and the German knights who settled in this region, and made for the evolution of the local branch of the Knights Hospitaller. It is paradoxical that due to this evolution the crusade tradition was almost completely renounced by this order.

Translated by Agnieszka Kreczmar

---

46 Maria Starnawska, 'Mnisi, rycerze, szlachta: Templariusze i joannici na pograniczu wielkopolsko-brandenbursko-pomorskim', *Kwartalnik Historyczny*, 99 (1992), 20, 29–31.

47 Radacki, *Średniowieczne zamki*, pp. 126–44, 153–8, 259–60.

48 Maria Starnawska, 'Die Johanniter in der Kirchenprovinz Gnesen und im Bistum Kammin gegenüber der weltlichen Macht: Amtsträger, Berater der Herrscher, Landesherren', in *Die Ritterorden als Träger der Herrschaft: Territorien, Grundbesitz und Kirche*, ed. Roman Czaja and Jürgen Sarnowsky (Toruń, 2007), pp. 239–44.

49 *Codex diplomaticus Brandenburgensis*, Part B, vol. 3, pp. 84–7.

Centres of the Knights Templar in Polish Lands

House or possession of the Order	Founder	Date of origin	Duchy	Centre existing till the suppression of the Order	Commandery of the Knights Hospitaller of St. John after the suppression of the Knights Templar
Grzybowo, Studzieniec, Milossovo	Ladislaus, son of Odo, duke of Great Poland	1225	Great Poland	no	no
Mała Oleśnica – Klein Öls	Henry the Bearded, duke of Silesia	About 1226	Silesia	yes	yes
Leśnica – Lietzen	Henry the Bearded	1225-1229	Region of Lubusz	yes	yes
Gniezno	Ladislaus, son of Odo	1232	Great Poland	no	no
Wielka Wieś	Ladislaus, son of Odo	1232	Borderland of Great Poland and the region of Lubusz	yes	yes (Łagów)
Chwarszczany - Quartschen	Henry the Bearded or Ladislaus, son of Odo	1232	Borderland of Great Poland and the region of Lubusz	yes	yes

House or possession of the Order	Founder	Date of origin	Duchy	Centre existing till the suppression of the Order	Commandery of the Knights Hospitaller of St. John after the suppression of the Knights Templar
Rurka - Rörchen	Barnim, duke of Western Pomerania	1234	Borderland of Western Pomerania and Great Poland	yes	yes
Orzechowo, Dręszew, Skuszew	Boleslaus, duke of Mazovia	1239	Mazovia	no	no
Szydłów - Schidlo	Henry the Bearded or Henry the Pious, dukes of Silesia	Prior to 1240	Region of Lubusz	no	no
Sulęcin - Zielenzig	Mroczko, the Silesian magnate	1244	Region of Lubusz	no	no
Wałcz – Deutsch Krone	Widow of Peter from Lank, the magnate from Great Poland	1249	Great Poland	yes	no
Łuków	Boleslaus the Chaste, duke of Cracow and Sandomierz	Prior to 1257	Region of Sandomierz	no	no
Czaplinek - Tempelburg	Przemysł II, duke of Great Poland	About 1290	Great Poland	yes	yes

PART VI
General Aspects and the Aftermath

Chapter 25
Templar Runaways and Renegades before, during and after the Trial

Christian Vogel

In this article, I will discuss problems of apostasy before, during, and after the trial by considering both different forms of apostasy and the regulations of the Templars' statutes on this subject. I will also give some examples in order to compare theory and practice.

During the investigations against the Templars, many Templars appeared before the inquisitors without beard or habit, thus without visible signs of their affiliation to the order of the Templars.[1] Most of these had been reconciled to the Church at provincial synods and received episcopal absolution,[2] which meant that they had distanced themselves from their former order and had abjured the heretical errors of which the Templars were accused. These men cannot really be denoted as fugitives or renegades, as they were driven out of their order rather than being runaways. Besides, because they acted on the demand of the ecclesiastical authorities, they were assured that they did not have to fear any unpleasant consequences as a result of their apostasy from their order. There was another group of Templars which also had little reason to fear consequences due to their escape, although they were real fugitives. Several Templars fled because they were afraid of the coming trial.[3] Many Templar witnesses in the trial proceedings spoke of other brothers of their order who had run away in order to escape the arrests.[4] The pope later ordered them to appear at the provincial synods within a year so that they could be reconciled with the Church.[5] Another group were those Templars who appeared before the inquisitors asking for permission to leave the order at this time. Some alleged that

[1] *PT*, vol. 1, pp. 187–93; cf. Malcolm Barber, *The Trial of the Templars*, 2nd edn (Cambridge 2006), pp. 146–7.

[2] For example, *PT*, vol. 2, pp. 1, 33, 63, 144, 147, 157, 159; *Le procès des Templiers d'Auvergne (1309–1311): Edition de l'interrogatoire de juin 1309*, ed. Roger Sève and Anne-Marie Chagny-Sève (Paris, 1986), pp. 69sqq.

[3] *PT*, vol. 1, p. 412; vol. 2, pp. 263, 265, 267; *PUT*, vol. 2, p.75; cf. Barber, *Trial*, p. 46.

[4] *PT*, vol. 1, pp. 200, 412, 509; vol. 2, pp. 1, 33, 144, 147, 157, 159, 241, 265, 266; *PUT*, vol. 2, pp. 337–9.

[5] Pope Clement V, *Considerantes dudum* (May 1312), *Reg. Clem. V*, no. 8784; see also Joseph Alberigo, *Conciliorum oecumenicorum decreta*, 3rd edn (Bologna, 1973), pp.

they would like to return to secular life.[6] Obviously they considered the trial to be a convenient opportunity to do this without penance. Others were more obedient to the Templar rule and asked for permission to enter another religious order in order to save their souls there,[7] in accordance with the order's statutes, which allowed brothers to leave the Templars under exceptional circumstances as long as the departing brothers entered a stricter order.[8]

However, runaways from religious orders were not a phenomenon which had been known only since the beginning of the trial, neither had it been a peculiarity of the Templars.[9] The vows taken by monks and friars when entering a religious order were binding for life. Considering that joining a monastery was frequently not a result of careful consideration, but rather the consequence of external, such as familial, pressure, it is not really surprising that many monks or friars found no other way to escape the life-long bond of their vows than by running away.[10] An example from the inquiries into the Templars shows the difficulties of leaving the order. Brother Americus Cambellani wanted to leave the Templars and join another order instead, but he was unable to do so because his family forced him to stay.[11]

On the other hand, we find examples of Templars who obtained permission (or were even commanded) to leave their order to enter another order which followed a stricter rule, and to save their souls there. This happened to a Knight Templar at the time of Pope Boniface VIII. However, this Templar, an Aragonese named Peter de Sancho, did not wish to leave his order. Although he was excluded because of malpractice, he successfully appealed against the decision, and the pope obliged the order to take him back.[12]

347–9; six years later, his successor John XXII gave a similiar order to those Templars who had not yet returned to a monastic life: *EUT*, pp. 293–4 (Urkundliche Beilagen, no. 21).

6 Aymo de Pratini: *PT*, vol. 1, pp. 138–9; cf. Barber, *Trial*, p. 135; Jean de Primeyo, cf. Barber, *Trial*, p. 131.

7 Nicolas de Boncelo: *PT*, vol. 1, p. 83; cf. Barber, *Trial*, p. 131.

8 For a discussion about what is meant by 'stricter', see Alan Forey, 'Desertions and Transfers from Military Orders (Twelfth to Early-Fourteenth Centuries)', *Traditio*, 60 (2005), 143–200, here 147–161.

9 Cf. Francis Donald Logan, *Runaway Religious in Medieval England* (Cambridge, 1996); Albert Joseph Riessner, *Apostates and Fugitives from Religious Institutes* (Washington D.C., 1942); concerning the military orders, see Forey, 'Desertions and Transfers', passim.

10 Forey, 'Desertions and Transfers', 161sqq., describes apostates' lack of vocation and disobedience to the vows.

11 *UT*, vol. 2, p. 45: *Interrogatus quare non exivit, dixit super animam suam, quod nescit, quia erat ita turbatus, et multotiens rogavit consangineos suos, nobiles homines, quia ipse nobilis est, quod transferrent eum ad aliam religionem, sed ipsi nolebant facere.*

12 *PT*, vol. 1, p. 170.

The flight from one's religious order was a common evil in the monastic world of the middle ages. With regard to the Templars, this becomes obvious when one considers papal mandates from the twelfth century commanding the prelates to support the Templar authorities in recapturing renegades.[13] Members of religious orders who unlawfully deserted their position committed a grave offence against ecclesiastical law.[14] In the early thirteenth century, Pope Innocent III had prohibited religious from leaving their order and ruled out the possibility of a dispensation, which was accepted by Innocent IV. Instead, Innocent III had opened the possibility of a *transitus*.[15] These papal decrees were also put into practice by the Templars, although Pope Eugenius III had decreed especially for the Templars that no-one who had once entered the order and professed could leave this order, neither to go back to secular life nor to enter another religious community, because of the Templars' vocation as defenders of the Holy Land.[16] But this had been in 1151, and times had changed.

As in any other community living under a religious rule, Templars were generally forbidden to leave the order once they had entered it.[17] Leaving the order was only permissible in exceptional cases, and only with the permission of the superiors who were in a position to give permission with the consent of the chapter.[18] Without permission, a fugitive or recaptured apostate was sentenced to lose his habit for a year and a day. As another way of leaving, it was possible to

---

13 *Papsturkunden für Templer und Johanniter, Vorarbeiten zum Oriens Pontificius I, Archivberichte und Texte*, ed. Rudolf Hiestand (Göttingen, 1972), no. 15 (March 1151), pp. 221–2; ibid., no. 191 (February 1186/7), p. 375; no. 209 (February 1189), p. 387; no. 211 (February 1189), p. 388.

14 *Corpus iuris canonici*, ed. Emil Friedberg (Leipzig, 1879), part I, dist. 50, c. 69 (vol. 1, col. 203); part 2, causa 16, qu. 17 (vol. 1, col. 765), causa 27, qu. 1 (vol. 1, col. 1047), qu. 18 (vol. 1, col. 1053–4), qu. 19 (vol. 1, col. 1054).

15 cf. Logan, *Runaway Religious*, pp. 42–3.

16 Hiestand, *Papsturkunden*, no. 15: *nullatenus sibi de cetero liceat sub obtentu maioris sive minoris religionis ad alia loca transire vel alium habitum suscipere. Cum enim ipsi defendam orientalem ecclesiam et paganaorum sevitiam reprimendam relictis pompis secularibus in Die sint servitio mancipati, si transeundi ad alia loca et sumptum habitum reliquendi daretur eis licencia, magnum ecclesie Die posset exinde contingere detrimentum.*

17 Cf. Christian Vogel, *Das Recht der Templer: Ausgewählte Aspekte des Templerrechts unter besonderer Berücksichtigung der Statutenhandschriften aus Paris, Rom, Baltimore und Barcelona* (Münster 2007), pp. 216sqq.

18 Cf. Logan, *Runaway Religious*, pp. 42–3; for the Templars: *RT*, art. 429; Judi Upton-Ward, ed., *The Catalan Rule of the Templars: A Critical Edition and English Translation from Barcelona, Archivo de la Corona de Aragón, Cartas Reales, MS 3344* (Woodbridge 2003), section 11.

be expelled from the order. Expulsion was the sentence for serious crimes such as heresy, murder, theft and sodomy.[19]

But any way of leaving the order usually had to be followed by the former Templar being received into another order with a stricter rule.[20] If he did not enter another order within 40 days, the Templars caught him and sentenced him to perpetual prison,[21] otherwise the order could lose standing in the public because of the bad behaviour of its former members. Depending on the crime, perpetual prison was frequently the immediate result of an expulsion from the order.[22] Nevertheless, this does not seem to have been strictly enforced, because we can see from the statutes that there had obviously been some brothers who tried to bring about their own expulsion by accusing themselves of offences they had never committed.[23]

Once the Templars had let a brother go, whether they had permitted him to go or excluded him, they would not take him back.[24] This was also the case for the former members of the Hospitallers and other military orders. Templars and Hospitallers came to a mutual agreement regarding their former members. Both orders committed themselves not to receive ex-members of the other order.[25]

But nevertheless there are examples of Templars who entered the Hospitaller order after leaving the Templars.[26] Even the statutes mention some Templars going to the Hospitallers, in these cases obviously without the permission of their superiors. The statutes deal with non-permitted departures from the house with the intention of leaving forever and mention explicitly the Hospital as a place where

---

19 See the different lists within the statutes: *RT*, arts 224–32, 417–430; Upton-Ward, *Catalan Rule*, sections 73–83.

20 *RT*, art. 429: *quar en toute relegion plus etroite puet entrer por sauver s'arme*; Upton-Ward, *Catalan Rule*, section 9: *hom li det doner congé de aler salver sa arma en altra religió ... ço est a entendre a l'ordre de Sent Agustí o de Sent Benehet*. For all religious orders, cf. Logan, *Runaway Religious*, pp. 43–4.

21 *RT*, art. 437: *et sachiés que tout frere a qui l'on done congié de notre maison se doit rendre au plus tost que il porra en autre religion et en plus estrete. Et se doit faire en toutes manieres, se il puet, dedens XL jors, et se il ne se voloit rendre, et li frere le puent trover, il le doivent prendre et metre le en fers*.

22 *RT*, art. 267; Upton-Ward, *Catalan Rule*, section 120; cf. Vogel, *Das Recht der Templer*, p. 150.

23 *RT*, arts 238, 595; Upton-Ward, *Catalan Rule*, section 90; cf. Vogel, *Das Recht der Templer*, p. 199.

24 *RT*, art. 474; Upton-Ward, *Catalan Rule*, section 38.

25 *RT*, art. 429: *fors que en la relegion de l'Ospital de saint Johan, douquel fu establi en tel maniere, par acort des freres dou Temple et de ceaus de l'Ospital, que ja nus frere qui issist de l'Ospital ne venist au Temple en maniere qu'il preist l'abit de lor maison*; cf. Vogel, *Das Recht der Templer*, pp. 61–2.

26 *PT*, vol. 1, p. 187. In *PT*, vol.1, p. 647 a certain brother Julianus asked the Hospitallers to receive him, but then joined the Premonstratensian order. *PT*, vol.1 p. 140 gives a hint of conversions to the Hospitallers: *Appar ensi pour li frere qui ont esté deu dit ordre tresportés en autre, c'est à savoir en l'Ospital et en l'ordre de sans Lorens*.

fugitives were going.[27] One of the examples refers to a brother leaving the house and going to a castle under the command of the Teutonic Knights,[28] another is about a fugitive who left the Templar house at Tortosa (in the east) and went to the Hospital. His sentence was mitigated because he repented and returned the same day.[29] A brother who went to the Hospitallers' castle of Krak was expelled from the order because he took weapons when he left the house and lost a sword.[30]

Let us now return to the consequences of any non-permitted departure from the order. The Templar statutes exactly regulated the consequences of an unauthorized departure from a Templar house. These covered not only flight from the order, meaning that a Templar left the house with the intention of leaving for ever, but also cases of a brother leaving the house without permission for a period only. The sentences established by the statutes varied according to the length of the absence.[31] Moreover, the sentence was made more severe if the fugitive took with him certain property which he was not allowed to take away when leaving.[32] This was carefully checked. When the absence was noticed, the *aumosnier* (almoner) wrote down everything that the runaway had left in the house.[33] This was one of three actions that caused expulsion from the order. The others were flight to the Saracens[34] and staying outside the order for more than two nights with the habit.[35] Otherwise, a temporary absence without permission was followed by sentences up to the loss of the habit for a year and a day. If a brother threw away his habit it was also regarded as a kind of a symbolic flight and therefore followed by the loss of the habit.[36] Even the request for permission to leave was already regarded as despicable and therefore had its own consequences. A Templar who had asked for permission to leave was henceforth excluded from taking part in the election of the grand master or from carrying the banner.[37] But only crimes that were serious

---

27 Upton-Ward, *Catalan Rule*, section 114: *si ffrere pasa la porta per entenció de laxer la maisó, & puis se'n repent, hom li poria aler a l'àbit. Si il va a l'Ospital o altre loc fora la maisó, l'àbit est en la volenté deus ffreres*. See also section 147; *RT*, arts 261, 602; art. 261: *se frere passe la porte par entention de laissier la maison, et puis se repent, om li porroit aller a l'abit ; e se il va a l'Ospital, ou en autre luec fors de la maison, l'abit est en la volenté des freres ou dou prendre ou dou laissier*.

28 *RT*, art. 570; Upton-Ward, *Catalan Rule*, section 162.

29 Upton-Ward, *Catalan Rule*, section 182.

30 *RT*, art. 582; Upton-Ward, *Catalan Rule*, section 157.

31 Cf. Vogel, *Das Recht der Templer*, pp. 216–8.

32 *RT*, arts 561, 621; Upton-Ward, *Catalan Rule*, sections 115, 156.

33 *RT*, art. 491.

34 *RT*, arts 422, 603; Upton-Ward, *Catalan Rule*, section 198.

35 *RT*, arts 426, 558: with the habit; art. 262: two nights outside.

36 *RT*, arts 263, 463; Upton-Ward, *Catalan Rule*, section 116; for religious orders in general, cf. Logan, *Runaway Religious*, pp. 25–6.

37 *RT*, art. 631; cf. Vogel, *Das Recht der Templer*, p. 199.

enough could be sentenced by expulsion. Otherwise a brother could only be requested to ask for permission to leave, but could not be forced to do so.[38]

Some examples of fugitives can be found in the Templar statutes. The worst form of flight for a military order was surely not flight from the enemy but flight with the intention of deserting to the enemy.[39] That is what George le Masson did. He left the order's house in Acre and went to the Saracens. But the Templars managed to catch the deserter, who was wearing secular clothing under his clothes, and put him in prison.[40] A betrayal in the year 1268 resulted in severe consequences. An anonymous Templar went to the Saracen sultan, Baybars, taking with him the keys to the castle of Gaston. This action helped to bring about the defeat of his former comrades.[41]

The more harmless cases were those of runaways who tried to escape from living in chastity under a rule because of a woman. A certain Pons de Gusans left a Templar house in Provence and got married. After the death of his wife he decided to return to his order.[42] He used an excuse common in such cases,[43] arguing that he had not been regularly admitted to the Templar order before, so that it was not illegal when he left. We know similar cases from the trial investigations. Jacques de Troyes and Jean le Bergonhons left the order in the year 1306, both in order to live with a wife.[44] We also know of another brother, Andreas Armanni de Monte Oderisio, who had been admitted to the Templar order with the consent of his wife, but at a later point in time changed his mind and left the order.[45] We do not know if he returned to his wife. John of Plantarosa was married, too, when he entered the order. But he had concealed the fact that he was married when he had been received into the order. During the 1250s, he left the order in the east and returned to his wife in southern Italy. After her death, he wanted to re-enter the order, but he was expelled, not because of his apostasy, but because he had concealed his marriage when he was received. It has to be remarked that in this case a discussion arose among the brothers of the judging chapter. It seems that some brothers did not believe him and suggested that John had lied in order to take leave of the house.[46] As mentioned before, marriage as a reason for an invalid reception was a common excuse to leave a religious order.

---

38 Upton-Ward, *Catalan Rule*, section 11.

39 Cf. Forey, 'Desertions and Transfers', 167sqq. Forey interprets this kind of flight as a sign of discontent within a military order rather than a rejection of the faith.

40 *RT*, art. 603; Upton-Ward, *Catalan Rule*, section 198.

41 Upton-Ward, *Catalan Rule*, section 180.

42 Upton-Ward, *Catalan Rule*, section 183.

43 Cf. Logan, *Runaway Religious*, pp. 16–18.

44 *PT*, vol. 1, pp. 253–5; cf. Barber, *Trial*, p. 150 and *PT*, vol. 1, p. 76; cf. Barber, p. 131.

45 *The Trial of the Templars in the Papal State and the Abruzzi*, ed. Anne Gilmour-Bryson, (Vatican City, 1982), p. 39, pp. 145–55.

46 Upton-Ward, *Catalan Rule*, section 178.

There are more examples of fugitives who wanted to return to secular life because of a woman, or because they were unsatisfied with life in a religious order. A witness of the trial investigations, Stephen of Troyes, escaped but with little success. He was re-captured by the Templars after six years of serving a feudal lord. He was lucky, because his mother paid for his release, and the Templars let him go.[47] This was quite an irregular procedure, clearly against the law, but obviously possible. The reason for his flight is not mentioned in the sources, which corresponds to the statement of two other witnesses in the investigations, who also did not know the reasons for flights from the order, which – according to them – were numerous.[48]

But we can also find an example of a regular departure. A Templar named Adam de Wallaincourt left the Templars with permission and went to the Carthusians. Later on, he returned to the Templars, which was not possible – at least if we believe in the statutes. He obviously had influential relatives who supported him, and therefore he was readmitted but punished for his earlier departure: for a year and a day he lost his habit.[49] This was the same sentence as if he had left without permission. As outlined above, it was not possible for a brother to return after leaving the order with permission. But we have just heard of other examples where there were differences between the theory of the statutes and reality, for example, the case of the abovementioned brother whose mother paid for his freedom, or cases of long absences of several years.

There were often cases of brothers leaving the order and taking a wife, which was not only apostasy but also an offence against the vow of chastity. Nevertheless, such brothers were readmitted and punished only by the sentence of a year and a day, whereas the statutes required expulsion for an illegal absence longer than two nights, at least, when the brother kept his habit during his absence from the house.

Now let us consider the motives of runaways for leaving their order. Pope Gregory IX complained about the military orders often receiving criminals.[50] Some of the witnesses asserted during the trial investigations that the Templars received simoniac and excommunicated persons because of the money they paid.[51]

---

[47] *PUT*, vol. 2, p. 336: *exivit ordinem et stetit in seculo per sex annos cum comite Britannie usque ad mortem ipsius. Tamen cum quadam vice visitaret matrem suam, ceperunt et tenuerunt eum captum per V septimanas, donec mater sua redemit eum de ducentis libris, pacto, quod secure deinceps remaneret cum matre et ex toto stetit secure ab ordine*; cf. Barber, *Trial*, pp. 99–100.

[48] *PT*, vol. 1, pp. 192, 200; cf. Barber, *Trial*, pp. 146 – 7.

[49] *PT*, vol. 1, p. 204; cf. Barber, *Trial*, p. 149. Adam himself was a *nobilis miles*, and his family attended the Ceremony of his reception: *presentibus pluribus nobilibus, consanguineis et amicis suis* (*PT*, vol. 1, p. 204).

[50] *Les registres de Grégoire IX*, ed. Lucien Auvray et. al. (Paris 1896–1955), vol. 2, p. 916, no. 4148.

[51] *PT*, vol. 1, pp. 36–9; cf. Barber, *Trial*, pp. 127–8.

The reception of unwilling persons was much worse. We hear about Templar knights recruiting new members by persuasion. A non-Templar witness said during the investigations that 25 years earlier his uncle, who was a Templar, had come with another Templar knight from Aragon and had persuaded many to enter their order, although they did not really want to become Templars.[52] Because of such membership, it is not surprising that some Templars could not live up to the ideals of a religious order. In Spain, for example, it happened that the complete membership of some Templar houses disobeyed their authorities and broke away from the order in a kind of collective flight. We know about this from a papal letter of the year 1286 to the bishop of León, instructing him to take measures against the Templar rebels.[53] The most prominent example of a runaway is Roger de Flor. After the fall of Acre in May 1291, he had to flee because he was accused of having embezzled the property of the order. He then lived as a pirate in the Mediterranean, and served King Frederick III of Sicily for some years. But after the peace of Caltabellotta in 1302, the pope demanded that Roger be handed over to him, so he departed to serve the Byzantine emperor Andronikos II.[54]

The situation after the trial and the dissolution of the order was no better. Although we would not expect fugitives because the order did not exist anymore, nevertheless there were former Templars who caused scandal. A certain Berengar of Pulcronisu continued to live on Templar estates in Aragon; it annoyed the Aragonese king that he was living a secular life there with a woman.[55] For many Templars before him this had been a motive for leaving the order, but Berengar was now able to live on the Templars' former estates, using their revenues, without the need to leave the order. Some other examples from Aragon can be mentioned: Martin de Frigola became a criminal, and Bernard de Fontibus made use of his contacts and served the Muslim prince of Tunis.[56]

---

[52] *PT*, vol. 1, p. 176. On fugitives' motives, see Forey, 'Desertions and Transfers', 161sqq.

[53] *EUT*, pp. 94, 291–2 (Beilagen); *Les registres de Boniface VIII*, ed. Georges Digard et al. (Paris 1907–39), p. 170, no. 490.

[54] For Roger de Flor, see David Agustí, *Los almogávares: La expansion mediterránea de la Corona de Aragón* (Madrid, 2004). The main source for the life of this famous Templar is the chronicle of Ramon Muntaner, in *Les quatre grans cròniques*, ed. Ferran Soldevila, 2nd edn (Barcelona, 1983), pp. 665–1000. Some letters of Roger de Flor give evidence of his career as a pirate in the western Mediterranean: *Diplomatari de l'Orient Català (1301–1409): Collecció de documents per a la història de l'expedició catalana a Orient i els ducats d'Atenes i neopàtria*, ed. Antoni Rubio i Lluch (Barcelona, 2001), nos 2–7. For Roger in the service of the Byzantine emperor see also Pachymeres, books 11 and 12, in *La version brève des relations historiques de Georges Pachymérès* (Paris, 2002), ed. Albert Failler, vol. 2.

[55] *EUT*, p. 316, no. 9 (Urkundliche Beilagen IV).

[56] Cf. Barber, *Trial*, p. 239; *PUT*, vol. 1, p. 383 and vol. 2, pp. 226–7.

Although the order no longer existed, these final examples have to be characterized as renegades, because the dissolution of the order did not mean an exemption from the order's vows which were binding for life.[57] The problem of the renegades increased with the dissolution of the order because its internal executive power had collapsed. Until the trial, it was the master who sent brothers to pursue and catch a fugitive.[58] But after the trial these procedures could no longer continue; as the order was no longer in existence, there was no pursuit by the Templar authorities. In the case of Berengar de Pulcronisu, who was still living on the Templar estates, pursuit was not even necessary. Moreover, the internal Templar jurisdiction that would have assured obedience to the vows no longer existed.

However, the status of the ex-Templars was not clarified in the course of the dissolution. The estates were given to the Hospitallers by Pope Clement V who decreed that all fugitives were to appear before the provincial councils within a year, but he left the problem of the ex-Templars to his successor.[59] John XXII ordered the Templars to return to their assigned places.[60] Usually the Templars were given an income from Templar estates and then expected to enter a monastery. But the pope mentioned explicitly such Templars who had taken wives and lived a secular life, which shows that these were not occasional cases.[61] Alan Forey has noted in his article about ex-Templars in England that probably a number of Templars lived out their years in freedom after the trial, protected by either friends or family.[62]

The abovementioned examples of long absences make clear that it was not easy for the Templars to catch a fugitive, although the statutes give some examples where they did. George le Masson was caught by Templar brothers who were sent

---

57 *EUT*, p. 293–4, no. 21 (Urkundliche Beilagen II): *quod per professionem, quam ingressu dicti ordinis emiserunt, ad continentiam et alia religionis substantialia sic se perpetuo obligarunt, quod post sublationem dicti ordinis factam in generali concilio Viennensi nequaquam fuerunt a votorum observantia absoluti.*

58 *PT*, vol. 1, p. 218: *quod incarcerati fuissent si qui exivissent dictum ordinem et capti* [sic] *potuissent ab eis*. See also *RT*, art. 603; Upton-Ward, *Catalan Rule*, section 198, similar: section 181.

59 Alberigo, *Conciliorum Oecumenicorum decreta*, pp. 347–9.

60 Guillaume Mollat, *Jean XXII (1316–1334), Lettres communes* (Paris 1904), vol. 1, pp. 429–30, no. 4670.

61 *EUT*, p. 293, no. 21 (Urkundliche Beilagen II), John XXII (17 December 1318): *Sane ad audientiam apostolatus nostri pervenit, quod nonnullis fratres ordinis quondam militie Templi Iherosolimitani post sublationem ordinis memorati inconsulto mentis affectu ... divinum retorquentes vestes presumunt induere laycales seque gerunt pro laycis ... Quidam eciam eorundem se amplius mundi voluptatibus inmergentes de facto matrimonia contrahunt, que potius contubernia dici debent, et publice ducunt uxores*; *PUT*, vol. 1, pp. 384–5.

62 Alan Forey, 'Ex-Templars in England', *Journal of Ecclesiastical History*, 53 (2002), 18–37, here 36.

by the master.[63] A brother from Provence of whom we read in the Catalan version of the statutes was also caught, but he managed to escape again because his catchers forgot to lock the door of his room.[64] Usually help from the ecclesiastical and secular authorities was necessary.[65]

And finally, we have seen that even if pursuit was successful, the case was not always handled in accordance with the statutes. We can come closer to an explanation for this difference between law and reality when we consider that the statutes were not a widespread statute book but a collection of the order's laws and customs as well as commentaries and examples. Admittedly, there were probably other reasons, such as the support of fugitives by ecclesiastical or secular powers. I will not consider these points here, for Alan Forey has already elaborated on them in detail.[66] Instead, one important argument for the difference between the ideal of the statutes and reality has to be added once we consider the order's legal system. The order's laws and judgments were mainly passed on to the members by oral tradition.[67] In the case of a novelty it was necessary to appeal to the general chapter.[68] But if such an appeal failed to occur, the unity of the order's justice could not be guaranteed. One of the examples from the Catalan rule tells us about the provincial master of France, Guido de Basainvila, who did not know how to judge a certain case. He went to the general chapter in the east to get advice.[69] In addition, different opinions sometimes arose in the chapter meetings over how to handle a certain case.[70] In conclusion, we have to consider that the laws and customs of the Templars were handled in a flexible way, so that this may be an explanation for the differences between reality and law.

63 *RT*, art. 603; Upton-Ward, *Catalan Rule*, section 198.

64 Upton-Ward, *Catalan Rule*, section 181.

65 Cf. Forey, 'Desertions and Transfers', 188–90.

66 Forey, 'Desertions and Transfers', 200.

67 Cf. Vogel, *Das Recht der Templer*, pp. 125sqq., 143sqq.

68 *RT*, art. 527.

69 Upton-Ward, *Catalan Rule*, section 176.

70 For example, Upton-Ward, *Catalan Rule*, section 174.

Chapter 26
Priests of the Order of the Temple: What Can They Tell Us?

Anne Gilmour-Bryson

We have remaining to us about nine hundred depositions made by members of the order of the Temple during their examinations at various trials or hearings between 1307 and 1311.[1] Most, if not all of these, were examined at the council of Vienne, 1311–12.[2] Others have obviously been lost.[3] Trained notaries licensed by secular or ecclesiastical authorities wrote down these depositions in Latin, usually translated into the witness's own vulgar language prior to confirmation. The manuscripts I have edited contain the writing of up to four notaries, each confirming that what the other man had written down was correct. Many renowned scholars of the military orders have written on the still unresolved question of Templar innocence or guilt.[4] My intention here is to discuss not the testimony of Templars as a whole, but to focus on priests or chaplains of the order, permitted by the bull *Omne datum optimum* of 1139.[5] These clerics took the three vows of poverty, chastity and obedience, as did all members.[6] Because priests were at least minimally literate, possessing some education, their opinion of the Templar order is particularly important. After considering all depositions, I will consider here

---

1 See Malcolm Barber, *The Trial of the Templars*, 2nd edn (Cambridge, 2006), a completely revised and updated version of his similarly entitled work of 1978. The bibliography to the new version lists all primary sources and a vast and superb secondary list as well. Numbers of men interrogated are uncertain since in several cases individuals with the same name testified in the same or different hearings. Consult also Alain Demurger, *Les Templiers: Une chevalerie chrétienne au moyen âge* (Paris, 2005).

2 On Vienne, see Barber, *Trial*, pp. 259–71.

3 The only full published trial in English is my *The Trial of the Templars in Cyprus: A Complete English Edition* (Leiden and New York, 1998), hereafter cited as Gilmour-Bryson, *Cyprus*. Many extracts may be found in Barber, *Trial*, and his *The Templars* (Manchester, 2002), with Keith Bate; hereafter cited as Barber, *Templars*, a superb collection of sources in translation.

4 The best overview of historians' opinions on this topic is to be found in Barber, *Trial*, pp. 294–311. See also Jonathan Riley Smith, 'Were the Templars Guilty?', in *The Medieval Crusade*, ed. Susan J. Ridyard (Woodbridge, 2004), pp. 107–24.

5 See key provisions of *Omne datum optimum* translated in Helen Nicholson, *The Knights Templar: A New History* (Stroud, 2001), p. 154.

6 Nicholson, *New History*, p. 124.

only priests for whom reasonably full testimony is given: 71 Templars, or about eight per cent of those testifying.[7]

I shall begin in 1307 with the early French hearings. Peter Moreti in Cahors confessed to spitting on the crucifix meaning to disrespect the Lord Jesus Christ. He did not admit to erring in consecration of the Eucharist.[8] The other four priests were not fully reported.

In Chaumont, Conrad of Mainz [*de Mangoncia in Alemannia*], a Templar chaplain[9] received by the German master, begged three times for admission and joined to gain remission of his sins, for God, the Blessed Virgin Mary, and to help the Holy Land. No illicit acts took place, and Conrad reacted angrily when asked about the denial, spitting on the cross or improper kisses.[10]

Fifteen clerical depositions were heard at the Paris trial beginning in October, 1307, continuing until 24 November of that year. John of Fouilleyo, the first, also testified in Poitiers. His testimony is discussed below.[11] Peter of Bologna, procurator and future defender of the order, admitted in 1307 that he had denied the image of Christ on the cross and spat upon it.[12] He added that in spite of the admonition that sex with the brothers was licit, he believed it to be a *peccatum horribile* which he never committed.[13] He admitted to kissing the receiver not only on the mouth but also on the navel and *in vili parte inferiori*.[14] He did not explain why he committed these despicable acts. These very serious admissions are contradicted totally by his celebrated defence of the order in 1310, in which he stated that: '[t]his is a holy order, pure and free from stains … without the filth or dirt of any vice … [the postulant] is received with the pure kiss of peace … this is the one profession … observed throughout the whole world … Whoever says

---

7 I have omitted most of the testimony in Hans Prutz, *Entwicklung und Untergang des Templelherrenordens* (Berlin 1888), hereafter cited as *EUT*, and in Heinrich Finke, *Papsttum und Untergang des Templerordens*, vol. 2 (Münster, 1907), hereafter cited as *PUT*. I have not dealt with the Aragonese evidence found in Alan Forey, *The Fall of the Templars in the Crown of Aragon* (Aldershot, 2001), which is not reproduced in full.

8 *PUT*, pp. 317–18.

9 *EUT*, p. 327.

10 Ibid: *cum rubore et signo maximo indignationis dixit se nichil scire et nunquam fecisse aliquid de ordine*.

11 His name also appears as 'Folliaco' in Poitiers: *UT*, vol. 2, pp. 35–8; and 'Folligny' in Barber, *Trial*, pp. 117–18, and see index, p. 389; Malcolm Barber, *The New Knighthood: A History of the Order of the Temple* (Cambridge, 1994), see index, p. 431. See his testimony in Jules Michelet, *Le Procès des Templiers*, vol. 2 (repr. Paris, 1987), hereafter cited as *PT*, pp. 277–8.

12 Testimony in *PT*, vol. 2, p. 349.

13 Ibid. The next three priests contributed nothing unusual.

14 Ibid.

otherwise or believes something different is totally mistaken, commits a mortal sin and strays completely from the path of truth'.[15]

According to John of Sivriaco,[16] after the usual ceremony, when he was taken behind the altar, he kissed the receiver on the backside. Immediately, the man fell down before him almost dead, unable to go any further with licit or illicit acts. An act of God perhaps? Milo de Sancto Fiacrio, received by a one-time papal chamberlain,[17] admitted to the usual illicit acts, believing that all receptions were carried out in this manner since he knew of no new law on the matter.[18] A seventy-year old priest insisted that he had refused to spit on the cross, saying: 'Holy Mary, why would I do such a thing'?[19] The receiver then relented and said he would be spared on account of his age. He insisted he would not have entered the order had he known what it was like. John of Gisi was spared the indecent kisses because the receiver was a relative and because of his own priestly status.[20] Since some men were spared illicit acts, it leads one to think that the indecent acts had no serious purpose. Otherwise, these men would not have been allowed to refuse.

The hearing in Poiters in 1308 heard only one priest. John of Folliaco or Fouilleyo, mentioned above, received in Paris four years earlier by the treasurer of the Temple.[21] He was forced into performing the denial, stating, nevertheless, that he denied *deum paganorum*, the god of the pagans.[22] After the receiver grabbed him threatening him with jail, John shouted only *abnego te*, denying the receiver and not God. He neither spat on the cross, nor gave or received illicit kisses, nor knew of any same-sex acts. He claimed that when the grand master (James of Molay) came from overseas he carried with him 150,000 golden florins and other monies which he divided up after he had been in Provence.[23] He testified that dying Templars confessed their sins and received the Eucharist, although he had not personally heard their confessions, nor given them communion. Why not, one wonders?

The hearing in the Auvergne in 1309 heard from five priests who confessed guilt and two clerics who did not.[24] The most detailed deposition was that of

15 Barber, *Templars*, pp. 299–300; Barber, *Trial*, pp. 160–61. The Latin may be found in *PT*, vol. 1, pp. 164–9.

16 Testimony in *PT*, vol. 2, pp. 367–8.

17 In the diocese of Meaux.

18 Testimony: *PT*, vol. 2, pp. 393–4.

19 Testimony: *PT*, vol. 2, p. 407.

20 Testimony: *PT*, vol. 2, p. 414.

21 Testimony: *Der Untergang des Templerordens mit urkundlichen und kritischen Beiträgen*, ed. Konrad Schottmüller, 2 vols (Berlin, 1887), vol. 2, pp. 35–8; hereafter cited as *UT*. On this testimony, see also Barber, *Trial*, pp. 117–18._

22 *UT*, 2, p. 36.

23 Ibid., pp. 37–8.

24 *Le Procès des Templiers d'Auvergne (1309–1311): Edition de l'interrogatoire de juin 1309*, ed. Roger Sève and Anne-Marie Chagny-Sève (Paris, 1986).

Bernard de Villars.[25] He performed the denial of God or Christ and spat beside, not on the cross. He strangely stated that he failed to remember whether he had been told that Christ did not die for our sins or whether he denied the Virgin Mary or any of the saints. It is scarcely credible that he would not have remembered such significant and heretical acts. He had witnessed other receptions at which similar denials had taken place but had not, nevertheless, forced others to commit such acts. Upon becoming a priest four years after his reception, he was told to omit the words of consecration, which he did not do.[26] He did not believe lay absolution was lawful. He suggested that the denials and spitting took place because of the Templars' promise of obedience, not because of menaces or threats. (The claim that postulants performed illicit acts because they had just taken a vow of obedience is a fairly frequent one.) He was present when 34 brothers confessed their errors to the bishop of the Auvergne.[27] He had confessed to two Dominicans and had heard that many had confessed before the pope and others worthy of faith.[28] He believed that the errors crept into the rules and statutes after the order's foundation, primarily because postulants swore obedience.[29] The notary added, unusually, that Brother Bernard had testified truthfully, directly, without changing colour, sermonising or becoming obscure. We can deduce from this long recital that the inquisitors considered his testimony particularly carefully because of his priestly status. It is also evident that his testimony was much more complex, detailed and potentially damaging than the brief answers recorded for most others.[30]

Bartholomew Vassales, received five years earlier, claimed that he had to give money to the visitor Hugh of Pairaut before he consented to receive him, an unusual statement.[31] Peter Aureille was interrogated for a second time.[32] After the standard admission of the denial and spitting, he said that absolution in chapter meetings was only for transgressions or disobedience.[33] Sacramental absolution had to be sought from priests of the order, Carmelites or other priests if permission

25 Ibid., pp. 111–18. He was priest-commander of La Roche-Saint-Paul.

26 Ibid., p. 113. See also Bartholomew Vassales, ibid., p. 150. John of Menat gave basically similar testimony on this and other major issues, ibid., pp.124–7.

27 Ibid., p. 117, and mention of the cords, kisses and acquiring goods unlawfully. And see testimony of other priests who state no one asked them for sex, nor did they engage in sex acts with their brothers.

28 Ibid.

29 Ibid., p. 116.

30 Ibid, p. 89, for a discussion of the evident lack of impartiality shown by the inquisitors and notaries in the treatment of these witnesses.

31 Ibid., p. 152. Charging money for entry to a religious order was forbidden by canon law.

32 Ibid., pp. 218–20. We have no information on his first, probably not guilty, deposition.

33 On this matter, see also Peter Rose, ibid., p. 224.

had been granted to do so.[34] He had been told that permission for sex acts with brothers had been a rule of the order from its beginning.[35] Peter Rose, the first priest in the Auvergne to claim innocence, had been a Templar for 30 years.[36] He denied all illicit acts and asserted that the secrecy of reception was the cause of great suspicion of the order. The other innocent priest added nothing.

Twelve priests testified in hearings in England and Ireland between 1309 and 1311.[37] Ralph of Barton, custodian of the Templar chapel in London, denied any knowledge of any of the serious allegations, claiming they were all false.[38] Templars met together, in secret, but not for nefarious reasons. Brothers could only leave the order if granted permission and only for a stricter order.[39] The secrecy of reception did not cause suspicion since it had long been a custom in the order and did not derive from any illicit cause or action.[40] He knew nothing about idols. Receptions took place by day, not at night.[41] He insisted that Templars never promised to disinherit other Christians unjustly, as alleged.[42] This accusation was rejected by virtually everyone. He was asked about the death of Walter Bacheler, former preceptor in Ireland.[43] This man, he said, had been jailed in irons, suffered great hardship and died. Walter was not buried in the Templar cemetery because he had been excommunicated for unstated disobedience.[44]

Roger of Stowe had left the order for unspecified reasons and became a secular priest.[45] Two other priests said nothing significant. John of Stoke was the only priest in England to provide any guilty responses during his several interrogations.[46] In 1311, he implicated James of Molay in the illicit acts he committed after reception. In the presence of two sword-bearing serving brothers, Molay said he would have to give proof of obedience.[47] When asked about the image on a crucifix, John answered that it was 'Jesus Christ who died on the cross for the redemption of mankind'. The master responded: 'You are misspeaking. You are wrong. He was the son of some woman, crucified because he called himself the Son of God and

---

34 Ibid., p. 219.

35 Ibid.

36 Testimony, ibid., p. 224.

37 I am using the printed partial edition found in *Concilia Magnae Britanniae et Hiberniae,* ed. David Wilkins (London, 1737), vol. 2, hereafter cited as Wilkins, cols 329–401.

38 Wilkins, cols 335b–336a; Barber, *Trial*, p. 221.

39 Wilkins, col. 337b.

40 Wilkins, col. 336b.

41 Wilkins, col. 337a.

42 Ibid.

43 Wilkins, col. 337b and see Barber, *Trial*, pp. 226–7.

44 Wilkins, col. 337b.

45 Ibid., col. 342a.

46 Testimony: Wilkins, cols 345b–346a, 387b–388a, and see Barber, *Trial*, p. 226–7.

47 Wilkins, cols 387b–388a.

you have to deny him'.[48] When he asked in whom he ought to believe if not in Christ, he was told to believe in 'the great omnipotent God who created heaven and earth, and not the crucified one'.[49] In my view, stress, long imprisonment, fear and possibly torture impelled this confession. The six priests questioned in Lincoln and York confessed nothing significant.[50]

We rarely hear of the Irish trial in 1310, which, nevertheless, heard from 14 Templars as well as a number of non-members of the order.[51] The only priest was William of Kilros.[52] He confirmed that when the grand master heard the confessions of the brothers, he would advise the chaplain to absolve them. In other words, the grand master was not absolving brothers himself, as alleged. William believed that suspicion had arisen against the order some time ago caused by the friendship and dealings the Templars had with the Saracens.[53] It was very rare indeed for the Saracens to be mentioned in anyone's testimony. He also stated that a brother, whose name he did not know, was a sodomite, placed in the infirmary where he died.[54]

Among the seven Templars questioned in the papal state and the Abruzzi in 1310, only one, William of Verduno, was a priest.[55] Later on the day of reception, two men, William and Dominic, took him into a closed room and told him to deny Christ.[56] He did so because one of the men held a drawn sword and threatened him.[57] He insisted, nevertheless, that he had always believed, and still did believe, in salvation by Jesus. When ordered to trample a crucifix, he refused. One of the two men made a cross of two straws on the floor, threatening William with death if he refused to tread on it. Out of fear, and presumably because the straw cross had no sacramental significance, he trampled it.[58] Like most witnesses, William said he had done nothing *in vituperium Christi* or of the orthodox faith.[59] He had consecrated the Eucharist correctly. He did not believe any layman could absolve anyone from sin.[60] He knew nothing about illicit kisses. When asked about why he did not correct errors, he responded plausibly that he had no way to correct them.[61]

---

48 Ibid.

49 Ibid., col.388a.

50 Testimony, Wilkins, cols 368a–373a.

51 Wilkins, cols 373a–380a.

52 Testimony, Wilkins, col. 377b.

53 Ibid.

54 Ibid.

55 *The Trial of the Templars in the Papal State and the Abruzzi*, ed. Anne Gilmour-Bryson (Vatican City, 1982), hereafter cited as Gilmour-Bryson, *Papal State*, pp. 171–86.

56 Ibid., p. 173.

57 Ibid., p. 174.

58 Ibid., p. 175.

59 Ibid., p. 175.

60 Ibid., p. 176.

61 Ibid., p. 180.

He had heard Dominic's deathbed confession, at which time he asked him: 'Why do you not confess what you made me do, namely the denial of Christ and forcing me to trample and spit on the cross?' Dominic answered: 'It was told to me what you had to do'. To which William responded: 'Why do you not confess about the sins which you led me into?' Dominic answered only: 'Do what you have to do'.[62] This answer implies that Dominic did not consider himself guilty. He merely followed orders.

William had confessed his sins two days later to a Franciscan friar, confessor to the pope, in St John Lateran. Were this true, the papacy ought to have been aware of what was going on. Although the secret of the confessional existed, a priest should have informed his superior, even if not in detail, of any such egregious behaviour on the part of members of a religious order. '[I]f he [the priest] needs sage advice, let him seek it cautiously without mentioning the person'.[63] In spite of what William had done, he still believed that everything the grand master legislated was *licita et honesta*.[64] The fact that he did not confess to knowledge of any brothers who left the order because of improper acts may relate to his own fear of leaving.

The hearing in Cyprus in 1310 heard from 76 Templars, two of them priests, who all claimed complete and absolute innocence.[65] Richard 'the Englishman', as he was called,[66] admitted that receptions were secret and that brothers could discuss them among themselves. He insisted that chapter meetings happened at dawn, not at night.

Stephen, described as priest and prior of the Limassol house, had been received by James of Molay in Nicosia 15 years earlier.[67] He believed that if the master had confessed, as most of them knew he had, 'he has confessed against the truth'.[68] On the matter of the key illicit acts, he stated that: 'the reception of brothers was carried out legitimately, for good and not evil. And if there were such errors … he would not have entered the order [and if the errors came about later] he would

---

62 Ibid., pp. 180–81.

63 On confessional secrecy, see Gratian's *Decretum*, secunda pars, distinctio VI, causa II; and the 1215 Fourth Lateran Council, canon 21, which seems to allow seeking counsel from a superior on troubling matters heard in confession without revealing the individual's name, *Readings in Medieval History*, ed. Patrick J. Geary (Peterborough, Canada, 2003), pp. 126–7. Thomas Aquinas seemed to take the same position in the *Supplementum,* q. 11.

64 Gilmour-Bryson, *Papal State*, p. 185.

65 Gilmour-Bryson, *Cyprus*, or, for a shortened version of the Latin text, *UT*, vol. 2, pp. 143–400. Only 75 Templars gave the long, fuller deposition.

66 It is unclear exactly who this man was. See Gilmour-Bryson, *Cyprus*, pp. 81–2, n. 34. Testimony: ibid., pp. 81–2, 175–8.

67 Ibid., pp. 116–17.

68 Ibid., p. 289.

have already left … but they did not exist nor do now'.[69] 'If there is a scandal', he retorted, 'it is not from any misdeed of the order'.[70]

Probably the most important hearing was that of the papal commission in Paris which examined or re-examined witnesses, including 21 priests, from 1309 until 1311.[71] Walter of Buris had served for eight years prior to capture.[72] He had already testified and been reconciled by the bishop. Were he now to profess innocence, he would have risked being treated as a relapsed heretic, which could bring a death sentence once the person was turned over to the secular arm. At his reception he swore first to obey orders from his superiors. Next, he was ordered to deny Christ; stupefied, but obedient to his oath, he did so, followed by spitting not on the cross but on the floor. He was spared the immoral backside kiss as he was a priest[73] and told he could be imprisoned if he revealed these acts. He confessed, nevertheless, to the bishop of Langres who was amazed at his revelations but finally absolved him after imposing a penance.[74] Walter had never heard of sodomy or idols existing in the order.[75] He related that Paris chapter meetings occurred at night, in secret, with a guard on the door.[76]

Stephen of Divione[77] told a similar tale of being ordered to deny Christ 18 years earlier and to spit on the cross seemingly because of his previous promise of obedience.[78] Inquisitors seemed suspicious that he and the preceding witness might have colluded, an accusation which he denied. He testified that the order was cutting back on charity and that they did not take in paupers, only guests.[79] The order was not required to act as a hospice. He stated that many of the brothers quit the order, but not because of errors.[80] Odo of Dona Petra, a twenty-year veteran, had confessed his sins committed at reception to the bishop of Troyes who spent

69 Ibid.

70 Ibid., p. 291.

71 Testimony: *PT*, vol. 1, entire volume, and vol. 2, pp. 1–274. The first priest appeared on 19 December 1310, followed by 20 others until 13 May 1311.

72 Testimony, *PT*, vol. 1, pp. 296–301.

73 A similar story was told by the next two witnesses, also priests, ibid., pp. 301–11.

74 The bishop ordered him to fast on bread and water on *sextas ferias* for seven years, *PT*, vol. 1, p.298.

75 Ibid., p. 299. All priests heard here agreed on these matters. John Penyet, a priest, said that 'he did not believe that sodomy was committed in the order': *Nec credit quod crimen sodomiticum committeretur in ordine*, *PT*, vol. 2, p.72.

76 *PT*, vol. 1, p. 300. See also Stephen, ibid., p. 305.

77 Testimony: *PT*, vol. 1, pp. 301–6.

78 This same rationale for obeying the command to deny Christ or spit on the cross was given by many others, see among others, Matthew of Monte Lupello, *PT*, vol. 2, p. 176.

79 *PT*, vol. 1, p. 305, an opinion shared by the next priest.

80 Ibid., p. 306.

three years with the Templars.[81] The bishop finally absolved him and imposed a penance after keeping him waiting at least one day.[82] Aimery of Buris, a Templar priest for one year and three weeks before capture, gave additional information about the reception.[83] He was told not to enter a house in which a woman was giving birth, nor to become a godfather. He was not permitted to drink in a tavern with laypersons.[84] He explained that having been told to allow other men into his bed when travelling overseas, had nothing to do with immoral acts, but rather with the shortage of beds.[85] Not only did he believe in the sacraments, but also so did many of the others since they took communion twice a year.[86] He never swore, as alleged, not to leave the order. He did not believe the accusations regarding sodomy or idols. He had confessed and been absolved by a Dominican, confessor of the bishop of Langres.[87]

Raynald of Tremplaio, a twenty-year veteran, was curate of the Templar church in Paris.[88] He insisted from the outset that he did not intend to deviate from the confession he had made to the bishop of Paris. Recanting was, as stated above, an action which could result in death. He underwent the usual denial and spitting, but no illicit kisses. He had heard many Templar priests saying mass and had never heard anyone omit the words of consecration.[89] He elaborated on the matter of lay absolution confirming that the layman presiding over a chapter meeting would say: ‘Regarding those things which you did not confess out of bodily shame or from fear of punishment … we accord you the indulgence that we can … and our chaplain will absolve you’.[90] Raynald knew lay absolution was not licit. Giles of Rotangi described the usual reception including denial and spitting, nevertheless, insisting that he had attended both licit and illicit receptions.[91] He added concerning lay absolution that the presiding officer would ask that ‘God make to you and to us the same indulgence he gave Mary Magdalene’.[92]

John of Gisi[93] had been received along with a serving brother. He was required to affirm that he did not have any serious infirmity, had not been excommunicated

---

81 Ibid., p. 307.

82 The rest of his testimony echoed that of the first two priests.

83 Testifying late in 1310, ibid., pp. 316–20.

84 *PT*, vol. 1, p. 317.

85 Ibid.

86 Ibid., p. 318. See also John of Gisi, ibid., p. 568.

87 Fasting on bread and water on 13 Fridays and reading the psalter nine times, ibid., p. 319.

88 *PT*, vol. 1, pp. 421–4.

89 Ibid., p. 423.

90 Ibid.

91 *PT*, vol. 1, pp. 463–8.

92 Ibid., p. 466, a probable reference to Luke 7:48, ‘Your sins are forgiven’, given the medieval belief that that episode referred to Mary Magdalene.

93 Ibid, p. 567.

and did not have debts he needed to pay off. The serving brother swore that he was neither a serf nor promised in marriage. [94] John asked the man receiving him why the denial and spitting were required. The man responded that he had no idea; it was just a custom of theirs.[95] My reading of the testimony of all men for whom the depositions remain has convinced me that most of those responsible had no idea whatsoever as to why peculiar and/or illicit practices had ever become required, if in fact they had. The acts had nothing to do with belief in any heresy.

John Peynet,[96] who had attended many other receptions, stated that nothing illicit took place at them,[97] however, he presumed that as in his case the illicit acts occurred later.[98] He did not celebrate mass himself again until after his confession and absolution by the bishop of Beauvais.[99] John said he had been told that priests of the order 'had more power over them [the brothers] than others due to an apostolic privilege' – a common misconception.[100] The octogenarian William of Textor had been in the order for only eight years. Accepting a priest of more than 70 years of age must indicate a shortage of clerics in the early-fourteenth century. The secular priest to whom he originally went for confession refused him absolution, which he gained soon after from a Friar Minor.[101]

In 1310, four Templar priests gave evidence in the Elne. The longest deposition came from Bartholomew of Turri, a chaplain and Templar for 29 years.[102] He insisted that he had never heard of anyone denying Christ or spitting on the cross. He personally believed 'Jesus to be the word of God the Father, his humanity provided by his time in the holy womb of his Virgin mother where he was conceived by the Holy Spirit and not by manly semen. He did not die for his sins but for ours and on the third day he arose from the dead'. [103] In spite of the honour he felt for the lord pope and the cardinals, he did not believe that James of Molay had confessed as alleged.[104] Concerning same-sex acts between brothers, he answered: 'As far as other brothers are concerned, he did not know, nevertheless he said and believed that none of the brothers did this, because in committing such a sin, those lacking

---

94 Ibid.

95 '...*erat consuetum fieri*', ibid., p.569. He confessed his illicit acts to a Friar Minor receiving absolution and various penances: ibid., p. 570.

96 Testimony: *PT*, vol. 2, pp. 71–4.

97 Additionally, see Guy of Ruppe Talhata who also witnessed legitimate receptions, *PT*, vol. 2, p. 155.

98 *PT*, vol. 2, pp. 72–3.

99 Ibid., p.73.

100 Ibid. Priest Matthew of Monte Lupello added that by apostolic privilege Templar priests had the same powers of absolution as a monastic abbot: *PT*, vol, 2, p. 176.

101 Testimony: *PT*, vol. 2, pp. 129–32.

102 *PT*, vol. 2, pp. 428–35.

103 Ibid., pp. 428–9.

104 Ibid., p. 429

in faith would bring down on themselves the wrath of God'.[105] Since no errors existed, persons were not negligent in failing to correct them. At their receptions, men were told to obey only the old or new good precepts and good usages of the order and to avoid evil.[106] He gave a long and full description of his entirely licit reception which conformed precisely to what reception in the order should be.[107]

Bernard Guerrerii, a Templar priest for 12 years, testified emphasising the correct way in which the liturgy was recited.[108] The only kisses exchanged at reception were those on the mouth.[109] Any Templar acquiring goods unjustly, or discussing chapter meetings with those not present, would lose his habit and be expelled.[110] He stalwartly insisted that he did not believe that any brother had confessed sins before any court whatsoever.[111]

The chaplain John of Coma explained that brothers wore the red cross upon their clothing in commemoration of Christ Jesus.[112] It was because of their reverence for the cross that they removed their mantle, upon which the cross was inscribed, when they went to the latrine.[113] All words of the consecration of Christ's body and his precious blood were recited just as they appeared in the missal. The only idols he had ever heard about were those mentioned in Scripture.[114]

In conclusion, I have been able to discuss here only a fraction of the testimony of the 71 priests whose evidence was reasonably complete. Their depositions are frequently longer and more detailed than those of serving brothers and of many nobles. Their higher educational status enabled them to give more information on all aspects of the accusations related to liturgy or ecclesiastical matters. Their evidence enriches our knowledge of the order and its practices. They confessed guilt or innocence in about the same ratio as other Templars heard in the same places: threats, imprisonment, torture or lack of it apparently significantly influencing the responses.

It is obvious that most of those testifying, even those who imposed illicit acts upon others, had no idea whatsoever for what reason these acts existed. They were obeying a command to do so. These men were not heretics in any true sense of the term. They were believing Christians. Furthermore, the fact that far more priests than those of other ranks were spared certain illicit acts convinces me that those responsible did not take the acts seriously, if indeed they occurred.

---

105 Ibid., p. 430.

106 Ibid., p. 433.

107 Ibid., pp. 433–4.

108 Testimony: *PT*, vol. 2, pp. 442–6.

109 Ibid., p. 443.

110 Ibid., p. 445.

111 Ibid. He believed that any of the mentioned dignitaries who had supposedly confessed had done so falsely.

112 Testimony: ibid. pp. 463–6.

113 Ibid., p. 463.

114 Ibid., p. 464.

I do believe that improper acts may have occurred at some places belonging to the order of the Temple, particularly in France or Italy. Far more often, in my view, such acts were invented by the prisoners out of fear of torture or its actual application to them. Much more importantly, I have found no evidence that the order was infected by heretical beliefs. Heretics, such as Cathars or Waldensians, have a developed set of beliefs which vary in important ways from those of the Catholic Church. They do not willingly attend regular masses and take the Eucharist. Nor would they consecrate the elements and distribute them to others. These unfortunate men were, as I have said above, believing, practising Christians.

Chapter 27

The Assimilation of Templar Properties by the Order of the Hospital

Theresa M. Vann

After the spectacular arrest and trial of the order of the Temple, the question arose of the fate of the order and its properties. Pope Clement V convened the council of Vienne in October 1311 to discuss this matter, together with crusades to the Holy Land and the reform of the Church. At the council, the pope suppressed the Templar order and transferred its properties to the order of the Hospital.[1] Clement's decision at Vienne shaped the future of the order of the Hospital.[2] Acquisition of the former Templar estates substantially increased the Hospitallers' holdings, emphasized the order's responsibility for recapturing the Holy Land and subsidized the order's convent on Rhodes and, later, Malta. At the time, however, the order of the Hospital's immediate concern was the legal opposition the brothers encountered when they tried to claim their new properties. In the interim between the Templars' arrest and suppression, almost every royal and ecclesiastical authority in Europe had manoeuvered to obtain the Templar properties for themselves. The Hospital endured years of litigation to claim its property rights. The fragmentary nature of the Hospitaller main archives for this period provide little evidence of any kind of a centralized administrative process that the order developed to transfer the Templar properties into its possession. Even so, enough materials remain to reconstruct some administrative practices that the order developed during the transfer. The order's administration of the Templar properties illuminates the relationship

---

1 *Decrees of the Ecumenical Councils,* ed. Norman P. Tanner, vol. 1 (Washington, D.C., 1990), pp. 333–80; for *Ad providam*, see *Reg. Clem. V*, vol. 6, pp. 65–71, nos 7885–6. Also see Christopher M. Bellitto, *The General Councils: A History of the Twenty-One Church Councils from Nicaea to Vatican II* (New York: 2002).

2 Joseph Delaville le Roulx, *Les Hospitaliers à Rhodes jusqu'à la mort de Philibert de Naillac (1310–1421)* (Paris, 1913), pp. 31–78, remains the most complete overall description of the effect of the acquisition of the Templar lands upon the priories of the Hospitaller order. See also Malcolm Barber, *The Trial of the Templars* (Cambridge, 1978; 2nd edn, 2006); also Anthony Luttrell, 'The Hospitallers of Rhodes: Prospectives, Problems, Possibilities,' in idem, *Latin Greece, the Hospitallers and the Crusades, 1291–1440* (London, 1982), article I, pp. 250–3; idem, 'Gli ospitalieri e l'eredità dei Templari: 1305–1378', in idem, *The Hospitallers of Rhodes and Their Mediterranean World* (Aldershot, 1992), article III, pp. 67–86.

between the master and the priories during the early fourteenth century, and offers some insight into the Hospitallers' financial difficulties during the same period.

At the council of Vienne, Clement V ruled in the bull *Ad providam* (1312) that only the pope could reassign the order of the Temple's lands because it was an exempt order. Therefore, in accordance with canon law, Clement gave all the properties the Templars had at the time of their arrest to the order of the Hospital, because the original donors had given this property to the Templars to subsidize their work in the Holy Land. Now that the Templars were unable to fulfil the wishes of the donors, these gifts had to be returned or reallocated to an equivalent order.[3] The Hospitallers' recent capture of Rhodes, Clement stated, demonstrated that they continued to fight across the seas in defence of the faith. Therefore the Hospitallers would use the former Templar lands for recuperation of the Holy Land and do the work of the Templars in these possessions. Clement only exempted the Templar properties in the kingdoms of Castile, Aragon, Portugal and Majorca, because their rulers had petitioned the pope to give the lands to the native military religious orders or to establish new ones. Although Clement acknowledged the assertions of Iberian rulers that they fought the Muslims within the peninsula, at the same time *Ad providam* ignored Philip the Fair's similar request to create a new military religious order in France.[4]

Clement's determination to fight a holy war shaped the rhetoric of *Ad providam*, and it laid a heavy burden upon the Hospitallers to fight to regain the Holy Land. Fulk de Villaret, the master of the Hospital, realized this, but he also thought Clement's action at Vienne was a privilege, a manifestation of good fortune and high favour for himself and his order.[5] Clement publicly insisted that his decision showed no special favour to the Hospitallers, only recognition of their mission, and informed Fulk's procurator, Albert of Schwarzburg, that he gave the Hospitallers the properties not out of a special fondness for the order, but so they would be used in the service of God.[6]

Clement's decision upheld the papal prerogative over proprietary religious orders, but he erred when he assumed that all the lands in the Templars' possession had been given to the order *donatio sub modo* (a conditional gift under Roman civil law) to support the Holy Land. Clement's decision ignored the fact that not all donations and transfers contained diplomatic formulae indicating the specific intent of the donor, and that the Templars had also acquired properties by purchase or other means. Neither Clement nor his successors revoked this legal premise,

3 *Ad providam*, pp. 65–6, no. 7885; Barber, *Trial*, pp. 230–1; 2nd edn, pp. 271–3.

4 *Ad providam*, p. 67, no. 7885; Barber, *Trial*, p. 227; 2nd edn, p. 270.

5 Sebastiano Paoli, *Codice diplomatico del Sacro militare ordine gerosolimitano oggi di Malta* vol. 2 (Lucca, 1733–37), p. 36, for Fulk's appointment of Albert of Schwarzburg as procurator (1313); Valletta, National Library of Malta, AOM 16, no. 11, Fulk's appointment of Léonard de Tibertis as procurator (1314).

6 Abbé de Vertot, *The History of the Knights Hospitallers of St. John of Jerusalem* (New York, 1981 [Edinburgh, 1757]), p. 33; *PUT*, vol. 2, p. 219.

even when the initial gift was not conditional. For example, when the Hospitallers received the Templar lands in Castile in 1319 (after a royal minority prevented the kingdom of León-Castile from creating a new native military religious order) the order found itself in extensive litigation with the orders of Alcantara and Calatrava over the castles of Capilla and Almorchon.[7] Fernando III had given the castle of Capilla to the order of the Temple in September 1236 in return for services rendered to the crown that probably consisted of a loan.[8] Since the castle was in the middle of landholdings dominated by the order of Alcantara, Fernando III's donation created a region of mixed jurisdiction over lands and castles between two different military religious orders. Before the year was over, the two orders appeared before Fernando disputing lordship over castles around Capilla.[9] As part of the settlement, Fernando awarded the Templars an additional castle, Almorchon. The dispute resurfaced in 1241, when Fernando defined the boundaries between the Templars' holdings of Capilla and the lands of the order of Alcantara.[10] There the matter stood until 1309, when Fernando IV gave the castles of Capilla and Almorchon to the order of Alcantara. Benedict XII ruled in favour of the Hospitallers in 1335, citing the intent of Fernando III's original donation to support the Holy Land.[11] The Hospitallers arrived at a financial settlement with the orders of Alcantara and Calatrava to settle the case.

This particular episode demonstrates another legal flaw in Clement's initial bull: *Ad providam* transferred the Templar lands to the Hospitallers without due consideration of any encumbrances, prior claims or lawsuits. Clement, however, acknowledged this error and corrected it. He recognized royal and episcopal claims upon the properties, enabling Philip the Fair and his successor to insist upon just compensation for the expenses of the trial and for the upkeep of the Templar lands before releasing them to the Hospitallers.[12] Similar suits upon Templar properties materialized. Some claimants attacked the Hospitallers themselves as unworthy.[13] French prelates questioned the Hospitallers' exemptions and petitioned to bring all the Hospitallers' European commanderies under diocesan jurisdiction. Only the

---

[7] Carlos Barquero Goñi, 'El conflicto por los bienes templarios en Castilla,' *En la España medieval*, 16 (1993), 37–54; Barber, *Trial*, p. 236; 2nd edn, pp. 275–6.

[8] Julio González, *Reinado y diplomas de Fernando III*, vol. 3 (Córdoba, 1980), pp. 93–6, no. 575.

[9] Ibid., vol 3, pp. 100–101, no. 579.

[10] Ibid., vol. 3, pp. 226–8, no. 680.

[11] Benedict XII, *Lettres secrètes et curiales (étranger)*, in *Ut per litteras apostolicas* (Turnhout, 2000–), searchable database based on *Registres et lettres des papes du XIVe siècle*, 48 vols (Rome, 1899–), internet resource, www.brepolis.net: Avignon, 6 May 1335; source: Reg. Vat. 130, fol. 38r, no. CLXXXIII; Reg. Aven. 48, fol. 205v; Reg. Vat. 119, no. 369, Litt. patens.

[12] Pauli, *Codice diplomatico,* vol. 2, p. 34.

[13] Helen Nicholson, *The Knights Templar: A New History* (Stroud, 2001) p. 231; Pauli, *Codice diplomatico,* vol. 2, p. 26, no. 23.

Templars' Cypriot lands were immediately turned over to the Hospitallers without incident in 1313; by 1317, these lands paid Rhodes an annual responsion of 60,000 bezants.[14]

Fulk de Villaret, busy with the conquest and settlement of Rhodes, sent procurators to Europe to represent him in the lawsuits. His first procurator, Albert of Schwarzburg, the grand preceptor of the Hospital, arrived in Avignon in March 1313 and represented the order in England in November of that same year.[15] Fulk gave Albert sweeping powers that, in addition to litigating for the Templar properties, permitted him to conduct visitations, investigations and disciplinary actions against the European Hospitallers, and collect the responsions. The scope of Schwarzburg's authority suggests that Fulk expected his procurator would have to answer to the order's critics and undertake the reform of the Hospitaller European priories as part of the process of claiming Templar lands. His second procurator, Léonard de Tibertis, prior of Venice, received more specific powers in November 1314 to negotiate with all the rulers of western Europe over the Templar properties on behalf of the master.[16]

The high-level negotiations of Schwarzburg and Tibertis, however, only confirmed the Hospitallers' claims to the Templar properties; they did not settle every pending lawsuit. A case-by-case scrutiny of individual Templar properties reveals any number of encumbrances that prevented the Hospitallers from immediately exploiting their new wealth. For example, the royal commissioners transferred the Templar properties in Auvergne to the prior in May 1313.[17] The cartulary of the Hospitaller house of Velay (in Auvergne) shows that it settled a lawsuit against the Templars over the rights of justice in 1329[18] and concluded another lawsuit against the Templars over land and grazing rights in 1335.[19] This last suit had to have been pending over 20 years.

The assimilation of the Templar properties created huge logistical problems for the western Hospitaller priories. The Templars had one-half to two-thirds as much French and Catalan property as the Hospitallers.[20] The order of the Hospital made structural and administrative changes to accommodate the influx of Templar

---

14 Anthony Luttrell, 'The Hospitallers in Cyprus after 1291,' in idem, *The Hospitallers in Cyprus, Rhodes, Greece, and the West 1291–1440* (London, 1978), article II, pp. 167–8; Peter Edbury, *The Kingdom of Cyprus and the Crusades, 1191–1374* (Cambridge, 1991), p. 136.

15 Delaville le Roulx, *Les Hospitaliers,* pp. 32–3.

16 Valletta, National Library of Malta, AOM 16, no. 11.

17 *Cartulaire des Hospitaliers (Ordre de Saint-Jean de Jérusalem) du Velay*, ed. Augustin Chassaing (Paris, 1888), p. 123 no. 71.

18 Ibid., p. 149, no. 79.

19 Ibid., p. 159, no. 85.

20 *L'enquête pontificale de 1373 sur l'ordre des Hospitaliers de Saint-Jean de Jérusalem: Le prieuré de France*, ed. Anne-Marie Legras, vol. 1 (Paris, 1987), p. 73. Jaime II of Aragon feared the increased influence of the Hospitallers in Aragon and Catalonia

properties by creating new priories: Toulouse (1315) and Catalonia (1319). Pope John XXII created two more priories, Aquitaine and Champagne, at a general assembly of Hospitallers held in Avignon in 1317. In addition, French Hospitaller documents identified and tracked Templar properties separately from their other holdings through the fourteenth century; some continued the practice until the eighteenth century.[21] The Hospitaller house of Velay, for example, distinguished between their recently-acquired Templar properties and their 'ancient' Hospitaller properties. The bulls of Master Roger des Pins, written in Rhodes in 1358, described commanderies in Toulouse, France and Cyprus as former Templar properties. Likewise, the papal inquest of 1373 identified and tracked the Templar properties separately from the ancient Hospitaller properties.[22] This suggests that the papacy and the Hospitallers recognized that either the nature of the acquisition of Templar properties or particular legal encumbrances attached to each required special administrative notations in the written records. Certainly the legal claims filed against the Templar lands taxed the resources of the Hospitaller order, and scholars have suggested that the numerous lawsuits the Hospitallers settled over the Templar lands were one of the reasons for the order's indebtedness in the early fourteenth century. This theory supposes that the monetary settlements that the Hospitallers made on behalf of the Templar properties came from the order's common treasury. Instead, whenever possible the settlements came from the sale or other distribution of the Templar lands. For example, Fulk de Villaret settled a Templar debt with merchants who came to Rhodes from Marseilles in 1314 by selling a Templar vineyard in Marseilles, not by paying out of the Hospitaller's common treasury in Rhodes. [23]

The accounts that the priory of England rendered to the common treasury in 1338 best demonstrate Hospitaller documentation and accounting of former Templar properties. The English priory recorded how much revenue the Templars had received from the property and compared it with the revenues the Hospitallers collected. These revenues were applied to the legal responsibilities the Templars had incurred for those properties, such as pensions and annuities. The English Hospitallers recorded that the Templar properties brought in 5,739 marks, 4 shillings and 6 pence.[24] They paid out 67½ marks and 100 shillings in Templar

---

because of the large numbers of Templar castles in his realms: see Alan Forey, *The Fall of the Templars in the Crown of Aragon* (Aldershot, 2001), pp. 156–8.

21 Jean-Marc Roger, 'Les differénts types de commanderies du prieuré de Champagne au Xve siècle,' in *La Commanderie: Institution des ordres militaires dans l'Occident médiéval,* ed. Anthony Luttrell and Lèon Pressouyre (Paris, 2002), pp. 30–1.

22 *L'Enquête*, ed. Legras, p. 93.

23 Valletta, National Library of Malta, AOM 16, no 9.

24 *The Knights Hospitaller in England: Being the Report of Prior Philip de Thame to the Grand Master Elyan de Villanova for AD 1338*, ed. Lambert B. Larking, Camden Society, 65 (London, 1857), p. 202.

pensions[25] and satisfied other Templar financial responsibilities by the sale, lease or transfer of former Templar properties. The priory listed all of the goods that belonged to the Templars that had not been transferred to the Hospital, which came to a sum of 10,259 marks, 3 shillings and 1 pence. The priory must have received the Templars' financial records (now lost) to know these details.

There is additional evidence that even within the Hospitaller order the status of Templar properties was not clearly established. The master of the order periodically attempted to exercise direct control over the Templar properties. One of the charges brought against Fulk de Villaret in 1317 was that he favoured a crony by awarding him the commandery of Cyprus, which had been considerably enriched by Templar properties, and assessing his responsions at a lower rate than that paid to the Templars' treasury.[26] The oldest surviving volume of the *Liber bullarum* provides evidence that Master Roger des Pins awarded Templar commanderies in Toulouse and France to his chaplain and other associates on Rhodes in 1358.[27] In this instance, des Pins not only claimed the magisterial right of revenue from vacant commanderies; he also claimed the right to bypass the priory and appoint new commanders directly to former Templar properties.

For their part, the western priories did not use revenues from the Templar properties to pay their yearly responsions to the central convent on Rhodes. There may have been questions about the nature of the Templar properties; the revenue may have been held up by lawsuits; or it may have been thought that the Hospitallers had a legal responsibility to use the Templar lands only to recover the Holy Land, and therefore the former Templar revenues could not support the *Sacra Infermeria* on Rhodes. Whatever the reason, it appears that any additional Templar income had remained in the priory and was not transferred to the coffers of the common treasury. Such withholding severely threatened the financial stability of the central convent on Rhodes.

Part of the difficulty in understanding the full extent of the problem lies in the incompleteness of the archival records from Rhodes between 1308 and 1330. The enactments of chapters general for the period between 1308 and 1330 do not survive, although there is fragmentary evidence that the general chapter met during those years.[28] The earliest surviving volume of the *Liber bullarum*, the register of magisterial bulls, dates from 1346. We do not know what the order's financial

25 Ibid., p. 209.

26 Vertot, vol. 2, pp. 103–4. This would allow the crony to pocket more income than previous tenants of Cyprus.

27 Valletta, National Library of Malta, AOM 316, fols 55v–56.

28 The original text of the enactments of the meetings of the general chapters that met between 1308 and 1330 have disappeared. *CH* published the earlier statutes of the order, which Edwin J. King, *Rule, Statutes, and Customs of the Hospitallers (1099–1310)* (London, 1934), translated into English. Valletta, National Library of Malta, AOM 69 contains statutes collected by Master Roger de Pins in 1357; ibid., AOM 16, no. 11, was issued during a meeting of the general chapter in Rhodes in 1314. Also see Charles L.

position was before the arrest of the Templars, nor can we track how much money the central convent in Rhodes received or spent during that period of time. Instead, we have snippets of information. When Helion de Villeneuve became master of the order in 1319, he found the common treasury in debt, stemming from the large sums Fulk de Villaret had borrowed to finance the capture of Rhodes (completed by 1312) and its resettlement. At the meeting of the general chapter in 1330, the order's Italian creditors and European critics demanded payment, particularly in view of the Hospitallers' recent acquisition of Templar lands.[29] Villeneuve ordered each priory to pay the debt according to its means. The assessment of the priory of France, which contained most of the Templar lands, was 41,000 florins; St Gilles and Toulouse, 40,000; Aquitaine and Auvergne 14,000.[30] In comparison, other priories paid 8,000, 4,000, or as little as 100 florins. Villeneuve then reviewed the yearly responsions and assessed the priory of France at 13,000 gold florins, and the priories of St Gilles and Toulouse at 14,000.[31]

The priories did not receive explicit orders for the collection and remittance of revenues of the former Templar properties until Roger des Pins' statutes of 1357 established that former Templar properties had the same responsibilities to support the central convent by paying responsions.[32] But even after Pins' statutes, collection of responsions remained an ongoing problem that resisted resolution. For this the treasury's accounting system, which tracked the responsions from each commandery in a number of different currencies, bore some of the blame. In addition, it is not inconceivable that the priories kept separate account books to record the responsions to Rhodes. Michael Gervers has found evidence that the English priory kept separate accounts for the income of the prior himself from his own lands, and Anthony Luttrell has found that commanders kept their personal finances separate from that of their commanderies.[33] To be fair, these practices probably were not intended to defraud the treasury, but rather reflected an accounting system more akin to separate purses for each expense than a computer spreadsheet. Still, most of the excess wealth generated by the Templar properties remained within the priories, and the central convent on Rhodes found it very difficult to collect and utilize that wealth. The only Templar properties that directly enriched the central convent on Rhodes were the ones on Cyprus, possibly because of proximity, or because the lack of legal challenges permitted faster assimilation.

Tipton, 'The 1338 Chapter General of the Knights Hospitallers at Montpellier', *Traditio* 24 (1968), 293–308.

[29] Tipton, '1338 Chapter General', 298–300.

[30] Ibid., p. 302.

[31] Ibid., p. 304.

[32] Valletta, National Library of Malta, AOM 69, fol. 20v.

[33] *Cartulary of the Knights of St. John of Jerusalem in England, Part 2, Prima Camera, Essex*, ed. Michael Gervers (Oxford, 1996), pp. lxvi–lxvii; Anthony Luttrell, 'The Finances of the Commander in the Hospital after 1306', in *La Commanderie*, p. 278.

There is no doubt that the order of the Hospital benefited materially from the misfortune of the Templars. Clement's decision to transfer the Templar properties to the Hospitallers enriched the order and brought it to greater prominence. But it also entailed greater responsibilities and scrutiny, directed towards the central convent in Rhodes. The master of the order, now held solely accountable by the pope for the defence of the Holy Land, faced additional expenses. But the master did not control the Templar properties directly, only through the priors. The European priories, while substantially enriched by the Templar properties, also encountered additional administrative tasks. Lawsuits over Templar properties had to be handled on a case-by-case basis, so the priories kept separate accounts to settle legal claims, to pay pensions and other sums the Templars had originally allocated and to draw these sums from their Templar funds. The priories resisted sending what they considered to be Templar revenues to the common treasury unless the master demanded it for warfare against the Muslims in the Levant. This fulfilled the original intentions of the donors, but led to more than a century of hair-raising fiscal adventures.

Chapter 28
'The Templars Are Everywhere': An Examination of the Myths behind Templar Survival after 1307

John Walker

The arrest of the Templars in 1307, the suppression of the order in 1312 and the execution of Jacques de Molay in 1314 saw the end of the order in the eyes of academic historians. However, for conspiracy theorists, writers of pseudo-history and many of their readers the dramatic events of the early fourteenth century were simply the beginning of a new era in Templar history. In the second half of the twentieth century, and at an increasing rate with the rise of the internet, this speculative history of Templar survival has created an alternative to the orthodox version of events seen in most academic literature.[1] Despite little or no evidence to support their theories, many writers have persisted in perpetuating rumours that some Templars survived the calamitous events of the early fourteenth century and, indeed, that the order still survives to this day. In this study, some of the elements of this vast speculative literature will be examined, focussing particularly on the supposed connections that the order had with Scotland, before analysing the reasons why such literature seems to be accepted by so many people beyond the academic community.

One of the first books in the modern era to suggest something other than the official line recorded by historians was *The Holy Blood and the Holy Grail*, originally published in 1982. This book caused a storm of protest from the Christian Church and was largely dismissed by historians. The book's contents range over many themes, but in terms of the Templars the following quote gives an idea of the thinking of the authors.

---

[1] The vast amount of speculative Templar history includes: Michael Baigent, Richard Leigh and Henry Lincoln, *The Holy Blood and the Holy Grail* (London, 1982); Andrew Sinclair, *The Sword and the Grail* (New York, 1992); Lynn Picknett and Clive Prince, *The Templar Revelation* (London, 1997); Steven Sora, *The Lost Treasure of the Knights Templar: Solving the Oak Island Mystery* (Rochester, 1999); Eric Haagensen and Henry Lincoln, *The Templars' Secret Island: The Knights, the Priest and the Treasure* (Moreton-in-Marsh, 2002). A starting point for Templar speculation on the internet is www.templarhistory.com.

> Persistent but unsubstantiated rumours speak of the [Templar] treasure being smuggled by night from the Paris preceptory, shortly before the arrests. According to these rumours, it was transported by wagons to the coast … loaded into eighteen galleys, which were never heard of again.[2]

Speaking of the execution of Jacques de Molay and Geoffroi de Charnay, the authors go on to say,

> With their execution, the Templars ostensibly vanish from the stage of history. Nevertheless, the order did not cease to exist. Given the number of knights who escaped, who remained at large or who were acquitted, it would be surprising if it had.[3]

The idea that some of the French Templars and their treasure escaped the arrests and subsequent persecution was taken up by Andrew Sinclair in 1992. In his book, *The Sword and the Grail*, he wrote,

> Although King Philip's seizure and destruction of Jacques de Molay and the French Templars was as efficient an operation as Hitler's coup against Roehm and his Brownshirts, there is no record of his finding the Templar treasure in Paris or the secret archives of the order or its fleet, based mainly at La Rochelle in Brittany. Much evidence and some tradition points to the removal of the treasure and most of the archives on ships, with refugee Templars taking these to Portugal and to the west and east coasts of Scotland, where they were welcomed.[4]

Leaving aside the confusion as to the location of La Rochelle, Sinclair's work speculated on the possible destinations of the renegade Templars and their treasure. The clear inference from these two works was that there was no doubt in the minds of the authors that at least some members of the order got to safety in 1307 and the following years. This theme was followed by Lynn Picknett and Clive Prince in 1997 when they published *The Templar Revelation*. This book contained some of the same themes as *The Holy Blood and the Holy Grail* and also developed other ideas relating to the paintings of Leonardo da Vinci, the role of John the Baptist, and the person and role of Mary Magdalene. In the section on the Templars, the authors were very clear about their views on the survival of the order. They wrote,

---

2 Baigent, Leigh, and Lincoln, *Holy Blood*, p. 72.

3 Ibid., p. 73.

4 Sinclair, *Sword and Grail*, pp. 41–2.

> historically there is slender evidence that the Knights Templar were ever effectively killed off … It is very likely that knights [both rank and file and the elite] went off and founded their own underground movements …[5]

The view that the Templars did not disappear in the period of 1307–12 was brought to a mass audience in 2003 with the publication of Dan Brown's fictional *Da Vinci Code*, which suggests what many believe as fact, that fraternities of Templars are still in existence to this day.[6]

Once people had accepted the theory that the Templars and their treasure did escape the attentions of the French king, the debate about where they actually went to (and what happened to their treasure) was the next logical question to answer, with possible destinations including locations in Europe and northern and central America.[7] Michael Baigent and Richard Leigh, writing in *The Temple and the Lodge* in 1989, suggested that the three most likely destinations for members of the order were Scandinavia, the Muslim world and Scotland. Although their former co-author, Henry Lincoln, in collaboration with Eric Haagensen, suggested very close connections between the Templars and Scandinavia, Baigent and Leigh dismissed the region as a possible place to escape to because they believed that the arrival of Templars in such a sparsely populated area would have attracted too much attention. In a similar vein they also dismissed the Muslim world because they argued that Muslim writers would have recorded their former foe's arrival with great enthusiasm and used it for propaganda purposes. Having dismissed these two areas, Baigent and Leigh argued that the only location that was a safe haven for members of the order was Scotland.[8]

At this point it should be noted that there is a documented history for the Templars in Scotland which is recorded by a small number of historians including Aitken and Edwards, and more recently, Cowan, Mackay and Macquarrie, who have charted this history as comprehensively as the limited evidence allows. Following the foundation of the order in c.1119, Hugh de Payens came to England in 1128. King David of Scotland invited him to come north of the border and probably gave him land at Balantrodoch, to the south of Edinburgh. This is now known as Temple, and is where one of the order's two Scottish preceptories was founded, the other being Maryculter on the River Dee to the south-west of Aberdeen. In addition, we know that the order also had possessions in Lothian, Falkirk and Glasgow. We can also trace the suppression of the order which saw the examination and absolution of two knights at Holyrood on 17 November

---

5 Picknett and Prince, *Templar Revelation*, p. 163.

6 Dan Brown, *The Da Vinci Code* (London, 2003), p. 220.

7 Haagensen and Lincoln, *Secret Island*; Karen Ralls, *The Templars and the Grail* (Wheaton, 2003), pp. 172–3; Sora, *Lost Treasure of the Knights Templar*.

8 Michael Baigent and Richard Leigh, *The Temple and the Lodge* (London, 1989), pp. 105–6; Haagensen and Lincoln, *Secret Island*.

1309. In Scotland, like the rest of Europe, the history of the order of the Templars ended with these events.[9]

However, Scotland has also provided a rich vein of material for the after-history of the Templars, and Baigent and Leigh are only two of a number of writers who have suggested a range of unsubstantiated connections relating to the order's relationship with that country in the early fourteenth and subsequent centuries. These myths include the flight of the Templars from France (and other countries including England) to Scotland; the settlement of members of the order in western Scotland, specifically Argyll and Kintyre; the significant participation of a Templar force at the battle of Bannockburn in 1314; and the connections of the order to Rosslyn Chapel near Edinburgh. There are other myths relating to the development of freemasonry but there is not enough space to consider them here. Overall, little has been written to directly challenge the absurdity of these theories, although Oxbrow and Robertson have begun this process in *Rosslyn and the Grail*, published in 2005.[10]

There are several stories in circulation relating to the flight of the Templars from France. However, the story that has most support is that produced by Baigent and Leigh which argues that the renegade Templars sailed from France and headed for the west coast of Scotland. They provided a detailed explanation of the escape routes that Templar ships would have taken around the west coast of Ireland, collecting men, arms, and equipment along the way, and landing in Kintyre and Argyll. They argued that they would have been welcomed there by nobles who supported Robert the Bruce, who was ready to accept any refugees who might help in his struggle against the English King Edward II.[11] In reality, although Baigent and Leigh's idea is certainly possible, there is no contemporary evidence for these adventures at all. Given the danger of sailing round the west coast of Ireland, particularly in autumn or winter, and the debate surrounding the question of whether the order actually possessed a substantial fleet by the late thirteenth century, it seems highly unlikely that this escape actually took place.[12]

The second myth suggests that once the Templars arrived in Scotland they settled along the west coast. There are various debates among pseudo-historical writers as to where exactly this settlement would have taken place. In the mid-eighteenth century, Baron Karl von Hunt, the creator of the Strict Templar Observance, suggested that some Templars, led by Pierre d'Aumont, escaped to

---

[9] Robert Aitken, 'The Knights Templar in Scotland', *The Scottish Review*, 32 (July 1898), 1–36; John Edwards, 'The Templars in Scotland in the Thirteenth Century', *Scottish Historical Review*, 5 (1908), 13–25; Ian Cowan, P. Mackay and Alan Macquarrie, *The Knights of St. John of Jerusalem in Scotland* (Edinburgh, 1983), pp. xviii–xxvi.

[10] Mark Oxbrow and Ian Robertson, *Rosslyn and the Grail* (Edinburgh, 2005), pp. 115–36.

[11] Baigent and Leigh, *Temple and the Lodge*, pp. 106–10.

[12] Oxbrow and Robertson, *Rosslyn*, pp. 122–3; Helen Nicholson, *The Knights Templar: A New History* (Stroud, 2001), pp. 192–4.

Ireland after the arrests and suppression, then moved to Scotland where they settled on the Island of Mull. There they were joined by other renegade members of the order from Scotland and England led by George Harris and survived under the leadership of Harris and D'Aumont, the latter being included in a list of grand masters created by Hunt and shown as the successor to Jacques de Molay.[13] It should be noted that Hunt has been described as a 'self-deluded fanatic', and he was one of a number of people from the mid-eighteenth century onwards who created their own brand of Templar organisations and were keen to trace links back to the medieval order by creating false lists of grand masters.[14]

Baigent and Leigh dismissed the Mull theory and suggested that the Templars settled in Argyll from the early fourteenth century. Although there is no written record of the order ever having possessions in this part of Scotland, they argue that the discovery at Kilmory Knap, Kilmartin and Kilneuair of grave slabs marked with supposed Templar images is proof of Templar existence in the region during the fourteenth century. The images themselves include crosses, swords, ships, knights and various tools taken to have masonic connections.[15]

It is true that a number of the grave slabs have been dated to the fourteenth century from the sites mentioned. However, the images are similar to many found in the western Highlands and relate to the warriors who fought for the lords of the isles in this period. Knights and swords are very common images and may have been based on weapons actually carried by warriors in the region. The depiction of ships in that area is also a common feature, and the ships are typical of Highland galleys from this era. Furthermore, the supposed masonic images are workmen's tools or shears, another common grave motif in this region.[16]

The third myth connecting the Templars to Scotland is rather more dramatic. A number of writers, including Baigent, Leigh and McKerracher, have developed the role of the order in Scotland further by suggesting that the Templars provided Robert the Bruce with a ready-made fighting force which helped change the course of Scottish history at the battle of Bannockburn on 23 and 24 June 1314.[17] The date of the battle is particularly significant for Templar pseudo-historians because 24 June is the feast day of St John the Baptist, and a number of writers

---

13 Baigent and Leigh, *Temple and the Lodge*, p. 112.

14 Peter Partner, *The Templars and their Myth* (Rochester, 1990), pp. 117–19.

15 Baigent and Leigh, *Temple and the Lodge*, pp. 19–35.; Sinclair, *Sword and Grail*, p. 45.

16 James Drummond, *Sculptured Monuments in Iona and the West Highlands* (Edinburgh, 1881); Kenneth A. Steer and John W.M. Bannerman, *Late Medieval Monumental Sculpture in the West Highlands* (Edinburgh, 1977); Oxbrow and Robertson, *Rosslyn*, pp. 122–3.

17 Baigent and Leigh, *Temple and the Lodge*, pp. 61–5; Archie McKerracher, 'Bruce's Secret Weapon', *The Scots Magazine*, 135, no. 3 (June 1991), 261–8.

have developed theories linking the order with this particular saint. Interestingly, most of these writers ignore the fact that the battle actually started on the 23rd.[18]

This myth suggests that Robert the Bruce had little experience of pitched battles and only had a small Scottish army of circa 6,000 which was exhausted after eight hours of fighting on 24 June and had done little to inflict damage on the strong English force of circa 20,000 which benefited from heavy cavalry. The turning point came when a supplementary force appeared behind Bruce, and the English panicked and fled. Bruce was able to seize the initiative, go on to win the battle and establish himself as an effective king of Scotland.

McKerracher and others suggested that the cavalry charge that seemed to do the damage at Bannockburn was in fact led by Templar knights, driving fear into the English. In 1991, he wrote,

> I suggest that what broke Edward [II's] army was the sight of the men who led [the Scottish forces], … perhaps no more than 50 or 60 in number; men who wore their hair close-cropped and their beards long … They marched beneath their black and white banner called the Beauseant, and were instantly recognisable to the front rank of the English as ... Knights Templar.[19]

The objection that the Templars are not referred to as being at the battle by any contemporary writers is countered by the argument that Bruce kept their involvement quiet because he did not want to offend his ally Philip IV or the pope.[20]

This version of events is dismissed by historians, and modern accounts of the battle ignore the Templars almost completely. It is true that there is much that is unclear about the events of 23 and 24 June, including the actual location of the battle, size of the respective forces and chronology of the battle, and this vagueness has inspired some writers to fill in the gaps and speculate as to what might have happened. However, the absence of any contemporary or near-contemporary references to the Templars at Bannockburn should be enough to put an end to this speculation. As far as the role of the supplementary force goes, many historians accept that this extra force was made up of camp-followers, servants and cooks, who charged into the battle on horseback from Coxet Hill. They suggest that the English were already in retreat by the time the camp-followers appeared over the hill to look for plunder, and that it had no impact on the outcome of the battle. Although it is possible that a few individual Templars may have found their way to join Bruce's or even Edward's armies in 1314, it seems highly unlikely that a large force could have been there. In any case, given Edward II's relatively

18 Picknett and Prince, *Templar Revelation*, p. 131.

19 McKerracher, 'Bruce's Secret Weapon', 262.

20 Baigent and Leigh, *Temple and the Lodge*, pp. 64–5.

lenient treatment of the order it would seem strange for the order to have turned against him so quickly.[21]

The fourth Scottish myth concerns Rosslyn chapel, situated eight miles to the south of Edinburgh and close to the original Templar preceptory of Balantrodoch. More than any place in Scotland it is probably the most closely linked to the Templars. The chapel was founded by Sir William St Clair in 1446, third and last St Clair earl of the Orkneys. It was originally intended to create a large cruciform building with a tower at its centre. Its purpose was to serve as a collegiate chapel where colleges of priests could sing perpetual masses for the souls of the St Clair family. However, only the chancel and parts of the east transept walls were completed, and after Sir William's death in 1484 his successors did not continue his work.[22] While the exterior of the chapel is rather plain the interior is remarkable, with a collection of carvings, sculptures and other decorations covering every surface. The many images have attracted a huge amount of attention as people have tried to discover their hidden meanings. In particular, it has come to be associated closely with the holy grail and is believed to be one of the possible locations for its burial.

As far as the Templars are concerned, many writers, including Andrew Sinclair, have suggested strong Templar connections with the chapel.[23] Some of the links are focussed on the supposed relationship between the order and the Sinclairs, inspired partly by the later freemasonry connections of the family. In particular, one legend has it that Hugh de Payens, one of the original founders of the Templars, and Katherine St Clair, an ancestor of the Sinclair founders of Rosslyn, were actually married. Speculation also surrounds the possibility that William St Clair (who died in Spain in 1330 taking Robert the Bruce's heart to the Holy Land and whose grave slab is in the chapel) was a member of the order. It is argued that William was a member of the order because the grave slab contains various supposed Templar symbols including a cross, a chalice and a sword similar to those discovered by Baigent and Leigh in Argyll. In addition, Templar imagery is seen by many people in the sculptures contained in the chapel including a knight on horseback and an array of stars, crosses and doves. Finally, the idea that the order used Rosslyn chapel as a safe place to hide their vast riches, whether the grail or other sources of immense wealth and power, is the final seal on the supposed connection with the order.[24]

---

21 Geoffrey Barrow, *Robert Bruce* (London, 1965), pp. 326–7; Aryeh Nusbacher, *The Battle of Bannockburn* (Stroud, 2002), pp. 87, 141–2; Oxbrow and Robertson, *Rosslyn*, pp. 124–5.

22 Colin McWilliam, *The Buildings of Scotland: Lothian except Edinburgh* (Harmondsworth, 1978), pp. 409–11; Earl of Rosslyn, *Rosslyn Chapel* (Rosslyn, 1997), p. 2.

23 Sinclair, *Sword and the Grail*, pp. 1–7.

24 Picknett and Prince, *Templar Revelation*, pp. 167–8; Sinclair, *Sword and Grail*, p. 3; Ralls, *Templars and the Grail*, pp. 175, 187–90; Sora, *Lost Treasure*, pp. 116–19.

In reality, as with the other myths that have been considered, there is no evidence for, or truth in, any of these suggestions. The links made between individual Sinclairs and the Templars are pure speculation. The sculptures are not Templar and have been interpreted, rather like the Argyll grave slabs, by people who wanted to link the chapel to the Templars and who appear to have simply interpreted the carvings in a way that would support their theories.[25]

Having considered the nature of the myths surrounding the order in Scotland after the arrests and suppression, it is worth considering where these stories originated. As Partner has demonstrated, the after-history of the Templars really began to develop with the rise of freemasonry in the early eighteenth century. As masonic writers tried to establish links with the distant past the Templars were seized upon as potential ancestors. The idea of a Templar flight to Scotland was certainly propounded by George Frederick Johnson (d.1775) in a period when a number of Templar myths appear to have been concocted.[26] This was the era when Karl von Hunt created his Strict Templar Observance, and it is likely that the Bannockburn myth appeared at this time and was then further developed during the nineteenth century.[27] Again, as is the nature of myths, once created they flourished although it is probably fair to say that it was not until the late twentieth century that they took a firm hold in many people's minds. Certainly, the huge number of internet sites devoted to the Templars and their history and after-history has allowed these myths to be developed to an almost unimaginable extent.

The final question to consider is why these myths are accepted by so many people who appear to be willing to ignore the contemporary evidence (or lack of it) and the works of academic historians in favour of something which is lacking in proof and any credibility. This is a phenomenon examined (although not in relation to the Templars) by Michael Shermer in *Why People Believe Weird Things*, published in 1997.[28] Part of the answer lies in the nature of the order itself and its dramatic end which has served to grab hold of people's attention in the first place in a way that is not the case for the other military orders. The story of the Templars is a classic tale of humble beginnings, a rise to power, wealth and influence and then a dramatic fall from grace. The brutal end to the order heightens this interest and creates questions that cannot be answered with absolute certainty in many people's minds. Why were the Templars persecuted? Were they really as innocent as is now generally accepted by historians? Could they have managed to survive the persecution in some form? Furthermore, the fact that there are so many gaps in Templar history serves to encourage speculation. The loss of the

25 Oxbrow and Robertson, *Rosslyn*, pp. 127–36.

26 Partner, *Templars and Their Myth*, pp. 101–14, 119.

27 *Statutes of the Religious and Military Order of the Temple as Established in Scotland with an Historical Notice of the Order* (Edinburgh, 1843), pp. vii–viii; Anthony Haye, *The Persecution of the Knights Templar* (Edinburgh, 1865), p. 114.

28 Michael Shermer, *Why People Believe Weird Things* (New York, 1997).

Templar archives means that there is a good deal that we do not know about the development of the order. This is seen, for example, in the vagueness about the origins and foundation of the order in the early twelfth century, a vagueness which has resulted in the creation of a vast range of alternative foundation stories.[29] The gaps are filled, and because there is no evidence to contradict the theories, they flourish and are accepted. This is clearly the case with myths about the order in Scotland where the lack of evidence allows speculation to be rife among the writers of pseudo-history, as we have seen.

Another factor which encourages people to accept the Templar myths is summed up by Dan Brown's statement in *The Da Vinci Code* that 'everyone loves a conspiracy'.[30] The dramatic events of 1307–14, followed by the deaths of Philip and Clement shortly after the execution of Jacques de Molay, have helped to stoke conspiracy theories relating to the Templars which continue to this day. The idea that the order could cease to exist is simply not accepted by many, in the same way that huge numbers of people still cannot accept that Princess Diana was probably killed because she did not wear a seatbelt and was in a car being driven too quickly by a driver who may have been under the influence of alcohol. The Templars have always been an ideal vehicle for conspiracy theories and renewed interest in such theories goes a long way to explain the acceptance of the fact of their survival against all odds.

Finally, but importantly, the style of writing which seems to be prevalent among many of the pseudo-histories of the Templars also explains to a great extent why their contents are accepted. This style often creates an air of mystery and intrigue surrounding the researching and writing of the particular work, serving to attract interest and draw readers into the subject matter. Writing in 2002, Evelyn Lord referred to a 'Templar genre of literature' to describe this feature of Templar writing.[31] It includes a story-telling style of writing where the authors describe their personal experiences as they research and write their work. This is seen classically in *The Holy Blood and Holy Grail* and *The Temple and the Lodge*. Very often the researchers encounter problems along the way whether it be evidence going astray, or something as mundane as the inability to rent a boat! These 'problems' serve to heighten the mystery and accentuate the possibility of a cover-up.[32]

This style of writing does not follow traditional academic 'rules', so when looking for evidence, anecdotes and false assumptions are given the same weight as contemporary source material, and pseudo-histories are regarded as having

---

[29] See for example, Baigent, Leigh and Lincoln, *Holy Blood*, pp. 83–91, 116–19; Picknett and Prince, *Templar Revelation*, p. 130; Ralls, *Templars and the Grail*, pp. 141–63.

[30] Brown, *Da Vinci Code*, p. 500.

[31] Evelyn Lord, *The Knights Templar in Britain* (Harlow, 2002), pp. 280–81.

[32] Baigent, Leigh and Lincoln, *Holy Blood*, pp. 1–22, 103–4; Baigent and Leigh, *Temple and the Lodge*, pp. 19–35.

more authority than standard academic works. In any case, even when a lack of evidence is admitted this does not appear to be a problem.[33] It often seems that the lack of any corroborating evidence to substantiate particular claims is irrelevant as it merely proves how powerful potential conspirators are and how successful they have been in covering their tracks. As a result of this rather 'different' treatment of evidence it is not surprising that writers often move from theorizing to statements of fact rather more quickly than might be expected. Thus a hypothesis becomes a fact within the space of a chapter, a page, or even the same paragraph.[34] Following on from this, it should not come as a surprise that mainstream academic works are often discredited and viewed as being part of a cover-up either deliberately, through ignorance of the 'truth', or fear. This latter factor presumably accounts for the fact that some writers of pseudo-history claim to have the support of an anonymous academic who will not publicly support their theories because they are afraid of damaging their academic reputation.[35]

A final characteristic of this style of writing can be seen in the apparent unwillingness for writers to admit to errors. Believers in the paranormal have been described as 'unsinkable rubber ducks' and this phrase could easily be applied to those who speculate about the Templars.[36] However much alternative theories might be attacked or even discredited, devotees will continue to accept them and prefer to modify rather than discard them completely. This appears to be the case with the vast amount of literature produced about the Priory of Sion over the past twenty to thirty years.[37]

Despite the protestations of the academic world, the idea that the arrests of 1307, the suppression of 1312 and the execution of Jacques de Molay in 1314 saw the end of the Templars is simply not accepted by many writers and readers of pseudo-history. As we have seen, a number of different locations have been suggested as destinations for the Templars and their treasure after 1307, although a lot of writers do focus on the significance of Scotland. A dramatic escape followed by a daring and dangerous sea voyage, settlement in the remote western highlands followed by a dramatic role at Bannockburn and connections with Rosslyn chapel is the stuff of legends. That people accept these stories as fact and are happy to develop them to this day is not surprising given the nature of the order's history up to the early fourteenth century, the renewed and obsessive interest with conspiracy theories, the way these pseudo-histories are written and ultimately the tragic end of the order. Finally, the many gaps in our knowledge relating to Templar history leave many questions unanswered and mean that

---

33 Sinclair, *Sword and Grail*, pp. 2–3, 41–2, 220.

34 Baigent and Leigh, *Temple and the Lodge*, p. 96.

35 Picknett and Prince, *Templar Revelation*, p. 134.

36 Shermer, *Weird Things*, p. 72.

37 For changing views on the nature of the Priory of Sion see, Baigent, Leigh and Lincoln, *Holy Blood*; Picknett and Prince, *Templar Revelation*; Lynn Picknett and Clive Prince, *The Sion Revelation* (London, 2006).

pseudo-historical theories are impossible to disprove with one hundred per cent certainty. As a result, the tantalising possibility of Templar survival and a Templar after-history remains alive and well for many people in the twenty-first century.

Conclusion

Jochen Burgtorf, Paul F. Crawford and Helen J. Nicholson

The papers in this volume give a panoramic view of the background to the trial of the Templars, the events of the trial across Catholic Christendom and the fate of both the Templars' properties and reputation. The contributors have explored various possible motivations for the attack on the order including the evidence for the charges brought against it, the procedures used during the trial and the evidence given by the brothers. They have also considered various aspects of the government of King Philip IV of France which illuminate his attack on the Templars in October 1307 and the trial which followed. The papers here cover virtually every part of Christendom where there were Templars in 1307.[1]

We have not found any conclusive evidence that the Templars were guilty as charged, nor that the pope decided at Chinon in August 1308 that 'the strange profession ceremony was simply an entrance ritual' and forgave the brothers, as has been recently argued elsewhere.[2] David Bryson [8] notes that the original charges were centred on a very small area of southern France and could have resulted from the behaviour of a single commander of the order, pointing 'only to a particular and isolated instance of guilt'. Jochen Schenk [12] notes that family ties and even family control of certain Templar houses could have led to abuses within certain houses, but although 'nepotistic culture' could have been extremely detrimental to discipline and the quality of recruits to the order, even family ties could hardly have restrained rumours of blasphemy, sodomy and idol-worship, had such been common in Templar houses in the early fourteenth century. As Alan Forey [1] notes: 'even if abuses had been limited to certain houses, they were nevertheless likely to become sufficiently known to attract the attention of the ecclesiastical authorities'. Yet the ecclesiastical authorities had done nothing, indicating that they knew of no abuses. On the contrary, Thomas Krämer [6] argues cogently that the use of torture negates the value of any Templar confessions that such abuses had existed. And while there were certain discrepancies between the

---

1 The editors have not been able to trace any current scholarly experts on the German trial. See Marie Luise Bulst-Thiele, 'Der Prozess gegen den Templerorden', in *Die geistlichen Ritterorden Europas*, ed. Josef Fleckenstein and Manfred Hellmann, Vorträge und Forschungen, 26 (Sigmaringen, 1980), pp. 375–402, here p. 392 and notes 67–8. There were no Templars in the Netherlands in 1307: personal communication from Johannes A. Mol of the Fryske Academy, Ljouwert, 6 September 2008.

2 Barbara Frale, 'The Chinon Chart: Papal Absolution to the Last Templar, Master Jacques de Molay', *Journal of Medieval History*, 30 (2004), 109–34, here 127.

high standards set by the Templars' normative texts and the brothers' day-to-day realities, as Christian Vogel [25] shows in his paper on Templar 'runaways' and 'renegades', these discrepancies were a far cry from heresy or any other serious allegations.

Several papers in this volume address the contextual aspects of the trial against the Templars and thus allow us to view the event from a broader historical perspective. Dale Streeter [7] notes that Philip IV had in effect 'stacked' the episcopal tribunals in France to direct legal proceedings his way. Magdalena Satora [13] highlights the efficiency of the king's propaganda which was intended 'to create a picture of general support for the royal actions against the Templars'. Anne Gilmour-Bryson [26] suggests that the assumed higher level of 'literacy' of Templar priests rendered their depositions particularly useful to inquisitors. Showing the value of prosopographical research, Paul Crawford [11] analyses the role played by the masters of the University of Paris and explains their 'stakes' in the outcome of the proceedings. Both Crawford and Alain Provost [10] moreover illustrate that the Templar trial has to be seen in the context of other judicial showdowns in early fourteenth-century France, namely the trials against Marguerite Porete and Bishop Guichard of Troyes. While a wide-angle view does not explain the Templars' affair, it may suggest that such judicial attacks were common, rather than exceptional.

Although giving scant support to those who believe that the Templars must have been guilty of something, the papers presented in this volume do give some indication of what the Templars *were* doing in the early fourteenth century. Ignacio de la Torre [5] illustrates that the Templars in France performed useful financial services for their kings. Luis García-Guijarro Ramos [16], Jeffrey Hamilton [17] and Peter Edbury [20] demonstrate that the members of the order in Aragon, England and Cyprus were valued political allies of their respective rulers. In Poland, as noted by Maria Starnawska [24], they served as allies of the margraves of Brandenburg. Elena Bellomo [21] points to the Templars' 'positive relations with lay and ecclesiastical authorities and local society in general' in northern Italy. With regard to the kingdom of Naples and the kingdom of Sicily, Kristjan Toomaspoeg [22] notes the Templars' service as officers of the royal court. There is also some indication that the Templars were involved in plans for a new crusade. Sebastián Salvadó [15] points out that the objects of devotion venerated by the Templars of Aragon were focused on the Holy Land, while – as shown by Helen Nicholson [18] – the Templars of Ireland still had direct links with Cyprus, to judge from Brother Henry Danet's arrival there from Cyprus early in 1308. In his biography of Jacques de Molay, Alain Demurger has drawn attention to a letter of Pope Clement V of 13 June 1306, noting that the Templar Brother Himbert Blanc and Pierre de Langres, citizen of Marseilles and 'admiral of the galleys dispatched to aid the Holy Land', were launching a naval campaign against Muslims and the Christians who traded with them. Demurger suggested that this expedition was connected to the grand master's own crusade plan of 1306, in which he advised the pope to arm 10 galleys and send them to defend Cyprus and prevent Christians from supplying prohibited goods (such as weapons) to the Muslims.[3]

Yet, aside from these tantalising hints, little evidence survives of progress in Templar plans for a new crusade to the east. While Jacques de Molay may have undertaken to make reforms in the order – an obvious precursor to a new campaign in the east – Anthony Luttrell [2] points out that no definite records of such reforms survive. We may wonder why the Templars did not emulate the Hospitallers in attempting to find a new base from which to carry on holy war against Islam, perhaps on the frontier of Granada, or on one of the islands off the coast of northern Africa.[4] The Templars' temporary occupation of the island of Ruad/Arwad (1300–02), located off the coast of mainland Syria, just a few years before the trial, is often belittled as it ended in disaster for the order, but may have been more than a 'swan song'.[5] Although the occupation failed, western travellers to the region, even centuries later, were sure to point out the island's historic and strategic significance.[6] Perhaps if the Templars' grand master had more closely resembled the Hospitallers' ruthless and opportunistic Fulk de Villaret, the Templars would have been better able to exploit the opportunities which did exist for their order in the early fourteenth-century Mediterranean, and would not have fallen easy victims to charges of heresy.

In a few areas in the early fourteenth century there were indications that the Templars' political ties were not healthy for the long-term future of the order. According to Bernard Schotte [4], the Templars of Flanders were apparently involved with the Hospitallers and burghers of Flanders in warfare against the king of France, and Filip Hooghe's paper [23] suggests that, at least as far as Philip IV was concerned, the Flemish brothers of the order were no less elusive during the trial than they had been prior to 1307. In Portugal, Clive Porro [14] reveals, the king judged that the Templars had outlived their use in holy war and wished to recover former royal gifts from them. Nicholas Morton [3] draws attention to the fact that the Templars, although they were a supra-national religious institution, had close local ties that had once been essential for their survival, but could easily leave them at the mercy of local lordships. The apparently sudden demise of the order, which has so intrigued the conspiracy theorists of whom John Walker [28] writes in this volume, is less of a mystery when we take these political aspects into account.

---

[3] Alain Demurger, *Jacques de Molay: le crépuscule des templiers* (Paris, 2002), p. 210.

[4] For discussion of this question, see Paul Crawford, 'Imagination and the Templars: The Development of the Order-State in the Early Fourteenth Century', *ΕΠΕΤΗΡΙΔΑ* [Annual Review of the Cyprus Research Centre], 30 (2004), 113–21.

[5] Adrian J. Boas, *Archaeology of the Military Orders* (London, 2006), p. 218.

[6] See, for example, Henry Maundrell, *A Journey from Aleppo to Jerusalem in 1697*, ed. David Howell (Beirut, 1963), pp. 26–7.

This said, what future did the Templars have at the beginning of 1307, even before the moves against the Templars in Portugal and France? While 'virtual' or fictionalised history can be only speculative, it can sometimes cast light on actual events and highlight crucial factors. Even if the Templars had not come under attack from the king of France in October 1307, in order to survive as a military order they needed to revitalise their role in holy war. Given the reluctance of the monarchs of western Europe to invest in a new crusade to the east, without a new, independent base similar to the Hospitallers' base on Rhodes or the Teutonic order's base in Prussia, it seems unlikely that the order of the Temple could have continued to maintain its independence in the face of the political and financial pressure from these same monarchs. It would probably have continued down the slippery slope of secularisation, and become little more than a branch of royal government in the various kingdoms and states of Europe. Again, even if the Iberian Templars had been spared dissolution in 1312, as – according to Luis García-Guijarra Ramos [16] – the king of Aragon may have preferred, it seems unlikely that they could have survived as an independent institution. In the light of events in Portugal, and of later relations between the Hospitallers and the king of Aragon, it seems highly likely that a 'Templar order' surviving in the Iberian Peninsula would have gone down the same path as the Spanish military orders of Calatrava, Alcantara and Santiago: that is, as mere decorations controlled by the king, despite a continuing military role against the Muslims of Granada.

The studies collected here reveal that research into the trial of the Templars has expanded considerably over the last few decades. They also indicate areas where further work is needed. Jochen Burgtorf's analysis [9] of the trial inventories from France, and Sebastian Salvadó's analysis [15] of records from Aragon, offer a glimpse of the wealth of surviving material on Templar properties, which remains largely unexplored partly because of its sheer bulk. The inventories from Ireland have already been published in full, but scholars have made little use of them.[7] Alongside studies of the inventories, excavations at Templar commanderies can do much to illuminate the Templars' way of life.[8]

Although there has been some research into the passage of the Templars' former properties to the Hospital after 1312 – see, for example, the articles by Simon Phillips [19] and Theresa Vann [27] in this volume – much remains to be

[7] Gearóid MacNiocaill, 'Documents relating to the Suppression of the Templars in Ireland', *Analecta Hibernica*, 24 (1967), 183–226; cited by Evelyn Lord, *The Knights Templar in Britain* (Harlow, 2002), pp. 141–2; Helen Nicholson, *The Knights Templar on Trial: The Trial of the Templars in the British Isles, 1308–1311* (Stroud, 2009), chapter six. Helen Nicholson is currently working on the inventories of the Templars' estates in England.

[8] Recent publications of excavations include: Christopher Gerrard, *Paisaje y señorío: La casa conventual de Ambel (Zaragoza), Arqueología, arquitectura e historia de las Órdenes militares del Temple y del Hospital* (Zaragoza, 2003); Philip Mayes, *Excavations at a Templar Preceptory. South Witham, Lincolnshire, 1965–67* (Leeds, 2002).

said. For example, researchers can easily overlook the fact that a great deal of information about the Templars and their estates is contained in the later Hospitaller documents. Disputes arose over the customs and duties which had been attached to those estates during Templar tenure, but which the Hospitallers (it was alleged) had allowed to lapse. While the Hospitallers successfully refuted some of these claims, others were upheld by the courts and give an insight into the Templars' former relations with their patrons and their local communities.[9]

There is also a need for modern editions of the trial records. For example, there is no modern edition of the French Templars' testimonies. As noted by Anthony Luttrell [2], the manuscript in the Bibliothèque nationale, Paris, MS Lat. 11796, is the rough copy and that in the Vatican Archive, Archivio Vaticano Arm. D. 206, is the fair version produced for the pope. Jules Michelet, in producing his famous *Procès des Templiers* (1841–51), much cited in this volume, used only the Paris manuscript, 'which apparently has never been collated with the Vatican version'. At the time of writing, a new and complete edition of the trial proceedings in the British Isles is under preparation by Helen Nicholson; the summary of the testimonies sent to the papal commission differs in many respects from the full records of the testimonies which survive in the Bodleian Library, Oxford, and the British Library, London. On this basis, a careful comparison of the Paris and Vatican records of the French Templar testimonies may find many interesting and illuminating differences.

As regards other records of the Templars, there is a mass of uncoordinated material surviving at local levels all across Europe. In the early twentieth century, the Marquis André d'Albon collected a vast amount of material from Templar archives, which remained unpublished on his death in 1912 and much of which still remains unpublished – and hence under-used by scholars – in the Bibliothèque nationale de France. The collection comprises transcriptions not only of hundreds of documents from French local archives, but also of charters and letters relating to the Templars in Syria, the Iberian Peninsula and England, and letters from scholars to the Marquis d'Albon about documents relating to the Templars surviving in Germany, Austria, Hungary, Italy and Scandinavia.[10] The records of the trial in Germany, cited by Marie Luise Bulst-Thiele in her study of 1980, were published by François J.M. Raynouard in 1813 and Heinrich Finke in 1907;[11] a new edition of these documents complying with modern scholarly requirements is surely long

[9] See, for example, Simon Phillips, *The Prior of the Knights Hospitaller in Late Medieval England* (Woodbridge, 2009), p. 8; Helen J. Nicholson, 'Relations between Houses of the Order of the Temple in Britain and their Local Communities, as Indicated during the Trial of the Templars, 1307–12', in *Knighthoods of Christ; Essays on the History of the Crusades and the Knights Templar, Presented to Malcolm Barber*, ed. Norman Housley (Aldershot, 2007), pp. 195–207, here pp. 196–7, 199, 202–3.

[10] Émile G. Léonard, *Introduction au cartulaire manuscrit du Temple (1150–1317) constitué par le Marquis d'Albon et conservé à la Bibliothèque nationale* (Paris, 1930).

[11] Bulst-Thiele, 'Prozess', p. 392, notes 67–8.

overdue. There are further unpublished documents in many places, such as the archives of Barcelona, and in various Hospitaller archives across Europe. The archive in Perpignan, for example, has bundles of unexplored and un-inventoried documents.

Although some of this material is being examined by individual scholars, for there to be significant scholarly advance in knowledge of the trial of the Templars, it is necessary for scholars from different regions to work together. There are already regular international conferences on the military religious orders held at Toruń in Poland, Palmela in Portugal, and at Clerkenwell, London and Cardiff, Wales, where research can be exchanged and discussed, but what is needed is more international co-operation on an ongoing basis between these regular meetings. Such ongoing and long-term co-operation will enable an overall picture of the activities and condition of the order of the Temple in 1307 to be constructed, in addition to a full overview of the course of the trial in different regions and a clear view of the fate of the orders' members and their property.

It is also clear that historians of the Templars and the Templars' trial must have knowledge of many disciplines. In the past, many historians of the Templars have been primarily experts on the crusades; others have been primarily experts on national or local history, studying the Templars at a local or regional level. Some have specialised entirely on the study of the Templars to the exclusion of other religious orders or the rest of medieval society. The studies in this volume show that in order to research effectively into this subject, the historian must have specialist knowledge of the crusades and of national and local history, in addition to detailed knowledge of the inquisitorial procedures used against heretics, modern research on the psychological impact of torture, normal Latin Christian devotional practices of the early fourteenth century, theology and canon law – to mention but a few. Historians must use a wide range of sources, not only the narrative accounts produced by contemporary commentators and the records of the trial testimonies, but the inventories of the Templars' lands, the records of their possessions, including their art, contemporary charters and letters and a wide variety of other written records, both in Latin and in the vernacular. Only then can the history of events which involved virtually the whole of Latin Christendom and persons drawn from the whole spectrum of society be fully assessed and, perhaps, understood.

Select Bibliography

Primary sources

Annales Gandenses (Annals of Ghent), ed. Hilda Johnstone (Oxford, 1985)

'Annales de Terre Sainte', ed. Reinhold Röhricht and Gaston Raynaud, *Archives de l'Orient Latin*, 2 (1884)

Bernard of Clairvaux, *De laude novae militiae*, in *Sancti Bernardi Opera*, ed. Jean Leclercq and Henri Rochais, vol. 3 (Paris, 1963)

Bernard Gui, *Manuel de l'inquisiteur*, ed. Guillaume Mollat, vol. 1 (Paris, 1964); English translation: *The Inquisitor's Guide: A Medieval Manual on Heretics*, (trans. and ed.) Janet Shirley (Welwyn Garden City, 2006)

Calendar of Close Rolls Preserved in the Public Record Office, 1272–1509, 45 vols (London, 1900–1963)

Calendar of Documents Relating to Ireland, Preserved in Her Majesty's Public Record Office, ed. Henry S. Sweetman et al., 5 vols (London, 1875–86)

Calendar of the Entries in the Papal Registers Relating to Great Britain and Ireland: Papal Letters, 1198–1492, 15 vols (London, 1893–1960)

Calendar of Fine Rolls Preserved in the Public Record Office, 1272–1509, 22 vols (London, 1911–62)

Calendar of Patent Rolls Preserved in the Public Record Office, 1232–1509, 59 vols (London, 1891–1916)

Cartulaire général de l'ordre des Hospitaliers de Saint-Jean de Jérusalem, 1100–1310, ed. Joseph Delaville Le Roulx, 4 vols (Paris, 1884–1906)

Cartulaire des Hospitaliers (Ordre de Saint-Jean de Jérusalem) du Velay, ed. Augustin Chassaing (Paris, 1888)

Cartulaires des Templiers de Douzens, ed. Pierre Gérard and Elisabeth Magnou (Paris, 1965)

The Cartulary of the Knights of St. John of Jerusalem in England: secunda camera, Essex, ed. Michael Gervers (Oxford, 1982)

The Cartulary of the Knights of St. John of Jerusalem in England. Part 2, Prima Camera, Essex, ed. Michael Gervers (Oxford, 1996)

The Catalan Rule of the Templars: A Critical Edition and English Translation from Barcelona, Archivo de la Corona de Aragón, Cartas Reales, MS 3344, ed. Judi Upton-Ward (Woodbridge 2003)

Chartularium universitatis Parisiensis, ed. Heinrich Denifle and Emil Chatelain, 4 vols (Paris, 1889–97)

Chronica Walteri de Gyseburne: The Chronicle of Walter of Guisborough, ed. Henry Rothwell, Camden Society 3rd series, 89 (1957)

Chronicles of Flanders (1200–1500), ed. Véronique Lambert (Ghent, 1993)

Chronique de Guillaume de Nangis et de ses continuateurs, ed. Hercule Géraud (Paris, 1843)

La Chronique métrique attribuée à Geffroy de Paris, ed. Armel Diverres (Paris, 1956)

Chroniques d'Amadi et de Strambaldi, ed. René de Mas Latrie, 2 vols (Paris, 1891–93; repr. Nicosia, 1999)

Concilia Magnae Britanniae et Hiberniae, ed. David Wilkins, vol. 2 (London, 1737)

Councils and Synods with other Documents Relating to the English Church, vol. 2, part 2: *1265–1313*, ed. Frederick M. Powicke and Christopher R. Cheney (Oxford, 1964)

Cronaca del Templare di Tiro (1243–1314), ed. and trans Laura Minervini (Naples, 2000); English translation: *The 'Templar of Tyre': Part III of the 'Deeds of the Cypriots'*, trans. Paul Crawford (Aldershot, 2003)

Le Dossier de l'affaire des Templiers, ed. Georges Lizerand (Paris, 1923)

L'enquête pontificale de 1373 sur l'ordre des Hospitaliers de Saint-Jean de Jérusalem: Le prieuré de France, ed. Anne-Marie Legras, vol. 1 (Paris, 1987)

Excerpta e memoriali historiarum Johannis a Sancto Victore, in *Recueil des Historiens des Gaules et de la France*, vol. 21, ed. Joseph-Daniel Guigniaut and Natalis de Wailly (Paris, 1865)

The Fall of Acre: Excidii Acconis Gestorum Collectio, ed. Robert B.C. Huygens (Turnhout, 2004)

Florio Bustrone, 'Historia overo Commentarii de Cipro', ed. René de Mas Latrie as 'Chronique de l'île de Chypre', *Collection de documents inédits sur l'histoire de France: Mélanges historiques*, 5 (1886)

Foedera, conventiones, litterae et cujuscunque generis acta publica, ed. Thomas Rymer et al., new edn, 4 vols in 7 parts (London, 1816–69)

Gilles Le Muisit, *Chronique et annales*, ed. Henri Lemaître (Paris, 1906)

Inventaire des archives de la ville de Bruges: Inventaire des chartes, ed. Louis Gilliodts-Van Severen, vol. 1 (Bruges, 1871)

The Knights Hospitaller in England: Being the Report of Prior Philip de Thame to the Grand Master Elyan de Villanova for AD 1338, ed. Lambert B. Larking, Camden Society, 65 (1857)

Lettres communes de Jean XXII, ed. Guillaume Mollat, 16 vols (Paris, 1906–47)

Lettres inédites de Philippe le Bel, ed. Adolphe Baudouin (Paris, 1886)

'Le Livre de Guillaume Le Maire', ed. Célestine Port, in *Mélanges historiques: Choix de documents*, vol. 2 (Paris, 1877)

Monumenta Henricina, ed. António Dias Dinis, vol. 1 (Coimbra, 1960)

Papsttum und Untergang des Templerordens, ed. Heinrich Finke, 2 vols (Münster, 1907)

Papsturkunden für Templer und Johanniter, Vorarbeiten zum Oriens Pontificius I, Archivberichte und Texte, ed. Rudolf Hiestand (Göttingen, 1972)

Pierre Dupuy, *Traittez concernant l'histoire de France: Sçavoir la condemnation des Templiers avec quelques actes* (Paris, 1654; repr. Paris, 1978)

Le Procès des Templiers, ed. Jules Michelet, 2 vols (Paris, 1841–51)

Le Procès des Templiers d'Auvergne (1309–1311), ed. Roger Sève and Anne-Marie Chagny-Sève (Paris, 1986)

Regesta pontificum Romanorum ab anno p. Ch. n. 1198 ad annum 1304, ed. August Potthast, 2 vols (Berlin, 1874–5)

Regestum Clementis papae V, ed. cura et studio monachorum ordinis S. Benedicti, 9 vols in 7 (Rome, 1885–92)

Le Registre d'inquisition de Jacques Fournier, évêque de Pamiers (1318–1325), ed. Jean Duvernoy, 3 vols (Toulouse, 1965)

Registres du tresor des chartes, ed. Robert Fawtier (Paris, 1958)

Les Registres de Boniface VIII, ed. Georges Digard et al., 4 vols (Paris, 1884–1939)

Les Registres de Clément V, ed. Yvonne Lanhers, Cyrille Vogel, Robert Fawtier and Guillaume Mollat (Paris, 1948–57)

La Règle du Temple, ed. Henri de Curzon (Paris, 1886)

De Rekeningen van de stad Brugge, Tweede deel, eerste stuk 1302–1306, Tweede stuk 1306–1319, ed. Carlos Wyffels and André Vandewalle (Brussels, 1965–71)

Le Roman de Renart le Contrefait, ed. Gaston Raynaud and Henri Lemaître (Paris, 1914)

The Trial of the Templars in Cyprus: A Complete English Edition, ed. and trans. Anne Gilmour-Bryson (Leiden and New York, 1998)

The Trial of the Templars in the Papal State and the Abruzzi, ed. Anne Gilmour-Bryson, (Vatican City, 1982)

Der Untergang des Templerordens mit urkundlichen und kritischen Beiträgen, ed. Konrad Schottmüller, 2 vols (Berlin, 1887)

Urkunden und Regesten zur Geschichte des Templerordens im Bereich des Bistums Cammin und der Kirchenprovinz Gnesen, ed. Winfried Irgang (Cologne and Vienna, 1987)

Vitae Paparum Avenionensum, ed. Etienne Baluze, new edn ed. Guillaume Mollat (Paris, 1914–27)

William of Tyre, *Chronicon*, ed. Robert B.C. Huygens, 2 vols (Turnhout, 1986)

Secondary sources

Alaniѐce, Valerie, and François Gilet, *Les Templiers et leurs commanderies: L'exemple d'Avalleur en Champagne* (Langres 1995)

d'Alatri, Mariano, *Eretici e inquisitori in Italia*, 2 vols (Rome, 1986–87)

d'Alatri, Mariano, *L'inquisizione francescana nell'Italia centrale nel secolo XIII* (Rome, 1954)

Barber, Malcolm, 'Propaganda in the Middle Ages: The Charges Against the Templars', *Nottingham Medieval Studies*, 17 (1973)

Barber, Malcolm, ed., *The Military Orders: Fighting for the Faith and Caring for the Sick* (Aldershot, 1994)

Barber, Malcolm, *The New Knighthood: A History of the Order of the Temple* (Cambridge, 1994)

Barber, Malcolm, 'The Trial of the Templars Revisited', in *MO*, 2

Barber, Malcolm, *The Trial of the Templars*, 2nd edn (Cambridge 2006)

Bellomo, Elena, *The Templar Order in North-West Italy (1142–c.1330)* (Leiden, 2008)

Benavides, Antonio, *Memorias de Fernando IV de Castilla*, 2 vols (Madrid, 1860)

Biget, Jean-Louis, *Hérésie et inquisition dans le midi de la France* (Paris, 2007)

Bini, Telesforo, 'Dei Tempieri e del loro processo in Toscana', *Atti della Reale Accademia Lucchese di Scienze, Lettere ed Arti*, 13 (1845)

Boas, Adrian J., *Archaeology of the Military Orders: a survey of the urban centres, rural settlement and castles of the military orders in the Latin East (c. 1120-1291)* (London, 2006)

Boyle, Leonard E., 'Montaillou Revisited: *Mentalité* and Methodology', in *Pathways to Medieval Peasants*, ed. James A. Raftis (Toronto, 1981)

Bramato, Fulvio, *Storia dell'Ordine dei Templari in Italia: Le fondazioni* (Rome, 1991)

Bulst-Thiele, Marie Luise, 'Templer in königlichen und päpstlichen Diensten', in *Festschrift Percy Ernst Schramm*, ed. Peter Classen and Peter Scheibert (Wiesbaden, 1964)

Bulst-Thiele, Marie Luise, *Sacrae domus militiae Templi Hierosolymitani magistri: Untersuchungen zur Geschichte des Templerordens 1118/9–1314* (Göttingen, 1974)

Bulst-Thiele, Marie Luise, 'Der Prozess gegen den Templerorden', in *Die geistlichen Ritterorden Europas*, ed. Josef Fleckenstein and Manfred Hellmann, Vorträge und Forschungen, 26 (Sigmaringen, 1980)

Burgtorf, Jochen, *The Central Convent of Hospitallers and Templars: History, Organization, and Personnel (1099/1120-1310)* (Leiden, 2008)

Caravita, Renzo, *L'Arcivescovo di Ravenna Rinaldo da Concorezzo e il processo ai Templari* (Ravenna, 2008)

Carraz, Damien, *L'ordre du Temple dans la basse vallée du Rhône (1124–1312): Ordres militaires, croisades et sociétés méridionales* (Lyon, 2005)

Carraz, Damien, 'Archéologie des commanderies de l'Hôpital et du Temple en France (1977–2007)', *Cahiers de recherches médiévales*, 15 (2008)

Challet, Vincent, 'Entre expansionnisme capétien et relents d'hérésie: Le procès des Templiers du Midi', in *Les ordres religieux militaires dans le Midi* (Toulouse, 2005); new edition in *Cahiers de Fanjeaux*, 41 (2006)

Claverie, Pierre-Vincent, *L'ordre du Temple en Terre Sainte et à Chypre au XIII Siècle*, 3 vols (Nicosia, 2005)

Coste, Jean, *Boniface VIII en procès: Articles d'accusation et dépositions des témoins (1303–1311): Edition critique, introductions et notes* (Rome, 1995)

Crawford, Paul F., 'Imagination and the Templars: The Development of the Order-State in the Early Fourteenth Century', *Epeterida* [Annual Review of the Cyprus Research Centre], 30 (2004)

Crawford, Paul F., 'The University of Paris and the Trial of the Templars', in *MO*, 3

Crawford, Paul F., 'The Military Orders and the Last Decade of the Thirteenth Century', *Epeterida* 33 (2007)

Croix, Arnaud de la, *L'ordre du Temple et le reniement du Christ* (Paris, 2004)

Cumps, Lieven K., *De tempeliers in Vlaanderen* (Tielt, 1976)

Delaville Le Roulx, Joseph, 'Un nouveau manuscrit de la règle du Temple', *Annuaire-Bulletin de la Société de l'Histoire de France*, 26 (1889)

Delfos, Leo, *Het avontuur van de Liebaards 1297–1302–1304: Geschiedenis van een Vlaamse opstand 'omme die defense van den lande'* (Tielt, 1952)

Delmas, Jean, 'L'inventaire des biens de la commanderie de Sainte-Eulalie du Larzac en 1308', in *La Commanderie: Institution des ordres militaires dans l'Occident médiéval*, ed. Anthony Luttrell and Léon Pressouyre (Paris, 2002)

Delisle, Léopold, *Mémoire sur les opérations financiéres des templiers* (Paris, 1889)

Demurger, Alain, *Vie et mort de l'ordre du Temple* (Paris, 1985, 1993)

Demurger, Alain, 'Encore le procès des templiers: A propos d'un ouvrage récent', *Revue Historique*, 97 (1991)

Demurger, Alain, *Chevaliers du Christ: Les ordres religieux-militaires au moyen âge, XIe–XVIe siècle* (Paris, 2002)

Demurger, Alain, *Jacques de Molay: Le Crépuscule des Templiers* (Paris, 2002)

Demurger, Alain, 'Outre-Mer: Le passage des Templiers en Orient d'après les depositions du procès', in *Chemins d'Outre-Mer: Etudes sur la Méditerranée médiévale offertes à Michel Balard*, ed. Damien Coulon et al., vol. 1 (Paris, 2004)

Demurger, Alain, *Les Templiers: Une chevalerie chrétienne au moyen âge* (Paris, 2005)

Dondi, Cristina, 'Manoscritti liturgici dei templari e degli ospitalieri: Le nuove prospettive aperte dal sacramentario templare di Modena (Biblioteca capitolare O.II.13)', in *I Templari, la guerra, la santità*, ed. Simonetta Cerrini (Rimini, 2000)

Edbury, Peter W., *The Kingdom of Cyprus and the Crusades, 1191–1374* (Cambridge, 1991)

Edbury, Peter W., 'The Suppression of the Templars in Cyprus', *St John Historical Society Proceedings* (2003)

Eubel, Konrad, *Hierarchia catholica medii aevi* (Münster, 1898)

Favier, Jean, *Un conseiller de Philippe le Bel: Enguerran de Marigny* (Paris, 1963)

Favier, Jean, *Philippe le Bel* (Paris, 1978)

Forey, Alan J., *The Templars in the Corona de Aragón* (London, 1973)

Forey, Alan J., 'The Military Orders and Holy War against Christians in the Thirteenth Century', *English Historical Review*, 104 (1989)

Forey, Alan J., *The Military Orders: From the Twelfth to the Early Fourteenth Centuries* (Basingstoke, 1992)

Forey, Alan J., 'Towards a Profile of the Templars in the Early Fourteenth Century', in *MO*, 1

Forey, Alan J., 'Literacy and Learning in the Military Orders during the Twelfth and Thirteenth Centuries', in *MO*, 2

Forey, Alan J., 'Letters of the Last Two Templar Masters', *Nottingham Medieval Studies*, 65 (2001)

Forey, Alan J., *The Fall of the Templars in the Crown of Aragon* (Aldershot, 2001)

Forey, Alan J., 'Ex-Templars in England', *Journal of Ecclesiastical History*, 53 (2002), 18–37

Forey, Alan J., 'The Charitable Activities of the Templars', *Viator*, 34 (2003)

Forey, Alan J., 'Desertions and Transfers from Military Orders (Twelfth to Early-Fourteenth Centuries)', *Traditio*, 60 (2005)

Forey, Alan J., 'Women and the Military Orders in the Twelfth and Thirteenth Centuries', in *Hospitaller Women in the Middle Ages*, ed. Anthony Luttrell and Helen Nicholson (Aldershot, 2006)

Forey, Alan J., 'A Templar Lordship in Northern Valencia', in *Die Ritterorden als Träger der Herrschaft: Territorien, Grundbesitz und Kirche*, ed. Roman Czaja and Jürgen Sarnowsky, *Ordines Militares: Colloquia Turonensia*, 14 (2007)

Frale, Barbara, *L'ultima battaglia dei Templari: Dal codice ombra d'obbedienza militare alla costruzione del processo per eresia* (Rome, 2001)

Frale, Barbara, *Il papato e il processo ai Templari: L'inedita assoluzione di Chinon alla luce della diplomatica pontificia* (Rome, 2003)

Frale, Barbara, 'The Chinon Chart: Papal Absolution to the Last Templar, Master Jacques de Molay', *Journal of Medieval History*, 30 (2004)

Fried, Johannes, 'Wille, Freiwilligkeit und Geständnis um 1300: Zur Beurteilung des letzten Templergroßmeisters Jacques de Molay', *Historisches Jahrbuch*, 105 (1985)

García-Guijarro Ramos, Luis, 'Los orígenes de la Orden de Montesa', in *Las Órdenes Militares en el Mediterráneo Occidental (siglos XIII–XVIII)* (Madrid, 1989)

García-Guijarro Ramos, Luis, 'The Development of a System of Commanderies in the Early Years of the Order of Montesa, 1319–1330', in *La Commanderie: Institution des ordres militaires dans l'Occident medieval*, ed. Anthony Luttrell and Léon Pressouyre (Paris, 2002)

García-Guijarro Ramos, Luis, 'The Growth of the Order of the Temple in the Northern Area of the Kingdom of Valencia at the Close of the Thirteenth Century: A Puzzling Development?', in *Knighthoods of Christ: Essays on the History of the Crusades and the Knights Templar Presented to Malcolm Barber*, ed. Norman Housley (Aldershot, 2007)

Gilmour-Bryson, Anne, 'L'elezione di Bertrand de Got (Clemente V) e l'incontro a St. Jean d'Angély', *Rivista di Storia della Chiesa in Italia*, 53, n. 2 (1999)

Gilmour-Bryson, Anne, 'The London Templar Trial Testimony: "Truth", Myth, or Fable', in *A World Explored: Essays in Honour of Laurie Gardiner*, ed. Anne Gilmour-Bryson (Melbourne, 1993)

Gilmour-Bryson, Anne, 'Testimony of Non-Templar Witnesses in Cyprus', in *MO*, 1

Gilmour-Bryson, Anne, 'The Templar Trials: Did the System Work?', *Medieval History Journal*, 3 (2000)

Given, James, 'The Inquisitors of Languedoc and the Medieval Technology of Power', *The American Historical Review*, 94 (1989)

Given, James, *Inquisition and Medieval Society: Power, Discipline and Resistance in Languedoc* (Ithaca, NY, and London, 1997)

Given, James, 'Chasing Phantoms: Philip IV and the Fantastic', in *Heresy and the Persecuting Society in the Middle Ages*, ed. Michael Frassetto (Leiden, 2006)

Guzzo, Cristian, *Templari in Sicilia: La storia e le sue fonti tra Federico II e Roberto d'Angiò* (Genoa, 2003)

Hefele, Karl Josef von, et al., *Histoire des conciles d'après les documents originaux*, 11 vols (Paris, 1907–52)

Hosten, Jan, *De tempeliers: De tempelorde tijdens de kruistochten en in de Lage Landen* (Amsterdam, 2006)

Housley, Norman, *The Avignon Papacy and the Crusade* (Oxford, 1986)

Housley, Norman, ed., *Knighthoods of Christ: Essays on the History of the Crusades and the Knights Templar Presented to Malcolm Barber* (Aldershot, 2007)

Jordan, William Chester, *Unceasing Strife, Unending Fear: Jacques de Thérines and the Freedom of the Church in the Age of the Last Capetians* (Princeton, 2005)

Juillet, Jacques, *Commanderies sur le chemin de Rocamadour* (Saint-Yrieux-La-Perche, 1975)

Lalou, Elisabeth, 'Les assemblées générales sous Philippe le Bel', in *Recherches sur les états généraux et les états provinciaux de la France médiévale, Actes du 110e congrès national des sociétés savantes, Montpellier, 1985* (Paris, 1986)

Lalou, Elisabeth, 'Templerprozeß', *Lexikon des Mittelalters*, vol. 8 (1997)

Lalou, Elisabeth, *Itinéraire de Philippe IV le Bel (1285–1314)* (Paris, 2007)

Léonard, Emile-G., *Introduction au cartulaire manuscrit du Temple (1150–1317) constitué par le Marquis d'Albon et conservé à la Bibliothèque Nationale suivie d'un tableau des maison françaises du Temple et de leurs précepteurs* (Paris, 1930)

Loiseleur, Jules, *La doctrine secrète des Templiers: Etude suivie du texte inédit de l'enquête contre les Templiers de Toscane et de la chronologie des documents relatifs à la suppression du Temple* (Paris, 1872)

Lord, Evelyn, *The Knights Templar in Britain* (Harlow, 2002)

Lüpke, Helmut, 'Die Wüstungen Grossdorf und Giemeln im Lande Sterneberg', *Die Neumark: Mitteilungen des Vereins für Geschichte der Neumark*, 9 (1932)

Lüpke, Helmut, 'Das Land Tempelburg: Eine historisch-geographische Untersuchung', *Baltische Studien*, 35 (1933)

Lüpke, Helmut, 'Untersuchungen über den sagenhaft überlieferten oder fälschlich vermuteten Besitz der Tempelherren in Deutschland', *Jahrbuch für Brandenburgische Kirchengeschichte*, 31 (1936)

Luttrell, Anthony, 'The Aragonese Crown and the Knights Hospitallers of Rhodes: 1291–1350', *English Historical Review*, 76 (1961), and in idem, *The Hospitallers in Cyprus, Rhodes, Greece and the West 1291–1440* (London, 1978), article 9

Luttrell, Anthony, 'La Corona de Aragón y las Órdenes Militares durante el Siglo XIV', in *VIII Congreso de Historia de la Corona de Aragón*, vol. 2.2 (Valencia, 1970) and in Anthony Luttrell, *The Hospitallers in Cyprus, Rhodes, Greece and the West 1291–1440* (London, 1978), article 12

Luttrell, Anthony, 'The Hospitallers in Cyprus after 1291,' in *Acts of the I International Congress of Cypriot Studies, II* (Nicosia, 1972), and in idem, *The Hospitallers in Cyprus, Rhodes, Greece, and the West 1291–1440* (London, 1978), article 2

Luttrell, Anthony, 'The Hospitallers of Rhodes: Prospectives, Problems, Possibilities,' in *A History of the Crusades*, ed. Kenneth M. Setton, vol. 3, *The Fourteenth and Fifteenth Centuries*, ed. Harry W. Hazard (Madison, 1975), and in Anthony Luttrell, *Latin Greece, the Hospitallers and the Crusades, 1291–1440* (London, 1982), article 1

Luttrell, Anthony, 'Templari e Ospitalieri in Italia', in *La chiesa di San Bevignate a Perugia,* ed. Mario Roncetti, Pietro Scarpellini and Francesco Tommasi (Perugia, 1987), and in Anthony Luttrell, *The Hospitallers of Rhodes and Their Mediterranean World* (Aldershot, 1992), article 1

Luttrell, Anthony, 'Gli ospitalieri e l'eredità dei Templari: 1305–1378', in *I Templari: Mito e Storia – Atti de Convegno Internazionale di Studi alla Magione Templare di Poggibonsi-Siena (29-31 maggio 1987)*, ed. Giovanni Minnucci and Francesco Sardi (Siena, 1989), and in Anthony Luttrell, *The Hospitallers of Rhodes and Their Mediterranean World* (Aldershot, 1992), article 3

Luttrell, Anthony, 'Gli Ospitalieri di San Giovanni di Gerusalemme dal continente alle isole', in *Acri 1291: La fine della presenza degli ordini militari in Terra Santa e i nuovi orientamenti nel XIV secolo*, ed. Francesco Tommasi (Perugia, 1996)

Luttrell, Anthony, 'The Finances of the Commander in the Hospital after 1306', in *La Commanderie: Institution des ordres militaires dans l'Occident médiéval*, ed. Anthony Luttrell and Lèon Pressouyre (Paris, 2002)

MacNiocaill, Gearóid, 'Documents relating to the Suppression of the Templars in Ireland', *Analecta Hibernica*, 24 (1967)

Mallia-Milanes, Victor, ed., *The Military Orders*, vol. 3: *History and Heritage* (Aldershot, 2008)

Melville, Marion, *La Vie des Templiers* (Paris, 1951)

Menache, Sophia, 'Contemporary Attitudes Concerning the Templars' Affair: Propaganda's Fiasco?', *Journal of Medieval History*, 8 (1982)

Menache, Sophia, 'A Propaganda Campaign in the Reign of Philip the Fair, 1302–03', *French History*, 4 (1990)

Menache, Sophia, 'The Templar Order: A Failed Ideal?', *The Catholic Historical Review*, 79 (1993)

Menache, Sophia, *Clement V* (Cambridge, 1998)

Menard, Léon, *Histoire civile, ecclésiastique, et littéraire de la ville de Nismes avec des notes et les preuves, suivie de dissertations historiques & critiques sur les antiquités & de diverses observations sur son histoire naturelle*, vol. 1 (Paris, 1750)

Miguet, Michel, 'Le personnel des commanderies du Temple et d'Hôpital en Normandie', in *La commanderie: Institution des ordres militaires dans l'Occident médiéval*, ed. Anthony Luttrell and Léon Pressouyre (Paris, 2002)

Miller, Thomas W., 'Long-Term Effects of Torture in Former Prisoners of War', in *Torture and Its Consequences: Current Treatment Approaches*, ed. Metin Başoğlu (Cambridge 1992)

Miret y Sans, Joaquím, 'Inventaris de les cases del Temple de la Corona d'Aragó en 1289', *Boletín de la Real Academia de Buenas Letras de Barcelona*, 42 (1911)

Mollat, Guillaume, *The Popes at Avignon, 1305–1378*, 9th edn, trans. Janet Love (London, 1963)

Nicholson, Helen J., *Templars, Hospitallers and Teutonic Knights: Images of the Military Orders, 1128–1291* (Leicester, 1993)

Nicholson, Helen J., ed., *The Military Orders*, vol. 2: *Welfare and Warfare* (Aldershot, 1998)

Nicholson, Helen J., *The Knights Templar: A New History* (Stroud, 2001)

Nicholson, Helen J., *The Knights Hospitaller* (Woodbridge, 2001)

Nicholson, Helen J., 'Relations between Houses of the Order of the Temple in Britain and their Local Communities, as Indicated during the Trial of the Templars, 1307–12', in *Knighthoods of Christ; Essays on the History of the Crusades and the Knights Templar, Presented to Malcolm Barber*, ed. Norman Housley (Aldershot, 2007)

Nicholson, Helen J., 'The Testimony of Brother Henry Danet and the Trial of the Templars in Ireland', in *In Laudem Hierosolymitani: Studies in Crusades and Medieval Culture in Honour of Benjamin Z. Kedar*, ed. Iris Shagrir, Ronnie Ellenblum and Jonathan Riley-Smith (Aldershot, 2007)

Nicholson, Helen J., *The Knights Templar on Trial: The Trial of the Templars in the British Isles, 1308–1311* (Stroud, 2009)

Nuyttens, Michel, *Krijgers voor God: De orde van de tempeliers in de Lage Landen (1120 – 1312)* (Leuven, 2007)

Paker, Murat et al., 'Psychological Effects of Torture: An Empirical Study of Tortured and Non-Tortured Non-Political Prisoners', in *Torture and Its Consequences: Current Treatment Approaches*, ed. Metin Başoğlu (Cambridge 1992)

Partner, Peter, *The Templars and their Myth* (Rochester, 1990)

Perkins, Clarence, 'The Trial of the Knights Templars in England', *English Historical Review*, 24 (1909)

Perkins, Clarence, 'The Knights Templars in the British Isles', *English Historical Review*, 25 (1910)

Perkins, Clarence, 'The Wealth of the Knights Templars in England and the Disposition of It after their Dissolution', *American Historical Review*, 15 (1910)

Perkins, Clarence, 'The Knights Hospitallers in England after the Fall of the Order of the Temple,' *English Historical Review*, 45 (1930)

Peri, Illuminato, *La Sicilia dopo il vespro: Uomini città e campagne, 1282–1376* (Rome and Bari, 1981)

Peters, Edward, *Torture* (Oxford, 1985)

Phillips, Simon, 'The Recycling of Monastic Wealth in Medieval Southern England, 1300–1530', *Southern History: A Review of the History of Southern England*, 22 (2000)

Phillips, Simon, *The Prior of the Knights Hospitaller in Late Medieval England* (Woodbridge, 2009)

Provost, Alain, 'La procédure, la norme et l'institution: Le cas de Guichard, évêque de Troyes (1308–1314)', in *Les procès politiques (XIVe–XVIIe siècle)*, ed. Yves-Marie Bercé (Rome, 2007)

Prutz, Hans, *Die geistlichen Ritterorden: Ihre Stellung zur kirchlichen, politischen, gesellschaftlichen und wirtschaftlichen Entwicklung des Mittelalters* (Berlin, 1908)

Prutz, Hans, *Entwicklung und Untergang des Tempelherrenordens* (Berlin, 1888)

Raynouard, François J.M., Monumens historiques, relatifs à la condamnation des chevaliers du Temple, et à l'abolition de leur ordre (Paris, 1813)

Riley Smith, Jonathan, 'Were the Templars Guilty?', in *The Medieval Crusade*, ed. Susan J. Ridyard (Woodbridge, 2004)

Riley-Smith, Jonathan, 'The Structures of the Orders of the Temple and the Hospital in c.1291', in *The Medieval Crusade*, ed. Susan J. Ridyard (Woodbridge, 2004)

Rogghé, Paul, *De Orde van de Tempelridders en haar geschiedenis in het oude graafschap Vlaanderen* (Ghent, 1973)

Rubió, Jordi, Ramon d'Alós and Francisco Martorell, 'Inventaris inèndits de l'Orde del Temple a Catalunya', *Anuari de l'Institut d'Estudis Catalans*, 1 (1907)

Salvadó, Sebastián, 'Interpreting the Altarpiece of Saint Bernard: Templar Liturgy and Conquest in Thirteenth-Century Majorca,' *Iconographica: Rivista di iconografia medievale e moderna*, 5 (2006)

Sans i Travé, Josep Maria, 'L'inedito processo dei Templari in Castiglia (Medina del Campo, 27 aprile 1310)', in *Acri 1291: La fine della presenza degli ordini militari in Terra Santa e i nuovi orientamenti nel XIV secolo*, ed. Francesco Tommasi (Perugia, 1996)

Sans i Travé, Josep Maria, *El proces dels Templers catalans* (Lleida, 1991)

Scharff, Thomas, 'Auf der Suche nach der "Wahrheit": Zur Befragung von verdächtigen Personen durch mittelalterliche Inquisitoren', in *Eid und Wahrheitssuche: Studien zu rechtlichen Befragungspraktiken in Mittelalter und früher Neuzeit*, ed. Stefan Esders and Thomas Scharff (Frankfurt a. M., 1999)

Scharff, Thomas, 'Seelenrettung und Machtinszenierung: Sinnkonstruktionen der Folter im kirchlichen Inquisitionsverfahren des Mittelalters', in *Das Quälen des Körpers: Eine historische Anthropologie der Folter*, ed. Peter Burschel, Götz Distelrath and Sven Lembke (Cologne, 2000)

Schenk, Jochen, 'Aspects of Non-Noble Family Involvement in the Order of the Temple', in *The Military Orders*, vol. 4: *On Land and by Sea*, ed. Judi Upton-Ward (Aldershot, 2008)

Selwood, Dominic, *Knights of the Cloister: Templars and Hospitallers in Central-Southern Occitania c.1100–c.1300* (Woodbridge, 1999)

Shermer, Michael, *Why People Believe Weird Things* (New York, 1997)

Somnier, Finn et al., 'Psychological Consequences of Torture: Current Knowledge and Evidence', in *Torture and Its Consequences: Current Treatment Approaches*, ed. Metin Başoğlu (Cambridge 1992)

Starnawska, Maria, 'Crusade Orders on Polish Lands during the Middle Ages: Adaptation in a Peripheral Environment', *Quaestiones Medii Aevi Novae*, 2 (1997)

Starnawska, Maria, 'Military Orders and the Beginning of Crusade in Prussia', in *The Crusades and the Military Orders: Expanding the Frontiers of Medieval Latin Christianity*, ed. Zsolt Hunyadi and Jósef Laszlovszky (Budapest, 2001)

Starnawska, Maria, 'Notizie sulla composizione e sulla struttura del ordine del Tempio in Polonia', in *I Templari: Mito e Storia – Atti de Convegno Internazionale di Studi alla Magione Templare di Poggibonsi-Siena (29-31 maggio 1987)*, ed. Giovanni Minnucci and Francesco Sardi (Siena, 1989)

Strayer, Joseph R., *The Reign of Philip the Fair* (Princeton, 1980)

Suedfeld, Peter, 'Torture: A Brief Overview', in *Psychology and Torture*, ed. Peter Suedfeld (New York, 1990)

Tipton, Charles L., 'The 1338 Chapter General of the Knights Hospitallers at Montpellier', *Traditio* 24 (1968)

Tommasi, Francesco, 'Interrogatorio dei Templari a Cesena (1310)', in *Acri 1291: La fine della presenza degli ordini militari in Terra Santa e i nuovi orientamenti del XIV secolo*, ed. Francesco Tommasi (Perugia, 1996)

Toomaspoeg, Kristjan, 'Le patrimoine des grands ordres militaires en Sicile, 1145–1492', *Mélanges de l'Ecole française de Rome, Moyen Âge*, 113.1 (2001)

Toomaspoeg, Kristjan, 'Le ravitaillement de la Terre Sainte: L'exemple des possessions des ordres militaires dans le royaume de Sicile au XIIIe siècle', in *L'Expansion occidentale (XIe–XVe siècles): Formes et conséquences, XXXIIIe Congrès de la Société des Historiens Médiévistes de l'Enseignement Supérieur Public (Madrid, Casa de Velázquez, 23–26 mai 2002)* (Paris, 2003)

Toomaspoeg, Kristjan, *Templari e Ospitalieri nella Sicilia Medievale* (Bari, 2003)

Toomaspoeg, Kristjan, 'La fine dei Templari in Sicilia (1305–1327)', in *Religiones Militares: Contributi alla storia degli Ordini religioso-militari nel Medioevo*, ed. Anthony Luttrell and Francesco Tommasi, Biblioteca di 'Militia Sacra', 2 (Città di Castello, 2008)

Tyerman, Christopher, *England and the Crusades, 1095–1588* (Chicago, 1988)

Upton-Ward, Judi, ed., *The Military Orders*, vol. 4: *On Land and by Sea* (Aldershot, 2008)

Valente, José, 'The New Frontier: The Role of the Knights Templar in the Establishment of Portugal as an Independent Kingdom', *Mediterranean Studies*, 7 (1998)

Valois, Noël, 'Deux nouveaux témoignages sur le procès des Templiers', *Comptes rendus des séances de l'Académie des Inscriptions et Belles-Lettres* (Paris, 1910)

Verbruggen, Jan Frans and Rolf Falter, *1302: Opstand in Vlaanderen* (Tielt, 2001)

Vilar Bonet, Maria, *Els béns del Temple a la Corona d'Aragó en suprimir-se l'orde (1300–1319)* (Barcelona, 2000)

Villari, Litterio, *Templari in Sicilia* (Latina, 1993)

Vogel, Christian, *Das Recht der Templer: Ausgewählte Aspekte des Templerrechts unter besonderer Berücksichtigung der Statutenhandschriften aus Paris, Rom, Baltimore und Barcelona* (Münster 2007)

Wood, Charles T., ed., *Philip the Fair and Boniface VIII: State vs. Papacy* (New York, 1967)

Indexes

The following abbreviations are used: archbp. (archbishop), bp. (bishop), card. (cardinal), H (Hospitaller), kg. (king), T (Templar), TK (Teutonic Knight), univ. (university)

Index of Persons

Index of Places

Index of Subjects